ISBN 978-1-330-91447-2
PIBN 10120813

1 MONTH OF
FREE
READING

at

www.ForgottenBooks.com

By purchasing this book you are
eligible for one month membership to
ForgottenBooks.com, giving you
unlimited access to our entire
collection of over 1,000,000 titles via
our web site and mobile apps.

To claim your free month visit:

www.forgottenbooks.com/free120813

THE

NORTH AMERICAN

REVIEW.

RE-ESTABLISHED BY ALLEN THORNDIKE RICE.

EDITED BY LLOYD BRYCE.

VOL. CLIV.

Tros Tyriusque mihi nullo discrimine agetur.

NEW YORK:

No. 3 EAST FOURTEENTH STREET.

1892.

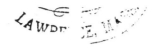

NORTH AMERICAN REVIEW.

No. CCCCXXII.

JANUARY, 1892.

MR. SPEAKER.

BY THE HON. ROGER Q. MILLS, REPRESENTATIVE IN CONGRESS
FROM TEXAS, AND THE HON. THOMAS B. REED, EX-
SPEAKER OF THE HOUSE.

MR. MILLS:

WHETHER the Speaker of the House of Representatives, when a record vote is being taken, can add to, subtract from, contradict, vary, or explain the record, is an American and not a European question. It arises out of the construction of a specific provision of the constitution, which creates the House and the Speaker, and its decision must be determined by that constitution and the interpretation it has received from the speakers who have presided over the House during its existence, and not by the practice of European assemblies or the opinions of European statesmen.

Our constitution, in section 5, article I., says : "Each house shall be the judge of the elections, returns, and qualifications of its own members, and a majority of each shall constitute a quorum to do business." What is meant by doing business ? Certainly doing nothing is not doing business. The business of a legislative body is to debate, to make motions, to elicit the expression of the will of the body, and to vote. To do business is to act, and act in the line of duty prescribed by law. Members who retain their seats, and refuse to speak, make motions, or vote, are not doing business. The constitution takes no notice of the man who is present but abstains from acting. It is only those who are present acting and doing business that it regards. Members present doing nothing imperil no right, and do no injury to any one ; but members present who attempt to make laws affecting the rights and liberties of the whole people may do infinite mischief to millions. Therefore the constitution requires that a majority of the House shall do whatever is done.

Our government is founded upon the immovable conviction in the minds of our people that freedom is their birthright, that governments are instituted to secure it, and that to be rightful they must exist by the consent of the governed. In every line of our organic laws jealousy of power is written, and in all questions of doubt our creed is : He who stands still stands best. When affirmative action is to be taken, when the *status quo* is to be abandoned, it must be done by the consent and coöperation of the greater part. Our whole history is an indictment against excesses in the legislation and administration of other governments. The Declaration of Independence proclaimed to the world that we held that we were endowed by our Creator with certain inalienable rights. These we cannot permit any government to take from us, nor can we voluntarily surrender them. Here is defined a boundary beyond which no government can go.

When the constitution was formed, governing power was divided and subdivided among many agencies, and closely laced within the corsets and stays of federal and State constitutions. The constitution lays down clearly and explicitly the principle of majority rule,—not a majority of a minority, but a majority of the whole,—and this principle is as clearly and explicitly ignored by the parliamentary assemblies of Europe. No government in Europe stands upon the inalienable right of its citizens or subjects. None of them stand upon the equal rights of all before the law. England for many generations has been looking through a glass darkly at the freeman with equal rights and privileges. France catches a meteoric glimpse occasionally, when it throws her into transports and leaves her in blood. Switzerland sees a little spot and retains that little by the aid of the friendly mountains that surround and protect her in her enjoyment. But the Americans alone see the inalienable right of the person, enfortressed in the very citadel of the constitution and secured there by an intelligent, virtuous, and courageous manhood. No people dread and abhor arbitrary power as they do, and none love liberty with their steady devotion. Here the people are supreme, and they confer whatever amount of power they think necessary to enable the government to secure them in the enjoyment of their rights, and no more.

As to that which they delegate, they prescribe just how it is to be exercised, and all other modes are forbidden. In conferring legislative power on the House they have enumerated a few things which it may do and many things which it may not do; and that which it is authorized to do is required to be done by a majority of the House. No bill can have the power of law unless it is passed by a majority of the whole House doing business. It may not have a majority of the whole House voting for it, but a majority of the whole House must vote, and a majority of those who do must vote for it. The majority principle is the ruling principle of our legislative assemblies. When the majority act within the authority of the constitution, then, as Mr. Jefferson says, "absolute acquiescence in its decisions is the vital principle of the republic."

But the majority of the whole is not omnipotent. The individual citizen is the only repository of supreme power in this land. There are limitations beyond which no majority can go, however large it may be. The people in their organic laws have placed the majority under the ban of suspicion. They have bolted and barred all the gates around them against its advance across its boundaries. A majority of Congress can raise and support an army, but it cannot raise and support a church; it can create a court, but not an establishment of religion; it can suppress an insurrection, but not a newspaper; it can close our ports, but not our mouths. No power in government here can do these things by counting a quorum or otherwise. The jealous love of the people for their liberties has invested the government with certain power, and set "bounds to its habitation." The same jealousy that withheld from Congress all power of interference with freedom of speech, press, and religion, prescribed to them that, when they did interfere where they were authorized, it should be by the act of a majority of the whole body attending, deliberating, and voting. They interdicted all rule save that by the majority of the whole.

This has been the uniform construction of the constitution for a hundred years. No Speaker from the First to the Fiftieth Congress ever held otherwise. Speaker Reed himself, prior to the last Congress, held the same view as all his predecessors. In 1880, when this very question was before the House, he said: "The constitutional idea of a quorum is not the presence of a majority of the members of the House, but a majority of the members present and participating in the business of the House. It is *not the visible presence of members,* but their presence and *their votes,* that the constitution calls for." He never gave expression to a different view until party exigency demanded revolutionary methods to stay the fleeting fortunes of that party of which he was a distinguished leader. Then with a breath he swept away the settled law of a century. The Hon. George M. Robeson, another distinguished and able leader of that party, said in the same debate : " It is necessary, under the constitution, that a majority shall be present doing business before there is a quorum of any kind, and no rule can make it otherwise." Such has been the interpretation of all parties in the country from the origin of the government to the present time. If the uniform construction of a century can settle anything, it is settled that a majority to do business is the majority of the whole House attending and participating in the business. The position is too clear and too long settled to remain in the domain of controversy.

It is contended that the Speaker, to meet the constitutional requirement of a quorum, may count the members present not doing business as present doing business. That is, he may nullify the constitution. If he has the power, he may, at his discretion, use it or abuse it. This is not a government where rights of the people depend on the discretion of any one man, but upon the laws passed in pursuance of the constitution which they have made, and which they declare to be the supreme law of the land. If the Speaker has the power to count, he may count the absent as being present ; which very thing occurred under this new rule during the last Congress. If he has that power, he may have the names of a hundred or more absent members entered on the journal as present, and thus have a bill passed by a minority instead of a majority. How is that wrong to be corrected ? He makes the record, and as he makes it it stands, whether true or false ; and a bill so enacted would not be a law passed in obedi.

ence to the constitution, but, like the laws of many European assemblies, one passed by a rump.

This mode of procedure may be in accordance with the principles of European governments, but it is not in harmony with the principles of our free government, where the liberty of the citizen is protected from oppression by checks and balances in every direction. Such counting may be proper in France, where, Mr. Stanton tells us, the assembly is composed of 745 members and the quorum is 200. It may be proper in England, where the Commons consists of 670 members and 40 is a quorum. But it is not proper in this country under our constitution, which requires a majority of the whole House to constitute a quorum to do business. There is no legislative body in Europe precisely similar to ours, whose power is so hedged in with limitations and interdictions. The practices of European assemblies are as inapplicable here as are their dogmas of hereditary aristocracy, primogeniture, and entailment. Our quorum, as Cushing says in his treatise on parliamentary law, is a majority of the whole number of which the House may consist, and not a majority of the number of which it does in fact consist. Our whole number is 332, and a quorum to do business is 167. If any number of these die, or resign, or be voted out, the quorum is not changed. It is still 167 members, and no smaller number can do business.

There are three ways of voting in the House : one when the Speaker counts, one when tellers count, and one when the clerk counts. When the Speaker puts the question to the vote by sound, he decides whether the ayes or noes have it. If he doubts, he calls upon the House to divide, and if a member challenges his decision he calls for a division, and the ayes rise and remain standing till counted. The ayes are then seated, and the noes rise and remain standing till counted. If the Speaker's count on a division is doubted, tellers are called for by a certain number of members, and one member on each side of the question is appointed by the chair, and the ayes pass between them and are counted by the tellers, and then the noes pass between them and are counted by the tellers, who report the numbers as they have counted them to the Speaker, and he announces the vote to the House and decides the question according to the count of the tellers. This vote by tellers is had by the House to ascertain if the Speaker's count is correct, and he has nothing to do with it but to announce it and act on it. He cannot revise it, nor add to nor take from it. It is the law to him just as it is to every other member of the House. If the Speaker could say, "The chair saw present a number of gentlemen who did not vote, and he will add them to one side or the other, or count them to make a quorum," the vote by tellers would be no verification of his count. It would only be a motion for a new trial before the same court. The whole matter would still be in the control of the Speaker, and selecting one member on each side of the question to see a fair count would be of no avail.

These two votes are provided for by the rules of the House. The third vote, by roll-call, is required by the constitution to be taken when one-fifth of those present so desire. When this vote is taken, the clerk calls each member by name, and enters his vote on the journal, as the constitution demands. The Speaker has nothing whatever to do with this vote but to announce it as reported to him by the clerk. The Speaker cannot officially know whether a member has voted or not. It is not his business to know. It is the duty of the clerk to know and to report to the Speaker, not for his revision, but simply for him to announce the vote to the House, and render the decision which the vote has made necessary. If he has the right to count, he can render the constitutional provision wholly nugatory. For after the vote is taken and no quorum has done business, he can add to the journal as many names as he pleases, whether the members are present or absent, and make a quorum on the journal though it is not in the House.

This would, indeed, be a great scandal; but there would be no way to correct it, if the Speaker can do with the journal as he pleases. When Speaker Blaine was urged to count a quorum when the roll-call showed there was none voting, he indignantly refused, and said that there could be no appeal from the record of the yeas and nays, and that when such a rule was adopted the House would stand on the brink of a volcano. The House adopted it in 1890, and in November the volcano poured forth a volume of lava that blew the House into "innocuous desuetude." He further said that that very principle had been the foundation of probably the greatest legislative frauds ever committed, and that where speakers had declared a quorum present against the result of a roll-call in State legislatures, the proceedings had brought scandal on their names.

Mr. Blaine seems not to have been alone in holding that opinion, for the States in recent years have been making these frauds and scandals impossible by providing in their constitutions the rule that had for a century been observed in the national House of Representatives. The constitutions of Alabama, Arkansas, Colorado, Illinois, Iowa, Kansas, Maryland, Michigan, Missouri, Nebraska, Nevada, New Jersey, Oregon, Pennsylvania, Tennessee, Kentucky, California, New York, and Georgia require a majority of all who may be members to constitute a quorum to pass bills. They refuse to let their speakers go behind the roll-call to count a quorum. Here is overwhelming authority as to the correctness of the practice of all the speakers preceding Speaker Reed, and of the correctness of the interpretation of the constitution which for a century they gave. These provisions would never have appeared in these constitutions if it had not been for the scandals and frauds that had occurred in some legislatures by reason of the rule that permitted the speakers to count a quorum present when the record showed it was not present. If the Republican party should continue in power in the House, these frauds and scandals would appear in the federal as they did in the State legislatures.

Happily for the country, the volcanic eruption of November, 1890, has made that impossible, and the next House will return to the constitution and the footprints of the fathers.

It is asked, if a majority does not vote and members cannot be made to vote, and cannot be counted as present to make a quorum, what good can be accomplished by compelling the attendance of absentees ? The answer is that when all absentees are present there must be a majority on one side or the other of every question. A majority of those present are always ready to act without compulsion, but they are not sufficiently numerous to make the constitutional quorum. Compulsory attendance supplies the requisite number, and that acts of its own volition. If those who are opposing a measure find, when their numbers are full, that they can defeat it by voting against it, they will do so without compulsion; if those who are advocating it find, when the House is full, that they can pass it, they will do so without compulsion and end the struggle. The compulsory attendance, therefore, is to produce the constitutional quorum, and let the advocates of the measure take to themselves the whole responsibility for its passage, instead of compelling those who oppose it to supply the quorum and share with its friends the responsibility for a measure which the minority hold to be fraught with the direst mischief.

All this controversy about a quorum is produced by the absenteeism of those who advocate the measure over which the conflict occurs. Its friends present, not having the constitutional number required to pass it, try to do so by making their opponents do a part of the necessary work to accomplish it ; and that the latter refuse to do. The Representative who abstains from voting feels that he can best represent the interests of his constituents by withholding his vote, and that right never should be usurped or surrendered.   .

No rule of any parliamentary assembly in this country should ever compel any member to vote or abstain from voting. Whether it is right for him to do the one or the other is a matter over which his constituents should have exclusive jurisdiction. The Representative will know the wishes of those whom he represents and his duty to them, and our government is founded on the idea that he is capable of performing it, and will do it better when left to himself than when acting under the constraint of others.

Those who deny the right of the Representative to withhold his vote say that it delays legislation and prevents the majority from attending to public business. That it delays legislation deemed to be hurtful and mischievous is not denied ; and that it only occurs as against measures which the opposition regard as revolutionary is equally true. In the language of a distinguished Republican statesman, a measure "should not be passed until it is systematized and reduced in the alembic of deliberation, through the slow processes prescribed by the rules."

All legislation, to be wise and beneficent, should be well considered, and accomplished after thorough deliberation. Wild, revolutionary, and unconstitutional legislation should be resisted by all the means which parliamentary tactics can supply. Rules are not only intended to provide for the enactment of proper legislation, but to hinder, obstruct, and check all revolutionary schemes which parliamentary assemblies may attempt to pass. An extraordinary measure provokes extraordinary opposition, which cries "check," and shelters itself under constitutional power to protect constitutional rights. From reckless and unbridled majorities inflated with ambition to retain power, right or wrong, the opposition appeals to " the sober second thought of the people," upon whose immovable foundation all our institutions rest.

ROGER Q. MILLS.

MR. REED:

IT IS the fault of most discussions which are decided incorrectly that they are decided by the misuse of terms. Unfortunately, words have very little precision, and mean one thing to one man and a different thing to another. Words also are used with one meaning and quoted with another. When men speak of the rights of minorities and claim for them the sacredness of established law, they are correct or incorrect according as they interpret the word " rights."

A man has a right to an estate in fee simple, a right to land, and there is no right more indisputable under our system. Nothing but the supreme law can take the estate away, and then only after compensation. The same man has a right of passage over land used as a highway, but his town or county can take that privilege away from him without his consent and without compensation. In both cases the man has rights, but the rights are entirely different, and the difference arises from the nature of things. It is good for the community, or at least it has been so thought, that a man should have unrestricted right over his land. On it he can build as high as heaven or dig as deep as a prob· able hereafter. This is not because it is pleasant for the man, but because it is best for the community. Therefore his right to build or dig is limited by the right of eminent domain—the right of the whole people to take his property at any time for the common benefit on paying its value.

For the same reason the right of a man to walk over the land of a roadway is an inferior right which may more easily be taken from him ; for if it be more convenient for the whole community that nobody should walk over that land, each man's right, which is a perfect right while it exists, is taken away from him, and he alone bears the loss.

It is hardly neeessary to multiply examples in order to lay a foundation for the assertion that the rights, so called, of any man or set of men have their foundation only in the common good.

There is no such thing as an unrepealable bill of rights. Even the constitution of the United States can be changed by due process of law. So long as that instrument remains unchanged, the rights secured under it remain fixed. When it is changed, the rights obliterated cease. By that constitution the majority voluntarily limited its own powers. But this limitation was not for the sake of the minority, but for the good of the whole nation. No system of government could long exist which sacrificed the many to the few.

During the last Congress there was much talk by the Democratic press, and much haranguing on the floor of Congress, about the rights of minorities. Most of the talk and about all of the haranguing were based upon the false idea that the rights in question were real estate in fee simple, not to be diverted, instead of public rights of way, to be changed any time the majority deemed it to be for the good of the community.

Another source of error in all this loose and unsatisfactory haranguing was the notion entertained that a minority in Congress is always a political minority. Three-quarters of the questions which arise are not political. One-half at least of the bad results of disorder and wilfulness on the part of the few against the many were not political. The worst filibuster I ever knew, except that which by killing the Force Bill years ago handed over the Southern Republicans to the tender mercies of their foes, was against the refund of the direct tax, which had been reported by a Democratic committee in a Democratic House, where it had a two-thirds vote, or nearly so, ready to be cast whenever it could be counted. The question of the settlement of the debt of the Union Pacific road was not at all a political question. Men divided without any reference to party. But a hearing on the bill was refused, not because any political minority opposed it, but because two Representatives were allowed to stifle it in the supposed interest of the farmer politicians, to whose subsequent vengeance both these gentlemen fell victims.

When our government was formed, there were two contending elements, the same two which fight everywhere and at all times—conservatism and progress ; but at that time both elements faced each other with more than the usual definiteness of purpose. The ideas which finally culminated in the French Revolution had been gradually spreading over the world, and had been imbibed by certain of our statesmen ; but they were much modified by the pride of locality and the great desire on the part of each and all of the great commonwealths to retain untouched as much of their unfederated power as was possible, consistent with making a suitable front to the foreign world.

Frank, outspoken, open government of the people by the people was a very novel experiment. The most intelligent men had grave doubts of the wisdom of the masses. In fact, the idea of really letting out of chains all the people, giving them unrestricted power, had not much more support than it would have to-day in Russia. Hence the constant striving for checks and limitations. While progress ran to all lengths in the Declaration of Independence, conservatism held its own in the constitution of the United States.

If the House of Representatives can be readily brought to book every two years, the President, with his tremendous veto power, can be dislodged only at the end of four years, and even the House itself defeated by the people survives its own defeat an entire session. When four years have elapsed, and both House and President have been swept away by the popular vote, it often happens that the public have to reckon with a Senate which cannot be displaced. All these things and many others were consciously or unconsciously concessions to that conservatism which distrusted the people, and built itself upon the idea that the intelligence which is held by the minority, and comes from birth and books, is superior to the intelligence which is held by the majority and comes from practical life.

The same circumstances which made our constitution have contributed to preserve it nominally unaltered in most respects. Nevertheless, while the constitution has been preserved, it has been much stretched, and otherwise, by wearing, more or less fitted to the young giant which it covered in many places rather too tightly. If the constitution had not been persuaded sometimes by judicial interpretation, and sometimes by legislative interpretation, to grow up with the country, if there had not been a very great chance to let out at the seams on the general-welfare and taxation and other like clauses, it is to be feared that the country would have been cramped or the constitution burst.

If by the aid of any witch of Endor one of our forefathers could have been beguiled from the New Jerusalem to listen to

Mr. Reagan expounding the Inter-State-Commerce Act, he would have returned heavenward in a paralysis of amazement, after learning that all that millennium was to be accomplished under the power to regulate commerce between the States. Or if he had been present when the needs of our farming community demanded protection against oleomargarine, he would have been startled to find that adulteration of food could be dealt with by the Union, and that, too, under the taxing clause.

These are but examples of how the public welfare gets taken care of by the insistence of majorities whenever the demand is sufficiently imperative.

This constitution of ours is, however, the only charter of the rights of minorities. The rights therein secured are in their nature like the right of ownership of real estate. They cannot be directly attacked. What are called the rights of minorities in deliberative assemblies are like the right of any individual in a highway, subject at all times to the control of the whole community. Strictly speaking, they are, like the rights in a highway, bestowed not for the benefit of the minority, but solely for the benefit of the whole.

A few examples will make this very clear, and will show how many of the discussions of the last two years were mere misuse of terms.

Among the most cherished so-called rights of minorities is the right of debate. But is that in any sense a right of minorities as such? What is debate, and what is it for? It is not merely a display of the vocabularies of orators. It is not a sacred privilege of talk for no purpose. It is permitted solely to guide the whole assembly to right conclusions. Men join in debate, when they fulfil honestly its mission, for the purpose of pointing out the advantages of the thing proposed or the objections which exist against it. Debate is intended to throw light on the subject from all directions, so that there may be no delusions arising from the shadows. Now, what is all this for? For the benefit of those who in the result turn out to be the fewer in number? By no manner of means. All this light is thrown, not to enable the minority to prevent conclusions, but to enable the majority to come to right conclusions. It hardly needs more than this statement to show that any right of debate which prevents results by obstruction, instead of guiding to correct results by enlightenment, is a perversion of honest purpose which ought to receive condemnation and repression.

Some also of the rights of minorities are supposed to reside in the rules of a deliberative body. These are said to be the charters of the power held by the fewer. The same quiet examination of the nature of rules will dispose of that assumption as readily as considerations from the nature itself of debate have disposed of that right of the minority.

What are rules for ? What are rules ? The constitution uses the full expression, and says that each house may determine the "rules of its proceedings." How does a house proceed ? Solely by majorities. Rules, then, are only methods of procedure established, not for the benefit of the few, but to enable the whole body to accomplish in an orderly and systematic way its duties and purposes. What can it be but a perversion of words to claim that in rules of procedure are sacred rights of non-procedure ? that a systematic way of doing something gives the right to a systematic power of preventing the very thing the rules were established to accomplish ? It is perfectly true that while rules exist they should be followed ; not, however, because of the minority, but because, having been established by the whole body, only the whole body can abrogate them. Whenever the whole body choose to change them, no one has any right of complaint. And if in the rules themselves there are provisions for their own suspension or temporary modification, no one has any right to find fault.

Yet when in the Forty-seventh Congress, after full, exhaustive, and exhausting debate, the House determined to change its rules, the whole Democratic press of the country burst into one wild shout against the outrage ; and one would have thought that liberty lay dead at the base of her own altar. When in the Fifty-first Congress the Committee on Rules, to suppress factious opposition, used the power granted them for that very purpose, and gave the whole body an opportunity to decide whether the obstruction should cease, there was language used which the horrors of the French Revolution would not have justified. No doubt half the people thought there must have been some stretch, at least, of power. Men in general know so little of how business is done in Congress, and how it is prevented from being done, that any outcry receives at least half-credence.

In fact, the lack of knowledge on the part of the public, their ignorance of their own affairs, is the great reservoir from which the Democracy always draws. It takes time to expose lies, and they always seem so trivial to those who are acting the truth that only after they are well embedded in the popular thought do the friends of truth realize what a potent thing a lie is in an imperfect world. Sometimes only the logic of events can dislodge a lie. In truth, it is doubtful if argument ever did do it.

When, less than a year ago, the whole Democratic party, the entire Democratic press, and all the shop-keepers, actuated by an honest desire to sell goods and pressed by tight money, were proclaiming, on the advent of the McKinley Bill, a carnival of high prices that would deprive the poor man of his tin dinner-pail, and strip from the backs of the women their woollen frocks, and otherwise play Moloch to the Hebrew children, no argument could meet it, and hundreds of good men went down with the avalanche of lies. To-day the logic of facts is justifying the wisdom of the doctrine of protection in its latest manifestation, and the farmer is finding plenty of chances for his bushel of wheat. Yea, even his barrel of pork may find lodgement somewhere.

The doctrine of the right of the majority to rule in legislative assemblies cannot hope to escape the general danger of misrepresentation. There are many interests which are concerned to perpetuate the rule of the few. The Southern men are fearful that this nation will some day awaken, as it has once before awakened, from the false idea that commerce is all, and that peace and quietness ought to be purchased at any price, to the nobler idea that human liberty is beyond all price, and that the government of all by all is the very foundation of our system. There are some men who desire, when this happens, that the few shall be so intrenched in forms and usages that they may keep the many entirely out of control. The same may be said of all vested interests and vested wrongs. These are all enlisted on the side of repression.

But the great immediate power which has for so many years prevented the manifestation of the power of the majority—the power which has kept the control in the hands of the few—is the combination or concert of old members, who, knowing the rules and being skilled in all the arts of killing bills without being caught, and of depriving the community of what it wants while exhibiting zeal the other way, are enabled to govern the House and perpetuate their own rule.

It will be an interesting spectacle in the new House to watch the process by which the new members will be persuaded to surrender their rights, to go gently under the yoke, and to witness their wonder and perplexity when they find that somehow or other they cannot do what they want to do, even after they have convinced the majority that it will be the right thing to do. They will then find that the gentlemen who have so sedulously hedged them in to protect. them against the wicked Republicans have reserved for themselves a veto power greater than is intrusted by the wisdom of the constitution to the wisdom of the President. They will also find that there is no greater fallacy than the idea that majority and minority are predicated of political parties only. It will soon become evident that many questions on which parties divide—questions which concern the welfare of the entire community, and which are of all questions the most suitable to be decided by superiority of numbers—will be really under the control of some minority with a crank for a leader, whom the rules of the House will make victorious over numbers and sense alike. Then there will be wailing and wagging of tongues.

Conservatism is, of course, not to be undervalued. The advantages of time and reflection cannot be overestimated. Things ought not to be done rashly or hastily. But in this country, with the fullest power of control by majorities in either house of Congress, things cannot be done hastily or rashly. Too many currents of power have to join forces under our constitution to make the determination of legislative action anything but the consensus of the people. The States, both great and small, have two Senators each. No Senator can be disturbed during six years. If the Senators, representing States, and the members of the House, representing populations, both agree, there is a double guarantee, each for the other, against the idea that rash or hasty action has been had. If, then, the President agrees, though elected at a different time and by a different system from either house, we have another safeguard. Indeed, we have so many safeguards that the wonder is how anybody dared tie up the people so tightly.

If to all these be added the divine right of a minority to stop all business, surely this government, of which we have made rather frequent and obtrusive boasting as being a government of the people, is only an irresponsible despotism. For despotism was never anything more than the rule of the few over the many.

It is a curious fact that while we have relaxed none of our conservative safeguards, but rather have striven to add to them, even to the very verge of unreason, the world outside, the abode of the " worn-out and effete dynasties " has become more and more progressive until many European governments are as fairly representative of the people and responsive to their will as our own, and some much more so.

In England the House of Commons may vote out a ministry and change the whole policy of the country, domestic and foreign. This the members do as representatives of the people, for if a ministry think the people are not with Parliament, they may go to the people by a general election and must abide the result.

With us the new House will overwhelmingly try to reverse the policy of its predecessor, and the President and cabinet and the Senate will move on, let us hope, as serenely as if nothing had happened. Of course this new House was elected with full knowledge that the Senate and President would hold them in check. But even if the people had very determined intentions, and had meant a complete overthrow, they could have accomplished nothing, because of the constitutional system of checks on popular power. While our constitutional checks can command much to be said in their favor, yet they have many disadvantages, and not the least of them is the undecisive nature of our elections. Men vote with less regard for results in proportion as the natural results are made uncertain.

However that may be, the checks and balances of the constitution are enough to preserve us without setting up a divine right of minorities and still further depriving the people of power. All other countries are growing more and more every day into the sound belief that common-sense is the best sense, that a government on the general level is the soundest government, and that the people as a whole are wiser than the most learned men. The United States also ought to keep pace, within the limits of the constitution, with the progress of the race, and at least demand that in its legislative assemblies the majority shall have the right to control to the extent of the full powers of the body to which they belong, and that the public business shall not be left at the mercy of obstructive politicians who have at heart the rule of party rather than the rule of the people.

THOMAS B. REED.

THE QUESTION OF THE QUORUM.

BY THE LATE MANUEL ALONZO MARTINEZ, PRESIDENT OF THE SPANISH CHAMBER OF DEPUTIES.

In the last legislative session of the House of Representatives of the United States, the majority, on the proposition of the Speaker of the House, added a new article to the regulations, which provides that, when it is desired to know whether there is a quorum of members present, the total number of Representatives present at the time of voting, not only those who vote, but also those who do not vote, shall be counted.

The opinion of the undersigned has been asked : (1) On this reform of the rules of the House of Representatives of the United States. (2) On the general question of the quorum in Spain.

I.

Although an eminent writer of ancient Spanish America [1] defines parliamentary law, from a purely theoretic point of view, as that branch of science which investigates the principles to which the constitution and procedure of legislative assemblies should conform,[†] he is, nevertheless, obliged to recognize that this science is so new that it may be said to be in course of formation, and that, though Jefferson, Erskine May, Cushing, Pondra y Piene, Franqueville, Mancini y Galeoti, and other authors have given us valuable information upon the matter, their works have been all confined to a simple exposition of parliamentary procedure as current in North America, in England, in France, and in Italy. He holds that they have rendered a signal service in thus preparing the way for scientific investigations upon this branch of law, by the accumulation of material, but that they have made no theoretic progress in the science.

In the opinion of the author cited, Bentham alone consecrated

[*] " El Poder Legislatif," by Justino Jimener de Aréchaga, Vol. II. Published by A. Beneiro y Ramos (Libreria Nacional), Montevideo, 1890.
[†] Ibid, p. 9.

himself to the study of the principles to which parliamentary constitution and procedure should conform, his essay on "Parliamentary Tactics," published near the beginning of this century, being a veritable treatise on the science of parliamentary law ; but, adds Señor Jimener de Aréchaga, as is generally the case with works which initiate a special order of investigation, a very incomplete one.

In fact, the essay on "Parliamentary Tactics " is so incomplete upon the point now under consideration that, although Bentham devotes the whole of the eighteenth chapter to it, he only says, in substance, that if satisfactory statutes were enacted to prevent non-attendance, there would be no need of recourse to the quorum or the determination of the number of representatives necessary to constitute an assembly ; that the principal aim of the quorum is to compel attendance through respect for public opinion ; that those who direct assemblies are forced to take vexatious measures to insure the presence of a complete number ; and that rigorous measures are excusable if the negligence be extreme ; adding that the quorum is the last expedient to which recourse should be had to obtain the desired result.

As will be readily seen, there is nothing in these remarks of Bentham resembling a scientific principle capable of theoretically solving, apart from considerations of time and place, the questions which arise on the establishment or reform of the quorum in any legislative assembly, and there is nothing rash in the belief that the ideas so vaguely expressed by the illustrious English jurisconsult were inspired by the recollection of the words of a certain Speaker of the House of Commons who, closing the sitting for the first time on April 26, 1729, because there were not forty members present, declared that "members who abandon the discussion of the most grave affairs of state to amuse themselves in taverns and gaming-houses are unworthy of the position they hold as members of this House."

In the absence, therefore, of established scientific principles admitted of common accord by legal writers, and of authorities to aid us in judgments upon this matter of the quorum or on any other point of parliamentary law, any opinion formed upon the two subjects proposed at the head of this paper should take into account the circumstances of each country, not only as to the relation of the constitutional régime, whether it be representative or parliamentary, to the fundamental laws of the constitution—generally different upon the question of the attendance of representatives at the meetings of the legislative chambers—and to the constitutional means of obtaining or exacting their attendance, but also in relation to temporary circumstances, which rightfully exercise so large an influence in politics considered as the art of government, and on the resolutions of the governing body or its constituent elements.

Things being as they are, it would be a vain presumption on the part of the undersigned to pretend to as thorough a knowledge as his interrogator—an eminent writer of the United States—possesses of the customs of the representatives of that country, so distinct from all the nations of the old world ; and consequently the opinions here expressed have been formed without the aid of that certitude which is the capital element of all verdicts, and which largely rules judgment in political matters.

To the undersigned, limited to the knowledge which he has obtained from books, and starting with the general principle that the regulations of the legislative assemblies of a country should be inspired by the same spirit and reasons as govern its constitution and its fundamental laws, it does not appear hazardous to maintain that in countries where the representative régime is in force—of which the great North American republic is the model—it is more necessary than in countries subjected to the parliamentary régime—as are almost all European monarchies and republics—to insist that the assiduous and constant attendance of a majority of members of the assemblies devoted to the exercise of legislative functions is of transcendent importance to the rights and dues of the nation at large, and to maintain that the constitution of the United States differs from the fundamental laws of all other countries in regard to the quorum by the means it assures the legislative assembly of imposing its authority upon the members who compose it.

By virtue of one section of that constitution only a majority constitutes a deliberative quorum ; but a smaller number may adjourn from day to day, and are authorized to compel absent members to put in an appearance, by what means and under what penalties each house may determine. The second clause of the same section provides that each house may decide upon its own rules of procedure, may punish its members for bad conduct, and, with the assent of two-thirds of its voting members, may expel the offenders.

In accordance with these provisions of the fundamental law, the regulations of the lower house decree that every member shall be present in the legislative building during the sessions of the assembly unless he has been excused, or in a case of unavoidable absence ; also that he shall be under an obligation to vote on all questions unless he has been freed from this duty on a motion presented before the division or the roll-call has commenced and the debate closed, and unless he has a personal or pecuniary interest in the matter under discussion. It is also enacted that if a quorum be not present, fifteen members, inclusive of the Speaker, may compel the absent members to appear ; to this end, at every roll-call the names of absent members should be recorded, the doors closed, and those members in whose name no sufficient excuse has been presented may, by virtue of an order of the majority of the members present, be sought for—wherever they may be— by officers appointed for the purpose by the sergeant-at-arms, arrested, and conducted to the legislative assembly, which then decides on what condition they shall be released.

All this, which is in perfect harmony with the constitutional provisions already set forth, and which is completed by the large privileges which the Representatives enjoy by virtue of this same constitution and of other more recent laws, is quite foreign to European parliamentary law and procedure ; but we cannot do less than to take account of it, in judging the reform concerning the quorum with which our first question deals.

Certain words employed by my interrogator in formulating his question seem to indicate that what has occasioned the excitement produced by the reform of the regulations of the North American House of Representativas is the fact that, to render the working of the quorum regulation satisfactory when its application is necessary, the total number of members present in the House at the time of voting is counted—not only those who vote, but those who do not vote—for the reasons given above, and this resolution does really appear very strange ; but, in the opinion of the undersigned, it is less strange than it is taken to be at first sight, not only in North America, but in parliamentary Europe, whose constitutions, laws, regulations, customs, and usages differ so much from those of the United States of America.

In the United States the right of demanding a quorum has two objects. First, to insure that whatever may be voted shall be voted by a majority of the Representatives who represent to the country the majority of her citizens, and to insure that the Representatives shall perform the duty of presence which the constitution imposes upon them under penalty of the punishments which the assembly has the right to inflict and has decreed in its regulations ; which explains the unity of the law established by the reform of the regulations here under consideration. The reform has also another distinct object, which, like the previous one, is in conformity both with the letter and with the spirit of the constitution of the United States of America. Otherwise it would be necessary to consign to oblivion the discussion of the subject of which something was said at the beginning and which it is convenient to explain somewhat more fully at this point.

As Jefferson notices in his " Manual of Parliamentary Practice," the name quorum is derived from the custom, which still exists in England and in the Roman Chancellorship, of giving to certain acts of the government the name of the legislative actions they decree or of the formulæ which are proper to them. Jefferson also considers it a reasonable hypothesis that the name given to the number of members who suffice to constitute an assembly originated in some formula which commenced with the word quorum. Since April 26, 1729, not only the word but its signification and the parliamentary customs derived from it have spread from England to all assemblies of the old and the new world.

Well, from the day when, for the first time, the Speaker closed the session of the House of Commons with the remark that there were not forty members present, and from the 5th of January, 1640, when in the same chamber the question arose whether there were or were not a sufficient number of members present to open the session, and it was decided negatively because there were not forty members in attendance, up to the present time, every individual member of the House of Commons is entitled, and may use his right at any moment of the session, either when it has been announced that a vote is about to be taken or during a discussion, to demand that the number of members present shall be counted, thus often delaying by many hours and sometimes by several days the taking of a vote.

In such cases a sand-glass is placed upon the table, and during the two minutes its upper cavity takes to empty, electric bells are rung in all the precincts of the chamber. Thereupon the members who are in the corridors, in the library, or in the refreshment rooms repair promptly to the chamber. The sandglass run out, the Speaker counts the number of members present ; if the total is less than forty, he closes the session, or, rather, adjourns it to the following day ; if the total exceeds forty, the session continues.

From these facts it may be inferred that the function of the quorum, both originally and in its developments, as practised by the nation which, at least in Europe, passes for an authority on these matters, is in itself independent of the vote, inasmuch as the validity of this latter necessitates the existence of a quorum, which varies infinitely in different countries and even at different epochs in the same country.

In virtue of these considerations, having had no opportunity of acquiring an intimate knowledge of the customs of the members of the House of Representatives of the United States of America, which may have induced the Speaker to propose and the majority to approve the reform of its regulations which has been adopted, I think that this reform is not in opposition to, but is in harmony with, the letter and the spirit of the constitution, and with the regulations in force in the House of Representatives, and also that it is in conformity with the spirit and general meaning of the quorum of the British Parliament, which, since 1729 and 1640, has been adopted by all the legislative assemblies of the world.

II.

When, in 1836, the constitutional and parliamentary régime was definitely established in Spain, the royal decree dated August 21, 1836, convoking the Cortes, contained, in accordance with the constitution of 1812, a clause to the effect that the deputies should perform their duties gratuitously until the Cortes had determined upon the best course to be taken with regard to article 102 of the said constitution, in which it was provided that the provinces should pay their respective deputies the salary which the representatives then forming the Cortes voted to subsequent parliaments.

This clause, amplified and confirmed by article 58 of the electoral law of July 18, 1837, provided that, as long as senators and deputies performed their duties gratuitously, they might resign their mandate whenever they so wished, even after having accepted it and having commenced to exercise their functions. The principle of unpaid parliamentary representation has survived in the Spanish political Right, and to it is chiefly due the opinion that the assiduous attendance of senators and deputies at their respective chambers cannot be and ought not to be rigorously exacted. It has on several occasions caused the rejection of the proposal that non-attendant members should be subjected to an efficacious judicial punishment ; it being pointed out that non-attendance might be considered as a renunciation of functions on the part of the senator or deputy who absented himself under such circumstances as might determine the necessity of imposing upon him a punishment for the said absence.

An immediate result of this opinion is the existence of articles 202 and 203 of the regulations of Congress, which provide that, if any deputy has occasion to absent himself for more than eight days, he must request the permission of Congress, explaining his motives in writing and stating the time during which he desires to absent himself, so that Congress shall consider his request and accede to it if it be judged warrantable ; but that, since it is essential that at all sessions the number of deputies which the constitution indicates as necessary to formulate laws should be in attendance, leave of absence shall never be accorded to more than a third of the number in excess of the number of members necessary to form a quorum. In the generality of cases, however, members absent themselves without requesting leave of absence, and it is not the custom to make any kind of remonstrance with regard to such absences.

The same thing happens in the Senate, although articles 59 and 60 of its regulations reproduce in substance the provisions of articles 202 and 203 of the regulations of Congress, cited above.

As to the quorum, the regulations which govern its application in the Spanish chambers may be resumed in the following terms:

According to article 43 of the constitution it is essential for the validity of the laws passed by each of the legislative bodies that one more than half the total number of individuals composing the body shall be present ; a principle which, in turn, inspires article 214 of the regulations of the Senate and article 179 of the regulations of Congress, whose purport is that the constitutional mandate is applicable only to the final voting of laws, and not to votes which are taken merely on individual articles.

In computing the total number of individuals who compose each legislative body—both in the Senate and in Congress—only those senators and deputies are counted who have not been simply admitted, but have in addition taken the oath.

The constitution is silent as to the number of senators and deputies necessary to definitely constitute either of these legislative bodies, and the omission in the fundamental laws is filled up by the respective regulations of the Senate and of Congress.

By virtue of and conformably to article 30 of the regulations of the Senate, in the first legislative session succeeding the renewal of the elective portion of this chamber, the examination of acts and measures of the second category being terminated, if afterwards one more than half the total number of senators present is admitted, the definite constitution of the Senate is, by common consent, proceeded with ; whereas, conformably with article 34 and the concordant articles 10 and 11, when the legislature has undergone neither a complete nor a partial renewal of its elective portion, the Senate is definitely constituted as soon as fifty senators are present to nominate the four secretaries.

Articles 37 and 15 of the regulations of Congress require for its definite constitution in the first legislative session of each parliament that there shall be admitted at least as many deputies as are necessary to vote the laws, and in the second and succeeding sessions at least that same necessary number of deputies shall be present.

To open and continue the sessions of the Senate, according to article 109 of its regulations at least thirty senators must be present, and forty suffice to pass any resolution excepting the definite adoption of a project of law.

In Congress, conformably to article 107 of its regulations, at least seventy deputies must be present to open the session, and this number suffices to pass any resolution excepting the definite adoption of a project of law ; but the presence of no given number of deputies is required to continue the session, when once opened, or to maintain a debate.

The Senate, like Congress, is divided into sections ; and, according to article 68 of the regulations of the first of these assemblies, to open the session in each of these sections at least ten senators are required to assemble, but if, fifteen minutes after the hour appointed, it is found that the president, vice-president, secretary, and under secretary are absent, they may be replaced, for that session only, by substitutes chosen among themselves by the members present.

The regulations of Congress contain no rule concordant with article 68 just mentioned.

On the other hand, in order that decisions arrived at upon the validity or nullity of laws classed as important may have a definite character, article·36 of the regulations of Congress requires that the number of deputies present shall in no case be less than one hundred and forty ; whereas the regulations of the Senate do not require the attendance of any particular quorum for the passing of important laws.

The principal regulations which require the attendance of senators and deputies at the deliberations of the legislative corps to which they respectively belong, and the various quorums proper to each of these assemblies, having been indicated, it should be added that, excepting the quorum necessary to pass laws and to definitely constitute Congress,—which increases and diminishes in proportion to the number of individual members of whom, according to the constitution, the chamber may be composed, or to the number who actually compose it at any given time,— these quorums do not represent the quotient of a dividend and divisor previously established, but, as far as Congress is concerned, a figure decided upon many years ago, when the number of deputies who formed the assembly was far less than it should be according to the electoral law annulled by that of June, 1890, which reëstablished universal suffrage.

Notwithstanding that by this last law the number of deputies may be augmented, there is to-day no current of opinion in Spain in favor of an increase in any one of the quorums already mentioned.

As to the establishment of new regulations to insure the constant attendance of senators and deputies at their respective chambers, the common opinion is that it is best to have recourse to indirect means of obtaining attendance ; but it is certain that no measures framed with a view to forward this end by the imposition of penalties for non-attendance could be proposed without encountering serious opposition.

The utmost ever obtained in this matter, on two distinct occasions, separated by an interval of twenty-two years, was the establishment of the custom of noting down the names of the deputies on their arrival at the Congress House. As soon as the number of seventy was reached, the session was opened with the reading of the list thus formed, which was then published in the journal of the sessions (*Diario de Sesiones*); but the presidents who adopted this plan were never able to maintain it for any considerable time, and to-day it would be no longer possible to put it into practice without running directly counter to public opinion, which would repel this kind of moral coercion were it applied to the representatives of the nation.

The advocates of the parliamentary régime grieve over the fact that but a scanty number of deputies and senators take part in the discussion and adoption of projects of great importance to the country, and over the difficulties so frequently experienced in obtaining the attendance of a sufficient number of members to open the session ; yet they would themselves disapprove any measures of a more energetic character than a suave admonition made by the president in open session, and formulated in such general terms as to render it entirely free from the character of a correction administered to any single individual.

The undersigned considers, therefore, that, as long as the services of senators and deputies continue to be rendered gratuitously, public opinion will demand no alteration or reform whatsoever in the regulations relating to the quorum in the Spanish legislative bodies.

MANL. ALONZO MARTINEZ.

FRENCH NOVELS AND FRENCH LIFE.

BY ANDREW LANG.

Do FRENCH novels give a fair picture of French life ? According to Madame Adam they do not. But I never knew people yet who admitted that any written account of their own life and of themselves was true. Consider the sorrows of Mr. Froude, and remember how the colonists arose up and did not call him blessed. No English traveller's account of America is admitted to be true ; no American traveller's account of England. These things are written by strangers. But I never was acquainted with a literary Scotchman whose written Scotch was accepted as good Scotch by his countrymen at home. You cannot satisfy people by pictures of their manners and peculiarities. There is no novel of life at Oxford which Oxford men recognize as correct. The critics, who are also to some extent the characters, invariably say that they are misrepresented.

Thus Madame Adam may possibly overstate her case, unless she is superior to an almost universal kind of sentiment. She tells us that the laboring classes of Paris decline to see themselves as M. Zola sees them. He is, indeed, such a fantastic and romantic writer that he always exaggerates, and, probably, represents the exception as the type. It is not in nature that an honest and kindly *ouvrier* should like M. Zola's drunkards and debauchees ; still one may guess that there is an element of likeness in the caricature. Now, an element of likeness, a resemblance more or less close, is all that we can hope for in any picture. Every picture will be colored by the artist in accordance with his own eyesight. M. Zola, like Turner in old age, will see things in yellow. George Sand saw them in rose. Her peasants are not absolutely true to nature, nor are the very different peasants of Balzac. It is a question of degree, of the less or more ; and so it must be in all studies of human life.

These are obvious, but necessary, considerations. For the rest, to a foreigner who seeks information from Madame Adam her interesting essay seems too abstract. It is certain, as she says, that Paris draws to herself all literary France; that men are almost obliged, if they would be known, to leave their country towns; and that they do not love their country towns is very probable. Literature is their profession; their interests are in literature. They cannot, as a rule, find like-minded people in Poictiers or Tours any more than I could expect to find many of of them in Kelso or Elgin.

Again, at home their view of society is limited by class. If they are of the middle class, it is nearly as difficult for them to know the workmen as to know the *noblesse*. We all regret these gulfs, but they exist, and even in pure socialism there will inevitably be "sets," just as there are in the peerage, where, if anywhere, all are peers. The son of a notary, who can write and wishes to write, may love his kindred and their friends at home, but he cannot confine his observations to them, nor perpetually put his aunts and cousins into his novels. He must go to Paris, where there is a good deal of variety, and so, as Madame Adam says, novels are written in Paris, for Parisians, by Parisians. There is no getting out of that fatal circle, and we must remember that French novels represent life less as it is than as Parisians like to have it represented. Moreover, we must allow for the choice of situations and sentiments new rather than true, and fashionable rather than permanently human.

We must always make these deductions; but, when they are made, do French novels, on the whole, give a true picture of French life? A foreigner can only ask the question. Here it is that he finds Madame Adam's account too abstract. For example, take the broad differences between French novels on one side and English or American novels on the other side. In our fiction (by "our" I mean that of the English-speaking people) almost all the love is between bachelor and maid, and the goal is the altar. In French fiction almost all the love is between man, married or single, and the wedded wives of other men. What we wish to know is this: Does the absence of honorable love-making between the young people of French fiction correspond in any degree, and, if so, in what degree, to its absence in real life? Again, does the preponderance of lawless love in French fiction answer in any degree, and, if so, in what degree, to a like preponderance in actual fact?

Naturally I am not pretending that we Anglo-Saxons are more " moral " than the French. Scandal for scandal, " appalling revelation " for " shocking disclosure," perhaps we have the worst of it. But if there is as much honorable " courting " in France as in England or America, the fact does not come out in French fiction. Perhaps the French do not find it interesting to read about; or, again, they may consider it too sacred a theme for the novelist's art. It is only plain that there is a great difference of taste between French and English novel-readers: how far that difference of taste answers to difference in life we cannot tell, and Madame Adam does not tell us.

In our own life it is obvious that, in some classes, high and low, a certain commandment is no more honored than it is in France. But we do not wish to read about intrigues in our fiction, and our difference in taste must not blind us to something very like identity in morals. Thus, just as there is plenty of intrigue in some sections of English life, though very little of it in English novels, so there may be plenty of prenuptial affection . in French life, though in French novels we seldom find it sympathetically handled. But, then, if it exists in a large degree, why is it so systematically ignored? That is one of the things about which we aliens desire information.

A French critic may ask, in reply, wherefore, if we have plenty of loose living, we do not represent it in our fiction. Is it because we are prudes and hypocrites? Not altogether. We have an impression that, however much guilty passion may be abroad, it would not be diminished, but rather increased, by pictures of its indulgence. The set of public opinion is decidedly against such intrigues; and the examples of it which occur are not calculated to alter that which is decidedly the general sentiment. I do not mean to hint that the general sentiment is less honorable in France; but I do think that French novels might lead one more or less into that opinion. To that extent, then, French novels may be misleading, and, in studying them, we must allow for the influence of an old tradition and for the special taste of certain circles in Paris. Again, of course, the liberty of our girls is so great that it would be hard to keep any English novels from them. Thus our novelists, as some of them complain, have the fear of the young girl before them. In France girls are held more strictly in hand, and it is understood that they only read Walter Scott. Their condition is the more gracious, but here the difference in novels does rest on a difference in social usages.

When we are asked, Do French novels represent French life? we must, of course, distinguish. Nobody supposes that French life is all baccarat, murder, duels, *horizontales,* gay breakfasts, and amateur detectives, as in M. Fortuné du Boisgobey, nor all dirt, drink, curses, and the rest, as in some naturalistic books. Nor is it all compact of parties in country houses, and escapades in the wrong bedrooms, and wit, and raillery, and riding, and shooting, as in the dialogues of Gyp. Xaintrailles is manifestly a caricature, and a caricature is the detestable minor poet in " Un Raté," and one can only hope that Eve is a good likeness. Even a foreigner can see all this plainly enough. Even a foreigner knows that all Academicians are not a set of libidinous *crétins,* as in "L' Immortel"; and it is but in human nature to behave quite like the miners in "Germinal." We do not suppose that all members of *la haute finance* are ill-mannered and corrupt, nor that all French women of fashion are akin to Madame de Flirt. The blue boudoirs of M. Paul Bourget must shelter many duchesses who are not constantly hurrying across Paris to a rendezvous. I decline to believe that many French gentlemen are so forlorn of occupation as to stand about like amateur sentries, without even a dry sentry-box, after the manner of the hero of M. Guy de Maupassant's " Notre Cœur." Paulette is plainly an exceptional little person, nor can there be so many young milliners of beauty and virtue, and high birth, as those who, in M. Xavier de Montépin's legends, are so perpetually kidnapped by miscreants.

Mr. Ruskin has written with a good deal of indignation about French fiction, and, for a moralist, Mr. Ruskin's knowledge of his theme is " extensive and peculiar." But people are not, after all, so very bad. In those endless romances of M. Xavier de Montépin, popular sympathy is always with virtue in distress. The heart of the people, the heart of all peoples, is in the right place. As to the fiction, we see that there is everywhere an immense deal of exaggeration. Engineers are not so clever as M. Ohnet's engineers ; Brazilians are not so unscrupulous as M.

Boisgobey's Brazilians ; *ouvriers* are not such blackguards as
M. Zola's *ouvriers* ; marchionesses are not in so coming-on a humor
as the *marquises* of M. Bourget ; literary men are not so " sair
beside themselves " about hateful actresses as M. Bourget's literary men ; peasants are not so sordid as almost everybody's peasants, and the whole world is not so sentimentally profligate as
nearly the whole world of popular French fiction. " Every one
has a sane spot somewhere in his mind," and even the seventh
commandment has intervals of security and repose.

When we ask whether novels represent life, let us remember
that only an infinitesimal fraction of any people reads novels, or
any other literature. In France, we may be sure, there is a great
worthy middle-class population which never reads. They do not
know the novelists, nor the novelists them. They are unrepre-
sented. Again, those who do read like to read about something
alien to their experience. Alien to it is all that exaggerated profligacy of romance ; so alien that they no more dream of imitating
it than you or I dream of imitating Tiberius, or Chaka, or the
Artful Dodger. To them it is, essentially, a fairy tale, remote,
unenvied, but entertaining. To be sure, if we carried this argument far, we might find ourselves maintaining that the morality
of a nation is in inverse ratio to the immorality of its fiction.
We border on Charles Lamb's perilous theory about the comedies
of the Restoration. Still, there is a certain amount of truth in
our contention.

To most readers, not to all, novels are fairy tales. Thus, allowing for exaggeration, for the taste of the capital, for the *remoteness* of fiction, for the really small number of persons who
read and who are written about, we may decide that French
novels in the mass do not give a truly accurate description of
French society in the mass. For example, I this moment chanced
to look at Miss Price's account of life in Anjou (*Longman's
Magazine*, October, 1891). Now, no French novel had revealed
to me that beautiful survival of the existence of the old *noblesse* at
its best. Gyp's *noblesse* live very differently from Miss Price's.
Their existence seems far too good to last, a fragile relic of what
· was noblest and simplest of old. Good go with it, one hopes ; but
Miss Price's picture is a new and strange picture to at least one
reader of French fiction.

Doubtless fiction does not represent many other noble aspects of French existence. One regrets these omissions, and there are sins of commission too which one regrets. As far as the bulk of French fiction has any influence on young French people (old people are safe), it is seldom excellent except in so far as it is always patriotic. The republic has not killed in France that old chivalrous virtue of patriotism, nor has fiction soiled it, nor commerce nor cynicism laughed it to scorn. The flag is the flag still, be it white or be it tricolor, and I wish that the same spirit were as strong in another country.

To end, as far as a foreigner can determine, French fiction exaggerates much in French life that is evil, and omits much that is noble. Thus its picture cannot be correct; yet, on the whole, novels show what way the popular wind blows, and help a little to produce the modes of action and sentiment which they describe.

Andrew Lang.

WAGES IN MEXICO.

BY M. ROMERO, MEXICAN MINISTER TO THE UNITED STATES.

I HAVE often heard it stated, as the chief reason for advocating restrictions on this country's trade with Mexico, that we pay low wages to our laborers, who are sometimes called paupers or peons, and that the maintenance of the high wages prevailing here requires that the free entrance of Mexican products similar to those of the United States be forbidden. As this reason is repeated whenever it is proposed to adopt liberal measures to promote trade between the two neighboring republics, it seems to me that I might render a service to their better understanding of each other and to their increase of trade, reciprocally advantageous, if I should give an idea of the wages which are paid in Mexico ; of the causes which control their amount; of the manner in which these causes affect the cost and therefore the price of the commodities we produce ; and of the price of Mexican articles obtained with low wages, compared with the same commodities produced here with high wages. I should be very glad if I could in this way help to dispel the mistaken ideas which prevail in this country in regard to the labor and wage system of Mexico, and which stand in the way of measures tending to increase our mutual trade.

The broken surface of Mexico gives us all the climates of the world, frequently at very short distances from each other, and enables us to produce the fruits of all the zones, while placing at our disposal, at the same time, an immense hydraulic power, of which for the present we hardly avail ourselves. But, on the other hand, it makes transportation very expensive ; and this fact renders exceedingly difficult the interchange of products. The obstacles to communication between the various sections of the country, and the diversity of conditions existing in each, cause a great difference in the wages paid in different localities.

The Department of Public Works of the Mexican Government has been for some time collecting exact data regarding the wages paid to field laborers, and during my last visit to the City of Mexico I obtained a summary of these data. It is very difficult to present it in a complete and correct form, because there are several systems of wages. In some places a fixed amount is paid for one day's work ; in others a given sum is paid for a certain amount of work done; in some others, besides the wages, rations are given, which consist of a certain quantity of grain, sufficient for the subsistence of the laborer and his family ; the quality and quantity of these rations vary, as well as their value, for grain has different prices in the various localities ; and all these causes render it very difficult to make an entirely accurate *résumé* of the official data. The most complete that I have been able to prepare is the following, which embraces the maximum and minimum field wages paid in the different states of the Mexican Confederation, in cents and per day :

States.	Minimum. Cents.	Maximum. Cents.	Average. Cents.
Aguas Calientes	.18¾	.18¾	.18¾
Baja California (T.)	.50	.50	.50
Chiapas	.25	.75	.50
Chihuahua	.18¾	.25	.21⅞
Coahuila	.31¼	.75	.53⅛
Colima	.25	.37½	.31¼
Durango	.25	.75	.50
Distrito Federal	.31¼	.37½	.34⅜
Guanajuato	.18¾	.31¼	.25
Guerrero	.18¾	.50	.34⅜
Hidalgo	.12½	.37½	.25
Jalisco	.18¾	.50	.34⅜
Mexico	.12½	.37½	.25
Michoacan	.15½	.75	.45¼
Morelos	.25	.75	.50
Nuevo Leon	.18¾	.18¾	.18¾
Oajaca	.18¾	.50	.34⅜
Puebla	.18¾	.50	.34⅜
Queretaro	.18¾	.37½	.28⅛
San Luis Potosi	.18¾	.25	.22¼
Sonora	.30	$1.00	.65
Tabasco	.37½	.50	.43¾
Tamaulipas	.25	.50	.37½
Tepic (T.)	.25	.50	.37½
Tlaxcala	.25	.50	.37½
Vera Cruz	.25	.62½	.43¾
Yucatan	.25	.37½	.31¼
Zacatecas	.18¾	.50	.34⅜
Total average	.23⅛	.50	.36

I do not know that a statement similar to the preceding one has been made concerning the wages paid to laborers in factories, in mines, and on railroads, but I understand the Mexican Government is now collecting such data. I am sure, however, that these laborers earn wages considerably higher than those paid to field hands, as those working on railways on the coast and on the frontier receive as much as $1.50 per day.

Before giving an account of the causes of the diversity of wages paid in Mexico for field work, and showing why these wages are so low, it is opportune to state that it is not in Mexico only that such diversity of wages exists, for something similar takes place in this country. According to the latest information published by the Wisconsin Labor Bureau, a common laborer in Atlanta earns 7½ cents per hour, while the same laborer in Galveston, which is another Southern city, earns 25 cents per hour, or three times as much.

As I have just stated, the broken surface of Mexico makes transportation very expensive, there being comparatively few wagon roads. On the one from Vera Cruz to the City of Mexico, which was the best constructed, the average freight in normal conditions was $68.75 per ton of 2,200 pounds for a distance of only 263¼ English miles, or more than 26 cents per mile and ton; and in extraordinary circumstances, as during the French intervention in Mexico from 1861 to 1867, the freights were as high as $330 per ton, or over $1.25 per mile and ton.

Nothing shows more plainly how high freights have been in Mexico than to state that, in accordance with the Mexican laws, the company to which a grant was given in 1857 to build a railroad between Vera Cruz and the City of Mexico forfeited its charter because of services rendered to the French intervention ; and when the national government returned to the City of Mexico, in 1867, and revived the grant, among the new restrictions agreed to by the company, a maximum freight was fixed of $62 per ton of 2,200 pounds, or 24 cents a mile per ton ; and this rate was then considered quite reasonable.

The common way of transporting merchandise was on the backs of mules or donkeys, the former carrying from three to four hundred pounds and the latter about one hundred pounds, both making about fifteen miles a day, and where there were no mule-paths goods were carried on the shoulders of Indians. The high cost of transportation allowed only the exportation of gold and silver, because the precious metals, having great value in comparatively small volume and weight, could bear the expense. These metals were, therefore, almost the only articles of export from Mexico for about three hundred years, excepting a few other high-priced products, like cochineal and indigo, which, before the progress of chemistry, were almost the only materials used to dye in red and blue colors, and for this reason commanded a very high price. Even now, when Mexico has in operation over 5,000 miles of railways, and when the depreciation in the value of silver has established a bounty of about 30 per cent. on the exportation of commodities, the total amount exported from Mexico during last year was, in round numbers, $40,000,000 in precious metals and only $20,000,000 in commodities.

Merchandise could not be transported from one place to another in Mexico, whenever there was any distance between them, without increasing the cost very largely. Sugar, for instance, which in some localities was produced at the cost of 1 cent a pound, was sold in others at 25 cents a pound. Such a condition of things reduced the consumption and consequently the production to a very narrow limit, and very often a year's abundant crops amounted to a calamity to the farmers, as the abundance of products without an increase of consumption caused a great fall in prices. Under such circumstances the wages paid to the field laborers had necessarily to be low ; and although they now begin to improve with the greater demand for labor brought about by the construction of railroads, and the consequent material progress of the country, they are yet far from being what is desired, and what I am sure they will be before long.

It is a fact that wages in Mexico are far lower in many cases than those paid for the same industries in the United States; but this ought not to seem strange when it is considered that this country pays probably the highest wages in the world ; and not even the foremost manufacturing nations of Europe, as England, France, Germany, and Belgium, can compete with it in this regard. Yet while it is true that labor in the European countries is not so well remunerated as in the United States, it must be taken into account that it does not produce there as much as it does here. I am assured by competent persons that a bank-bill printer, for instance, does not print in England more than 1,500 sheets per week, while the average work done by the American workman is 6,000 sheets per week ; and it is stated in the *Journal des Economistes* that a French weaver can take care of only four looms, a Belgian of five, an English weaver of six, and one from this country of eight. But the actual production during a given working time is in Mexico far less than in the United States or even in Europe. The day's work of a Mexican laborer very likely represents only one-fourth of what is accomplished during the same time by a laborer in the United States. A Mexican laborer working from ten to eleven hours a day, for instance, accomplishes less work, or produces less, than a European or an American laborer in nine hours, and in some instances the disproportion is as great as 1 to 5. I have been assured that a Mexican bricklayer in eleven hours' work does not lay more than 500 bricks, while a bricklayer in the United States lays 2,500 in nine hours ; and that a Mexican weaver cannot attend to more than two looms. Under such conditions the high wages of $3 a day paid in the United States are no higher than the wages of 50 cents paid in Mexico, so far as the product of labor is concerned.

The principal causes for this difference in working capacity are, in my opinion, the following : (1) the Mexican laborer is not so well fed and paid as his brother in this country ; (2) he generally works until he is exhausted, and his work is not, therefore, so productive ; (3) he is not, on the whole, so well educated as the average laborer in the United States ; (4) he has fewer wants to satisfy, and therefore less inducement to work. Perhaps there is, besides these causes, at least in some localities, a climatic influence, due to the enervating character of the tropical climate and to the high altitude above the level of the sea, and the consequent lower atmospherical pressure, where a large portion of the population of Mexico is located. I am inclined to believe that this is a factor in the case, as a similar difference is noticed among animals. A plough drawn by one horse in this country would in Mexico require two or three horses to accomplish the same work in similar localities ; and this shows that the difference in working strength may be due, at least in part and in some places, to natural causes or climatic influences.

The impression prevailing in this country regarding the Mexican peon is an erroneous one. It is supposed here that peonage is equivalent to slavery, and that it is spread throughout the whole country. I must state at once that it exists principally in a comparatively reduced area where laborers are very scarce, and this fact shows that, while the system is liable to abuse, it has some advantages for the laborer.

The largest portion of the Mexican population is located on the mountains, central table-lands, and other high regions, which enjoy a cold and healthful climate, on account of their elevation above the sea level. Only the products of the cold zone can grow there, and they used to be cultivated on a limited scale, solely for local consumption, however, as the high cost of transportation prevented their being carried to any distance. In this region labor is abundant, and exceeds considerably the demand. Consequently the wages are low, and the peonage system only exists to a small extent ; and, as the number of working hands is greater than the demand, the laborers are exposed to disadvantages that fortunately are now disappearing as the progress of the country increases the demand for labor.

The temperate region embraces the lands located from three to five thousand feet above the level of the sea, and it is sparsely populated ; but its products are valuable, like coffee, sugar, and other tropical fruits. It is very difficult to find in this region the necessary hands to till the land on a large scale. For these reasons, and, above all, because of the high cost of transportation, such articles cannot be grown for export, except in a few places favorably located, and then in a limited quantity. This explains why some of these products command a higher price in some localities of the country where they are produced than in foreign markets, where they are transported from great distances. Sugar, for instance, which is retailed in New York at 4½ cents a pound, costs in the city of Mexico from 12 to 18 cents, and it is not so well refined as the article sold here, although for that reason it has a greater amount of saccharine matter.

The hot region, which embraces the coast on both oceans and low valleys situated in the interior of the country, is very sparsely inhabited : labor is therefore very scarce and wages are higher than in any other region. While in the high and cold regions wages are often 12½ cents a day and rations, on the coast they are sometimes $1.50 a day. The inhabitants of the cold and temperate regions do not come down to the warm zone, because they are exposed to sicknesses prevailing there, such as yellow-fever and intermittent and remittent fevers, and because they are terribly annoyed by mosquitoes, and can hardly endure the heat. If at any time they do go there, it is only for a few days, and they return home very soon afterwards.

It has been thought, because the lowlands are the most fertile and rich, and almost uninhabited, that they could only be cultivated by means of negro or Asiatic labor; and this idea has induced some Mexican planters to try Chinese immigration, as article 11 of our constitution grants to all men the right freely to enter and leave Mexico.

The laborers living on the warm lands have, on account of the scarcity of their number, advantages which are not shared by their brothers inhabiting the higher regions. The first of these advantages is, as I have already stated, larger wages; the second is that they can obtain advances, in reasonable amounts, for any needs they may have, as marriages, births, sickness or death in their families, since the small amount of their wages does not allow them to economize for such emergencies, and these advances are willingly made by their employers on account of future services, without interest or security. But, unfortunately, these very advantages are the source of great abuse on the part of some employers, of which the laborer is sometimes the victim on account of his ignorance and complete destitution, on one side, and the influence and wealth of his employer, on the other.

I speak of this subject from personal experience, because, having spent several years as a planter in the department of Soconusco, state of Chiapas, where these conditions prevail, I saw practically the workings of the peonage system. It was not possible there to obtain a laborer either as a domestic or a field hand without paying beforehand the debt he had contracted with his former employer, which was from one to five hundred dollars; so it is easy to understand what an expenditure of money was required before a large number of hands could be obtained. Lapse of time increases the debt instead of diminishing it, since the laborer asks each week, as a rule, for more than the amount of his wages. Whenever the hands are displeased with their work,—either because they quarrel among themselves, because their employer does not treat them well, because they do not get all the advances they ask for, or for any other reason,—they have full freedom to offer their services to anybody else, who willingly pays their debt, as everybody is always in need of help; but often, and especially in the case of persons who do not live permanently in the country, as happened to me in Soconusco, laborers whose debts reach a considerable sum conceal themselves, fly to another district where they are not known, or in some other manner evade the payment of their indebtedness ; and the result is that it is lost to their employer.

These are the practical results of the peonage system, so far as my experience goes, although I do not deny that it is liable to great abuse on the part of the employers, who are favored in a few cases by the tolerance of some local authorities and by the ignorance and poverty of the laborers.

There are some places—especially in the states of Tabasco and Campeachy, where fine woods are cut in uninhabited spots, which change as the wood is exhausted—where the employer assumes, in the absence of any authorities or magistrates, and generally through an overseer, for he himself seldom remains at such places, all the powers of government. There, of course, the opportunities for doing wrong are very much increased, in view of the fact that there is hardly any responsibility for abuse of authority. In most of these cases the employer is obliged to set up, for the convenience of his laborers,—as I have heard, never having seen such a thing personally,—a store where they can provide themselves, there being no other near by, with groceries and such dry goods as they need in the ordinary course of life, paying for them with the scrip issued to them in settlement of their wages by the employer over his signature. It is easy to see how greatly this system is liable to abuse, since the laborer has to purchase at the store of his employer everything he wants, and at such prices as the owner may think fit to charge, losing all the benefits of competition.*

But the peonage system has no legal existence in Mexico, be-

---

* It seems that something similar to this is done in the United States, as is shown by the following extract from Gen. Rush C. Hawkins's article, entitled "Brutality and Avarice Triumphant," published in the June number of THE NORTH AMERICAN REVIEW, page 660: "One of the most facile means in the hands of avarice for cheating the poor and helpless is the ' corporation and contractors' store.' It is usually owned by corporations whose employees are the only patrons, and the rule is to sell the poorest possible quality of supplies at the highest price obtainable. In many instances employees are given to understand that they are expected to trade at the company and contract stores, or, failing to do so, will be discharged. This oppressive method of cheating is not confined to any particular part of the country, but prevails, with varying degrees of malignancy, wherever under one management, either corporate, partnership, or individual, any considerable number of employees are assembled together. Since the close of the Civil War many thousands of igno-rant blacks have been make the victims of this common and heartless swindle, which has absorbed their scant earnings. At the end of each month, year in and year out, it has proved to their untrained minds an astonishing fact that the longer and the harder they worked the more they got in debt to their employers."

cause article 5 of our constitution of 1857, enacted for the purpose of abolishing it, provided that "nobody should be obliged to render personal service without proper compensation and his full consent," and forbade the law to authorize any contract which might have for its object the "loss or irreparable sacrifice of the freedom of man through work, education, or religious vows." This article was amended on the 25th of September, 1873, with the main view of prohibiting the taking of religious vows in Mexico, and of making it more explicit, and it reads now, so far as work is concerned, as follows : "The state cannot allow the fulfilment of any agreement, contract, or covenant which may, in any manner, impair, destroy, or irrevocably sacrifice man's liberty, either through work, education, or religious vows."

The Catholic clergy of Mexico encouraged the system of having a great many feast-days, because they were quite productive to the church. Over one-third of the year, not counting the Sabbath, was given up to religious festivals, during which all work was stopped. So objectionable were the results of this system that, when, in 1858, the laws of reform were enacted separating the church from the state, the feast-days were reduced by law to a very limited number— about six only in a year; but, as happens with all legislation in conflict with the actual habits of the people, the law has not been faithfully complied with, especially because it does not provide any punishment for the offenders. This fact makes foreigners in Mexico consider native labor unreliable.

It is time now to speak of the prices of Mexican commodities and to compare them with such as are produced here. The Department of Public Works has been for some time collecting data as to the prices of agricultural products in Mexico, and during my recent stay in the capital of the republic I obtained a *résumé* of such data, which I give on the next page, reducing the weights and measures used in Mexico to those used in this country, and stating the price of each article in each country.

It has been very difficult to make this table, for the complete accuracy of which I cannot vouch, notwithstanding that I have used much care and availed myself of all the means within my reach to make it as complete as possible ; but the difficulty of obtaining the average price of certain articles in both countries is very great, and no less the reduction to a common standard of the weights and measures used in each. So far as commodities in the United States are concerned, I have taken as the basis for fixing their price the data contained in No. 12 of the Statistical Abstract of the United States for the year 1889, prepared by the Bureau of Statistics under the direction of the Secretary of the Treasury, and sent by him to the House of Representatives on the 4th of December of the same year. In regard to such commodities as were not embraced in that document, I have used the data contained in the thirty-second annual report of the Chamber of Commerce of the city of New York for the fiscal year 1889–90, and in the report of the Produce Exchange of New York for the same period, and such other as I have been able to obtain from reliable sources.

Articles.	Prices in the City of Mexico.		Prices in the United States.	
Bacon	50c.	per lb.	20c.	per lb.
Beeves	8c.	per lb., gross weight.	4½c.	per lb. gross wt.
Coal	$16.00	per ton.	$3.18	per ton.
Coffee	22c.	per lb.	19c.	per lb.
Corn	2c.	per lb.	⅘c.	per lb., or 43c. per bushel of 56 lbs.
Cotton prints	10½c.	per yard.	3⅘c.	per yard.
Cottons	19c.	per lb.	10c.	per lb.
Flour	5c.	per lb.	1½c.	per lb., or $2.75 per barrel of 196 lbs.
Ham	50c.	per lb.	18c.	per lb.
Hogs (live)	9c.	per lb., gross weight.	3¾c.	per lb., gross wt.
Iron, pig	$32.00	per ton.	$19 00	per ton.
Lard	18c.	per lb.	8⅛c.	per lb.
Meats:				
Beef	12c.	per lb.	7c.	per lh.
Mutton	14c	per lb.	8¼c.	per lb.
Pork	11c.	per lb.	5¾c.	per lb.
Paper, printing	15c.	per lb.	5c.	per lb.
Prints	8½c.	per yard.	6¼c.	per yard.
Rice	7c.	per lb.	5c.	per lh.
Salt	7c.	per lb.	4c.	per lb.
Sheep	9c.	per lb., gross weight.	5c.	per lb., gross wt.
Sugar	21c.	per lb.	5c.	per lb.
Tallow	15c.	per lb.	4⅜c.	per lb.
Tobacco	24c.	per lb.	6¼c.	per lb.
Wheat	3c	per lb.	1⅜c.	per lb., or 83c. per bushel of 60 lbs.
Whiskey	$16.00	a cask of 20.0787 galls., or 80c. per gall.	36c.	per gall. in bond.

One reason why Mexican products are so high is that when they reach the markets they have paid the local duty levied in coming into the cities. Unfortunately the internal commerce of Mexico is not free, as in the United States, where such freedom has contributed greatly, in my opinion, to the marvellous prosperity of the people. Our constitution of 1857 prescribed the abolition, from the 1st of July, 1858, of the interior duties and custom-houses throughout the whole country; but unfortunately it has not as yet been possible to comply with that provision, and the time has been extended by amending the constitution. The railroads have come to demonstrate practically the great inconvenience of the system of trammelled interior commerce, and the Mexican Government is now endeavoring to bring the different states to an agreement to replace such duties with some other tax less objectionable.

The reciprocity treaty of January 20, 1883, contained a provision, which was, I think, little commented upon or appreciated here, whereby complete immunity from all local, state, and municipal taxes was granted to merchandise from this country imported into Mexico ; giving it the same freedom as it enjoys at home. My object in agreeing to the above clause was not only to encourage and promote the development of trade between the two countries, but also to undermine the present obnoxious legislation, which, by interposing so many obstacles, makes traffic almost impossible. The moment foreign merchandise was exempted from all local duties and barriers, domestic merchandise was left in such an unfavorable condition as to demand imperatively a change for the better.

I expected in this instance a repetition of what took place with our postage rates, which up to 1874 were almost prohibitory,—25 cents per quarter of an ounce,—thereby considerably encouraging evasion. Our Minister to Berlin was appointed a delegate from Mexico to the Universal Postal Union Congress which met in Paris, and he was one of the signatories of the convention concluded June 1, 1878, whereby the international postage rate was fixed at five cents per sixteen grammes, or half an ounce. When the Mexican Government ratified that convention, the old postage rates could not be kept up, and a few years later they were finally reduced to ten cents per half-ounce, and the number of letters forwarded in the Mexican mails has since immensely increased, the revenue therefrom having augmented fourfold.

When economical errors of long standing prevail in a country and become imbedded in the people, the most effective way to eradicate them is sometimes to make their remedy a subject of stipulation with a foreign country, giving it thereby a special force ; otherwise, if the remedy is enacted by one Congress, another can repeal that measure, as has been the case in Mexico with the *alcabalas* excise. We have great respect for international agreements, and hold that the legislative branch of the government cannot abrogate them, unless with the consent of the other party or in case of war.

It is now time to show that the low wages paid in Mexico do

not produce cheap commodities, and could not therefore, by' competition, lower the compensation of labor, or the cost of similar manufactured articles in the United States.

We pay at home, in several cases, wages amounting to about a sixth of what is paid here for similar work, and yet the production in Mexico, with such low wages, is a great deal more expensive than the production of similar articles in the United States, with probably the highest wages in the world, and with prices consequently higher.

It is true that wages are one of the principal factors in the cost of production of all kinds of merchandise, but they are not the only, and in many cases not even the principal, one. The question of wages is very complex, and it seems that, in comparing the wages of this country with those paid in Mexico, two important factors are overlooked : first, the cost of living in each country, or the purchasing power of the currency in each ; and, second, the amount of commodities produced in each country by the same unit of work, either on account of the greater fitness or greater physical strength of the laborer, or through the use of machinery, which increases the amount of production and cheapens it enormously. When these two circumstances are taken into account, it will be found that the high wages paid here are often no higher for the work performed, perhaps in some cases even lower, than those paid in Mexico and in other countries ; and only in that way can we explain how this country with its high wages can produce many articles—for instance, watches and clocks—which compete successfully with those made in Switzerland, where wages are comparatively low.

The cost of production, too, depends on other circumstances, different in each country, all of which must be considered for a proper appreciation of the subject. I would need more space than I can reasonably use in this article to mention all the causes which affect wages, and to show how far they influence the cost of production ; and I shall only present some practical and suggestive examples taken from the preceding table, to show that the same commodities produced in this country, with high wages, cost less, and therefore are sold at a lower price, than similar articles produced in Mexico with low wages.

One of the best illustrations of the correctness of this statement is the working of mines in both countries. Although wages in Mexico are probably one-fourth or one-fifth of those paid in the United States, the production of silver costs much less here than there. Mr. Thomas H. Carter, late member of Congress from Montana, and a very competent judge, stated, during the first session of the last Congress, that miners' wages here were $3 a day, while he fixed at fifty cents per day the wages of Mexican miners. I do not think his statement correct so far as Mexican mining wages are concerned, as miners there earn larger wages than field hands. That our production of silver is more costly than it is here is shown by the fact that mines similar to those which we abandon because it does not pay us to work them on account of the low grade of silver, or for other reasons, are operated in the United States with profit. This is in a great measure because mines are worked in this country by machinery, which diminishes the cost and increases the production ; but this very fact shows that wages are not the only factor affecting the cost of production, and also that with high wages it is possible, and even easy, to produce at a less expense than with low wages.

Cotton-culture is another example. I am aware that the cotton-growers of the United States hold that what they call their cotton belt has peculiar conditions for the production of their staple, which in their opinion do not exist in any other portion of the world, and they believe, therefore, that nobody can compete with them in this regard. Without any intention on my part to belittle the advantages of the cotton belt of this country, I am of the opinion that there are in Mexico lands as well adapted for the production of cotton as the best in this country, and in some of our regions perhaps even more so ; yet, notwithstanding these advantages and although our wages are low, cotton is produced cheaper in this country, and is sold with profit by the planters for one-half the price that it commands in Mexico. So great is the difference in the price of this staple in the two countries that notwithstanding an import duty on cotton of 8 cents per kilogram, or almost 5 cents per pound, which is equivalent to 50 per cent. ad valorem, we import from this country almost one-half of the cotton used in our home manufactures. I do not overlook the fact that cotton is raised here by negro labor, which is considerably cheaper than white labor ; but, even assuming that wages in this case be the same in both countries, the difference in cost is so great that labor is not the only factor in the expense of production.

Something similar happens with sugar. Here it is produced with high wages, and—although its culture in Louisiana is an artificial one, since frosts prevail there, since the cane has to be planted every year or two, and the ground cultivated at considerable expense several times a year, so that such culture is almost as artificial there as coffee-culture would be in New England —yet the Louisiana planters sell their sugar in New York with profit at from 6 to 7 cents per pound, while in the City of Mexico and other places in my country it commands twice and even three times that price.

The same is the case with tobacco. Although the climate and soil are very likely better fitted for its culture in Mexico than in this country, tobacco costs there, on an average, 24½ cents per pound, while it is sold here at 8½ cents per pound.

I shall not speak of the products of the cold climate, like wheat, barley, oats, etc., because the climate and soil of this country are naturally adapted for such culture, while for tropical products the conditions are decidedly in favor of Mexico ; but despite the fact that we also have cold regions in Mexico, and not-·withstanding the difference in wages, wheat is worth there twice as much as here, and there is about the same difference in the price of corn.

It is much the same with manufactured articles, like common printing-paper, which in the United States is worth about 3 cents a pound and in Mexico 15 cents, although we have abundant raw material and water-power for its manufacture. To encourage the making of paper, we established an import duty on foreign unsized and half-sized paper of 10 cents per kilogram, or over 5 cents per pound, equivalent to over 100 per cent. ad valorem, which was reduced by our present tariff to 5 cents per kilogram for the unsized, keeping the duty of 10 cents on the half-sized paper ; and notwithstanding this we import printing-paper from this country, where the wages are so high compared with ours. Something similar happens with cottons and cotton prints, the former being worth 5 cents per yard in this country and from 10 to 15 cents per vara of 33 English inches in Mexico, and the latter, which are sold here at 8 cents per yard, being worth in Mexico about 20 cents per yard.

I believe that the preceding facts show beyond all doubt that, unless there is a material change in the present conditions of Mexico, there need be no fear of competition in the United States from Mexican manufactures in articles produced by us with cheap labor.

My country, too, has adopted the protection system, and we have carried it considerably further than it ever was carried in the United States. We established it originally, as it was established here, for the purpose of obtaining the means to defray the expenses of the government, and it was developed under the supposition that the higher the import duties the larger would be the revenue yielded ; but we failed to consider that smuggling is, in the nature of things, and especially in countries, like Mexico, well adapted for its operation, the regulator of prohibitory or exceedingly high duties. Under the protective duties, several industries have been established at home which are now greatly interested in the permanency of the present system. The import duty upon common cotton goods, which is the material worn by the largest portion of the Mexican population, is from 9 to 17 cents per square metre, or over 100 per cent. on the price of the goods in England. Flour pays 10 cents per kilogram, or more than 5 cents per pound, equivalent to 350 per cent. upon its value in New York. Printing-paper pays, as already stated, 5 and 10 cents per kilogram, or over $2\frac{1}{2}$ and 5 cents per pound, equivalent to from 100 to 200 per cent. ad valorem. I could multiply similar instances of high duties ; and yet we have not succeeded in cheapening our products or in perfecting our manufactures.

A very suggestive instance where high duties encouraged smuggling came under my personal observation. Mexican tobacco could not reach the northern states of Mexico on account of the high rates of transportation, to which I have alluded, and it could not be raised close by because its culture was for several years a government monopoly. Therefore the inhabitants of that region used tobacco raised in the United States, which they bought at a moderate price. Our import duty on tobacco up to the year 1878 was $1.25 per kilogram, or about 66 cents per pound, and although tobacco from the United States was consumed in all the frontier of Mexico, and that was the only tobacco imported in the free zone, which at that date was limited to the state of Tamaulipas, and although the yearly importation exceeded one million pounds, yet there hardly appeared in the treasury any revenue collected on this article. At that time I had the Treasury Department of Mexico under my charge, and, having observed this fact, I obtained the sanction of the President, who then had full authority from Congress for that purpose, and reduced the duty on tobacco to the comparatively moderate amount of 16 cents per kilogram, or less than 8 cents per pound ; and from that time we derived some revenue from foreign tobacco. I could mention many other instances as forcible as this one.

As the system of collecting import duties ad valorem is liable to many frauds, Mexico has adopted specific duties, or a fixed amount per weight, unit, or measure. Although this system has the disadvantage that the duty is not proportionate to the price of the merchandise, as is theoretically the ad-valorem duty, it is not liable to so many frauds as the other, and for that reason, I understand, it has been adopted by most of the European nations.

Agricultural products of this country, like wheat, cotton, and other farm products, notwithstanding the high wages paid here to field laborers, compete in the English and other free foreign markets, and successfully sustain a sharp competition with similar foreign products obtained with low wages, in some cases even lower than in Mexico, as in the case of China and the East Indies. There need, therefore, be no fear of competition from Mexico.

I believe that the people of the United States have the necessary pluck and fitness to compete with any other people in the world in the production of manufactured articles. It is true the high wages paid here, the import duties upon raw materials, and the higher price of coal than in some other countries, enhance the cost of the production of certain commodities as compared with similar ones manufactured in England, France, Germany, and Belgium ; but it must at the same time be remembered that the application of machinery, which is used here on a much larger scale than in any other country, cheapens production so greatly that it enables this country to manufacture many articles at a less cost than any other. An instance of this is the manufacture of steel rails in the Edgar Thompson factory, at Pittsburg, Penn., where, the entire production being mechanical, few hands are employed and where natural gas is used as fuel.

High duties collected in Mexico, amounting in some cases to

even 300 per cent. ad valorem, have not increased or cheapened our production. Our imports in the fiscal year ended on the 30th of June, 1889, the last one for which official data have been published, amounted to $40,024,894.32 ; if we deduct from this the free articles, valued at $13,506,230.23, we shall have as the dutiable merchandise $26,518,664.09, yielding a revenue of $22,477,962.95, or an average of 84.7 per cent., which is larger in proportion than that of any other American nation, and almost double that of the United States, where the average was 44.41 per centum for the fiscal year ending on the 30th of June, 1890 ; the value of the dutiable articles amounting to $507,511,-764, and the import duties to $226,540,037. Notwithstanding all this, and although our wages are lower than those in this country, our production is considerably dearer.

I should be very glad if the explanations made in this article result in dispelling the errors prevailing in this country in regard to the conditions of labor in Mexico ; and hope that, in case restrictions against Mexican trade are discussed, they will not be urged on the ground that our articles are produced with peon labor. I sincerely hope that both countries, instead of acting in a way contrary to the ends of nature, which has placed one beside the other, and has given them different climates, productions, and possibilities, will coöperate with the purpose of nature, and not interpose other obstacles to reciprocal trade than those absolutely necessary for their mutual well-being and progress.

M. ROMERO.

THE PARDONING POWER.

BY THE HON. DAVID B. HILL, GOVERNOR OF NEW YORK.

The propriety of the existence of some power to pardon persons convicted of crime is recognized in every well-regulated government. This essential attribute is based upon the conceded imperfection of human action in the punishment of offenders. The Marquis Beccaria said that the power of pardon does not exist under a perfect administration of the laws, and that the admission of the power is a tacit acknowledgment of the infirmity of the course of justice. Story speaks of this power as "a benign prerogative." Montesquieu regarded it as "the most glorious attribute of sovereignty." Chancellor Kent says that "a power to pardon seems, indeed, indispensable under the most correct administration of the law by human tribunals; since, otherwise, men would sometimes fall a prey to the vindictiveness of accusers, the inaccuracy of testimony, and the fallibility of jurors and courts." Hamilton, as early as 1788, said in *The Federalist* that "the criminal code of every country partakes so much of necessary severity that, without an easy access to exceptions in favor of unfortunate guilt, justice would wear a countenance too sanguinary and cruel."

Jeremy Bentham, speaking of the exercise of this prerogative in England, expressed the sentiment that "the power of pardoning is often said to be one of the brightest jewels in the royal crown; it is burdensome as it is bright, not only to those who submit to the crown, but still more so to him also who wears it."

This important function of government seems to be securely established, because public sentiment rebels at the idea that the determination of a criminal court should be absolutely and forever irrevocable. It may be regarded as the true province of a government that it should provide for mercy as well as for justice

—for reformation as well as for punishment. A learned modern law-writer, treating of this subject, has asserted that "the idea of justice, stern, certain, and unappeasable, is inconsistent with the better impulses of our nature, repugnant to the teachings of our religion, and in conflict with those influences of our civilization which are fast changing our prisons from penitentiaries to reformatories."

In monarchical countries the power of pardon is vested in the crown. There the king is usually the prosecutor of all offences against the criminal laws of the realm, and in his name all actions are brought; therefore it is appropriate in theory that he should have the power to remit any punishment inflicted for the vindication of public justice. In this country all power is in the people and criminal offences are deemed committed against the public, but nevertheless the constitution of the United States provides that the President "shall have power to grant reprieves and pardons for offences against the United States, except in cases of impeachment." In the States the power is usually vested in the Governor, either alone or by and with the advice of his council or a board or court of pardons. In at least twenty-eight States the power is reposed in the Governor alone. In at least seven States the power is conferred upon the Governor acting with a board, court, or council. In one State the power is expressly retained in the Legislature. In two States the Governor and Senate may exercise the power. I am not advised as to the other States.

In the State of New York it is provided in its constitution that "the Governor shall have the power to grant reprieves, commutations, and pardons, after conviction, for all offences except treason and cases of impeachment, upon such conditions and with such restrictions and limitations as he may think proper, subject to such regulations as may be provided by law relative to the manner of applying for pardons." This authority, upon its face, would seem to be more essential and beneficial than that conferred upon the President. While a cursory perusal might lead to that conclusion, a more careful examination, however, proves otherwise. While it is true that the clause conferring authority upon the President does not expressly mention "commutations" and is silent upon the matter of "conditions, restrictions, and limitations," which the Governor is expressly at liberty to impose, yet the President has, in fact, the same powers, because it has been adjudicated that the general power of pardon includes the lesser power of commutation, and that it also carries with it the implied authority to impose any conditions which the President may desire to impose. The recital of these two powers, therefore, in the New York constitution, may now be regarded as unnecessary verbiage. Besides, the Governor's power to pardon is restricted to cases " after conviction," while the President's power, being general and unlimited, may be exercised at any time after the commission of the offence, whether before or after an actual conviction. It will be observed that the Governor cannot pardon for the offence of treason or in cases of impeachment, while the President may exercise his prerogative in every case except impeachment cases. The right to grant a pardon for the offence of treason was wisely conferred upon the President. For obvious public reasons it is essential and appropriate that the Chief Executive of the nation should always be in a position to promptly extend amnesty in all proper cases, pending a rebellion or insurrection, or subsequent thereto. No other official can so well understand the situation, or appreciate the motives of public policy which induce and require action in such emergencies. There is no legal distinction between a pardon and an amnesty. Amnesty, however, is said to be "a compact rather than a grant, and is addressed to a population instead of an individual." A pardon includes amnesty.

There is no restriction to the "conditions" which an Executive may attach to a pardon, except that the courts have held that they must be reasonable. It is, of course, implied that he cannot impose impossible conditions. The most usual conditions are as follows : first, where the crime was committed in a state of intoxication, the convict is frequently required to abstain from the use of intoxicating liquors for a certain period of time, generally five years—sometimes for life, especially in cases of homicide ; second, where it appears that the public interests will be peculiarly subserved or the best interests of the convict promoted, he is often required to leave the State or country either permanently or for a stated time. It may be safely asserted that experience has demonstrated that the conditions exacted have been generally fulfilled in good faith. It is believed that the requirement in regard to abstaining from the use of liquors has been productive of much benefit. Many instances can be recalled where the convict has been thoroughly reformed and where he not only remained sober during the allotted period, but ever afterwards. In some cases convicts thus released have become conspicuously earnest in their zeal for the temperance cause, and have afforded practical testimony as to the wisdom of such a condition. It cannot be denied that drunkenness is a fruitful source of crime, and any restriction which tends to lessen the evil should in proper cases be freely imposed and rigorously enforced, not only for the good of the convict, but also for the protection of society.

The utility of the other condition is not so obvious, and it has seldom been imposed in New York in recent years. It may well be doubted whether it is good policy for the Executive of each State to seek to make some other State the asylum for its criminals or to unload them upon other countries. It would seem to be preferable that each State and country should keep within its own borders its own pardoned criminals, maintaining over them such surveillance as prudence may dictate. A general policy of expulsion towards the recipients of executive clemency in one State is likely to induce a similar course in another State by way of retaliation, and a system is thereby inaugurated of compelling unfortunate convicts to find a refuge in places other than their own homes. Unless there are extraordinary circumstances to justify exceptions, it is believed that, as a general rule, a condition requiring a convict to leave the State where he was convicted should not be attached to a pardon. Not long since a peculiar and interesting case was presented to me, as Governor of New York, where insistence upon such a condition seemed desirable.

A bright young man, scarcely twenty years of age, had been sent to this country from Liberia by his parents, who were reputable and well-to-do people, to finish his education. Being somewhat wild, he fell among evil companions in New York city and was soon led astray. He stole some money and was sent to prison. In consideration of his youth, his previous good character, and other circumstances, I pardoned him, upon condition that he return immediately to Liberia with the messenger whom his parents had sent to accompany him home. It was regarded as appropriate in this case that such a condition should be insisted upon, not especially for the protection of the State, but in the hope of effecting a reformation by restoring him to the custody of his par-

ents in his own country.   He returned to Liberia, and the information which reaches me is that he is now leading a correct
life.

In whom the power of pardon should be vested is a question
upon which there is much difference of opinion.   The framers of
the federal constitution and of most of our State constitutions
came to the conclusion, after much discussion and deliberation,
that the prerogative properly belonged to the Chief Executive.
There has been a tendency of late years towards the establishment
of a council or board in which should be reposed at least some advisory functions pertaining to pardons.   It has been strongly
urged that the power is a judicial function, and that its lodgement
in the Executive or in the Legislature is an anomaly in our institutions.   It has also been argued that the power is too important a one to be reposed in a single official, especially a Chief
Executive who is usually overburdened with administrative duties,
and who must find it impossible to devote the necessary time for
the proper consideration of the numerous cases which are constantly before him.   On the other hand, it is said that there
ought not to be a division of responsibility in such matters.   It is
suggested that, while the responsibility is fearful to contemplate,
its very magnitude induces scrupulousness and caution.   It is
contended that a tribunal of four men can better evade, shift,
and shirk responsibility than can one official, and that the latter
is less likely to be moved by extraneous influences than is a
council or board.   Hamilton, who was well versed in the science
of government, reached the conclusion that "one man appears to
be a more eligible dispenser of the mercy of the government than
a body of men."   The force of that conclusion is much augmented if it be conceded that the one man is conscientious, independent, and resolute.

It must be admitted that there have been some scandals connected
with the discharge of this power by councils or boards in certain
States, while there has been no serious allegation that the power has
ever been abused by an Executive.   Whether favoritism, prejudice,
and sympathy, in the execution of this high function, can better be
avoided by a body of officials than by a single official is a question not
free from difficulty, and there are plausible, if not reasonably satisfactory, arguments on both sides.   It is probably
true that the trend of public opinion is against the "one-

man power." The majority of magazine contributors and many modern law-writers join in the opposition. It is very likely the popular side. But after an experience of seven years in the administration of this great trust, I feel constrained to say that it is my deliberate conviction that our fathers were wise when they provided that the pardoning power should be lodged in the Chief Executive alone, and, in my opinion, it ought not now to be transferred.

I am aware of the criticism which a single official evokes in the fearless performance of his duty ; of his liability to err ; of the vast responsibility which he assumes, involving frequently the momentous question of life or death ; of the antagonisms which he necessarily creates ; of the severe strain and labor which a conscientious and intelligent discharge of his duties involves ; and yet, even in the light of these considerations, I am still inclined to believe that the public interests are, as a general rule, better subserved where the responsibility is not divided. I realize the fact that other Executives, emerging from several years' discharge of such arduous duties, have taken a different view of the matter. I have great respect for their opinions, but I am compelled to differ with them. I recall the instance where a most distinguished and able Governor of a Western State, at the close of his official term, issued a pamphlet earnestly and vigorously arguing against the possession of the pardoning power by the Executive of the State, and advising the creation of a board to assume that function. Under the constitution of his State he was deprived of the veto power, neither could he approve bills, and he had no voice in the legislation enacted, while his principal duties, aside from the exercise of the pardoning power, consisted in the appointment of notaries public ; and yet he seemed to have been so impressed with the responsibility assumed that he actually advocated a transfer to another tribunal of about the only important duty which invested the office of Governor with dignity and character.

In other States, where Governors are busily occupied with important legislative and other duties, the suggestion that they are unable to give the necessary time and attention to pardon cases is not without weight ; but with the assistance of a competent and faithful pardon clerk, who is usually, and always should be, provided, it would seem as though a painstaking and diligent Executive should be able to exercise the high prerogative reposed in him in a reasonably satisfactory manner, and with honor and credit to the commonwealth.

It has been asserted that the exercise of clemency is a semi-judicial act, and that inasmuch as Executives have, as a general rule, no authority to summon witnesses or to take testimony in a formal way, their examination of pardon cases must necessarily be imperfect and to a large degree ex parte and unsatisfactory, and that, therefore, additional reasons are furnished why such functions should be discharged by a court expressly created for that purpose. There is some force to this contention, because cases are constantly arising where a searching oral examination of witnesses is indispensable to a proper determination of the merits of the application. But this objection does not apply to New York, where, in 1887, at my instance, the Legislature passed an act (chap. 213 of the laws of 1887), providing for the sub-pœnaing of witnesses and the production of books and papers in any matter arising before the Governor upon an application for executive clemency, and also authorizing the Governor to appoint a referee to take any testimony which may be offered. I regard such a statute as a valuable contribution to the facilities required for a proper and just administration of the criminal laws.

What are the precise grounds upon which clemency should proceed ? It is easier to ask than to answer this question. It may be assumed that clemency should be based upon public considerations. General and consistent rules should be observed as far as possible, although each case must largely depend upon its own particular circumstances. It is seldom that there are any two cases exactly alike ; and this fact opens up a large field of discretion to be wisely exercised. It is clear that the constitutional provisions to which I have referred are so broad that the pardoning power must be deemed to be absolutely discretionary. It is doubtful whether even the courts have the authority to compel an Executive simply to *decide* a pardon case. He may, by reason of the peculiar circumstances surrounding the application, regard his duty as best discharged by holding the case without final determination at all. It is difficult to discover how his course in that respect can be reviewed by any judicial or other tribunal. He should always act from the highest motives of public policy and regardless of personal consequences ; without trepidation, fear, or favor ; unaffected by political or other improper influences ;

unawed by public clamor or prejudice ; with courage, integrity, and good judgment.

There may be occasions when he should interfere as an act of political justice, where some corrupt and unworthy judge, unmindful of his duty, has undertaken to serve the ends of partisanship by the improper exercise of arbitrary powers in cases involving political consequences. Such instances are rare, however.

There is a vagueness and indefiniteness surrounding the pardoning power which renders it a most delicate and thankless duty to discharge—a task usually not thoroughly appreciated by the public. It is governed by no fixed or arbitrary rules. It is controlled by no higher authority. The popular idea is that it may be exercised at the mere caprice of the Executive, and that he is not obliged to expose his reasons. But the constitution of New York, as well as the constitutions of several other States, requires that the Governor "shall annually communicate to the Legislature each case of reprieve, commutation, or pardon granted, stating the name of the convict, the crime of which he was convicted, the sentence and its date, and the date of the commutation, pardon, or reprieve," and a long-established custom seems to demand that the reasons upon which his decision is predicated shall accompany his report. There can, therefore, very properly be no secrecy concerning his action. It is a public and not a private proceeding. The Legislature and the people, while unable to reverse his action, may judge of its merits themselves.

It is well said that "a pardon is purely an act of grace." No one is entitled to it as a matter of strict right. Mere sympathy should not dictate its allowance, but considerations of mercy alone are sometimes sufficient. Shakespeare's *Portia*, "a young and learned doctor to our court," is made to say that the quality of mercy

> "becomes
> The throned monarch better than his crown."

How far mere mercy may be the controlling motive for granting a pardon is a question addressed solely to the conscience of the Executive. There can be no just cause of complaint "when mercy seasons justice," if the act proceeds not from a mere whim, but is approved by an honest and sound discretion. It has been tersely said "that the very notion of mercy implies the accuracy of the claims of justice."

There are a few general rules or principles which may be laid down as safe to follow in these cases.

1st. The Executive should not interfere to correct mere errors of law which may be remedied by an appellate court.

2nd. He should await the *final* determination of a criminal case.

3rd. The findings upon disputed questions of fact decided by a jury should usually be regarded as conclusive.

4th. Newly-discovered evidence of the innocence of the prisoner may be accepted, provided relief based upon it cannot be had in court.

5th. Cases should not be considered where the term of imprisonment does not exceed a year, except upon the allegation of entire innocence. (This rule is necessary to relieve the Executive from the multiplicity of small cases arising under sentences from the minor courts.)

6th. The prisoner's conduct while in prison must have been good.

It may be interesting for the public to know the routine course which is generally taken when an application for a pardon is entertained. A petition must be presented from the convict, or in his behalf, setting forth the nature and circumstances of the conviction and the grounds upon which' executive interposition is asked ; and upon its filing a letter is sent to the district attorney who prosecuted the case and to the judge who presided at the trial, asking for a statement of the facts of which they have official knowledge, and for their opinion of the merits of the application for pardon. Another letter is sent to the warden of the prison where the convict is confined, asking for a report in reference to the conduct of the prisoner since his incarceration ; and when replies are received from these three sources, the case is ready for examination by the Executive.

Naturally the opinions of the judge and district attorney are entitled to considerable weight in the consideration of the case, although they are by no means conclusive. Sometimes the facts upon which clemency is sought have arisen since the trial, and these officials have no knowledge concerning them. Where both concur in recommending the pardon, it is ordinarily, though not always, granted. If their opinions differ, the case usually receives further and more careful consideration. If the case is otherwise meritorious, but the conduct of the prisoner while confined has been bad, the application is denied. This seemingly harsh course is essential to preserve the discipline and good order of the prison.

The cases which are very difficult satisfactorily to decide are those where the prisoner is concededly more or less guilty, but where the punishment which has been imposed seems to be excessive. Some contend that a merely excessive sentence presents no proper ground for executive interference. It is urged, not without some force, that it is not the province of the Executive to revise the sentences of the courts simply because the opinion of the Executive may differ from the opinion of the judge as to the punishment needed. The judge who sees the witnesses and hears all the evidence is certainly more competent, usually, than a stranger to determine what the proper sentence should be. Yet, while all this is true, it is evident that a judge unconsciously is often unduly influenced by the prejudiced atmosphere of a court-room and the unreasonable clamor of a community, and hastily inflicts a sentence which in his cooler moments he would not deliberately approve ; and injustice would clearly result if a general rule should be observed which forbids sentences from being commuted, although concededly excessive. Let me give an illustration.

A young man scarcely twenty-one years of age, living in a rural county in the western part of the State of New York, left his home to find work upon a farm, his parents moving at about the same time to Buffalo. Unable to find steady work, he roamed about the country, and unfortunately fell into the company of a hardened criminal, who persuaded him to accompany him, when one day they entered a dwelling-house, the family being absent, and secured something to eat, and the young man stole a dollar and two cents. They were subsequently arrested, and they both pleaded guilty to burglary, the young man refusing to give his true name for fear his parents would hear of his disgrace. His companion being shown to be an experienced burglar, indignation in the county ran high against the two. Without making any particular inquiry as to the previous history of the young man, the judge sentenced him to *twenty-six years' imprisonment* in the State Prison. This was in September, 1888, and his parents did not learn of his misfortune until about June, 1891, he being all the mean time in prison. His parents then presented an application for a commutation of his sentence, which was entertained. The district attorney wrote that since the conviction he had "investigated the case more thoroughly," and had "come to the conclusion that the sentence was *somewhat* excessive." The judge attempted no justification, and simply wrote : "I think, on the whole, it would be a wise thing to extend to him executive clemency." It was shown that the young man had never been arrested before and that his previous character was excellent. I promptly commuted his sentence, and he was immediately released from prison. His sentence was an outrageous one and wholly indefensible. He should have been sent to the Elmira Reformatory, and not to prison. The case fittingly illustrates the necessity for executive interposition in instances where excessive sentences have been thoughtlessly or unfairly imposed.

The fatal illness of a prisoner is a constant source of embarrassment to the Executive, because it is made a very common ground of application for the commutation of sentences, and presents many difficulties. There is a sort of prevailing notion among the people, or some classes of them, that any prisoner ought not to be allowed to die in prison, but that he should be released whenever his illness is believed to be fatal. Such people argue that the public interests cannot suffer if the prisoner should be allowed to die outside of prison walls, and that the dictates of humanity require that himself and his friends should be spared the alleged disgrace of such an ending of his life. They seem to forget that both he and they have been, in reality, as much disgraced by the original sentence and imprisonment as they can possibly be by the simple death of the convict in prison ; yet the fact cannot be disguised that, either from superstition, prejudice, or whim, the popular idea is that to such a prisoner ought not to be refused the poor privilege of dying among his friends and outside of prison scenes. The denial of such a request does seem cruel and apparently heartless ; yet in seven cases out of ten it is probably true that the accommodations of the prison hospital and the skilled attention which the prisoner receives are far better than would be afforded him among his own friends.

It seems quite impossible to establish an arbitrary rule in this class of disagreeable cases. Where the sick prisoner is serving out a life-sentence, the request for release upon the sole ground of his fatal illness may be more easily denied than when the sentence is for a term of years, because a life-sentence contemplates the death of the convict while in prison, but a fatal illness during a short term is an unexpected event. A practical difficulty arises sometimes when the prisoner is ill and the physicians think he cannot recover and his friends are urging the necessity of speedy action. The Governor must act promptly and upon the information before him, and is liable to err. An instance is on record in the State of New York where one of my distinguished predecessors pardoned a very sick convict upon the sole ground that he was likely to die, and, though the medical representations were abundant that his illness would prove fatal, he subsequently recovered and is alive to-day. It might be a questionable exercise of power, or at least a violation of propriety, to make it a condition of granting a pardon that the convict should die or else be returned to prison. Public sentiment would probably revolt at such an obnoxious and unusual condition.

In July, 1888, I commuted to imprisonment for life the death-sentence of an Italian woman named Chiara Cignarale, who had been convicted of murdering her husband, and among the grounds for my action which were stated at the time, in my "Public Papers" of that year, appears the following : ". . . it is certified to me by eminent physicians, in whom I must place confidence, that the prisoner is and has been for some time seriously ill, and that in all probability she cannot survive over a year at the most, and is likely to die at any time." One of the most celebrated physicians in the country wrote : "In my opinion, it is impossible for her to live longer than a year at the utmost." Yet she is alive to-day, and is understood to be enjoying fair health in the New York Penitentiary.

Where a sentence is for a short term and a prisoner is so dangerously ill that his recovery is believed to be impossible, the exercise of clemency may be justified in the interest of humanity, although there may be no other grounds upon which to support it. Yet even this safe rule subjects the Executive to the constant importunities of friends who, unnecessarily alarmed at the illness of a prisoner, besiege the Executive for immediate favorable action.

The desirability of some general rule of action in these cases is very apparent. Their proper disposition occasions more anxiety and annoyance to the Executive, and demands greater circumspection, than almost any other class of cases.

Whether executive clemency should be freely or sparingly exercised has given rise to much discussion. I have conversed at different times with Governors Seymour, Tilden, Robinson, Fenton, Cornell, and Cleveland, of my own State, upon this point, and the impression which I derived from such interviews with all of them, except Governor Cornell, was that, if they had any criticism to express in regard to their own action, it was that they had not exercised the pardoning power freely enough. As I understood it, they would have preferred to give pardon cases more consideration, but were unable to do so because of numerous other important duties which constantly engaged their attention.

Another source of embarrassment to an Executive arises where a jury finds a prisoner guilty of murder in the first degree and at the same time recommends him to the mercy of the court. Such a recommendation is without legal effect and cannot be considered by the court in mitigation of the sentence which the law imperatively requires shall be imposed. But it is made the basis of an appeal to the Executive for clemency, and must be respectfully considered. It has been ignored in many cases, but in a few it has been regarded as of sufficient weight, in connection, however, with other facts, to require executive interference. It is believed that such recommendations should not be encouraged. They enable a jury to escape or evade the just responsibilities which attach to their position. They secure verdicts which otherwise would not be rendered. They unduly stimulate appeals to clemency and arouse expectations which ordinarily cannot be realized. Neither should courts, in my judgment, anticipate or prejudice executive action in their determination of criminal cases. I have known of one or two cases where convictions for murder in the first degree have been affirmed, and yet the court has seen fit to suggest that the case was a proper one for executive interposition.

The exercise of the pardoning power should be so regulated as to subserve the best interests of the State and at the same time to secure, if possible, the reformation of the offender. Clemency may often be wisely extended where a deserving convict has not long to serve and steady employment shall be guaranteed immediately after his discharge. One great reason why there are so many second-term convicts in our prisons arises from the fact that upon a discharge from his first term the convict can find nothing to do, and easily returns to a career of crime. There is, naturally, a prejudice among the people against the employment of persons who have served a term in prison ; but what are the poor convicts to do and what is to become of them if no employment shall be opened to them ? They must starve, beg, or steal, if they can-not find work. This thought leads to the suggestion that benevolence and philanthropy can find no better field for their exercise than in securing employment for discharged convicts who are deserving. An effective society organized for such a beneficent purpose could accomplish much good, and, in my opinion, it is one of the needs of the hour. I commend the sug-gestion to the consideration of those who have the means and disposition to inaugurate so desirable a movement, which can be productive of so much benefit. Who will start it ?

DAVID B. HILL.

THE DARKER SIDE.

BY LADY HENRY SOMERSET.

THE poor of all great cities may be broadly divided into two classes. First, those who work for wages, miserably low but fairly regular, whose earnings keep them from starving, though never sufficient to remove them from the verge of famine ; whose good fortune may be summed up in the expression that they are not chronically in a state of utter destitution. The second class includes those who are. The rookeries in which they live are the plague-spots of great towns. It is an army wretched and weary, recruited from the refuse—if so cruel a word may be used—of every country under heaven. Their continued existence is a standing wonder and a standing menace,—a wonder because how the gains of their sweated labor and petty peddling can support them is a mystery ; a menace because no public peace or morality can be secure with such a class in our midst.

My definition of this second class almost excludes comparison ; utter destitution knows of few degrees. In America 'food is cheaper, and fewer meet their death by starving ; and, indeed, among the native American population of New York few are wholly destitute ; while in London the casual dock laborer, the "unemployed," the captives of the sweating-den, in spite of our vast mass of Jewish labor, are English or Irish, and form the bulk of the pauper outcasts.

Undoubtedly, however, the cosmopolitan character of New York has produced within its precincts samples of the vices of all nations. In London we have nothing parallel to Chinatown and the Arab quarter. When I visited the former of these, I saw an American girl lying senseless in an opium den, surrounded by the heathen authors of her shame ; herself, their fellow victim, in the toils of that relentless vice. As I looked upon that scene, which seemed to give the lie to one's belief in the divine spark that exists in every human heart, another girl passing me where I stood, with a faint blush of shame that spoke of the memories of a brighter past, covered that poor degraded child with a newspaper that lay at hand.

The curse of poverty is great, but in no country has anything struck me as so horrible as this reënforcement of the evil that we know by the unspeakable horrors of the heathen world. It is not my purpose here to linger on this subject. It is one to tax all the enthusiasm and eloquence that man or woman could muster to denounce as the vilest, the most unnatural, and the most festering evil of modern times.

To pass to the first of my two classes of the poor. In London what strikes one most is their immense number and low individual calibre. Their long subjection has so robbed them of ambition and self-respect that the one thing that would raise them—the wish to rise—has to be instilled, instead of helped. Such is the work of centuries of neglect ; such the nemesis that the apathy of our fathers has brought upon us.

Whitechapel is the district which has generally been taken to be the worst in our English metropolis. Really it is only typical of a score of areas such as South Lambeth, St. Pancras, Southwark, and Soho. But Whitechapel will serve as an example, and for choice let us take our stand in the Mile-End Road.

This is a magnificent thoroughfare running through all East London from the heart of the city to its confines at Bow—a street wider than any I have seen in New York, with pavements on either side almost as wide as the roadway itself. Here, one would think, was the great opportunity for a popular boulevard, green with trees, and bright with flowers and little lawns, showing in its splendor some of the wealth the daily toil of its teeming millions produce. Alas ! it is far otherwise. The wealth is gone to deck the lazy West End, and the only gayety is the ·garishness of vice. On a Saturday night, here in the heart of London, in this great artery of its system, what shall we see ?

The wide street brilliantly lit, brighter than any street in all the town ; but not by the public gas-lamps. The sidewalk alive with the passing crowd ; but this is not the throbbing pulse of industry. The air resounds with the voices of men and of women ; but there is nothing human in the sound.

The brightness is the glare of the gin-palace lamps. We can see forty on the opposite side of the street in less than a quarter of a mile. The beat of the shuffling footsteps is the march of hopeless fellow creatures sullenly tramping to Saturday's sorry saturnalia. The cries that strike through the cold night air fall like a whip upon our hearing, for over all there rings the shrill shriek of women lost to womanhood; and I know no more dreadful sound than the outcry, indecent and profane, of a drunken woman. In this fearful pandemonium there are many such. The shadows on the gin-shop doors are the shadows of mothers drinking at the bar within, drinking with their babies sometimes at their breasts, drinking their children's food and lives away. It is here that girls are led by drink to forget their virtue, and then to forget their vice ; and—shame upon us that this is so !— it is by the hands of women, mostly young, that the poison is handed across the bar.

Here at a moment's glance you may see the distinctive curse of London's poor. The women drink. Mothers, daughters, sisters, wives, grown women, children of tender years—the gin-shop is open to all, and all go to it. Nowhere in New York did I see or hear of women not utterly abandoned habitually frequenting saloons. Nowhere in London is there a public house but the women will be as good (?) customers as the men. It is impossible to overrate the influence, the soul-destroying influence, this has had upon the homes of the poor ; for it is by this, I am convinced, that the idea of right and wrong has come to be hopelessly confused where it is not absolutely lost. It is not uncommon to find a mother who since marriage has been a faithful wife, and perhaps before that a virtuous girl, looking on with indifference while her daughter "goes on the streets," and is lost in the unnumbered legion of victims hourly sacrificed to the demon of vice. She may regret the fact, as a mother in a wealthier station might regret her daughter marrying beneath her, but there is no shock, no natural horror, at the wanton marring of God's fairest handiwork, a woman's soul. In our long worship of mammon, the shame of poverty and the shame of sin have got confused : to the poor in their misery the burden of disgrace is but a slight addition to the load they already carry.

It is this demoralization that makes the case so serious ; this that differentiates them from their compeers in misfortune in

New York. There, for the present at least, public sentiment amongst themselves forbids open drinking and open drunkenness amongst the women; but the terrible amount of unlicensed liquor-dealing that goes on, unless promptly checked, must soon rob them of this superiority.

Whether drink causes poverty, or poverty drink, is a matter over which philanthropists may wrangle. For my part, I have never had a doubt, and this is what my experience has taught me : let a man or woman give up the public house, and within three months his or her whole environment will have changed ; in six he or she will have forever left the slum where hitherto he or she lived contentedly. It is by the poorest wage-earners that the public houses are maintained, and probably the meanest could not sub-sist with a custom of less than £2,000 yearly. If so,—and this is a minimum amount,—the forty I have mentioned in four hundred yards of Mile-End Road must mean an annual tribute of £80,000, say $400,000, from the poorest of the population. Spent in their material benefit, what would not this sum effect ? what the moral gain with this incentive to evil gone ?

New York seems to me to have the advantage of England in three respects. Her quotum of submerged poor is smaller ; they are individually more self-reliant ; their women are more self-respecting. And yet so wretchedly is this class housed that all these advantages seem to be in a fair way of being lost in the vice of the system that herds them together. I have spoken of the unlicensed drinking that I fear is undermining the self-respect of the women. It needs little of the spirit of prophecy to foretell what must be the future of a city that packs its infant life in tenements such as those that disgrace the East Side.

It is only within the last score of years that London has at all realized how great her evils were. Considering that we have had to make up the omissions of centuries, it is marvellous how much has been done. Private benefactors and the public law, ground landlords and the county council, all have joined hands in the work of rehousing the poorer artisans ; and, although much remains to be done, so educated is public opinion that 5 per cent. is the accepted maximum interest that ought to be expected from capital expended in such dwellings, if in any way they are to prove a benefit to the tenants. The middleman in London may still exact an exorbitant rent from his single-room tenant in the slum ; but, thank God ! his trade is being made harder every day, and the worst tale of London is better than what I saw in this city a week ago.   Three men sleeping in a cellar, their beds a few boards stretched across the barrels that held the fruit they hawked by day ; the floor of mud, with pools of filthy water here and there ; and for the privilege of sharing such quarters with the rats each was paying thirty-five cents a week—eighteen pence of English money ! It is probably only within the last few years that New York has awakened to the fact that the down-town back alleys can eclipse in horror the worst purlieus of Liverpool and London.   When disasters such as the fire in Madison Street alley occur, Fifth Avenue learns for the first time " how the other half live."

Here are evils that must be faced and manfully grappled with. In London the fact that the evil is of old standing, the lack of field for labor, the daily addition to the pauper class by foreign immigration from abroad and native immigration from the impoverished rural districts, all make the problem more complicated and more difficult of solution.   New York is a modern city —I understand its rapid growth dates from 1812—standing on the threshold of a continent whose wealth and enterprise are the wonder of the world.   To her the task of dealing with her poor should be as easy as it is urgent.   What kind of citizens must conditions such as I have alluded to produce ?   The very glory of New York's democratic liberty will be the guarantee of future disaster.   A race of paupers would be a mocking offset to the great achievements of the world's greatest republic.   In America an hereditary class of idlers strikes one as an anomaly—at whichever end of the social scale it may occur.

ISABEL SOMERSET.

"NINETY MILES IN EIGHTY-NINE MINUTES."

BY THEODORE VOORHEES, GENERAL SUPERINTENDENT OF THE
NEW YORK CENTRAL AND HUDSON RIVER RAILROAD.

"ANOTHER record broken. A remarkably quick trip from Jersey City to Washington." These are the headlines that appear in the morning papers, and call attention to the latest fast, long-distance special train. The account goes on to say that the distance, 227 miles, was covered in exactly four hours' running time, and that "the party aboard was delighted at breaking the record."

Of those who read this account, how few gave a thought to the real merits of the feat and the fine organization necessary to make it possible ! Even of those who were passengers on the train in question, how few, aside from the professional railway men who may have been of the party, appreciated the details of the effort that was being made for their benefit ! To make such a trip possible required, first, a road-bed, solid, substantial in every respect, free from bad curves, guarded from all liability of obstruction, and protected by reliable signals. Next, that the rolling stock and motive power be in perfect order and of ample capacity to do the work assigned. And, finally, after the most careful preparation, all would have gone for naught had not the actual handling of the train been put in charge of engineers whose experience, skill, nerve, and courage fitted them for the work. Such men are rare and by their employers valued, but by the public seldom appreciated.

The technical knowledge required to handle a locomotive engine is not a difficult matter to acquire. Ordinarily a boy, after spending a preliminary year or so in the round-house or shops, is put on an engine as a fireman. His period of service in that capacity varies greatly according to the natural ability he may display and the exigencies of the service. From a fireman he is promoted to the first or lowest grade of engineer, *i.e.*, on a yard or shifting engine. From that he is promoted, in due time, to the next grade, that of freight engineer, and finally he is put in charge of a passenger locomotive.

A man, to fill this position, should have had sufficient experience to know exactly what to do in any case of emergency; should be prompt and quick in decision, clear-eyed, alert, watchful for any indication of danger, free from fear or nervousness, forgetful of self if danger does confront him. To the credit of American locomotive engineers, it must be said, our records show that we have many such men in active service to-day.

Yet a man may be all this and thoroughly competent to handle a regular passenger train, who would still be unfit for such record-breaking service as has been of late the subject of newspaper comment. " Ninety miles in eighty-nine minutes !" "One hundred and forty-two miles in one hundred and forty minutes without a stop !" One can hardly appreciate what this means until one sits by the engineer's side and sees it done.

The skill and judgment come from long experience; the coolness, the watchful eye, and the nerve are born in the man and cannot be acquired. Great generals are born, not made. So it is with fine engineers. No amount of experience will produce them unless they possess the special qualities needed.

Sometimes it happens that a single accident will destroy the future of a capable man. Some years ago there was a young engineer employed on a railway in the State of New York who was in every way fitted for his position. Intelligent, quick-witted, with a thorough knowledge of the locomotive, he was prudent, watchful, prompt in emergencies, and capable of performing any duty required. One dark night, while running a regular passenger train and passing over a specially crooked portion of the line, there suddenly appeared before him the headlight of an approaching locomotive on the same track. No time to do more than shut off steam and apply the brakes, and the collision occurred. Both engines were overturned and badly wrecked. The fireman had had a moment's warning from the engineer and jumped. The engineer stood by his work, and went down in the wreck. When picked up, his shoulder was dislocated, but no bones were broken, and he was soon able to be sent to his home. His principal trouble appeared to be from the shock. After a few weeks he gradually recovered. He got out, and after a further time reported for duty. He was put back on his former train. He appeared to be quite well and as fit for duty as ever. The train started and all went well during daylight. The return trip was made at night. As the train approached the crooked piece of road, the fireman noticed that the engineer seemed to grow white and nervous, and involuntarily to shut off steam. The train drew nearer and nearer the scene of the accident, and the engineer grew more and more nervous. Finally when the exact spot was reached, he fell over. He had fainted. His career was at an end. He never stood on the footboard again.

To drive a locomotive at a very high speed continuously for a considerable distance undoubtedly involves the exercise of great skill and judgment on the part of the engineer. That it necessarily involves a great strain on his nerves or endurance does not follow. On the contrary, very many cases occur in the daily working of our railways where men are put in positions trying by reason of the risk to be encountered rather than by any speed required.

The calling of a locomotive engineer is one involving a certain hazard. The degree of danger involved depends very greatly on the nature of the service.

Regular trains, that are duly advertised and shown on the schedules of the road, that are run regularly day after day by the same men, are by far the safest service. The men running them become used to them and perform their daily work with the regularity of machines. They think as little of danger as the passengers in the trains behind them. Many a man to-day is running the same train he ran ten, fifteen, even twenty years ago, and will continue to run it for years to come. With such service the question of speed counts but for little. Provided the work be regular, uniform, day by day the same routine, it soon becomes a matter of custom or habit, and with good health it cannot be said to involve any special strain on the system.

Not long since the engineer of a limited train "pulled out" from a station where the train had made a regular stop. Within the next two miles he brought the train to the precise rate of speed called for by the schedule, about forty-two miles per hour. After that, save for an occasional glance at his gauges, he apparently did nothing for nearly two hours. He did not move the throttle-valve nor touch a lever. Except for his watchful look ahead one would not have thought him on duty. Approaching the end of his run, he got off his seat, took off his overalls, and had the fireman give him a basin of water, with which he washed his hands. A few minutes later he gradually shut off steam, and then with the air-brake brought the heavy train to a stop at the end of an eighty-one miles run, exactly on schedule time. Such coolness and accuracy can only be acquired as a result of daily habit and long experience.

The recent exceptionally fast service between New York and Buffalo, involving, as it does, a speed of a mile a minute for the greater part of the distance, has proved no more trying to the engineers who run the train than to those of other regular trains of the same line. The speed is a question of power and weight —the power of the locomotive to do its work easily and the weight of the train. The chief anxiety of the engineer is as to whether his engine is in first-class condition, capable of doing the work called for without crowding. He knows that every man on the line is alert and looking for his train, that every possible precaution is taken to insure him a clear track, that the chance of any obstruction is reduced to a minimum. He drives his engine, conscious that he has the best "run" on the road, that he has a position eagerly sought after, with no thought of possible danger, but with a feeling of pride that his engine is capable of such work and that he is identified with a road where such work is possible.

Irregular or special train service is accompanied with more risk of accident than regular service. It constantly happens that the requirements of the business necessitate special service, often on very short notice. Such work always involves a certain risk, and is proportionately trying to the engineers. Especially is such service dangerous when performed at night or in a storm or dense fog. To drive an engine "running extra" on a dark night or through a driving snow-storm or heavy fog is as unpleasant a duty as can be assigned to an engineer; the chief danger being, not the risk of collision, which even in fog is but slight, but the danger of striking some trespasser walking on the track—a danger which unfortunately is ever present to our engineers.

The annual reports of the various State Boards of Railway Commissioners give the number of persons who each year lose their lives while trespassing on railway tracks. Of the far greater number of persons who daily walk on the tracks and narrowly escape death we hear nothing. And yet the narrow escape is almost as trying to the engineer as the real accident.

The engineer will often on rounding a sharp curve meet a long freight train on the opposite track. Directly ahead and but a few feet distant stands a woman on the track waiting for the freight train to pass. The noise of the passing cars prevents her hearing the approaching train. The engineer reverses his engine, applies his air-brake, and pulls his whistle-lever, knowing all the time that he cannot possibly stop in the short distance. The most hardened veteran at such a moment will feel sick and faint. It may happen that at the last moment the woman sees the engine and leaps backward. She is safe, but will not recover from the fright for hours, while the engineer sweeps on and does not recover his composure for some time to come.

It is not alone the trespasser on the track ahead that requires the close attention of the engineer. There is a constant succession of signals, switch targets, train or station indicators, etc., all of which require his watchfulness.

It would be difficult to convey an adequate idea of the number and variety of details that go to make up a single run of an engineer, or the full degree of responsibility that rests upon his shoulders. The greater number of our roads, even those with the heaviest traffic, have but a single station at each point. All passengers habitually walk across a track to take a train going in one direction. Overhead bridges or under passage-ways are almost unknown. Even where they are provided the public rebel and evade their use by every means in their power. The result is that one ever-present danger which our engineers have to guard against is that of running over passengers who may be entering or leaving a train on the opposite track. This, while it may seem a matter of course, often involves the exercise of great judgment on their part.

Highway crossings at grade are a constant source of danger. Accidents often occur that are absolutely beyond the power of the engineer to prevent, and yet in very many cases the men are held accountable and the company held liable.

Horses and cattle break through fences and appear suddenly in front of a train. Such a case occurred but a few days ago, where a pair of horses came off a farm-crossing directly in front of a train. The result was that the engine was thrown in the ditch bottom side up, the fireman killed outright, and the engineer and one other employee seriously injured.

That all signals must be promptly obeyed is a matter of course. This becomes a sort of second nature to an experienced engineer. He will shut off steam and apply the air-brake at the sight of a danger-signal long before a novice who may be riding on the locomotive with him will have caught sight of the signal. To aid the engineers in this respect, where signals are liable to be obscured by smoke or escaping steam, auxiliary audible signals are sometimes used—torpedoes on the rail or gongs.

Accidents from a direct failure to properly observe and obey fixed visual signals are very rare. Yet when they do occur the consequences are so serious that the attention of inventors has been especially turned to the subject. Several very ingenious devices have been suggested to supplement the action of the engineer when passing a danger-signal, and, in fact, to do his work for him in case of negligence. One of the most ingenious proposes to use the compressed air of the air-brake, and by that power, called into action by a guard-rail on the track and certain electrical connections, automatically to shut off the steam on the engine and apply the brakes on the train, in case of any neglect on the part of the engineer.

The locomotive engineers of this country, from the necessities of the case, are a picked body of men. They are prudent, trustworthy, sober, and intelligent in a very high degree. In nothing is this better shown than in the success that has been attained by them in the organization known as the Brotherhood of Locomotive Engineers, which comprises the great majority of the engineers in the United States. This is a form of trades-union which, under the wise and skilful guidance of its grand chief engineer, has for many years upheld and advanced the best interests of its members throughout the country. That the Brotherhood has made some mistakes its best friends will not deny. But it has proved of incalculable benefit to the widows and orphans of hundreds of its members. And in one especial feature its policy should be commended. Differing from many so-called labor organizations, which seek to level all their members to the grade of the least efficient, the Brotherhood has always recognized the necessity and value of classification ; urging that different men be paid according to their experience and the duties required of them, and so using its influence to elevate and promote its members, by degrees, to the highest grade of proficiency, instead of holding all down to the level of the least efficient.

What· becomes of old engineers ? There is a certain fascination in the occupation that unfits many men for any other work. They have no ambition, but are content to live and die engineers. On the other hand, many are promoted to the higher positions in the mechanical department of the railways. They become round-house foremen, engine-despatchers, master mechanics, etc. Exceptional men make exceptional advancement in this as in other callings. Some of the most able men in the railway service of the country to-day began life in the shops and worked their way up from the foot-board of the locomotive.

Many very useful and valuable devices have been the invention of locomotive engineers. In fact, the efficiency of the American locomotive may be said to be in a large measure the result of such inventions. It is by reason of their skill and ingenuity that the American locomotive is so efficient and is able to perform an amount of work that is the wonder and admiration of our friends abroad.

With these locomotives American railway managers move on our railways—the greater number of which have but a single track, and many of which can hardly be said to be more than half finished—a traffic which in volume, rapidity of transportation, and economy is a constant marvel.

But no efficiency of our locomotives would accomplish this result were it not for the fidelity, skill, ingenuity, and trustworthiness of the men in charge of them—our locomotive engineers.

THEODORE VOORHEES.

THE FIRST COST OF SHIPS.

BY CHARLES H. CRAMP.

NOT long ago a metropolitan newspaper quoted me in an "interview" as saying that the higher classes of ships could be built as economically in this country as in Great Britain.

This observation called out a number of inquiries and requests for more specific information; among which was a letter from the editor of THE NORTH AMERICAN REVIEW offering the pages of that eminent periodical for any elaboration of the subject suggested that might seem proper.

In availing myself of that offer, it is proper to say that I do so, not from desire to provoke controversy, but with a view to clear away some prevailing misapprehension as to the relative state of the shipbuilding industry in this country and abroad, and as to the effect of the alleged or supposed difference in first cost upon the growth of our merchant marine.

The scope suggested by this inquiry is naturally much beyond the limits of a single magazine paper, and, besides, the pressure of daily duties precludes such exhaustive treatment as I should like to give it. Therefore, the tenor of this paper will be that of a cursory survey of the most recent achievements in shipbuilding and their effects upon the conditions of ocean steam traffic.

A review of the comparative history of British and American shipbuilding from the foundation of our republic would be interesting and instructive, as showing a steady tendency to superior workmanship and more elaborate finish on the part of American builders, class for class and rate for rate, whereby a factor of greater first cost was established, independent of any other conditions; but space and time forbid anything more than reference to it as a fact.

Coming immediately to the subject matter of the existing state of things, it may be said that there is perhaps no topic which so many men discuss, and so few comprehend, as the technique of shipbuilding. This fact is gratifying as an evidence of growing public interest, but it often gives rise to amusing *contre-temps*. For example, the frequenters of the smoking-room of one of our great trans-Atlantic liners, in a recent passage, had been treated to a voluble disquisition on the comparative " lines ' of certain rival steamers. Persons not familiar with the subject were profoundly impressed with the belief that this gentleman was an authority. Finally one of the listeners interrupted the discourse to inquire what the gentleman understood the term "lines of a ship " to mean. He was unable to define the term at all. It is this fact of limited public knowledge that makes misapprehension so easy, and accurate information so hard to convey.

The simple question, Can you build a ship as cheaply in the United States as in England ? is as impossible of direct positive or negative reply as would be the question, Can a man be educated as cheaply in one country as in the other ?

The absurdity of the latter question would be manifest, because any one could see that it depended partly on the man and partly on the education. In different ways, but in a similar generic sense, the principle would apply to the first question, and the answer would be that it depended partly on the ship and partly on the builder.

With regard to the simpler and plainer types of vessels, such as are used for freighting mainly, it is not worth while to discuss them here. The question solves itself to any one of average intelligence who will go aboard and compare the workmanship, style, finish, and general range of seaboat qualities as between any freight vessel like those of the Metropolitan Line or the Morgan Line or the Clyde Line, for example, and the usual English tramp of approximately equal burthen.

Put the plans and specifications of the average English tramp in the hands of an American shipbuilder, and he could not duplicate her. He would build a better vessel, of superior workmanship and neater finish in every respect; for the reason, to put it broadly, that the mechanics who make up an American shipyard organization are trained to a grade of performance which they could not reduce to the standard of tramp-construction.

Under these circumstances this branch of the subject may be dismissed summarily, with the statement that an English freight ship of the usual type could not be duplicated in this country at any cost. Whether our superior standard in vessels of this class is an advantage or a disadvantage in competition I will not attempt to decide.

Coming to the highest class of vessels,—that is to say, the most recent trans-Atlantic liners, which are rated first in speed and accommodations,—the attention of the world is now directed to certain conspicuous ships. These are the " Columbia," the " City of Paris" and " City of New York," and the " Teutonic " and " Majestic."

In model these vessels show no improvement over the best American or British model of thirty years ago. Dividing them and the types which they represent into three groups, we find them distinguished by marked differences of form and construction, and also of machinery detail, but there is little difference in outfit or engine performance.

The recent award by the Cunard Company of the contract for a new ship to the Fairfield works, of which Dr. Elgar, late superintendent of dock yards, is naval architect, will probably develop a fourth type.

It is not my purpose to go into an exhaustive analysis of the peculiarities of these several types, and I have introduced the fact of their existence partly because I have seen no previous reference to it and partly to preface some remarks more directly pertinent to the main points of my theme. Thus, when one uses the term " British ships " for purposes of comparison with "American ships," it is calculated to mislead, because the inference would be that all " British ships" were alike ; or, at least, that the similarity of type, model, mode of construction, cost, etc., class for class, was sufficiently close to make the national designation alone an adequate basis for comparison.

Nothing could be further from the truth. Every great shipyard, of long existence and extensive output, acquires methods, systems, and practices peculiarly its own, and these in turn express themselves in the characteristics of vessel which it designs and builds.

The result is that, while there may not be much difference in the average performance between vessels of the same class by different builders, so far as speed, endurance, cost of operating, and annual expense of repair are concerned, there will be material difference in the means and methods by which these results are reached, and hence a corresponding disparity in estimates of first cost. A Harland & Wolf ship will not be a Thomson ship, nor a Laird ship, nor an Elder ship ; and the same rule will apply to further comparisons between the others.

An error quite prevalent is the supposition that whenever a trans-Atlantic steamship company decides to add a new first-rate vessel to its fleet, complete plans, specifications, etc , are prepared and submitted to a number of competent shipyards for competitive bidding, after the fashion of the United States in its navy contract work. As a matter of fact, this sort of thing never occurs. As a rule, each company has its particular or favorite builder ; and often they are associated financially.

The builders' type of ship becomes the company's standard for service. The excellences of the type have been ascertained by experience, and opportunity has occurred to detect and remedy any defect. Hence the steamship company and the builders work together, and their coöperation results in the growth of a fleet having a reputation of its own and with it, to a very great extent at least, a settled class of public patronage.

In short, the business, in a certain way, is governed by the general commercial rule that public patronage is largely a matter of habit, and that in making use of ships, as of other wares, people continue to patronize that which has suited them once.

There are many shipyards in Great Britain ; more than in the rest of the world combined; but, so far as my observation enables me to judge, there are not more than three or, at the outside, four yards which would be considered by any of the great steamship companies in connection with a first-rate modern vessel such as is now required for trans-Atlantic mail and passenger service.

As before intimated in referring to the diversity of types, vessels of this class involve specialties of model, motive power, structural character, and quality of equipment, which, it may be said, make them *sui generis,* and in many particulars it is impossible to form an advance estimate of cost without a very liberal margin for contingencies. These facts are well understood in England, and their logic is invariably observed in negotiations for building such ships. It often happens that, after the general scheme and approximate price have been agreed upon, achievements elsewhere make expedient certain departures from the original.

In this connection it is worth while to bear in mind that during the construction of the "Majestic" and "Teutonic" at the Belfast yards, for the White Star Company, work was suspended for several months pending consideration of material changes, some of which were adopted and others rejected.

But these conclusions were not hastily reached, and were based upon actual observation of the behavior of rival ships built elsewhere. Under an iron-clad contract, with arbitrary fixing of specifications and price, this could not have been done without friction. It may be that there are good reasons why the United States Government should to a great extent tie both its hands and those of the contractors by inflexible written stipulations under bond and penalty ; but no such conditions are imposed in transactions between steamship companies and shipbuilders of established rank, for the simple reason that both would be subject to probable or possible embarrassment thereby, and experience demonstrates that it is better to leave the mass of detail to the operation of the common rules of business as encountered in the progress of the work.

From these observations it ought to be tolerably clear that the question, for example, Can you duplicate the "City of New York," or the "Majestic," or the "Columbia"—using the word "duplicate" in the purely structural sense—for the cost of those vessels in Great Britain ? would be putting the matter in an impracticable form. The "City of New York" is a product of the peculiar methods, practices, and systems of the Thomsons, of Clyde bank ; the "Majestic" similarly represents the Belfast yard of Harland & Wolf, and the "Columbia," the Lairds, of Birkenhead.

In each case the vessel is of a special type, and embodies idiosyncrasies which no other establishment could imitate—at all events, not at equal cost.

The proper form in which to put the question is : Can you build a ship to do the work of the "City of New York" or the "Majestic" or the "Columbia," in all respects, for the same cost ? To that question I would reply : Yes, or within as small a margin as would be likely to prevail in a similar case between any two British shipyards.

Our ship might differ from the "City of New York" in the ratio of principal dimensions, in the type of machinery, in style of finish, in fittings, equipment, and accommodations, and in many other things, as sanctioned by our experience or approved in our particular practice; but she should exhibit at least equal performance in speed, seaworthiness, comfort, durability, and, all other things being equal, in economy of operation.

But the point which I wish to accentuate is that the ship would be of our type and our model, and would embody our methods, our systems, and our practices; she would not be a duplicate or an imitation of any other ship, whether British or otherwise. A proper apprehension of this point and an adequate realization of the importance of its bearing upon any question as to the comparative first cost of high-class vessels in this country and in England are absolutely essential to practical or valuable knowledge on the subject.

In this connection I will refer briefly to a phase of the subject which I have exploited at other times in the numerous inquiries that have been made by committees of Congress.

That is the fact that the "first cost" of ships is not only not a prime factor, but it is not even a serious factor, in any competition that may occur between this country and Great Britain for a share of the traffic of the ocean.

My views in that direction are, perhaps, well enough known to make repetition of them here unnecessary, and I do not know that I could say anything that would affect any differences of opinion which may exist.

I simply state the fact as such, in order to preface the further and more important statement that growth of demand for new ships, with its resultant development of contributory industries in steel and iron and other materials of construction, its enlargement and improvement of plant and personnel employed, its natural incentive to greater energy and enlarged enterprise, and, above all, its assurance of security and perpetuity in the business, would speedily wipe out any small margin that may now exist against us in the matter of first cost, generally speaking.

Whatever else may be needed to restore the United States to its footing as a maritime power I leave to the patriotism and wisdom of our legislators to determine.

Referring, in conclusion, to the inquiry as to the relative cost of construction for navy account in the two countries, it must be borne in mind that disparities in bases of comparison exist in that direction even greater than in merchant shipbuilding.

In Great Britain public patronage in great amount has been

constantly and consistently extended to private enterprise, from time immemorial. Here, excepting the abnormal period of the Civil War, government patronage of private shipyards is a thing of recent growth ; not more than seven or eight years old.

The evolution of the modern war-ship in England was a steady and natural growth ; the strides of progress were short and easy, and all contributory industries were concurrently developed by equally easy stages. There was no sudden transition ; no leap into unknown or untried fields. From the first iron war-ship of any note—the old " Warrior," in 1857—up to the " Hood ' and the " Royal Sovereign," first-rate battle-ships of 1891, there was a rate of progress the steps of which were as regular as the ticking of a clock. At all times and under all conditions the shipbuilding industry of Great Britain has been of paramount national importance ; recognized as such by every public authority and fostered as such by every public power.

The advantageous effect of such a state of affairs may be best apprehended by contrast with the conditions under which American shipbuilders undertook, a few years ago, the task of rebuilding the United States Navy.

On November 7, 1881, just ten years ago at this writing, the first Naval Advisory Board reported a general scheme of naval reconstruction. The assembly of this board was one of the acts of the Garfield administration. From it may be dated the prevailing consistent policy of the new navy, though actual construction was not begun until about two years later.

At the outset it was resolved that we must have ships of the latest approved standard in every respect of material, armament, and equipment. When the work began, there were, say, three shipyards that the Navy Department considered competent to undertake it. But there was no steel-mill that had ever made plates and shapes of the quality required by the government specifications ; no foundry that had ever made steel castings of that standard ; no forge capable of making the steel shafts, or the tubes, jackets, and hoops required for the motive power of the ships or for the built-up breech-loading rifled cannon of large cal. ihre wherewith to arm them ; and no plant able to even entertain a proposition for the heavy armor-plates necessary in the construction of fighting ships. To such an extent was this true that the steel shafts for the earlier ships, the forgings for the pioneer eight-inch guns, and the compound armor for the turrets of the monitor "Miantonomoh" were all imported.

Without going into tedious detail of these preliminary operations, it may be said in bulk that we not only had to build ships of even a higher grade than their contemporaries abroad, with no commensurate, initial resources, but we had to create a new group of industries in every branch of the art of steel-making to supply us with the necessary material.

Under these circumstances American shipyards have built or are building about forty naval vessels of numerous rates and types, all of the very highest and most effective class in the world; and this development has been crowded into a space of about seven years. To put the case a little stronger, you may say that, with only the existing authorized construction in view, this country will have the third navy in the world within less than ten years, from a starting-point which may be described as at zero !

By that time we will have four first-rate battle-ships, six powerful double-turreted monitors, two heavy-armored cruisers, thirteen large protected cruisers, two of which are the fastest and most effective in the world, and fifteen smaller vessels of from 2,000 tons down to first-class torpedo boats.

In addition to these achievements we have developed on our own soil forging, foundry, and rolling plants with capacity of production, as to size or quality, equal to any in the world ; and all this has been built, you may say, literally " from the ground up."

To state the case in another phrase, we have, in a comparatively brief period. accomplished practical results commensurate with those due to steady growth during many years abroad.

Manifestly it must have been impossible to carry all these things along together at such a rapid pace and to surmount so many initial difficulties with such celerity at a normal cost. No one conversant with the laws of trade would expect it. But it is a well-known and admitted fact that a decrease in cost per ton of displacement, or per indicated horse-power of machinery, or per foot-ton of ballistic energy in our guns, or per unit of effective resistance in our armor, has quite kept pace with our growth of facilities and our enlargement of output.

The disparity in cost of naval ships between our yards and those of Great Britain, ton for ton, gun for gun, and performance for performance, has dwindled in seven years until, in the case of the three latest battle-ships, the margin between our prices and those of similar constructions abroad may be expressed by a very small figure. To illustrate the rapidity of progress in this direction I will call attention to the fact that Congress, by an act approved June 30, 1890, authorized the construction of three battle-ships of "about 8,500 tons' displacement," to cost "not more than four million dollars each, exclusive of armament"; and the vessels now building under the provisions of that act are of 10,400 tons' displacement, or nearly 25 per cent. larger and more efficient than those contemplated by Congress, with a margin on each ship of over $800,000 for fixed armor and other necessary deductions.

Gratifying as this prodigious development of new and great industries may be in the warlike sense, and in view of its guarantee of our independence as a nation for defence or for offence, its peaceful significance is still more profound.

At this writing there are plants and organizations in the United States capable of producing in any quantity, and of the highest quality, any structure in steel or iron or brass, or any other metal, that can be produced anywhere ; a state of things which did not exist seven years ago, and the present existence of which is a direct outcome of the enterprise and energy called forth by the rebuilding of the navy. In my opinion it must be a pretty poor American who is not proud of such achievements in so short a time.

With regard to the character of the vessels built or building for the navy, so much has been said about it in the daily press, and public interest has been so constantly and so cordially expressed in every form, that comment here would seem unnecessary. Suffice it to say that it is the universal testimony, both of our own sailors who have been abroad in the new ships and of candid foreigners who have seen them, that they are excelled by none and equalled by but few in their respective classes anywhere.

If the current policy of naval reconstruction be pursued for another decade, coupled with a vigorous and consistent execution of the measures recently enacted in behalf of the merchant marine, the question which forms the subject of this paper will be asked no more ; unless, indeed, its point should be reversed and Englishmen be asking one another, Can we build ships as economically as they can in the United States ?

CHARLES H. CRAMP.

THE BEST BOOK OF THE YEAR.

BY SIR EDWIN ARNOLD, GAIL HAMILTON, AGNES REPPLIER,
AMELIA E. BARR, THE REV. DR. CHARLES A. BRIGGS,
JULIEN GORDON, AND DR. WILLIAM A. HAMMOND.

SIR EDWIN ARNOLD:

You have done me the honor to invite me to mention which is the most remarkable book I happen to have read during the past year, and to give my reasons for the choice, as well as some account of the particular book.

Ordinarily this would be rather difficult, for I am a varied and omnivorous reader, and should be puzzled in most years to pick out the special work which had made the most impression upon me. But now it chances to be an easy answer which I shall make. I brought on board the "City of New York," when starting for this country, four volumes to beguile the brief voyage. These were a pocket copy of the Greek "Odyssey," a Russian grammar, a Japanese fairy-story book, and "La Bête Humaine," by Émile Zola. Beyond doubt it is the last mentioned which has most forcibly impressed itself upon me of late, and which I shall associate always with that wild and wintry voyage across the Atlantic.

I take it that anybody who pretends to keep at all abreast of modern literature must read, and does read, whatever Zola writes. I myself have certainly gone through every word of his writing : some of it with disgust, much of it with deep pain, and much of it, from the point of view of literary art, with profound admiration. There can be no question but he is one of the greatest masters of fiction in past or present times, and will stand forth in times to come the chief representative of the realistic school of novels. With how subtle a skill, for example, does he not open the grim and dismal story of " La Bête Humaine " ? Before two or three pages are perused we find ourselves familiar with Roubaud, the deputy station-master, and with Severine, his wife, whom he has married from the house of the Chief-Justice Grandmorin, his god-father and guardian. Nothing more tender, pretty, or idyllic could begin a book than the telling of the railway official and his wife meeting in the little upstairs room of the Rue d'Amsterdam, and one almost hopes that M. Zola is going to give us at last a glad and clean book, such as he knows well how to write. But suddenly a little slip on the wife's part about a ring that she is wearing tears the veil away from the jealous eyes of her husband ; he discovers that she had in by-gone days improper relations with the chief justice ; and in a frenzy of rage and anguish he forces her, after a scene of frightful violence, to write a note to M. Grandmorin, which brings that aged debauchee into the train going back from Paris to Havre. During the passage of that train, Roubaud murders M. Grandmorin, obliging Severine to assist in the deed ; and from that hour forward the whole volume seems to be written in blood, so full are its red pages of the shadow of evil passions, assassinations, envies, hatreds, malice, and all uncharitableness.

It is not long before we make the acquaintance of Jacques Lantier, the driver of a locomotive engine named *La Lison*, which figures in the story as quite a special and living character. Jacques is the son of Gervaise, of "L'Assommoir," is perhaps the central personage of the book, and the one who links it with those previous volumes of Zola in which the fortunes of the Rougon-Macquart family have been evolved in that dark, gloomy, fateful chronicle so well known to M. Zola's readers. Jacques Lantier is a special example of that heredity on which Zola dwells so constantly. He is born with a latent passion in his blood to kill—a passion always specially aroused by the presence of any woman who awakens desire in him. It is not fair even to read or quote M. Zola in anything except French ; his style is one of his great attractions, being in the highest degree lucid, strong, and flexible. Moreover, most of his translators do him very poor justice, *traduttore traditore.* " La Bête Humaine," for instance, should by no means be rendered " Human Brutes," the title given it in the American version, but, rather, " The Brute in Man"; and, to be brief, half the wonderful force of the French realist exhales when you strip him of his Gallic garb. But here is, so far as it goes, a passage in English defining the curse that lies upon Jacques Lantier :

"So it had opened again, that odious ulcer of his life,which he thought at last closed and healed! Once more that insane impulse to kill, to kill a wo. man, just as a desire of her began to overpower his senses, that impulse which he had carried within him from his childhood up, had returned as the impla. cable plague of his existence. How well he remembered its first appearance : that little girl at Plassans, who had once kissed him on the lips with a kitten-like, caressing gesture. He had scissors then in his hands, and had to throw them away quick, quick, or he would have sunk them in her delicate pink and white neck. Who was he to have such a destiny meted to him? His mother, Gervaise, bore him when hardly fifteen, and, before him, his brother Claude, the painter, also strange and wild in his mood. Later Etienne, another diseased branch of that same tainted tree. They all seemed ill balanced, with an hereditary insanity creeping out under one form or another. It appeared, at times, that he was not himself, but some one else, over whom he had not the least control, one who was leading him, in spite of all resistance, to shame and murder. Perhaps whole generations of fathers and grandfathers, drunkards and debauchees, were bound to bear such fruits, spoiled in the germ, and never to grow whole and healthy. He dared not touch alcohol, as one glass was enough to drive him crazy. But he felt. all the same, that the drunkard's blood coursed in his veins, dragging him back, with its all-powerful grasp, to the savage instincts of the wild beasts of the field, to that first state of the primeval man, brutal and blood-thirsty.

"Indeed he hated them not, these wretched women he had so often felt like strangling or stabbing to death. He hardly knew them sometimes; chance acquaintances of the street; neighbors at some theater or stage; scarcely spoken to, but always bringing home to him, with the first desire of possession, the stronger craving for immediate murder. A strange dul-ness would creep over his brain, and it seemed then as if he had to avenge some far off insult made to one of his race, in centuries past, by some woman who had left the hatred of her sex in the blood of the insulted one's race ; and he thirsted for that revenge, as if he had but to slay his victim, to throw her panting body over his shoulder, and to walk into the wilderness, the deed done, his task accomplished."

The masterly art of Zola is seen in this volume, as much as in any other of his extraordinary series, by the way in which he makes his story grow out of the business along the railway line, and brings into its scope all the daily and weekly incidents of a great main steam road. Just as the novel " L'Assommoir " had for its focus the life of the Paris workman, and that entitled "Au Bonheur des Dames," the life of the Paris shopwoman, and "La Terre," again, the low and earthly desires and ideas of the French peas-ant, so this volume is a faithful mirror of railway existence and work ; and it is with an amazing dexterity that the author weaves the daily passage of the trains and the traffic of the line into the terrible web of the sins and passions and sorrows of his charac-ters. Incidentally one learns the working of trains, the actual routine of the officials who manage them, and it almost might be said, indeed, that the line from Havre to Paris is like an iron thread upon which are strung the lurid events and low crimes which blot the book from end to end with tears and blood. Sev-erine and Roubaud keep their bad secret close, but, as in the case of that other absorbing story by the same author, "Therese Ra-quin," their crime has killed in their bosoms all love, and Rou-baud turns to gambling, while his wife takes up with Jacques, the engine-driver.

There is an ugly, lonely house along the line, at the mouth of a long tunnel, which we get to know and shudder at as the mys-terious centre of all the crime and misery of the story, *La Croix de Maufras*. Round this point a group of new characters gather: Flore, the signal-girl ; Misard, the pointsman ; Cabuche, the quarryman, and Pecqueux, the stoker, who in conjunction with Jacques drives the locomotive *La Lison*. This engine is the real mistress of Lantier ; he is never tired of cleaning and polishing her, or of lavishly satisfying her eternal passion for oil, and we almost feel with him that she lives and has an existence and disposition of her own in the scenes where Jacques drives her through the piled-up snow, or in the last frightful catastrophe of her career, when Jacques tries to avoid the fatal collision which Flore has prepared for him in order to be avenged against Severine. The signal-girl smashes up the train, but fails to kill Jacques, and afterwards, in a fit of remorse and disappointment, goes into the tunnel and stands up full front on the line to meet the express, which crushes her. The evil current of the narrative presently draws Jacques and Severine into an absorbing desire to get rid of Roubaud, and it is while the engine-driver is waiting at the *Croix de Maufras* to assassinate her husband that the sudden impulse to slay, which always mixes with his brutal love, constrains him to turn upon Severine and to kill her with the very same knife which she had given to her husband, and with which the Chief-Justice Grand-morin had been put to death in the train.

The gloomy and miserable atmosphere of the book—never for one instant relieved except by the accurate pictures of railway life and the working of this great road—becomes more and more darkened by the low avarice of Misard, who slowly poisons his wife to get hold of a thousand francs, which she has hidden, and by the vulgar quarrels and vile amours of the railway-staff people at Havre, Rouen, and Paris. With Severine's death, the hereditary curse lurking in the blood of Lantier is fulfilled, and here is such a translation as I find to hand of the feelings of the man, as Zola depicts them :

"So, at last he had satiated himself; he had killed! Yes, he had done it! A boundless joy, a monstrous feeling of contentment, filled his whole being, in the triumph of the accomplished deed. He enjoyed a fierce surprise of satisfied pride ; he was indeed the male, lording it over the minor race. That woman—he possessed her at last, as he had always dreamed to possess her ; he had her whole self, even to annihilation. Never could she belong to any other. And he remembered also the corpse of Chief-Justice Grandmorin, lying on the track, limp and rag-like. Just such a wretched object she was now ; a mere puppet, empty and worthless ; a stab of a knife had made that of a human, living creature. Was it not in the presence of the other murdered body that he had sworn to himself to taste these acute delights of killing? While leaning over the dead man's remains, he felt running through his whole being a thirst for blood and murder. Oh! to know now that he was no coward! that he had had the courage to plunge the knife into that throat! The craving had grown in him slowly and surely. For a year he had marched, step by step, toward the inevitable deed. Upon the throat of the woman stretched before his eyes the two crimes had met, as it were, brought together by the implacable logic of fate."

But the baneful influence of the *Croix de Maufras* is not yet exhausted ! Jacques has got a new engine, *La Lison* having been broken to pieces ; and has taken up with a new mistress in Philo-mène, the companion of Pecqueux, the stoker. This man who was, beforetimes, faithful and devoted as a dog to Lantier, and always associated with him on the foot-board and the locomotive and in the station lodgings, becomes possessed of a fierce jealousy and hatred towards him, and there occurs a very powerful description of the last ride these two men take together, conducting from Havre to Paris a train full of soldiers who are going to the war with Prussia. One may deny many merits to Zola, but never that of dramatic force. It is beyond measure impressive to read those last pages, where the two men, now become bitter enemies, struggle to the death on their flying engine, hurling each other at last in a fatal embrace on to the track, where both are cut to pieces, while behind their abandoned engine those eighteen cars, full of drunken, singing, and shouting "food for powder," fly along the line through the night to a fatal smash-up. Most skilfully does the author make his blind, mad, runaway locomotive an image of Fate dragging the victims of his genius through blood and woe unspeakable to their wretched destiny. In the last paragraphs of this terrible book its characters and the express train seem to be whirled together out of sight into a black cloud of woe and wickedness which closes over all. To quote once more the very imperfect translation published in America :

"But now all the telegraphic bells upon the line were ringing, all hearts were wildly beating, at the news of the phantom train which had just passed Rouen and Sotteville. There was a great shudder of deathly fright. No doubt the express ahead would not by any chance escape. And the train, like a wild boar in a thicket, rolled on, mindless of signals or dynamite fuses. It almost upset a pilot engine at Oissel; it terrified Pont-de-l'Arche as it passed the station with undiminished speed. And, disappearing again, it rolled on, it rolled on, to the mysterious over-there !

"What mattered the victims the engine crushed on her way ! Did she not drive on toward the future, heedless of the blood that poured like water ? Without a driver, in the night, like a blind and deaf brute let loose among the dead and dying, she rolled on and on, ever dragging behind her that flesh to the cannon pledged, these soldiers stupefied by wine and fatigue— who sang."

A clean sweep is thus at last made by the author of his *dramatis personæ*. Grandmorin, Severine, Flore, Lantier, Pecqueux, Misard's wife, Cabuche, are all killed or dead ; Roubaud is gone to the galleys for life, and the express train full of howling soldiers rushes in the very last line out of sight to a ghastly catastrophe. Horrible from beginning to end, the book leaves upon the mind an overpowering sense of "the beast in man," and, for my part, as soon as I had finished it I went to the side of the steamer and hurled it as far as I could into the sweeping billows of the Atlantic, with a feeling that no other eyes should have the pain of perusing it.

Nevertheless, as a man of letters myself, I must acknowledge, and do acknowledge, the marvellous power of this great master of fiction. Zola's theory of human life is detestable ; his choice of subjects is repulsive ; his treatment of them is too often needlessly and aggressively coarse and offensive ; and he exaggerates to the point of monstrosity the evil in humanity at the expense of the good. His study is a dissecting-room, where nothing interests or engages that poisoned scalpel, his pen, except the cadaverous and the diseased. Even allowing all the importance he claims for this great and well-established principle of heredity, it is still the case that good is as much inherited as bad, and is so vastly a pre-dominating force in the universe that in the working of these two rival principles nature is always rooting out and healing the inherited evil. M. Zola forgets, or for the purpose of his art ignores, the fact that virtuous propensities are bequeathed from generation to generation, as well as vicious. As far as human life is concerned, and its true study, we might as well take the incurable ward in a great hospital as a specimen of the daily existence of mankind, and leave utterly out of sight the pure and happy homes, the bright society, the glad and graceful inter-course, the countless unrecorded brave and unselfish deeds, the gentle general flow of human existence. I find in a local journal, this very morning, the Detroit *Tribune*, some observations which are very much to the point on this head as regards novels and newspapers. The journal remarks :

"Look over your morning paper and you receive the impression that the world is filled with crime and disaster. You lay it aside with a feeling almost of despair. But you were abroad all day yesterday, threading miles of streets and mingling with thousands of people, and you saw no crime committed. You did see, however, enough of duty done, of kindly helpful-ness, of cheerful self-sacrifice in time, convenience, and service, to have filled a dozen newspapers with the recital of them. Here are columns of the papers filled for weeks with the doings of one woman who is said to have poisoned her husband. Well, you know of some wife whose daily self-sacri-fice for a helpless husband would furnish materials of noble heroism for a volume; but such devotion is so common as to pass without comment. Wifely devotion is not ' news,' while wifely infidelity is news, and there is a deep, hopeful, reassuring meaning in it. It would be a bad world if it had to be raked all over every day to find good deeds sufficient to fill a news-paper."

Nevertheless, incurable wards do exist in our hospitals, and taints of hereditary insanity do affect the blood, and sin and selfish-ness and wild, low passions do exist among us too widely and too palpably to be ignored ; and I am not one of those who would for one moment deny to M. Zola the right to choose these sombre themes for his extraordinary art. I do not even think his books immoral. If they be immoral in the sense of being mercilessly outspoken, coarse, revolting, and painfully true to our lowest nature, he would still have a right, in my opinion, to paint upon his rough canvas whatever picture suited him best, so long as he did not paint for the sake of pruriency or the amusement of the vile-minded.   Art *quâ* art has nothing whatever to do with the bound-aries of morality as they are laid down in Sunday-schools and Young Men's Christian Associations.   It violates its own truest rules only when it depicts the truth, as a pander, not as a painter.   In the cellars of our British Museum in London are justly hidden away some works in marble, of such superb execution, such life-like creation, that nothing above ground in public sight approaches them for artistic excellence.   They were the em-bellishments of certain rich Roman villas at Capri and Naples in days when the best Roman art lent itself to the worst desires.   In these splendid, but wicked, works, art has dethroned herself, be-cause her motive was unroyal and disloyal ; but I do not think such can be said of M. Zola and his books.

Weak minds would be much more easily corrupted by " Madame De Bovary " or " Mademoiselle De Maupin," the well-accepted works of Flaubert and of Gautier, than by even the brutal " La Terre" or the terrible "L'Assommoir" of our author ; nay, I consider some of his books as distinctly and powerfully of a most moral tendency ; for example, " Therese Raquin," which could not be read even by a criminally-minded man without a shudder at himself and his inclinations.   As for the subtle charm of Zola's style, I well remember bringing that book from Paris on a stormy day to read as I recrossed the Channel.   The sea was rough, the rain and spray flying, and in my not very comfortable corner on deck I commenced the perusal of that awful book. After some time, when everybody had gone below seeking refuge from the weather, I felt rather cold myself, and looked at my watch, but, making a mistake, mistook the hour, and imagined that we had been at sea only some fifteen minutes.   I therefore went on reading the passage which absorbed me at the close of the volume, and suddenly heard the cry " Dover ! Dover ! " showing that eighty minutes of time had passed away like eight minutes without my notice, under the spell of Zola's wonderful genius. In regard to philosophy and the theory of human life, no man can be farther away from my views than this cynical and un-sparing French pessimist; but I recognize with admiration his stupendous genius as a realist, and I am quite sure that posterity will keep, as painful but precious memorials of our time, the dark and dismal studies that he has made of this our humanity, which, if it touches heaven on one side, certainly plunges deep into its native clay on the other.

I flung "Therese Raquin" into the Channel, as I threw "La Bête Humaine" overboard into the Atlantic; so that I am no propagandist of the ideas of M. Zola; but those who can read him in the French, in which alone he should be studied, know nothing at all of criticism if they style him less than a great master; and I have here at least candidly answered you as to what book has impressed me most painfully, but most permanently, of all those that I have chanced to read during the past ten or twelve months.

EDWIN ARNOLD.

GAIL HAMILTON:

THE most impressive book that I have ever seen is The Modern Iphigenia, an English story by an English author whose name has not been known to American literature. The work owes its power to no charm of style, no artistic grouping of details, no dramatic development of cause and effect; but to the deadly distinctness with which it reveals the sombre, sacrificial fires of pagandom glowing on Christian altars.

The glory of the English race is its self-government. The glory of the English occupation of India is its splendid organization. A crowned conqueror, England submits to the laws which it has imposed upon the conquered. Before its majesty the lowest pariah is on a level with the highest nabob—nay, with the haughtiest ruler of the ruling race.

Yet in this England, our mother land, the home of justice, the light of Asia, an altar of savage lawlessness is reared and Iphigenia lies thereon, bound and speechless, yet

> "Dimly can descry
> The stern, black-bearded kings, with wolfish eyes,
> Waiting to see her die."

And over those kings a Queen whose white hands, calm and cruel, —please heaven, unconscious of their cruelty!—bind the slow cords into their final knot of torture.

For Iphigenia is no myth, of doubtful origin or reality. She is a living woman, and her altar is the prison of penal servitude.

A living woman with the habits and associations of ancestral culture ; a mother, of passionate devotion, torn from her children, who are robbed even of her name and given to another woman ; a daughter, the sole comfort of a mother whose moans should move the pitying skies—" Would God I could die for thee, O my child ! my child ! "

The modern Iphigenia is an American girl, become an English subject by a marriage at eighteen to an Englishman of twice her age, who dies eight years afterwards. The brothers-in-law come out of the dying man's room with a will professing to have been signed by him, leaving them sole control of his property and his children. They, who have already thrust his wife from his bed-side, a servant who has already foully betrayed her mistress's trust, a meddlesome, middle-aged gossip who was once betrothed to the young woman's husband, and who is now divorced from her own, concoct a theory that the young wife poisoned her husband. A mysterious illness falls upon her some hours before her husband's death, and holds her speech-less and unconscious for many hours after, during all which time the conspirators are balefully busy. The police are introduced, not to make discoveries, but to adopt the discoveries which the conspirators allege themselves to have made, and the theory of guilt which they have already framed. The doctors swallow the poison of asps placed under their lips, though they frankly swear they had never suspected or thought of poison until it was suggested to them by the conspirators. The dead body is explored, but no poison is found. Nevertheless, the stern, black-bearded kings, with wolfish eyes, of whom the rapacious brothers-in-law are chief, surround the bed where the foreordained victim lies, still dazed and prostrate, with no friend of her blood near, and summon her from the Valley of the Shadow of Death with the announcement that she is under arrest for murder !

Forcibly restraining her natural convulsion at the shock, even to laying their coarse hands upon her bared and shrinking limbs, they snatch her from the bed, from the arms of her too late sum-moned mother, to the hideous gaol. Another and more deter-mined exploration is made into the exhumed body of the dead, and is rewarded by the desired "find"—a minute particle of arsenic, harmless, medicinal, of such widely-distributed sort as the eminent Parisian chemist Raspail declared he could find in the judge's arm-chair—even beyond that, abundantly accounted for by the husband's well-known habit of taking arsenic, or by the doctor's drugs prescribed to him in his last illness,—but still arsenic.

The young mother is haled before the judge, and the judge casts her into prison.

"It is necessary to an unfavorable verdict that the man died of arsenic," is the judicial principle laid down at the outset to the jury.

The trial does not prove that he died of arsenic. The overwhelming evidence is that he did not die of arsenic. But he must! The stern, black-bearded kings, with wolfish eyes, will wait in vain to see their victim die, if her husband were not murdered.

The adroit judge shifts his ground. He no longer asks : "Was this man poisoned to death ?" He asks : "Why did this woman poison him?" He no longer says to the jury: "You must prove that the man died of arsenic." He says : "You must *not* merely consider whether this man did or did not die of arsenic according to the medical evidence. . . . You *must rely upon your knowledge of human nature* as to the results at which you will arrive "!

The jury heeds the hint. Abandoning the evidence, this English jury of farmers and bakers and milliners and plumbers betake themselves to their "knowledge of human nature," and on that knowledge bring in a verdict that this young mother poisoned her husband to death.

It is incredible, but it is contemporary English history. It is not a myth. It is in the records of English law which are collected in this book.

"The bright death quivered at the victim's throat," but the horror of a great people quenched the gleam. The law was forced to call a halt upon itself by the popular revolt. The executive officer dared not execute. The bright death quivered, but the man who held it dared not thrust it in for fear of the people ; yet dared not unbind the victim for fear of the judge : so he smothered sentence and reprieve alike in sophistry.

"It is essential that the man died of arsenic," had pronounced the judge.

"There is a reasonable doubt whether he died of arsenic," pronounced the executive.

What, then, was the only righteous course ? The judge himself had indicated it in his charge to the jury : "Are we sure,
beyond all reasonable doubt, that she is guilty ? If she is not,
she is—NOT GUILTY."

The executive says : " There is reasonable doubt whether she
is guilty ; but she is—GUILTY."

And the throat which they dare not pierce, they clutch. Her
youth is blasted with a curse, and she is cut off from hope in
that sad place which yet to name my spirit loathes and fears.

If England is a pagan nation, what sword shall sever the cords
of innocence upon the altar of sacrifice ?

If England is a Christian nation, who shall roll us away the
stone from the door of this sepulchre wherein a living creature
lies enshrouded ?

But not only, not even first, is the individual suffering. It is
the menace to order, it is the peril to life and liberty and free
institutions ; it is the temptation to revolution ; it is the defiance
of law by the law-makers ; it is the mockery of justice by its administrators ; it is the crime against society by the leaders of
society ; it is the obtrusion of heathenism into Christendom,
that makes this outrage ominous.

Victoria !

> " Not alone in the East is she greatest and best.
> We own the sweet sway of Victoria, West.
> By her womanly worth, without contest or cost,
> She has won back the empire her grandfather lost.
> Her white hand was peace when our trouble was sore :
> By that sign she is queen of our hearts evermore.
> The ligeance of love sea nor sword shall dissever—
> God's blessing be on her forever and ever ! "

Thus we sang, thrilled with her high thought and honorable
words to us in our time of storm and stress. We resent upon
that white hand, that mother's hand, that friendly hand, the
stain of innocent blood, besmeared thereon by lawlessness in the
masquerade of law. Out, damned spot ! All the perfumes of
Arabia will not sweeten that little hand. It will, rather, the multitudinous seas incarnadine that roll between. The ligeance of
love sea nor sword shall dissever, but no ties can resist the dis-
solving force of wrong perpetrated and perpetuated. " The
Queen can do no wrong " is the fiction of monarchy. The conviction of republicanism is : The Queen is Queen, our Queen, only
so far as she does right.

Thus my book. It is not *called* The Modern Iphigenia. It borrows no romance from the past. It bears the dry legal title of "The Maybrick Case." It is by that most unhomeric of heroes, a London lawyer, whose canny Scotch name is Alexander MacDougall. But, for all its legal reasoning and repetition, it is vital with unquenchable fire; that eternal revolt of the human heart against tyranny crushing helplessness which has lent passion to poetry, and stimulus to passion, and purpose to life through all the ages of history, but which in our day and our race flames up against a tragedy which is an anachronism.

GAIL HAMILTON.

MISS REPPLIER:

EVER since the first printers with misguided zeal dipped an innocent world in ink, those books have been truly popular which reflected faithfully and enthusiastically the foibles and delusions of the hour. This is what is called "keeping abreast with the spirit of the times," and we have only to look around us at present to see the principle at work. With an arid and dreary realism chilling us to the heart, and sad-voiced novelists entreating us at every turn to try to cultivate religious doubts, fiction has ceased to be a medium of delight. Even nihilism, which is the only form of relief that true earnestness permits, is capable of being overstrained, and some narrowly conservative people are beginning to ask themselves already whether this new development of "murder as a fine art" has not been sufficiently encouraged. Out of the midst of the gloom, out of the confusion and depression of conflicting forms of seriousness, rises from London a voice, clear, languid, musical, shaken with laughter, and speaking in strange sweet tones of art and beauty, and of that finer criticism which is one with art and beauty, and claims them forever as its own. The voice comes from Mr. Oscar Wilde, and few there are who listen to him, partly because his philosophy is alien to our prevalent modes of thought, and partly because of the perverse and paradoxical fashion in which he delights to give it utterance. People are more impressed by the way a thing is said than by the thing itself. A grave arrogance of demeanor, a solemn and self-assertive method of reiterating an opinion until it grows weighty with words, are weapons more convincing than any subtlety of argument. " As I have before expressed to the still reverberating discontent of two continents," this is the mode in which the public loves to have a statement offered to its ears, that it may gape, and wonder, and acquiesce.

Now, nothing can be further from such admirable solidity than Mr. Wilde's flashing sword-play, than the glee with which he makes out a case against himself, and then proceeds valiantly into battle. There are but four essays in his recent volume, rather vaguely called " Intentions," and of these four only two have real and permanent value. " The Truth of Masks " is a somewhat trivial paper, inserted apparently to help fill up the book, and " Pen, Pencil, and Poison " is visibly lacking in sincerity. The author plays with his subject very much as his subject, " kind, light-hearted Wainewright, ' played with crime, and in both cases there is a subtle and discordant element of vulgarity. It is not given to our eminently respectable age to reproduce that sumptuous and horror-laden atmosphere which lends an artistic glamor to the poisonous court of the Medicis. This " study in green " contains, however, some brilliant passages, and at least one sentence—" The domestic virtues are not the true basis of art, though they may serve as an excellent advertisement for second-rate artists "—that must make Mr. George Moore pale with envy when he reflects that he missed saying it, where it belongs, in his clever, truthful, ill-natured paper on "Mummer-Worship."

The significance and the charm of Mr. Wilde's book are centred in its opening chapter, " The Decay of Lying," reprinted from The Nineteenth Century, and in the long two-part essay entitled " The Critic as Artist," which embodies some of his most thoughtful, serious, and scholarly work. My own ineffable content rests with " The Decay of Lying," because under its transparent mask of cynicism, its wit, its satire, its languid mocking humor, lies clearly outlined a great truth that is slipping fast away from us,—the absolute independence of art—art nourished by imagination and revealing beauty. This is the hand that gilds the grayness of the world ; this is the voice that sings· in flute tones through the silence of the ages. To degrade this shining vision into a handmaid of nature, to maintain that she should give us photographic pictures of an unlovely life, is a heresy that arouses in Mr. Wilde an amused scorn which takes the place of anger. " Art," he says, " never expresses anything but itself.

It has an independent life, just as Thought has, and develops purely on its own lines. It is not necessarily realistic in an age of realism, nor spiritual in an age of faith. So far from being the creation of its time, it is usually in direct opposition to it, and the only history that it preserves for us is the history of its own progress." That we should understand this, it is necessary to understand also the "beautiful untrue things" which exist only in the world of fancy; the things that are lies, and yet that help us to endure the truth. Mr. Wilde repudiates distinctly and almost energetically all lying with an object, all sordid trifling with a graceful gift. The lies of newspapers yield him no pleasure; the lies of politicians are ostentatiously unconvincing; the lies of lawyers are "briefed by the prosaic." He reviews the world of fiction with a swift and caustic touch; he lingers among the poets; he muses rapturously over those choice historic masterpieces, from Herodotus to Carlyle, where "facts are either kept in their proper subordinate position, or else entirely excluded on the general ground of dulness." He laments with charming frankness the serious virtues of his age. "Many a young man," he says, "starts in life with a natural gift for exaggeration which, if nurtured in congenial and sympathetic surroundings, or by the imitation of the best models, might grow into something really great and wonderful. But, as a rule, he comes to nothing. He either falls into careless habits of accuracy, or takes to frequenting the society of the aged and the well-informed. Both things are equally fatal to his imagination, and in a short time he develops a morbid and unhealthy faculty of truth-telling, begins to verify all statements made in his presence, has no hesitation in contradicting people who are much younger than himself, and often ends by writing novels that are so like life that no one can possibly believe in their probability." Surely this paragraph has but one peer in the world of letters, and that is the immortal sentence wherein De Quincey traces the murderer's gradual downfall to incivility and procrastination.

"The Critic as Artist" affords Mr. Wilde less scope for his humor and more for his erudition, which, perhaps, is somewhat lavishly displayed. Here he pleads for the creative powers of criticism, for its fine restraints, its imposed self-culture, and he couches his plea in words as rich as music. Now and then, it is true, he seems driven by the whips of our modern Furies to the verge of things which are not his to handle—problems, social and spiritual, to which he holds no key. When this occurs, we can only wait with drooping heads and what patience we can muster until he is pleased to return to his theme ; or until he remembers, laughing, how fatal is the habit of imparting opinions, and what a terrible ordeal it is to sit at table with the man who has spent his life in educating others rather than himself. " For the development of the race depends on the development of the individual, and where self-culture has ceased to be the ideal, the intellectual standard is instantly lowered, and often ultimately lost." I like to fancy the ghost of the late rector of Lincoln, of him who said that an appreciation of Milton was the reward of consummate scholarship, listening in the Elysian Fields, and nodding his assent to this much-neglected view of a much-disputed question. Everybody is now so busy teaching that nobody has any time to learn. We are growing rich in lectures, but poor in scholars, and the triumph of mediocrity is at hand. Mr. Wilde can hardly hope to become popular by proposing real study to people burning to impart their ignorance ; but the criticism that develops in the mind a more subtle quality of apprehension and discernment is the criticism that creates the intellectual atmosphere of the age.

AGNES REPPLIER.

MRS. BARR:

THERE was once a pope who desired to destroy all the books in the world except 6,000, which number he averred would contain all of human wisdom worth preserving. This computation would give about an average of one good book every year. Is there any one living whose taste and acquirements are so catholic, so judicial, and yet so sympathetic, that he might be safely intrusted with the selection of the book of the year ? The answer must be a universal " No."

For over half a century my intercourse with books has been constant, but during 1891 we have been on a holiday together. During this year I have begun to read newspapers, and to defend my lapse of mental dignity by saying that but for newspapers many things could only be known at a cost too great to pay. I have also required six magazines every month, and have felt it to be necessary to supplement these by reviews that supplied history, social science, literature, and philosophy put up in portable forms. For at sixty years of age it strikes one forcibly that life is shorter than ever in proportion to what has to be crowded into it, and that our minds are not more capacious. I have even come to a good opinion of the funny newspapers. I believe they are one of the best popular antidotes for the dead-alive, serious sensuality of bad novels. A hearty laugh blows into thin air romantic animalism, and all that mock sensuality which depicts men and women who call their vices by the names of passions.

Yet, amid much desultory reading, there is in every student's mind an inner circle, to which none but really good books are admitted, and the most charming of these intimates of 1891 has been the Rev. Adam Sedgwick's " Life and Letters." I invited the book because in my girlhood the great geologist was such a familiar figure about the mountains and towns of the English lake district. And through it we have had delightful conversations about people and times that will never return—grand old " statesmen " riding along the mountain roads, with their wives on the gorgeous family pillion, and their pretty daughters, in long flowing scarlet cloaks and silken hoods, stepping briskly at their side ; of the old ways and celebrities of Cambridge; of the burial of Porson ; of the ringing of a dumb peal at St. Mary's for Trafalgar ; of the mail coach coming into Lowestoft streaming with ribbons, and carrying a sailor on the top waving the Union Jack, while the guard threw down to the cheering crowds the *Gazette Extraordinary* of the battle of Salamanca. And what stirring descriptions of the geological " meets " when sixty or seventy undergraduates met before the Senate House, and then all off together for a grand " field day " among the fens or up to the northern mountains ! In those days the Cambridge liverymen charged extra for horses used for " jollygizing," and no wonder ! Through this book I could feel the enthusiasm with which men listened to the first words of the new science of geology, and to those wonderful lectures on " The Great Irish Elk," and on the " Dragons of the Prime," while Sedgwick's eloquence

" rolled like a deluge retiring,
Which mastodon carcasses floated."

I am not sure if this delightful biography has been reprinted in America ; if not, some publisher will doubtless soon find it out.

Another book of 1891, but of a decidedly different character, has made a very marked impression upon my mind. Its name is unattractive, and, until the book is once read through, seems to have no special significance. Its binding is rigidly plain and there is nothing whatever to point to its author. "God in His World"—this is the title, and one is apt to think the writer must be a clergyman, until startled continually by such sentences as the following : " There is no need of an atonement to reconcile God unto man. . . . [Christ] is the Lamb of God, not the scapegoat" (p. 138) ; or, "Justice is not a divine attribute. It has in it no divine quality, no vital meaning, either as applied to Nature or to the kingdom of heaven " (p. 140) ; or, " Even though the church should die, the kingdom will live. . . . The Father worketh in all humanity and not in a chosen part. What if he raise up children unto his kingdom from among the children of this world, seeing that they are in their generation wiser than the children of light, in that they more readily throw aside tradition and show a quicker and more vigorous life ? What if he seek his own among them that are repelled by the dead forms and artificial solemnities which he himself abhorreth ? " (p. 255.)

There is a sequence in writers as in everything else, and this book is a carrying-forward of that spirit of natural religiosity which evoked its remarkable predecessor by Professor Drummond. And that I am not able to define the serious and peculiar charm of " God in His World " takes nothing from it. A person may not be able technically to distinguish between good wine and bad wine, but when it is set before him he will drink more of the good than of the bad, having an inarticulate consciousness of the difference. So in a book we may not be able to explain the very excellence which has yet most impressed us.

In fiction I have read many short stories, and very good most of them appeared to me. Our fathers followed the stars of their gods, Scott, Dickens, Thackeray, etc. ; and we have our own idols. Tolstoï has been one of mine, but this year—and last year too— he has disappointed me. I make him welcome still ; but I no longer salaam to him. He is too many Tolstoïs. I had just begun to admire his dry realism, when I found out he was not a realist, but a mystic. The gloomy horror of the "Kreutzer Sonata" debased him from the altitude of mysticism ; and in his last work, " The Fruits of Enlightenment," he pays a visit full of sardonic mirth, in which spiritualism and microbes are leading motives. It is clever, but not what I expected from Tolstoï; and his excessive versatility makes one unavoidably remember the elderly naval man that "was a cook, and a captain bold, and the mate of the Nancy brig, and a bo'sun tight, and a midshipmite."

During 1891 no one has sung a song for me ; perhaps that is because I have grown too old, and the singing birds have no message to bring. For now I like the old songs best, and I have a fancy that, though the gods never permit poets to be mediocre, modern publishers do. I feel kindly, however, to every book I place upon my shelves. I get out of my library that confused, soothing influence a man gets out of his pipe. The books shine with kindliness and mild gravity ; they diffuse an atmosphere of stillness and gentle warmth ; and I love to sit quietly among them, just speculating as to whether the spirits of books disembodied ever clothe themselves again in paper and calf and morocco, or retain any traceable connection with their former selves. And any thinker can tell how delightful such questions and speculations may be, without individualizing a single volume.

AMELIA E. BARR.

PROF. BRIGGS

THE year 1891 has been fruitful in great theological writings. Oxford has produced no less than three of these, by Canon Driver, Principal Gore, and Canon Cheyne. Canon Driver gives a masterly exposition of the present state of opinion as to the criticism of the entire literature of the Old Testament. Principal Gore gives an able and brilliant statement of one of the most important topics of Christology. But the Bampton lectures of Canon Cheyne on the " Origin and Religious Contents of the Psalter, in the Light of Old Testament Criticism and the History of Religion,"* constitute, in our estimation, the most important theological work of the year. These lectures were delivered in 1889, but first appeared in print in the summer of 1891. The author is somewhat cramped by the form of the lecture; but he has managed by numerous notes and appendices to give the freshest, richest, and most fruitful piece of criticism that has appeared for many a year ; showing an amount of original research and a

* Kegan Paul, Trench, Trübner & Co.

wealth of knowledge that can hardly be surpassed by any biblical scholar now living.

Canon Cheyne, in his introduction, gives a sketch of the development of his own critical experience. He tells us, in a frank, modest, naïve, and charming manner, his progress through those periods of criticism which have been under the spell of Ewald and Kuenen; and of his loneliness in Great Britain until W. Robertson Smith and Samuel R. Driver came to his support. Now the mass of biblical scholars of Great Britain are with him in spirit and methods, if not agreeing with him in all his results. Cheyne has throughout his career kept in touch with the religious life of the Church of England and also with the evangelical piety of the school of Delitzsch ; so that his growth has been steady and comprehensive. This is doubtless due in great measure to his earliest teacher, to whom he attributes " the example of a mild and yet fervent Johannine religion and a Pauline love of the Scriptures." Any one who knows Cheyne will recognize that these qualities are essential constituents of his character. Notwithstanding all that he has learned from Continental scholars, he has ever been an independent, painstaking student, never accepting anything without submitting it to fresh, independent investigation ; brave and frank, and yet shy and cautious ; true to the instincts of an Anglican scholar. He, more than any one else, has been the pioneer of Old Testament criticism in England. He is entitled to speak in its interests, for he has passed through its various phases. Even when we may differ with him, his words are those of a master who must be respected.

The Psalter is in some respects the most interesting book in the Old Testament. It is used in the devotions, public and private, of synagogue and church throughout the world. No book awakens a more general interest. The critical movement of modern times has for the most part left it aside, doubtless on account of the extreme difficulty of the problems, as any one must recognize who has given any attention to the subject. It has long been evident that the Psalter was the key to the Old Testament. Bibical criticism will never attain its end with regard to Penta-teuch or prophets until the Psalter has given its witness and the whole Old Testament speaks in unison the last word. Cheyne deserves great credit for undertaking this difficult problem and for opening it so bravely and so well.

The traditional opinion for centuries was that David was the author of the Psalter, as Solomon was the author of the Wisdom literature, and Moses was the author of the Pentateuch. Criticism has resolved all these into groups of writings of different authors and different periods of composition. After the traditional theory was abandoned, there was a rally about the five books into which the Psalter has been divided from the most ancient times, and the titles of the psalms were supposed to give a number of authors, such as David, Asaph, Solomon, Moses, and the sons of Korah, and to leave a number of psalms orphaned, without designation of author. But this theory soon proved untenable. The groups assigned to Asaph and the sons of Korah have certain features that justify their grouping under these names; but the internal evidence of these psalms showed that they belonged to different periods, and could not have been written by Asaph and the Korahites of the Davidic period. The psalms assigned to David also represented widely different periods of composition. Do these ascriptions represent conjectures of later editors as to authorship, or do they simply mean that these psalms were taken from earlier collections that bore the names of David, of Asaph, and of the Korahites ?

Cheyne holds that the five books represent, in the main, successive layers of the Psalter ; only he very properly states that the division between books 4 and 5 was an afterthought ; and he really does away with the distinction between books 2 and 3, and divides the whole Psalter into three sections representing, in the main, the Persian, Greek, and Maccabean periods. Cheyne also represents that the ascription to David meant nothing more, originally, than a group of psalms gathered under the name of the poet-king ; but that afterwards not a few psalms were ascribed to David by mistaken conjectures of later editors. It seems to us that Cheyne halts in his criticism at these points. Doubtless there are mistaken conjectures as to authorship in the titles of the psalms ; but, on the whole, the titles seem to represent three earlier minor psalters, which were named after David, Asaph, and the Korahites, a greater Psalter made up chiefly of selections from these, called the Director's Psalter, besides a number of groups such as the Hallels and the Pilgrim psalms. We cannot see anything more in the five books than a liturgical division to correspond with the Pentateuch. When the divisions are very properly reduced to three, they do not then represent different layers of the Psalter, but divisions made by the Maccabean editor prior to the division into five books.

The critical study of the Psalter has resulted in the constant pushing of the psalms into later periods in the history of Israel. Cheyne goes farther in this direction than any previous writer. Most scholars now recognize that there are Maccabean psalms as well as Davidic psalms, and that the Psalter represents the psalmody of Israel in all that intervening period. But the number of Davidic psalms, and, indeed, preëxilic psalms, has been steadily diminishing in the closer study of the Psalter. Even the more conservative critics feel themselves forced to give up the antiquity of one psalm after another. Cheyne seems to take an extreme position when he represents that we have no preëxilic psalm save a portion of the eighteenth, and that we must also give up exilic psalms, and when he distributes the psalms over the Persian, Greek, and Maccabean periods.

We have no space to follow him into the details of his argument. He tries to give the psalms their historic setting in those times and circumstances which seem to be the most appropriate for the purpose. All the resources of history, comparative biblical theology, and the religions of Babylon and Persia, are used to cast light upon the composition of the psalms and the gradual evolution of the Psalter. The argument from language is not neglected, but it is not employed with much effect. It will doubtless appear to some that Cheyne does not sufficiently estimate the editorial changes that have been made to adapt earlier psalms to the later use of the synagogue ; and that the imagination is too freely employed to color the psalms with the hues of the history of the times in which he places them ; and that, in a measure, the same mistake is repeated that was made by the older scholars, who strove to find the historical occasions of the psalms in the life and experience of David. And yet the careful reader will be convinced that in a large number of cases Cheyne has put psalms in their most appropriate historic circumstances, and that he has given them a new and richer meaning.

There is doubtless a sad loss and a strain upon the faith of those who have been accustomed to look upon the Psalter as David's psalm-book, or as the expression of the experience of worshippers in the temple of Solomon. But criticism has made it evident that David composed but few of the psalms, to say the least; and that the Psalter was not a temple hymn-book, but a hymn-and prayer-book for the synagogue wherever the different psalms themselves may have been composed. It matters little, therefore, where you place these psalms in the historic development of Israel. Wherever they seem most appropriate to the evolution of life and thought of the Jewish people, there they will take on the richest coloring and the fullest meaning. If, as Cheyne supposes, the Psalter represents the religious experience of Israel after the restoration in the Persian, Greek, and Maccabean periods, then the chasm that used to be regarded as separating the Old Testament from the New Testament is filled up; and an unbroken continuity of divine revelation in sacred writings takes its place. This is more in accord with what one might expect from the living and true God. He would not abandon his people for centuries after restoring them to their own land. He would continue to guide them and teach them. This would be a gain that would far out-weigh the loss in the supposed greater antiquity of the Psalter.

One of the most interesting and valuable parts of Canon Cheyne's work is his study of the Persian religion and the influence that it had upon the psalms and other postexilic writings. The student of biblical history and of biblical theology, in our day, must take into consideration the ethnic environment of the biblical writers. He must recognize that the holy people as the kingdom of priests, called to mediate redemption for the nations of the world, not only had something precious to give, but also some gifts to receive in return, and that there were action and reaction in the relation of Israel to the nations in all that long period in which Israel seemed to be the foot-ball tossed to and fro between them.

C. A. Briggs.

JULIEN GORDON:

When invited to express an opinion on the book of the year, one is met at the outset with peculiar difficulty. One asks one's self, in this age of many writers and numberless readers, if it is a public verdict one is to voice or an individual predilection. Of a book people make such different—nay, divergent—uses. The moralist seeks a sermon, and demands that he shall be taught a lesson. The doubter craves a new *Credo* ; the scientist, a fresh problem solved, or at least suggested ; the æsthete, a work of art that shall please his fancy and warm his imagination ; while the frivolous desires only to be entertained for a half-hour. In this clash of sentiments and wants, it is assuredly no light task to select a work that can meet or has met the general requirements.

A treatise which touches upon topics of immediate moment were perhaps the fittest to dub " the book of the year." It alone can be considered important and authoritative. I think in Mr. Herbert Spencer's " Justice," Part Fourth of his " Principles of Ethics," we have such an *exposé*.

Since the death of John Stuart Mill, that pioneer of the cause of woman, England has produced no such leading thinker as Herbert Spencer. There is not to-day in France, in Germany, or in America, any writer upon sociology who can even be compared with him. A new book by this great philosopher may therefore be viewed with the interest which is evoked in a politically disturbed country by a manifesto emanating from its sovereign or its prime minister. It cannot be denied that in " Justice " Mr. Spencer considers questions of burning and urgent import. He has something to say, in his opening chapter, of " animal ethics," of ethics considered not merely as calling forth sentiments of approbation or reprobation, but of ethics considered objectively, as producing good and bad results to " self or others or both." He tells us that a bird who feeds his mate while she is sitting is regarded with approval ; while for a hen who declines to look after her eggs there is aversion. The egoism of animals is deplored, and their altruistic acts are admired. This may give food for thought to those advanced naturalists who insist upon the higher intelligence of what we are now pleased to call " the dumb creatures," and who believe we shall soon learn to exchange ideas with our dogs and horses by means of learning to understand their now incomprehensible volapük. When this is done, we shall study them with even greater interest than those queer animals men and women study each other in modern drawing-rooms.

He tells us, in his chapter upon the " Idea of Justice," that this idea is developed from the recognition of inequality. If, therefore, there were no inequality, justice would be a mere word, a term, no more. He glances at the " right of physical integrity," the value and protection of the person, the sanctity of human life. He carries us from the days when the rude Wends and Herulians killed their aged and sick parents, to the present time, when the growth of civilization has awarded to the citizen a claim against his fellow citizen for bodily danger, not only willingly inflicted, but for bodily danger caused by careless actions or inactions.

He has some pregnant words to say upon the " Rights of Property," and of incorporeal property, wherein the demands of authors and artists for proper remuneration for mental labor are broached.

The "Rights of Free Belief and Worship" are dwelt upon. He would here accord absolute liberty, except where the beliefs entertained and practised would diminish the powers of defence against hostile societies, or imperil subordination to the government, thus paralyzing its executive powers. He prophesies that complete freedom of belief will exist only when industrial life has become preëminent, and has displaced the military régime.

In a cursory review of this admirable book there is one topic which peculiarly meets the anxiety of the hour, and of which I would speak at somewhat greater length. Mr. Spencer gives us a brief sketch of the gradual progress and emancipation of woman since Fulc the Black amused himself burning his wife— unmolested, and, in fact, all German rulers bought their wives, and might sell or slay them at their good pleasure In those happy days English brides were purchased and haggled over, their own desires counting for nothing in the bargaining.

He points out—with some felicity in sustaining his own opinions expressed later—that it was only in those tribes where women shared in the dangers of war that they gained some degree of liberty. In other words, brute force was the law of gained freedom. Mr. Spencer realizes the infinitely delicate handling needed to compare in detail the capacities of men and of women. He accepts the unquestionable fact that, whatever the fiat of averages may be, there are some women physically and mentally stronger than some men, healthier, more vigorous, endowed with a larger and richer intelligence. Generosity aside, he avers that justice demands that women, if they are not artificially advantaged, shall not, at any rate, be artificially disadvantaged. Hence, if men and women are to be regarded as independent beings, each one of whom is to do the best he or she can for himself or herself, no restraint should be placed upon women in regard to whatever career or profession they choose to adopt.

So far so good ; but—in the last page—Mr. Spencer goes on to point out what he seems to consider the emphatic disability of women. He asks us if the political rights of women are the same as those of men,—realizing that the assumption is now widely made, —and if their only duty of citizenship is to consist in the casting of a vote. How shall one portion of a community, he argues, assume the rights of government without incurring any of its risks ? Men have to man war vessels, to shoulder the musket in times when the public peace is threatened. Are women not only ready to do so—are they able ? He concludes with the statement that, if they are not, it is useless to prate of their political rights, unless, indeed, we lived in a state of permanent peace. Here then in a nut-shell lies the gist of the whole matter, the opinion of the greatest of living philosophers. Women are unqualified for governing because they are unqualified for fighting.

It may here be said that it seems, indeed, a pity that women should be so unqualified. Women are by nature quicker to resent injury than men, more fiery, more easily roused to indignation at the sight of wrong, more combative. The last word is proverbially the feminine one. Then, they are more dramatic than men, and therefore more prone to be thrilled and stirred by the heroic. They are courageous, and they are cheerful under physical pain. No one will deny that in their narrow sphere—and why not, then, in a wider one ?—they are diplomatists, strategists, and tacticians ; eminently, therefore, fitted for the subtleties of the art of war. One cannot doubt that morally they would make excellent soldiers As to endurance ! only watch the evolutions of the maiden *à la mode*, at one of our great watering-places ; the veriest unbeliever would be persuaded, nay, converted. She will be up with the lark, swim all the morning, attend a " girls' luncheon " at noon, be in the saddle all the afternoon, dine at eight, and dance till three, and this for a period of six months of summer heat ; and she will not look much the worse for the régime !

Octave Feuillet, in one of his recent novels, paints with his poignant and piquant satire the fatigue of the enervated and dyspeptic man of the world who tries to emulate and follow a Parisian great lady in her exhausting and exhaustless round of

pleasure ; pleasure which necessitates unflagging physical prowess, as well as the alertness of a keen and wide-awake *esprit*.

But here come the doctors and the men of science to dispel
and refute all the illusions of superficial observers. The late Dr.
Clark, of Boston, contends that for physiological reasons, associated with woman's function of maternity, she is unfit for that
military service which, in the last resort, is the supreme duty of
every citizen.

The other day a distinguished German anatomist declared
that, from a careful study of the conformation of a woman's
knee, he has arrived at the conclusion that it is not constructed
for the maintenance of an upright posture, or of movement under
heavy weights for any protracted period. Women, therefore, are
barred out, in his opinion, from those forced and fatiguing
marches which form an essential feature of every campaign.

It is a curious fact that Mr. Spencer was formerly an advocate
of female emancipation. He now declares himself against it. The
Liberals were, until lately, the hope and trust of the female suf-
fragists. They, indeed, were once on the verge of passing a resolution on the question through the House of Commons. Recently,
however, they appear to have grown tired of the women, and the
Conservatives have taken them up. These have passed a resolution at Birmingham in favor of female suffrage. When Mrs.
Fawcett—the widow of the blind Postmaster-General, and mother
of the Miss Fawcett who beat the senior wrangler in mathematics
at Cambridge—addressed the convocation, she said that the Gladstonians feared that the women would reënforce the party of
order and the upholders of the indissoluble union between Great
Britain and Ireland.

It is odd that Spencer should desert the female emancipators
just as the "Primrose dames" have rendered such solid service
to the Tory leaders as to convince a large portion of them that the
ballot ought to be granted to them.

That women cannot go to war seems a poor and idle plea for
refusing them a voice in public affairs. Men who have passed the
age of military duty are permitted to vote, and since the days of
Homer particular respect has been given to their decisions. It is
only in countries where the conscription prevails that weight
would be attached to women's inability for militant services. In
England and the United States armies are formed by voluntary

recruitment. In the last century the recruiting system was almost universal. All countries would probably revert to it if women voted. Who shall say that the reversion would not be a good thing for civilization ?

JULIEN GORDON.

DR. HAMMOND:

I AM not quite sure that the book I am about to mention as the best published during the year is strictly inside the limits laid down by the editor of THE REVIEW within which a choice is to be made, but with free scope embracing the entire literature of the world during the year 1891, and excluding technical works, there is no doubt in my mind that the " Century Dictionary " stands preëminent. If it were an ordinary dictionary, or even merely the best of the class hitherto published, it would certainly not be entitled to this exalted position ; but it is such a great advance upon everything of the kind yet given to the world, and so different from all else in its extent and detail, and embraces so much of science, literature, art, philosophy, and, in fact, every kind of knowledge, that its influence upon mankind must necessarily be of the most direct and powerful character. If it were a mere compilation, however excellent it might be, this praise would not be justified ; but it is full of originality from beginning to end, and is so comprehensive and far-reaching that one cannot turn over its pages without being almost appalled at the magnitude of the work, and astonished at the thoroughness and exactness with which it has been accomplished.

Of course any well-educated and intelligent person with a competent corps of assistants can make an encyclopædia or dictionary. There are a great many remarkable examples of the truth of this assertion ; none more to the point than the wonderful " Grand Dictionnaire Universel du XIXème Siécle" of Pierre Larousse, certainly the greatest work of the kind which the mind of man has ever conceived or executed. But this is not only a dictionary ; it is an encyclopædia of history, geography, literature, science, art, and, in truth, every branch of human knowledge. It is a library in itself. Its cost, however, to say nothing of its bulk, is so extreme as to place it entirely beyond the reach of the majority of those who might need to consult its pages.

But the " Century Dictionary " is essentially a dictionary, and

not an encyclopædia, although it has several encyclopædic feat·
tures. Its first object is to treat of words, and the fact that 7,000
pages are required for this purpose is due, not so much to the
extent of the information in regard to persons, places, and things,
as it is to the number of words and the amplitude of its defini-
tions, its etymologies, and the citations of authorities illustrative
of usage and meaning. In the matter of derivatives and compound words, no dictionary that I have ever seen can make any
pretence to approaching it. Take, for instance, the word "powder."
I have found under this head reference to every kind of substance
to which the word powder is ordinarily applied, even to those
which are used in medicine. I have discovered only one notable
omission, and that is "succession powder," the substance used
during the latter part of the middle ages, especially in Italy, by
expectant heirs to get rid of those who stood in the way of their
inheritance. But then I do not find "succession powder" in any
other dictionary, which is somewhat strange, for various other
powders of analagous classes, such as the "powder of sympathy,"
for instance, are given by these others, and with great fulness by
the "Century."

With the extension of education into all classes of life, words
which a few years ago were regarded as being peculiar to science
have now become commonplace, and a dictionary with pretensions
to general usefulness must bring them within its scope.

In dictionaries hitherto published there seems to have been
no rule governing the principle of acceptance, but merely a notion
based upon the idea that this or that word was not of sufficient
importance as an integral part of the language to warrant its
being incorporated with others in regard to which no doubt existed.
Thus, all dictionaries gave the word "opium," but none except
those pertaiming to medicine or botany contained "apiol," which
word is fully defined in the "Century." "Stramonium," a word
indicating a substance certainly of no greater importance than
"physostigma," has been recognized for several years by all the
prominent dictionaries ; but this last-named receives no notice,
while the "Century" devotes several lines to its consideration,
giving its pronounciation and etymology, a description of the
botanical characteristics of the genus of plants to which it refers,
and an account sufficiently full for the general reader of the medical properties of the only species of the *physostigma venenosum.*

With all living languages there is danger that expressive words, better for some purposes than others of like meaning, and always useful in our efforts to avoid that mean fault, tautology, will die merely because there is not a sufficient number of writers to perceive their value and to employ them. It is as a preserver of such words that the "Century Dictionary" stands preëminent among all works of its kind. The reader of Chaucer, of Spencer, of Shakespeare, and of other writers to whom the English tongue owes so much of directness and force, requires a glossary in order to understand fully the meanings sought to be conveyed. Indeed, he needs one such help for Chaucer, another for Shakespeare, another for Piers Ploughman, another for the "Morte d'Arthure," and so on for a dozen or more others. A few examples will suffice to show that with the "Century Dictionary" the reader of early English literature requires no other aid for the elucidation of the text. Thus the word to *kemp* is not found in any of the dictionaries in common use, but the "Century" treats of it as follows :

Kemp (kemp), *v. i.* [A var. of *camp* (after *kemp, n.*) : see *camp, v.*] To strive or contend in any way ; strive for victory, as in the quantity of work done by reapers in the harvest-field. [Scotch and old Eng.]

> There es no Kynge undire Criste may *kempe* with hym one !
> He wille be Alexander ayre, that alle the erthe lowttede.
> > Morte Arthure [E. E. T. S.] I. 2634.

"Gurl" and its adjective, "gurly," are not given in either Webster or Worcester, but the "Century" cites them as follows :

Gurl (gerl), *v. i.* [ME. *gurlen;* a transposed form of *growl*, D. *grollen*, etc.: see *growl.*] To growl ; grumble. [Prov. Eng.]

As a mete in a man that is not defied bifore, makith man bodi to *gurle* [var. *groule*].
> > Wyclif, Select Works (ed. Arnold), II. 249.

Gurly (ger'li), *a.* [Also *gurlie;* a transposed form of *growly:* see *gurl.*] Fierce ; stormy.

> The clouds grew dark, and the wind grew loud,
>   And the levin fill'd her ee;
> And waesome wail'd the snaw-white sprites
>   Upon the *gurlie* sea.
> > The Daemon Lover (Child's Ballads, I. 204).

> Iberius with a *gurly* nod,
> Cried Hogan ! Yes, we ken your god.
> 'Tis herrings you adore .
> > Allan Ramsay, The Vision. (Mackay.)

In a book of old English nursery rhymes which was familiar to me in my childhood, and many of the poems of which I still call to mind, is the following :

> " To market ride the gentlemen;
> So do we, so do we.
> Then comes the country clown
> Hobbledy gee.
> First go the ladies mim, mim, mim,
> Next come the gentlemen, trim, trim, trim,
> Then comes the country clown
> Gallop a trot, trot, trot."

Now, I have never had the slightest idea of the meaning of "mim," and, on looking for the word in Webster, Worcester, Stormonth, and other dictionaries in my possession, have been unable to find it. Doubtless it occurs in some of the glossaries of old words, but I am quite sure that no considerable number of the readers of THE NORTH AMERICAN REVIEW have any clear notion of what William Black means when he says in "Far Lochaber " : " Lightning-storms seem to come quite natural to you, for all as prim and *mim* as you are."

But, turning to the " Century," we find that *mim* is an adjective, "a minced form of *mum*, silent," and that it means " primly silent; prim ; demure ; precise ; affectedly modest ; quiet ; mute"; and that it is also used adverbially; and then a quotation from Burns and the one from Black just cited are given as examples of the use and signification of the word.

In these times, when writers, either from a disposition to rescue good words from oblivion and to bring them again into use, or from affectation of knowledge easily acquired, are searching for quaint and little-known modes of expression, a dictionary that does not contain a full assortment of the words used at the present day, as well as of those that have fallen by the wayside, is deficient in one of the most essential qualities of a lexicon. The " Century" does this, and a great deal more. If I were writing a review, I should be tempted to consider at some length several of these excellences. But I am only telling what I consider the best book of the year, and I must close with a reference to one single additional point ; and that is that the " Century" rectifies many errors which have been transmitted from dictionary to dictionary, and which have thus been productive of a great deal of harm. For instance, take the word "coca." Coca is defined by Worcester as "the dried leaf of the *Erythroxylon Coca*, a native plant of Peru ; it is a very stimulating narcotic and more pernicious than opium." By Webster coca is said to be "a highly stimulating narcotic, the dried leaf of the *Erythroxylon Coca*, a plant found wild in Peru." By Stormonth coca is said to be "the dried leaf of a plant having highly narcotic quantities, used by the Peruvians."

Now, coca is not a narcotic and never has been so regarded. Turning to the "Century," we find it defined as "the dried leaf of the *Erythroxylon Coca*, natural order Linnaceæ, a small shrub of the mountains of Peru and Bolivia, but cultivated in other parts of South America." Then, after a few lines of description, it is said to be "a stimulant, bearing some resemblance in its effects to tea and coffee, and has long been used as a masticatory by the Indians of South America. It relieves feelings of fatigue and hunger, and the difficulty in breathing experienced in climbing high mountains. The habit of chewing coca is an enslaving one. . . . It yields the valuable alkaloid cocaine." And all this is correct.

The "Century" is excellent reading for one fond of learning, even in a mild form, while for the scholar, though it may contain little that is new, it will inevitably, by saving him trouble, take a place that a hundred other dictionaries, glossaries, and such like would be required to fill.

So far, therefore, as my limited information extends, and in accordance with the condition imposed by THE REVIEW of excluding strictly technical works, I regard the "Century Dictionary" as the "best book of the year."

WILLIAM A. HAMMOND, M. D.

NOTES AND COMMENTS.

THE PRESENT AND FUTURE OF MEDICAL SCIENCE.

MEDICINE—I take the term to mean that science, or art, if you will, that essays to effect the cure of diseases by means of substances administered to human beings—may be said to have advanced in a sort of spiral manner. Starting at a point, it has circled about it, slowly increasing the diameter of its rings. It has from time to time gradually enlarged and improved its old methods of diagnosis and treatment; but it has added very few new and original discoveries of value.

Until quite recently our pharmacopœia contained scarcely any remedial agents that were not known in some form one hundred years ago. Indeed, many of them were familiar to the ancients. During the past decade we have seen medicine eclipsed by the advancement of all the other arts and sciences. Surgery has made its greatest strides. Electricity has taken its place as a practical science. Chemistry has given us wonderful discoveries. The fruits of the other arts and sciences have afforded a rich harvest. It seems, in fact, to have been a ripening time for these.

Medicine has not kept abreast of its correlated sciences. In point of fact, it is far in their rear. The reason for this, I think, is two-fold. Medical science rests upon a foundation built of stones taken from the other arts and sciences. The first advances in materia medica were the outcome of discoveries in organic chemistry. The chemist extracted the alkaloids, and the physician then recognized them as the active principles of the drugs from which they came.

The discoveries in synthetical chemistry marked another epoch in medicine. By grouping elements obtained from certain organic compounds, chemistry produced for us new substances having medicinal properties of great value. Experiment has proved some of these to have specific curative effects. Electricity has furnished us remedial agents, and has enlarged our means of diagnosis. Improvements in the art of manufacturing microscopic lenses have enabled us to see the germs of diseases, and have opened up to us the great field of bacteriological chemistry that now engrosses the attention of the medical world.

Through the agency of the microscope we are now beginning to understand the real cause of disease processes, and the chemico-vital forces evolved by nature to effect their destruction.

In short, the dependence of medicine upon the other arts and sciences has kept its development in their wake. But there is another reason for the tardy development of medicine—an even more powerful one than that just given. It is the great difficulty of proving that certain effects are due to certain causes ; whether the result of the given medical procedure is *post hoc* or *propter hoc*. So many factors operate to produce effects that it is often impossible to determine the real causative one. In no other science is it so easy to mistake coincidence for cause.

The proverbial disagreement of doctors is due to this. Homœopathy, faith cure, and other medical crazes are fathered by it. The anti-vaccinists, the anti-contagionists, find their arguments in mistaken premises. It is on account of this that medicine is, and probably always will be, an inexact science, and that theory has been productive of so little.

The few specifics (by specific I mean a medicine that has a certain curative effect upon a particular disease) have all been the outcome of experience from chance observation, and not of theoretical work. No science, however, is so rich in theories. It is significant that these in the main have been advanced to account for empirical facts. Innumerable have been the theories endeavoring to account for the action of cinchona, a drug for the existence of which we are indebted to the instinct of the Peruvian Indians. The theories attempting to account for the action of every medical agent and for the contagion of every disease are legion.

The differences in the so-called "temperaments" of individuals must always tend to prevent the exact in medicine. The old adage " One man's food is another's poison " finds its origin here.

It seems probable that in the near future the hypodermic syringe will be the principal means of administering remedial agents. This little instrument has already done something towards reducing the inexactness of medicine to a minimum.

The most remarkable thing in medical science to-day is the fewness of specific remedies. The comparatively recent discoveries in physiology and in the causes of diseases have not brought forth medicines that will act as sure cures. We are almost as powerless to cure the more severe types of diseases to-day as we were ten or twenty years ago. Our immense credulity is a witness to this, however strongly some of us may deny it. We are ready to accept the wildest assertions as proved facts. We have believed that condurango would cure cancer; that an elixir of life had been discovered ; and now we think the specific for tuberculosis is in our hands, and this opinion is based almost on the assertion of one man. * The great wish that these things should be true is the father of the thought that they are, and it makes us deceive our very selves.

I know of no more trying position than that of the physician who, having in vain exhausted all the means known to him to save his patient's life, is compelled to watch him die without being able to do anything to avert the end. Is it to be wondered at that in our helplessness we grasp at straws? I would not be taken in these statements as belittling medical science and conveying the impression that the physician is useless. Far from it. We hold in our hands much that the test of time and experience has shown to be of great value in ameliorating diseased conditions.

The future of medicine, and especially of preventive medicine, seems very bright. It seems probable that the so-called "preventable diseases "— that is, the contagious and infectious maladies—will in time be actually avoidable.

* Written January, 1891,

The " preventive viruses " originated by Jenner in the discovery of vaccination, and added to by Pasteur in the discovery of anti-rabic and anti-charbon* virus, will play a most important part. The causes producing and the conditions favoring these diseases are well known. It seems probable that the bacilli causing them produce in some way poisons that are destructive to themselves, and that we shall sooner or later be in possession of means whereby we can isolate and utilize these principles, not only as preventive, but also as remedial, agents.

It is not likely, however, that our old methods will be superseded, or that any of them will be abandoned. It is not improbable that all the acute diseases, and many of the chronic, will be found to be caused by germs. I do not think we need fear that new maladies will appear to take the place of those that we may in the future be able to control, and so keep the results of beneficent discoveries from effecting good.

Recent researches have shown that nature effects the destruction of germs in several ways. The phagocytes, whose function was comparatively recently discovered by Metchnikoff, are probably the most powerful of these. The phagocytes are found in the blood. They are whitish spherical bodies, considerably larger than blood-corpuscles. They are found in great abundance in and about the seats of inflammation, and were here first observed by Metchnikoff to absorb and destroy the bacteria causing the disease processes. The experiment made by him to prove his observation is most interesting and ingenious.

It is not unreasonable to predict that we will learn how to favor the production of these organisms, and in this way assist nature in her fight against disease more directly and to the purpose than at present. The soluble ferments are thought by competent observers to be inimical to the bacilli of diseases. We may possibly be able to apply the means whereby these may be produced in infected systems. We can only conjecture, at the best, what the harvest of the discoveries in the field of bacteriology will be. Let us, at any rate, hope that our dreams of its richness will be realized.

We must not let our hopes deceive us into expecting too much, for it has been said, " Thus far shalt thou go and no farther " ; and it would seem as though obstacles had been placed in the way of medical science which all the force of man is powerless to remove. The most difficult thing on earth for a man to understand is himself. The wonderful machine of brain and muscle, and the strange chemico-vital forces that supply energy to it, must, it seems to me, in the very nature of things, always remain to man more of a mystery than anything else material that he may have to do with.

After all has been said, it must be admitted that a proper observance of the rules of personal and public hygiene on the part of every individual belonging to the civilized world would do more to effect a reduction of the death-rate, and prolong the average duration of life, than any discoveries in the cure of diseases that at present seem within the bounds of possibility.

CYRUS EDSON, M. D.

RESCUE WORK AMONG FALLEN WOMEN.

"RESCUE homes are premiums on iniquity ; by assisting girls to conceal their shame, they encourage them to repeat their offences." " They are establishments for the maintenance of the idle." " It is impossible to reform fallen women."

* Malignant pustule.

Such expressions are common. Have they any justification in fact?

It is true that depraved women who have no intention of reforming sometimes seek admission to the homes simply that they may be fed, clothed, and sheltered; yet there is always the possibility that they may be reached by a good influence. The managers are aware that some applicants endeavor to deceive them, and they are watchful.

A form in substance like the following must be signed by applicants for admission to many homes :

"Desirous of forsaking a life of sin, I apply for admission to the Ottawa Home for Friendless Women. agreeably to the following conditions :

"Not to leave the home without the matron or some other responsible person, until a situation or another home is obtained.

"To live quietly and peaceably with the inmates.

"To obey implicitly the orders of the matron."

In most cases the homes are partly self-supporting, and the idle have no place in them. Those in charge appreciate the necessity of occupation for mind and body.

The receipts of the New York Magdalen Benevolent Society from laundry and sewing-room for twelve months were $3,058.20. Reports from a large number of homes in the United States and Canada show that a good income is derived from the labor of the inmates. In some institutions instruction is given in millinery, dressmaking, fine sewing and embroidery, and different branches of domestic service. Many who seek refuge are physical wrecks, unfit for hard work, and some light occupation must be provided. The majority have little knowledge of the use of the needle when they are admitted.

At St. Michael's Home, Mamaroneck, and other country homes, gardening is a profitable recreation, the vegetables for home consumption being raised by the inmates.

A superintendent writes : "Anything and everything that will develop a hearty self-respect must be called for and used. The truest charity is simply tiding over a time of need and then expecting a return of the bounty conferred. In my own experience it has been a great gain to my girls to know that they would be expected to repay all moneys loaned them for imperative needs, to pay, at cost price, for clothing, medicine, etc."

Girls who long ago left that home return to repay a loan or to make a thank-offering.

The charge that fallen women will not reform has some show of reason in the fact that reformation is rare among those who have grown old in sin ; but this is not true of the younger women.

The Toronto Prison-Gate Mission and Haven gives this testimony : "In the fourteen years of our existence we have had some very hopeful cases of reformation, particularly among the young mothers. With our maternity cases we have learned the sacred value of requiring the mother to nurse her infant, and so learn to love and care for it. Among the more hardened in sin we have not such an encouraging report to give, but we can mention a few cases of older women who have not returned to abandoned lives. Among the inebriates reform is very slow, requiring years of patient work and trial. The more experience we have among this class, the more necessity we find for a home where they can be kept and given work in an industrial department. They are not fit for domestic service, but young mothers often become valuable domestics."

The majority of abandoned women are intemperate. A report says: "In all our experience we have not found one who was not a victim of intemperance."

Experience shows the vital importance of separating the younger offenders from the more hardened. The Wayside Home of Brooklyn says regarding this : "Let any place of detention, it matters not how well it may be conducted, take in both these classes, and if they have any contact whatever, the younger and more impressible will imbibe from the others, and such places become schools of vice."

Among older offenders who have reformed may be mentioned one who said that when she sought the shelter of the home she had no clear knowledge of the difference between right and wrong. Through her influence a woman who had kept four houses of ill-fame was led to forsake her sinful life. The two opened an evening mission for rescue work.

When the Home of the Friendless at Hamilton, Ontario, was enlarged, some of the former inmates expressed a wish to make a "thank-offering," and contributed money for furnishing.

A girl who had been sheltered by the Florence Mission of New York in a measure resumed her reckless career, but repented and returned to the mission. As a thank-offering she gave the beautiful furniture from her home of sin to the "Door of Hope," a newly-organized mission for fallen women.

The best results are obtained in homes where there are careful classification, seclusion of the inmates, regular employment and recreation, and a long course of training.

A lady interested in the work of the "Retreat" in Cleveland, Ohio,—one of the most successful of reformatories,—says with regard to the last point: "I think there should be an earnest protest against sending girls from the homes too soon. A decided sentiment prevails that you can change the whole course of a girl's life and thought in a few months. Our most shining examples are those who have stayed in the home two or even three years."

This point was particularly emphasized by the sisters in charge of St. Michael's Home. They desire to keep their girls not less than two years, and longer if possible.

The managers of other institutions appreciate the value of a long residence ; but many homes in large cities, endeavoring to meet a continual demand for assistance and to accommodate as many as possible, can offer temporary shelter only.

In no other undertaking are more wisdom, patience, and Christian charity needed. It must be a work of daily struggle, of resolute and persistent effort. The spasmodic compassion that moves the public when some particularly interesting case is brought to its attention is not the quality that is demanded for workers in rescue homes. Compassion they must have, zeal they must have ; but their zeal especially requires to be tempered with discretion. In judgment they must remember mercy, but in mercy they must not forget judgment. Taking into account all the weakness, all the temptation, they must avoid treating the offender as an interesting moral invalid or an injured heroine. A good deal of cheap and unwholesome sentimentalism appears in the reports of criminal trials, and lends a glamor to sin.

Not long ago the trial of a young woman, whose case was certainly sad enough to touch any heart with pity, was made the occasion for an outburst of sentimentality, and, following her acquittal, the announcement was made that she would soon appear on the operatic stage. The harmful nature of such notoriety is too obvious to require much comment. Its tendency to lower the standard of morality can hardly be questioned ; but it is surely illogical to claim that a similar result is effected by the rescue work which seeks to raise the sinner. The compassion for a fallen woman is born of reverence for pure womanhood, and does not mitigate the loathing of the sin.

The pity of it is that the sin is irrevocable ; that no repentance, no forgiveness, no later uprightness, can make it possible for the woman to live the life that has no darkness to hide, or to forget that she has fallen. Yet she may deserve our affection, our sincere respect ; by her victory over sin she may pass on the upward way those who once held out to her their sustaining hands.

Any one who contrasts the repulsive, almost brutalized, countenances of those who have grown old in vice with the comparatively innocent face of the girl who has but lately set her feet in evil ways, must shudder at the thought of the terrible retribution.

A report pleading for the rescue of girls just entering a career of crime says : " This is a need that affects the future of our city ; for those whom we would save are soon to take their places among the mothers ; and not to meet the need is to pursue a penny-wise and pound-foolish policy, which puts to shame the business foresight of a modern American city."

And further : " Every life rescued from vice, vagabondage, and despair, and established in the ways of upright living, is so much gain to our civilization. But only when to this is added the higher Christian motive of the infinite value and far-reaching possibilities of each human soul can the full significance and importance of this rescue work be realized."

M. Bourchier Sanford.

THE SOLDIER AND THE CITIZEN.

WHEN the soldier's malevolent critics shall have ceased their unjust and ungrateful aspersions in magazine, journal, and stump speech, the trite subject of his heroism and sacrifices may be dropped for a while at least, but not, in justice, until then.

While the surviving "bummers and mendicants," the "skulkers and hospitalers," of the war are held up to public reprobation, the saving clause is sometimes condescendingly appended, that so large a body as the veterans form must necessarily represent all classes and conditions of men. But we refuse to admit the truth of this saving clause. There were several classes who were not represented, and never could be represented, in any army like that which conquered the rebellion. The blind, deaf, and halt, dwarfs, lunatics, and idiots (save those whom faithful service and terrible suffering made such), were not represented. There were men whom no inducement could persuade, no force could compel, to face the fearful hazards of war ; men who, if their own firesides were attacked by an armed foe, would flee without striking a blow ; who, if their own wives and children were in danger, would first seek a place of safety for themselves. No sudden fever of patriotism, no noble love of adventure, no thirst for martial glory, not even a princely bounty, could tempt these men where bullets were hissing and shells were shrieking. Were they drafted ? There were substitutes to be bought, or, if this were too expensive a means of escape, there was a sure refuge beyond the St. Lawrence—at least there was the *dernier ressort* of self-inflicted disability. Were they tricked into enlisting while in their cups, or did they go through the form of enlistment to escape other penalties for their misdeeds? The first roll-call showed them among the "missing."

There were other men who were not represented in the army, men to whom the war, with all its horrors to others, was but one tremendous flood-tide bearing on to fortune. What business had they at the front, when each day of those four years was literally one long chain of "golden" moments? And there were still others, men who, though they were not brave or self-sacrificing enough to leave their own States and enter the ranks of their country's would-be destroyers, yet hated with all their souls her friends and saviours, who did all in their power—consistently with their personal safety—to give aid and comfort to her enemies. Some of these very men are prominent enough *now* in their relations with the army. Of all the malcontents at the nation's liberality to her defenders, they are the most active and bitter.

With these modifications, the "saving clause" quoted at the beginning of this paper may be accepted as true. It goes without saying that the bravest, noblest, and manliest, the most unselfish and patriotic,—in short, the flower of the virtue and strength of the land,—were represented in the army; quite as fully, it may be safely added, as they were represented at home. There were men of brilliant genius, of ripe scholarship, men of the highest standing in social, religious, political, and business circles. There were also, as a matter of course, men of the lower orders of intelligence and morality; loafers, shirks, drunkards, wife-beaters, blacklegs, and jail-birds. Cowards and "skulkers" are usually included in the black-list, but there were bad enough men and enough bad men in the army without special mention of these—by the stay-at-home critics, at all events. The cruel and bitterly unjust mistake, either intended or made unthinkingly, is to place the worst representatives of the veterans in the foreground. If his censors are to be believed, the typical veteran is a shirk, a "beat," a pension-beggar. The truth probably is that the rank and file of the army were not much better, and certainly no worse, than the average body of citizens, and that its survivors are no more greedy or grasping now than men in general would be in their place.

How does the average citizen look upon the soldiers? We all know how he regarded them during the war; we all know, too, with what generous enthusiasm he welcomed them home to the security and prosperity they had won for both themselves and him, how he threw up his hat, shouted himself hoarse, and freely contributed his dollars for bunting and hot coffee.

But generous enthusiasm is like rich perfume—volatile. Little by little, the "brave defenders" have come down from their pedestals in the citizen's estimation. Not all of them, of course. The strong of body and mind, the wealthy, the cultured—in short, the self-supporting in general—still retain his respect and a more or less latent residuum of grateful recognition for their old-time heroism. But the disabled, the poor, those whom advancing years render incapable of supporting themselves and their families, are fast becoming a burden and a bore.

· It is true that the burden and the bore are still borne with little effective opposition; that, though there is much ill-natured grumbling from many sources, the enormous and increasing drafts which the soldiers make on the national treasury are still honored,

But cannot this strong, free, prosperous nation, made so by these men who now in their turn look to it for succor, continue for a few years longer *uncomplainingly* a recognition which, despite its falling-off in fervor of sentiment, has thus far surpassed that of any other nation in history? What if the tax is great? It is utterly insignificant in comparison with the deserts of those for whom it is levied; for, be it remembered, while it can last but a few years longer at most, the rich fruits of all that suffering and sacrifice will last to the end of time.

A SOLDIER.

NEEDS OF THE NAVAL RESERVE.

IT IS no news to any well-informed ¡person that the United States has not at present enough seamen to man its war vessels. That is a condition which will at some time disappear, for it is not conceivable that Congress will permit an aged law to cramp the vigorous youth of our new defensive policy. But it is equally inconceivable that we shall ever maintain the navy in time of peace on a war basis. That being the case, it is obvious that we must rely on the possession of a thoroughly drilled and experienced reserve force to call upon in the case of any sudden outbreak of hostilities. The nucleus of that reserve force has been formed, and it is composed of good material. It is true that the First Battalion, Naval Reserve Artillery, is not prepared to man a harbor-defence vessel to-morrow, but it is beyond disproof that it can be made ready in thirty days.

The preparation of the battalion for active service is in the hands of the people. The State of New York has given the organization a legal name. What it needs now is a local habitation. There is a good deal of difference of opinion as to whether the Naval Reserve ought to have an armory or a ship. It is pointed out that for the State to provide a ship would be equivalent to its maintaining a navy, which is unconstitutional. On the other hand, it is said that the Naval Reserve has no use for an armory. The truth, as usual, lies midway between extremes ; or, rather, in this case, it includes both. There should be an armory and a ship. The force needs both, and has a right to expect both. It should have an armory with a model ship's side erected in it. Along one side of the armory, say ten feet from the wall, should be built a light wooden model of one of the bulwarks of a man-of-war, the armory floor being the deck. At convenient positions in this bulwark should be erected dummy models of 5- or 6-inch breech-loading rifles, mounted on fixed pivot carriages. At other points there should be one Hotchkiss 3- or 6-pounder rapid-fire, one Hotchkiss revolving cannon, and one Gatling. These secondary guns should be genuine, and not models.

The remainder of the armory would be clear for cutlass, field-gun, and infantry drills. The field artillery and infantry drills are a part of the man-of-war's man's education, and there is not room enough for them on the deck of a ship. All winter long, when the weather would be unfit for outdoor work in boats or aboard ship, the men of the Naval Reserve would be perfecting themselves in their duties in their armory, housed, protected, and on an equal footing with the regiments of the National Guard. To provide this armory, then, it seems to me, is the plain duty of the State of New York. To provide it without the appurtenances necessary for the special instruction of naval artillerymen would be to deprive the new force of its distinctive value, and make it an unnecessary addition to the National Guard.

In warm and pleasant weather the Naval Reserve imperatively requires training in "cutting-out" drills, distant boat service, and actual handling of guns aboard ship. The last-named training, which includes target-practice, is indispensable to the perfection of the force as an efficient auxiliary to the navy. It is beyond question that the men must have some experience in firing from the rolling deck of a vessel under steam at a mark moved about by the heave of the sea. Otherwise, if called suddenly into service, they would be confronted with conditions wholly new to them. Gunnery from an earthen or stone barbette is very different from gunnery on a deck which has not a fixed level and not even a permanent angle of inclination.

It is not necessary that the State of New York should build a ship for the training of its Naval Reserve forces. There is no reason to doubt the readiness of the national government to furnish the vessel. In a recent report Secretary Tracy urged upon Congress with great earnestness the necessity of building coast- and harbor-defence vessels, and he added that such craft would be of much value in training naval-reserve forces. The complete delivery of any one of these vessels into the hands of any reserve body was, of course, not contemplated by the Secretary, because there would be legal as well as practical obstacles in the way of such a transaction. But, on the other hand, the harbor-defence vessel might be maintained at a very economical cost to the national government with a very small force of officers and men—just enough to man her engines and boilers, and to take care of the vessel at her berth in a navy-yard. When taken out into the bay or its adjacent waters, she would be fully manned by a Naval Reserve battalion, whose men would be wholly equal to the task of handling her batteries, her boats, and her ground tackle.

This plan, or one not very dissimilar, must eventually be adopted for the full development of the possibilities of the Naval Reserve. It is, like every war-ship's company, an amphibious organization, designed to serve both ashore and afloat. To confine it to an armory would be to invite it to "hang its clothes on a hickory limb and not go near the water." To bid it seek all its instruction aboard a United States war-ship would be to cripple the organization and to impose upon the national government a burden which ought to rest on the shoulders of the State. The Naval Reserve is worthy of good treatment at the hands of both. Two nurses will not be too many to take care of such a promising infant.

W. J. HENDERSON.

THE NEXT AMENDMENT.

THE men who devised the framework of the government of the United States intended and proposed that it should be capable of adjustment to the needs of any changed conditions not then by them foreseen. It is for this declared reason that the Constitution provides, guardedly, for its own amendment. The unforeseen changes have from time to time demanded such action as was provided for, but the aggregate popular mind, which expresses its supreme will in the terms of the Great Charter, is conservatively slow to recognize and respond to these consecutive demands. This conservatism was manifested, almost ruinously, in the tardy and convulsive advances to the constitutional settlement of the fundamental slavery question.

As the constitution now stands, and as it must, in form at least, remain, new States may be added, in a kind of creation, even by the division of old States, but no provision exists or can be made for the obliteration of any of the existing commonwealths of the Union. However small may be the area or the population of any member of the federal family, or however grotesque may seem its vested right to equal rank and power in the Senate with its greater associates, that rank and power cannot be directly interfered with by any process yet invented. That there is here a defect presenting matter for serious consideration has long since been generally admitted. It becomes more glaring, it attracts more attention, and it threatens to become a source of more dangerous irritation, year after year, as the disproportion, for example, between New York and Delaware requires more and more offensive figures to declare its political arithmetic.

So great a defect implies a discoverable remedy, and there are signs that one is in due process of discovery by means of a species of normal evolution, every way preferable to revolution.

If much of the party and partisan history of the country is associated with State geographical boundary lines, more attaches to the action, in combination or semi-combination, of the States adhering politically in groups. The history of the Civil War presents the most perfect illustration, and is also full of instructive suggestions as to the nature of the practical remedy. At the outset of the war, the cotton States led off, as a group, acting almost as one State. The Atlantic Southern States followed as another, and the refusal of the border States to follow promptly and effectively prepared for the failure of the Confederacy. Each group drew its membership together in obedience to a natural law of American politics, plainly written in our history, but not defined or utilized in our constitution.

In the school geographies of the last generation, the natural grouping of the States at that time was set forth as the New England, Middle, Southern, and Western. The existence of the political fact was recognized and was taught to all children.

If, now, for an inquiry into one phase of this subject we select the New England States, we may find that this group has undergone changes latterly, but that these are less apparent to the eye than are some of the mutations of the other groups. There are, however, very readable indications of one irresistible tendency. The school-books said that it consisted of Maine, New Hampshire, Vermont, Massachusetts, Rhode Island, and Connecticut. All of these old commonwealths retain their boundaries, their nominal State organisms, and their representative power in the Senate of the United States. If, however, it is true that Maine and Massachusetts are at this day States, in the full definition of the term, what is to be said of the progressive conditions of the others? If they could be considered as the asserted roots of a great national tree, would it not be nearly correct to reply that they are rather so many bunches of rootlets, attaching permanently to several central or main roots? Are their boundary lines upon the map entitled to the political significance which the constitution accords to them?

The present examination does not contain any necessity for now indicating the precise composition of a new group which might be constructed, for purposes of reformed administration and federal representation, as the New England group. The pertinent suggestion is that one might well be created, that it yet will be created, and that it will enjoy, measurably, the powers, or some of them, which are now exercised by one of the existing States. Without attempting the elaboration of details, the new organism, of whatever allied elements, will be a State as to its relations with the federal government, without too great a disturbance of existing forms of local self-government. In adjusted correlation with other groups, it will be entitled to representation in a reorganized national Senate and House. In the former body there will then be no such monstrosity as a fictitious equipoise between Rhode Island and Pennsylvania.

It is manifest that the powers of the central, national machinery, acting at and from Washington, would be relieved of clogging and pressure, but in no manner diminished, by the successful working of groups, operating as States within the limits assigned to them. The reformed mechanism, in part and in whole, will be entirely in accord with what is called the "genius"—that is, with the integral principles—of our complex idea of representative republican government.

The Middle State group was said by the school-books to consist of New York, New Jersey, Pennsylvania, Delaware, and Maryland. It is evident that this old listing offers hardly an indication of the constituent parts of a new, self-governing independency in union, with New York as its main stem.

It is assuredly premature to discuss the future, in this relation, of the British provinces north of us, or to surmise what parts of them might, for instance, be well associated with Maine in a Northeastern group, or how the other provinces would prefer to be associated or severed.

There is an area related to Pennsylvania of which the natural State membership would fall into correct relations and position as readily as do the pieces upon a chessboard. Somewhat the same is true of the Atlantic States, south of the Potomac; of the central States between Pennsylvania and the Mississippi, north of the Ohio; of a corresponding group south of the Ohio; of the southern and southeastern cotton States; of the Gulf group; the group immediately west of the Mississippi; of the Northwestern group proper; of the Far Northwest; of the Mountain group; of the Pacific Northern; of the Pacific Southern; and, eventually, of the Southern Mountain group.

Leaving indefinite all questions of absolute selection, there are at least eighteen probable groups, much exceeding in number the cluster of stars upon the first flag of the republic. Each of these ideal associations has already distinctive interests, progressively becoming more apparent and more plainly acknowledged by its citizens. It is more and more commonly understood and asserted that these interests demand, for their proper care, both legislative and executive capacity exceeding that of the present local organisms, State or municipal, but which cannot be transferred to or undertaken by the overburdened, far-away, and practically unappreciating central government at Washington. The truth demands very full recognition that this country is too vast for successful centralization, however absolute is its need for permanent, unassailable nationality in its representative union. Its fast-increasing parts must therefore be governed through adjusted and adjustable machinery, both adapted to and developed from the fundamental idea of the original, existing organism. The machinery now in use announces, in every creak of its patriotic helplessness, that it is forced to bear too much and that, unless it shall be relieved, it must shortly break down.

The presentation of a political necessity and of its attendant problems to a self-governing, intelligent people, carries with it not only a demand for, but a rational assurance of, eventual action and successful solution. All growths of public opinion, all questions of methods and details, are sure of elaborate counsel and discussion, but there is no necessity for the discovery

or invention of anything novel, which would be popularly offensive as foreign.   The actual grouping of the States has gone on from the beginning,
from an earlier day than, for instance, the birth of George Washington, and
the British provinces of North America acted in groups when the Dutch
held New York and the French held the Canadas.   The same action goes on
now, increasingly, and the natural affinities and political necessities producing it only require something of boldness and wisdom in applied statesmanship in order to produce a reform which would assure the best results locally, and would, at the same time, give more firmness and stability, as well
as greater freedom and effectiveness of administration, to the national
government.

WILLIAM O. STODDARD.

NORTH AMERICAN REVIEW.
No. CCCCXXIII.

FEBRUARY, 1892.

HOW TO ATTACK THE TARIFF.

BY THE HON. WILLIAM M. SPRINGER, CHAIRMAN OF THE
WAYS AMD MEANS COMMITTEE OF THE HOUSE
OF REPRESENTATIVES.

DURING the first session of the Fiftieth Congress the House of Representatives was Democratic and the Senate was Republican. Mr. Cleveland was President. The first session of that Congress assembled on the first Monday in December, 1887, and adjourned on the 20th day of October, 1888. The presidential election occurred in November thereafter. The Committee on Ways and Means of the House of Representatives of that Congress reported a measure for a general revision of the tariff, known as the Mills Bill. The general debate on that bill began in the House on the 17th day of April and occupied twenty-three day-and-evening sessions. In all, 151 speeches were made during the general debate. The debate upon the bill by paragraphs began on the 31st day of May ; and twenty-eight days, or 128 hours and 10 minutes, were occupied in the five-minute debate. The vote was taken upon the passage of the bill in the House on the 19th day of July.

The bill then went to the Senate, where considerable time was spent in so-called "hearings" by the Finance Committee of that body. The result was inevitable from the beginning ; namely, that there was no tariff legislation enacted, and the session of Congress was prolonged until the 20th day of Oc-

VOL. CLIV.—NO. 423.   9

tober, as already stated. As the presidential election occurred within a few days thereafter, there was no time whatever for the proper consideration of this measure by the people. Whatever may have been the cause of Democratic defeat at that election, it must be conceded that the introduction and passage through the House of a general bill of tariff revision did not produce the effect which the friends of the measure had earnestly desired, namely, the choice of a Democratic President and a Democratic Congress at the ensuing election.

During the last Congress, which was Republican in both branches, and during which time there was a Republican President, a measure for a general revision of the tariff, known as the McKinley Bill, was passed at the first session and was approved on the day of adjournment, October 1, 1890.

It is conceded that the time necessary for the preparation and passage through both Houses of Congress of a carefully matured revision of the tariff required both of the preceding Congresses to consume upon that subject the time which was actually occupied, and which in both cases resulted in the prolongation of the session until the 20th and the 1st of the month of October, respectively.

The Republicans in the late Congress, at its beginning, were undoubtedly of the opinion that the interests of their party required that there should be a general revision of the tariff passed during that session, and fondly hoped that such general revision would bring success to their party at the ensuing congressional election. They were sadly disappointed. The result of the ensuing election for Members of Congress was most disastrous to the party that was responsible for the passage of the McKinley Bill ; the Democrats and Independents, both opposing that measure, having elected a majority of 158 over those who supported it.

However meritorious the Mills Bill may have been from a Democratic standpoint, or however meritorious the McKinley Bill may have been from a Republican standpoint, it is nevertheless true that the time which elapsed between the passage of each bill and the ensuing election was not sufficient to enable the people to become sufficiently familiar with the provisions of either measure, and, being in doubt, caution doubtless suggested the preservation of the *status quo.*

In view of these precedents in tariff legislation, what should be the policy of the Democratic majority in the House of Representatives of this Congress ? If both branches of Congress and the President were Democratic, there would be grave doubt as to the propriety of attempting a general revision of the tariff immediately preceding a presidential election. The disastrous results to the Republican party which immediately followed the passage of the McKinley Bill ought to teach Democrats to avoid the rocks upon which their opponents were dashed to pieces. But when we consider the fact that the Senate is Republican, and that there is a Republican President, and that any such measure which might pass the House would not have the slightest prospect of success, it seems almost self-evident that a general revision of the tariff should not be attempted during this session. As recently stated by a distinguished tariff-reform organ in the city of New York, " to propose in the House at this session, on the eve of a national election, a general revision of the tariff, might be magnificent, but it would not be war, such as must be waged for victory. It would in no sense advance the object professed ; it would not make the devotion of the party to the principles of industrial and commercial emancipation a whit clearer than it is now. It would not make the necessity or advantage of the triumph of those principles any more obvious. It is not at all requisite to inform the country what the Democratic party believes in and is working for. It would be simply a tactical error of the gravest possible kind. It would be to abandon a strong aggressive position for a position of defence that would not be strong. It would instantly invite the concerted opposition of every interest now depending on the favors of the present tariff, and give to the opponents of every item in the bill the combined strength of the opponents of all." These propositions are absolutely unassailable.

While a general revision of the tariff should not be reported and passed at this session of Congress, yet it does not follow that nothing should be done on this subject. The Committees on Ways and Means and on Manufactures should proceed at once to a careful investigation of the practical workings of the McKinley Bill and of the conditions of our manufacturing industries. This information should be utilized in the preparation of a measure of general relief upon this subject ; but as such measure could not be passed except by a prolongation of the session,—even if it were desirable to pass it at all at the first session,—in view of the precedents of the past, sound policy would require that it should not be reported to the House until the beginning of the next session. Some progress could be made during that session in its consideration, but a definite line of policy to be pursued at that time would depend upon the result of the presidential election. If either branch of the Fifty-third Congress should be Republican,—a fact which will be determined at that election,— it would be futile to attempt to pass a measure of general revision during the remainder of this Congress or during the next Congress. If, however, the Fifty-third Congress should be Democratic, and a Democratic President should be elected, the new Congress might with great propriety be called in extraordinary session on the 4th day of March, 1893, and the work of tariff revision could then be begun in earnest, with a certainty of practical and successful results. Such early revision at the beginning of a presidential term would enable the country to become thoroughly familiar with the great advantages of a genuine revision of the tariff prior to any general election, and the party which was responsible for such revision might confidently expect the continued support of a majority of the American people in subsequent elections of Congresses and Presidents.

There are several features of the McKinley Bill which may be amended or repealed during this session. The Republican Senate and the President would hardly take the responsibility of refusing some of the measures of relief which may be brought forward and passed by the House of Representatives. The particular measures which should be selected for passage through the House should be determined either by the Committee on Ways and Means or by a caucus of Democratic members. There are several, however, which have already received favorable mention in the press of the country: such as placing wool on the free list and repealing the compensatory duty on woollen goods ; placing on the free list binding-twine, cotton-ties, lumber, salt, and raw materials generally. The discussion in this article of particular subjects which should have consideration at this time would perhaps be unprofitable ; but there is one measure which is of overshadowing importance, and which should receive immediate and favorable consideration.

The placing of wool on the free list and a corresponding reduction of the duties on woollen goods are a matter the importance of which cannot be overestimated. The duties on woollen goods were increased by the McKinley Bill from an average of 67.15 per centum to 91.65 per centum. The increase on wool was from 34.32 to 40.66. The duties imposed on woollen goods are of a two-fold character: first,· there is a duty per pound or per square yard, which is intended to compensate manufacturers for the higher price which they claim they must pay for wool by reason of the tariff; and second, a duty ad valorem, being, as is alleged, imposed to compensate for the higher-priced labor of this country as compared with foreign countries. The duties per pound or per square yard are especially burdensome upon the cheaper grades of goods worn by the masses of the people. These specific duties frequently amount to over 100 per centum of the value, and, in some cases, to over 200 per centum. If these specific or compensatory duties are repealed, the ad-valorem duties only will remain, and these do not exceed in any case 60 per centum, and are frequently as low as 35 per centum; the average, perhaps, would amount to 45 per centum. This is the amount of protection which the friends of the protec· tive system have adjudged is necessary to prevent injurious competition from abroad. But if wool is placed upon the free list, and the compensatory duties upon woollen goods are repealed, the manufacturers of woollen goods will have no reason to complain of their new conditions; on the contrary, while the people will get the benefit of a reduction of more than one-half of the tariffs on woollen goods, manufacturers will have the benefit of cheaper material and will be enabled to sell their products abroad in competition with the products of other countries. Thus, a larger market will be secured for woollen goods; there will be a greater demand for labor in establishments of this kind; and new industries, it is confidently expected, will spring up in all parts of the country.

It is next to impossible to estimate accurately the amount which the consumers of the United States pay annually on account of woollen goods. The amount of such goods made in the woollen mills for the census year 1890 was valued at $344,000,000. This does not include the output of ready-made clothing establishments for men and women; nor does it include the cost, to consumers, of the work done by tailors and dressmakers; nor the labor bestowed in the manufacture of woollen goods in the families of the country. The amount of woollen goods imported into the United States for the year 1890 was valued at over fifty-six millions of dollars, and the average duty paid upon these goods was 67 per centum,—the McKinley Bill not having been passed at the close of that fiscal year. The output of factories and ready-made clothing establishments, and the amount of goods imported, with the tariff added to them, is given at factory or wholesale prices. The amount paid by consumers will undoubtedly be increased at least 25 per centum over such prices.

When all these facts are taken into consideration, it will be seen that the consumers of woollen goods in the United States paid during the census year of 1890, in money and in labor, at least $750,000,000 for the woollen goods actually consumed and purchased. Just how much of this amount is due to the tariff on wool and woollen goods cannot be estimated with accuracy, but it is reasonable to assume that not less than $150,000,000 of this cost is due to the tariff on wool and woollen goods. At least half of this amount would be lifted from the shoulders of the people annually by placing wool upon the free list and repealing the compensatory duties on woollen goods. This estimate does not take into consideration the large increase in the tariff on wool and woollen goods made by the McKinley Bill.

So far as wool is concerned, the McKinley Bill has completely failed to accomplish the object which its authors claimed they had in view. In the report which accompanied the bill, when it was brought into the House of Representatives, it was stated that in every case of increased duty, except upon tin-plate and linen fabrics, "importations would fall off." It was stated to be the aim of the committee to fix the duties upon manufactured goods and farm products so as to discourage the use of like goods and products and give our producers the benefit of the home market ; and also to afford ample protection to the farmers of the country engaged in wool-growing. The protection on wool, which the bill secured, was claimed to be sufficient, beyond a doubt, to enable the farmers of the United States, at an early day, to supply substantially all the home demand. This was the argument made by the authors of the bill to justify the imposition of increased duties upon wool, and, as a compensation for this, increased duties on woollen goods.

Time is a cruel arbiter. It is no respecter of persons. It visits upon false theories and false pretences the judgments which they deserve. The statement of the imports of the United States, furnished by the Bureau of Statistics of the Treasury Department, shows that the imports of wool for the ten months ending October 30, 1890 (the McKinley Bill took effect October 6, 1890), amounted to 88,000,000 pounds, while the imports for the ten months the ending October 30, 1891,—the ten months next after the passage of that bill,—were over 119,000,000 pounds, an increase of over 30 per centum. Thus are the theories upon which the McKinley Bill was constructed crushed by the irresistible force of facts.

But this is nᵣ ᴊll. The increased duties on woollen goods were, as claimed, made necessary by the increased duties on wool. The manufacturers of woollen goods were satisfied with the old law ; but if the duty on wool was to be increased, they must be compensated by an increased duty on woollen goods. The increase was made, as stated above. The statistics show that for the ten months ending October 30, 1890, the imports of woollen goods were valued at over $49,000,000, while those for the ten months ending October 30, 1891, were valued at only $29,000,000, a decrease of over 41 per centum. It also appears that the price of wool has averaged from two to three cents a pound less since the passage of the McKinley Bill than it was when the bill passed. The only beneficiaries of the measure are the manufacturers of woollen goods, and it is doubtful whether they will, in the end, receive substantial benefit therefrom. The wool-growers and consumers of woollen goods have not been benefited ; on the contary, they have been greatly injured thereby.

Legislators who regard the interests of the people cannot disregard these facts. It is their duty to apply a remedy for existing evils, and to correct the blunders of their predecessors. Every consideration of the public weal demands that wool shall be placed on the free list, and that the compensatory duties on woollen goods shall be repealed. If the present Congress does not respond to this demand, it will be derelict in duty.

A measure which would bring such immediate and substantial relief will not be regarded with indifference. It would " bring relief to the consumer as well as the manufacturer, and redound to the prosperity of the wage-worker as well as the capitalist."

The other measures which may be passed by the House of Representatives during the first session of this Congress, and to which reference has already been made, will attract universal attention and be received with great favor.   They will remove the most glaring inequalities of our tariff laws, and bring immediate relief to those most entitled to consideration.   They will be especially aimed at monopolies and other combinations to limit production and oppress labor.

It is futile to attempt that which cannot be accomplished.   A good general will not waste his ammunition and resources in assaults upon an impregnable fortress when there are forces of the enemy encamped upon the open field within convenient reach.   The friends of tariff reform should waste no time in endeavoring to secure that which is beyond their reach.   Their time can be well employed in attacking the weak and exposed points of their enemy's lines.   By pursuing this course there will be no step backward in the cause of genuine tariff reform.   Everything should be done, and will be done, to bring about a thorough and complete revision of our tariff laws at the earliest time practicable.   Such revision should be in the interest of the consumers of the country, but brought about by such conservative methods as will not embarrass any legitimate industry in the conntry, or deprive labor of one day's employment or of one cent of its just remuneration.   On the contrary, any revision of the tariff ought to be followed by increased stimulus to industries, increased demand, and better wages for labor ; and by lower prices for manufactured articles which are most necessary to the health and comfort of the people.

Some objection has been urged to any effort being made by the House of Representatives to secure the passage of separate measures upon the subjects indicated, for the reason that the credit for the beneficent results which would follow would be claimed and shared, perhaps, by the Republican Senate and the Republican President.   Such considerations should not have the slightest weight with legislators who desire to promote the best interests and welfare of the people.   Should Democrats refuse to give sanction and support to only such measures as Republicans will oppose ?   If so, only measures of partisan advantage should be supported, while such as would commend themselves to men of all parties should be avoided.   Even if the Republicans should be entitled to equal credit for any measures of reform that might be passed by this Congress, Democrats should not hesitate on that account to press those measures to a final and successful issue.

But, in view of the fact that the Republican party is thoroughly committed to all the provisions of the McKinley Bill, any repeal or modification of its provisions which might originate in the House of Representatives and be favorably considered by the Senate and President would be regarded as a Democratic measure, the credit for which would be accorded to that party almost exclusively. If, however, any measures which may pass the House should fail in the Senate, or, having passed the Senate, should be vetoed by the President, the labor spent upon them would not be in vain. The National Democratic Convention could make a direct issue upon them before the people at the presidential election; and, having failed to pass during the first session, they would, in all probability, be successful at the second, after the people had, in effect, demanded their passage in the election of a Democratic President and a Democratic Congress.

An issue thus directed to the weakest points of the McKinley Bill would be much easier of comprehension and more conducive to successful, aggressive warfare than one encumbered by the endless details of a general revision of the tariff, requiring defensive arguments, and arraying the whole protected industries of the country upon the weakest points of the measure. The importance of preserving the McKinley Bill as a distinctive issue in the Presidential campaign should not be lost sight of. Its general provisions are wholly indefensible ; it deprives labor of its just reward, fosters monopolies, and encourages combinations of capital to limit production and to control prices. It was enacted in the interest of the favored few and for the oppression of the masses of the people. Opposition to the objectionable features of this measure, coupled with a demand for genuine tariff reform, should be the paramount and overshadowing issue in the Presidential contest ; and, upon that issue, the Democratic party is already assured of success, not only in the election of a President, but of a Congress Democratic in both branches.

WILLIAM M. SPRINGER.

A CLAIM FOR AMERICAN LITERATURE.

BY W. CLARK RUSSELL.

UNTIL Richard H. Dana and Herman Melville wrote, the commercial sailor of Great Britain and the United States was without representation in literature. Dana and Melville were Americans. They were the first to lift the hatch and show the world what passes in a ship's forecastle ; how men live down in that gloomy cave, how and what they eat, and where they sleep ; what pleasures they take, what their sorrows and wrongs are ; how they are used when they quit their black sea-parlors in response to the boatswain's silver summons to work on deck by day or by night. These secrets of the deep Dana and Melville disclosed. By doing so, they — the one by a single volume, the other by four or five remarkable narratives—expanded American literature immeasurably beyond the degree to which English literature had been expanded by, say, the works of two-thirds of the poets named in Johnson's " Lives," or by the whole series of the Waverley novels, or by half the fiction, together with much of the philosophy, theology, poetry, and history, that has been published since the death of Charles Dickens.

For compare what the vast proportion of poets and novelists and philosophers and the rest have done with what these two men did. Dana and Melville created a world, not by the discovery, but by the interpretation of it. They gave us a full view of the life led by tens of thousands of men whose very existence, until these wizards arose, had been as vague to the general land intelligence as the shadows of clouds moving under the brightness of stars. It came about in the case of one of them thus : A young gentleman of Boston, being at Cambridge, fell ill of a malady that affected his sight. His father's means were slender ; the lad— he was but a lad—knew that whatever he was to get must be of his own earning. How was he to recover the power of his eyes ? He determined on making a sea voyage—such a voyage, indeed, as must either kill or cure. So on the 14th August, 1834, this fine-spirited young fellow, Dana, carried his chest on. board of a little bit of a brig called the " Pilgrim," for which he had signed as a sailor before the mast. He sailed round the Horn to the coast of California, where he shifted into a full-rigged ship called the " Alert," and arrived at Boston September 22, 1836, having been absent rather more than two years.

The sea appears to have quickly cured his eyes : certainly he used them very promptly ! With what sagacity of observation, with what keenness of sympathetic inquisition, he had exercised his vision, was not to be conjectured until 1840, in which year was published the famous " Two Years Before the Mast," the most memorable of all contributions to the literature of the sea ; excelling as a faithful and perfect picture of one vast side of the ocean life—a side to which no man heretofore had attempted to give expression or even heed. What was the representation this forecastle artist invited us to view ? Something was it after the school of Smollett ? Something was it to triumphantly compare then or presently with the fine sketches of Michael Scott, the delightful stories of Captain Marryat, the yarns of our old friend Fenimore Cooper ? What was it all about ? Did it deal with the almond-white decks, the white lines of hammocks, the black dogs of thunder of the man-o'-war, with the leaning, distant, gleaming chase, the blasts of tiers of ordnance, the hauling-down of sieve-like bunting, the proud mounting of the spangled banner or John's crimson cross, as the case might be ? Did it tell of wide and airy 'tween-decks, of hurricane choruses and flowing cans, of the loves of Bet and the bos'un bold, and of many similar matters, all which had found their chroniclers, some of whose works survive and many of whose works you shall never behold though you offered down to the bottom dollar of your pile for a fleeting view of but one—but one ?

Dana lifted the curtain and showed you the sort of life hundreds and thousands of those fellow creatures of ours called " sailors " were living in his day, had been living long prior to his day, and will go on living whilst there remains a ship afloat. No Englishman had done this. Marryat makes his Newton Foster a merchant sailor ; but Marryat knew nothing of the hidden life

of the merchant service.   He had passed his sea life in ships of
the state.   When he wrote he held command in the Royal Navy,
and knew no more of what passed in a merchantman's forecastle
than I of what goes on in a steamer's engine-room.   Fenimore
Cooper came very near to the truth in his Ned Myers, but the
revelation there is that of the individual.   Ned is one man.   He
is a drunken, swearing, bragging Yankee *only* sailor; very brutal,
always disgusting.   Cooper's book is true of Ned Myers ; Dana's
of all sailors, American and English.

His narrative disclosed an unsuspected state of human existence.   Never before had the land-going world beheld such a picture of ocean life as Dana submitted.   For be it clearly understood that what happened in the " Pilgrim " and the " Alert "
happens in all ships : years may have wrought a few changes, but
the picture of 1840 will stand for the picture of 1891.
I speak not, to be sure, of steamers.   Dana wrote of the
sailing ship, and it is of the sailing ship that I am writing.
When you.talk of sailors, you do not think of steamers.   If you
inquire for a seaman, you are conducted to a ship that is not
impelled by machinery, but by the wind.   You will find the seaman you want, the seaman Dana wrote about, the generic seaman
whose interpretation I count among the glories of literature, seeing how hidden he had been, how darkly obscure in his toil and
hourly doings,—*this* seaman you will find in the deck-house or
the forecastle of the sailing ship.   He is not thrashed across the
Atlantic in six days.   He is not swept from the Thames to the
uttermost ends of the earth in a month.   He is afloat for weeks
and weeks at a spell, and his life is that of the crew of the " Pilgrim."   Do you ask what manner of life it is ?   Read " Two
Years Before the Mast," and recognize the claim I make for
American literature by witnessing in that book the faultless picture of a scene of existence on whose wide face Richard Dana was
the first to fling a light.

Herman Melville, as I gather from an admirable account of
this fine author by Mr. Arthur Stedman, a son of the well-known
poet, went to sea in 1841.   He shipped before the mast on board
a whaler and cruised continuously for eighteen months in the
Pacific.   He saw much ocean life, and his experiences were wild
and many.   I will not compare him with Dana : his imagination
was soaring and splendid, yet there are such passages of pathos

and beauty in Dana's book as persuade me that he might have matched Melville's most startling and astonishing inventions, had taste prompted him or leisure invited. There is nothing in Melville to equal in simple, unaffected beauty Dana's description of an old sailor lying over a jibboom on a fine night and looking up at the stirless canvas white as sifted snow with moonlight. Full of rich poetry, too, is Dana's description of the still night broken by the breathing of shadowy shapes of whales. Melville is essentially American : Dana writes as a straight-headed Englishman would ; he is clear, convincing, utterly unaffected. A subtle odor of the sea freshens and sweetens his sentences. An educated sailor would swear to Dana's vocation by virtue of his style only—a style as plain and sturdy as Defoe's. In truth, I know of no American writer whose style is so good. Yet are Melville's pictures of the forecastle life, his representation of what goes on under the deck of that part of the ship which is thumped by the handspike of the boatswain when he echoes in thunder the order of "All hands !" marvellously and delightfully true. I will not speak of his faithful and often beautiful and often exquisite sketches of the life and scenery of the South Sea Islands, nor of his magnificent picture of Liverpool, and the descriptions of London and of English scenery in "Redburn," and the wonderful opening chapters of "Moby Dick." I link him with Dana ; I place the two side by side as men of genius, but sailors first of all, and I claim, in their name, that to American literature the world owes the first, the best, and the enduring revelation of the secrets of one great side of the ocean life.

"When I go to sea," Melville says in "Moby Dick," "I go as a simple sailor, right before the mast, plumb down into the forecastle, aloft there to the masthead." His "Redburn" supplemented Dana's book. It is a further upheaval of secrets sheer through the forescuttle into the eye of the landsman. No such book as that was to be found in literature in the English language. Plenty there was, and always was, about the navy, royal and republic. One might have thought that Melville, having read Dana's famous work, had said to himself : "I, too, have suffered and seen and know ; I will help to brighten the glittering beam this fine fellow* has darted into the ocean parlors ; which

---

*Mr. Melville, I know, greatly admired the genius of Dana. His praise of "Two Years Before the Mast" half fills a letter I possess.

has even now made all English readers understand that we merchant seamen form a great world of human beings of whom nobody that takes pen in hand appears to know anything at all, who
are carefully neglected by British naval writers because, from the
elevation of a man-o'-war's decks, even the biggest merchantman
looks to sit low, humanly speaking very low indeed, and who by
the inexpert are hideously muddled under that vague term of
' Jack,' confounded with the blue-jacket, and elbowed in with the
'longshoreman."

   Melville wrote out of his heart and out of wide and perhaps
bitter experience ; he enlarged our knowledge of the life of the
deep by adding many descriptions to those which Dana had
already given. His " South Seaman " is typical. Dana sighted
her, but Melville lived in her. His books are now but little read.
When he died the other day,—to my sorrow ! for our correspondence had bred in me a deeper feeling than kindness and esteem,—
men who could give you the names of fifty living American poets
and perhaps a hundred living American novelists owned that they
had never heard of Herman Melville ; which simply means that to
all intents and purposes the American sailor is a dead man, and
the American merchant service to all intents and purposes a dead
industry. Yet a famous man he was in those far days when every
sea was bright with the American flag, when the cotton-white
canvas shone starlike on the horizon, when the nasal laugh of the
jolly Yankee tar in China found its echo in Peru. Famous he
was ; now he is neglected ; yet his name and works will not die.
He is a great figure in shadow; but the shadow is not that of
oblivion.

   Mr. Charles Francis Adams, in his recent biography of R. H.
Dana, tells us that on the publication of " Two Years Before the
Mast " the young author received many cordial congratulatory
letters from such men as Rogers, Brougham, Moore, Bulwer, and
Dickens, and the first man Lord Althorp visited on his arrival in
the States was the sailor of the " Pilgrim " and "Alert." Dana's
revelation was instantly accepted and enjoyed in Great Britain.
Would not Charles Dickens, in particular, marvel that the hidden
life and spirit of the great maritime industries of Britain and the
States had never before been so much as hinted at by the many
writers who professed to know the sea and who had dealt with it ?
Yet one ought not to be surprised that America should have fore-

reached on and outweathered Great Britain, in a literary sense, in
this matter of the merchant sailor. As seafarers whilst they
were or had occasion to be seafarers, the Americans shot distinctly ahead of the British. The whole country took such an\
interest in maritime affairs, in all that pertained to the sea, as
must have been sought for in vain amongst the English even in
the height of their wars. We cheered Jack and made much of
him in our songs and dreams. Oh, yes ! the Jack of the frigate
and the liner was a wonderfully noble creature indeed whilst he
fought for us ; but we thought nothing of breaking his skull to
secure his services, of flinging him bleeding and mutilated into a
tender to lie in stinking quarters till he was drafted, of leaving
him to starve on wooden legs when he could fight no more. The
Americans were governed by wise theories of equipment. They
provided that their service should be coaxing and relishable.
That to begin with : patriotism might follow. When the
" Chesapeake " was to be manned, some time, I think, in 1813,
houses of rendezvous were opened, every man who offered received a dollar and was taken by an officer to the ship, where he
was examined as to his knowledge of seamanship, his age, the
state of his health, and so forth, by a board of officers consisting
of the master, surgeon, and others ; if he was approved, he signed
the ship's articles and stayed ; if rejected, he went ashore with a
dollar in his pocket. Many boatloads went ashore. There was
no need for the bludgeons of the press-gang. No man was torn
from his home or employ, from his ship or his wherry, and forced
to fight for the principles he abhorred, against states, such as
France, whose spirit of revolution and liberty he loved.

In shipbuilding the Americans most assuredly showed the
English the road. William James, the historian, in his " Naval
Occurrences," published, I think, in about 1817, after he had
been a prisoner in the United States, has a passage worth quoting
on the speed of the American ships. " They are," he says,
"proverbially swift sailers, and the ' President,' with such uncommon topsides, one of the swiftest among them. The quality
of sailing depends chiefly upon the form of a ship's bottom,
aided by her length. The Americans had, according to Char-
nock, discovered this early in the war of 1776 ; and they have
now proved clearly that swift sailing is not incompatible with
the strongest construction." James hated the Americans ; it

was worse than sweating blood with him to flatter them; his compliments are contrasts designed to explain why it was that the Yankee successes at sea were many. Assuredly while they were a maritime people the Americans built better than the English, saw into the sea life more clearly, perceived with more foresight and sagacity its needs and obligations, commercially and humanly; and they taught us fifty valuable lessons, all of which we were very slow and reluctant to learn.

Take, for instance, the rivalry between the two countries in the China trade. In 1845 a number of splendid ships were despatched from New York and Boston to Whampoa. The English had nothing like them. Their hulls were low, their beam great, their lines wonderfully fine, and their spread of canvas fit to have driven a "Royal George" through it with foam to the hawsepipes. The English followed suit in 1846, and launched at Aberdeen one of the swiftest of schooners, named the "Torrington." We continued to build when we found this schooner a success; but it was the Americans who had shown us what to do and how to do it. Again, the Americans were always in advance of us in the care they took of their seamen. The late Mr. Lindsay, in his "History of Merchant Shipping," says that in the rules and regulations drawn up for the internal management of their marine "the Americans were able at the commencement of their independence to adopt from other nations such laws, even to their most minute details, as appeared to them the best fitted for their position." This is wisdom that was rendered characteristic by the whole of their policy in relation to the discipline and governance of their commercial marine. Lads were highly educated before they were sent to sea; and the American merchantman was often commanded by a gentleman with a college education. Wages were sometimes threefold greater in the American than in the British merchant service. It is asserted that an ignorant American native seaman was as rare as the ignorant British seaman is common; there was scarce a hand in a Yankee forecastle but could read, write, and cipher.

And now, after all these years, the few Britishers who take an interest in their commercial marine and who deplore that English forecastles should be filled with the drainings of the Yaw Yaw clans, the dregs and lees of the Scandinavian populations, are beginning timidly to make proposals which, even if they should be fully matured and executed, would still leave the deck-house of the red flag out of the running with the forecastles of the stars and stripes when that brilliant bunting had scores of peaks of its own to soar to. Alas! where be those peaks now? Dana, on his arrival for the first time in England, dwells with delight on the hundred American flags flying the length of the docked Mersey. I own I could scarcely credit the accuracy of the historian of "Merchant Shipping" when I read that, whereas in 1815 the tonnage of the United States was not more than one-half that of Great Britain, it had risen by 1850 to over three and a half million tons, as against less than four and a quarter million tons of British shipping, whilst ten years later the United States owned a larger amount of tonnage than the United Kingdom—that is, inclusive of lake and river steamers : almost as much, indeed, as Great Britain and her colonies combined. In some trades, so supreme was the domination of the Americans by virtue of such perfect ships as the " Oriental, " " Challenge, " "Sea Witch, " " Flying Cloud, " and many others, that competition seemed almost hopeless. We built and throve and rose triumphant afterwards, but the Americans had been first ; once again Jonathan had shown the greatest maritime nation in the world what to do at sea.

I cannot speak with conviction on the subject of the American forecastle dietary; but if the provisions served out to the American seamen in the heyday of the stripes and stars were not good, most assuredly they could not have been worse than the victuals on which the unhappy English sailor has had to support life while on the ocean ever since Britannia arose at heaven's command. References to food in Dana's and Melville's books are few. Dana speaks of tea as " water bewitched," and of sea biscuit and cold salt beef as forming the sailor's meal. But the question is not, How much do they give you ? but, Can you eat it when you have got it ? Tom Cringle somewhere says that no monarch could wish for sweeter fare than a piece of virgin cold salt beef, a crisp sea biscuit, and a glass of old Jamaica rum. And Tom Cringle was right : and no sailor would ever dream of murmuring were the salt beef and the biscuit as good as Tom Cringle had in his mind when he talked of them as a dish fit to set before a king.

In the English merchant service nothing has ever proved so

fruitful of mutiny as the provisions served out to the forecastle. I had no other desire in writing the "Wreck of the Grosvenor" than to exhibit and tragically accentuate the owner's ghastly and disgusting indifference to the health and wants of his crew. I heartily wish that Mr. Dana, in his magnificent revelation of the hidden parts of the sea life, had dwelt on this subject of food. Melville romances somewhat when he approaches the galley; and you are scarcely sure that he quite means all he says. In "Omoo," for example, he describes the "Julia's" provisions; the pork looked as if preserved in iron rust and diffused an odor like a stale ragout. Of the beef the cook told a story of a horse's hoof with a shoe on having been fished up out of the pickle of one of the casks. The biscuit was like gunflints full of little holes, as if the worms in boring after nutriment had gone through and come out on the other side without finding anything fit to eat. This ship was a whaler; she had been long a-cruising, and the provisions aboard her might very well lack relish. Fortunately for American tradition in respect to the excellent provisioning of Yankee whalers, the "Julia" was an English vessel—that is to say, she was owned by a house in Sydney, New South Wales. Davis, in his excellent and powerful "Nimrod of the Sea," an American whaling story full of fine touches, old sea jokes, and useful information, is very express in the matter of provisioning. The stores of his ship were first-rate; it may have been always so with the whaler.

However, I will not here assert that the Americans have taught us any particular lesson in the direction of forecastle fare. They invented the double topsail yards; they invented the "chanty," the inspiring choruses of the windlass and the capstan, such hurricane airs as "Across the Western Ocean," "Run, Let the Bulljine Run!" "Shanadoah," "Old Stormy," "Bully in the Alley," "Cheerily, Men!" and scores besides; they were the first to lighten the sailor's labor by bidding him lift up his voice when he hove or shoved; they imported into their commercial marine fifty useful time- and labor-saving ingenuities, all which we on our side, blind with the scaly salt of centuries of dogged seagoing, were very slow to see, to apprehend, and to apply. But the imaginations, the inventions, of the American nautical mind seemed to have come to a stand at the Sign of the Harness Cask.

American judgment in matters maritime showed strong at a

very early period in the history of the republic. We believed on our side that we had reason to laugh at the Yankees' pretensions as sailors, and a bloody lesson was the penalty of our royal naval scorn. That we should have underrated their courage and seamanship is the more extraordinary in that, after some of our ships had been sunk or taken, we discovered that the majority of the fighting crews of the enemy were British seamen! Now, there is no question that a large number of British sailors did enter the American Navy at the beginning of the century. Many British ships were paid off during the short peace of 1803, and numbers of English seamen from these vessels entered under the flag of the republic at the various seaport towns in the United States, at Cadiz, and the Mediterranean ports. Scores of these gentry fought against their country in 1812 : it cannot be denied. But I observe this inconsistency in the statements of the historians of that time : when the English are beaten, the opposing ship is more than half manned by British sailors ; when the American ship surrenders, her crew are discovered to be, to within a man or two, splendid examples of the pick of American seamen ! In the case of the " Chesapeake " and the " Shannon," James is not satisfied with the swift and signal victory ; he tells us that the " Shannon's " crew were men below the middle stature, and numbers of them old or elderly : the " Chesapeake's " men, on the other hand, were the finest that ever graced a ship's decks ; and as a proof of their noble proportions " the handcuffs that had been placed upon the ' Chesapeake's ' deck ready to secure the British crew as soon as the ' Shannon ' was captured, caused, when applied to the wrists of the Americans, many of them to wince with pain." So in the case of the action between the U. S. S. " United States " and H. B. M. S. " Macedonian," in which the British were defeated ; we affirm— or we allow Mr. William James to affirm for us—that the crew of the " United States " consisted of picked seamen, all young and vigorous, and a great proportion " were known to be British sailors." But when the U. S. S. " Frolic " hauled down her flag to H. B. M. schooner " Shelburne " without firing a shot, " happily no British sailor was discovered on board the ' Frolic.' Her crew consisted of native Americans, and in appearance a finer set of men than even the ships of war of the United States usually sailed with." The English of all this is that when we are beaten

we must be beaten by our own men—renegados if you will, but—
British sailors.

The truth is, the American sailor was every jot as good as the
English sailor. It is a distinction without a difference to speak
of Englishmen and Americans in 1812 and in 1776. The American is far removed from the Englishman now : in those old fighting years they were cousins ; they were brothers in a sense considerably different from what is meant by " kinsman " in its
current mawkish and insincere application. The rival Jacks might
have been born in the same English towns, might have drained
the breasts of sisters, so close were they in blood *then.* Yet there
is this to be said of those wars, and more particularly of the War
of 1812, kinsmen or no kinsmen : the Americans, by capturing
the " Guerriere," made us look to ourselves ; determined us upon
an era of renovation: we found it desirable to improve our ships
in men, gunnery, and appointments. The Americans were before
us and fired several ugly broadsides of lessons into our massive
and self-complacent understanding.

It is consistent that the nation which rose with marvellous
celerity to the marine commercial supremacy that is indicated in
the tonnage statistics of the United States of 1860 should have
produced for her literature the men whose revelations, as I choose
to call them, are a distinct ennoblement of letters, whether
English or whether American, in the name of art, and in the
name of genius, and in the name of humanity. "Two Years
Before the Mast " should have been written by an Englishman :
nothing of the kind was ever attempted by an Englishman. Was
it because we have a trick of snubbing the sailors of the merchant
service on our side, so that no man of Dana's and Melville's genius
would dream of taking the little forecastle of a brig seriously as a
theatre for his comedy or tragedy ? Was it because it was felt
that the people of the greatest maritime country in the world
are, were, and ever have been, and methinks will be, unable to
distinguish between the common sailor who serves the state and
the common sailor who serves the private owner, and that the
effort to discriminate could but tend to a groping confusion of
the public mind? Or was it because the English take no possible
interest whatever in the calling of the merchant-mariner, in all
that that calling implies of tyranny, cruelty, frightful indifference to life, food at which a dog would hiccough, sleeping

abodes from which a water rat would fly lest he drown, a wage which yields no hope beyond the workhouse, and a working-day of twenty-four hours ?

Two American sailors, men of letters and of genius, seizing the pen for a handspike, prized open the sealed lid under which the merchant-seaman lay caverned. The light of heaven fell down the open hatch, and the story of what had been happening for centuries in the British service, for years in the American, was read. Did any good come of it ? I should have to ask your patience for a much longer paper than this to answer *that* question. But as a literary feat ! in an age, too, when men thought most things known. Americans ! honor your Dana and your Melville. Greater geniuses your literature has produced, but none who have done work so memorable in the history of their native letters.

W. Clark Russell.

CAN OUR NATIONAL BANKS BE MADE SAFER?

BY THE HON. EDWARD S. LACEY, COMPTROLLER OF THE CURRENCY.

THE national banking system was organized under an act of Congress passed in 1863, upon the recommendation of the Hon. Salmon P. Chase, then Secretary of the Treasury, who chiefly sought to create a market for bonds of the government and to provide a uniform bank-note currency, national in its character, and amply secured, which would circulate at par in every part of the Union. Two years later (October 2, 1865) 1,513 national banks were in operation, possessing an aggregate capital of $393,157,206 and $723,281,252 of deposits. The growth of the system has since been continuous and its success conspicuous. It is worthy of note, however, that the rapid payment of the bonded debt and the consequent high premium commanded by government bonds have rendered the issue of circulating notes upon pledge of these securities unremunerative, so that this feature of the system, so important when inaugurated, is yearly becoming less so. As banks of discount and deposit, however, the associations constituting the national system have become indispensable to the commercial and business interests of the country.

On the 25th day of September, 1891, 3.677 national banks were in operation, having in paid-up capital $677,426,870, and in surplus and undivided profits $330,861,160, with deposits aggregating $2,040,633,924. The system has been in operation for nearly twenty-nine years, and during that period has passed through all the vicissitudes of war and peace, adversity and prosperity. It will be pertinent, therefore, to inquire as to the degree of success achieved, before endeavoring to answer the question submitted for consideration. On the 31st of last October 4,648 banks had entered the national system, 164 had become insolvent, and 791 had gone into voluntary liquidation, paying their liabilities in full. The failures were equal, numerically, to about 3½ per cent. for a period of twenty-nine years. Of insolvent banks the affairs of 102 had been finally settled, representing $28,544,992 of proved claims, upon which the creditors have received $21,172,956, leaving a net loss to depositors of $7,372,036. The affairs of 62 banks are in process of settlement, representing claims proved to the amount of $29,247,036, on which has been paid $17,456,167, leaving assets estimated at $3,702,925 yet to be distributed, involving a loss to creditors of $8,087,944. It will be observed that the losses to creditors of national banks during the twenty-nine years of the existence of the system, taking into account the amounts ascertained and the amounts estimated, aggregate $15,459,980, or an average of $533,103 per annum. The average amount of the liabilities of all national banks since 1863 approximates $1,055,434,022, and upon this sum the annual average loss to creditors for the period of twenty-nine years has been only one-twentieth of 1 per cent. The creditors of banks whose affairs have been finally closed have received, on an average, 74.17 per cent., the cost of administration being 9.28 per cent. Of those closed during the last five years the creditors have received, on an average, 90.65 per cent., the attendant expenses being 4.08 per cent.

In considering the security of national banks, as compared with others, we are embarrassed by the fact that official data are not accessible as to banks other than national. The report of Comptroller of the Currency Knox for 1879, however, contains statistics, from partly official sources, showing the failure of 210 State banks during the three years ended January 1, 1879, having liabilities of $88,440,028, with losses to creditors of $32,616,661, or an average loss of $10,872,220 for each of these years. A prominent commercial agency* furnishes a list of 117 institutions, consisting of bankers, brokers, savings-banks, trust companies, and banks other than national, which failed during the year ended June 30, 1891, representing losses to creditors of $17,477,419, an amount in excess of the total losses of all the banks of the national system for twenty-nine years.

* Bradstreet's.

It is worthy of note that under the National Bank Act we have what is known as free banking, it being competent for any five reputable persons, acting in good faith, to procure a franchise. While this provision is in harmony with our free institutions and is a necessary feature of any enactment calculated to meet the approval of the public, it nevertheless renders it reasonably certain that the management of these associations will sometimes be committed to persons lacking in experience, and occasionally to those wanting in integrity. Again, banks may be organized with a capital of only $50,000, which facilitates the establishment of associations in places too small to give adequate support, and occasionally tends to promote unhealthy competition. These features may not be conducive to the very highest degree of safety, but they prevent monopoly and enable the general public, even in sparsely-settled regions, to enjoy the advantages afforded by well-conducted banks. The growing popularity of the system is an evidence of its conspicuously faithful service. The annual average accessions during the past five years have numbered 213, which is 53 in excess óf the annual average for the entire period since the inauguration of the system. These cover the entire country, new organizations, however, being most numerous in the undeveloped portion west of the Mississippi River. The speculative spirit which has prevailed in that region has not contributed to the safety of these new associations, and the recent reaction has been a potent factor in precipitating the disasters of the year just closed. Nevertheless, the losses recorded above appear inconsiderable when contrasted with the immense volume of business transacted.

In the report of the Comptroller of the Currency for 1891 it is shown that the amount of domestic exchange drawn by all national banks during the year ended June 30 last aggregates $12,782,212,495. This vast sum represents the transfer of bank credits necessary to simply adjust the balances arising out of trade relations between the various sections of the country. Comptroller Knox in 1881, and the writer again in 1890, procured reports from all national banks, stating their receipts upon given days, so classified as to show the proportion of actual money which entered into their daily transactions. The facts thus elicited, taking the average of two days in 1881 and two days in 1890, show that only 6.94 per cent. of actual money was employed, the remainder being represented by checks, drafts, and other substitutes for money. It appears, therefore, that of the transactions liquidated through these banks, 93.06 per cent. is accomplished by the use of bank credits. Further use of data thus obtained enables us to make an intelligent estimate as to the magnitude of the business transacted by these associations. It is shown that the receipts of 3,364 national banks on the first day of July, 1890, aggregate $421,824,726. If we take $421,000,000 as an average of their daily transactions and multiply this by 307, as the number of business days in the year, it will be found that the total receipts of these banks for a single year aggregate $129,247,-000,000, or a sum greatly in excess of the estimated value of all the real and personal property of Great Britain and the United States combined. If we consider with what economy and safety the immense business thus outlined is transacted, it will be apparent that we have already reached a condition of safety in banking not heretofore realized. The ideal bank is an institution of absolute security. Although the operations of more than a quarter of a century have demonstrated that associations organized under the National Bank Act approximate more nearly than any other to this ideal condition, it may be admitted, without humiliation, that further progress in this direction is attainable. Those whose duty it has been to administer the provisions of the act in question, as they have studied them and watched their application to actual business, have been more and more impressed with the great wisdom of its authors.

In the consideration of measures looking to the greater safety of national banks, it should be borne in mind that 96½ per cent. of these associations have in this respect met the requirements of the most exacting ; hence any new restrictions to be imposed should be directed toward preventing loss to the creditors of the remaining 3½ per cent., without imperilling the general success attained. As previously stated, under present conditions no᾿ material profit can accrue to national banks by reason of the issue of notes for circulation, and therefore any onerous restrictions might cause many national associations, now successfully and honestly managed, to withdraw from the system and incorporate under the laws of the several States. Similar consideration must be bestowed upon various propositions submitted for greatly increasing the liability of directors for losses which occur under their management. It is well known that bank directors are not salaried officers and that their services are usually rendered gratuitously ; hence, in the large cities especially, it is with great difficulty that men of high character and great ability are induced to accept these positions, because of the labor involved, the loss of time, and the grave responsibility. Any enactment that would unnecessarily increase the pecuniary responsibility of directors, and place in jeopardy their private fortunes, would no doubt cause the withdrawal from these positions of those most efficient, and cause their places to be filled by men in every way their inferiors, thus aggravating, instead of palliating, the evil resulting from the present lack of attention and efficiency on the part of directors. Certainly no radical innovations should be adopted under the pressure of temporary excitement at the risk of destroying the most effective system of which we have any knowledge.

As a general proposition it may be stated that the success of a bank is dependent upon the integrity and ability of its active officers. Neither legal enactments nor official supervision can create these qualities, although the former serve to deter the wrong-doer and the latter to educate the inexperienced. Whatever, therefore, tends to induce greater care in the selection of these officers by boards of directors will enhance the safety of the system. Experience demonstrates, also, that safety is promoted by a proper distribution of shares. In a general way success is jeopardized where the holdings of capital stock are so widely distributed as to prevent the active supervision of intelligent proprietorship, or so concentrated in the hands of a few as to make possible selfish or corrupt control. Safety ought to be the paramount consideration in bank management. As a rule, this principle is recognized by managers. The exceptions, however, are made so conspicuous by disaster as to give them more prominence than their relative importance warrants. Many dangers menacing these associations are due to mistakes in judgment entirely consistent with complete integrity and the scrupulous observance of legal requirements. Loans are always an accomplished fact before they come to the knowledge of the Comptroller or examiner, and hence serious losses have often become inevitable before official action could be taken. It is obvious that the governmental authorities cannot conduct a banking business,

—they can only inspect and supervise. The National Bank Act is mainly confined, so far as it relates to the transaction of the business of banking, to the imposition of restrictions, leaving the managers of an association free to act within established limits. So long, therefore, as bank officers are deficient in judgment or integrity failures will occur. That system is best which reduces these disasters to the minimum.

In order that we may more intelligently select the remedies to apply, it will be well to consider the prominent causes of failures and their relative importance, as disclosed by an investigation of the affairs of national banks which have heretofore become insolvent. These are stated below in the order of their relative importance, which is indicated by percentages :

1. Depreciation of securities 27.0
2. Injudicious banking.. 22.7
3. Fraudulent management 18.3
4. Defalcation of officers.............. .... 9.0
5. Excessive loans to officers and directors.............. .... 7.1
6. Real estate and real-estate loans 6.8
7. Excessive loans to customers............................. .... 5.0
8. Failure of large debtors 4.1

100.0

The classifications adopted are necessarily general in their character, but are sufficiently explicit to facilitate the grouping of certain remedies suggested by experience, and herewith submitted in outline for consideration.

DEPRECIATION OF SECURITIES.

The law should forbid the purchase by national banks of shares of any incorporated company as an investment, and should require the prompt sale of all shares taken to secure doubtful debts. Investments in bonds issued by such corporations should be subject to the same limitations as to amount as may be applied to direct loans to individuals.

INJUDICIOUS BANKING.

Injudicious banking includes, in a general way, such violations of the rules of good banking as do not involve disobedience of law. The remedy rests with the boards of directors, who should exercise greater care in selecting officers, and employ greater diligence in instructing and supervising them.

FRAUDULENT MANAGEMENT.

The presence of fraud taints far too many failures. This indicates the existence of over-confidence on the part of directors and the necessity of more exhaustive examinations. A proper division of duties, occasional changes of desks among employees, and a systematic and thorough audit of the affairs of the bank by expert accountants of known skill and integrity, will greatly reduce the losses from this cause.

DEFALCATION OF OFFICERS.

Considering the vast sums handled by and the confidence necessarily reposed in bank officers, defalcations are comparatively rare. The severe condemnation visited by the public upon criminality of this character is the best proof of its infrequency. Crime, like disease, is usually insidious in its development, and often exists for years unsuspected. No panacea in such cases can be provided. It is a significant fact that, aside from cases of accidental discovery or voluntary confession, crimes of this character are almost invariably detected by the bank examiner, whose visits are brief and infrequent, and not by the directors, whose continuous supervision is too frequently superficial and perfunctory. The antecedents, habits, associations, and financial necessities of those who handle bank funds must be patiently investigated by directors who would do their whole duty, and severe discrimination enforced against those who fail to meet the most exacting requirements. Only unremitting vigilance and unrelenting prosecution of the guilty can be relied upon to limit an evil that cannot be entirely eradicated.

EXCESSIVE LOANS TO OFFICERS AND DIRECTORS.

Losses from this source may be largely curtailed by the adoption of an amendment to the present law forbidding the active officers or employees from becoming liable, directly or indirectly, to the bank with which they are connected. The liability of directors also should be, by law, made subject to reasonable limitations as to both loans and discounts, inclusive of indorsements and guarantees for the accommodation of others.

REAL ESTATE AND REAL-ESTATE LOANS.

As original loans upon real estate are forbidden by law, and the purchase of real property confined to such as is taken for debt or purchased for use as a banking-house, it seems clear that losses stated under this head result in the main from securities taken as a last resort to secure doubtful debts originally made upon personal security. It is impossible to wholly prevent losses of this character. In my opinion, however, a limitation should be placed upon the amount which may be lawfully invested in banking-houses, as serious loss and sometimes insolvency result from locking up an undue proportion of the capital in realty, which is thus rendered unavailable at critical periods.

EXCESSIVE LOANS TO CUSTOMERS.

The liability to an association of any person, company, corporation, or firm for money borrowed is now limited by law to one-tenth of the capital paid in. This provision is in the main salutary, as applied to interior banks, but inapplicable to the conditions existing in many reserve cities. Its uniform enforcement is rendered difficult on account of the failure to provide an adequate penalty for its violation. The limitation should be based upon the combined capital and surplus, and made more liberal in reserve cities when applied to loans upon certain lines of first-class securities, including in this category warehouse receipts for staple commodities. This would more fully utilize the very best securities for bank loans and greatly facilitate the periodical movement of farm products so necessary to the general welfare of the entire people. Having properly adjusted these limitations, such reasonable penalty should be provided as would make practicable the uniform enforcement of the law, thereby promoting the safety of the banks and the interests of the general public.

FAILURE OF LARGE DEBTORS.

Under this classification are placed those losses which result from the discount of large lines of commercial and business paper, including bills of exchange drawn against actually existing values, as to which no limitation is now imposed by law. In my opinion, this omission should be supplied, and such bounds put upon transactions of this character as will make imperative a proper distribution of loans and discounts, thus preventing the solvency of a bank from being dependent upon the success or failure of one or more of its chief customers.

Having briefly considered the causes of failure and made such suggestions as seem pertinent, it may be proper to say that the most serious obstacle encountered in all endeavors to promote sound banking has been the inefficiency and inattention of directors. Whatever may be said of the legal aspect of the matter, in the light of recent decisions it is clear that the general public will continue to hold that power and responsibility are inseparable, and that no director can be morally justified in accepting an office and then utterly neglecting to discharge its duties. While it would undoubtedly be unwise to so increase the responsibility of directors as to render it impracticable to secure or retain the services of those most competent, it is nevertheless due to both stockholders and creditors, as well as to directors themselves, that the duties of the office should be by law clearly defined. Vast interests are intrusted to their care, and commensurate responsibility should rest somewhere. No plan for increasing the safety of our banks which permits directors to abdicate their powers while retaining office, and to avoid the responsibility for losses resulting from disobedience of law by pleading ignorance which could only result from the most persistent neglect, can meet the requirements of the situation.

The supervision exercised by the Bureau of the Currency is of very great value in promoting the safety of national banks. Under its direction the organization of an association is properly completed and the capital actually paid in. It is charged, among other things, with the duty of enforcing those provisions of law which require that loans shall be made upon personal security only ; that a lawful money reserve shall be maintained ; that a surplus fund shall be accumulated ; that dividends shall not be declared until earned ; that the total liabilities of any person, company, corporation, or firm for money borrowed shall not exceed one-tenth part of the capital paid in ; that no association shall make any original loan or discount on the security of the shares of its own capital stock ; that no check be certified in excess of the drawer's deposit ; that reports of condition be made and published at least five times in each year ; that circulating notes be issued and redeemed ; that real estate taken for debt be disposed of within five years from date of acquirement ; that any impairment of capital be made good by assessment upon shareholders ; and that insolvent associations be promptly closed, and their assets converted into money and divided among creditors with diligence and economy. These salutary requirements have the sanction of the highest authority, and the unremitting efforts put forth by the Bureau, through correspondence and otherwise, to insure their enforcement, have largely contributed to the safety for which the system is conspicuous.

In addition to the supervision exercised by means of correspondence, every association is visited at least once in each year by a bank examiner, who has power to make a thorough examination into all its affairs, and, in doing so, to examine any of the officers and agents thereof on oath. He is required to make a full and detailed report of the condition of the association to the Comptroller. This agency is more potent for good than any other at the command of the Comptroller. These examinations have for twenty-nine years been undergoing a process of evolution made necessary by the exigencies of the service, and it is believed that they are to-day more effective than ever before. The ingenuity of unfaithful bank officers is constantly employed in inventing new devices for concealing their unlawful acts. Hence increased vigilance and improved methods are being constantly demanded of examiners. The most valuable service performed by these officers consists in arresting dangerous and unlawful practices at the threshold. The extent to which the safety of the system is due to this timely interposition is, unfortunately, unknown to the general public. It is to be regretted that only failures can be publicly discussed.

So, also, the grave responsibilities devolved upon the Bureau of the Currency are very imperfectly understood. It is charged with the supervision of nearly 4,000 banks, covering a vast area of country in all stages of development. These associations are managed by persons of all grades of ability and experience, and are exposed to dangers of every type and character. In addition to interpreting and administering the law, a vast school of instruction is conducted. Inexperienced managers are instructed; the careless are warned; the indolent aroused, and the unscrupulous restrained. The best and the worst of bank management are daily passed in review, to the end that the good may be commended and the bad reformed. During years of severe business depression, like the one just closed, the financial disasters of a continent are epitomized in its correspondence and reports. The efficiency with which it has met these exigencies can be safely left to the decision of those who intelligently and dispassionately investigate recorded results.

It will be observed that the measures suggested as necessary to a greater degree of safety on the part of our national banks are neither numerous nor radical. The system has long since passed the experimental stage, and, despite ephemeral and injudicious criticism, it to-day stands firmly established in public confidence, and recognized as indisputably superior to any hitherto known.

In closing it may be said that its safety will be best promoted by adhering with increased fidelity to those sound principles which experience has approved, and which of necessity underlie all true success. To a marked degree these salutary maxims are found embodied in the law governing the national system. Local and exceptional conditions have made minor amendments desirable ; yet, taken all in all, it has proved admirably adapted to the changed conditions developed by the experience of a quarter of a century, and well suited to the wants of the inhabitants of widely-separated States, living under varied social conditions, with customs as dissimilar as climatic and race conditions can produce upon this continent.

EDWARD S. LACEY.

FIRES ON TRANS-ATLANTIC STEAMERS.*

BY THE RIGHT HON. EARL DE LA WARR.

WITHOUT being too much a *laudator temporis acti*, it may perhaps fairly be said, within the limits of truth, that accidents from travelling, attended often with loss of life, are far more frequent in the present day than in times gone by. No doubt a cause can readily be assigned for this. Facilities of locomotion formerly unknown are now offered to all classes, and thus increase the chances of casualties in an almost infinite degree. It cannot, however, be supposed that any one would desire to lessen or check the means of intercourse between one country and another, or to underrate the commercial benefits which it affords, the civilizing influences which it exercises, and the useful tendency which it has in overcoming national prejudices and antipathies; but what may reasonably be expected, while science and skill are almost daily increasing the means of communication between the nations of the world, is that the dangers consequent upon these advantages should not be disregarded and lost sight of.

To come, therefore, to the point which we wish to bring under public notice, it might be asked, Is it not somewhat difficult to understand that, in a matter affecting the lives of so large a number of persons, as well as property to a great extent, and which is at the same time immediately under the daily observation of trading companies involving large shipping interests, there should still exist a doubt as to the cause of one of the most destructive and calamitous disasters which can befall a ship,—a disaster which may result in its total loss, together with that of a valuable cargo, and—what is more—the sacrifice of hundreds of lives ? In connection with this it is a startling fact that about

---

* The observations made in this article are emphasized by the recent burning at
sea of the steamship "Abyssinia."—EDITOR N. A. R.

200,000 cabin passengers leave the port of New York alone for Europe every year, of whom a large proportion are liable to dangers such as those to which the passengers of the "City of Richmond" were recently exposed.

It cannot be for a moment supposed that science or skill will ever overcome the special perils of the sea; but what reasonably may be looked for is that scientific knowledge should be made use of to prevent disasters such as that which took place on board the Inman liner "City of Richmond," so that the reproach may be wiped away that in the British Parliament in the year 1891 no satisfactory explanation of the cause of these fearful accidents could be given. That such should have been the case is the more extraordinary in these days when the application of scientific knowledge to practical purposes has been of such a marked character. It is not as if it had been a solitary instance or an accident of rare occurrence. When we find that in the last ten years there have been no less than one hundred and seventy-one fires in cotton-laden ships from America to British ports, that nearly four hundred lives were lost through cotton fires in holds of steamers in the year 1890, that there were during the years 1889 and 1890 nearly sixty fires of a serious nature on ocean-going steamers, besides numerous instances, frequently terminating in the total destruction of the vessels, of cotton fires on board American river and coasting steamers, and that not less that £150,000 is the estimated cost of insurance of cotton imported to England from America, it is certainly not a little surprising that more information is not available, and that more attempts have not been made to arrive at the causes of these serious calamities, so damaging to commercial interests, and so perilous to the lives of the many thousands of passengers who every year cross the Atlantic.

Since, then, there are such grave doubts as to the origin of fires in cotton-laden ships, there seems to be good reason for specially drawing attention to the serious danger to which passengers in those ships are exposed, and also to point out that, unless the causes of those fires can be discovered and remedies applied, it may become the duty of the legislature to take some steps to regulate, or, if necessary, to prevent, the carrying of passengers in ships laden with cargoes of inflammable substances.

Let us now briefly refer to the accident on board the "City of

Richmond." This vessel left New York on the 3d of June, 1891, bound for Liverpool, with a crew of 146 hands and 298 passengers, with a general cargo, consisting chiefly of 1,000 quarters of fresh meat and 2,082 bales of cotton. It appears from the report of the surveyor of the Board of Trade at Liverpool that a large proportion of the cotton was carried under the cabin floor, and that the length of the space on fire was about one hundred feet. After the vessel had been seven days at sea, on the 10th of June, in latitude 46 degrees 9 minutes north, longitude 35 degrees 34 minutes west, at midnight, when a heavy sea was raging, a passenger gave an alarm of fire, and smoke was seen issuing from the cabin. The ship was soon found to be on fire in the hold where the cotton was stowed, under where the passengers were sleeping, and had not the deck over the cotton been of iron, it is believed that the vessel could not have reached a port of safety. The imminent danger is described by a passenger as follows :

"Whilst the storm was at its height, about midnight, a lady passenger was awakened from her sleep by the intensity of the heat and by the fumes of smoke. She immediately called a steward, and it was found that the floor was so hot that a fire of some kind was in the hold near by. . . . Portions of the crew endeavored to get at the burning bales of cotton, but the men were almost suffocated in their endeavors to do so. . . . Captain Redford, being aware of the serious nature of the fire, now ordered the stewards to rouse all the passengers and get them up on deck. . . . When I got up on deck, the crew were running to and fro preparing boats for launching, and the stewards were providing six days' rations for each passenger. It was a fearful night. The wind was screeching as it swept through the vessel's rigging, and seas were washing across the decks. . . . The suspense all through that night was something terrible."

Providentially, at length ships were sighted, and after four days the " City of Richmond " was brought to Liverpool without loss of life, with the fire still burning.

Now, it is probable that few of the many hundred passengers who cross the Atlantic are aware of the danger they are incurring. It is a danger not apparent ; a danger far more to be dreaded in its probable consequences than the ordinary perils of the sea ; a danger unthought of, because unknown ; a danger, it is supposed, which a drop of oil or a current of air may originate and cause to burst forth at any moment. But great as may be the difficulty of arriving at any satisfactory results as regards the causes of cotton fires in ships, we confess that we are at a loss to understand how it is that more attention has not been given to the subject; how it is that the great interests affected by it remain almost quiescent when the safety of many lives are involved in it, and when so large an amount of property and insurance is concerned. If it had not been brought to our attention by the recent discussion in the British Parliament that comparatively little is known with regard to the causes of fires in cotton-laden ships, we might have hesitated to believe it possible that the trading interests of America, India, and other cotton-growing countries should have been so long contented, in these days of advancement in scientific knowledge, to leave such an important question unsolved. We are aware that there are laws compelling passenger steamers that leave ports in the United States to be fitted with pipes for injecting steam into their holds in the event of fire occurring in them, and that British passenger steamers have adopted the same system ; but this provision has been found insufficient in the case of American as well as of British vessels. As an instance of this, it may be noticed that in the case of the "City of Richmond," after the injection of steam for several days, upon opening the hold after the arrival of the ship at Liverpool the fire was found to be raging fiercely.*

Now, in connection with this it is important to observe that the interests of underwriters do not seem to lie in the direction of assisting in the introduction of means of doing away with one of the principal dangers which it is their business to insure against, and there is reason to believe that a somewhat similar view is taken by passenger steamship companies—that it would not do for them to adopt expensive apparatus for extinguishing fires unless it was made compulsory upon all to do so. Upon the whole, it seems that the conclusion must be come to that there has been no very serious endeavor to ascertain the true cause of these disasters, which, it would seem most probable, have arisen from more causes than one. It has been stated that the mode of packing may account for some cases of cotton fires, and in support of this view it is found that the fires occur but rarely in shipments from India. It appears that about 6,000,000 hundredweight of cotton is shipped yearly from India to England, that during the nine years up to 1887 only four fires

* It would be wrong to suppose that no attempts have been made to grapple with this serious danger, especially in cotton-laden ships. The successful experiments made with Carver's apparatus for extinguishing fires in ships' holds must be well known by all who have given their attention to the subject.

occurred in ships with cotton cargoes, and that since then there has not been a single fire in any cotton cargo from India. Relative to this the Parliamentary Secretary of the Board of Trade recently said in the House of Lords :

" I am inclined to infer that the danger is not necessarily inherent in the cotton, but is probably due to some different circumstances of treatment or packing. It is an absolutely admitted fact by almost every court of inquiry held under the Board of Trade, by the committee of Lloyds', and by committees which have sat in America, that the packing of cotton there and its transit from the cotton-growing districts to the port are not nearly so satisfactory in America as in other places, especially in India."

Evidence of a similar kind to this was given not long ago at the Board of Trade inquiry into the loss of the National liner " Egypt." It was stated that in the previous two seasons there had been seventy-seven fires in ships carrying cotton, and that forty-four had broken out after the vessels had sailed. The imperfect packing and banding of American cotton, and also the method of sampling, the cutting into the bales and leaving the exposed places in a rough state, were considered to be one of the causes of fires, and it was said that a more closely woven material for packing, closer pressing, and the use of an increased number of bands, as is customary in the Egyptian and Indian cotton trades, would prove an effectual check.* Various other causes of danger in connection with packing have been suggested, such as contact with some kinds of oil or grease, also cotton waste, so much used in steamships, and especially cotton-seed oil, the production of which has been much increased, and which is liable to rapid oxidization and consequent combustion. But none of these suggestions seems to solve the question in a satisfactory manner, and little has comparatively been done.

The important fact ought, however, to be mentioned, that about a century ago fires were of far more frequent occurrence than now in ships with cotton cargoes from India. In 1842 it is recorded that four cotton ships were burnt in Bombay Harbor. It is also a fact worthy of notice that out of one hundred and seventy-one fires which occured in ships carrying cotton from America in the last ten years, eighty-one occurred in the port of lading, forty-five in the port of discharge, and forty-five during the voyage. But although we are almost driven to the conclus-

* Liverpool *Journal of Commerce*, Dec. 20, 1889.

ion that cotton will at times, under certain circumstances, generate sufficient heat to produce combustion, notwithstanding the experience of years we seem to be almost as far as ever from knowing the actual cause, and therefore from being able to prevent it or to apply the proper remedy in the event of a fire taking place. It seems that in the case of the " City of Richmond " the vessel was fitted with apparatus for injecting steam into the hold where the cotton was stowed, and, though it had the effect of checking, it did not extinguish the fire, which broke out afresh when the ship arrived at Liverpool.

From what has been stated, especially as regards the difference in the number of fires which occur in cotton cargoes from America and India—that, while in ships from America the number is large, fires are of rare occurrence in ships from India—it is not unlikely that a comparison of the modes of lading and stowage might lead to important results, and show that while in the one case the ship is carrying, as it were, the means for her own destruction, which may almost at any moment be brought into action, and which, in case of a passenger ship, may place many lives in the most imminent peril, there would in the other case be comparative safety. The comparison might also tend in some measure to remedy the evil by showing that it is not inherent in the cotton itself, but rather in the mode of packing and stowage, and that it results from circumstances external to it, which might be regulated or rendered harmless. The subject is one of the greatest importance when it is borne in mind that about two hundred thousand cabin passengers leave the port of New York alone for Europe every year in ships carrying cotton ; and when we find that the imports of cotton from the United States in the year ending December 30, 1890, amounted to 2,888,997 bales, the value of each bale being about £10, the magnitude of the trade, and the necessity of its régulation with regard to the safety of passengers and the security of property, may in some measure be realized.*

In conclusion, we may express a hope that the serious accident which befell the " City of Richmond," and which was prov-

---

* It is said to be not an uncommon thing for the White Star liners " Majestic " and "Teutonic" to leave New York Harbor with over a thousand souls on board. As a matter of fact, the " Majestic " sailed from New York in July, 1890, with 1,500 souls on board. These giant steamers generally carry large cargoes of cotton. In August, 1890, a fire occurred on board the " Majestic," amongst the cotton cargo, a short time before the vessel sailed.

identially terminated without loss of life, may not be without some good result, and that the shipping and trading companies who have such great interests at stake will themselves adopt measures that will render unnecessary any legislative interference, and at the same time restore confidence in the public mind as regards the safety of passengers crossing the Atlantic on the powerful and well-appointed ships which form the links of social and commercial intercourse between Europe and the great continent of the West.

DE LA WARR.

THE DUTY AND DESTINY OF ENGLAND IN INDIA.

BY SIR EDWIN ARNOLD, KNIGHT COMMANDER OF THE INDIAN EMPIRE AND COMPANION OF THE STAR OF INDIA.

ISOLATED by their self-completeness and continental seclusion, the inhabitants of the great republic possess, I think, only an imperfect comprehension of the extent and importance of India, and of the nature and scope of British administration in that Asiatic world. They themselves touch no Oriental races, are perturbed by no Oriental problems, and in their national policies have no account to take of Oriental feelings and aspirations. The "Indians" of whom alone they know are as different from the people of Hindustan as one branch of the human tree can possibly be from another ; and those other " colored persons " with whom they have to do—Africans, not Asiatics—represent only for them the memory of a great historical fault, and of a sublime and sorrowful expiation ; as well as perpetually presenting to them a dark and difficult problem for the future. There is next to no trade between India and the United States, and the wonderful peninsula itself is, as far as geographical remoteness goes, at the longitudinal antipodes for all travelling Americans. Thus, it is not surprising if somewhat confused ideas are held here regarding the Indian dominions of Queen Victoria ; and if erroneous and sometimes even unjust notions upon the British occupation exist among the public writers of the States.

Yet it is extremely desirable that the vast, powerful, and enlightened trans-Atlantic portion of the Anglo-Saxon family should truly understand what is the magnificent charge laid in Asia by Providence upon the shoulders of the cis-Atlantic portion of the breed, and how that charge has been, and is being, fulfilled. Personally I could wish with all my heart that many, very many, Americans, instead of few, as at present, would visit the land. The majority of them would come back, I know, full of a new sense of the noble task which England performs towards all those scores of millions of their Aryan relations—since the people of India proper are really very nearly akin to our Anglo-Saxon blood ; much more closely, indeed, than, say, the Hungarians, the southern Italians, or the Russians. Many a word in constant use among New Yorkers or Bostonians is of direct Sanskrit origin ; many an intimate, familiar philosophical or religious thought has come straight to them from the scrolls of the Vedas or the teachings of ancient Hindu sages ; and if it were possible, at a stroke, to cancel from daily life in these American cities, or in our own, the elements due to Indian metaphysics and Indian mental influences, the gap caused would enormously astonish the unreflecting. Moreover, on the friendly and imperial side, as a sister people of our speech and of our mighty common line, the American Republic has a special share in the British control of India, and in the prodigious effect which our sway over it exercises on the imagination of the world and upon the fate of Asia. For these reasons, and others, it is heartily to be desired that the public opinion of your great country should rightly comprehend the duty and destiny of England in India, and I gladly avail myself of the honor of an invitation from the conductor of THE REVIEW to offer herewith a humble contribution of facts and generalizations towards such an end.

For example, I have read during the recent talk about India, in connection with the temporary trouble in the Pamir, articles in American papers, lightly and carelessly—but, of course, cleverly —penned, as if it were an indifferent matter to civilization generally, and to Americans in particular, whether Russia should ever seriously challenge the British possession of India and perhaps even some day succeed in ousting us from the peninsula. In reality, such an event, could it befall, would prove the direst occurrence for human progress—and indirectly for the United States themselves—since the overthrow of the Roman Empire by the barbarians. It would be the triumph of the Slav over the Saxon, and would set back the development of Asia, and the advancement of the human race generally, at least a thousand years. I can imagine some of the clever young newspaper men, whom I have been everywhere glad to meet, responding in familiar local phrase to this : " Well, but it would not be *our* funeral ! " In this respect they would find out their mistake if they should live long enough. The loss of India to England would mean the breaking-up and decay of our ancient empire ; the eventual spread of Slavonic and Mongolian hordes all over the vacant places and open markets of the world ; the world's peace gone ; again, as in days of Belisarius, the march of sciences, arts, religions, arrested as when Omar burned the Alexandrian Library ; and history once more put back to the beginning of a new effort, under novel and gloomy auspices, to effect that which is the perpetual object of its course and its combinations—the final amalgamation of all the peoples of the globe under one law and one common faith and culture.

That " real estate " in Kansas City, where I am writing these pages, would suffer from a decisive victory won over Her Majesty's troops by a Russian army inside India is more, indeed, than I venture to affirm ; but I am quite sure of two facts : one that such a disaster would be as bad a thing for Americans in the long run as for Englishmen, for Hindus, and for the people of Islam ; and the other that it will not happen, because—thanks be to God !—Her Majesty Queen Victoria's strength in India, material and moral, is amply sufficient to-day to guarantee the security and tranquillity of the stupendous charge it bears there against any force, and any combination of forces, likely to be brought forward in challenge of the Empress of India.

The way in which we acquired this immense appanage of the British Empire is often made a matter of reproach, and not, of course, without grounds ; but chiefly by those least thoroughly informed of all the facts. If there is to be no statute of limitations in history ; if all the title-deeds of states are to stand vitiated when any ancient wrong, or violence, or selfishness, or insincerity can be proved against them, then, indeed, I should have to own our Indian possessions forfeit, and the map of the world must be also remodelled from pole to pole. Not alone Clive, Warren Hastings, and Lord Dalhousie must be arraigned and condemned at the bar of international equity, but the Pilgrim Fathers, and Penn the Apostle, and Columbus himself.

In point of fact, our Indian Empire was forced upon us by the irresistible current of events. It began in the utmost simplicity, with a merchant's charter and with a doctor's prescription ! Some London traders got a monopoly of buying and selling goods at the mouth of the Ganges, as well as at

Bombay and Surat ; and were doing a quiet wholesale and retail business when one of their doctors cured the Great Mogul Ferozeshah of a boil on his back, and the princess, his daughter, of a, fever. For a fee he received the land where Calcutta now stands, and sold it cheap to his company, who erected a factory there called Fort William. After that the merchants became princes in spite of their earnest effort to remain brokers. To protect themselves against the misrule and lawlessness of the Bengal Sonbadhars, culminating in such terrible and unfortunate outrages as the "Black Hole," they were obliged to build strongholds, occupy stations, and enlist soldiers. They were drawn into wars against their will, successively with the French, the Mahrattas, the Mohammedans of the Carnatic, of Beejapore, of the Northwest, etc., not less than with roving Pindarries, restless Madrassees, and powerful piratical enemies on the sea. As they grew perforce greater and richer, and the central business house in London appointed, one after the other, those famous satraps, called governors-general, it is notable and almost comic to read how the court of directory, upon his nomination, strictly charged each of these magnates in succession to keep out of conflicts, and not under any circumstances to acquire any fresh territory ; and how each of them, having stoutly protested at the farewell banquet in the "House" on Cornhill that he intended to bring home an undrawn sword, sent despatches after a year or two, by the long sea route, to say with deep contrition that he had been obliged to defeat a formidable potentate and to annex a splendid province.

In this reluctant and fated way the "Company Bahadur," augmenting time after time by kingdoms and states, increased to its later imperial and commanding proportions, until it ended by gaining the golden prize of Indian sovereignty from all the eager aspirants who had disputed it : from the French, the Portuguese, the Mogul, the Mahratta, the Madras Islamites, the Punjab Sikhs, the predatory robber princes, and even from some of these dangerously allied. The Olympic garland of all the world's glories, contended for from the days of Alexander the Great to those of Avitabile, Lally, Dupleix, and Tippu Saheb, thus fell at last to that band of respectable and pacific city merchants, who started an empire with a physician's prescription, and established a commerce of hundreds of millions sterling with an original

order to their agents at Calcutta " to procure a dozen lbs. of
the best tay ye can gett." Nor did they undeserve or misuse
that extraordinary and brilliant fortune to any serious or criminal
extent. The eloquent thunders of Burke and Sheridan against
the great lieutenants of the company were, in reality, largely
rhetorical. Clive was better justified than the casual student of
history deems when he exclaimed, referring to his impeachment :
" By God ! I am astonished, when I look back, at my own moderation !" Their grand succession of illustrious rulers—Corn-
wallis, Amherst, Wellesley, Auckland, Elphinstone, Munro, Dalhousie—all took, in their degree, the enthusiasm of service with
which India inspires a man, gave solid peace and safety to
the teeming population, and rooted out from the land innumerable ancient cruelties and abuses. It is notable how the recollection of those great and valorous servants of " John Company "
still lives with gratitude and reverence among the people of Hindustan. In many a town and village you may see shrines and
religious monuments erected to them, where the simple peasants
offer daily gifts of rice and flowers, and you may hear to-day in
the bazaars of Calcutta the black mothers singing to their children:

> " *Hathi par howdah, ghora par jin,*
> *Juldi bahir jata Warin Hastin*";

which means :

> "The howdah on the elephant, the saddle on the steed,
> And soon will Warren Hastings go riding forth with speed."

It was under that marvellous and masterful " John Company" that India silently but gratefully saw abolished " *sati*," the
burning of Hindu widows ; " *thuggi*," the organized assassina-
tion of travellers by the *roomal*, the handkerchief, of the Thugs ;
the dreadful and common practice of infanticide, once a general
custom in certain provinces ; the celebration of the *Meriah*, or
human sacrifices to propitiate the gods of rural fertility ; the
countless and fantastic tyrannies practised by cruel princes on
their subjects ; the bitter tortures and exactions with which
traders who had amassed wealth were persecuted ; the holocausts
of dying victims drowned daily in the name of religion on the
banks of the Hoogli, and many other enormities of the preceding
times. Generous in a princely way to their servants, easy with
their subjects, liberal and large-minded in council, fearless and im-

placable in war, well-meaning and conscientious in administration, the "Company Bahadur" made for itself in its one hundred years of Oriental sway a name which has rendered commerce imperial, and has, as before in Corinth and Venice, robed traffic in the purple of royalty. It became among the natives a majestic abstraction, something divine, mysterious, and omnipotent, which they worshipped like *Kali*, the Goddess of Power and Terror. It shared with the British throne the task of ruling the Asiatic Empire, and its proconsuls regularly reported, mail after mail, by "double entry," to the sovereign at St. James's and to the chairman of the Honorable East India Company in the City. But the sword which it had forged to serve and sustain it—the Sepoy Army—broke in its still vigorous grasp through carelessness and inadvertence ; and the home government, which was obliged to step in with all the might of the realm to save it, succeeded inevitably to the lapsed estates of its sway.

I myself had the never-to-be-regretted and never-to-be-forgotten honor of serving the Honorable East India Company in its Educational Department, and was present at the table of the Governor of Bombay, Lord Elphinstone, on the memorable night when, at Kirkee, in the Deccan, he read aloud to a brilliant company of administrators, public officials, and military and financial officers collected round him, the proclamation transferring British India from the company to the crown. Deep as our devotion was to the Queen's Majesty, and grateful as we all were that those two years of darkness and danger lately traversed had passed away, bringing safety, sunshine, and stronger securities than ever, the emotion produced by that ceremony was extraordinary. I wistfully saw, on that proud and sad evening, renowned old veterans of the wars weeping openly, and gray-haired officials of the famous company, when attempting to speak, choked with their crowding memories. It was the demise of a veritable and mighty potentate at which we assisted ; the passing-away of an association of empire-making traders, greater than the proud burghers of the Hague, than the Hanseatic Leaguers, nay, than the Council of Ten itself when, from ocean-throned Venice,

"Thrice did she hold the gorgeous East in fee."

I was in India during that great mutiny of 1857, and, of course, saw and heard things which I prefer now to forget; for we were but a few "Saheb lôk" among many and ferocious enemies, and the typical Englishman "cornered" is no saint. But, also, I saw and heard at that dark time things good to remember in the way of perfect fidelity and fast affection between the races ; and, as a matter of fact, the population at large were never, for a moment, against us. Had they been, we must have disappeared as sand castles do before the roll of the sea breakers. A Mahratta *shikari*, one of my hunting servants, casually remarked to me once in the jungle, when we were chatting about the "Sircar": "If we should spit at you altogether and with one mouth, Saheb! we should drown all you English"; and of course that was coarsely true. The mutiny was, however, not Indian, but Mohammedan in origin and essence, and only by the scandal of the "greased cartridges" through the pampered spirit of the high-caste Hindu soldiers, did the Muslims get the Hindus to act with them for once, albeit, if successful, they would have instantly set to work to cut each others' throats. Such an event as that alliance, and the consequent outbreak, is next to impossible again, because communications are now made perfect, the British forces in India are maintained at a scale commandingly strong, and the artillery ever since the mutiny has been kept wholly in British hands.

Moreover, with that mutiny and with the rule of "John Company" terminated the era of annexation ; and, partly on that account, ever since then the independent native princes have become heartily loyal, and will remain so, while we deserve their loyalty by our strength, our justice, and our resolution to maintain the peace and prosperity of the land. The Queen's name is to-day far greater and more potent in Hindustan than was even the company's, and "*Maharani Kajai*"—"Victory for the Empress!" —is a battle-cry which would be shouted joyfully by all the warlike races of Rajpootana, Kattiawar, the Punjab, the Deccan, and even the Mohammedan Northwest, if in any crisis Her Majesty chose to admit the chivalry of the native courts to her active service. The regular native army, by which I imply our Sepoy regiments, horse and foot, is in excellent condition to-day as to drill and discipline, and side by side with its English comrades, and led by British officers, would perform doughty deeds of valor, albeit the English officers are by no means numerous enough.

As to the courage of the Sepoy, it is not to be doubted, so long as he has white leadership. I sat once with a detachment of the 25th N. Infantry of Bombay, just returned from the mutiny campaign under Sir Hugh Rose and Havelock. One among the gallant fellows had lost a hand. He did not tell me himself how it happened, but a comrade explained that Govind had led a party of stormers to a fortress gate, one of those which opened, after the Indian fashion, by a heavy wooden bar which you lifted through a hole. Putting his left hand through the hole to move the sliding latch, it was shorn clean off by the blow of a sabre-blade inside, whereupon the brave soldier thrust in his right hand, opened the gate, and was the first to rush the entrance and take the fort. A hundred similar examples of national valor live in my mind.

With the transference of India to the Crown came advantages and disadvantages. Among the former was the direct impress given of imperial modes of government, through the hands of such eminent and experienced statesmen as Lords Lawrence, Northbrook, and Dufferin ; and among the latter the mischief of getting India " meddled and muddled " by entanglement with the House of Commons debates. With the true good sense which ever distinguishes His Royal Highness, the Duke of Cambridge once remarked to me : " How can you expect India to be well governed any more when the Viceroy has always at his elbow a button which communicates straight with the India Office in Westminster, and with the lobby of the House of Commons ? " Another result has followed which is of mixed evil and good. Education has been largely extended, with excellent consequences in many directions, but baneful ones in others. Instruction in the vernacular, conveying by native language the simplest and most solid truths and achievements of Western schools, goes on very widely indeed, and is an unmixed good. But in the colleges and high schools, where degrees are conferred or prepared for, the custom has too much been to impart a superficial acquaintance with English literature, which is of no use to the student unless he obtains government employment, and not of very much utility even then. The Brahman, dispossessed of his old authority and influence in the land, has taken largely to these curricula of polite sciolism, and becomes " a fish out of water," utterly helpless and malcontent, except he gets into some department of official work. This has mischievously bred a large and restless class of discontented young men, principally of high caste, who receive in the government colleges and high schools a superficial instruction in

English language and literature, which turns them out conceited, but unfitted for the duties of life. As they are far too numerous to be all of them received into the service, the large balance of the disappointed Brahmans constitute a collection of people who agitate and raise political questions for which India is not ripe.

These young smatterers are known on the Bengal side as Baboos, but there are plenty of them to be found on the Bombay side and in the vicinity of every government college. These are they who agitate in the native press, in public meetings, and among foolish and thoughtless circles in England itself, for representative institutions and other absurdities, with ever larger share in the government of India on behalf of themselves and their fellows. I have been myself to some extent guilty of creating a considerable number of these intempestive spirits, since I was president for several years of the Sanskrit College at Poona, in the Deccan, which, with the Elphinstone Institution, constituted the University of Bombay. But my 500 students were almost all Mahrattas, who are of a sturdier type than the Bengali Brahmans. These latter, when they have learned English and dabbled a little in Scott's poems and other ornamental literature, have really nothing that they can do except to turn clerks in a government establishment. They are full of a certain narrow capacity, and when Lord Dufferin once asked me what was the most striking sight I had seen in travelling through India, my answer was, to have beheld a Calcutta Baboo prime minister to the Maharajah of Jeypore. But even in my time we had begun to rectify the mischief of this too genteel education by doing that which ought to be done and will now be done, and in the future, all over India. Technical and practical instruction, with reading, writing, and arithmetic, ought to be rendered as common and easy as can be ; but *belles lettres* should be made expensive and comparatively unattractive, so as to divert the minds and thought of the rising intellect of India to botany, mineralogy, chemistry, and the more useful branches of learning, the fruit of which would be that we should gradually get the immense natural resources of India better developed.

In connection with this class of youthful and disappointed agitators, one hears sometimes the government of India reproached for not advancing quicker on the path of social progress and political reform of the modern type. The Marquis of Ripon was hailed with delight by these well-meaning but hasty people, because he took his inspiration from the Calcutta Baboos and their friends, and tried to rush ahead with what was justly called at the time a "breathless benevolence." But he confessed himself, on returning home, to a friend of mine, that he had no real supporter in that premature policy among English residents in India, "except his Scotch gardener at Simla"; and if one understands the land, it will be seen how rash and precipitate it is to apply to her the constitutional or democratic principles of the West. Patriotism is a word that has not and cannot have any universal meaning in that vast peninsula, which is a continent and not a country. India has never governed itself, and has never once been governed by one supreme authority until the time of the English rule. Consequently, there never was and there never could be that common sentiment among its inhabitants which is the necessary basis of the feeling of patriotism. There never even existed one comprehensive native name for the peninsula, regarding it geographically from Comorin to the Indus. Realize what India is! In the immense territory enclosed by the great mountains on the north and the oceans on the south, it contains nigh upon three hundred millions of souls, divided into innumerable races and classes, and speaking many more than a hundred different tongues and dialects. No countries in Europe, none in North and South America, are more widely divided from each other, in blood, religion, customs, and speech, than the Sikhs, say, from the Moplas of Calicut, or the Mahrattas of Poonah from the Mohammedans of Bhopal.

What has always helped to keep India from becoming homogeneous is her village system, which prevails everywhere. The towns and cities, of which, of course, there are many, are all entirely unconnected in interests and business ; and live apart from each other as much as if they were islands in the sea. Between these lie, in the huge interspaces of the rural districts, innumerable villages, each of them constituted on the same plan, and each of them forming the little centre of the agricultural district radiating far round it. These villages are of immense antiquity, and possess an identical system of civil life which probably dates from days long before Moses and the Pharaohs. They never grow smaller or larger, for if the population increases, it migrates a few leagues off and opens up some new jungle or hill.

There are the Patel or chief of the village, the Brahman astrologer, the blacksmith, the carcoon, or accountant, and the low-caste man, whose business it is to deal with corpses, human or animal, and to skin the cattle when they die. There is also always in these "gaums" a panchayet, or council of five, which acts as the little village court, and settles small local questions, under the sanction of the authorities. Amid these countless small centres of Hindu existence the English collector or his assistants go round annually, taking from the cultivators the light assessment which makes the government land tax, and holding among them a perambulating court of justice, which deals with more serious civil and criminal cases, or else refers them to the higher tribunals.

If all India were composed entirely of these villages, and the villages were tenanted by exactly the same sort of people, there might be such a thing as a homogeneous peninsula, for which its children might feel that sentiment of patriotism which is evoked with us by the mere name of England, and which unites all the States of America, in spite of their different and sometimes discordant interests, under the star-spangled banner. But the numberless millions of that land are split up in every direction, so that the human strata cross and recross each other, and show a hundred lines of cleavage. There is, first of all in the whole region, the broad distinction to be ever borne in mind between Hindus and Mohammedans, the proportion between these being, as nearly as I can remember, about seventeen to one. Yet this proportion gives Queen Victoria so many Muslim subjects in India that she rules, taking them into account with the same religionists in Ceylon, Malay, Africa, Arabia, and elsewhere, three times as many of "the faithful" as the Sultan of Turkey himself. These Indian Mohammedans represent and are derived from the old governing dynasty of the Mogul. They largely retain, except down in Madras, the ways and feelings of a lordly and dominant race ; constantly quarrelling with the Hindus upon religious questions, and always ready to fly at their throats but for the strong restraining hand of the English Government. As matters stand in the great Indian cities, we have occasionally the "work of the world" to keep the peace between the Mohammedans and the Hindus, especially at the chief festivals ; while every now and then, between whiles, the Hindus will throw the carcass of a pig into a Mohammedan mosque-court, or the Mohammedans will openly slaughter a cow, each of which unkind acts sets a whole province thirsting for blood. Nothing is more certain than that, if our power were withdrawn, these two main classes of Indian inhabitants would wage a war of mutual extermination.

And while this main division exists, the Hindus themselves are, first of all, cut up into four chief castes, with countless other and minor divisions, which keep them definitely apart, and will do so, it appears, for centuries to come. Up to this date modern civilization and the ideas introduced by us have had little or no effect upon that antique institution, which is supported by the vast bulk of Hindu opinion. The high-caste soldiers who fill our regiments of horse and foot, and who would cheerfully follow their English officers to death in battle, would fling away their half-cooked dinner if even the shadow of their commanding officer should fall upon their cooking-place; and this out of no disrespect for him, whom they often love and always revere, but because of an immemorial religious prescription. I had myself as a friend a native officer, who fell very sick, and to whom I said one day : "Luximan, I could restore you to health if I might give you, without your knowledge, a pint of strong beef-tea every day." He made me a feeble salaam, and answered : "Saheb, when I recovered, if I had found out what you had so kindly done, I should want to kill you at the first opportunity." This is enough to show that socially there is no unity among the inhabitants of India, nor any possibility of it, while they are further split up by geographical and natural limitations, and by old distinctions between the many kingdoms of India; so that, as I hav remarked, the Rajputs are more remote from the people o Cuttack, and the Todas of the Blue Mountains less akin to the mountaineers of Thibet, than the New Yorkers are distinguishable from the Esquimos, or the Southerners of Richmond from the red Indians of Winnipeg.

Since the time of Alexander of Macedon and of King Asoka, we are the first whose large and undisputed authority has practically brought India under one sceptre. Indeed, the renowned Macedonian never even saw the Ganges ; and Asoka, the famous Buddhist monarch, with all his widespread influence, did not rule a tenth part of the peninsula. It lies now, from north to south and from east to west, under the benignant hand of the "Maharani," Her Majesty the Queen of England. And perhaps by the net-work of railways established, and the good roads which far and near link the large territories of the country, as well as by the electric wire and the postal service, India is at last becoming, as far as the thing is possible, a country and not a continent.   Nor is it without hopeful foresight of such future amalgamation that we have everywhere instituted and encouraged a municipal system in the towns, which will help to teach Indian citizens the art of self-government.   But when folks talk of ready cut-and-dried representative systems for India, and a hasty adoption of the civil and social methods of the West, they talk the "breathless benevolence" of ignorance.   Modern institutions are not yet possible in that vast and varied world, which for many and many a year to come wants nothing so much as the immense tranquillity, the *burra choop*, which the Queen's government secures to it.

With what far-off and final object, then, it may be asked, does that government hold rule ?   And what do we propose to ourselves as the outcome of our continued guardianship ?   First of all, they do not ask these questions in India.   The Eastern mind, never restless like the Western, is thoroughly Christian in this, that it "takes little thought for the morrow."   It loves well to live along, waiting for history and destiny—which is the will of Parabrahm—to develop things.   For it is necessary to understand the mind of India, as well as the face of the beautiful land and its immemorial divisions.   India, even in her rural and least-educated districts, is metaphysical and philosophical to an extent unrealized by the practical and material West.   This comes by inheritance.   The Hindu peasant succeeds by an unconscious birthright to profound and far-reaching ancient ideas which make life's facts present themselves to him in quite a different light from the aspect which they bear for us.

Take, for example, the familiar question of the remarriage of Hindu widows, very much discussed and advocated by the "breathless-benevolence" school.   Now, nothing would, on the surface, seem more reasonable or more seasonable than that all kindly people in England and America should denounce the present Hindu system.   Under this, at five years of age the little Indian maiden is publicly betrothed to a Hindu boy of seven or eight, of whom she is from that time, in social regard, the wife.   When they are thirteen and seventeen, respectively, they will live together in the house of the bridegroom's father.

But if the bridegroom should die before this, or die shortly after the marriage, the Hindu girl must remain a child-widow for all her life, her ornaments taken from her, her hair cut short, and wearing, not the glad garments of crimson and gold, or purple and silver, which mark the happy state of an Indian wife, with gold and silver bangles and the bright vermilion mark on the forehead, but clad in the sad white *sari* of her loneliness. Nothing can seem more deplorable. But if you understand Indian ideas, you will see at once how serious a matter, socially speaking, any rash reform might become. The universal Hindu belief is that so great a calamity as the death of her husband could only befall any hapless child or woman because of some great offence committed by her in a previous existence, and that patient solitude is the right expiation.

Of course the Western reformer will immediately exclaim: " We have no patience with such fantastic beliefs. Why, in the name of sober sense and of the Christian government that rules India, should millions of these poor females be compelled to lead a solitary and mournful existence for so doubtful a tenet as this of expiating by patience and loneliness the wrong deeds done in some former life ? " True ! I warmly agree. But consider a little how this thing works socially. The little maid, from and after the time of her betrothal, wholly belongs to the family of her bridegroom, and is wholly chargeable to that family ; so that—since every girl not deformed, sick, or lunatic, is betrothed as early as possible in India—there is no such thing as a woman in that land without protection and subsistence among all the immense numbers to whom this rule applies. For the sake of the dead husband or bridegroom, his family or its collateral branches will faithfully support her ; and does support her to the end of her life. But if you take away that supreme motive of regarding her as belonging to her dead consort, and destined to rejoin him by virtue of her patience and fidelity, if you allow any or all of these young widows to remarry,—or, rather, compel Hindu civil law to allow it,—it will soon be nobody's business to shelter and protect one who is disputed, like the woman in the New Testament, by different husbands. The consequences of such a reform would be that in a few years you would have millions of Indian women absolutely destitute, and for the first time you would establish, what does not now exist in the peninsula, a pauper class.

I remember astonishing one of our English ministers of state, who was president of the Poor-Law Board, by asking him if he had ever studied the Indian poor-law system. "No," he said, "but I wish greatly to do it, since there must be much to learn from a country with so vast a population. Pray tell me what it is." I replied : "There is none at all !" And that is the case. In India, as in Japan, there prevails the very peculiar and very admirable custom, immensely convenient to a government, of what is called by Hindus the *bhaobund.* Under this, anybody out of means goes right away to his nearest relative who happens to be fairly well off, and will be cheerfully maintained by him until such time as he can find something to which to turn his hand. In the same really Christian spirit, among the Japanese people also, if the police see any one begging for alms, they make inquiries at once as to his friends and relatives, and carry him off to the person who may be most reasonably called upon to take heed that he does not degrade his family by asking charity. Religious mendicants abound in both countries. But that is a different matter altogether ; and under the existing system in India nobody ever saw a woman of the three higher castes stretch out her hand to the passer-by to ask for help. She has and can have no need ; but would soon sink into it if in our reforms we did not regard the peculiar bearings of religious thought in the land.

This example is cited only to show how necessary it is, in any beneficent councils conceived for the sake of the Indian population, to have regard to the peculiar manners and beliefs of the people. Far be it from me to desire to maintain such a system, which links the living too severely to the dead, and is, indeed, a continuation under another form of that rite of *sati,* or the burning of widows, which, while it had a beautiful and sublime side, was a social evil which we did well to abolish from the land. Herein also much misconception prevails, however, for *sati* was at no date very prevalent in India. As far as I could ascertain, there never occurred more than about a thousand instances in a year throughout the land, even when, as at first, the English Government did not interfere with it. Martyrs are not so common as some imagine, even in India itself.

The duty of the English Government to India is, beyond all question, to administer that great special and separate Asiatic world for its own good and for its own sake, and not for the profit of the mother country. It is not to be denied for a moment that we derive, directly and indirectly, immense advantages from our possession of Hindustan. First of all, it gives us, in the eyes of the world, an imperial prestige that nothing can surpass ; and I have said before, and repeat, that the loss of India, if that were possible, would mean the sure and speedy decay of the British Empire, and the falling-away, one by one, of our great colonies. Next to the place which India fills in the imagination of the world may be ranked in importance the large commerce which we carry on with her ; the very considerable revenue derived from her people; of which, although most goes to the necessities of the country, it is not to be forgotten that a considerable portion supplies the salaries of that numerous civil service, covenanted and uncovenanted, which performs the duties of government ; and that pension and other funds drawn from the same source sustain a great many English families in comfort and even in distinction. But right nobly does that civil service repay to India the funds which it thus derives from it. No one acquainted with the subject will gainsay me when I state that there does not exist a more accomplished, competent, or devoted body of men in the whole world than the civil servants of India.

From the earliest times until now this illustrious company of hard-worked officials has preserved unbroken the tradition of a perfectly spotless and unsparingly energetic administration, so that, as in the case of the judges of England, the "civilians" of India, almost without exception, have come to place themselves beyond the reach of suspicion or of reproach. In the by-gone times son and grandson succeeded father and grandfather in this official hierarchy, almost as a matter of course. And the method had this benefit in it, that it preserved an unbroken habitude in Indian affairs, so that we had seldom or never in the ranks of this perpetual dynasty of duty what is called "a Queen's bad bargain." Later in the day there came in that movement which abolished purchase in the army and appointment by favor to the Indian civil service. Nominations and promotions are all effected now by the universal plan of examination, which, while it does away with nepotism, and insures a due supply of brains for this most exacting work, gives us sometimes not quite the ideal man, as regards physical qualities and that custom of command which used to attach to the "Indian" and aristocratic class from which we drew our Indian servants. Sir Charles Trevelyan and his son, Sir George, were the main agents in that great reformation ; but I myself heard Sir Charles once say at the table of his son : " We have altered the system, but I am, nevertheless, delighted to observe that the old familiar names are still constantly coming up in the lists of candidates obtaining appointments in India under the new competitive plan." And true it is that something in the magnificent surroundings of that service, in the dignity of its duties, in the inspiration of its imperial tasks, seems to turn almost all new comers into the old masterful and serviceable mould ; so that the Queen's justice is still carried purely and faithfully to the door of every hut in India, and the collector's camp, as it passes through the districts, is still the recognized and trusted centre of clemency, equity, and consideration for the villagers, and a cause of terror only to the tigers which decimate their cattle ; for wherever there is an Englishman in India, there is almost sure to be a passionately eager and enthusiastic sportsman.

The clear duty of England, therefore, towards India is to legislate and administer for her good, regardless of selfish considerations, and only careful not to lose step with the slow progress of the Asiatic mind by adopting the restless paces of Western reform. From the beginning until to-day that duty has never been put out of mind. Seventy years ago when somebody found Mountstewart Elphinstone sitting in his tent at night surrounded with piles of school-books and asked the Governor of Bombay what he was doing, he—one of the most devoted of administrators —replied: "I am paving our way out of India." I do not believe the English Government would hesitate at any measure, even if it involved the eventual loss of India, could it be made clear to them that that measure was for the sure and lasting benefit of the millions committed to our charge in those wide regions. But it is their opinion, and it is honestly mine, who love India as well as I love England, that the connection between the two peoples is one ordained by Divine Providence itself, and that the issues of that long strife that gave the great country to us, out of the hands and above the heads of so many fierce claimants, was a happy result for India, first, and after that for England ; but chiefly for her in the noble duties and in the majesty of the mighty and onerous charge laid upon her.

Nowadays the Indians have become fellow subjects of the Queen, with general rights equal to the rights of those who live nearest the throne. An Indian Parsee gentleman has been a candidate for Parliament, and might have sat in it. Indian princes are among the highest knights of the English orders; Indian attendants accompany Her Majesty everywhere; and it is well known that the heart of Queen Victoria is attached to no part of her boundless dominions more closely than to those in India; whose people,—to speak what is the truth,—high and low, rich and poor, reverence the Empress, in return, as a sort of incarnation of power and goodness. It has come, indeed, to this, that India belongs to England, because England belongs to India; and having buried in her soil so many thousands of brave, devoted women and tender children, as well as gallant men, the title-deeds of my country to that proud and faithful guardianship are written almost more clearly in tears than in blood.

If a country like Russia challenges this long and faithful protectorate, it certainly is not and never has been upon the pretence that she could administer the country better, or be more in honest and useful sympathy with its people. Although the Muscovites have learned to treat with policy and consideration their vanquished Mohammedan races in Samarcand, Bokhara, Khiva, Merv, Kashgar, and elsewhere, they are not a tolerant race, as has been only too sadly shown by their conduct of late towards the Jews. In fact, Russia makes no affectation of political beneficence in approaching the gateways of India; she obeys two imperative impulses of national yearning and state necessity—one of them being the ever-pressing instinct to get down from her icy isolation to the sunshine and the sea; the other the never-forgotten mandate of Peter the Great not to rest till Constantinople is possessed. So obvious is the force of these two motives that the patriotic and sagacious Turkish statesman, Fuad Pacha, was wont to say: "Were I Russian, I would shake the world down to gain Stamboul!"

In half-conscious pursuit of these objects, Russia has pushed along from the Caspian to Merv, always thinking to use a real or menaced attack upon India as a flank diversion for her main assault upon the Bosphorus. We have stopped her again and again, on both wings of her advance; and from the political point of view the reason of this is clear, when your readers reflect what the Queen's Mohammedans would think and feel if we ever abandoned Stamboul to the Slav. While Britain continues a first-class power, Russia will never hold Constantinople, and will never enter the gateway of India except to be rolled back, in confusion, blood, and ruin, all the way along her track of advance, to Krasnovodsk and the Caspian marshes. If ever she defies in earnest the British Lion couched at Quetta and at Attock, the strife will not end until the Romanoff dynasty has been ruined,· and Russia broken up. This is so well understood that the most peaceful men on both sides are those who command affairs, and best understand the momentous problem.

But English policy must follow the course of events, and His Imperial Majesty the Czar is served upon the frontier by restless and enterprising officers, who, after doing what mischief they could on the Afghan frontier, have of late opened up new troubles on the eastern slope of the Pamir, where they have instigated certain hill tribes to provoke the British border guards. The Pamir passes are impracticable for warfare. Anybody who will read M. Bonvalot's book will perceive that only small parties, and those with difficulty, can cross the inhospitable and dreadful *cols* of that "roof of the world." Moreover, in recklessly wandering towards Cashmere, by the Pamir Mountains, the Muscovites provoke and alarm China as well as England ; and, briefly, they will most assuredly have to retire. It is an instance of the erroneous statements that are current to notice the Russian journals accusing England of annexing Cashmere by recent sinister measures ; whereas, if they knew the facts, they would be aware that Goolab Singh, the former ruler of the country, freely offered it to us after the second Punjab war, and we refused it then and have since always refused it, the country being sufficiently at all times under our influence. The recent *alerte* was directed against the frontier of Cashmere, but there is no military road into India by that path ; and the affair must be considered, unless it takes far larger proportions, as a mere diversion and piece of mischief, which Lord Lansdowne will know very well how to checkmate.

The invader who means earnestly to dispute India with the British must come by different roads and in a less furtive manner. If ever Russia has the will and the power to knock in serious purpose at the northern gates of India, she will come by Merv and Herat ; and the great battle outside the frontiers of Hindustan will take place at Girishk upon the river Helmund. We must not lose that battle, and we shall not lose it, for all India will be watching at our backs ; and we owe to them, as the first guarantee of our fitness to be their rulers and protectors, the spectacle of our fearless and sufficing might. But if we lost it, we should be far, very far indeed, from losing India. The command of the sea, the guardianship of Egypt, the possession of those important sea stations, Malta and Gibraltar and Aden, are what really give us power to hold India against the world. And while we are masters of the sea, India will never be forced to change her allegiance. Even in the great mutiny there was never any real danger of our expulsion. An old Hindoo astrologer told me that the prince of his state con suited him as to the course that should be adopted towards the then struggling and apparently overmastered Sahebs. " What did you say, Shastri ? " I asked. He answered : " I told the Maharaja, without even consulting the stars, that if we killed every one of you all but the last, he would bring the rest of the nation back upon us across the water."

The real pith of the problem lies deeper. India is well contented, safe, tranquil, and prosperous. Not actively grateful to us ; for no people ever are grateful for being well governed ; but deeply assured, as far as her masses think on the subject at all, that the " Queen's peace " in India is the truest blessing she ever had from the gods, and most desirable to maintain. India is well contented, and will flourish so long as England's strength suffices, along with justice purely administered, and tolerance truly maintained, and reforms seasonably introduced and fostered, to keep unbroken that deep peace, the first which India has known in all her history. To day, at least, the strength of England is abundantly adequate by land and sea to hold the country against any challenge.

But—and here comes the point—the question of questions is whether the democracy of Great Britain, our household-suffrage men, who have of late come to supreme power in the realm, comprehend their Indian Empire and care to maintain it. Undoubtedly, if they did comprehend, they would care ; for no nobler charge was ever laid upon a people than thus to repay to India—the antique mother of religion and philosophy—the immense debt due to her from the West. There are, of course, many collateral considerations which ought to move the popular mind ; such as commercial benefit, colonial advantage, and national prestige ; but these are weak in comparison with the force which ought to be exercised upon the general imagination by the sublime duty laid upon Great Britain, if ever any duty was sublime, by the visible decree of Providence itself, and it may be said, consecrated to the pride and fidelity of succeeding generations of Englishmen, as well as, in past days, by the brightest valor, the noblest devotion, the highest capacity, and the most unflinching discharge of duty.   Upon this it all turns.

I believe myself that the people of England, who from all ranks of the home country have themselves furnished the soldiers, the officers, the administrators, and the statesmen that have built up British India, hold at heart, as a cherished principle, the maintenance of that glorious Oriental empire until such time as our duty is fully and finally done to the great and wonderful land.   Nothing on the political horizon as yet even begins to proclaim that the task of England is accomplished towards India and her countless peoples ; and therefore nothing, in my mind, at present so much as even threatens the manifest destiny of England to pass insensibly and happily from the position of the mistress and protectress of the peninsula to that of its first friend, its sister, and its ally, in some far-off day when the time is come for India to manage her own happy destinies.

EDWIN ARNOLD.

A PERILOUS BUSINESS AND THE REMEDY.

BY THE HON. HENRY CABOT LODGE, REPRESENTATIVE IN
CONGRESS FROM MASSACHUSETTS.

WHEN Burns wrote his famous lines,

> " Man's inhumanity to man
> Makes countless thousands mourn,"

he probably had in mind only that direct inhumanity which is unfortunately but too well known, and which has been the source of
so much grief in the world. Yet there is a kind of inhumanity,
indirect and unintentional, certainly much less obvious than that
of the familiar verse, which is nevertheless the cause of almost as
much suffering. The failure of Congress to act in the case of the
trainmen is an instance of this latter sort. Three times has the
President of the United States asked Congress to do something
to protect the lives of trainmen by securing uniformity in couplers
and the adoption of train brakes on freight trains. A committee
of the Senate has held an extensive hearing upon the subject.
The Railroad Commissioners of the country in their national convention have discussed the question, and appointed a special committee, with Mr. Crocker, of Massachusetts, at its head, to secure
action. Yet Congress has done nothing. It would be going too
far to say that nothing has been accomplished, for the efforts of
the Railroad Commissioners have awakened public interest and to
a certain extent formed public opinion. But the body which has
the power to actually do something effective has not yet stirred.
This inaction is inhumanity, unintentional and thoughtless no
doubt, but none the less the cause of many deaths, of much pain,
and of widespread suffering, which might be mitigated, if not
stopped, by intelligent legislation.

I desire here to state the case briefly, merely bringing figures
and facts together in such fashion that they shall tell their story,
and, if possible, help forward the work of proper legislation. The

story is a simple one, and any one who will take the trouble to read the figures will, I think, be convinced that something practical ought to be done and done quickly.

The following table gives all the really essential facts :

Kind of accident.	1890.		1889.	
	Killed.	Injured.	Killed.	Injured.
Coupling and uncoupling	369	7,841	300	6,757
Falling from trains and engines.	557	2,348	493	2,011
Overhead obstructions....	89	343	65	296
Collisions................................	236	1,035	167	820
Derailments..........	150	720	125	655
Other train accidents	154	894	189	1,016
At highway crossings..............	22	32	24	45
At stations	98	691	70	699
Other causes....	749	8,250	539	7,729
Unclassified......	27	236	....	......
Total ......·............	2,451	22,390	1,972	20,028

The totals in these tables are really appalling : 22,000 men were killed and injured in the railroad service of the United States in 1889, and 25,000 in the following year. Of these, in round numbers, 2,000 were killed in 1889 and 2,500 in 1890.

Let me try now by a comparison to bring home what these figures mean. At the battle of Sedan, which sealed the fate of the Second Empire, the loss on both sides in killed and wounded was a trifle more than the killed and wounded among our trainmen last year. At Gravelotte, where the loss was heaviest in the Franco-Prussian War, the Germans lost 20,577 men. Wellington won Waterloo and Meade Gettysburg with a loss of 23,185 and 23,003 respectively, and the total loss on both sides at Shiloh in two days' murderous fighting did not reach 24,000. These were all great battles. They decided the fate of nations and were fought bravely and obstinately with the purpose of destroying human life. Yet the winner's loss and sometimes the loss of both victor and vanquished never equalled the loss in killed and wounded suffered by our trainmen in the pursuit of a peaceful calling during a single year. I think these figures from a few battles show in a very striking manner what a terrible loss of human life and what a frightful maiming of human bodies, with all the consequent suffering, occur among the trainmen of the country.

The proportion of killed to wounded is larger in battle than in the case of the trainmen, but the chief difference in these

figures is that the losses in battle were concentrated into a few hours. So it happens that while we glow or shudder over a battle, with its heroism and its slaughter, the trainmen picked off or maimed one by one do not strike our imaginations. Of course the percentage of killed and wounded in battle, as compared with the numbers engaged, is greater than the percentage of killed and wounded on trains compared with the numbers employed. But the object of soldiers in battle is to kill and wound. They are there for that purpose. The object of train-
• men is to carry on safely the railway traffic of a great country. Yet they suffer as if they were fighting a war, and the percentage of loss to numbers employed, if not so high as with soldiers, is frightful enough. For the year ending June 30, 1889, among all railroad employees there was one death for every 357 and one injury for every 35, while amongst trainmen alone there was one death for every 117 and one injury for every 12.* For the year ending June 30, 1890, the secretary of the Inter-State Commission, Mr. Moseley, informs me that for all employees there was one death for every 306 and one injury for every 33 men employed.

If nothing can be done to lessen the dangers which bring such results, it is only possible to regret deeply that so much suffering and death among vigorous men should be necessary in order to carry on the business of transportation ; but if anything can be done to lessen them, it is little short of criminal not to do it. That improvement is possible is shown at once by the fact that in England there is among all employees only one death for every 875 and one injury for every 158 men employed. Such evidence, however, is really needless, for every one who has considered the subject at all knows that a great deal can be done to stop this killing and maiming in at least two directions —the coupling of cars and the braking of freight trains. It will be observed by examining the table already given that to these two causes 37 per cent. of the deaths and 45 per cent. of the injuries recorded are due, so that anything which cuts off these two sources of danger would largely reduce the total losses of life and limb.

How, then, is it to be done ? The accidents under the first head now arise for the most part from the use of what is known as the old link-and-pin coupling. What is desired is to replace the old system with uniform automatic safety couplers or draw-

* "Statistics Railways of United States," 1889, p. 37.

bars. Two conditions are absolutely necessary for improvement —safety couplers and uniformity in their use. At the hearing before the Senate committee representatives of various railroad systems spoke. They opposed legislation on the ground that the movement towards the uniform safety coupler was going on as rapidly as possible by the action of the railroads themselves ; that the requirement of a given type of coupler would lead to the establishment of some single patent and the consequent advance in its price, and that, in any event, an act of Congress would put the railroads to heavy expenses, and was not required.

There is no reason to suppose that the managers of the railroads are not as anxious as any one else, from motives both of economy and of humanity, to check the frightful loss of life and limb arising from the two causes which have been mentioned. The able management of great roads, like the Pennsylvania and the Chicago, Burlington, and Quincy, as was shown at the hearing, are now doing everything in their power upon their own lines to secure protection for their trainmen in the matter of couplers. Mr. Haines, president of the American Railway Association, said also at a meeting of the committee of the commissioners in New York, last November, that our railroads are at this moment making a wider application of safety appliances than is the case in Europe. I think this is perfectly true, despite the fact that the English Board of Trade during the past summer have issued orders defining and requiring train brakes on freight trains, and that the percentage of loss of life and limb is less in England than with us. Yet, after conceding to the railroad management of the country all that is claimed in the way of humanity and progress, it seems clear that their objections to legislation of a proper kind are not valid.

When the committee of the commissioners was appointed last March, it issued a set of inquiries to presidents of different railroads designed to elicit information on the matter of couplers. The results of this inquiry are condensed and tabulated in the following report made by Mr. E. A. Moseley, the secretary of the Inter-State-Commerce Commission, who is an expert on this subject, and were presented by him to the committee of the commissioners at its November meeting :

" The following is a summary of the replies received from the presidents of the different railroads in answer to the circular sent them regarding equipment. The replies in many cases are very vague and incomplete, but the following is as a clear statement as could be made of them.

"The total number of freight cars owned, leased, or controlled, 978,161. The total number equipped with automatic couplers, 129,304. The number of couplers used and the number of cars equipped with each, as well as could be prepared, is as follows: Of the M. C. B. type : Janney, 40,231; Gould, 23,357; Hinson, 42,061; designated simply M. C. B., 13,279. Of the Safford type there are reported 12,207, and couplers specified other than those named, 33,965.

"Owing to the imperfect manner in which the replies were made, we cannot tell whether the sum of the differences between the totals above mentioned of cars equipped with different couplers—190,090—and the total number of freight cars owned, leased, or controlled, viz., 978,161, would make the number having the link and pin 788,071 ; but this is the only conclusion which can be reached from the data furnished, as many of the replies state that they have no automatic couplers ; and where they have done so, and have not indicated any other couplers used, we have concluded that the link-and-pin was the one in use.

" Of the total number of cars reported, 110,127 are equipped with train brakes as follows: Westinghouse, 97,238; Eames, 30; Boyden, 304; other types, 12,555. The balance of the cars, we conclude, are equipped with hand brakes only, as there is nothing to show to the contrary.

"The number of locomotives owned, leased, or controlled is 27,159, of which 17,000 are shown to be equipped with driving-wheel brakes.

" The replies to the question regarding the best means of bringing about uniformity in safety car-couplers are not at all clear in many cases, but the following is a statement which has been prepared, showing as nearly as possible the position of the roads :

" ' Sixty-nine roads, representing 13,014.24 miles of road operated, are in favor of national legislation; eighty-eight roads, representing 46,791.09 miles of road operated, are in favor of voluntary action by the railroads; two roads, representing 139.09 miles of road operated, are in favor of State legislation; seventeen roads, representing 11,915.88 miles of road operated, are in favor of the M. C. B. type of coupler; ten roads, representing 4,829.83 miles of road operated, are in favor of different couplers; fifteen roads, representing 9,407.79 miles of road operated, express the opinion that the matter is still in the experimental stage, while 145 roads, representing 38,985.59 miles of road operated, have expressed no opinion in regard to the best means of bringing about uniformity in automatic couplers.'

" A number of the roads in favor of voluntary action and some of those which are silent in relation to the best means of bringing about uniformity in automatic couplers have shown a preference for the M. C. B. type.

" The Atchison, Topeka, and Santa Fé Railroad Company and its auxiliary lines, together with one other road, expressed themselves in favor of the Safford coupler."

This report shows what might have been expected—that, however well-intentioned the railroads, it is not possible for them by their own unaided efforts to obtain any uniformity of action on this subject within any reasonable time. Still less is it within the power of the separate States to obtain it. Freight cars belonging to different companies are scattered all over the country. They can be reached only by a legislation of equal extent.

In other words, to obtain uniformity in freight couplers we must invoke the law of the United States.

The question of what couplers should be used, about which there has been, perhaps, more discussion than about anything else, is in reality secondary. Some type, that of the master car-builders or some other, could easily be agreed upon by the railroads, if it was once fixed by law that they must have some kind of uniform safety couplers. The main thing is uniformity, for where cars having the old link and pin have to be coupled with others having safety couplers, the danger is increased instead of diminished, as the advancing rate of loss from 1889 to 1890 painfully shows.

What we want, therefore, is an act requiring the adoption of uniform safety couplers by the railroads throughout the country. A reasonable time should be given to enable the roads to make this change, and they ought to have at least five and perhaps ten years, which is the average life of a freight car, to complete it. Then at the expiration of the time fixed by law the use of uniform safety couplers ought to be compelled under penalty.

The question of a type could be left to the railroads themselves, for when the railroads found that they would be forced under penalties to have uniform safety couplers, they would soon agree on the best and cheapest kind. If they did not, further legislation on this point could be easily obtained, vesting the necessary authority in the Inter-State-Commerce Commission.

As to the other prolific source of casualties, hand brakes on freight trains, the case is simpler. The heading in the statistics describes these accidents as "falling from trains," which occurs almost wholly on freight trains where the brakeman is required to pass along the top of the cars and to climb to and from the roofs in order to reach the brakes. The danger of this work is obvious. Running along the roof of a moving car by night, with the boards covered perhaps with ice or snow, in the midst of storms and darkness, which hide from sight the coming bridge, it is little wonder that so many meet death in the performance of this duty. In this case all that is required is to follow the directions of the English Board of Trade defining and requiring train brakes which are worked automatically from the engine, and with which we are already thoroughly familiar in our passenger service.

The case is such a plain one that it hardly seems to need argument. No possible political feeling can be involved in it, and no very complicated legislation is required to bring about the desired result without placing a ruinous expense on the railroads. It is simple inhumanity not to take prompt action. The total number of killed and wounded is increasing from year to year, and so is the proportion of loss to the total number of men employed. Uniformity in the use of safety appliances and of train brakes on our freight trains will save hundreds of lives, stop the maiming of thousands of men, and preserve the bread-winners to thousands of families. Such uniformity can be obtained only by legislation which will reach into every State and every territory. The Congress of the United States alone has the power to pass such legislation, and it is high time that the power was exerted.

HENRY CABOT LODGE.

A YEAR OF RAILROAD ACCIDENTS.*

BY H. G. PROUT, EDITOR OF THE "RAILROAD GAZETTE."

EVERY intelligent reader of the newspapers must have thought more than once during the year just ended that it would be a year memorable for the loss of life in railroad accidents. In Europe two of the worst accidents recorded in the whole history of railroading occurred in 1891. On June 14, at Mönchenstein, Switzerland, 73 people were killed and 130, or more, injured by the fall of a bridge under a train. On July 26, at St. Mandé, near Paris, 48 persons were killed and 180 injured in a collision. Up to this time there had never been more than thirteen railroad accidents in which 40 or more persons were killed. In the United States there were no such serious single accidents, but the railroad history of the year has been bloody enough to draw the attention of the most superficial reader.

In the first month of the year there were five collisions of passenger trains in which eight passengers were killed. In February occurred the Fourth Avenue tunnel accident in which six persons were killed and seven injured, and the circumstances of the accident gave it extraordinary prominence. It occurred within the limits of the greatest city of the continent, on the tracks of one of the greatest railroads of America, and fire added to the horror of the occasion. In the same month five persons were killed by a derailment. Then the months followed with no serious accidents until July, in which month 54 passengers were killed on the railroads of the United States. All of these were in four accidents ; 49 of them were killed in three accidents, and 21 in one accident. These figures alone are impressive, but their effect

*The statistics used in this article have all been gathered by private enterprise, and are necessarily incomplete. The totals of casualties are below the facts, but they are the best that can be had for the whole country. The figures gathered by the Inter-State-Commerce Commission do not go back far enough for comparison, and none have been published by the commission since those for 1889. Moreover, the classification adopted by the commission has been faulty and misleading as to train accidents. The figures here given are sufficiently correct for purposes of a general comparison

upon the mind is increased by the contrast with the customary course of events. The average number of passengers killed in one month for four years, 1887–1890, was 13.8. To suddenly increase this number to 54 was startling, and it was even more so from the fact that so many passengers had not been killed in any one month since October, 1888, when 70 were killed. In August, 1887, the month in which the Chatsworth accident took place, 80 persons were killed. Aside from these two months, the fatal_ ities in July, 1891, were greater than they had been in any one month for five years. But July was followed by a month of almost equal mortality. In August 42 passengers were killed, 18 of them in a malicious wreck and 14 in a collision, the result of gross negligence on the part of the trainmen. Fortunately, in the next three months there was no great single accident, but in December came the Hastings collision, in which 13 persons were killed or fatally injured. This again excited intense interest, not only because of the number of deaths, but because it was on a very rich railroad with a great volume of business, and because public attention had very lately been drawn towards that railroad by the remarkable efforts that it had been making to increase the speed of passenger trains. The total number of accidents in December cannot now be told, as the statistics are not yet made out, but probably the deaths of passengers in the month will be found to be not less than 20. So the year began and ended with some startling accidents, and contained two months in which the death rate was very unusual. It is of interest to inquire whether or not 1891 has been more fatal in this particular than preceding years.

Before we begin comparisons, we must know what we compare. I shall consider train accidents alone,—that is, accidents which involve more or less injury to a moving train,—and shall confine the examination, so far as possible, to accidents involving passenger trains. Anybody using the figures must remember that the casualties to persons on railroads from train accidents alone are only about 8 or 9 per cent. of the total casualties. Further, of all persons killed on the railroads of the United States, about one-half are trespassers on the tracks and right of way of those railroads. It will be seen, therefore, that the branch of the subject to which this inquiry is limited is unimportant if measured by the relative number of casualties to persons.

I have said that the statistics of December, 1891, are still incomplete ; therefore, I shall compare the first eleven months of that year with the first eleven months of 1890. In that period there were, in 1890, 1,939 train accidents of all classes, including freight trains. It is impossible to separate the passenger-train accidents without a greater amount of labor than the result would justify. In the corresponding eleven months of 1891 there were 2,215 train accidents. If the December, 1891, average is main- tained, the year's accidents will be considerably above those of 1890 ; but 1890 itself was an exceptional year in this respect. For nine years, including 1882 to 1889, the train accidents have averaged 1,452 a year. In 1890 there were 2,146. The greatest number of accidents in any one year before that was 1,935, in 1888. So, considering only the number of train accidents, 1891 has been the worst year in the history of railroading in the United States. In the number of casualties to persons, however, it does not compare unfavorably with 1890. In the first eleven months of 1891 those killed in train acci- dents were : passengers, 160 ; employees, 488 ; total, including others . than passengers and employees, 705. In the first eleven months of 1890 the killed were : passengers, 159 ; em- ployees, 534 ; total, including " others," 753. But 1890 was also a year of unusual fatality. The following little table gives the deaths of and injuries to all persons, including passengers, em- ployees, and others, from train accidents in the nine years 1882 to 1890 inclusive. The figures include freight-train accidents, as do the totals given above.

	Killed.	Injured.		Killed.	Injured.
1890	806	2,812	1885	307	1,530
1889	492	1,772	1884	389	1,760
1888	667	2,204	1883	473	1,910
1887	656	1,946	1882	380	1,588
1886	416	1,409			

It is quite obvious that both 1890 and 1891 were years of ex- traordinary fatality to those who travel by rail. Necessarily, railroad accidents must increase with the increase of railroad business, but whether or not they have increased relatively faster than the volume of railroad business has increased is hard to say. It is difficult to make an accurate comparison of one year with another, because where the figures are so small as those with which we have to deal, one extraordinary accident affects the total so greatly as to vitiate averages. There is another consideration ; the records of railroad accidents in the United States are very incomplete. On the other hand, we have means of measuring accurately the progress in the growth of the volume of railroad business. In an attempt to ascertain whether or not railroad accidents have increased in greater ratio than the causes which might lead to such accidents have increased, the increase of miles of railroad operated would not be a fair measure, for as the length of railroad operated increases, the density of traffic on each mile may diminish. The best measure, probably, is that of train-miles. This gives us the total number of miles run by all trains, and this total depends upon the number of trains running, as well as upon the distance run.

It will be seen that the number of accidents ought to increase a good deal faster than the number of trains running. This is so because every additional train on a railroad adds the chance of accident due to its own journey, and also increases the chances of accident to each train which immediately precedes it, to each one which immediately follows it, and to every train that it meets on its journey. If the number of accidents increased in any given time in no greater ratio than the train-miles run, we should be justified in considering that the danger of railroad operation had been very much reduced in that time. If the number of accidents did not increase considerably faster than the train-miles, we should still be justified in assuming that a greater degree of safety had been reached. From the little table given above, it will be seen that 58 per cent. more persons were killed in the three years 1888 to 1890 than in the three years 1882 to 1884. The increase in the train-miles run in the same two periods was 42 per cent. From these figures it is impossible to say whether or not train accidents are *relatively* fewer than they were in 1882 and 1883, but I think that anybody at all familiar with the conditions of railroad operation in the United States will believe they are. It does not follow at all that the railroads of the United States have done all that they can do and ought to do to secure safety in operation. Some estimate as to how far they have done this may be made by taking up some of the more important accidents to passenger trains during the year. We cannot pretend to examine them all, nor would it be profitable to do so. The examination will be limited practically to such accidents as have caused the death of passengers.

In the first six months of the year 25 passengers were killed.

Eight were killed in January in five collisions.   One of these was a butting collision on a single-track railroad, the result of a mistake in transmitting or reading orders ; one was a collision in a station yard, the result of carelessness on the part of the yardmen.   Another collision was between a freight train crossing over from one track to the other and a passenger train running on the second track.   This was an example of a class of accidents which could be provided against with almost absolute certainty by the well-known device of interlocking the switches with the signals which protect those switches.   But further than that, such an accident should be provided against, first, by the orders under which the trains were running, and, second, by a proper protection of the train movement by the crew of the freight train. The other two collisions in this month were rear collisions—that is, an engine ran into the rear of the train in each instance. These collisions occurred on crowded tracks in or near the city limits of Chicago, and should have been provided against by block signals.

In February seven passengers were killed.   Of these, five were killed in a derailment at Newton, North Carolina.   The derailment occurred on a trestle which was wrecked by the shock, and the train fell thirty feet.   There seems to be little doubt that the fatal results of this accident were due to the fact that the trestle was weak, or that its floor system was defective.   In this month, also, occurred the well-known Fourth Avenue tunnel collision in New York city, in which no passengers were killed, but six employees of the road were killed and seven injured.   A train of passenger cars was being hauled to the yards, and the engine of a train following crashed into the rear of these cars, in which the employees were.   The result was a bad wreck, which took fire, and it is generally believed that several people lost their lives in the fire.   The tunnel is well protected by block signals, but the engineman ran past the signals which were set to danger, for which he was blamed by those who carefully investigated the case.   It seems unjust to hold the railroad company responsible for this collision, for the tunnel was protected at least as well as could have been required by the "state of the art" of signalling.   The company has, however, been blamed, and justly so, for the use of stoves in the cars. Another remarkable accident occurring in the month of February fortunately caused no deaths, although nine passengers were injured. This was on the Canadian Pacific. An axle broke near a high trestle; the train was derailed, and a sleeping-car fell off the trestle, landing ninety feet below. Of the fifteen passengers in this car nine were more or less injured, but none fatally. An incident which occurred in the same month, although it had nothing to do with an accident, shows the sort of service which railroad men must be prepared for, and is an instance of fidelity which is worth mentioning. During a severe storm a Union Pacific passenger train was blockaded for thirty-six hours. The storm was so furious that the passengers did not dare leave the cars to go even the shortest distance without forming a line. The conductor went back to flag a following fast train and was badly frozen—an almost inevitable result. It is possible, at least, that his courage and devotion to duty prevented an accident.

In March six passengers were killed, four in derailments and two in collisions. One of these derailments, in which two passengers and one trainman were killed, was caused by a broken rail. The wreck took fire from a stove in a baggage car and was entirely consumed. The derailment was one of a class extremely difficult to prevent. A track-walker had gone over the track shortly before the accident, but did not detect the broken rail. The night was dark and rainy, and the rain froze on the track as fast as it fell. One derailment, in which one passenger was killed and ten injured, was caused by a broken wheel; another by a switch being carelessly thrown.

In April no passengers were killed, but there was one disastrous passenger-train accident. At Kipton, Ohio, on the 24th, a butting collision took place between train No. 21, westbound, and train No. 14, a fast mail train, eastbound. This resulted in the death of the two engineers, six postal clerks, and one fireman. Train No. 14 had the right of way, and was running at about fifty miles an hour; No. 21 was going slowly for the purpose of entering a siding to allow No. 14 to pass. The immediate cause of this accident was that No. 21 was behind time and should have stopped at the preceding station, but the conductor decided to run for Kipton, the usual passing-place. He and the engineman were held responsible for the accident, as they should have been, but behind this is the responsibility of the railroad company; for the accident would have been prevented had the road been worked under the absolute block system.

In May two passengers were killed ; the accidents in which they were killed had no special significance. There was, however, one sensational accident in this month. A work train, carrying a gang of men to fight forest fires, was derailed where the rails had been warped by the heat of the fires, and several cars were thrown upon a pile of burning logs. Six men, including the superintendent of the road, were killed or burned to death. A singular and pathetic event in this month was the killing of a child, a passenger in a sleeping-car, by a stone thrown through the window. Unfortunately, the miscreant who threw the stone was never captured.

In June five passengers were killed. Two of these were killed and eleven were injured by a derailment near Coon Rapids, Iowa. The train was derailed on a trestle approaching a bridge over the Coon River by a tie which had been fastened between the rails. The baggage car and four cars following it fell about forty feet. The case was undoubtedly one of malicious wrecking, but the wrecker was never caught. Another accident in this month, in which one passenger was killed and about thirty injured, was to an excursion train the engine of which was running tender first. The tender was derailed by a broken wheel, causing the wreck of the train. This was an example of bad practice in running the tender foremost, which, however, it is sometimes difficult to avoid.

We come now to the disastrous chronicle of July, in which month fifty-four passengers were killed and 120 injured. Twenty-three of these were killed and 27 injured in the accident at Ravenna, Ohio, July 3, at half-past two o'clock in the morning. A passenger train was stopped at a station several minutes beyond the usual time. While standing there, a train of twenty-four loaded refrigerator cars ran into the rear of it. There was a down grade approaching the station where the passenger train stood, and the freight train was not fitted with air-brakes, so that, although the passenger train was partially protected by a man who had gone to the rear with a lantern, the engineman of the freight train did not get the warning in time to prevent the accident. Several persons have been blamed for this accident ; the flagman of the passenger train for not going back far enough, and the engineman of the freight train for running too fast approaching a station when he knew that he was pretty close to the passenger train's time. Doubtless there was fault of this sort, but back of it all is the fact that under the block system this dreadful accident would have been prevented, and the accident was followed almost at once by measures on the part of the railroad company looking towards equipping the road with block signals. A further lesson is that freight trains should have air-brakes. The next morning, July 4, the two rear cars of a passenger train ran off a trestle bridge eight miles west of Charleston, West Virginia, and fell about twenty feet. The conductor and seventeen passengers were killed, and forty-seven passengers and a mail clerk were seriously hurt. It is said that but one passenger in these two cars escaped uninjured. The cause of this accident has never been precisely determined, but it is said to have been the spreading of the rails from the partial destruction by fire of the cross-ties on the bridge. There seems to have been reasonable inspection of the structure, for it was customary every day for a section-man to walk over the bridge an hour later than the time at which the accident occurred. The other very serious accident in July was a singular one. An excursion train which was being switched at Aspen Junction, Colorado, was struck obliquely by a freight engine approaching on a side track. The car which was hit was little injured, but a check-valve on the side of the locomotive boiler was broken off, and a stream of steam and hot water from the boiler was poured into the car, scalding the passengers so that six were killed on the spot and two died afterwards. In this case the railroad company may properly be blamed, for there are well-known devices by which, in case of such an accident, a check-valve on the inside of the boiler shell is closed, preventing the escape of steam and hot water.

In August forty-two passengers were killed and 186 injured. Thirty-six employees were killed also. On the 27th a passenger train was derailed approaching a bridge near Statesville, North Carolina. The whole train ran off the bridge and fell about eighty feet to the bed of a small stream below, making a terrible wreck. There were 85 passengers in the train, of whom 18 were killed and 15 injured. Four trainmen also were killed, and two badly injured. The water in the creek was dammed by the wreck and some of the victims were drowned. This accident was, almost without question, another malicious wreck. A rail had been either removed or unfastened. The August accident next in importance was at Montezuma, New York, where 14 passengers and 2 employees were killed. That was a rear collision. Before daylight in the morning an express train ran into the rear of a preceding freight train, which was just entering a side track. There was a dense fog, and the engineman of the passenger train did not see the lantern of the freight trainman who went back to warn him ; in fact, the lantern was only carried back a very short distance. Fourteen passengers were killed and sixteen injured. The flagman did not do his duty by going back as far as he should have done even had the night been clear ; as it was foggy, his duty in the case was still more apparent. But beyond all this is the fact that the accident would have been prevented had the road been operated under the block system. In this case the defect is still more noticeable because a portion of the same road has been worked under block signals for years. On the 5th of this month a butting collision took place at Champlain, New York, between a regular passenger train and an excursion train, in which three passengers were killed and 10 or 11 injured. The railroad company was blamed by the coroner's jury for employing trainmen who were not familiar with the road. On the 31st, near Tell City, Indiana, a train was derailed by a broken wheel on the front truck of the locomotive. Four passengers were killed and 20 injured.

In September six passengers were killed and ninety-five injured. One was killed in California by a freight train running into the rear of a passenger train which had been stopped on a steep grade by a land-slide. The rear of the train was not properly protected by the train crew. Near Pickerell, Nebraska, one passenger was killed and one injured by a butting collision due to the failure of an operator to deliver orders. At Kent, Ohio, one passenger was killed and 24 injured in a butting collision which was caused by neglect on the part of the crew of a freight train to observe the signals carried by the preceding passenger train ; that is, a passenger train was being run in six sections, carrying a large number of excursionists. When the fifth section passed the siding on which the freight train stood, the trainmen of the latter assumed that it was the sixth, and pulled out on the track. None of the other accidents of this month was remarkable except one in which a train of ten cars, carrying 700 passengers, was derailed and several of the cars were overturned into a stream. By remarkable good luck, however, no one was killed, although 18 passengers were injured.

In October thirteen passengers were killed and seventy-four injured. Only three were killed in the cars of a passenger train, and two of these were killed in a derailment which has never been explained. Six passengers in a caboose at the rear of a freight train were killed at Thorson, Minnesota, the result of gross negligence on the part of the trainmen of a freight train following an extra which was running very fast, contrary to orders. On the 15th, near Crete, Illinois, a passenger train ran through a misplaced switch and into a round-house, a portion of which fell and crushed the cab of the locomotive. The engineer and three newspaper reporters, who were riding on the engine, were killed. These men had gone out on the engine of a fast train to write up a run. This accident was followed, a few days later, by another one of a very similar character near Monmouth, Illinois. In this latter case a passenger train again ran through an open switch and several of the cars were overturned and badly wrecked. Two passengers, the engineman, and a travelling engineer were killed; the fireman and 19 passengers were injured. In both of these cases it has been claimed that the switches had been tampered with, but, whether or not this is true, the railroad companies are not relieved of the responsibility for the accidents, because there is a very well-known and widely-used method of preventing just such accidents—that is, by the protection of switches by distant signals. Signals are placed at such distances as to give ample warning of the condition of the switch, and these are so connected to the switch that it cannot be thrown without first throwing the signal. Another accident occurring in this month resulted in the death of no passengers, but a brakeman and an express messenger were killed, and three postal clerks and a baggeman injured. This was a butting collision between an express train and a freight train, and was the result of an extraordinary combination of circumstances. The point was properly protected by block signals, but the operator on one side had fallen asleep and left a clear signal for the westbound train. The signals were set against the eastbound train, but the engineman failed to observe them. There was a dense fog at the time.

In November seventeen passengers were killed and sixty-four

were injured. The worst accident of the month was at Toledo, Ohio, where, early in the evening of the 28th, nine passengers were killed and about twenty injured. The situation was a complicated one. One passenger train had stopped about one hundred and eighty feet east of a short tunnel. A passenger train following ran into the rear of this standing train. The accident happened within the "yard limits," where orders require all enginemen to keep such speed that they can stop within the range of vision. The tunnel was somewhat obscured by smoke, and the engineman of the second train was blamed, and justly, for running too fast and not keeping a sharp enough lookout. He should have been able to stop in one hundred and eighty feet if he had been running at twenty miles an hour or less, and it is clear that his speed was too high, or that he did not apply the brakes as soon as he ought, or both. But behind all this is the old fault, insufficient signalling. At Perry, New York, a car was derailed and went down a bank into a stream and one passenger was drowned,— cause, broken rail. Near Medina, Tennessee, one passenger was killed in a butting collision between a passenger train and a freight,—cause, mistake of orders or disobedience. The other passengers killed this month were on freight trains.

December opened with a rear collision of an express train with a local passenger train standing at Tarrytown station, New York, in which no one was killed, as the passengers had been warned and had left the standing train,—cause, defective signalling. On December 3 an express train ran into the rear of a gravel train near Pennington, New Jersey, killing four employees and injuring 15 passengers ; and on the 4th, at East Thompson, Connecticut, two freight trains were wrecked by a collision, a passenger train ran into the wreck, and a second passenger train ran into the rear of the first. One passenger is supposed to have been burned in the wreck, but, wonderfully enough, there were no other deaths. This complicated accident and the one at Pennington would have been avoided by proper signalling. In the East Thompson accident the wreck of the freight trains would have been prevented by block signals, but after that took place the wreck of the first passenger train could not be prevented. The freight wreck fouled the passenger track, and there was not time to send out a flag before the first passenger train arrived. The flagman of this train was thrown to the ground and stunned, and before this was known the fourth train was in the wreck. Finally, the year of railroad accidents came to a dramatic end on Christmas eve with the dreadful disaster at Hastings, New York. One express train, which had come to an unexpected stop, was run into from the rear by another express going at about forty miles an hour. Thirteen people were killed outright or have since died. The immediate cause was the failure of the flagman to do his duty. The ultimate cause was one that has been generally recognized —the lack of proper signals.

I have cited only thirty-six accidents out of several hundred. The number of passenger trains involved in accidents during the year was not far from 850 or 900, but the number of accidents was, of course, somewhat less, as there were a good many collisions involving two passenger trains each. But those thirty-six accidents are characteristic. The first great fact that appears is that twenty-two of them might have been prevented had employees obeyed orders. They were not called on to exercise wit or judgment in alarming emergencies, but simply to obey orders. Space and time are lacking to discuss the measures that operating officers take to maintain discipline and the difficulties that they encounter. It is enough to say that this is the most troublesome part of their duties, and that the·unions, instead of helping, have made matters worse. We may hope that this is a passing phase of trade-unionism, and that, as the men learn more of their proper relations to the rest of the world, they will discover that it is for their own interest to weed out the insubordinate, the inefficient, and the drunken.

The next striking fact is that nineteen of these accidents would probably have been saved by block signals and interlocked switches and signals. I would not say unqualifiedly that every one of the roads on which these accidents happened should at once equip its tracks with block signals and interlock all of its switches. There are reasonable limits within which they must work ; but it may be said without qualification that it is poor railroad economy to operate a road having a heavy and fast traffic without block signals and interlocking for the protection of switches. It can be proved by the statistics of cost of accidents that a judiciously-planned block system pays in money, and generally on a crowded road it actually facilitates the movement of trains. In fact, there is a good deal of nonsense talked and written about the cost of establishing, maintaining, and operating block signals. Some of these accidents could have been prevented, and more would have been mitigated, had freight trains been fitted with air-brakes.

It is some comfort to see that so few of these fatal accidents were due to defects of track and equipment; and it will, no doubt, surprise many people to know that one-twelfth of the whole number were malicious. It is humiliating, but should be encouraging, that only about half a dozen of these thirty-six accidents were without fault on the part of the railroad officers or employees. This is encouraging, because it shows that many of the fatal accidents of the year would not have happened under conditions of operation which we may expect will be realized before many years have passed.

H. G. PROUT.

THE OPERA.

BY EDMUND C. STANTON.

No ONE will deny that America has made, during the last decade, vast and important strides in matters musical and operatic. With the story of the latter's progress I had, fortunately for myself, a close connection during the period of seven seasons when grand opera in German held sway at the Metropolitan Opera House ; and I do not think it will be considered out of place on my part to say that opera reached with us a development, after the several seasons, that demands the completion —that is to say, the carrying-out to the fullest the artistic completeness—of these great principles in operatic arts of which Richard Wagner must always be acknowledged the great representative. In saying this I do not wish to be considered in any way a Wagnerite, pure and simple ; but we must all admit that to ignore Richard Wagner and his magnificent work in raising up opera to the highest artistic possibilities, while compassing what he has styled the Music-Drama,—that is, the cohesion of all the arts in the splendor of music,—would be to place ourselves, at the very least, a decade back in our artistic and musical tastes and operatic enjoyments.

Italian opera is again with us at the Metropolitan, and it will be interesting to note how far the charms of the operatic entertainments, that have given so much pleasure to generations ever since opera became a fashionable feature of social life, still hold in a generation of opera-goers that has had the advantage of hearing the works of the greatest composers of nationalities abroad.

In the concert hall it is certain that a list of the numbers copied from a fashionable programme of twenty years ago would not be tolerated by modern concert-goers. The same may be said in regard to opera, and any attempt to revive anything more than a passing enthusiasm for the works embraced in what may be styled the old repertory, without paying attention to the modern productions in the realm of opera, must inevitably result in artistic disappointment, even if interpreted by the greatest of singers. I do not say that the old favorite operas should be excluded from the modern repertory. They demand a place in it for the sake of those of the younger generation who have not heard them. But the works of modern composers can be relied on to satisfy the demand for all the melodious charms on which the fame of the old repertory so long rested, because of the added grandeur of modern orchestration and dramatic and poetic completeness. The orchestra of to-day is vastly different from and a grander organism than that for which the old Italian masters wrote their works. Brought to its present standard by the artistic demands of the symphony, it has taken its natural place as a majestic, collective, interpretative organism in the Music-Drama, and in modern opera in general, from which it can never more be removed.

But opera in Italian will always be listened to with pleasure for one reason : Italy still retains her preëminence in the art of song, even though her singers are only for the smaller part of Italian nationality. During the reign of the Wagnerian opera the gentler beauties of the human voice were undoubtedly oftentimes sacrificed to an unnecessary extent ; though this was due to faulty vocal methods prevalent among some German singers and to a misunderstanding of the lyrical-dramatic nature of the Music-Drama. Solo singing was too often made to take a secondary part in Wagnerian interpretations, and the Wagnerian conductors too frequently allowed the orchestra to run riot in the attempt to reach the utmost possibilities in dramatic climaxes. But at the Metropolitan, season after season, the methods of interpreting Wagner underwent a beneficent change, and the advent of the pure lyric tenor and the smooth, suave, baritone, in place of the so-called heroic singers of a decade ago, brought out beauties in the Wagner scores that had remained obscure to German audiences.

The objection to the declamatory and heroic styles, falsely imagined by many singers and critics to be the expression of dramatic feeling and intensity, was not only artistically justified, but was a sign of the unerring and delicate appreciation of true artistic work on the part of our highly-strung, nervous American audiences. Art to the American, especially to the American woman,—who must always remain the final court of appeal in matters musical and operatic,—is not noise or coarseness, but beauty and chasteness and naturalness ; in other words, Art in its absolute simplicity beautifies and idealizes all that it touches. It would be quite impossible for us to understand the enthusiasm that greeted the lyrically charming and artistically simple and natural beauties of "Siegfried" or the deep, tender, emotional truth of "Fidelio," if we did not admit the intuitive power of artistic appreciatiation which, if not born with, is at least second nature with, cultured American women.

This intuitive artistic feeling of Truth in Art is a glorious boon that has been developed in our country and nurtured by many positive, if indistinct, influences. Sprung from diverse stock, the American woman has won recognition not only for personal beauty, but for high literary, artistic, and musical taste and intelligence, throughout the civilized world. In Music she has had the advantage of training under the most capable masters, sent to us in periods of revolution and overcrowding by the most cultured of European nations. The pupils of our schools and seminaries have had the benefit of the ripest scholarship and the highest artistic training imparted to them by the best of European teachers. They have enjoyed the incalculable advantage of being initiated at once into the highest results of musical production and training of the age in which they live, without having had to undergo the ordeal of unlearning and shaking off the vitiated inheritance of decades of commonplace in music and opera through which Europe had to pass.

Then, to assist this natural, inherited appreciation of the highest art presented to them, came the benefits of travel and leisure, and years of study and education in the great European capitals, enjoyed by those whom wealth has fortunately made the great supporters of our opera. Audiences at the Metropolitan are essentially cosmopolitan. They have heard all that is best in the great opera-houses of the world, and if they cannot go into raptures over the memories of the singing of the great artists of the past, they have heard, and enjoyed, and become permeated with, all that is artistic and beautiful which Europe has had to offer of late years, and they could no more sink back into the enthusiasms that satisfied the audiences of a quarter of a century ago than could our modern theatre-goers applaud the mouthings and struttings of the dead histrionic heroes of melodramatic fame. They have spent seasons in Munich, where the Wagnerian operas used to be given in such beautiful and artistic completeness. They have made their pilgrimages to Bayreuth and seen the great music-dramas produced under the eye of the master. They have seen all the glories of spectacular in Meyerbeer, as given at the Grand Opera in Paris, and the ballets of Milan and Vienna given in all their glitter and magnificence.

Long before the Wagner seasons at the Metropolitan, the great American audience was ready to receive, and to appreciate to the fullest extent, the marvellous creations of the prophet of Bayreuth and his new revelations in operatic art,—the Art Work that embraces Drama and Song, Painting and Poetry, Architecture and Music, welded into a wonderful artistic whole,— and I believe it to be the universal testimony of those who have followed the history of Wagnerism here and abroad that nowhere has the reception of the Music-Drama been so spontaneous and heartily enthusiastic as here. Nowhere has Wagner been more deeply and truly understood in the poetic, dramatic, and . musical compass of his splendid genius. All this, thanks to the beneficent influence of the American woman upon matters artistic and musical in America.

This brings me to the discussion of a fundamental principle of true operatic exposition—the necessity of good all-around casts and the exclusion of the system of stars. It must not be imagined for a moment, however, that good all-around excellence in casts should exclude the highest art in singing. During the seven seasons of grand opera in German at the Metropolitan, singers were heard who surely will stand comparison with the stars of the great Italian seasons. In devotion to true artistic principles, in the fervor of dramatic exposition, they were, for the most part, superior to their Italian confrères,—at least to those of the old school,—though no one would venture to deny that the beauty of art in song is still royally held by the Italians. But singing is only one important accompaniment in the operatic performance of to-day and of the future. To produce an opera in the style that shall meet the requirements of a modern American audience, which has seen the best that Europe has to present, which knows its Wagner and Beethoven by heart, whose musical taste and education have evoked the praise of a Von Bülow and a Tschaikowsky, demands a vastly greater artistic capacity than in the olden days.

The production of the art-effects that Wagner demanded, this blending as far as possible of Music, Singing, Painting, and Drama, requires not only the assistance of a small army of skilful and artistic people, drilled under the most competent direction, but infinite patience in unceasing work, beginning with the separate rehearsals of chorus, orchestra, and soloists, and ending only after weeks of hard and earnest labor, when all the forces are brought together for the final rehearsals upon the stage. Then the work of the stage-manager has to be attended to, and scenic effects given in such a way that they shall agree with the intentions of the composer, so that the artistic results in the presentation of the scenes shall enhance the artistic enjoyment of the entire performance. It is not always the most expensive *mise-en-scéne* that produces the greatest artistic results. The cost of the second act of " Tristan and Isolde" was astonishingly small, yet infinite trouble and patience and great artistic knowledge in the manipulation of lights were necessary before the work could be properly presented to the public.

What infinite patience is needed before the elaborately built-up scenes of " Rheingold "—one representing the bed of the Rhine with its flowing waters, with its elaborate machinery for the swimming Rhine maidens; another with its towering walls of Walhalla, its scenes of storm and lightning after the gathering of the clouds at the command of Loki ; another with its rainbow bridge over which the Teutonic gods pass on their way to their heavenly home—can be revealed to the public in artistic beauty and completeness ! What a vast amount of patient working is demanded, again, for the production of scenic illusions, even for the simplicity of the second act of " Siegfried," when the hero is discovered resting under the forest tree, and where the dancing effect of sunlight upon the sward has to be imitated from nature in order to harmonize with the exquisite Waldweben music of the orchestra, where scenery and music must combine to produce that delightful dream of idealic charm and loveliness ! Only with the assistance of artistically competent heads of departments, the devotion of principals, and the willing obedience of supernumeraries, could the great Wagnerian art-works have been produced at the Metropolitan, even with the aid of the large sums of money furnished by the box-holders and subscribers. Only an organization having some degree of stability and permanence can possibly hope to present modern opera in a way that can satisfy the demands of American audiences in the future.

And the work before the operatic intendant of the future will be, I think, even greater than that which was accomplished during the seven years of grand opera in German, when nearly all the great works of the greatest composer of modern times were so successfully and brilliantly produced. The work done during those seven seasons would have tasked to their utmost the efforts . of even the most experienced of European operatic organizations. Through the German and their own language American audiences were enabled to enjoy for the first time, presented and sung in a way that compared more than favorably with the productions in the great German capitals, the four operas composing " The Ring of the Nibelung," namely, " Rheingold," "Walküre," " Siegfried," and " Götterdämmerung," besides " Die Meistersinger," " Rienzi," and " Tristan and Isolde," in which appeared artists like Materna, Lehmann, Brandt, Schroeder-Hanfstaengel, Ritter-Goetze, Mielke, Niemann, Vogl, Reichmann, Gudehus, Robinson, Emil Fischer, Alvary, and a host of others who had won fame as Wagner singers in Germany or in Bayreuth.

Besides the Wagner works, there were produced during those seven seasons, for the first time on this side of the Atlantic, Victor Nessler's "Trumpeter of Säckingen," Spontini's "Ferdinand Cortez," Weber's " Euryanthe," Cornelius's " Barber of Bagdad," Franchetti's "Asrael," Smareglia's " Vassal of Szigeth," Goldmark's "Queen of Sheba" and "Merlin " ; then came the magnificent revivals of Beethoven's " Fidelio," Meyerbeer's " Prophet " and "L' Africaine," Weber's "Freischütz," Rossini's " William Tell," Auber's "Stumme von Portici," and Halévy's " Jewess," besides several ballet operas, a style of entertainment which had never before been introduced here on the grand operatic stage. It is true that there gradually arose a demand for change ; and the filling of this demand by the present season of Italian opera is the legitimate outcome of an artistic catholicity of taste which I should be the last to condemn.

It is this catholicity of taste in matters musical and operatic, in fact, that will demand in the future a repertory that shall embrace the operatic productions of all the musical countries of the world. To meet the demand of the catholic, cosmopolitan, and international spirit of our musical taste, the operatic purveyors of the future will have to search through the world for what is highest and best. Italy must yet be considered non-productive, so far as operas of the newer school are concerned. Even Verdi, who attempted, but failed, to assimilate and Italianize the Wagnerian idea, can no longer draw audiences as of yore. Boito, one of the moderns, has failed to fulfil the promises of his early genius, and only Mascagni in his "Cavalleria Rusticana" and "L' Amico Fritz" seems to promise the beginning of a new and glorious era for Italian opera once more. His smaller work has been accepted with enthusiasm, and the welcome given to it is assuredly justly deserved, for he has been able to carry out to completion the Wagnerian ideas, the wedding of poetry, drama, and music, in his own way. His genius is apparently born of true, simple, natural inspiration, derived from the subject treated ; his every musical phrase throbs with the poetic and dramatic significance of the emotional situation ; he is a modern Italian composer to whom the world bows in willing homage.

But the impresario of the future will not confine himself to Italy or to Germany. The Slavic countries and Hungary have already produced operas of sterling merit and startling originality. And what a splendid operatic mine has yet to be exploited for our benefit in Russia, which can boast of not only a national but of an international operatic repertory, including works by composers of all countries, not excepting Wagner, and which has symphonic and operatic composers like Rubinstein and Tschaikowsky. Turning to Bohemia, there is Dvorák, whose cantatas alone are known to us, but who has written several interesting operas for the Bohemian stage; while England has produced of late years several grand operas by her native composers, some of which have been adopted in the German operatic repertory. France, too, has many modern writers of opera, whose works have not yet been heard here, but which have found brilliant interpretation, for the most part in Brussels.

Why, then, should the operatic repertory of New York be confined to the works of Italian and French composers of a quarter of a century or more ago, worn out, and only revived to enthusiasm with the assistance of exceptional singers, demanding exceptional prices and necessitating the curtailment of expenses in every other direction, thus prohibiting the production of opera as an Art-Work ? The operatic repertory of the future must of necessity be cosmopolitan and international in character. During the last season of grand opera in German the directors of the Metropolitan made a beginning in this direction, and only the constant and pressing demand on the part of the public for the Wagnerian repertory compelled a postponement in carrying out the plans to completion.

Such a repertory will embrace all nationalities and all schools, more especially the modern. We are essentially a cosmopolitan people, and should not, if we wish to develop further in musical and operatic taste, confine ourselves slavishly to the production of the operas of any one school or country. In what language this international repertory is to be sung is yet a matter of earnest thought and discussion. It seems probable that we must eventually adopt the English, but, for the present, we can hardly afford to prohibit by our language the engagement of the many great singers of the world who cannot do, and never will be able to do, themselves or their art justice in our vernacular. This difficulty will presumably settle itself in good time. Fortunately, we can feel assured of this : that whenever opera is presented in New York in its artistic completeness, the audiences will not fail to give it the necessary support, not because the opera-house is a centre of fashionable resort, but because they are themselves imbued with the true artistic spirit of appreciation of what is high and true in musical and operatic art.

EDMUND C. STANTON.

LOTTERIES AND GAMBLING.

BY ANTHONY COMSTOCK, SECRETARY OF THE NEW YORK SOCIETY
FOR THE SUPPRESSION OF VICE.

WHAT the Louisiana Lottery Company is doing for the State of Louisiana by corrupting officials, bribing public servants, destroying public morals, breeding crime and dishonesty, wrecking homes, and impoverishing the laboring classes, the pool gamblers of New York and New Jersey are doing for these two States.

Betting and gambling were denounced by the recent Methodist Ecumenical Council as two great vices of the age, and the necessity of suppressing them by vigorous legislation was most strongly urged. One of the morning papers, in commenting upon the action of this council and the gentlemen who made addresses upon this subject, made this very strange criticism :

> "Laws are made, not to promote the spiritual welfare of men and women, but for the protection of society. Morality is very wisely left to the churches. . . . The church, not the state, must reform the gambler."

If this means anything, it means that the state should not interfere with the gamblers of the day. But this sentiment every thoughtful man will dissent from and protest against.

Any act against public morals is a breach of the peace and indictable at common law. We find this principle laid down and established more than a century and a half ago under the common-law decisions of the English courts.

Any person who will reflect a single moment cannot but feel and see that the corrupting of public morals, either by intemperance, lotteries, gambling, or lewd and unclean publications, must be attended with the most disastrous consequences, and our courts of justice are, or ought to be, the schools of public morals.

Gambling and lotteries, obscene publications and houses of ill-fame, are all classed together by law-writers and courts as vices

which "tend to destroy public morals." Wherever these questions are discussed, either singly or grouped together, by the
courts of any civilized nation, *what tends to corrupt public
morals* (especially of that class in a community whose character
is not so completely formed as to be proof against these corrupting influences) "is declared to be indictable."

This principle has been unanimously affirmed by the Court of
Appeals of this State in many cases, and particularly in the case
of The People *vs.* Muller, reported in the 96th New York Reports.
The courts have been as emphatic and uniform in adjudging gambling in its various forms, including pool-selling, bookmaking, and lotteries, to be against public morals, as they have
been in their denunciations of obscene and criminal publications.

The English Parliament in 1699 declared all lotteries a
common and public nuisance, making void all lottery grants, and
providing that parties conducting them henceforth should be
prosecuted as *common rogues.* (1698, 10 Will. III., C 23.)

In the same year a body of ministers in Boston, Mass.,
denounced lotteries as " cheats," and the managers as " pillagers
of the people " ; and that sentiment has grown until every State
in the Union but one has either laws or constitutional enactments
against lotteries. From the highest to the lowest courts in this
land, lotteries and the keeping of common gaming-houses have
been declared "a public nuisance." The late Chief-Justice
Waite, in delivering the decision of the Supreme Court of the
United States, said:

" That lotteries are demoralizing in their effects, no matter how carefully
regulated, cannot, in the opinion of this court, be doubted. Experience has
shown that the common forms of gambling are comparatively innocuous
when placed in contact with the widespread pestilence of lotteries. The
former are confined to a few persons and places ; but the latter infects the
whole community ; it enters every dwelling ; it reaches every class ; it preys
upon the hard earnings of the poor, and it plunders the ignorant and
simple." (Stone *vs.* State of Miss., 11 Otto, 814.)

Again says the Supreme Court of the United States, in construing the constitution of Maryland concerning lotteries :

" The object to be accomplished was the suppression of a great moral
evil, and to effect so praiseworthy and laudable a purpose the construction
should be a benign and liberal one."

Bishop's " Criminal Law " places lotteries in the same category as the selling of untaxed liquors and houses of ill-fame.

The Supreme Court of the United States has repeatedly held "that nuisances injurious to public health and morality are among the most important duties of government to suppress." (Phalen *vs.* State of Va., Howard's Prac., p. 168.)

The State of Louisiana stands upon the threshold of what threatens to be a bloody conflict. On the one hand are a few unscrupulous men managing a lottery enterprise; on the other hand are those who have lived in hopes that at the end of the twenty-five years of chartered life this monster would be buried out of public sight. Instead, however, with millions of ill-gotten gain at its command, this hydra-headed monster now has clutched the throat of the body politic of the State of Louisiana and cries, "Give! Give! Give!" even to the very last remnant of respectability and common honesty, and seeks to enforce its demands by an offered bribe of $31,250,000.

For twenty-five years it has paralyzed industrious habits wherever its contagious touch has been felt. Public officials have been bribed and large sums of money have been offered by this lottery company, or its representatives, in order to intrench itself under police protection in communities where the laws prohibit its existence.

The very preamble of the charter of this lottery company condemns lotteries and witnesses against their demoralizing effects. It says: "Whereas, many millions of dollars have been withdrawn from and lost to this State by the sale of Havana, Kentucky, Madrid, and other lottery tickets, policy combinations, and devices, and fractional parts thereof, it shall hereafter be unlawful to sell, or exhibit for sale, any of them, or any other lottery," etc. The second section, authorizing a plundering scheme of their own, says that its objects and purposes are "the protection of the State against the great losses heretofore incurred by sending large amounts of money to other States and foreign countries for the purchase of lottery tickets and devices, thereby impoverishing our own people." It would be difficult to surpass this bold and daring demand of one State by official enactment proposing a legalized system of wholesale plunder upon sister States.

Louisiana proclaims to all other States by its enactment: "Lotteries are frauds. By their operation the people are plundered. None of you shall sell tickets in any of your lotteries in the State of Louisiana. But we propose to defy your laws and send our tickets into every State in the Union, regardless of State rights, enactments by constitution, or laws prohibiting such traffic."

To show the greed of these public plunderers, we have but to call attention to the fact that a few years ago the price of their tickets was $2 a ticket for ordinary drawings and $10 a ticket for extraordinary drawings, making the total receipts each year of the tickets sold in all the drawings $4,000,000. By the terms of their charter, 1 per cent., or $40,000, was to be paid to the State of Louisiana each year. This sop to charity was nothing but an apology for the existence of this monstrous fraud.

Year by year they have increased the price of tickets, until now the ordinary ticket is $20, and the extraordinary ticket is $40. Tickets for ordinary drawings are divided into twentieths, each fractional part of a ticket being sold at $1. Reckoning that all of these tickets have been sold, the income of this company has been thus increased from $4,000,000 to $28,000,000 per year. It was supposed that this vast increase of wealth would satisfy the demands of the unscrupulous board of managers. Not so. At the last meeting of the General Assembly of the State of Louisiana a bill was introduced to amend the present constitution, which prohibits all lotteries after 1893 (when this lottery charter expires), so as to extend the present charter another twenty five years.

This atrocious attempt to prolong the existence of this public scourge aroused the loyal element in the State of Louisiana, and for a time it looked as if there was no possible prospect of such a measure passing the General Assembly. When it seemed as if it must fail, one of the managers boldly offered a bribe of $31,250,000, payable $1,250,000 annually for the next twenty-five years, provided the constitution be thus amended.

When this question came to final vote, it was found that the lottery company had just sufficient votes in the Assembly to carry it through the Assembly, and just sufficient votes in the Senate to carry it through the Senate. It went to Governor Nichols, and was vetoed in a ringing message by him. After the Governor vetoed it, it again had just enough votes to carry it through the Assembly, but when it reached the Senate it would seem as if Providence interposed to prevent its passage, as the member who was to give the necessary vote died, and the measure failed to pass the Senate after the Governor's veto. Then it was brought by the lottery company before the Supreme Court of Louisiana on mandamus proceedings to compel the Secretary of State to publish this act. The Secretary of State contended that, as it had failed to pass over the Governor's veto, he was not obliged to publish it with the other acts of the General Assembly. The constitution of the State of Louisiana requires that all amendments to it, after passing the Legislature, shall be published a specified time before going to the people to be voted upon.

When the Supreme Court of Louisiana came to deliver its decision, it was found that the lottery company had just sufficient votes to carry it through the Supreme Court. One of the Supreme Court judges who voted in favor of this lottery scheme is the lottery candidate for Governor of the State of Louisiana at the coming election.

Only a few weeks ago the Democratic convention was held. The majority of the delegates who went to that convention were anti-lottery men when they went there, but when they came to organize it was found that the lottery company had just enough votes to organize in their interests. Now the issue is between the honorable citizens of Louisiana, on the one hand, and this organized band of public plunderers, on the other.

A prominent merchant fron New Orleans a few days ago related to the writer an incident that illustrates how lost to shame, how utterly unprincipled, these lottery advocates have become.

In electioneering for the primaries recently in New Orleans, a procession was gotten up in the lottery interest, and it is said that nearly or quite six thousand men and boys were in line, each one supplied with a tin cup, and kegs of beer were carried along in the procession, while certain saloons along the line of march displayed signs of " Free Beer," and there the rabble could go in and swill beer without charge.

It would seem as if every spark of manhood had been quenched, as if those working for the perpetuation of this nefarious business had sunk all self-respect, all regard for decency and morality, in their zeal to reëngraft this cursed thing into the body politic of that State. This nation owes it to itself to wipe out this disgrace and end this infamy. Such tactics are but a bid for revolution and lynch law. They are too exasperating to be tolerated by decent men. The manhood of Louisiana is not only dragged in the mud, but is stamped upon by such outrages.

The administration of justice in the city of New Orleans, so far as the lottery interests are concerned, is a mockery and by-word. Public servants bend their necks to do the bidding of this lottery company. The managers boast that they have six millions of dollars in the banks of the city of New Orleans to be spent to carry through their amendments at the coming April election.

Anti-lottery societies have been organized, and prominent men are to-day, in the city of New York, endeavoring to secure help and sympathy for those in the State of Louisiana who have determined that this disgraceful sale of the State of Louisiana to an organized band of public plunderers shall not be consummated.

This nation is humiliated by the spectacle. There is need to be alarmed, for if this organization can collect together millions of money each year without returning any just or fair equivalent therefor, and can spend six millions to corrupt a single State election, what may it not do in the matter of corrupting and controlling national elections, where it requires less than three millions of dollars to meet the legitimate expenses of all parties to a Presidential election ? Is it not time for something to be done to stay the wholesale bribery of officials and the corruption of the elective franchise ? Is it not time for the moral people of the community to awaken from their lethargy and indifference, and take some decided steps to crush out this crime-breeder that has been for nearly a quarter of a century fattening upon the credulity of the people ?

For five years this lottery company successfully prevented amendments to the acts of Congress concerning the transmission of lottery matter through the mails. But the last Congress enacted stringent laws despite their efforts, and the President promptly signed the enactment closing the mails effectually to all correspondence of every description relating to lotteries.

It would be difficult to picture the impoverishment of the poor of Louisiana ; the demoralization of the young men ; the beggaring of women and children, and the increase of crime, growing out of this monstrous swindling enterprise. The same demoralization that exists to-day in the State of Louisiana, like a slow paralysis is creeping over the States of New York and New Jersey through the policy gambling and betting on horse races. This nation is fast earning an unsavory reputation because of gambling propensities. Moral and religious influences seem to have no effect in checking this degrading passion. Year after year the gambling fraternity are becoming more and more strongly intrenched, while continued success renders them more and more arrogant and unscrupulous. Political leaders in both the Republican and the Democratic party, in localities where gambling is especially carried on, appear to be hand in glove with the principal "boss" gamblers.

The halls of legislatures are crowded with men intent upon amending liquor laws and gambling laws, so as to legislate away the rights and liberties of the people, and give the liquor traffic and the gambling fraternity the freest license to scatter their vicious influences.

Coming down from the halls of legislation, this dishonest and piratical crew enter the halls of justice and demand that the laws shall not be enforced against the members of their various fraternities. The hands of prosecuting attorneys are fettered by the command of political "bosses," or corrupted by the "hush-money" of those who grow rich by violating the laws of the land.

Underneath the surface, hidden from public view, there seems to be a positive understanding between political leaders and gambling "bosses" that if the gambling "bosses" pay liberally of the funds dishonestly taken from others, in support of local politics, the members of the fraternity so paying shall have immunity from interference or punishment by public officials.

The newspapers are brought under the same controlling influence by this fraternity, and while one column will give a sensational account of some murder, suicide, embezzlement, or defalcation growing out of the gambling craze, another column in the same paper will contain an account of the race-track and city pool-room gamblers, giving aid, support, and encouragement to these dishonest schemes by a daily publication of "tips" upon the various races.

Illegal liquor traffic, the banking gambling game, the policy-shop, the pool-room, the vendor of filthy publications, each and every one has maintained its existence by a system of paying political blackmail levied by political leaders or officials in the district where it belongs.

The time has come when thoughtful men should arouse themselves to the dangers that threaten the future of this nation from these degrading influences. The demoralization flowing from these schemes has entered the marts of trade, honeycombed commercial institutions, and undermined the stability of banking corporations. Our young men are rendered dishonest and ruined by thousands each year. Many a beautiful home has been wrecked by the downfall of a once honored father and husband. A blight has fallen upon public interests. Disorder and crime run rampant, while the ceaseless miasma arising from these putrid streams poisons the atmosphere which surrounds the rising generation.

A few months ago in Albany a prominent society man with a family of five motherless children committed suicide. He occupied a position of great responsibility. Up to the time of his death he enjoyed the confidence of his employers and received a handsome salary. After his death it was found that he was a defaulter in a sum of more than $100,000 ; that he had betrayed the trust of the company which employed him, and had embezzled its funds to gamble with. After his death, although his orphan children resided in a large and beautifully furnished house, it was found that there was not sufficient food to supply their wants in the house, and neighbors had to contribute to their support.

One of the daily papers a few days ago contained an account of a young woman who, with her husband, had been " playing the races." The husband lavished his money upon the professional gambler at the race-course rather than support his wife. She became desperate, went out upon the street, and in cold blood murdered her husband, because of his failure to support her.

Defalcations, embezzlements, forgeries, thefts, robberies, breaches of trust, suicides, and murders are breaking out in our midst as the harvest of this seed-sowing. Yet when these professional gamblers are brought into court they almost invariably escape with a nominal fine, and that, too, under a law which fixes a maximum punishment of two years' imprisonment and $1,000 fine.

ANTHONY COMSTOCK.

TAMMANY HALL AND THE DEMOCRACY.

BY THE HON. RICHARD CROKER.

No political party can with reason expect to obtain power, or to maintain itself in power, unless it be efficiently organized. Between the aggressive forces of two similar groups of ideas, one entertained by a knot of theorists, the other enunciated by a well-compacted organization, there is such a difference as exists between a mob and a military battalion. The mob is fickle, bold, and timid by turns, and even in different portions it is at the same time swayed by conflicting emotions. In fact, it is a mere creature of emotion, while the drilled and compacted battalion is animated and supported by purpose and scientific plan. It has leaders, and these leaders are known to every man in the ranks and possess their confidence. It is thus that a single company of infantry is able to quell almost any popular outbreak in a city; and a regiment is completely master of the situation, even if it be outnumbered by the malcontents in the proportion of ten or twenty to one.

The value of organization in the case of politicial parties does not appear so obviously upon the surface ; but in point of fact organization is one of the main factors of success, and without it there can be no enduring result. In the immense republic of the United States, which is really a congress or union of over forty separate republics, each having its interests more or less dissociated from those of the others, and yet acknowledging the bond of a common political interest, the organization of a national party must, to a large extent, be based upon a system of deferential compromise, and be an aggregation. The Democrat of New York and the Democrat of Iowa are agreed on certain fundamental doctrines, and in order to put these in action they

forbear to press the acceptance of ideas as to which they are at
variance. They only vote for the same candidate once in four
years ; at other elections they choose Governors, Representatives,
etc., who are at liberty to entertain widely different views as to
the extent to which certain political theories should be made to
operate. Thus an *ultra* tariff-reformer from Nebraska and a
very mild tariff-reformer from some redeemed district of Pennsylvania or Massachusetts may each be an excellent Democrat at
home ; and they may vote harmoniously as Congressmen on national questions ; but the two are are not as strong and effective
as if they were both members of some political club with one
watchword and one purpose.

No great army ever has the cohesive power of a regiment. The
larger the mass the less perfectly do its members know the habits
and purposes of its leader, having no close personal contact with
him ; but in the regiment, which is the unit and type of military
strength, every private knows his captain and his colonel as
well. In the course of service he sees all his comrades and officers
in array ; he sees the officers advance and salute the commander
and that salute returned, and thus experiences the spirit and purpose that animate the entire body. This feeling of common purpose is the supreme aim of military organization in the direction
of effectiveness ; and a compacted and select political club or
society is governed by the same processes.

It does not detract at all from the truth of this statement,
that local political organizations composed largely of depraved
men of revolutionary tendencies have often been powerful engines
in government. It rather proves the essential verity of the principle, and indicates the necessity of a sound political basis.
Cavalry is an important and powerful factor in war, whether it
consist of a horde of Scythian robbers following some incarnate
fiend of strife, or of a gallant " Six Hundred " charging down
some Valley of Death in obedience to a mistaken order and led
by a fearless and trained leader. When we consider the ghastly
turmoil of the French Revolution, we cannot fail to admire the
success, the influence, the resistless power of the Jacobin Club,
not because the club was praiseworthy, since its actions were ab-
horrent, but because it was skilfully organized and handled.
When its representatives sat in the convention, they knew their
orders, and they were also conscious that it was their business to

carry them out. They acted upon the principle that obedience to orders is the first duty of the soldier, and that "politics is war." Chess is war; business is war; the rivalry of students and of athletes is war. Everything is war in which men strive for mastery and power as against other men, and this is one of the essential conditions of progress.

The city of New York to-day contains a political organization which, in respect of age, skilful management, unity of purpose, devotion to correct principles, public usefulness, and, finally, success, has no superior, and, in my opinion, no equal, in political affairs the world over. I mean the *Tammany Democracy.* I do not propose to defend the Tammany organization; neither do I propose to defend sunrise as an exhibition of celestial mechanics, nor a democratic form of government as an illustration of human liberty at its best. In the campaign of 1891 almost the only argument used by the Republicans against the Democrats was the assertion that Flower was the candidate of a corrupt political club, and that club was named Tammany. Tammany was accused of every vice and crime known to Republican orators; it was a fountain-head of corruption; it was because of it that every farmer throughout the State could not at once pay off his mortgages; it took forty millions annually from the citizens of New York and gave them nothing in exchange for it. To the credit of the Democrats let us note the fact that, while this torrent of abuse was being poured upon the heads of voters, Democrats did as the inhabitants of Spain are said to do when the clouds are opened,—"they let it rain." Nobody apologized for the misdeeds of the alleged malefactor; the Democrats went before the people on legitimate issues, and the result of the affair was expressed in the figures, 47,937 majority. I doubt if the Democracy would have fared anything like as well if they had defended or apologized or explained away. "He who excuses himself accuses himself" is a time-worn proverb. They let Mr. Fassett shout himself hoarse over "Tammany corruption," and they won the victory.

In fact, such a defensive attitude would have been wholly at variance with the basis on which the Tammany Democracy acts. A well-organized political club is made for the purpose of aggressive warfare. It must move, and it must always move forward against its enemies. If it makes mistakes, it leaves them behind and goes ahead. If it is encumbered by useless baggage or half-hearted or traitorous camp-followers, it cuts them off and goes ahead. While it does not claim to be exempt from error, it does claim to be always aiming at success by proper and lawful methods, and to have the good of the general community always in view as its end of effort. Such an organization has no time or place for apologies or excuses; and to indulge in them would hazard its existence and certainly destroy its usefulness.

The city and county of New York comprise a population of nearly two millions and furnish the business arena for near-by residents who represent two millions more. The political party, then, that is uppermost in New York legislates locally for the largest municipal constituency on the planet, except one. The task is clearly one of enormous magnitude, and demands a combination of skill, enterprise, knowledge, resolution, and what is known as " executive ability," which cannot be at once made to order, and cannot be furnished by any body of theorists, no matter how full may be their pockets or how righteous may be their intentions. Since the Whig party went out of existence the Democrats have administered the affairs of New York County, rarely even losing the mayoralty except on personal grounds ; always having the majority in the Board of Alderman, and as a rule the Sheriff's and County Clerk's offices. And at the same time the guiding force of the New York Democracy has proceeded from the Tammany organization.

As one of the members of this organization, I simply do what all its members are ready to do as occasion offers, and that is, to stand by its principles and affirm its record. We assert, to begin with, that its system is admirable in theory and works excellently well in practice. There are now twenty-four Assembly districts in the county, which are represented in an Executive Committee by one member from each district, whose duty it is to oversee all political movements in his district, from the sessions of the primaries down to the final counting of the ballots after the election polls are closed. This member of the Executive Committee is a citizen of repute, always a man of ability and good executive training. If he were not, he could not be permitted to take or hold the place. If he goes to sleep or commits overt acts that shock public morality, he is compelled to resign. Such casualties rarely occur, because they are not the natural growth of the system of selection which the organization practices; but when Tammany discovers a diseased growth in her organism, it is a matter of record that she does not hesitate at its extirpation.

Coincident with the plan that all the Assembly districts shall be thoroughly looked after by experienced leaders who are in close touch with the central committees, is the development of the doctrine that the laborer is worthy of his hire; in other words, that good work is worth paying for, and in order that it may be good must be paid for. The affairs of a vast community are to be administered. Skilful men must administer them. These men must be compensated. The principle is precisely the same as that which governs the workings of a railway, or a bank, or a factory; and it is an illustration of the operation of sophistries and unsound moralities, so much in vogue among our closet reformers, that any persons who have outgrown the kindergarten should shut their eyes to this obvious truth. Now, since there must be officials, and since these officials must be paid, and well paid, in order to insure able and constant service, why should they not be selected from the membership of the society that organizes the victories of the dominant party?

In my opinion, to ask this question is to answer it. And I add that the statement made by the enemies of Tammany that "Tammany stands by its friends," is, in fact, praise, although intended for abuse. Tammany *does* stand by its friends, and it always will until some such change occurs in human affairs as will make it praiseworthy and beneficial that a man or an association should stand by his or its enemies. We are willing to admit that the logical result of this principle of action would be that all the employees of the city government, from the Mayor to the porter who makes the fire in his office, should be members of the Tammany organization. This would not be to their discredit. And if any one of them commits a malfeasance, he is just as responsible to the *people* as though he were lifted bodily out of the "Union League" or some transient "Citizens' Reform Association," and he will at once find himself outside of the Tammany membership also.

Fearfully and wonderfully made are the tales that are sent out into the rural districts touching the evil effects of "Tammany rule." The trembling countryman on arriving in New York expects to fall into a quagmire of muddy streets, and while struggling through these quicksands he fears the bunco man on one side and the sandbagger on the other. Reaching some hotel, he counts on being murdered in his bed unless he double-lock his door. That his landlord should swindle him is a foregone conclusion. And when no adventure happens, and he reaches home in safety, he points to himself, among his neighbors, as a rare specimen of a survival of the dangers that accompany the sway of a Democratic majority in New York.

The facts are that New York is a centre to which the criminal element of the entire country gravitates, simply because it offers at once a lucrative field for crime and a safe hiding-place. Therefore, to preserve social order and "keep the peace" in New York demands more ability and more policemen than are required in country solitudes. It is safe to say that any right-minded citizen who attends to his own affairs and keeps proper company and proper hours is as safe in New York as in any part of the globe, the most violently Republican township of St. Lawrence County not excepted. Our streets are clean and are in good order as to the paving, except where certain corporations tear them up and keep their rents gaping. Our city is well watered, well lighted, and well parked. It is conceded that we have the best police and fire departments in the world. Our docks are being rapidly improved, and will compare, when completed, with the Liverpool and London docks. Our tax-rate is lower than that of dozens of other American cities whose affairs are not nearly so well administered. Nor is the tax-rate low because the assessed values are high. If any real-estate owner claims that his property is overvalued, you can silence him at once by offering to buy it at the valuation. Practical real-estate owners know that the county of New York does *not* over assess its property-owners.

That the Tammany Hall Democracy will largely aid in organizing victory for the national ticket next November is beyond question. The national Democracy is free to choose whatever candidate it may prefer. Tammany has no desire to dictate or control the choice; its part in the conflict is to elect the candidate after he shall have been named. No matter what Republican majorities may come down to the Harlem River from the interior of the State, we propose to meet and drown them with eighty-five thousand majority from New York and Kings.

Richard Croker.

THE OLYMPIAN RELIGION.

I.—ITS SOURCES AND AUTHORSHIP.

BY THE RIGHT HONORABLE WILLIAM EWART GLADSTONE.

BY THE Olympian religion I mean the religion of the Achai ans, or Greeks of the Troic period, as it has been portrayed in the "Iliad" and the "Odyssey."

There are also partial indications in the Poems of circum-jacent worships. These, so far as they have been observed, have been sometimes strangely mistaken for proofs of a dual authorship. They are, in truth, sketches of systems prevailing beyond Achaian limits, interesting in themselves, and important from the light which they cast upon the Olympian scheme prop-erly so called. These exotic religions, of Troas, of the further East, and of the South, will require in their own place such notices as the text will warrant.

And the Olympian religion will also have to be examined on its practical and ethical side.

It follows, from the nature of the case, that I have not to be-gin with a discussion of what is known as the Homeric question, but simply to pass it by. We have now and here to deal with the whole of the religious presentations in the Poems simply as a collection of facts. They may embrace a mixture of fable and of truth, which we cannot always disentangle from one another; but both the fable and the truth are facts for the present purpose. They were human concepts; and every human concept is a fact at least of the conceiving mind. But they were also, as cannot be doubted, based upon what the Poet saw and learned of the human society or societies around him; and, as descriptions of prevalent usage or ideas, they are facts of human life, belief, and experience.

It would be unpardonable to present my inferences from the

Homeric text as being facts like those of the text itself ; and in placing them before the reader it will be my duty, to the utmost of my ability, to keep the two visibly distinct.   The utmost limit of my hope is that they may be found to be, in the main, probable inferences from the language of the text.   At least, they are conceived and offered with the intention of conforming in every case to the spirit of my original.   It may be right to add that, when I began the serious study of Homer, some forty years ago, I began it without theory or prepossession of any kind, and that my endeavor has been to let his text lead me by the hand.   I do not, however, deny that prepossession, even when not entertained at the outset, may be acquired during the earlier, and may thus give a bias to the later, stages of a pursuit.   If I have not throughout been able to tread the beaten path, it is because I think, and shall give reasons for thinking, that some of those who have preceded me have not always set out from the proper point or points of departure.

A treatment of the subject, thus composed of facts and of deductions from facts, is widely different from the method which has been sometimes adopted by recent writers.   That method is to lay down some theory, which they have been led by considerations extraneous to Homer to adopt, as to the origin of religion, and then to read the Homeric facts, and construe them, in the light of that theory.   I speak here of general theories, to which the text is made to bend ; for without doubt every inference may be called a theory on the point to which it belongs.   I speak, therefore, of wide and sweeping theories.   For instance, it is taught by some that all Aryan religions are founded upon nature-worship, and that Homer describes an Aryan religion ; consequently his deities all represent natural objects, and his text is to be construed accordingly.   I contend, on the contrary, that he is to be construed by the laws of grammar and history, and, next to these, by himself carefully compared with himself.

In another vital point I differ from the method which has been almost invariably adopted in writing on what is termed the classical mythology.   I claim to separate not only the Greek from the Italian *stoff*, or material, but also to separate that material which belongs to the classical and properly historical period from that which is Homeric ; and which may be called prehistoric, because it is anterior to chronology and continuous record.

I take the entire evidence of Homer, and claim that he be heard alone ; that he be allowed to tell his own tale, without being *in limine* contradicted, hustled, and shouldered out by other witnesses, who have another tale to tell. Their tale is Greek, but is not Achaian ; it is not his tale, because it proceeds from different times and men, and witnesses to altered, multiplied, and comparatively confused traditions.

No ingenuity can weld into a whole the Greek religion of the classical period. But I hope it will not for a moment be supposed that, when I ask for a severance of the Homeric from the non-Homeric material, I intend to disparage the mass of information which is to be gathered from Greek literature generally respecting the religion of that race. It may happen, nay, may often happen, that writers more recent than Homer may present to us traditions more ancient. For example, it seems plain, even from Homeric evidence, that Hesiod deals much more largely in pre-Hellenic material than Homer himself, and that, moreover, with every presumption of fidelity, and without any suspicion of having tampered with his materials for a purpose. This remark has its application to the later Greek authors when they have been in contact with channels of popularly transmitted belief.

It is matter of regret to me to appear as in some sort the censor of any writers whose method I seek to amend, but whose superiority to myself I readily admit : this is, in truth, the only regret I have had to feel in connection with a peculiar, delightful, and profoundly important subject. Those, let me add, from whom I may seem to differ, are well able to defend themselves, should they think that defence is required. They have also, I think, at present the advantage of being the majority.

Until the present century had counted several decades of years, the poems of Homer were loved and studied among us as magnificent romances with more or less of foundation in the world of fact. Distinguished scholars, like Cyril Jackson, the Dean of Christ Church, offered to his memory a worship alike steady and fervent. Still, the historical ingredient in these immortal works was afloat upon the great sea of prehistoric antiquity, like the island of Delos in the well-known legend, unmoored, and unrelated to any authentic records of the past. They had, indeed, been made the object of the fiercest disintegrating attacks ; and it is, perhaps, to these attacks that we are in great part indebted for that serious scrutiny of the text, upon the comparative method, which has been a characteristic of the more recent Homeric study. This examination opened to the recent inquirer fields of knowledge altogether new. As anatomy discloses to us, under the smooth unbroken texture of the human skin, a system of bones and sinews, of ducts and nerves, so under the surface of the Poems there has lain all along, and there is now perceivable, the entire framework of contemporary human life. The several ethnical factors of the newly-compounded Achaian nation became in some degree distinguishable one from another ; and with these distinctions there rose into view those differences of religious belief and worship which severalty of race and local origin implied. I admit that I have here to make an assumption, which must for the present be an assumption only. It is that the Achaian or Greek nation was a composite nation.

In the next place, it has also become clear that the celestial or preternatural portion of the great human dramas represented in the poems was not merely secondary or ornamental, but was, like the terrestrial portion, especially in the " Iliad," a work of consummate art, and a vehicle of rich and varied traditions, opening to us the religious beliefs and influences known at a very early date to a particular aggregation of men, which a long experience subsequently proved to be in natural gifts the most richly endowed of all known races. At the same time, so far as chronology is concerned, I apprehend that all research, based upon the text, has tended rather to lengthen than to shorten the interval supposed to lie between the date of the Poems and the classical period of Greece.

While a way was thus opened by which to penetrate further and further into the mine of the Poems of Homer by the light which they themselves afforded, new and powerful sources of information were most opportunely opened from without. The generous and life-long enthusiasm of Dr. Schliemann, now unhappily deceased, led him to undertake excavations which have contributed, in a certain manner and measure, to support the historical character of the "Iliad," and to establish a connection between prehistoric Greece and the Egypt of the monuments. Of direct and sweeping results in relation to religion we can hardly speak in connection with this generous toil ; but the general effect has been, in whatever degree, to accredit the Poems, and to favor the presumption of their high antiquity.

Much larger, in relation to the present subject, has been the knowledge derived from those researches in Egypt and in Assyria which, during the second and following quarters of the century, have carried light into wide regions previously most obscure, and have established as history much that was theretofore speculation. These systems of knowledge have required, and have justly obtained, the scientific names of Egyptology and Assyriology. Both of them, but the second in particular, have shed an altogether novel and unexpected light upon the Poems of Homer, especially as regards the subject of religion. They establish the eastern and southern derivation of a number of the elements which go to make up the Homeric system, and in so doing they may, perhaps, be found to supply in some degree a link between the Poems and the historical books of the Old Testament.

We seem, then, to have before us the outline at least of copious materials for a distinct and separate work on the religion of the Homeric Poems. And it is high time, as I contend, to recognize that we possess, in these Poems, a large treasure of knowledge, archæological in the widest sense, as a record of the ideas and beliefs, as well as the acts and characters, of the earliest fathers of the Greek nation. I believe it to be a record fuller and more instinct with life than any other equally ancient record that has been handed down to us ; attested from within by its own self-consistency, and now, after running the gantlet of so many ages, further attested from without by the results of Egyptian and of Assyrian or Babylonian discovery.

There are other and very special reasons for an endeavor to extricate the subject of Homeric religion from the confusing associations by which it has so long been fettered and deformed, and to secure for it its due place in the history of human thought as well as of human life.

What I claim for Homer is not supremacy or infallibility as a guide in our inquiries respecting Hellenic religion. Any such claim is to be repudiated, were it only because it is impossible to say, as we view the field before us, at what point in the general tissue of the Poems the work of literary manipulation ends, and the practical and historical record begins. Even in the Christian churches, resting, as they do, upon a strong dogmatic and historic basis, there is a wide space between the restricted theory of their necessary books, or documents, and the living and working system of their official teachers and disciples. Much more must we guard against precipitate assumption when we have to deal with the effort of a poet to present a systematic religion without the guidance of commanding authority, and in the face of the problems offered by national conditions as yet unadjusted. Yet, after every deduction, there is much to affirm. We have before us a witness independent, solitary, and of unsurpassed creative and constructive powers. In the wide range of his Poems, he speaks to us with a self-consistency not less remarkable than his consummate art. What he has to say, he only has to say. From the depths of a prehistoric period, and across the sea of centuries that separate him from classical Greece, he conveys to us utter-ances with which there is really nothing to compare. The Hymns called Homeric are evidently the product of a civilization different from his, seated in the Asiatic Greece, and built up after the Dorian conquest. Still less of his spirit, if more of his facts, can be found in the "Theogony" of Hesiod, which conflicts with Homer on a number of vital points, and which almost bears to the Poems of Homer the relation borne by an almanac to a his-tory.

My claim for Homer is that he is worth hearing for himself, and on his own ground, apart from the jangle of discordant voices. No one, early or late, except himself, has exhibited to us the early Achaian religion with comprehensiveness and elaboration. Nowhere else are its features so pronounced that their essential character is legible beyond mistake. All this is on the surface of the case. But we are also invited to mine below the surface, and to see whether, when we have classified his deities according to their ethnical relations, we may not find ourselves introduced to the actual process by which Achaian religion became what it was, and which gives to us an analysis of the nation, as well as of its thearchy, and assigns to each of its main ingredients its proper place and work in the formation of the compound. I seek, then, to extri-cate Homer and his testimony from the chaotic mass accumulated by so many countries and ages, and to see what lessons he may have to teach us. Not that he will teach us everything. But he will teach us something : whereas the method not uncommonly pursued seems to be a contrivance for destroying all hope of access to the religion of Greece in its embryonic and most plastic stages.

No great difficulty will perhaps be found in admitting that the testimony of Homer should be received as separate from and superior to that of the classical literature, with reference to the religion of Greece, on account of the wide and silent tract of time by which it precedes that literature. But still we may be asked to give some reasons why we are to demand a similar severance and precedence for the poet as against the Hymns commonly termed Homeric and the works of Hesiod, inasmuch as these, like the "Iliad" and the "Odyssey," partake of the prehistoric character. To this reasonable question I reply as follows.

Among the so-termed Homeric Hymns, that which is addressed to Apollo is the one which may best claim the title of so high a parentage on account of the touching passage cited by Thucydides,[*] and of the claim to Homeric originality which that passage itself seems to contain. But, as I conceive, I have elsewhere proved, by an examination of the text and contents of that Hymn, that it cannot possibly be the work of Homer, but belongs to a later author.[†]

The case of Hesiod, who has sometimes even been deemed, however strangely, to be older than Homer, requires a separate consideration.

Among the instances which may be adduced of misleading method, one of the most conspicuous is the practice of dealing with Homer and Hesiod as twin authorities for the Achaian religion. Thus Rinck[‡] speaks of "the ancient poets," and says that "in Hesiod and Homer"—there is not even the sorry preference of "Homer and Hesiod"—"we find the general structure of Hellenic religion completed." Now, it is true that a number of names and particulars found in Homer are also found in Hesiod ; but this is a very small part of the truth.

It seems probable that there was a period, immediately following the Dorian conquest, in which the poems of Homer had been ejected from the country together with the more civilized Hellenic tribes ; and the ancient tradition, which connects him with Lycurgus, may mean that he was reimported by that lawgiver, possibly from his being esteemed as a great war poet, which

---

[*] III., 104.   [†] See "Homeric Synchronism " (1876), Part I., Chap. IV.
[‡] " Religion der Hellenen," VIII. (Zurich, 1855.)

was apparently his leading excellence in the eyes of Aristophanes.*
Hesiod may have lived in Bœotia before Lycurgus, but probably
during this period. In any case, we find confounded together by
him all that in Homer was the subject of keen discrimination. The
Olympian religion of Homer was national, political, theanthropic,
and of highly scientific construction, all the parts of it standing
in due and orderly relation to one another. But the "Theogony"
of Hesiod is neither national, nor political, nor (in any distinctive
manner) theanthropic ; nor is it scientific in any sense higher
than that of a series of catalogues. Foreign and domestic elements, archaic and nascent or embryonic cults, are all set down
side by side without distinction. Above all, the Nature-powers at
large, including a multitude of abstractions such as Chaos, Erebos,
Night, and many more, whom Homer virtually deposes, are restored to their high places in the lineage from which the thearchy
is derived.

The comparison between the two poets is, indeed, extremely curious. Besides considerable coincidence, and very
great divergence, in direct statement, we may observe that Hesiod,
manifestly the more modern of the two, imitates Homer in a
multitude of particulars. He constantly uses "Olympian" as
an epithet for his divinities, but he has also imitations which are
much more specific. For instance, he introduces the name of
Iris, of whom we fail to find any trace in the religion of historic
Greece, and whom, accordingly, Hesiod could not well be led to
commemorate except, as I am tempted to say, in a rather blind
following of Homer. But his departures from Homer, in letter
and in spirit, are not less remarkable. In the well-remembered
meeting of Zeus and Herè on Mount Ida, Homer graces and also
veils the occurrence by introducing the immediate and spontaneous growth beneath them of flowers and fresh herbage ; the
tribute of Earth to the head of Olympos. Now in Zeus there
was, along with sensuality, a certain majesty, and even a certain
refinement. But Hesiod borrows the same figure first for Aphroditè,† who in Homer has no command over any natural agency
except that of impure passion, and secondly for Poseidon,‡ who,
in the Poems, notwithstanding his extraction and prerogatives, is
in character little better than an exhibition of sheer animal force
without any moral or transcendental element. It is not too much

* Aristoph., Batr., 1,034.   † Theog., 194.   ‡ Ibid, 277-279.

to say that the work of Hesiod, most valuable without doubt in its own sphere, is not only different from, but even alien to, the works of Homer.

The Earth,* or Gaia, repressed in the Homeric scheme, and divested of all but physical attributes, is the progenitress of the Heaven of Hesiod. Okeanos is their joint offspring; whereas he is in Homer the first ancestor of gods and men.† Hesiod, again, makes Earth the parent of Kronos, and with him of the strangest miscellany of abstractions and realities.‡ But in truth, and speaking at large, nothing can in spirit be more alien to Homeric ideas than to derive the Olympian rulers from Gaia, the most material, the coarsest, if I may so speak, among all the objects of the Nature-worship that he deposed.

For another instance, Briareus, in Homer,§ is the son of the exotic Poseidon, who is himself the son of Kronos. In Hesiod the son becomes the uncle, for Briareus is a brother of Kronos, as are the Cyclop family.‖ Again, the Erinues, in Homer a creation of singular nobleness, are in Hesiod sisters of the rebel Gigantes. It would be an endless task to note all the contradictions between the "Theogony," on one side, and both the letter and spirit of Homer, on the other. I will close with two instances which will stand *instar omnium*. The great Athenè is, in Homer, conspicuous for the universality of her gifts; and her being the war-goddess figures only as a kind of secondary attribute. But in the three lines of the "Theogony" which relate her birth and character, the whole description is one of war, tumult, and terror.

Again, when Hesiod introduces Iris,¶ the ethereal creation of Homer, the most remote of all his divine company from association with the nature-cult, he makes Thaumas, a son of Nereus, her father, and a daughter of Okeanos her mother; utterly confounding together the things which Homer labors hardest to keep apart.

Except that the rule of Zeus and his court is set forth as the actually prevailing system in both, the productions of the two poets confuse rather than illustrate one another; and the rural, local, industrial, pacific muse of Hesiod ** stands in a contrast almost ludicrous with the great works which Homer addresses for man to man, and which have conveyed the whole world of his day to all the worlds of all the succeeding generations. The "The-

---

* Theog., 126.   † Ibid, 133. Il., XIV., 201, 302.   ‡ Theog., 129–137.   § Il., I., 404.
  ‖ Theog., 139, 149.   ¶ Theog., 237, 265.   ** ' Works and Days," v. 19.

ogony " only touches Homer to darken him ; nor does it throw
npon the origins of Hellenic nationality or religion so much as a
single ray of light.   And these two, opposed at every point of
deeper meaning, even when the statements of fact seem to coincide, are treated almost as if they had been twin artists, jointly
employed in a common work.   This is the method of proceeding
which it seems to me necessary not only to renounce, but to
reverse, if we are ever to find any true and profitable meaning
in the old Olympian religion.

The work of Rinck, which I have quoted, is now of old date.
And it is well known that the German experts have, during the
present century, been so unequivocally the leaders of the world
in classical research that our debt to them is one perhaps needless to acknowledge, and certainly impossible to overstate.   But,
so far as I know, they, as well as the scholars of other countries,
have, with the one distinguished exception of Nägelsbach,* continued to treat the Homeric evidence as if it were simply part
and parcel of a homogeneous common stock, which continued in
a gradual course of accumulation down to and including the
Roman period.   I hope it is not inconsistent with gratitude,
or with respect, to say that this continuance can hardly be due to
a reasoned and deliberate conviction, but may have sprung from a
usage which needs only to be questioned in order to be discarded.

The severance now proposed of the Homeric from the later
Greek system of religion is, in truth, at once a necessity and an
advantage.   It is, in the first place, a necessity, for without this
no clear and consistent picture of the religion can be presented
either for the heroic or for the classical period.   If we take the
great human characters described by Homer, such as Achilles,
Helen, Odysseus, Hector, we find that in the historic time their
aspects were blurred and their outlines shifted, so that the general
effect was seriously or entirely altered.   And even so it is with
the Homeric deities.   In Homer we find portraits of them drawn
and finished with consummate care ; so drawn that a sculptor,
if deeply imbued with Homeric study, would be able to preserve
the individualities of the Olympian court as faithfully as those of
Agamemnon's council.   But with reference to the aggregate of

* Nägelsbach, "Homerische Theologie," Nürnberg. 1861. Preceded by the
"Nachhomerische Theologie bis auf Alexander," Nürnberg. 1857. The "Myth-
ologie der Ilias," by Dr. Von Sybel (Marburg, 1877), contributes little or nothing to
elucidate the subject.

the deities of the historic period, such an attempt would clearly be desperate. The Apollo is lowered and fundamentally changed ; the Arès and the Aphroditè are promoted, nay, almost pitchforked, into a new position ; the common properties of deity encroach on the distinctive ; all true personality is enfeebled. In the case of the Erinues, nothing less than a disastrous revolution is brought about. The ethical color is itself affected. So is the association, or polity. What is a true picture of the Olympian system of Homer, with its power and habit of collective action, would be an untrue picture for the classical period ; and *vice versâ*.

But there is also a great advantage in the separate treatment of the Homeric scheme of religion. In the examination of the prehistoric religions generally, it is felt that they extend over long periods of time in which great changes must have taken place. It follows that, in the mass of particulars presented to us, some are older, some newer ; but that we have no effective, or even possible, means of separating the old from the new. Now, let us suppose that in some one of these cases we should find that we were able to note a certain portion, or a certain form, of their particulars, as absolutely original, or, at any rate, as lying near the source ; again, as being thereby distinguished broadly from all the rest ; and as forming a point of departure from which the measurements of the rest could be taken. Is it not obvious that the gain would be immense ? and that new lights, decisive in their character, would or might be thrown upon the most important questions ? For example, we should obtain data of a positive character towards determining whether the history of ancient religion, as it grows older, exhibits at all, and, if so, in what particulars, the notes of an upward or of a downward movement. But this high vantage ground is exactly what is found ready to our hands, in the case of the Olympian religion, through the poems of Homer. He is the only primitive author who has treated the subject of religion systematically, and has presented it to us, first as an organic whole, and next as an organic whole that still carried upon it, in his day, the notes of its derivation from yet earlier sources. With this we should compare all the later forms, and it should supply a standard which forms an element of the case when we proceed to measure them.

W. E. GLADSTONE.

[TO BE CONTINUED.]

NOTES AND COMMENTS.

AN OPEN LETTER.

THE policy I have outlined in my article "How to Attack the Tariff," in this number of THE REVIEW, has already been received with great favor by journals representing the business industries of the country. It is conservative in its methods, and will not alarm any legitimate industries or tend to embarrass production or trade of any kind. On the contrary, it is believed that all industries will be promoted and general prosperity will result from the adoption of this policy.

It has the advantage of being easily comprehended. Those who have paid but little attention to economic questions will have no difficulty in comprehending the method of attack or of understanding the results which will follow. It has the further advantage of permitting a short session of Congress, and thus enabling Representatives to return to their constituents at the earliest time practicable. It will enable the House to fully map out and determine its line of policy before the meeting of the National Democratic Convention, so that confusion and uncertainty will be prevented, and the platform of the party which may be adopted at the National Convention can be in perfect harmony with the policy of the Democratic Representatives in Congress.

The Committee on Ways and Means is composed of fifteen Representatives, eleven of whom, including the five Republicans, reside in Northern States. No charge of Southern sectionalism can be alleged or maintained against this committee, or against any measure that it may recommend. The great manufacturing and producing States of the country are represented, and every measure produced will have in view the promotion of the best interests of the country, both manufacturing and agricultural.

WM. M. SPRINGER.

THE FLOUR OF THE FUTURE.

WHAT part has science in the making of bread? To what extent has this staple article of food been improved and benefited by the immense strides made in scientific knowledge, applicable to almost every other article? There seems a great lack of knowledge of the proper composition and nutritious qualities of flour ; of the process of fermentation ; of the generating of gases in baking ; of the effect of the absence or superabundance of any certain ingredient in bread. It is true that the bread of this century is whiter than that of our forefathers ; it may be lighter, from the addition of artificial baking-powders and similar compounds ; but is it better, more wholesome, nutritious, and digestible? Compared with the making and the composition of bread, which everybody consumes, there is ten times as much science employed in the making of beer. Recently Edward Atkinson, of Boston, whose pursuit of economical problems is a national advantage, said :

" What is the amount of scientific labor and application to-day bestowed on the proper regulation of the fermenting process in the brewing of beer? We all know that every brewer of any prominence has for his guidance a chemical laboratory; that the practical men intrusted with the management and superintendence of the process are picked and selected; have great experience, thorough training, and can command the highest remuneration for their work, when well performed. Millions of dollars per year are expended in the effort to make the beer as palatable as possible, and to insure a perfect uniformity and precise quality of the same."

In civilized Germany, the man who should venture to adulterate or even dilute beer goes to prison, followed by disgrace and the imprecations of his fellow citizens. The man who should take it into his head to adulterate bread might do so with impunity, as long as he avoids introducing poisonous substances.

The demand has been made for white bread; fashion calls for it; the millers have complied. Mechanical skill has come to their assistance, and every part of the wheat which would tend to darken the flour is being removed with a precision and thoroughness which are simply wonderful. But does this tend to make the bread better? Does it give the workingman a greater return for his hard-earned loaf? Does this refined milling process give to the convalescing invalid, to the growing child, more strength and nutriment than did the old-fashioned dark bread? The answer to the foregoing questions is decidedly in the negative. Indeed, on the other hand, it is impossible to estimate the injury done by the elimination of the most valuable constituents of the grain. A prominent English physician, when discussing this question, has recently said :

"Wheat and water contain all the elements necessary for man, and for the hardworking man, too. Where is the man that can exist on our present white bread and water? There is an old joke about doctors being in league with undertakers ; it would rather appear as if the millers and bakers were in the doctors' pay, as if, were it not for them, and for the white bread they are so zealous in producing, the doctors would have less to do. Separating the bran from the flour became fashionable at the beginning of the present century. This fashion created the dental profession, which, with its large manufacturing industries, has grown up within the last two generations. It has reached its present magnitude only because our food is systematically deprived of lime, of salts and phosphoric acid, the creators of nerve bone, and tissue, which especially are so signally absent from our modern white bread."

What we need is a reversal of the opinion which demands a white, starchy flour. We further need a milling process which will grind the whole berry of the wheat to such fineness that the grain will not act as an irritant on the membrane of the stomach and bowels. It is well known that the germ of the wheat contains a high percentage of ash and phosphoric acid, and also fat ; indeed, the germ contains almost all the fat of the grain, and it therefore becomes one of the most important elements of food. The slight discoloration of the flour which is caused by its presence has, however, condemned it, and in the modern system of dressing white flour it is discarded. For much the same reason the cellulose and the cerealine, which are part of the bran, are also unadvisably cast out. This cerealine is one of the most important of the soluble albumenoids in respect to the energy with which it attacks the starch of the grain and converts it into a species of sugar, called maltose or dextrose. It also has a diastatic action, which sets up a ferment wherever it is present, thus largely assisting in the digestion of other articles with which it comes in contact. It acts on the food much in the same way as the saliva or gastric juice. It is, in fact, one of nature's wonderful aids to digestion.

In spite of this, and of all the dyspeptic and constipated tendencies of our people, fashion has refused the bran a place in our daily dietary. We endeavor to replace the agencies of nature by a stimulating diet, forcing the heart to an unnatural action, or, if we are too poor to afford this, we are compelled to let the craving of the system go unheeded, and receive the punishment which is always meted out for transgressions against the laws of nature, by reduction of mental and physical vitality, which in due course of time is transplanted in the coming generations. Too much importance cannot be given to the serious mistake at present committed in discarding a considerable percentage of the nutritious elements in the grain, and especially of the agencies provided by nature to enable us to properly digest and absorb the purely nutritious portions of the wheat.

Attempts have been made in the United States to introduce a more rational and digestible flour, but they have all stranded against the unreasonable demands of the consumers for white flour and bread, and against the disinclination of leading millers and flour merchants to combat the prejudice and promote reform. It has, however, remained for Great Britain, so often foremost in practical common-sense and rational application of the results arrived at by theorizing science, to lead in this reform. In 1890 a company was formed in London for the manufacture of whole-wheat meal. It was a small beginning, but the results have been such that, within a comparatively short space of time, large numbers of leading bakers have commenced furnishing whole-wheat-meal bread and biscuits to a rapidly increasing host of consumers; sub-companies are being formed in the different cities, and sales have reached an imposing figure.

The process used in the manufacture of whole-wheat meal is novel, and, as originally carried out, was briefly described in the issue of *The American Miller* for March, 1891. The iron mill used is of exceeding simplicity, and acts by creating two exceedingly powerful revolving air-currents, by which the grains of wheat are thrown against each other, thus being reduced by attrition— bran, germ, and kernel—to a flour which, as soon as fine enough, is floated off on a rising air-current and deposited in the bin above the packer, without the necessity of submitting it to any bolting or sifting process. The grinding is done at low temperature ; the meal is perfectly dried and aërated by the circulating air-currents, and the whole grain is ground. Thus all the elements present in the wheat are also found in their natural proportions in the meal. The bread baked from this meal is not white, but assumes a warm golden-brownish tint. It is free from the rasping grittiness of the imperfectly-ground Graham bread, the bran in which, never having been thoroughly pulverized, acts as an irritant upon the delicate digestive apparatus. The bread made from whole-wheat meal has a richer, more palatable taste than ordinary wheat bread. Certainly its constituents, being those provided by nature, are calculated to assist the digestive powers, and especially to counteract any constipated tendencies. For the health of the whole people, as well as upon grounds of economy, it would appear to be a duty to better utilize the nutritious and digestive substances in the wheat.

This question of proper food is one that thinking physicians might discuss. If it is a fact that, by a simple reform in the grinding and preparation of an article of such universal use as flour, a great benefit can be effectually secured, no greater good could be achieved than by encouraging such a reform. It is important to create a popular feeling strong enough to carry reform and improvement over the strong fortifications which prejudice, ignorance, and habit have formed around the present starchy compound which we call wheat bread.

Erastus Wiman.

THE TOMBS IN WESTMINSTER ABBEY.

The time is within measurable distance when we may expect to find hung on the tower of Westminster Abbey a placard bearing the legend seen on the Paris omnibuses when they are full—" Westminster Abbey is *complet.*" To be precise, it is almost full of more or less illustrious dead, and for generations to come the accommodation that remains must needs be sparingly dealt with. The Royal Commission which sat this year (1891) to inquire into the matter discovered that by masterly contrivance, making use of every spot available for the purpose, ninety or even ninety-five interments might yet take place. If burials under this sacred rooftree went on at the ancient scale, this accommodation would be speedily exhausted. From a search through old records, happily kept with infinite care at the Abbey, it appears that in ten years from 1681 to 1690 there were one hundred burials in the Abbey itself, whilst one hundred and twenty-five more or less obscure persons were allowed to rest within the precincts. A hundred years later, in the corresponding decennial period, there were but thirty-one. Not that there were fewer great people to bury, but that there were fewer mediocrities upon whom the honor of sepulture in Westminster Abbey or its precincts was bestowed.

"Westminster Abbey or glorious victory!" Nelson cried when leading the boarders at Cape St. Vincent on to the Spanish three-decker "San Josef." It is not precisely the kind of remark in such circumstances one would expect off the transpontine stage. But Colonel Drinkwater Bethune declares the words were used, and the Colonel was there at the time. However that be, the phrase connected with Nelson's name shows how high is reckoned the distinction of being buried in Westminster Abbey. And yet even within the present century the cloisters and the Abbey have been used as a place of sepulture for people living obscure lives in humble circumstances. In jealously limiting admission to the illustrious dead, the Abbey authorities are reverting to the earliest intention of its founder and his successors. The first burial in the Abbey was that of Edward the Confessor, who built the earlier church with the special object of serving as a tomb for himself. The King was buried near the altar, and close by his grave on Christmas Day, 1066, William the Conqueror was crowned, and there on the selfsame spot every King or Queen who has since reigned in England has received the rite of coronation. At first only members of the royal family were buried at Westminster, and when Richard the Second ordered the interment, within the chapel of the Confessor, of John of Waltham, Bishop of Salisbury, his trusty minister, a thrill of horror ran through the kingdom as far as the story travelled. No one was surprised when such a King was dethroned by Henry of Bolingbroke, and presently done to death in Pontefract Castle.

The ground thus broken, Westminster Abbey slowly became the place of sepulture for men who had claims to eminence other than the adventitious circumstance of royal birth. In the last year of the sixteenth century Spenser was buried in the spot now known as the Poets' Corner. Next followed Beaumont, Drayton, and Ben Jonson. It is, however, in the present century that the Abbey obtained the peculiar place in English history which connects it with the roll of supremely great Englishmen. Pitt and Fox were both buried there within the same year. Brinsley Sheridan was buried in 1816. To what strange uses the noble fane might still be put is shown on turning over the record by finding that in the next year there was buried in the Abbey a still-born daughter of their royal highnesses the Duke and Duchess of Cumberland. Grattan was buried here in 1820 ; Canning in 1827 ; Wilberforce, 1833 ; Lord Chatham, 1835 ; Thomas Campbell, 1844 ; Stephenson, 1859 ; Macaulay, 1860 ; Outram and Clyde, 1863 ; Lord Palmerston, 1865 ; Dickens, 1870 ; Lord Lytton, 1873 ; Dr. Livingstone in the following year, and Lord Lawrence and Sir Rowland Hill in 1879, whilst in 1881 Dean Stanley, who during the term of his deanship had watched over the building with infinite solicitude, had a place found for him in Henry VII.'s chapel.

These are names familiar throughout the world, and the burial of such men in Westminster Abbey is appropriate enough. What is less known is the presence within the precincts of the Abbey of a long list of nonentities. As recently as the year 1817 there was buried in the cloisters George Wellington Francis Balthasar St. Anthonio, aged two years. The Royal Commission in vain inquired as to the identity of Master Anthonio, and the wherefore of the honor done to him, for which Nelson cheerfully perilled his life at St. Vincent. Nothing is known of him, only his name, under the weight of whose syllables the infant seems to have sunk ere yet he learned to walk. It is easy to understand why in 1801 Susanna Frances was buried in Westminster Abbey, for it is mentioned in the register that she was the widow of a sacrist. Similar honor was done in following years to George Schliemacher, "formerly servant to the Dean"; Elizabeth Newbegin, wife of the college butler ; Mary Barrow, widow of a chorister ; Ann Forster, niece of the Abbey carpenter, and Amelia Cook, daughter of the Abbey organist, were people connected, however obscurely, with the service of the Abbey, and were buried within its precincts. But persons having property in the neighborhood claimed the right, and generally had it admitted. Macpherson, the reputed author of "Ossian," died in Inverness. When his will was opened, there was found in it directions for his burial in Westminster Abbey on the ground that he had property near there. No objection was offered on the part of the authorities. Macpherson's body was brought by hearse all the way from the far north and buried in the Abbey close by Dr. Johnson, who when alive had not been reticent in his criticism on "Ossian." In the register one finds an entry of the interment of a lady with the explanation that it was "so ordered in her will,"—scarcely sufficient authority in these days for burial in Westminster Abbey. There exists at this day a curious claim to burial in the Abbey which the authorities are bound to admit whenever put forward. It belongs to the Duke of Northumberland's family, who claim a prescriptive right of burial in this Abbey dating back to the time when the Duke of Somerset married the heiress of the Percys. The Percy tomb is in the chapel of St. Nicholas, and when in 1883 Lady Louisa Percy died she was buried there. Naturally an end must come to this luxury. There are already twenty-five coffins in the vault, and scarcely room enough for another full-grown Percy. There is one other private vault in the nave, that of Atterbury. This good bishop, having been sent to the Tower on suspicion of high treason, and subsequently banished from the realm, left directions in his will that he should be buried in Westminster Abbey, adding the proviso that it should be " as far away as possible from Kings "—a foresight lacking in the case of Mac pherson, who never thought of Dr. Johnson when he desired to be buried in the Abbey.

One of the most curious discoveries recently made in connection with burials in Westminster Abbey came out in an accidental way. Workmen were engaged in the cloister garden making an engine-room. In digging for foundations they came upon a lot of human bones buried in the sand. They were lying carefully placed east and west, but there was no sign of coffin or of rust of nail ; only the bare bones. Evidence in connection with excava tions made clearly traced the burials back six hundred years, to the time of Edward I. A grassy space shaded by the walls of the Abbey is full at this day of the bones of coffinless, nameless subjects of Edward I.

The Abbey records do not, in respect of interments, go back in any completeness beyond the year 1600. Since that day 1,175 persons have been buried within the Abbey, and 1,811 in the precincts. In later years the Abbey doors have been opened to receive dead only under circumstances of exceptional merit. Dean Stanley was in office for eighteen years, during which time there were only twenty-one burials within the Abbey and five in the precincts. Dean Bradley succeeded in 1881, and up to the present time only seven interments have taken place. The last was that of Mr. Browning, and the search for room for his coffin brought into fresh prominence the narrow limits of the opportunities the Abbey possesses to-day for receiving the illustrious dead.

Mr. Wright, the clerk of the Works, gave some interesting evidence before the Commissioners, his business-like, off-handed manner of alluding to the details of his business recalling the style of conversation peculiar to gravediggers in *Hamlet's* time. He seems to have been much troubled in the pursuit of his business by coming in contact with concrete, brought on the spot in connection with the foundation of the building. There is still space for interments in the west aisle of the north transept which might have been available only for the inconsiderate action of Henry III. " It is a mass of concrete," Mr. Wright told the Commissioners. " Concrete was, as far as my judgment goes, rather carelessly and lavishly used by Henry III. '

Sometimes, driven by circumstances, Mr. Wright has been compelled to struggle with this concrete. It invades Poets' Corner, and when Browning was buried there it was necessary to fill up the grave with concrete instead of earth. Digging here, the men found traces of two other nameless bodies gone to dust, with the exception of just the main bones. No sign whatever of a coffin. " I found concrete here when I buried Spottiswood," said Mr. Wright, pointing to the map, "and there when I buried Browning. But when I buried Browning we got partly out of it."

Hamlet. How long will a man be in the earth ere he rot ?
First Clown. Faith if he be not rotten before he die he will last you some eight year or nine year. A tanner will last you nine year.

In this familiar strain Mr. Wright, all unconsciously, continued to speak. Asked if he knew of other interments in Poets' Corner made in concrete, he said : "There are two ladies, two Percys, and they are excavated out of concrete. I saw them when I buried Spottiswood by their side." Speaking of the vault where the Cecils were buried and answering a question from *Hamlet*—I mean from one of the Commissioners—he said : "You know, sir, it is a mixed party which is buried there." Living poets will hear with interest Mr. Wright's testimony as to the space remaining in their heritage of the Corner. "I have room for three or four more," he said, as if poets were packets of stationery or flagons of ink. "I know one spot to a certainty, and I know another spot or two beside Browning, two near Dickens and Macaulay." Taking up the staff and pointing to the map, he added : "I believe there is room for one here. I know there is room for two or three here. I am certain of one by the side of Browning."

In contravention of ordinary principles of political economy, the scarcer ground for burial grows in Westminster Abbey the price of interment decreases. In the receiver's office there is a musty book setting forth the funeral fees in 1717. From this we find that " a gent buried in the body of ye church" must needs have paid on his account a sum of £10, being fabric fee. Other fixed charges were :

	£	s.	d.
A Kt in the Body of yᵉ Church	13	06	8
Within any of yᵉ Chappells	20	00	0
A Baron	26	00	0
An Earl	30	00	0
A Marquis	35	00	0
A Duke	40	00	0
A Bp	30	00	0
An Archbp	40	00	0
All within the Tombs	20	00	0

A Ld by courtesy same as a Baron.

In addition there were fees to officers, the dean taking £2 12s., the prebends half a sovereign each, the sub-dean 13s. 4d., and the minister officiating a sovereign. The chantor and choir appropriated £8 3s. 4d. The receiver and the registrar had 10s. a piece, whilst the verger "left it to you." All above the rank of knight had to pay mourning-fees in accordance with the following ordinance:

	£	s.	d.
To the Dean, 10 yds. of cloth for a gown, cassock and hood, at 20s. a yd	10	00	0
His 4 Servants, 4 yds. each, at 10s. a yd	8	00	0
The Sub dean, 5 yds. for a gown and hood, at 20s	5	00	0
The Sub-dean's man, 3 yds., at 10s	1	10	0
The Chantor, 5 yds., at 20s., for a gown and hood	5	0)	0
The Vergers, 4 yds. each, at 10s	4	00	0
The Porter, 4 yds., at 10s	2	00	0
The 12 Almsmen, in lieu of mourning	4	16	0

Finally, there was £5 for the use of Jerusalem Chamber, a sum the dean pocketed. In all, a funeral in Westminster Abbey was not to be done under a minimum of 100 guineas, and ran up to £150. Persons buried in leaden coffins paid a fee of £6, if interred in the Abbey, and half that sum if buried in the cloisters. There was a £5 fine for burying in linen. When Pitt was buried, 90 pairs of gloves, at 3s. 6d. each, were presented to the choir.

In 1829 these fees were revised, but not largely reduced. It would still cost a duke or duchess £150 to be buried in the Abbey, whilst a commoner "could be done," as Mr. Wright would say, for £80. Dean Stanley introduced searching reforms into the scale of charges, reducing them, on the one side, as far as perquisites for officials were concerned, so as to increase the amount going to the fabric fund. Up to 1874 silk scarfs, hat-bands, and gloves were given to the clergy, officers, and choir. The value of these perquisites was submitted to solemn arbitration, and it was decided that in lieu thereof there should be made to the choir, organist, and servants a money payment amounting to £31 2s. 6d. Total fees for interment now charged are for the fabric fund, £26, £36 or £46, according to the decree of the person buried. The fees of the dean, canon, choir, officers, and verger are fixed at £34 2s. 6d., which, with the £31 2s. 6d. presented to the choir, organist, and servants, makes a total varying from £91 4s. 8d. to £110 4s. 8d. Formerly the scarfs, hat-bands, and gloves were charged in the undertaker's bill, and it will be seen that economies to that amount, which would certainly not be less than £31 2s. 6d., have been effected at the Abbey.

The conclusion arrived at upon the inquiry undertaken by the Royal Commission, assisted by the business aptitude of the clerk of the Works, was that, using every available space for the purpose, not more than ninety to ninety-five interments may in future take place. At the western end of the nave there is probably room for forty-five coffins; twenty more might be laid in the concrete which supports the wall at the northwest corner of the north aisle, and possibly a dozen more coffins might be added to the "mixed parties" in the larger vaults not yet full. That, taking the average of persons deemed eligible for admission to the Abbey in recent times, would provide for all the just needs of the next hundred years.

Of the various projects submitted for supplying adjuncts to the Abbey that might be used as charnel-houses, the commissioners recommend the erection of a monumental chapel on a vacant piece of ground, the site of the old refectory, lying immediately south of the great cloister and parallel to the nave of the Abbey. But there is not much enthusiasm in the recommendation, nor has there, since it was submitted to the Queen, been any movement towards carrying it into effect. There seems, in truth, a disposition to extend to the unborn future the privilege of burying its dead, already claimed for the dead past.

HENRY W. LUCY.

JEWS IN THE UNION ARMY.

IN THE December number of THE REVIEW, Mr. J. M. Rogers, in a reply to Isaac Besht Bendavid's statement that "on both sides in that conflict the American Israelites stood shoulder to shoulder with their fellow citizens of all other races and creeds," says that in all his eighteen months' experience in the army he never met or heard of a Jewish soldier, and "if so many Jews fought bravely for their adopted country, surely their champion ought to be able to give the names of the regiments they condescended to accept service in."

Did Mr. Rogers make this absurd statement in the hope that no champion of the Jews would lift his pen in refutation of his assertions? Who Mr. Rogers is, and what prompted him to attack the Jewish people, I am at a loss to ascertain. But that he has resorted to means unworthy of impartial historical record, and that his outraged feelings have played sad havoc with his sense of fairness,—rashly assuming that he possessed this virtue in some small measure,—I can most safely affirm. There is not a semblance of truth in the charges with which he attempts to impeach Jewish national pride; otherwise his indictment would imply the justice of Mr. Goldwin Smith's denunciatory branding of the Jews as a "parasitic race."

Many of my co-religionists, wrathful at this scurrilous attack, have ex-claimed : "Another page must be added to the historical record of the Civil War, telling of the heroic martyrdom the Jews rejoiced to suffer, to save their land from further degradation." And as a result of the agitation pro-duced by this article, I am happy to say that work has already been begun for the preparation of a complete history of the part the Jews bore in the late struggle.

Immediately upon reading the article referred to, I wrote to Mr. Thomas S. Townsend, compiler of the "Library of National, State, and Individual , Records," and received from him the following reply :

"NEW YORK, December 22, 1891.

"STEPHEN S. WISE, ESQ.

"MY DEAR SIR : Referring to the article in THE NORTH AMERICAN REVIEW on 'Jews in the Union Army,' to which you call my attention, I would say that I consider it both absurd and unjust, as I have in mind the names of many Jewish offi-cers who served in the late war with distinction and repeatedly received 'honorable mention' for bravery in the discharge of duty. To be more particular, I find by the most cursory reference to the 'Townsend Library of National, State, and Indi-vidual Records,' the following names of those who have done credit to their coun-try and their race : General F. Knefler, General Blumenberg, Major Alfred Morde-cai, Lieutenant-Colonel Neuman, David Ezekiel, Elias Leon, David M. Cohen, Edward D. Taussig, Captain Michaelis, J. S. Emanuel, Henry B. Nunes, Henry B. Nunes, Jr., J. R. Nunes, Emanuel Phillips, Jonas Barnett, Capt. J. P. Levy, Albert A. Michaelson, Levi M. Harby, Mark E. Cohen, Israel Moses, Isaac Moses, Mordecai Myers, and Colonel Asch. These instances recorded, and a host of gallant soldiers and sailors of Jewish extraction who have shed lustre on their race, will suffice to awaken a higher regard for their talents in a field hitherto unexplored. You are at liberty to examine my work at any time, and thus further substantiate my state-ments and demonstrate the injurious character of those in the article referred to. Very truly yours,

"THOMAS S. TOWNSEND."

Availing myself of this kind invitation, I found, upon reference to Mr. Townsend's work, the names of a large number of Jewish soldiers recorded in the "Roll of Honor" for specially distinguished and meritorious services ; among whom• are Lehman Israels, Sergeant Jacobson, Captain Asche, Samuel Benjamin, Colonel Hayman, Jacob Fry, Joseph S. Abraham, Nathan S. Benjamin, Isaac H. Dann, and Charles Abrams.

Simon Wolf, of Washington, D. C., without any attempt at elaboration, collates the names of eighty officers (some holding the high rank of general), the majority of whom distinguished themselves by the most reckless daring and zeal. Mr. Wolf states, and I am prepared to justify his claim, that the proportion of those of the Jewish religion who fought in the army is as large as that of any other faith.

Considering that the number of Jews could not have been greater than 140,000, and that at least 6,000 fought in the Union army alone, the percent-age is truly striking.

I will concede that Generals Lyons and Rosecrans were not Jews. This admission on my part is important, for it constitutes the only point in which I subscribe to the truth of Mr. Rogers's statements. Un-worthy of notice is his insinuation that wherever the Jews stood "shoulder to shoulder" with their fellow-citizens they were "promptly ordered out for speculating in cotton, and conveying information to the Confederates." Not-withstanding the fact that a number of soldiers were charged with the offence of "speculating in cotton" and that not a few Christians met with punishment, he deems the Jews alone, of all people, entitled to blame. It is no secret that General Grant repeatedly declared that his famous order No. 11, expelling the Jews from Paducah, Kentucky, was the result of carelessness; had he thoroughly investigated affairs before sending out this order, his action would have been different, and he never ceased to regret that he issued it. It was promptly revoked, and *The Times* of January 18, 1863, says : "Its immediate and peremptory abrogation saved the government from a blot and redeemed us from disgrace." Will it surprise Mr. Rogers to learn that a resolution censuring General Grant for his order expelling the Jews was the subject of much debate in the Senate, and that the fear that General Grant's influence with his soldiers might thereby be lessened saved him from the humiliation of censure ?

The issuing of General Sherman's order, similar to that of Grant, was confessedly prompted by a misunderstanding of the true status of affairs. Readily believing all that was told him, he issued the order, but its injustice he conceded, and he endeavored to make reparation by confessing that he was mistaken and deceived.

While Mr. Rogers deserves to feel mortified and humiliated, I cannot allow my interest in the subject to interfere with the lesson I hope he will derive from my exposure of his weak, silly, and contemptible statements, which he seems prompted to make with a view to casting odium upon my race; and I hope I have taught him not to make rash statements that he cannot substantiate. In conclusion, I think I have succeeded in disabusing the mind of the reader of any injurious impression that may have been created by the statement of the author of the article to which I reply.

STEPHEN S. WISE.

RAILROAD CONSOLIDATION.

It DOES not require any argument to demonstrate that consolidation, up to a certain point, in all business transactions, must be advantageous to the interests directly involved. Whether such consolidation will result in advantages to other interests, or to the general public, will depend largely upon circumstances. That large transactions, large purchases, the percentage of decrease in cost, not only in the original purchases, but in freight, insurances, and every other item which goes to make up the increase in the capital involved, and the resultant dividends, possess great advantages over smaller transactions, goes without saying. This is a matter of every-day demonstration. It goes to show that where great interests are consolidated in the hands of one man, with power to control them with the will of an autocrat, the object of those interests will be better attained than when those powers are distributed amongst half a dozen different persons. These latter are apt to become, on the slightest clashing of interests, such a "balky team" in commercial matters as General Grant once alluded to in military affairs. No reasonable man will attempt to deny that one railroad corporation operating a single road between Albany and Buffalo has immense advantages, and can transport passengers and freight better, more promptly, and more cheaply between those two points than half a dozen different companies could. But, in the absence of competition, does it follow that it will do it?

When the first Pacific railroad was in course of construction, and everybody in the country was wondering if it was going to be a success, hoping it would be, and almost holding his breath least the obstacles to be overcome should prove too formidable and the work suddenly cease, I remember having my indignation considerably excited by hearing a gentleman from "the States" exclaim: "What a terrible monopoly it will be !" Does any one to-day doubt what a monopoly it would have been but for the construction of other roads? Now, if all the Pacific roads were consolidated under one head, the monopoly would be worse than ever. The question, therefore, naturally arises whether consolidation may not be carried too far, and too many miles of road be placed under one head, just as too many soldiers may sometimes be placed un'er one general whose capacity for command is limited. This state of affairs was exemplified more than once during the Civil War.

All observing men will acknowledge that to properly manage a large railroad demands the very highest talent, and people who think of railroad presidents, superintendents, and managers only as personages who draw immense salaries, ride in sumptuous special cars, and live, when at home, in palatial residences, know little of what hard-worked people they are, and what sleepless nights and days of worry are constantly passing over their heads. Their work can be compared only to that of soldiers in an active field campaign when every faculty is kept on the alert night and day for thirty or forty days at a time. But for the soldier there *must* come rest, and it has been stated that a thirty days' active campaign is almost as much as human nature can stand without completely breaking down. For the railroad officials this rest *never* comes, and is seldom voluntarily enjoyed until by the constant wear and tear, not of thirty days, but of months and years, the man becomes a wreck, and is obliged by his physician to abandon all work or die. The instances of this are far too numerous in this country alone to raise the suspicion that this picture is a fanciful one.

Some one has said that one always writes and speaks in the language of his profession, and the impulse is irresistible to make a comparison between the railroad profession and my own. In both, the very highest talent in the upper grades is required, though, strange to say, in railroading the demand is so imperative that it is very unusual to see such serious blunders as are sometimes made in the military, where the grave exigencies of war can ill afford mistakes. These mistakes in the military are accounted for by the fact that the process of evolution in that service is confined in war to the short period of three or four years, and in our country, unfortunately, the evolution process does not go on in time of peace ; whilst in railroading evolution has gone on ever since railroads were invented, and when one leading light drops out another is ready to take his place. These leading lights command immense salaries, and it is curious to note the contrast between railroading and the military profession in this respect.

In the Civil War, at a time when the very existence of the country hung in the balance, and failure on the part of the military would have made railroad bonds and most other securities as worthless as the paper upon which they were written, the highest military talent commanded less pay than does the president of a second-class railroad, whilst that of the constitutional commander-in-chief of the army and navy was only about one-half of that paid to the presidents of first-class roads !

Consolidation or concentration is as important in railroading as in military operations, but there is no reason why the one should not be as much governed by rule and law as the other. If the banking institutions of the United States are to be governed by fixed laws, there would appear to be no good reason why the intercourse between the States of this Union should not be governed in the same way, not only to protect and secure the public against imposition, but to prevent the clashings liable to arise between the different States.

Proverbially, corporations have no souls, and but too frequently individuals are their victims, and practically have no remedy worth naming. What remedy, for example. has a man who receives a telegraphic despatch stating that his wife or sister lies dead at a morgue, when no such thing is true? when a careless, reckless, or indifferent operator sends an important despatch to Vancouver, *B. C.*, when it ought to have gone to Vancouver, *Washington?* or when a poor, anxious officer of the army, looking eagerly for a despatch, is awakened at midnight with a telegram intended for a church dignitary of *nearly* the same name, conveying the intelligence that a bishop of the church has just died? None whatever that is of any practical value. Why should a despatch be paid for when not delivered, when delivery was easy and practicable? Why should not a ticket issued by a railroad company, and paid for, be good until used, just as a check on a bank is good until the bank pays it? And is there any good reason why these and similar matters should not be regulated by law?

"Why should not a very large number of the people who use these roads invest their money in such an organization and thus become, to a large extent, the owners and controllers of the railroads that they use?" The reason is that a very strong impression exists amongst a large number of the people that the value of railroad stock in this country depends not so much upon the intrinsic value of the railroad as upon the extraneous value given to it in commercial centres like Wall Street. In other words, an outsider always buys "a pig in a poke" and never knows, when he purchases railroad stock, whether he is paying twice as much as it will ever be worth or not. There is not much danger that he will ever pay too little, although those who are behind the curtain frequently do that and make their profits by the manipulations to which the stock is subjected, no matter whether it is really worth much or little. What remedy there may be for this state of affairs it is hard to say, since gambling in stocks seems to be inevitable; but the fact will always prevent the populace from investing in such stocks, as is suggested by Mr. Huntington in THE REVIEW for September last. Outsiders cannot but be timid about placing their money in stocks which are liable to be manipulated in this way: A prominent railroad official gives out in Wall Street that his road is sure, when the time comes, to declare the usual dividend, and in anticipation of this dividend the price of the stock remains steady. Suddenly, however, as the time approaches, it is given out that the railroad has not been doing as well as it ought and it is doubtful if any dividend will be declared this quarter. The usual time for the meeting of the directors comes. There is no meeting, and there is no dividend, and down goes the price of the stock. Then it is discovered that the prominent railroad official was "short" on stock and wanted the price to fall in order that he might make his millions by the change of price !

Were it possible to make railroad stocks as permanent and invariable in price as United States bonds, then we might expect the money of the multitude to flow into railroad securities; but as long as the condition of affairs remains as it is at present, such a direction to the currency of the country need not be expected, and unlimited consolidation would only tend to make matters worse.

It is simply idle to talk of the great transportation companies of this country not overriding the rights of the people—*if they had the chance.* Man is such a tricky animal that, give him the *power,* and the *rights* of other people disappear like mists before the rising sun ; and unfortunately *rights* have a heavy fight to right themselves against *power* when once in possession. This is sure to be the case, no matter in what country "power" gets the upper hand of "rights."

Unlimited consolidation, if good anywhere, is good everywhere. Suppose it were possible to do with the banks what Mr. Huntington proposes to do with the railroads of the country. Can it be doubted that, when an occasion arose, those who wanted to borrow money would be obliged to pay for it just what this consolidated bank demanded ? If it did not demand the highest price the first time, it would be simply because it would be thought bad policy to do so ; but it would only require a threatened war, drought, or famine to run the price of money up to the highest point deemed prudent to ask ; yet few will doubt that such a consolidated bank could be so conducted as to cheapen generally the price of money, and still pay a good dividend to the stockholders. But the same question still comes up, Does it follow that it would be done ?

JOHN GIBBON.

SUNDAY AT THE WORLD'S FAIR.

SOME of our people are already passing resolutions in their convocations and rolling up petitions to Congress asking that the World's Fair in Chicago may be closed on Sundays, and it is important that those holding opposite views should be heard.

To my mind the fair should be open for many reasons. It is the only day that the laboring masses can enjoy it, as they are practically excluded every other day by the necessities of their condition. When the vast army of men who will construct the magnificent buildings and beautify the grounds, who day by day will lift the heavy machinery and foreign exhibits in place, desire to bring their wives and children to the exposition, Sunday will be the only day they will have leisure to do so ; the only day, too, when farm-hands from the country, men and women from the workshops and the factories, clerks from the busy marts of trade, servants from their domestic vocations, can claim a few hours for recreation. When we consider the multitudes that comprise these classes and their immense value in the world of work, we appreciate the importance of their rights and interests in all the arrangements of society, whether for profit or pleasure. So far from the fair being closed on Sunday, it should be the one day especially reserved for the masses, when all those who have other opportunities should not crowd the exposition.

Though the Centennial Exposition in 1876 was closed on Sunday, yet favored statesmen, millionaires, and foreign diplomats visited every department on that day and viewed the exhibits at their leisure. Whether the fair is open or not, the city of Chicago will inevitably be crowded on Sunday. People will come from all parts of the State, to look at each other, at the exposition buildings, the parks, and to enjoy whatever attractions the surroundings afford. If the exposition is closed, they must necessarily crowd less desirable places of amusement; hence if it is the best interests of the people those in authority aim at, they will keep the fair open on Sunday.

It is said that "those who watch the exhibits and serve the public through the week should have one day of rest." As their labors are transient, lasting only a few months, and as their surroundings are varied, beautiful, and entertaining, the tax on their time and patience would be light compared with the dreary monotony of the lives of ordinary laborers who spend year after year in dingy workshops and dark offices, or with multitudes of young men, sitting with bent shoulders, writing by artificial lights, —a class as much to be pitied as those who dig in the mines, scarcely ever seeing the light of day.

Those who can dispose of their time as they see fit can hardly appreciate what a Sunday at the World's Fair would be for large classes of their fellow men. It is difficult to see from what standpoint those women viewed the happiness of their fellow beings, who, in convention assembled, passed resolutions in favor of closing the fair on Sunday.

That noble Quakeress, Lucretia Mott, seeing that the laboring masses were practically excluded from the Centennial Exposition, made her protest against the injustice by never passing within the gates herself. With fifteen added years of experience one would think all American women might have reached a similar standard of justice and common-sense.

. What is the duty of the State in this matter? Clearly, to do whatever conserves the welfare of the majority of the people. The minority have the right to stay away from the exposition on Sunday, but they have no right to throw obstacles in the way of a majority by influencing popular sentiment or securing legislative enactments to prevent them from enjoying that day in whatever way they may see fit, provided they do not infringe on the rights of the minority.

Again, in a financial point of view, the State has no right to cripple a great popular enterprise, wholly beneficial in its results, by any interference. The managers of the exposition, before everything is completed, must expend fabulous sums of money in realizing their ideal of what an exposition should be, and to close the gates the very day the greatest numbers could be there would be hostile to the interests of the managers as well as the happiness of the people. If to close the fair would drive the laboring masses to the churches, there to drop their dimes into the collection-boxes, there might be some reason for ecclesiastical interference. But the majority will not go to the churches, but rather crowd the drinking and gambling saloons, the restaurants, and the dance-houses, and make the city a pandemonium by night. But, after a long, well-spent day mid such fairy scenes as the exposition will present, wandering round the beautiful park or sailing on the lake, the majority would take the evening trains to their respective homes, with pleasant memories of all they had seen—enough to gladden the remaining days of the week.

If we would lift the masses out of their gross pleasures, we must cultivate their tastes for more refined enjoyments. The object of Sunday observance is primarily to give the people a day of rest and recreation, a change from their ordinary employments, a little space of time, in the hard struggle of life, for amusement. Sunday by common consent is the day set aside to use the best influences society possesses, to cultivate the religious emotions, the moral sentiments, to teach the dignity of humanity and the brotherhood of the race. It needs but little reflection to see what a potent influence in all these directions the World's Fair will be. The location is in every way most desirable. A magnificent park, whose shores are washed by an inland sea, vast buildings, that in grandeur and beauty of architecture have never been equalled, filled with the most wonderful productions of all that is new in art and science, from every nation on the globe—what an impressive scene this will be! With multitudes of men and women in happy companionship, now wandering through this museum of wonders, and now down the winding walks of the boundless park, now seated in that beautiful pavilion on the shores of Lake Michigan, watching the rolling waves break at their feet, or in the grand concert-hall listening to interpretations by Theodore Thomas, Seidl, or Damrosch, of the divine melodies of the old masters—where else could such a rare combination of pleasures, mid such surroundings, be so easily provided for the people?

Here, too, in shady nooks gifted orators might speak to the multitudes on popular reforms or religious questions, for there are no meetings more impressive than those held in the open air, and many assemblies might be held in that vast space without interfering with each other.

If, then, the influence of the exposition on the minds of the people, can be alike entertaining and instructive, we may well ask, Why should it be closed on Sunday?

.   ELIZABETH CADY STANTON.

MARCH, 1892.

ISSUES OF THE PRESIDENTIAL CAMPAIGN.

BY SENATOR JAMES MCMILLAN, OF MICHIGAN; REPRESENTATIVE
BENTON MCMILLIN, OF TENNESSEE; SENATOR FRANK HIS-
COCK, OF NEW YORK; REPRESENTATIVE R. P. BLAND, OF
MISSOURI; SENATOR EUGENE HALE, OF MAINE; REPRE-
SENTATIVE W. C. P. BRECKINRIDGE, OF KENTUCKY, AND THE
HON. W. R. MERRIAM, GOVERNOR OF MINNESOTA.

SENATOR JAMES McMILLAN:

IT IS difficult to tell in advance of the opening of a campaign
what its predominant issues will be; and just what phase of
a particular issue the people may take up is especially uncertain.
Yet there are three questions which are now uppermost in the
public mind, and which must continue to enter into every campaign, so long as opinions in regard to them differ widely, or until they shall be finally settled—if they ever can be settled.
These three are the tariff, the finances, and the franchise.

The tariff, like the poor, we have always with us. When the
First Congress embodied the protective principle in the first tariff act, the question of how duties shall be levied was made a continuing one. The United States has made a virtue of what was
at first a political necessity, and by means of a protective tariff
has been able both to diversify its industries, and to keep the
standard of wages comparatively high. But any tariff is of
necessity more or less arbitrary, and so is open to attack. As a

VOL. CLIV.—NO. 424. 17

consequence, while a very great majority of the people believe in a protective tariff, there is more or less diversity as to what articles should bear the duties. In the McKinley law, so-called, the theory of protection has been carried to its logical conclusion. Articles which can be manufactured or produced in this country in sufficient quantities to supply our own needs are brought under the shelter of a protective tariff, leaving competition among our own people to regulate prices. Those articles which from climatic or other reasons cannot be produced in this country in sufficient quantities to regulate the price,—in value equal to a little more than half the imports,—are put on the free list. The Republican party as a party believes this to be the true theory of a tariff. The party will go into the coming campaign prepared to maintain this theory, and will adduce the trade history of the country since the McKinley act went into effect to support its position.

More important, however, than the additional symmetry which the McKinley law is believed to give to the protective tariff, is the provision in that act which establishes the policy of reciprocity. The framers of the McKinley Bill, not being able to see their way clear to incorporate the reciprocity scheme in their measure, the Administration pressed the matter on the attention of the Senate, and Mr. Blaine took an appeal to the country. The response in the press and in public meetings was so quick and so satisfactory as to show the deep interest the people have in measures to extend our trade, where such extensions can be made on the basis of mutual concessions. With not only Mexico and the nations of Central and South America, but also Germany and England, for her dependencies, entering into reciprocal trade relations, new · commercial bonds are being established between nations. By the exchange each nation gains larger markets ; and, inasmuch as it is the surplus of one country that is exchanged for the surplus of the other, the question is not one that affects the protective principle, but simply the revenues. One great difficulty that has existed in discussing the tariff has been the lack of data which both sides could admit as authentic.

The extended inquiry now in progress under the auspices of the Senate Committee on Finance—an investigation that is being conducted in a scientific rather than a partisan spirit, and by experts—promises to supply information that may be relied on in regard to the cost of production, both at home and abroad, of the leading articles on which duties are levied. This information, when obtained, should make it possible nicely to adjust the import duties, so as to compensate for the discrepancy between the cost of labor in this country and its cost in other countries ; and to make this compensation is the true aim of a protective tariff.

The question of finances will be a disturbing one so long as there is anything essentially arbitrary in the additions made to the currency. The maintenance of the free coinage of both gold and silver at some fixed ratio is the only solution which could take the currency question out of politics ; but, unfortunately, the difficulties at present in the way of an effective restoration of silver to its former monetary uses are such as to make the free coinage of that metal by the United States alone, disastrous to the very people who are most ardent for it. Between those who clamor for free coinage and those who are anxious to have gold maintained as the monetary standard of the commercial world, there is a large class of producers who feel deeply the inconveniences of carrying on their business with an amount of money so out of proportion to the volume of credits. It has been the boast of our business world that so small an amount of money was necessary to carry on such an enormous volume of business, but when a commercial shock in Great Britain, like that of the Barings, sends its pulsations through every commercial city in the United States, it is time to consider very carefully some method for getting and keeping larger reserves of money as safeguards against those sudden convulsions which make everything, save money, well-nigh valueless for the time being. This large class of business men— very many of whom are also bankers—are concerned in having a larger supply of money on which to do business, but they see the dangers of free silver-coinage without such help from foreign nations as shall open up again to silver the place which a mistaken financial policy a few years ago closed to it. It is now the study of financiers both in this country and in Europe to maintain larger reserves. To this end business men in this country welcome the regular additions being made to the currency. They prefer to take the risks of a currency contraction which might result by Europe drawing our gold, rather than to put a stop to the expansion of the currency coincident with the natural growth of business. The present law is, of course, a more or less temporary expedient ; but the Republican party will maintain that it is the best possible solution of the financial question for the time being.

The practical defeat of the Lodge Election Bill in the Fifty-first Congress has had the effect of changing the attitude of the members of the Republican party, not in regard to the evils and the menace of the denial of the rights of citizenship to citizens for partisan purposes ; but in regard to the means which shall be taken to solve this very perplexing problem. Evidently, in the public mind, the day has gone by for a resort to stringent laws which, however just in themselves, must depend for their enforcement upon a power outside of and opposed to the prevailing sentiment in the States in which the colored vote is suppressed. Throughout the South there are industrial and educational forces at work to change the condition of the colored people. In time the property-owning, intelligent colored man will assert, obtain, and maintain his rights. The question now is as to whether this better day cannot be hastened by some legislative process in which the Southern States themselves will be glad to acquiesce. To meet this need President Harrison, in his latest message, has proposed a non-partisan commission to devise measures which shall insure free and fair elections.

The people who make up the Republican party are not exercised as to the particular manner in which the freedom of the ballot shall be brought about in the South ; but they do believe that some way can be found by which the present flagrant injustice may be remedied. While the existing condition of affairs at the South gives that section representation in Congress and in the Electoral Colleges out of all proportion to its voting strength, the franchise will not cease to be a national issue.

There are questions connected with pensions, with the use of the gerrymander, with the foreign policy of the Administration, with the building-up of a merchant marine, with the enlargement and improvement of the water-ways, which will play parts in the coming campaign, varying in importance with the events of the next few months, or with the locality. But the old issues of the tariff, the currency, and the franchise are too deeply rooted in the public mind to be thrust aside, even though party leaders may desire to eliminate one or the other of them. On these questions, as well as on the high character and business-like conduct of the present Administration, the Republican party will go confidently into the coming campaign.

JAMES McMILLAN.

HON. BENTON McMILLIN:

THE records' of the two parties have, in a great measure, made the issues of the campaign of 1892. The principles of the Democratic party are as old as the government. They are the defence of the citizen in his personal liberty; the upholding of the Constitution, and the support of the general government and the State governments in all their integrity. During the administration of President Harrison the Republican party has had control of every branch of the Government. Hence, the action of the party thus in full control and unrestrained may be taken as the most recent and, at the same time, most accurate exposition of the party's principles. They have further made that action their platform by indorsing it in their various State conventions and making their contests upon it.

What are the issues thus raised? It is impossible in so brief an article as this must be to discuss all of them; or to discuss any of them so minutely as would be most satisfactory. But public sentiment has taken so steady a course as to indicate that the following will be issues separating the two parties :

1st. Shall there be reckless prodigality, or wise economy in public expenses ?

2d. Shall the people remain free, or be enslaved through "Force Bills," by turning the elections of the legislative branch of the government over to the judicial ?

3d. Shall the people be robbed and commerce be destroyed by the imposition of excessive rates of duty ?

One of the complaints justly made against the Republican party is its reckless expenditure of public moneys. They found when they came into power a surplus of millions. They spent in two years a billion and nine millions of money and left a deficiency threatened, if not actual. The flood gates were lifted by the Fifty-first Congress, and the millions accumulated by unjust and excessive taxation, but husbanded by Democratic economy to extinguish our public debt, were squandered. Stale jobs were revived, and new ones devised, to get rid of the money and make an excuse for still higher taxation. The expenditures during two years of Republican rule can only be comprehended by comparison. They amounted to eight dollars per capita or forty dollars per family each year. The expenditures of that Congress—the Fifty-first—including indefinite and permanent appropriations,—amounted to sixteen dollars for every minute since the Declaration of Independence was signed. The excess of these expenditures of the Fifty-first Congress over the Fiftieth was one hundred and ninety-three millions of dollars, or about seven dollars per annum for every family in the land. The people are coming to regard this as too costly a luxury.

The effort to subvert the Government by passing the "Force Bill" and turning the elections over to the Federal Courts and to the appointees of federal power, was rebuked in the elections of 1890 and will be rebuked again in those of 1892. Appropriations to pay bounties and subsidies were made permanent to prevent their repeal. The taxing power was surrendered by the Congress to the President. The treasury was emptied. The taxes were vastly increased. The tendency of our people to resent wrong and smite the wrong-doer being known, it was determined by those in control of the Republican party to change the election laws so that complaint would be unavailing; to "put," as they boasted, "bayonets behind ballots," and thus control elections through power emanating from Washington. After the people had been robbed through unjust tariff taxation, they were to be enslaved. The "returning board"—that engine by which the will of the majority was thwarted in 1876, and Tilden's inauguration prevented—was to be again invoked. Forty-four returning boards were to be organized. Forty-four live thieves, turned loose from forty-four crosses on a helpless people, would not have been half such a curse. The right of the people through their laws to regulate and conduct their own elections will ever be contended for while we are worthy the elective franchise. This "Force Bill" proposition was defeated. But even yet many advocate it. It was defeated by the stubborn resistance of a solid Democracy, aided by many patriotic men of all parties who were unwilling to see the institutions of one hundred years perish to subserve temporary or mere partisan interests.

The Tariff issue is at the front, and will be the leading issue in the elections of this year. For a quarter of a century the people have struggled to relieve themselves from some portion of the high taxes imposed to carry on the most gigantic civil war of modern times. They had seen remitted the income, legacy, and other taxes which had been placed on the wealth of the country. These alone, if kept to this day, would have paid all the public debt, improved every river and harbor for which estimates have yet been made, and would have left the country out of debt. They had seen the manufacturer's tax repealed without the repeal of the compensating tax placed on manufactured goods. The Tariff Commission of 1883, composed of protectionists, had reported that the people were entitled to a reduction of 20 or 25 per cent., and had recommended it. All the political platforms of all parties had recognized the justness of their demand for relief. Yet the Tariff law of 1883 was an increase on the rates theretofore existing, and the act passed by the last Congress is a still greater increase on the bill of 1883. Verily, the people have "asked for bread and been given a stone."

Let us examine the act passed by the last Congress and see whether it is worthy of permanence. For the first time all disguise was thrown off, and the doctrines of the campaign were put into practical legislation. "The fat fried out" for campaign purposes had to be returned with "thirty, sixty, or an hundred fold." The average rate of duty was increased from about 45 per cent. to nearly, or quite, 60 per cent.; the increases being . greater on the coarser articles required for common use than upon luxuries.

The importer was dealt with as if he were a criminal. They legislated as if commerce were a crime ; as if ballast were the only commendable incoming cargo. The effort was made in earnest to put the "wall of fire around the country." Bounties were provided for to be paid out of the public treasury ; and the experiment entered upon of taxing directly one man to make another's vocation pay. The authors of this measure take to themselves great credit for having placed sugar on the free list. It is true near fifty millions of sugar duties were repealed ; but the same act which did this placed sixty-five millions additional duties on other things. "With one hand they put a penny into the urn of poverty and with the other took a shilling out." They repealed the duty which yielded eight-ninths of its exactions to the treasury and placed additional duties on other necessaries of life, where three-fourths of the increase went into the coffers of manufacturers and only one-fourth into the treasury. And, as before stated, this was not a free-will offering, for it went hand in hand with a measure giving bounties in lieu of the tariff repealed.

There is another feature of this monstrous measure, un-American and dangerous, deserving comment and condemnation. Nothing could be more at war with our institutions than the section of the present tariff law authorizing the President, "in his discretion," to impose a tax of ten cents a pound on tea, three cents a pound on coffee, and two cents a pound on sugar, and a tax on hides. He may impose and remit these taxes at pleasure. He may impose millions of taxes without convening Congress or consulting it if in session. To-day the President of the United States is threatening to impose these taxes, instead of referring the matter to the representatives of the people assembled in Congress. If he does, he will impose no more taxes after March 4, 1893. King George the Third was denounced, defied, and defeated in the Colonies for levying, even through Parliament, less tax on less tea. Did we rebel against the usurpations of George the Third in 1776 only to make an unmanly surrender of high prerogatives to Harrison the second in 1890 ? But it is insisted that by this surrender to one man of the right of the people's representatives to impose the taxes, they may get reciprocity and commercial advantages. Esau's excuse for the base bargain by which he sold his birthright and heritage for a mess of pottage was, that he was hungry. Yet even his spiritless imitators of modern times would hardly praise his accumulation of fat by such folly. They are denied here the pitiful palliation of empty stomachs which the "base Judean" had.

The highest tariff law this country ever knew—higher even than the war tariff—has now been in operation one year and four months. No one can point to a period of greater prostration than has characterized this. Strikes and labor troubles have been the rule, not the exception. Many manufacturing establishments have closed. Others have reduced the wages of the employees, others the time of employment. Much was said in behalf of the laborer when the bill was under consultation. Yet "eye hath not seen nor ear heard" of a laborer who has had his wages increased by the McKinley Bill. Favor to him was a mere pretext and sham. He has been forced to pay more for the clothes that cover his back, and for the roof that covers his head, and in hundreds of instances at the same time to accept a reduction of wages.

The Democ̃ratic party insists, and will insist in the campaign, that this enormous increase in the rate of tariff taxation is not a sufficient response to the people's demand for tariff reduction. They will be found ever battling against the robbery of the many for the enrichment of the few. The battle is on, and Democracy will stand where it has stood—in favor of the rights of the masses as against the exactions of the classes. There will be no shirking, no postponing, no evading this issue. Democracy could not avoid it if it would ; it would not avoid it if it could. Our cause is just, and will triumph.

BENTON McMILLIN.

SENATOR FRANK HISCOCK:

You ask me to "prophesy," for publication in·THE NORTH AMERICAN REVIEW, the issues that will predominate, and divide the two great political parties, in the presidential election of 1892. Leading Democrats can indicate them in detail with far more certainty than I, for the reason which will appear later on.

The representatives of the Republican and Democratic parties will convene in May or June next and adopt their platforms, and it is very easy now to outline the resolutions of each declaring their political faith. The legislation of the Fifty-first Congress fixing the present customs duties will afford the leading issue. The Republican convention will approve that legislation, and the Democratic convention will denounce it in both elaborate and pointed rhetoric ; but, in my judgment, the actual contention upon this great economic question will be made, not by the resolutions of the two conventions, but by the House of Representatives of the Fifty-second Congress. The Democratic party is largely in the majority there. The constituencies of the Demcratic members will expect, the Republican party will have a right to demand, and the country will exact of them, an expression, in the form of a bill agreed upon and passed by them, of the changes which they propose in our present tariff laws. The law-making power of the Democratic party must, therefore, make the issues of the next national election upon this subject.

In 1888 the House of Representatives was Democratic and passed what is known as the Mills Bill. A Republican Senate rejected it and proposed a bill which went to the country long enough before the election in November to be fairly understood by the people. This bill, amended somewhat, but not to the extent of changing its general character, was passed by the Senate at the short session of the Fiftieth Congress. Its provisions were practically those embodied in what is now popularly known as the McKinley Law. The bill which passed the House and that proposed to the Senate by the Finance Committee made the controversy of the presidential contest of 1888, resulting in the election of President Harrison. And again in 1892 will the candidates of the two parties be elected and defeated according as the people shall approve the bill which shall be proposed by the Democratic House of Representatives of the Fifty-second Congress, or the tariff legislation of the Fifty-first Congress.

I suppose I am expected to indicate somewhat more in detail the issues that will be made upon this dominant and all-absorbing question, the tariff, and there arise my difficulty and the occasion for my assertion that Democratic authority would be far more satisfactory than mine.

The revenue legislation of the Fifty-first Congress places sugar substantially upon the free list, resulting in a loss of revenue of nearly fifty-four millions of dollars annually. It provides for bounties to be paid upon domestic sugar requiring nine millions of dollars annually. The sugar legislation involved a loss and expenditure of revenue, therefore, of sixty-three millions of dollars annually.

The legislation also placed upon the free list other articles involving an annual loss of nearly six millions of dollars to our national revenues. No political party will restore sugar or one of those other articles to the dutiable list. With great confidence I express the judgment that the Democratic party will not go to the country in 1892 weighted with an increased duty upon sugar or a duty upon any article now on the free list.

Especially with reference to sugar and those articles is it true that customs duties upon them are a tax upon the consumer. Sugar, the most prominent, will serve to illustrate the entire line. It has become not only an article of luxury, but really of necessity, to our people of all classes, and is consumed in about equal proportions by all. From the fact that the American production is so small in comparison with the entire amount which we use, it cannot materially affect the market value of foreign sugar here; certainly, whatever is added in the way of customs duties to the importations is paid directly by the American consumer. A political party, if it did hesitate to remove the duties, will absolutely refuse to reimpose them. But the bill which the Democratic House proposes must of necessity provide ample revenues for the administration of the various departments of our government. With the loss of revenue which I have indicated, the framers of the tariff law of the future must bear anxiously in mind its effect upon the income of the government. If the present sugar legislation and the present free list are to be retained, the Mills Bill, as it passed the House of Representatives of the Fiftieth Congress, unchanged in other respects, cannot be made the platform of the national Democratic party in 1892, in my opinion, for the reason that it would not provide sufficient money for government use.

Retaining the present free list and legislation upon sugar, as I have already indicated,—it does not occur to me that the House of Representatives of the Fifty-second Congress will disturb it,—we are on the borders of the realm of speculation as to what attempt statesmen and political leaders will make against the present duties upon importations. I again call attention to the fact that the bill must provide sufficient revenue for the government. No political party will propose any other. Our people will not tolerate national bankruptcy. I am not, however, in the counsels of the gentlemen who have the difficult task before them of preparing a bill on the line I have indicated which shall provide sufficient revenue and at the same time reduce the present duties. I frankly admit my inability now to indicate how it might be wisely done either for the good of the country or a party success, even if we eliminate from the consideration of the question the policy of protection for our domestic industries.

Doubtless quite a large majority in the House of Representatives of the Fifty-second Congress favor, or would vote to open our mints for, the free coinage of the silver of the world. Still, I doubt if that question will be made important in the next presidential canvass. The electoral vote of the State of New York will doubtless be required for the election of the Democratic national candidates, and the Democratic majority in the House of Representatives will hardly care to handicap their party in New York by passing a free-coinage bill.   The exigencies of the situation, I believe, will suppress an expression of their political convictions in that form.   The Silver-Purchase Act of the last Congress will doubtless be approved by the Republican and challenged by the Democratic National Convention ; but in the tangible form of a bill passed by the present House of Representatives the free-silver issue will not be presented to the country.

The national Republican party will stand stoutly by the policy and acts of the present administration to promote reciprocal trade with foreign countries under the Aldrich amendment of the Customs Law of 1890.   I doubt if any attempt be made by the present Democratic House to repeal this provision.   The Democratic National Convention will, I apprehend, pass over that question with little more than an unfriendly allusion to it.

FRANK HISCOCK.

HON. R. P. BLAND:

UNDOUBTEDLY the question of tariff reform will be the most absorbing issue in the coming Presidential election.   But it will not be the only question presented.   The issues that grow out of our duplicate form of government, the conflicts arising between the jurisdiction and proper functions of the States and the Federal system, have in the past entered largely into the discussions involved in the Federal politics and will continue to demand attention.   The attempt of the Republican party in the Fifty-first Congress to take from the people of the States the control over the local and Congressional elections, under the plea of superior wisdom and virtue in Congress to secure honest results, called forth a determined opposition on the part of the masses of the people of the States.

The alarm bell had been sounded.   Home rule and local self government were put in jeopardy.   This attempted legislation, and the methods resorted to to accomplish it, did more than all else to send to the Fifty-second Congress an overwhelming majority of Democrats.   It is plain that a vast majority of the intelligent people of this country still adhere to the Jeffersonian idea of our institutions.   No political party can safely attempt to permanently establish the Hamiltonian theory for us.   It is true that during the war the Hamiltonian theories were the rule, and have been since ; but the people are now most emphatically calling a halt on the usurpations and encroachments of the Federal Congress. The laboring and producing classes of the American people thought they saw between the lines of the " Force Bill " an attempt on the part of centralized monopoly and organized selfishness to take from the people of the States the freedom of elections. The people are justly jealous of the powers of Congress. They have good reason to believe that centralization at Washington would attempt to control the ballot in the interests of centralized greed. Thus the issues, presented by Jefferson on the one hand and Hamilton on the other, have again become dominant in our politics. A partial truce has been called. Republican ascendancy means other and further attempts upon the liberties of the masses.

A protective tariff was but a part of the class legislation sought to be sheltered and protected by " Force Bill " ballots. The question of tariff reform has been taken by the Republican party from the domain of revenue. They declare it to be a necessity, independent of any question of revenue. Protection is the great object sought; revenue a mere incident to be considered.

Thus, the tariff as now presented is a war for markets. A certain class of our people clamor at the doors of Congress for a "home market." This class gained a complete victory in the enactment of the McKinley tariff. The tariff baron has secured to himself a monopoly of the American market in which both to sell and to buy. The law that gives him a monopoly of the home market in which to sell his wares also shuts in the farmer and other producers, compelling them also to buy and sell in the home market. The farmer in particular has now been forced into the arena of battle for markets. He is organized, well equipped, and freshly painted for the battle. He finds himself from year to year with an enormous surplus of products on hand, that the home market is wholly unable to consume. The market for him is but a limited market.

The American farmer knows his rights. He is now alert to his interests as never before. Woe be to the political party that opposes him in his material interests ! A flag of truce, or blind, thrown in his path, called reciprocity, will not do. As now outlined by his enemies, reciprocity means freer trade with agricultural countries that compete with him. He demands and will have freer trade with the peoples who will buy most from him and sell most to him. Any other reciprocity is a transparent cheat.

The money question, in the shape of the free coinage of silver, will not down at the bidding of either political party. The people will make it an issue. As to how this question may be met, is disturbing both political organizations. It may find its solution in the way the tariff question was met when Mr. Greeley was nominated for the Presidency by the Democrats; that is, leave it as an issue in the various congressional districts; the executive not to interpose his individual views as against the people as expressed at the ballot box, and crystallized into legislation by their representatives in Congress.

The evident effort on the part of the opponents of free coinage to commit both parties to a hostile attitude as respects silver by forcing a candidate on them who is pledged in advance to play Czar or autocrat in vetoing any bill Congress may send him, ought not to succeed. If the majority of the American people want free coinage of silver, they ought to have it. The question has been the subject of heated discussion for near twenty years; both parties are divided upon it, but neither party should be so manipulated or controlled as to cheat a fair expression upon the subject. Let it be understood that whoever is elected President, he will conform to the wishes of the people's representatives. All parties ought to be satisfied to abide by that determination. This is supposed to be a republican form of government, where the will of the people constitutionally expressed is, or ought to be, the law.

The opponents of free coinage profess not to desire the question agitated. Yet they are cunning enough to demand of both parties a nominee practically pledged in advance to veto any free coinage bill that Congress in its wisdom may send him.

The question of economy always ought to be a burning question for the taxpayer. Yet of late this question is practically submerged in the tariff. If it is true, as the doctrine of protection proclaims, that the foreigner pays the tariff tax, economy will be a lost art. What reason could my constituents have to complain should I vote to increase my salary to ten thousand a year instead of five thousand? Indeed, the argument for protection tells them that the foreigner bears the burden, that the more money I get the more I am likely to spend in employing servants and giving wages to labor, and by luxurious living buy more and spend more, and thus put money in circulation among my constituency. If the foreigner pays the tax, billion-dollar Congresses are billion-dollar benefactors. Judge Holman's economic resolutions are aimed to pauperize our own people and to relieve the foreigner. The more extravagant our appropriations, the more we draw from the foreigner. Inasmuch as a protective tariff is thus admitted to be organized selfishness, it cannot be wondered at that we have now a prodigal government.

Political parties on this theory are no longer accountable to our taxpayers. Congress has undisputed and absolute sway in dealing out favors. Since we have found a way to raise revenue without taxation, it must be expected that Congress will deal out bounties and subsidies, and lavish the money wrung from the foreigner upon political favorites ; like all freebooters, Congress must bountifully provide for the mercenaries and retainers who make up the army of spoils and plunder.

R. P. BLAND.

SENATOR EUGENE HALE :

THE Republican party will furnish the issues for the campaign of 1892. It began doing this for Presidential elections in 1856, and the history of the propositions touching the existence and the prosperity of the nation—which propositions it has victoriously maintained and embedded in the life of the Republic—makes the national record for the last thirty years. It will be no new thing for the party to see its advance contested and its way blocked up by the Democracy.

First, The doctrine of protection, as opposed to free trade in any shape into which the Democratic party may turn it, will have a front place in the contest. The temporary check which the party met in the elections of 1890, largely because the provisions of the McKinley Bill were not understood and their effect had not been demonstrated, no more decided the battle and delivered the victory to the free-traders than Marengo was lost to Napoleon at that stage where Dessaix appeared upon the field. The Republican party will take its chance before the people upon the doctrine of protection as opposed to free trade or what is called revenue reform ; but this doctrine, in 1892, will be enlarged and expanded and popularized by its new ally and handmaiden, reciprocity, which, when protection has built up the product of American labor, furnishes a market abroad for its overplus, without in the least endangering that product by the competition of foreign underpaid labor. The whole scheme of reciprocity, mainly directed to trade with the sister Republics of the American continent, goes hand in hand with protection. The Democrats pervert its meaning, deride its uses, and yet, it is plain to see, are afraid of it.

Governor Hill's convention in New York denounced it as a humbug, and his party associates, North and South, are plainly getting ready to oppose it. In the great battle between free trade and protection the centre of the Republican line will be reciprocity, and, so far from this being a concession of ground to the free traders, it is just the reverse. The two things mean exactly the opposite. Protection and reciprocity mean more manufacturing and more production at home and more sales abroad. Free trade means less manufacture and less production at home and more purchases abroad. Any man who has tried to do business, or any woman who has tried housekeeping, with more going out and less coming in, has easily enough found out which way the road leads.

Second, A sound, stable currency, maintaining gold and silver at par and utilizing both these American metals, under some such proposition as that embodied in the legislation of 1890, will be another issue that the Republican party will present to the American people. The party will have practically close ranks on this issue ; but it requires a seer's foresight to discern what will be the attitude of the Democratic party in national convention on this issue, where the dominating force in numbers, in delegations representing the States which must furnish a large majority of the votes which it can secure in the Electoral College in order to elect a President, is rabidly bent on nothing short of free silver.

Third, I look to see during the coming session of Congress a Republican issue clearly defined covering the restriction of criminal and pauper immigration. Whether the Democratic party will venture to oppose this, as it opposes reciprocity, may not yet be certain ; but the proposition will, I believe, be elaborated and adopted by the Republican party.

Fourth, The year 1892 will be a great centennial year. Sixty-five millions of people in the United States will hail it as the era of Americanism, and all the things which go to make a great, broad, inspiring American policy will be presented to the American people in the platform of the Republican party. The encouragement of American steamship lines by governmental benefactions, which 'have been tried so successfully by great European commercial nations; the rebuilding of the navy as an adjunct and protector of our growing commerce; and a diplomatic policy which makes the United States the centre and perhaps the arbiter of all peoples in this hemisphere—all these will be included in what may be called the American issue to be presented next year by the Republican party.

Going with these, not quite as an issue, but potential in reinforcing the issues, will be the record presented by the Republican party of an Administration which has shown itself patriotic, honest, practical, and able to grapple successfully with the largest questions that interest the American people. The President has shown himself thoroughly equipped for all the duties of his great place. The Secretary of State, so far from turning his department into a rallying place for jingoism, has maintained the honor and dignity of the Republic with calmness and wisdom, and in his encounters with the diplomatists of Europe, who have passed their lives in such controversies, has never come off second best. The heads of the Treasury department have managed the finances of the people with ability and integrity. In all the other departments of the Government the record has been one of unbroken success.

If with these issues the Republican party cannot prevail before the people in 1892, it may as well go out of political business.

EUGENE HALE.

HON. W. C. P. BRECKINRIDGE:

ASSUMING that the Democratic party has not already thrown away the Presidency, upon what issue can it win, and has it the wisdom to select and skill to compel the battle to be made upon it ?

There are fundamental differences between the Republican and Democratic parties, and a Democrat, in the technical sense of the word, will find in every contest ample justification for opposing Republican candidates, no matter what may be the particular declaration of policy announced. But as new questions of practical importance constantly arise, each canvass assumes a peculiar aspect, and in each Presidential contest there must be some leading issue or issues, and to select wisely and skilfully the issue to be made pre-eminent in a particular canvass is becoming more important because of the increase of those troublesome voters upon whom party ties sit lightly, but who reserve to themselves the privilege to vote as they please. And it is not exaggerating the importance of this increasing class of voters to say that they have much to do with the formation of issues in a given canvass. They hold the balance of power.

This is peculiarly true as to the Democratic party. To elect its candidates it must secure the electoral vote of the sixteen so-called Southern States, whose solidity has been compacted by the effort of a Republican Congress to pass a force bill, and, in addition, the votes of New York, Indiana, Connecticut, and New Jersey, for even the Michigan law renders our success too uncertain for us not to depend upon those four Northern States. We have in the last three years carried Iowa three times, Massachusetts, as to the Governor, twice, Wisconsin once, and have the delegation in Congress from Rhode Island and New Hampshire. It is true that in these States we have been aided by local influences. The engaging personality and popularity of Governor Russell, and the power of the group of young men around him, may account for the triumphs in that State. The skilful leadership of Governor Boies and the dissatisfaction at the stringent provisions of the prohibition legislation have won in Iowa. In Wisconsin local questions touching the right of parents over the education of their children aided there. In Illinois, the power and character of General Palmer were, no doubt, of great avail. But these peculiar local causes alone cannot account for the overwhelming victory of 1890, and for the maintenance of our ground in 1891. There must be some underlying reason, some general tendency caused by some question of interest alike to every section and held to be important by the people of all the States, that has enabled us to win these victories. It is clear that that is the reduction of taxation and a revision by Congress of the tariff laws. None of the States mentioned can be claimed to be surely

Democratic. They have simply indicated their willingness to become Democratic upon certain conditions.

It may be assumed that we cannot elect a President on the issue of free coinage ; that we cannot carry any one of those States on that issue, and that we endanger our success in New York, New Jersey and Connecticut. Economy in public expenditure is important, but it is scarcely possible to make it a national issue, and it must always remain an auxiliary rather than a preëminent issue.

In the approaching canvass, therefore, the main issue between the parties will be the question of taxation, and the success of the Democratic party may depend upon the earnestness and aggressiveness it shows in the present House on that question. We cannot win upon the do-nothing policy, for if the country gets it into its mind that our party in Congress is on dress parade, that its fight on the tariff is simply a sham battle that marks the evolution of an army in time of peace, and that we are firing blank cartridges, the Presidency is lost before the canvass begins. And if the Republicans are skillful enough to take advantage of our division on the money question to force that issue to the front, we may find it impossible to regain the confidence which we may thus lose.

As " the cruel war " with Chili is over, the Republican party will be compelled to make its fight upon some economic question. It may not be able or, indeed, anxious to avoid the issue upon which it claims to have won in 1888. Particularly will it be its policy to press the advantage if the Democratic party attempts to evade this. If no real, earnest and aggressive attack is made upon the McKinley Bill in the present House, the Republicans will put us on the defensive, and it will not be a contest between opposing principles, but a mere fight over details. It will be claimed that the Democratic party will not force the repeal of the McKinley Bill, and, in lieu of it, the enactment of a Democratic tariff bill carrying out the views of those who led the party on that issue from 1884 to 1891, and that all the country has to pass upon is whether certain details of that bill shall be changed, at the risk of disturbing the industries of the country and keeping in uncertainty its commercial interests. So that while the main issue in the approaching canvass will be the tariff, the particular form in which it will be presented will depend upon the action of the present House, and largely upon the past history and present views of the candidates selected by the Democratic party; and somewhat upon the platform adopted by our convention.

It would be well if the leaders of both parties, especially those who control the machinery by which delegates are elected and conventions constituted, could realize that the people understand this question : that they are in earnest about it, and that they cannot be fooled by careful but ambiguous declarations in platforms, or speeches in obscure oratorical and oracular phrases.

For two months the country has been in a condition of expectancy; thousands of independent voters in a state of uncertainty. This will not continue long, and that party will win which soonest impresses upon the country that it is sincere and will follow its convictions to their logical results.

We lost New York in 1880 and in 1888, and we have lost Indiana so often, and under such circumstances, as to make the party extremely anxious when her vote is necessary to success. It is, therefore, never certain that we can carry these two States. It dwarfs the party, and limits its choice, to depend upon these States for success. It is of importance to so frame the issue as to give hope for carrying enough electoral votes to render the Demcratic party hereafter more independent.

A sweeping victory this fall would give us the Presidency and both Houses of Congress for the first time since the war. This is the only year in which this has been possible, and if we do not accomplish this now it will scarcely be possible to win the Senate two years from now. This condition creates two distinct influences: One, to cause all Democrats to be more anxious to frame the issues so as to give hope of such a victory; the other, to cause each Democrat to be more tolerant of conduct in those who control the machinery of the party than he otherwise might be. In other words, the stakes are so high that men who would otherwise make open breach for conduct of which they disapprove hesitate even so much as to criticise this conduct.

But it is well to remember that this does not control those independent voters, who care but little as to the party which holds power and nothing as to the persons which fill offices, but much as to the success of views which they hold to be superior to party affiliations.

The administration of Mr. Cleveland put an end for all time

to any serious discussion of the sectional questions, or of the capacity of the Democratic party to govern ; not that it has put an end to the danger of force bills, to perpetuate the Republican party in power, but to the discussion on the stump or around the firesides of the olden charges that the Democratic party was the friend of treason, that the South could not be trusted, and that the Democratic party was incapable of governing. This canvass, therefore, if it does not degenerate into a mere scramble for office, where the contest is between the two machines, will be one of great earnestness, and based on sincere differences of opinion, and mostly, if not altogether, upon the entire revision of the present system of taxation, and the substitution for the McKinley Bill of a bill which will be satisfactory to those who believe in the principles laid down in the celebrated message of Mr. Cleveland, and in the teachings of those who are peculiarly known as the tariff reformers.

W. C. P. BRECKINRIDGE.

GOV. WM. R. MERRIAM:

As THE time draws nigh for holding conventions by the two great political parties of the country, the question of the political issues that are likely to arise becomes a very prominent one. It would seem at this distance as though the Republican party must stand by the two important questions now under consideration, and already assumed in the past, as party principles I refer to the question of free coinage, and of the policy of protection. I name them in this order, as I look upon the financial question as the more important issue at stake for the next campaign.

The Republican party in the past has always stood firmly and unitedly against the issuance of fiat money in any form, or of governmental assumption of a currency that was not based upon a coin redemption. It has firmly set its face against the issuance of any dollar that was not the equal of any other dollar. In other words, it has been uniformly in favor of honest money. It has determined to oppose the free coinage of silver, unless the nations of the earth agree upon some basis upon which the two metals can flow side by side. It can not, in my opinion, at this time afford to change its position upon this important question. Let it be understood that its policy will be persistently and continuously opposed to the coinage of silver whenever that metal is not at a parity with gold. It is a very grave question in the minds of many Republicans whether the present law is not practically, in effect, a leaning towards the free coining of silver, and many object to it on this ground. Whether it will be policy to attempt to change this law at present, is a matter for consideration. There will come a time, certainly, when this enormous mass of silver will have to be gotten rid of, and to offer it for sale in large sums for purposes of redemption will result in great loss to the Government.

It is undoubtedly a fact that, as the question of free coinage is agitated and considered by the people and the practical results that would arise from it understood, there is a constant tendency towards defeating any measure that would look to the unlimited coinage of the white metal. The Democratic party seems to be fairly committed to the policy of free coinage. During the last' session of Congress it passed a bill in the House, and the Democratic Senators, with one or two from the other side, voted for that measure in the Senate. It was made an issue in the Ohio campaign last fall, the Democrats declaring in their platform for an unlimited coinage of silver. The Governor of New York in his recent speech at Elmira practically means that he proposes to stand upon the platform of free coinage. Some of the great lights of the Democratic party have seen fit to declare their opposition to any measure of this kind, but a large number of the leaders, including some of the most influential, stand squarely upon a policy committed to the unlimited coinage of all the silver in the United States and elsewhere, if presented at the mints. So that, while there are conservative members of the Democratic party who would like to make this issue a secondary one, and some who are anxious to evade it, the majority, who do want free coinage, come out and state their position. It is evident that the Democratic leaders, as a whole, believe in the wisdom of attempting to place a silver plank in their next platform and the committing of their party to the so-called free-coinage policy, and the campaign will be, no doubt, largely fought out on this line : a campaign of financial questions that will be of real benefit to the country.

It is not unlikely, in addition, that the Democratic party will feel the desirability of fusing with the Alliance organization as far as it may do so with hope of success. Should this policy be adopted, with that decision will come the consideration of the so-called sub-treasury scheme. The Democrats may feel it to their interest, in order to control the Alliance vote, to subscribe to the idea of having the general government loan unlimited amounts of money to any one who can present security within certain prescribed limits.

The time is drawing nigh for the Republicans to stand on a platform for honest money—in favor, however, of utilizing silver whenever all the great nations of the earth agree upon some basis of issuance as between gold and silver, whereby they may be kept side by side in value ; but steadily against the free coinage of the cheaper metal which must result very soon in driving the gold coin out of this country and shrinking our circulation over six hundred million dollars. I am fully convinced that the Republican party can go before the country and safely present its side of the money question, trusting that the good sense of the people will guide them right in the solution of this problem.

The other issue that will be most prominent will, of course, be the question of protection. The great leaders of the Democratic party—those, at least, who stand highest in its councils—have practically determined to make the next contest upon the question of free trade, pure and simple. Mr. Cleveland and Mr. Mills—both eminent leaders—have outlined this as the party's policy. They would like to call it tariff reform, but, if we can understand Mr. Mills upon this question, there can be no doubt as to a declaration on the part of the Democratic party, as a principle, for a tariff upon such articles as are not produced in this country. This is about as near a free-trade standpoint as he could well hold, and if he represents a majority of his party, as it is fair to presume he does, free trade will be a plank of the Democratic platform in 1892. The question of the desirability of taking such strong ground is a matter for the Democrats to settle for themselves. It seems to me that for them at this time to take secondary ground in connection with the so-called tariff-reform movement, would be to lose what they have gained in the past.

Governor Russell, in a recent article, ascribes the victory this fall to the feeling on the part of many citizens of Massachusetts of the necessity of tariff reform, and he indicates that any departure from this principle must result in ultimate loss to the Democratic party. Should there be any temporizing by the present Congress with the question of tariff reform, or any desire to simply secure a little political capital by making a few changes in the rate of duty upon particular articles, it will be understood by the country as meaning that the Democrats desire to evade any real issue in the next campaign on the question of taxation, and do not dare stand by the policy set forth by Mr. Cleveland and other Democratic leaders.

The Republicans must adhere firmly to their policy of protection of home industries. They must stand squarely upon this plank of their platform. The party cannot afford to stultify itself and evade this issue. It has too often proclaimed as one of its cardinal tenets the policy of protection, and it must adhere to that idea. While it is generally understood that any tariff law will not be absolutely satisfactory to all parts of a country like ours, many of the Republicans have felt in the past, that on some of the items included in the McKinley Bill the rate of tariff is excessive, and there was a feeling among many Republicans, and is to-day, that certain schedules should be revised ; but these are simply individual opinions, and as a whole the Republicans feel the necessity of adhering to the principle of protection as exemplified by the provisions of the law.

It is well to have it understood that the people desire a revision of the tariff upon the lines of a reduction of taxation as the changes of conditions and the needs of the country will permit. There will be in the future, whenever the time is ripe for such a change, an adjustment of the rates to the point of compensation for the difference in wages between the labor of Europe and America. In levying taxes necessary to cover the expenses of the Government, it is well to collect as far as possible through the medium of indirect taxation and protection to our own labor. This seems to have been the idea of Garfield and Arthur and other Republican leaders in the past, and is the idea of Republicans of to-day. The Republicans must take and maintain strong and decided ground upon the question of protection to American labor.

William R. Merriam.

'DO WE LIVE TOO FAST?

BY CYRUS EDSON, M. D., CHIEF INSPECTOR OF THE NEW
YORK BOARD OF HEALTH.

WHICH one among us, as he looks abroad at the country he is
so proud of ; as he reads the history of the short national life ; as
he marks the deeds of Americans that have made its pages stand
out in the records of mankind ; as he thinks of the heroes and
patriots who have led and governed this people ; as he remembers
the furnace of civil war in whose glowing depths the manhood,—
aye, and the womanhood, too, of the nation were tried ; as he
ponders over the growth, the strength, the intelligence, the
wealth, the genius, the power of the United States,—which one
among us does not feel an added heart-beat of pride and exulta-
tation as he realizes that he is an American ?

It is trite to say the power of a nation is but the aggregate of
the powers of its individual citizens, yet it is none the less profoundly true. It is a physical law that the union of diverse stocks
will produce the strongest progeny. Under this law we should
have the strongest blood on earth, for no nation is composed of
so many and so diverse strains. In our government, which is but
the will of the people, we have absolutely no restraint on our
development. It is for us to will and then to do ; there is nothing we need fear, nothing that will be a bar to our advancement.
In material wealth we have one of the richest countries in the
world ; our resources have not yet seen ten per cent of their possible development. In geographical position we are absolutely
independent ; we are not cursed by neighbors whom we must
dread. We are as safe from attack as it is possible for a nation
to be. We have in our climate the very best range of the
temperate zone, and we have every reason to be healthy.
Individually the race of life is equally open to all ; its prizes,
honors, emoluments are for the man who can take them. Under

such circumstances, physical, social, and moral, we should produce the most effective race the world has ever seen. The question is, and it is a question of the most vital importance to one and all of us who love this land of ours,—are we producing that race ?

The distinguishing characteristic of the American of to-day is his practicality. He demands as a result of his labor a tangible reward, and for the most part he seeks it in material prosperity ; and the American pursues the Almighty Dollar with an energy, a zeal, a persistence, that is amazing. But he can sacrifice it as a duty or from sentiment. The civil war proved what Americans would do for their country; the pension lists speak loudly as to their gratitude ; the vast sums which have been raised for the unfortunate answer for their charity ; the billions of money spent for education show their sense of duty. In the main, though, the American strives for wealth as the great reward in life.

But the free competition and the social environment that make it possible have between them driven the pace up to a fearful speed. The American works harder than does any other man or woman on earth. His business is always with him, he has no rest, no cessation, no relief from the strain. Were he to reduce the effort, his competitors would pass him at once. This and the fact that the rewards are so rich, so sure, so quickly won, stimulate him to his greatest effort all the time. He has been aptly likened to a steam engine running constantly under a forced draught. His daily routine is one of intense and ever-present excitement. He must have a stimulus even in his recreations. The most exciting books, dramas whose gorgeousness of setting and sensational character of plot rival the dreams of Eastern tellers of tales, athletic games that demand the utmost effort, horses whose speed is that of railroad trains, yachts that fly over the surface of the sea,—these and a thousand other things, all intense, all startling, all sensational, are the occupation of his leisure hours.

What is the outcome ? To supply his rapidly exhausted system he is compelled to consume large quantities of rich food and to stimulate himself with alcoholic beverages. One of three results almost inevitably follows:

First, He becomes an inebriate and is destroyed by the alcoholic poison he consumes.

Second, Escaping the pitfall of acquired drunkenness, he rapidly impairs his digestive organs by his abuse of food, and in consequence of this his stomach and intestines no longer properly perform their functions. His system does not receive its proper nourishment and he soon literally burns out.

Third, He starts on his career with a robust digestion not easily deranged. The over-indulgence of his appetite crowds upon the excretory apparatus an amount of work that sooner or later embarrasses and disorders it. Matter that should be cast out is retained in the body and forms unwholesome tissue. Fat is accumulated. The muscular system undergoes what is termed "fatty degeneration." The heart may become affected. The kidneys may become diseased, or the overworked digestive system refuses to perform its functions. Now, the digestive organs are controlled by a very important system of nerves, and the nervous balance (if I may be allowed this term) of these is disarranged. This gives rise to all kind of nervous phenomena,— insomnia, neuralgia, and hysterical symptoms. The name "nervous exhaustion," or "neurasthenia," has been coined to describe the condition into which this overworked, overstimulated man gets.

The American has little time to attend to bodily ailments. If some urgent symptom or an acute attack of disease compels him to consult a physician, the latter is required to "patch him up" as soon as possible. Thus urged, the doctor treats his symptoms instead of the disease, symptoms which in the main are only danger signals set by nature to warn the patient of the deeper-seated, more insidious malady that threatens his well-being. The American physician differs in no respect from the rest of his countrymen. His aim is to produce direct and immediate results, to cut away the shackles that incapacitate his patient for the race. His patients are accustomed to expect much of him, and he does much—not infrequently too much. He is the most accomplished repairer in the world. He can tinker up a worn-out system and keep it running long after it should have been laid away for a thorough rest and a re-creation.

The specific ailments of American women not only manifest themselves locally, but they intensify these affections of the nervous system, and make more serious the train of nervous symptoms caused by the digestive disorders already described. For this American life of ours is far more wearing on women than on men. They take less exercise ; they have, as a rule, more nervous organization ; they are intensely affected by the strain. Two, or at the most three, children born, and the mother is a physical wreck, a curse to herself and a trial to those around her.   She ages soon, far sooner than she should—a chronic invalid, she drags her weary days along.   Oh, the pity of it ! Yet the physician is almost powerless, he can but look on and grieve.

The children of these nervous parents inherit their weaknesses and are even more nervous than their progenitors, but their abilities are more keenly practical and their ambitions are higher. They are precocious and burn with a brighter fire that soon consumes them.   Not infrequently, however, when the parents have been utterly "burnt out" before the little ones were born, the offspring are dull and stupid, or develop insane or criminal tendencies.   The children of remarkably brilliant men are rarely noted for their abilities.   That strength and virile power to which the children had the most sacred of claims, they have been robbed of by the rush, the struggle of our American life.

Not only does the American carry on his work under the spurs of food and climate, for this rich nitrogenous food of which he eats is a stimulant for a time ; he has in the modern magazines and newspapers a mental spur constantly applied, the effect of which it would be impossible to overrate.   For,—think of it a moment—every morning and every evening the sheets,—four pages, eight pages, sixteen pages—damp from the flying presses,—come to him filled with new thoughts, new events, new matter for the mind to dwell on.   The experience of the world during the day is gathered that he may think.   Facts ranging in importance from a block on the Elevated to the death of thousands of people by famine are there for him to read.   New mercantile enterprises, many affecting his business, his profits, his very place in life, and his ability to support those who are dependent on him, give him subject for anxious thought.

The strain of all this, the stimulation of the mind which comes from it, would be something wonderful to us were we not so accustomed to it.   The news alone is enough even if it be not personal.   It devours a large part of our nervous force ;—it is a fact that a portion of the strength we derive from our breakfast is expended while reading the morning paper.   It is necessary in many cases to give the brain rest, to deprive it of the stimulant our modern life over-doses it with. "To my mind," said Dr. George F. Shrady to me once, "one of the chief benefits a patient may derive from a trip to Europe is to be found in the fact that there are no newspapers published on ocean steamers."

I find it somewhat difficult to convey to my readers the importance which the stimulation of the brain by newspapers assumes in my mind. I can, however, illustrate it by quoting what a patient of mine said to me once. She was suffering from a form of disease too common among American women. She had been telling me of the work her grandmother, who was the wife of a New England farmer, had been accustomed to all her life, and I said, jokingly, "It's a pity you have not got your grandmother's strength. One per cent. of such work would lay you up for a month." She looked at me for a moment and then said, "Do you realize that my grandmother never read anything except her Bible and hymn book?" The question suggested an idea to me that was new and I asked her what she meant. "Why," she said, "If I find in the paper in the morning some horrible story of a crime or disaster, it interests me very much. I am sorry for the sufferers. I seem to feel their pain in some way. Well, after such a story I have less strength for several hours. I find I must lie down and rest before I can begin my work for the day. It actually tires me out exactly as a shopping trip will tire me."

With the body nourished by rich food, the whole being stimulated by the climate, and the brain spurred on by the news of the world, let us see what this man, so nourished, stimulated, and driven, has done in his pursuit of material good. The following table shows the wealth of the United States and the wealth per capita on the dates given :

Date.	Aggregate wealth.	Per capita.
1850	$7,135,780,228	$308
1860	16,159,616,068	511
1870	30,068,518,507	780
1880	43,642,000,000	870

In thirty years' time, less than half the Biblical allowance of man's life, the United States has multiplied its wealth six times, and has nearly trebled that per capita. What energy, what work, what unceasing effort has been needed to bring about this marvellous result !

What can we do to retard this development of the brain and nerves at the expense of the body? Obviously it is impossible to change our surroundings, to change our food, to lessen the drive of our modern life, to relieve the strain on the mind, to make the competition less fierce. It is apparent, then, that as we cannot lessen the strain, we must increase the ability to undergo it. We must, as a people, learn to understand this : that while we drive the brain we must build the body. The methods of doing this are so simple that they are apt to be overlooked ; they may be summed up in two words,—exercise and fresh air. We must teach our children to exercise until it becomes a habit, a second nature, a something that when omitted causes real physical distress, and we must choose a form of exercise which is adapted to persons of middle age as well as to children.

The form of exercises which I should recommend is one of three, the dumb bells, Indian clubs, or the chest weights. Of the three the last is the best, because every muscle of the body can be worked with them. They should be a part of the furniture of every house, and the children should be given half an hour at them morning and evening. These children should be taught, too, to use them properly ; to exercise the muscles of the arms, thighs, abdomen and legs in turn. Out-door sports and recreative pursuits should be judiciously encouraged. One month, at least, in every twelve, should be spent in rest. Sundays and other holidays should be observed as days of rest and recreation.

Fresh air and exercise are of even greater importance for the girls than for the boys, if such a thing be possible. The girls will find their reward for the work when they become young ladies in society, in the bright eyes, clear complexions, stately carriage, graceful walk and perfect health which they will enjoy. More than that, when the time comes in their lives that they need all their strength they will find they have a reserve which will not fail them, and their children will be healthy and strong.

Build up the body, build up the body ! In our modern life, this should be dinned into the ears of all until it is obeyed, for, verily, unless we build up the body, the strain on the brain will ruin the American people. The very elements in ourselves that have made us great, the push, the drive, the industry, the mental keenness, the ability and the willingness to labor,—these contain in them the seeds of national death. No race may endure that has not the stamina and power of the healthy animal. The American race has run too much to brain.

CYRUS EDSON.

THE ANTI-SLAVERY CONFERENCE.

BY HIS EXCELLENCY, THE BELGIAN MINISTER AT WASHINGTON,
ALFRED LE GHAIT.

Now that the recent ratification of the act of Brussels by the United States has happily become an accomplished and definite fact, I feel at liberty to give the readers of The North American Review the requested general information regarding the character and purpose of this great work.

The suppression of slavery and of the slave trade carried on in the vast and unexplored territories of Africa has been a subject of solicitude for the civilized world for many years, especially since the generous action on the part of the American hemisphere. Numerous efforts were made to extirpate the scourge, but, unfortunately, in spite of all the treaties and conventions they were, necessarily, too individual and limited in their sphere of action to hope for efficient results.

When the Berlin Conference, in 1885, had put the African organization on an international basis and consecrated the work, initiated, since 1876, by the King of Belgium, by placing him at the head of an independent State in Africa, the dark veil covering this continent was to be torn ; the benefits of civilization were to penetrate it ; a free commerce of all the nations was to be inaugurated ; but, before all, the *slave-trade*, with all its horrors, was to disappear.

When dawn approached on the social condition of this country, when the missionaries, the explorers, the first traders, returned to present to us the thrilling picture of thousands of victims succumbing almost daily to this outrageous hunt for man, a universal cry of terror rang through the civilized world ; the heart of every Christian, of every free man, swelled with pity, and a charitable and humanity crusade was preached everywhere. A moral obligation prevailed, in both the Old and New World, to hasten to the aid of a victimized race, to stretch out a fraternal hand to these human victims ! It was felt that, before thinking of our material interests in those countries recently opened to cupidity, we must free them from the oppressing infamous yoke. Morality demanded this ; prudence advised it, to assure universal commercial security.

The touching and persevering eloquence of Cardinal Lavigerie had moved the world for several years. The philanthropic and religious societies solicited the support of their generous efforts.

King Leopold—always at the head of movements of civilization—believed, in 1889, that the time had arrived for codifying and putting into practice the sentiment that touched every heart. He convoked, in accord with England, an international conference at Brussels for the purpose of establishing a common understanding among the powers, whose isolated efforts, or aspirations, had been powerless to efficiently prevent the horrors of the slave trade in Africa.

The enterprise was noble and generous, but gigantic and beset with great difficulties. There was a general accord as to the usefulness and necessity of the great aim, but a thousand obstacles obstructed the path.

England had outlawed the slave trade in 1807, and never ceased promoting its total abolition.

But it required nearly a century to convince the powers of the necessity of accord and of subordinating, in this matter, all other considerations to that of the welfare of an entire race. More than a hundred treaties were concluded for this purpose among the European, American and Asiatic powers. But what opposition had to be overcome, what interests to be conciliated, to obtain any action ! The Congress of Vienna (1815) and of Verona (1822), the treaty of the Five Allied Powers (1841), with long negotiations concerning the right of search ; the English treaties with the Sultan of Zanzibar (1873), with Egypt (1877), with the Ottoman Empire (1880), and, finally, the General Act of Berlin (1884–5), mark the stages of this great diplomatic work pursued concomitant with enfranchisement, the most memorable epochs of which are the years 1833 in England, 1848 in France, 1865 in the United States, and 1887 in Brazil.

The mandate of the Conference revealed in many respects a unique character, owing to the wide scope of its object, the age and diversity of acts and habits to be revised, the number of the powers interested, and, finally, the purpose in view. The legislation demanded in this Conference was not to be restricted to a single country, nor even to a group of States, but to the greater part of an immense continent, to a territory equivalent to twice the surface of Europe, increased by a large maritime zone in the Indian Ocean. It was to assist, in this vast area, a population of more than 125,000,000 of people subject to barbarities during hundreds of years.

The Conference was enabled to meet at Brussels on the 18th of November, 1889, in spite of political, economic, moral, and religious preoccupations manifested beforehand. Seventeen Powers were represented there, viz. : Germany, Austro-Hungary, Belgium, Denmark, Spain, the Independent Congo State, the United States of America, France, Great Britain, Italy, the Netherlands, Persia, Portugal, Russia, Sweden and Norway, Turkey and Zanzibar.

The Conference had been able to assemble, because it posed before the civilized world on a question of honor to be determined whenever raised, and because, when the Powers had been convoked, it had been agreed upon that all discussion foreign to slavery and slave trade should be excluded from its programme, especially the political or territorial questions. The Powers were not to discuss their possessions or protectorates in Africa, nor to sanction them mutually.

It is of the greatest importance to declare that this Assembly has never departed from this programme during its protracted and intricate discussions, and that the General Act resulting therefrom is exclusively limited to the suppression of the slave trade and the restriction of the use of alcohol. The protocols III., IV. and XI. prove this, and this is the reason why all the Powers —even those possessing nothing in Africa and foreign to the politics of that continent—have been able to take part in the Conference and to ratify its conclusions. They understood, then, that they had not to do anything there—nor did they—but to cooperate in a purely humanitarian work, in the repression of revolting atrocities no longer to be tolerated in regions opening to free commerce.

The labors of the Conference continued from November 18, 1889, to July 2, 1890, but they terminated entirely only in April, 1891, by the complete understanding of all the Powers interested in reference to the means of carrying out their decisions.

The Conference at Brussels closed its work by resuming its decisions in a *General Act* signed by the representatives of all the powers on July 2, 1890. It comprises one hundred articles divided in seven chapters. This General Act is completed by a *Declaration*, signed on the same day, furnishing (as will be seen later) to the powers having possessions in the zone exposed to the slave trade the means of carrying out the engagements entered into by signing the General Act.

The Conference, in elaborating its work, rigorously followed the march of the slave trade for the purpose of repressing it in every one of its features. It directs itself from the beginning, therefore, to the very heart of Africa, to the regions where the negroes are captured ; it will then follow the transports of slaves toward the coasts and on the sea, to regulate there the action of the cruisers.

The Conference determined upon a number of means of action to protect the victims and punish the guilty. Such are the creation of offices of control, of liberation, and publicity ; the regulation of the trade in spirituous liquors and arms ; the creation of financial resources for facilitating the action of the governments on the territory where the traffic is particularly to be suppressed.

I shall not attempt to give here, even in a résumé, the description of all the articles of the General Act of Brussels. Those readers who want to examine them will find the English text in " Report 3,134 " House of Representatives, Fifty-first Congress : " Slave Trade in Africa." *

Chapters I. and II. treat of the suppression of the slave trade in the localities of its origin and of the measures to be taken for the supervision of the roads taken by the caravans.

Chapter III. treats of an intricate point which gave rise to long discussions. It defines the general principles and the procedure for suppressing the slave trade on the sea, to the regulation of which matter forty-two articles are devoted. The right of search exists only for the powers bound by treaties in this respect. If the provisions of the General Act for repression on land and the supervision of the embarkations are fully carried out, this right is destined to lead, in a short time, to a new and universal administration regulating the concession of the flag and the verification

* Peuvent être également consultés avec intérêt les 2 volumes déposés à la Conférence, sur la traite des esclaves en Afrique et les actes internationales y relatifs.
                                                                                A. le Ghait.

of the papers on board. Three principles will henceforward guide the intervention of the squadrons. Their supervision is restricted to a circumscribed zone of the eastern coast of Africa ; it extends only to the vessels of less than 500 tons' capacity ; the right of asylum, finally, is absolute for slaves, at least on board of the men-of-war.

Chapter VI. does not, apparently, apply directly to the purposes of the Conference, but it is nevertheless considered as a means of exercising a great influence on customs, morals, and, consequently, on civilization in general. It is admitted everywhere—and in the United States perhaps more than elsewhere—that the abuse of alcoholic beverages is the worst of destructive agencies.

The aim of the Conference, after having suppressed the odious traffic in slaves, was to bring, by pacific benefits, civilization to these unfortunate people, to elevate, gradually, their moral and intellectual level. The black race should neither be conquered, nor subjugated, but liberated, and called upon to participate with the white race in all the labors and privileges of free men. The Conference had, in order to reach this aim, to occupy itself carefully with the alcohol question. Importation, sale, and manufacture of spirituous liquors are, henceforth, totally forbidden in an immense zone, that from the 20th degree of north latitude to the 22d degree of south latitude.

This is a great triumph for the cause of civilization, and the representatives of the United .States at the Conference have greatly contributed to it by their insisting upon absolute prohibition. The Conference was, however, compelled to make concessions for certain points of the African territory where the use of and commerce in spirituous liquors already exist, so that the protestations of countries dealing in alcoholic beverages in Africa had to be taken into account. A right of entry for fifteen francs per hectolitre, at fifty degrees (Centigrade), has been fixed upon for those limited regions ; an equal right of excise has been imposed on manufacture. This tax may be increased to twenty-five francs after three years, representing about 100 per cent. of value. This tax is very high when compared with the buying capacity and the means of those who will have to pay for it. The greatest possible satisfaction has thus been afforded by the Conference to the desires expressed by the plenipotentiaries of the United States.

The General Act of the Conference formulates, in establishing the general system of the work, the engagements acceded to by the independent States of Africa, or those of Europe having possessions there, for the purpose of attaining the humanitarian end generally pursued by all the powers. But these engagements required pretty heavy charges, duties, and responsibilities for certain states, for the benefit of all; the question was raised then in what manner these new expenses could be met.

The situation was particularly serious for the independent Congo State, which, owing to its geographical position, will have to support much more considerable charges than the others for combating the slave trade, it having been the focus of the slave trade for centuries. Owing to its being of a quite recent creation, it incurs greater obligations and has more limited resources than other countries which, being merely colonies, dispose of the resources of the mother land.

The delegates of the Congo State were thus forced to declare frankly in the Conference that their government—while enthusiastically accepting all the stipulations of the General Act—was not in a position to carry out the regulations, if financial measures were not adopted for supplying the means. The Conference recognized, unanimously, that, in consequence of the new obligations and charges imposed on the countries in the conventional basin of the Congo, it was just and necessary to authorize them (by revising Article IV. of the Act of Berlin in 1885) to impose duties on the importation of foreign merchandise.

This resolution of establishing duties was made the subject of a separate act, on the demand of the United States Government, which, not having adhered to the Act of Berlin, could not take part in the revision. It was signed on July 2, 1890, at the time when the General Act was signed by all the powers, except Holland, which did so afterward. This resolution was named the *Declaration of Brussels*, and forms an inseparable annex to the General Act, with the expectation that whoever desired the result should grant the means of obtaining it.

That declaration authorized the collection of very limited duties, not above 10 per cent. ad valorem, on merchandise at the port of importation, spirituous liquors being regulated by the special provisions spoken of above.

But the declaration was not, in itself, a definite act ; it had merely adopted a principle and fixed a maximum of 10 per cent. Customs tariffs had to be established in mutual accord on this basis. These tariffs have been definitely fixed upon—December 22, 1890, and February 9, 1891—both for the countries of the eastern and those of the western coasts of the conventional basin of the Congo. An examination of these tariffs shows that the maximum of 10 per cent. authorized by the Conference is stipulated for arms and munitions only ; also that many articles are free of entry, and that as to the remainder the duty amounts only to from 3 to 6 per cent.

The United States, being the only state represented at this Conference that did not need a revision of the Act of Berlin, accorded the principle of establishing duties by signing, on January 24, 1891, a treaty of commerce with the independent Congo State. It obtains thereby the treatment of the most favored nations in its largest sense.

Such are the important advantages assured by the United States in all the states of the conventional basin of the Congo, in addition to its participation in the civilizing and humanitarian work of the Conference.

The sovereign king of the Congo State has, in consideration of the new tariffs, decreed the diminution of direct taxes and export duties ; he has also taken liberal measures with a view of encouraging commercial transactions, to the benefit of all the nations.

I cannot refrain from pointing to the astonishing manner— unprecedented in the history of colonization—in which the work of civilization has been acknowledged and developed in the Congo, in consequence of the great insight, perseverance, and magnanimous disinterestedness of King Leopold.

If civilization penetrates rapidly in the Congo, it is due to the benefits of peace, commerce, and education, without the aid of iron, fire, or alcohol, and without shedding a drop of blood, except for the purpose of saving slaves from infamous kidnappers, and never with the intention of subjugating the indigenous race. The assured and grateful populations group themselves quickly around European posts advancing from region to region and forming centres which are to become cities ; 15,000 kilometres of navigable ways have already been opened and used by a commercial fleet. The route of the caravans turning around the cataracts will soon be replaced by the railroad already being built. Modern and liberal institutions pervade the land and open it to the commercial rivalry of all the nations. Nothing of all this was to be seen six years ago, when the state was founded and intrusted to the sovereign direction of King Leopold.

The United States has always favored the young state; its sympathy was manifested at every opportunity in viewing the work of the great king in opening up the black continent to civilization. May the moral support given by the United States to the opening of these distant regions be compensated by the advantages it will not fail to obtain there in a population of more than fifty millions of inhabitants as an outlet to its coming exuberance of production !

The two acts of Brussels are now ratified by all the governments. These ratifications have been deposited at Brussels, except that of Portugal, which has not yet been able to present these acts to its Parliament, and obtained a delay up to April 2 for depositing its ratification.

The French Chambers have approved the General Act only, with certain restrictions. They eliminated, provisionally, the articles relating to the right of search, leaving them for an ulterior subject of arrangement between the powers interested. This temporary reservation (accepted by all the other signatory powers) does not modify in any way the provisions of the General Act, since they remain applicable to the other contracting parties in their primitive form.

The United States Senate has approved the treaty of January 24, 1891, and the General Act of Brussels, but it added the following proviso, not bearing on any special point of the act : " Resolved, further, as a part of this act of ratification, that the United States, not having in African territory any possessions or protectorates, hereby disclaims any intention, in adhering to this treaty, to declare any interest in such possessions or protectorates established by other powers, or any approval of the wisdom, expediency, or lawfulness thereof, and does not join in any expression in the treaty which might be construed as such a declaration."

The powers, having formally stipulated before meeting in conference that all ideas of sanctioning their possessions or protectorates should be excluded, have been able to accept with satisfaction the great reserve of the United States against a danger imaginary, and eliminated beforehand ; and this reserve has been inserted in the protocol of the ratifications signed àt Brussels on the 2d day of February, 1892.

Although traditional policy made the avoidance of any interference in political questions abroad with the European powers incumbent on the United States, yet their generous and liberal aspirations, their glorious antecedents, and even the blood ˙they shed for the enfranchisement of oppressed races, inspired them with the desire and moral duty to join in the purely humanitarian act of the Brussels Conference.

The illustrious President of the republic, and the eminent statesman at present directing the foreign affairs of the country, understood from the beginning, with a prudent and patriotic insight, that the great American republic could not remain a stranger to this general uprising of the civilized world against the last horrors of barbarism. They sent skilled and zealous plenipotentiaries to the Conference, who strove for more than a year, with remarkable ability, to conciliate the interests and dignity of their country with the aims pursued in common by all the powers.

The names of President Harrison, of Blaine, Terrell, Sanford, Tree, and Sherman, will remain connected with the noblest, most generous, and philanthropic work of our century.

When a new era dawns on suffering humanity, and when the Conference at Brussels has done its work faithfully, it is but just to attribute a great part of its merits to the eminent statesman who presided over it and directed the long and arduous work with an ability and tact greatly appreciated by the representatives of all the powers, and who was always able to meet the many difficulties encountered in every stage of the proceedings.

Baron Lambermont many times saved the work of the Conference, as it became involved in serious difficulties. He displayed great subtlety, insight, prudence, and patience during those memorable debates, where so many divergent interests, diverse doctrines, inveterate prejudices, contended, and where it was so earnestly sought to conciliate the moral integrity and interest of modern civilization with the dignity, self-love, ambition, and ˙material interests of the powers. The protracted and arduous negotiations leading to the ratification of the acts of Brussels by all the powers, in which he was the guide and constant intermediary, were to him a new field of hard work, in which he displayed the high qualities that had won for him long ago a universal reputation as one of the most eminent statesmen of our times.

The General Act of Brussels has been resolved upon in the cause of a supreme interest of humanity and justice. It is the expiation of the gloomy errors of past centuries, a renewed affirmation of the principle of freedom of all men; it is, above all, a promise of material and moral civilization for the unfortunate African population.

Allow me to say here, in conclusion, that Belgium is proud of her King, who has so nobly initiated, pursued, and accomplished such a work, and that she is grateful to those powers which honored her by signing in her capital an act which promises such gratifying consequences for coming times.

A. LE GHAIT.

THE DEGENERATION OF TAMMANY.

BY THE HON. DORMAN B. EATON, EX-PRESIDENT OF THE UNITED STATES CIVIL-SERVICE COMMISSION.

TAMMANY, the Tammany Society, Tammany Hall, the Tammany Democracy, the Tammany Machine—whichever may be used to designate the most unique and enigmatical product of a cross between simple charity and corrupt politics—has more and more, of late, aroused the curiosity of the country. Its origin is as peculiar and interesting as its present character.

In 1783, William Mooney, an eccentric upholsterer of the then little city of New York, formed a society for aiding and burying its poor members, naming it, in part after an Indian chief, the "Tammany Society, or Columbian Order"—some mysterious order of civilization. Thus from the outset the society had in itself the conflicting elements of savagery and charity which it has never lost. In 1805 it procured a special law for its organization, in which are these words, declaring its only purpose : "For the purpose of affording relief to the indigent and distressed members of the association . . . and others who may be found proper objects of their charity."

From such an egg the huge crocodile of the municipal politics of our time has been hatched. The society was at first authorized to hold property of the yearly value of $5,000—a right enlarged, in 1867, to $50,000. No other change has ever been made in the charter. The Indian dominated in the official sphere from the outset, the chief officers being called Sachems, and the inferior being designated Wiskinski, Sagamore, or by equally barbaric names which yet survive. The civilized Christian prevailed in its little sphere of charity. Humbly, and innocently for a long time, the little society lived on. Politics had no place in its annals.

From a germ apparently so harmless there has been evolved the most mercenary and merciless despotism—the most extraordinary combination of the spirit of the Indian and the spoilsman known to municipal government. The society in the course of years secured a hall, funds, and an influential membership. The politicians saw their chances. But the leading politicians of Madison's time were not of the kind now known as Tammany politicians. Besides, in the slow descent of this society from the heights of charity to the spoils-system bog of Tammany politics, . it was for a time in the sphere of manly human nature, where statesmen and honest, patriotic methods were possible. At that period, when it was first subordinated to party, its name is associated with statesmen and it had a part in contests for principle. But the debasement, once begun, could not be arrested, especially after the spoils system had become potential in New York politics. The congeries of local organizations—known as the Tammany primaries—and the secret, central, and despotic body by which the society has become enveloped, have a long time since made its character unimportant, save in this vital particular, that its sachems, whom its members elect, constitute, in whole or in the majority, that despotic and irresponsible junto by which the Tammany Democracy is governed, and in obedience to which the Tammany Machine is operated. These sachems—this junto—at whose will the leaders of the twenty-four Democratic primaries in the city hold their places—are beyond the control of the primary membership, which is many thousands. Powerless democracy and potential despotism—like the Indian and the Christian at the outset—are now in the most vicious and unnatural union. The relation between them is that which Frederick the Great said existed between him and his subjects. "They," he declared, "can say what they please, and I do what I please, and so we get on admirably."

Nothing is now heard of the Tammany Society. Yet I was not correct in saying that a generation ago—save in the matter of making its sachems feudal lords over the Tammany Democracy —it became unimportant; for it owns a vast building, including a great hall, where the delegates of the Tammany primaries hold their meetings and say what they please. The strange contrasts, everywhere seen in Tammany matters, appear in the use of this hall, it being about equally shared by Tammany delegates and Tony Pastor's low-comedy company.

Among the lamentable consequences of the debasement of the

society from its once respectable to its present moribund condition are these—facts notorious in New York : that, for more than a generation, neither within the society nor in any one of the congeries of organizations by which its noblest life has been quenched, nor in all of them together, has there been produced, or brought forward, or steadily sustained even, one public officer, municipal or national, who could properly be designated a statesman, a patriot, or a public benefactor; nor have any of these bodies been the source or the strength of a single law, public measure, or policy, largely in the public interest, or which can justly find honorable mention in history ; nor has one of them been prominent in aiding the repeal of any bad law or the suppression of any great evil. From none of these bodies or their leaders, so far as I am aware, has a single publication gone forth which can hold a respectable place in the literature of either politics or charity. The Tammany sphere, for a generation, has been one of intellectual and moral barrenness—of Lilliputs in usefulness, of Brobdingnags in rascality. Let no one cite that able, patriotic citizen, Abram S. Hewitt, or S. S. Cox, or Mayor Grace, to the contrary, for none of them sprung from Tammany, and each of them was opposed by it to the extent of its courage. That most active of politicians whom the official life of the Empire State has lately seen—and whom every reader will recognize —has been the only high officer since the days of Tweed and Barnard to whom Tammany has been constant.

It is this Tammany of to-day which, over the name of Mr. Richard Croker—sachem and champion—is introduced to the readers of this REVIEW in its last number. If in this article I found nothing I cared to answer separately, the relations of Tammany to the great problem of city government are so important I could not refuse a request for these pages.

Prudence would have suggested to Tammany the danger of bringing its affairs before the readers of this REVIEW—most of whom they have often disgusted—and the advantage of keeping its methods as dark and mysterious as that mongrel union has been between a charity society and a partisan faction for office and spoils. Yet, as Mr. Clarkson had come into these pages to defend the spoils-system methods which the Republicans had borrowed from Tammany, why should not the old offender himself be indulged in a like indiscretion ? Coming here solely to apologize for Tammany,—in the very midst of an elaborate defence, and while its chieftain is unconsciously betraying a painful sense of the distrust of his readers,—he declares, with a curious simplicity, that he will make neither apology nor defence for Tammany, since to rush on and to fight its opponents, and not to explain or defend anything, is its genius and its mission.

This defence has the assurance to boast of the great age of Tammany—an age most of the years of which only make conspicuous those prostitutions and debasements at which its degenerate sons might more fitly blush. Yet, much as sneers at mere theorists and at rural virtue invite retort, such self-stultification should not be too severely criticised ; for rare are the genius and attainments which fit one for the Tammany arena and for these pages. Our author's no-apology theory has caused him to do grave injustice to Tammany itself, against which I feel a duty to defend it. For, referring to the charges against it, he declares that if, in the last election, it had "defended or apologized," the Tammany Democrats would not, to use his phrase, " have fared anything like so well." That this view— which places Tammany sachems and the horde behind them on a level with gamblers, thieves, and pirates, who never apologize and who certainly would be injured by any attempt at justificasion—is just to the lower strata of Tammany followers, I cannot deny. Yet it is a cruel wrong to many above them. There are vast numbers of Tammany's voters who are disinterested and patriotic. Not a few,—even of those who run with the machine, and whose war-whoops in Tammany Hall would drown the voices of Tony Pastor's clowns,—knowing no better, are as honest as their sachem chief in thinking Tammany a blessing to New York. The frenzy and blindness of party keep great numbers in its ranks who deplore its vicious theories and its corruptions. There are many men of character who reluctantly adhere to Tammany— let it not be asked how many from hope of office and profitable contracts—because they think the city Republicans are corrupt. Not knowing so well as the Tammany chief what corruption is concealed, they think explanations less dangerous than secrecy.

Tammany leaders are sagacious enough to comprehend, in part, the power of the higher public press and public opinion. From a fear of them they put some good men in office, and improved parks (Tweed did much of this) and streets, sometimes from better motives than the profits of spending vast sums.

Nevertheless, as a whole, the article is true to the Tammany spirit and theory, showing that organization, a crushing military discipline, adroit management of elections and voters, the tangible assurance of rewards, pecuniary and official, the love of contention and passion for victory—and not patriotism, nor principle, nor parties devoted to principle, nor any sense of public duty, nor ˙public opinion—are, according to Tammany, the potential forces of municipal government. "Politics is war," says the article ; and so it is in the hands of savage and venal partisans.

Such is the admiration of our author-chief for crushing discipline, municipal savagery, and mere success, that he says : " We cannot fail to admire the success, . . . the resistless power of the Jacobin Club, . . . because it was skilfully organized." The hordes of Tammany are partisan soldiers to obey leaders and earn their reward ; not free citizens to discharge their duty.

Organization, and not education, success, and not improvement, victorious war, and not glorious peace, are presented as the supreme aims of Tammany. The regiment is the model for the Tammany primary, and the " six hundred charging down the valley of death " are cited as an inspiring example for city politicians. The ideal duties and relations of fellow citizens in city affairs are not those of peacefully considering them according to their nature as so much business to be done—the making and care of streets, buildings, and parks—or as so much discretion and trained skill to be exercised concerning schools, police, grogshops, and public health,—with all of which quarrelsome partisan factions can have no relations but those of pernicious intermeddling,—but all these duties and relations are those of remorseless conflict, of partisan politics, and hence of endless war between hostile factions and camps. A more uncivilized, diabolic, and detestable theory of municipal government—one more destructive of municipal prosperity and morality—was never sketched.

As we read this sketch and imagine the great Indian chief, Tammany, with his paint and his feathers, leading his tribe to battle, we can see tomahawks gleaming between the lines and hear the war-whoop in the distance. It defends a despotism the king of Dahomey might envy, and a perpetual warfare over which the Yahoos and Sioux would whoop and dance for joy. It would be unjust to say that there is nothing but the didactic presentation of this theory of eternal and insatiable war. There is a variety as great as in the hues of a zebra or in the contents of a Bologna sausage. That bumptious and audacious, yet specious and soporific, oratory of which Tammany has a fountain, everywhere lubricates the merciless logic of the war code.

The spoils system is defended in its most despotic, repulsive, and vicious form. "All the employees of the city government," says our chief, "from the mayor to the porter who makes his fire, should be members of the Tammany organization." Hence, every poor laborer appealing for employment, and every youth seeking a clerkship, under the city, is without hope if he has not sworn fealty to Tammany and, we may add, paid bribe money to its treasury or its leaders.

If a young woman would be a public-school teacher, or a poor widow be a matron in a city hospital, she must accept Tammany's war theories and wield little tomahawks in its defence. Office, according to Tammany, is not a trust, but a commodity. Are we really living in a civilized age and under a free government?

Tammany is no party, and refuses allegiance to any. It has no principles or platform to pledge it to duty. It fights only for itself. It is most like the mercenary and partisan war clubs of Florence which led to a despot. Its governmental theory is simple. It counts absolutely on the ignorant, the venal, and the depraved voters, holding them with the adhesive and relentless grasp of an octopus. It never alienates the grog-shop keepers, the gamblers, the beer-dealers, the nuisance-makers, or the proletariat. Patriotism and a sense of duty count for nothing in its estimate of political forces. Party passion, selfishness, and hopes of victory and spoils are its supreme reliance. Its basis is as enduring as the selfishness and depravity of human nature. Thus, sure of a vast mass of voters, Tammany will go as far towards well-doing as it may without alienating that mass. Its chiefs and mercenaries are forever laboring to bring out this vote. I once battled a whole night with two Tammany officials to secure a fair count in a model Tammany district,—of ignorance and vice,—with the result of more than 700 votes for Tammany to less than 20 opposed. What a blessing inestimable it would be if Tammany would allow such voters to stay at home and forget the elections, as most of them would but for its bribery and coercion. Half the occupation of its chiefs and henchmen, if that liberty were allowed, would be gone.

What does history give us as the outcome from such a Tammany ? Swartwout the collector, Price the district attorney, Fowler the postmaster, who together defrauded the nation of more than a million, were Tammanyites. The authors, in the days of Tweed, of the stupendous City Hall frauds, and the partisan rowdies and judges who foisted thousands as illegal voters upon the voting lists, were to a man Tammanyites. Tweed was a Tammany sachem ; Connolly, who robbed the city treasury, Barnard, and the notorious judges who aided the work of corruption twenty years ago—these men—whose infamies filled two continents with the disgrace of the republic—were all Tammanyites.

If, of late, sterner laws and a more formidable press and public opinion have prevented offences so flagitious, yet the worst that has been done is the work of Tammany. It has caused the Civil-Service Law to be more feebly enforced in New York than in Boston or Washington. The aldermen who took bribes for a Broadway railroad charter were all Tammanyites. It has prevented New York from having a ballot reform nearly as effective as that of other States. Combining with the grog-shop keepers, Tammany has prevented excise reform in New York ; and bills it has now pending at Albany threaten the most salutary restrictions, and may open Sundays and midnights to grog-shop debauchery. The fear of Tammany methods and of those who imitate them drove the World's Fair to Chicago. Tammany defeated that able and patriotic mayor, Hewitt, who stood for the commerce, the philosophy, the education, and the statesmanship of New York, and put in his place one unknown to any of these great interests. The degradation of the police courts has followed, unworthy men, utterly ignorant of the law, gaining seats there even more readily than under King John and the feudal lords of the thirteenth century; for his Magna Charta says : "We will not make any justices but of such as know the law and mean duly to observe it." Even worse than this ; for Tammany now compels her candidates for judges, as well as other candidates for office, to, practically, pay in advance for their nomination, thus accumulating a vast fund by which leaders can be paid and voters bribed. Such is an independent Tammany judiciary ! Such are our impartial judges ! One shrinks from putting truths like these in print. It is to our shame that we tolerate such degradation, the account of which reads like extracts from the infamous histories of Charles I. and James II. Such is the Tammany of to-day. Is it any wonder that it has plenty of money for carrying elections, or that its chief thinks all attempts at defence or apology would be dangerous ?

DORMAN B. EATON.

THE WORLD'S COLUMBIAN EXPOSITION.

BY THE DIRECTOR GENERAL, GEORGE R. DAVIS.

WHEN the gallant mariner, Christopher Columbus, landed from the "Santa Maria," October 12, 1492, and planted the standard of Spain upon the shores of San Salvador, he little appreciated the extent and significance of his discovery.

At that time nothing was more improbable than the formation of a vast republic in North America stretching from the Atlantic to the Pacific and sweeping the commerce of both oceans. There were then in the nations of Europe, from which America was to be colonized, absolutely no materials from which such a product could be expected to spring. The democratic element was nowhere developed. Government by the people was an idea that did not even enter the human mind. The nations had scarcely begun to emerge from the darkness and barbarism of the middle ages ; dense ignorance was the marked characteristic of the masses of the people. The learning of the times was monopolized by the clergy; the convents, monasteries, and clerical establishments were its repositories. The laity were hopelessly illiterate, and even kings were unable to sign their names to state documents, as the records prove. So far from governing in any part of Europe, the people were scarcely emancipated from slavery. They had been for ages bought and sold with the land they cultivated.

At the time of the discovery of America by Christopher Columbus, England was the only country in which the people enjoyed representation in the national legislation, and there they had a voice merely to legalize and authorize taxation for the benefit of the crown and the nobility. Spain had just been consolidated into one nation, under the government of Ferdinand and Isabella, and every energy had been strained to the utmost in the struggle for the expulsion of the Moors. In the new monarchy which was established the only representation the people had in the government was the deputations from the cities; but in those deputations it was the wealth of the city, and not the population, that was represented. The state of things was no better in France. where both kings and nobles united to oppose the people. They dared not trust them with arms, and chose rather to depend on foreign mercenaries for military defence than suffer the people to learn the secret of their own strength. Matters were still worse in the other nations of Christendom, to say nothing of the admittedly barbarous nations.

This unequal distribution of learning and political privilege in the nations of Europe would probably have continued indefinitely, had not the discovery of the new world by Columbus suggested to the oppressed people of the old world possibilities of emigration and enfranchisement from the grievous burdens of the feudal system by adding two continents to the geography of the world—a hemisphere for the overflow of Europe.

However this may be, it is a matter of history that colonists from the old countries flocked to America by thousands, and, settling along its eastern shores, laid the foundations of the civilization that to-day invites the nations of the world to the Columbian Exposition at Chicago in 1893.

In giving a leading place to the discovery of America as the instrument of human enlightenment and progress, it is not my purpose to underestimate the importance to the world of the invention of printing from movable types and the long succession of inventions and discoveries of which it was the precursor and incentive. But Columbus was eleven years old when Peter Schaefer cast the first metal types in matrices, thus becoming the inventor of complete printing; he was about twenty when the first printed edition of the Bible was given to the world, and twenty-one when Maintz was taken and plundered, and the art of printing, in the general ruin, spread to other towns Therefore, when we consider the international antagonisms, the difficulties of intercommunication, and the total absence of methods for the rapid diffusion of intelligence, it is easily conceivable that Columbus may never have perused a printed book or paper when he entered upon his career of discovery, which unfolded a hitherto unknown world and put in train the succession of marvellous results which followed. His discoveries served to stimulate the employment of the newly-discovered art of printing.

These two events—the invention of printing and the discovery of America—joined hands to lead in the grand procession of intellectual, moral, and material development. Parenthetically let me note the remarkable fact, not less interesting because of its being so well known, that, while so much is due to the invention of printing in the way of human progress along all lines, the method of type-setting by hand, as first adopted, has remained in vogue until the present day; but now the dawn of a new era to the printer is just at hand. The landmarks of progress along the journey from the middle-age darkness to the present light were at first few and far between (often retrogressive, but, when so, reactionary), gradually increasing in number and interest. We find the first printing-press in Copenhagen in 1493; Gama reaches India in 1498; musical notes first printed, 1502; Pope Leo the Tenth publishes his indulgences, 1517; Magellan's circumnavigation of the globe completed, 1522; the Copernican system published, 1530; the Pope of Rome issues his bull declaring the natives of America to be rational beings, 1537; Calvin founds the University of Geneva, and John Knox makes headway as a reformer in Scotland, 1539; pins first made in England. 1543; orange-trees introduced into Europe, the Diet at Worms and the discovery of the mines at Potosi, 1545; knives first made in England, 1560; Kew originates the game of billiards and Growse teaches the art of making needles to the English, 1556; the victory over the Turks at Lepanto won, 1571; carriages introduced into England, 1580; tobacco first brought to Europe, 1586; the first newspaper in England, 1588. Then a century more of progress brings us to the Revolution of 1688, and still another century to the death-bed scene of the "Last Pretender" in the mother land, and the election of George Washington as the first President of the United States.

George Washington in his last days was contemporaneous with the infancy of men still living. The world's progress at the time of his death had already been marvellous; yet, to borrow the language of Mr. Locke, the witty editor of the Toledo *Blade,*

"We don't like to be irreverent, but would like to ask, what did our forefathers know? What, for instance, did George Washington know? He never saw a steamboat; he never saw a fast mail train; he never held his ear to a telephone ; he never sat for his picture in a photograph gallery ; he never received a telegraphic despatch ; he never sighted a Krupp gun ; he never listened to the ' fizz ' of an electric pen ; he never saw a pretty girl run a sewing-machine ; he never saw a self-propelling engine go down the street to a fire ; *he never heard of* 'Evolution'; he never took laughing-gas ; he never had a set of store teeth; he never attended an international exposition ; he never owned a bonanza mine ; he never knew ' Old Prob.' He—but why go on ? No ; when he took an excursion it was on a flat-boat. When he went off on a train it was on a mule train. When he wanted to talk to a man in Milwaukee he had to—go there. When he wanted his picture taken it was done in profile with a piece of black paper and a pair of shears. When he got the returns from the back counties they had to be brought in by a man with an ox-cart. When he took aim at the enemy he had to trust to a crooked-barreled old flint-lock. When he wrote it was with a goose-quill· When he had anything to mend his grandmother did it with a darning needle. When he went to a fire he stood in a line and passed buckets· *When he looked at a* CLAM *he never dreamed that it was any relation of his.* When he went to a concert he heard a cracked fiddle and an insane clarionet."

The remarkable thing about this humorous statement of fact is that had Washington lived half a century longer it would still remain almost equally true. Indeed, the world's progress since the middle of the nineteenth century has distanced all that had gone before, and the last four decades, beginning with the date of the first world's fair, have witnessed greater strides than all the previous years of the Columbian epoch combined.

To exemplify this development the world over, in all its de tails and ramifications, falls within the general scope and design of the World's Columbian Exposition of 1893 at Chicago. The accomplishments of both sexes and of all ages, the researches of the "Challenger" and the "Talisman," of those that have plunged into the gloom of mid-African forests or scaled Himalayan summits or neared the frozen poles, are all included. It aims to present the achievements of mankind in man's dealings with the products and forces of nature, as by an exhaustive balance-sheet.

The Congress of the United States, deeming it advisable to commemorate the four hundredth anniversary of the discovery of America "by an exhibition of the resources of the United States of America, their development, and the progress of civilization of the new world," provided, in the act of Congress approved April 30, 1890, that such an exhibition should be held, and that it "should be of a national and international character, so that not only the people of our Union and this continent, but those of all nations, as well, can participate," and the recognition of its international character and purpose is evidenced in the President's invitation to foreign nations, and the acceptance of this invitation by nearly all the nations of the world.

There are sixty-two foreign nations and colonies which have already formally expressed a determination to participate in the exposition, and their appropriations approximate four million dollars. So far as it has been possible to comply with their pressing demands, space for exhibits has been assigned to all these countries in the departmental buildings, and sites in the exposition park have been set aside for their official pavilions and government headquarters. The United States Government has appropriated thus far one and a half million dollars, of which four hundred thousand is available for its building alone, in which will be illustrated the functions of the government in peace and war.

The agencies authorized by the act of Congress to determine the plan and scope of the exposition, and make all the necessary preparations and successfully conduct the same, were a National Commission, whose members are representatives at large and also of the States and Territories and the District of Columbia, appointed by the President of the United States, on the one hand; and, on the other, a corporation organized under the laws of the State of Illinois, entitled "The World's Columbian Exposition of 1892," which name was subsequently changed to "The World's Columbian Exposition," by which said corporation is now known. The former body, the World's Columbian Commission, in fulfilling the requirements of the act, has appointed a Board of Lady Managers. This latter body has been organized with a view to securing a comprehensive, interesting, and instructive exhibit of woman's work in all lands. This spirit on the part of the managers constitutes a striking commentary, and as gratifying as it is striking, on the change which time has wrought in the condition of women.

The limits of my space forbid an indulgence of the strong inclination I feel to dwell upon this feature of the exposition. A retrospect of some twenty-five centuries presents to view another historic exhibition in Media-Persia, lasting, like ours, "many days, even a hundred and fourscore days," of all the nations of the then known world, "one hundred and seven and twenty provinces," stretching "from India even unto Ethiopia." What a significant fact that this first of all recorded world's fairs should furnish the conditions out of which was developed a "lady manager" whose matchless tact and beauty, whose endowments of head and heart, have tinctured the poesy, the song, the romance, the pictorial art of all these intervening years !

The National Commission met and organized in the city of Chicago on June 26, 1890. The Board of Directors of the Illinois' corporation finally tendered Jackson Park and the grounds adjoining as the site for the fair, which were accepted by the National Commission.

It early became evident that by reason of the constitution of these two bodies and the requirements of the act of Congress a conference between them was absolutely necessary in order to reach an understanding of the powers, limitations, and duties of each. A joint conference committee was therefore formed, consisting of eight members of each body, to take this vital question into consideration. The result of its deliberations was embodied in a report, afterwards adopted by both bodies in their separate capacities, defining their respective jurisdictions. This compact between the two bodies (the term by which it is generally known) outlines the plan of procedure for the harmonious administration of the affairs of the exposition, and provides that the work of the exposition shall be divided into great departments. It also provides that, to properly administer these departments, the director general shall appoint a head or chief officer for each, and all required subordinates. The appointment of these department chiefs must be confirmed by both bodies.

The departments thus constituted consist of the following: Department A, agriculture ; B, horticulture ; C, live stock ; D, fish and fisheries ; E, mines and mining ; F, machinery ; G, transportation exhibits ; H, manufactures ; J, electricity ; K, fine arts ; L, liberal arts ; M, ethnology and archæology ; N, forestry ; O, publicity and promotion ; P, foreign affairs.

Chiefs, or head officers, have been appointed to all these departments, and, with a single exception, have already entered upon their official duties. In selecting these chiefs the importance of securing the best available talent has been kept constantly in view, and they were chosen from amongst the noted men in their respective lines throughout the country at large. The importance of the interests they have in charge may be

,partially gathered from the plan and scope determined upon for the exposition, by which it was found necessary to erect magnificent and commodious buildings for each exhibit department, in addition to those required for administration offices and for the Board of Lady Managers, covering in the aggregate upwards of one hundred and thirteen acres, and, including stables for live stock, over one hundred and fifty-three acres. This obtains with all the departments, with the exception of the departments of manufactures, liberal arts, and ethnology. These three are joined in one magnificent building covering something over thirty acres.

A brief summary of some of the exhibits designed for a few of the exhibit departments will serve to illustrate the importance of each, and perhaps give a faint conception of the extent of the combined whole.

Take, for one example, the Department of Transportation Exhibits. For the first time in the history of world's fairs, the science of transportation in its broadest sense will have that attention to which its importance entitles it. The development of modern transportation, having had its beginning within the lifetime of men now in the vigor of manhood, has been so rapid that its significance is hardly yet understood. Yet its early history is fading out of sight, and in a fair way to be utterly lost. Judged by its relations to the every-day life of the world, no other industry surpasses it in utility or as a power in the progress of civilization. Considered from the standpoint of the amount of capital invested, it overshadows every other industry. It has been stated by eminent authority that the world's whole stock of money of every kind —gold, silver, and paper—would purchase only one-third of its railroads. Add to this the shipping of the world and all the means of conveyance from place to place throughout the world, and the interests represented in this department of the World's Columbian Exposition can readily be imagined. It falls within the plan and scope of this department to exhaustively present the origin, growth, and development of the various methods of transportation used in all ages and in all parts of the world. The means and appliances of barbarous and semi-civilized tribes are to be shown by specimen vehicles, trappings, and craft. Water craft, from the rudest forms to the modern giant steamship ; wheeled vehicles, from the first inception of the idea to the latest development of the luxurious palace car, will be illustrated by the machine itself, or, in cases where this is impossible, by accurate models, drawings, plans, and designs.

By keeping the historical feature clearly in view, the greatest exhibition of the actual means of transportation employed throughout the world to-day will stand out by contrast in high relief, and the wonderful achievements of later years will bear testimony to the genius of the age in which we live.

A large number of the leading railways of the world will make exhibits of their roadbed, track, and equipment ; and even cities owing their existence to transportation influences will be represented by elaborately-prepared models. Nothing will be overlooked bearing on the subject of transportation, terrestrial, aquatic, or aërial.

The building for the display of the exhibits of this department is located on the western bank of the lagoon surrounding the beautiful wooded island which occupies nearly the centre of the exposition. It is surmounted by a cupola reaching a height of 165 feet. Eight elevators will run from the centre of the main floor to the balconies surrounding the cupola, at heights of 115 and 118 feet. The view from the observatory will be beautiful in the extreme, and will give visitors an excellent comprehension of the whole plan of the exposition grounds at a glance. The total floor space devoted to the interests of this department, including the *entresol*, amounts to nearly nineteen acres. The annex will open into the main building in such a manner as to afford long and striking vistas down the main avenue and aisles.

The giant among the mammoth buildings on the fair grounds is that devoted to manufactures and liberal arts. Presenting a floor space of thirty-one acres, and including galleries encircling the interior, it will afford in the aggregate some forty-four acres of exhibit space. It is the largest building ever contemplated or erected for similar uses. This vast structure will be covered with an arched roof of steel and glass, affording ample light and ventilation. Broad avenues and other conveniences will be provided generously for the comfort of visitors. Galleries will encircle the interior, overlooking Lake Michigan, the government buildings and grounds, the pier, and the surrounding exhibition, State, and foreign buildings, presenting to the spectator a scene of unparalleled beauty and magnificence.

The exhibit of the Department of Manufactures is destined to be one of the very greatest interest, embracing, as it does, the products of the machine and man's unequalled handiwork in every form and design. A mere enumeration of the beautiful and useful works to be exhibited here would require a volume, and cannot be attempted. The constantly increasing interest among our home producers, and the ever-growing rivalry of inventive genius in the way of improved machinery, will be amply illustrated, and will form one of the most interesting and instructive features of the exposition.

The field of the Liberal-Arts Department is a broad one, covering nearly every phase of the higher development of the race. It includes education, literature, journalism, government and law, civil engineering, public works and architecture, hygiene, sanitation, medicine and surgery, commerce and trade, all processes of precision, research, and experiment, music and the drama.

The importance of these subjects has been recognized in the scheme for this department, which surpasses in scope and range all previous attempts. In this scheme the subject of education naturally takes a leading place ; perhaps no single interest in any department is more worthy of adequate showing. Fourteen million pupils and four hundred thousand teachers, four hundred and fifty-two million dollars of school property and capital invested in education, are here to receive due consideration. The most complete showing of the educational system of the country that has ever been attempted is proposed ; the programme covering the entire field of primary, secondary, and superior education. It provides for an exhaustive illustration of the methods of instruction in all grades, from the kindergarten up to the colleges and universities.

A section of this department of great interest will be that devoted to music. The history and theory of music will be illustrated, showing the music of primitive people, crude and curious instruments, music books and scores, portraits and biographies of great musicians, church music ; and the sacred music of all periods will be represented, as well as the ballads, folksongs, and national airs of all lands. The display of musical instruments will eclipse all previous attempts. It will cover everything from the mouth-harp to the pipe-organ.

In addition to the space given to liberal arts in the great

building already described, an immense music-hall will be erected for the use of this department, in which will be given concerts, recitals, oratorios, and other entertainments during the progress of the exposition.

The Department of Horticulture will embrace the most elaborate and complete classification of its peculiar interests ever presented, arranged in the most comprehensive manner, to display all rare and choice fruits and plants of the earth. Tropical fruits and berries of the central latitudes will be abundantly exhibited, and varieties or species not obtainable at certain seasons will be represented by wax or plaster-cast imitations. Fruits, dried, canned, glacéd, preserved by chemical or cold-storage appliances, manufactured into jellies, jams, or marmalades, will illustrate the most approved means of conserving surplus products. Methods of crushing and expressing juices of fruits will be shown, and literature and statistics will form an instructive feature of the exhibit. So much for the pomological group.

Equally interesting will be found the viticultural, the floricultural, the culinary vegetable, the arboricultural, and other groups. The floricultural alone will consist of twenty-five classes, embracing plants and flowers from all countries, and will undoubtedly surpass any previous display of its kind. The orchidaceæ will be one of the principal features, and, together with the palms, cycads, ferns, aroids, and other tender exotics, will be collected in the magnificently-proportioned Horticultural Hall, while the out-door display will comprise a profusion of. beautiful flowers and plants, rhododendrons, roses, and herbaceous plants. Dahlias, improved cannas, gladioli, and irises will play an important part in embellishing the grounds. Examples of unique and beautiful designs in budding plants will be illustrated by artists in this specialty. Superintendents of public parks in most of the large cities at home and abroad have already signified their intention to compete for honors.

In addition to a building one thousand feet long by two hundred and fifty feet wide, surmounted by a dome one hundred and thirty-five feet high, to be devoted to exhibitions of both fruits and plants, the wooded island, the most beautiful natural feature of the exposition park, will be wholly devoted to an out-door display of flowering plants and shrubs.

The chief of the Department of Fine Arts has been abroad

for many months visiting the galleries of all the nations of Europe, and paving the way for a display which promises a higher degree of excellence than any ever before achieved at any exhibition of fine arts.

American art in every department received a new impulse from the Centennial Exposition of 1876, and it will be a special aim here to show the extent of the advancement made in American art work during the intervening sixteen years. It will be the endeavor to make a retrospective exhibit of American paintings, representing each artist who has achieved prominence by characteristic work, all of which will show the changes in the production and methods of our art and the development of the various "schools" of expression. But however much we might desire to see American art take the foremost position in this great concourse of nations, it must be frankly admitted that our guests will stand at the head. Contemporary art will be represented on a scale not at all understood as yet by the nations themselves or by our own public. A single illustration will suffice. At the Centennial the total of wall space devoted to fine art was one hundred and twenty thousand square feet. The government of France alone has applied for and will admirably fill wall space to the amount of seventy-five thousand square feet in the World's Columbian Exposition.

One leading object of the department is to form a collection of art works which shall be in the highest degree interesting and instructive to the visitor to the exposition—such a collection as will give one a higher appreciation of art and a desire for further knowledge, which may be satisfied by a study of the collection; such a collection, also, as may enable one to become acquainted with the characteristics of the best art of all nations, induce comparison, and develop critical judgment.

Space will not permit further details, but these examples, taken at random, and by no means the most interesting, will serve to give some faint idea of the prospective colossal proportions of the exposition as a whole.

All the several departments are well advanced with their work, and applications for space already received warrant the assurance that the exhibits to be displayed will in every respect be equal to the expectations of the people and commensurate with the dignity and honor of the occasion.

The Department of Publicity and Promotion and that of Foreign Affairs are purely administrative. The former was organized about the middle of December, 1890, and the scope of its functions includes the preparation of matter and furnishing of reliable information for the daily press and all other kinds of publications, domestic and foreign ; the preparation and distribution of maps and a variety of pictorial illustrations ; the stimulation of congressional, legislative, corporate, and individual action favorable to the interests of the fair ; the supply of stationery and printing for the use of the exposition authorities and agencies ; and a preservation in an orderly, comprehensive, and available form of the evidence of the results accomplished by all the agencies of the exposition, not only at headquarters, but throughout the whole world. It is a novelty in the history of world's-fair organization in that its scope is so greatly enlarged as compared with that of any previous agency organized for the exploitation of a world's fair, and the results attained justify the anticipations which led to its creation.

The Department of Foreign Affairs bears relation to the director general of the exposition somewhat similar to that which the Department of State bears to the President of the United States. It conducts all correspondence with foreign governments and their commissions ; it has charge of matters pertaining to the procurement of foreign exhibits, and superintendence of all agencies engaged in securing such exhibits and interesting all people beyond the boundaries of the United States.

The Board of Directors of the corporation known as the World's Columbian Exposition assumed the responsibility of preparing the exposition grounds and constructing the buildings. The board, at an early period of its existence, created a committee, designated as the Grounds and Buildings Committee, to which this important work was assigned, appointed a chief of construction, and constituted a Board of Architects. Plans were prepared, submitted, discussed, and duly approved. The work, once inaugurated, has been pressed with notable vigor, and marvellous progress accomplished. All the great buildings are under contract and in process of construction. A complete transformation has resulted in the appearance of the grounds. The work has been pushed day and night, and thousands of workmen are kept constantly employed. Some of the buildings are already under roof, and all are so far advanced that assurance can now be positively offered that the grounds and buildings will be ready on time and in every way satisfactory. When completed, the exhibits installed, and the seven hundred acres of ornamented park, with its city of palaces devoted to exposition purposes, all thrown open to the public, there will be presented to the vision of the beholder a scene of grandeur and beauty and activity the like of which has not been witnessed in all the cycles of time.

Beautiful and imposing as the exposition on the borders of the beautiful Lake Michigan will be, the most interesting feature of the fair, to many, will be Chicago itself. Of all the wonders of the world Chicago stands out alone, unexampled and without a peer, a youthful giant among cities, with its business quarter, its traffic lively beyond description, its wide streets, and colossal palaces built of steel and stone, completely fireproof, and rising ten, twelve, sixteen, yes, over twenty stories—prodigious beehives of earnest humanity.

Men still live who were prominent in founding Chicago, and these men now behold, instead of the open and unsettled prairie of their youth, a city of a thousand streets and a million and a quarter inhabitants. The engineer still lives who surveyed the first line of railroad into Chicago, and now more than forty railroads centre in this queen city, situated in the heart of this vast continent, a thousand miles from Hell Gate and twice that distance from the Golden Gate. Chicago is the chief centre of the entire railroad system of the United States. Fifty thousand miles of railway, representing capital of over two thousand millions of dollars, are largely dependent upon Chicago, and the history of the building and development of these roads sounds like a fairy tale. On a single one of these tributary systems four hundred and fifty passenger and eight hundred freight trains now move daily. A single corporation controls over seven thousand miles of line—the greatest number of miles of railroad under one management in the world. A single general manager, with headquarters in Chicago, can marshal railway rolling-stock in greater number than the number of men that Grant could muster on the left bank of the Mississippi the day he set out on his matchless campaign south of Vicksburg, or that responded to Sheridan's rallying trumpet-call at Cedar Creek, or sprang forward at Wellington's "up and at 'em" at Waterloo.

Chicago is surrounded on all sides by a complexity of navigable rivers, canals, and lakes which connect it with tidewater at widely divergent points, and it is, moreover, the centre of a network of railway systems which embrace all portions of the North American continent. Her wide streets cross each other at right angles, looking on the east out upon the broad blue surface of Lake Michigan, and in every other direction leading into splendid parks and wide, shady boulevards which surround the city as with an emerald girdle. No other city in America can show such a large number of public parks. Space forbids an extended reference to her schools, her churches, her theatres, her elevators, her water-works, her foundries, her rolling mills, her manufactories, her wholesale houses, her stockyards, and other features in endless variety.

And this great central city of the foremost nation of the Columbian Hemisphere has already provided over ten millions of treasure in aid of the International Exposition designed to fitly commemorate the epic-inspiring and epoch-producing achievement of the peerless discoverer, and to make our government the munificent host at a peaceful fête of nations whose splendors will outshine all that has yet passed into history.

GEO. R. DAVIS.

SPENDING PUBLIC MONEY.

BY THE HON. T. B. REED, EX-SPEAKER OF THE HOUSE OF REPRE-
SENTATIVES, AND THE HON. W. S. HOLMAN, CHAIRMAN
OF THE COMMITTEE ON APPROPRIATIONS.

I.—APPROPRIATIONS FOR THE NATION.

BY THE HON. T. B. REED.

WHEN the charge was made during the campaign of 1891 that
the Fifty-first Congress was a Billion-Dollar Congress, the complete reply, the best in kind ever evoked, was that this is a Billion-
Dollar Country. The answer had both wit and wisdom. The
Fifty-first Congress voted a billion of dollars because the citizens
of this country, who are the rulers of it, demanded it by reason
of the growth of the country and by reason of certain issues which
had been fought out, settled, and determined by them.

The word economy has a pleasant and satisfying sound, and
there are those who think that they can, by pronouncing the
word often enough, make seventy-five cents do the work of a dollar, and thereby safely stint the honest and needed expenses of a
great and growing country. Nobody disputes the virtues any
more than they do mathematics. Economy, the just adaptation
of expenditures to national needs, requires no more proof than
that two and two make four. Nobody believes in spendthrift
government, in the waste of money, or the throwing of dollars
out of the window. You could no more justify national extravagance than you could justify the breaking of the ten command-
ments. But while we are all agreed in the praise of any virtue.
it does not follow that we all have it, or even that all of us understand what it is. Not every one who cries "Lord, Lord," enters
into the kingdom. Not every one who cries "Economy, Economy,"
on all the housetops, is necessarily more virtuous than his neighbors.

There are, moreover, several things which are called economy that are not economy at all. Penny wise may be pound foolish. To build fine public buildings, and then make every one who goes into them long to behold signs of the activity of the scrubbing-brush is no more economy than it is cleanliness. To let a navy rot, and build nothing in its place, is not economy. It is only stupidness. To leave great cities undefended, liable to pillage, to leave wide open great opportunities for national disgrace, which it might cost uncounted millions to wipe away, is neither economy nor sense. To clamor loudly all through a session for a service-pension act and an arrears-of-pensions act which would have cost $200,000,000, and then go about the country denouncing the pension extravagance of a Congress which voted only $40,000,000, is not a sound preaching of economy or a very startling exhibition of common honesty. It is singular how much more effective an epithet is than an argument. Mouth-filling abuse is much more powerful than mind-filling demonstration. All over the country the Democracy have girded at the last Congress because it wasted money, and yet no Democratic convention has ventured anywhere to specify a single item where money was wasted or the sin of extravagance committed. There was no charge of robbery, of undue influence, or bad conduct ; only one loud outcry about the Billion Congress. Appropriation bills, however, are not passed on party lines ; and yet, to hear the loud talk made on the stump, one would hardly imagine that some of the loudest-voiced economists of to-day had tried to increase the billion by at least $100,000,000 more.

It has probably escaped the attention of the country that Judge Holman, who is the new chairman of Appropriations, and from whom great things are expected in the way of economy and diminished expenditure, himself voted for the service-pension amendment which Mr. Springer, the new chairman of Ways and Means, advocated, explaining that the cost would be but the bagatelle of $144,000,000 per annum. If you look over the list (page 4,062, *Cong. Record*, Vol. 1, 1st Sessn., Fifty-first Cong.) of those who voted for this increase over and above what even a Billion Congress would do, you will find the name not only of Judge Holman, of economists the chiefest among ten thousand, but of the cheerful Governor of New York, a very possible Democratic candidate for the Presidency of the United States.

Now that the responsibility of making up the appropriations has fallen upon the Democrats themselves, they are looking about in much consternation to find some way of not paying the bills of "a Billion-Dollar Country." As they look about them and see the growing land and its growing wants, they think that some special machinery must be adopted to prevent their vast majority, every one of them an economical Democrat, from doing exactly what the wicked Republicans have done. Hence they have already had careful tables prepared which show that, when the Appropriations Committee was forced to let two bills pass into the hands of other committees, our expenses rose instantly by the astounding sum of one cent—one cent—for each and every citizen; which ought clearly to have shown to the discerning, economical patriot that that way danger lay. It is sad to say, however, that no heed was paid to the warning, and, therefore, in time the Committee on Appropriations had the Consular and Diplomatic Bill taken away, and also the Naval Bill, the Army Bill including the Academy Bill, the Indian Appropriation Bill, and the Post-Office Bill. Each of these bills was intrusted to another committee. A tabular statement and due calculation show that since this was done there has been an increase in appropriation of forty-eight cents per capita, without including pensions.

It is needless to say that this calculation was put forth by the Committee on Appropriations, which desired to regain its lost power—a power which used to be almost absolute, not only over the expenditures of the government, but over almost everything else. In the old days, before Mr. Morrison and Mr. Carlisle determined to lessen the greatness of Mr. Randall, whom they did not quite venture to dethrone, the chairman of Appropriations, by skilfully manœuvring his bills, could control the House in spite of the Speaker and of all other leadership. But Mr. Carlisle and Mr. Morrison would not have been able to strip the Committee on Appropriations of its bills merely because they wished to deprive Mr. Randall of power. Behind them and behind the movement were the growing needs of the country. When economy is carried to extreme and becomes parsimony, it is only a hindrance and a stumbling-block instead of a virtue. In 1885 economy had become parsimony, and the real needs of the country had been repeatedly sacrificed to a mere show of figures. So bad had the practice become in this race for popular favor by claims of economy that the House under Democratic management repeatedly refused to put into its bills appropriations which had to go there in order to carry on the government. The Senate was then obliged to insert these necessary items, and endure, in the next campaign, the charge of extravagance, because the figures of a Democratic House were increased. This habit was kept up even after the Democrats had possession of the Executive Department, and the Republican Senate was obliged to insist that the Democratic Executive should have money enough to carry on the government. This conduct on the part of the House called forth a most vigorous rebuke from Senator Beck, who was too honest a man to aid this economic fraud.

In other ways the need of a change became manifest, and the House, which was Democratic, ordered the change because it wanted less restriction and more freedom in its appropriations. In other words, the new committees of appropriation are not the cause of the appropriation increase, but the result, or, more exactly, the medium by which the result was attained. The House, representing the country, wanted larger appropriations, and took the proper course to obtain them. Since that day no one has seriously proposed to go back to the old way. The result has been larger appropriations. I imagine that if a sensible and judicious man were asked if he approved of larger expenditure, he would answer, if the country needed it, yes, and if it did not, no ; and that the only test was, not the total, but the items. If the items are all good, the total cannot be bad. A large total does not prove extravagance, and a small total does not argue economy.

Economy is not the withholding of money. Economy is not necessarily decreased expenditure. There are times when the wisest economy is large expenditure. In the quaint language of Scripture, " There is that scattereth and increaseth yet more, and there is that withholdeth more than is meet, but it tendeth only to want." I might further illustrate this subject by what has frequently occurred in railroads and has cost the simple people much hard-earned money. A railroad may be so economically handled as to ruin it. Railway managers quite often seem to be managing the road wonderfully. According to the bookkeeping, economy reigns triumphant, the road pays fat dividends, and the percentage of cost of running becomes phenomenally low. Everybody who does n't know any better thereupon praises the manager and buys the stock ; but the wise man, who has previously suffered, gives both a wide berth. He knows that the road is running down, and that a day of new rails, of new sleepers, and new rolling-stock, and vast expenditures of money is at hand. He does not buy the stock. He leaves that for the fools who pass on and are punished. There are tricks in all trades, even in railroading ; perhaps I shall shock somebody if I add even in politics. I have seen a judgment of the Supreme Court of the United States thrown out of an appropriation bill because a patriot wanted economy in the totals. Of course some other year had to pay. In the long run the United States has to pay most of its honest debts, but it usually costs the party something which does it.

While I think it probable that the distribution of the appropriation bills among the various committees which now hold them may somewhat facilitate the desire of the country that whatever is really needed for the development and government of the people of the United States should be expended, I am not at all sure that the same increase in appropriations would not have taken place had the old committee remained in charge of all the bills. The bills which they have retained show the same or a similar degree of increase, and the Pension Bill keeps pace with all the rest. It ought also to be added that there can be no more absurd test of increase than the per-capita test. To say that we ought at all times to expend the same amount per head is to ignore all increase of wealth and all growth in the wants of the people. Whatever the government expends is largely for the whole people, and all the facts show that everywhere a gradual increase in money per head is spent all over the world for the general good. Twenty years ago our cities were proud of their gas lights, and now, at increased cost, they demand at night almost the brightness of noon.

In 1860, New York State, with a population of 3,880,735, expended $4,376,167, or at least raised that sum in taxes. That was one dollar and seventy cents per capita. In 1889, with a population of six millions, the expenditures were seventeen millions and a half. In 1860, one dollar and seventy cents per capita seemed enough. It takes three dollars for each citizen in 1890.

Lest it should be supposed that this also is Republican extravagance, I add that in New York city, where the Democratic

majority is colossal, and where true economy must reign, if anywhere, a population of 814,000 required the expenditure of $3,-
385,000, or four dollars for each and every citizen, in 1860 ;
while in 1890 a population not twice as large expended thirty-
three millions, or ten times as much. Four dollars was enough
in 1860 to protect every citizen, to give him streets and parks
and keep them clean, to prevent every other citizen from assault-
ing him, to light him to bed, and otherwise to be a father to him.
Since that time the city of New York has found out so many
ways of being really useful to the citizen of New York that
twenty dollars by the year, economically administered, is spent for
his good.

From these examples—and I presume any State in the Union
can produce parallel figures—it will be seen that the increase of
expenditures of the United States, large as they are, are in no
way out of proportion to the increase in those States and cities
enjoying true Democratic economy.

It is not, of course, possible in this article to explain fully the
causes of increase, nor is it desirable to display statistics, which
everybody avoids. Nevertheless, a few figures will show the
nature of the increase made by the last Congress, and will show
also what we must expect from the present one.

The increase in the annual appropriations for 1890–91 over
those of the preceding fiscal year was, in round numbers, $75,000,-
000. The large items which went to make up this sum were five
in number and easily understood. Of this sum, $25,000,000 was
for the River and Harbor Bill, which had the sanction of both
parties, and which is likely to increase hereafter with the growth
of the country. Three millions went for coast defences. If
there should be a war, the only complaint likely to be made is
that such an increase was not made long ago. Thirty-four
millions of increase was made for pensions, and five millions for
extra deficiencies which the last House ought to have paid.
Two and a half millions were added to the naval appropriations to
enable the Navy Department to commence to build the big ships
which were needed to complete our naval defences according to
the scheme which had been approved by the department under all
administrations. Five millions five hundred thousand more were
imperatively demanded for the needs of the postal service, and so
readily were its claims recognized that the Postal Bill which

carried $72,000,000 went through the House with the approval of all parties in half as many minutes as there were millions. The appropriations for the next year were still further increased by about $40,000,000, which increase justifies itself as effectually as any that was ever made. Of this sum, $8,500,000 was devoted to the payment of money due the Indians, some of which debts were contracted to open up to settlement the fertile acres of Oklahoma ; to build ships $7,000,000 more was used, and $36,000,000 for the pensions voted the year before. Five additional millions for the postal service at once justify themselves, and, by showing the growth of the country, make good some other expenditures, including part of the increase of eight millions in the Sundry Civil Bill. All these items together amount to $69,000,000 ; but as there was no River and Harbor Bill, the net increase was only about $40,000,000.

It will be seen that by far the largest item of increase for the two years, amounting in all to seventy-five millions of dollars, was for pensions and pension deficiencies. In fact, if you add to the figures already given the pension-deficiency items passed by the second session of the Fifty-first Congress, you will swell the total increase so that there will be hardly anything left to charge extravagance to; perhaps not even the seven millions for ships and the ten millions for increase of postal facilities. Whatever be the judgment of any citizen as to the propriety of the increase by forty millions of our pension expenditures, he will be much less inclined to blame the then dominant party if he will but read the debate in volume 19 of the *Record* of 1891, at page 3,118 or thereabouts, and find that the only complaint the present chairman of Ways and Means had to make against the appropriation was that in giving the soldier forty millions instead of one hundred and forty millions we were giving him too little. " They ask for bread, and you are giving them a stone," was the emphatic language of Mr. Springer before he became steadied by responsibility.

The blame of the candid citizen will be still further mitigated when he turns to page 4,062 of this interesting volume and finds that Mr. Holman showed by his vote that he thought that the appropriation of forty millions was too small by the large sum of one hundred and four millions, and that the sanction of his highly economical name is attached to the proposition that the Republicans were too niggardly by a round one hundred millions of dollars. Undoubtedly Judge Holman will be somewhat less ready to vote large sums when he has the responsibility, and he will be the less ready while in the majority to urge large appropriations than when he was in the minority.

Growth of expenditures has not been confined to Republican rule. In 1880, the last year of the Forty-fifth Congress, the appropriations were one hundred and ninety millions. In 1882 they were two hundred and eighteen millions—an increase of twenty-eight millions. In 1885 one hundred and ninety-five millions were the total, while in 1887 two hundred and sixty-three millions were called for, and both these sums were appropriated while Mr. Randall was at the head of the committee in charge. At the end of the Fiftieth Congress twenty-three millions more had been added for 1890, making in all an increase of ninety-one millions from 1885 to 1890. The increase from 1888 to 1890 was thirty-eight millions. During these last two years there were no additional pensions. The increase from 1890 to 1892 was one hundred and sixteen millions. But when you take out seventy-five millions increase of pensions, and also the pension deficiencies saddled upon us by the House Democracy, you will find a gratifying improvement even in "retrenchment and reform" over the last two years of Democratic control.

Thus far the question has been considered on the basis of amounts appropriated ; but this is no test whatever of either economy or expenditure. Amounts appropriated for deficiencies, instead of being charged to any first session of a Congress, ought to be charged to its predecessor. It is one of the common insincerities of "economy and reform" in both parties to refuse what is needed before election and pay it the next session. This artifice serves a double purpose. It exalts your own virtue and brings into bolder relief the wickedness of the enemy. As a striking example of how the people may be misled by simply comparing the amounts appropriated, take the figures of 1884 and 1885. On the face of them, the Republican Congress in 1884 voted two hundred and thirty-one millions, and its Democratic successor only voted one hundred and ninety-five millions —a plain triumph of virtue to the extent of thirty-six millions. Yet if you will look at the figures for pensions of both years and the year previous, you will see that the Republicans in 1884 and 1883, owing to a miscalculation of the Pension Office, had appropriated eighty-six millions for pensions, whereof a large surplus was unused. Of this the Democracy had the benefit the next year, and so had to appropriate only twenty millions for that object. This enabled them, before the unthinking, to score a victory for retrenchment and reform of thirty-six millions. The other thirty millions, which were a real increase of expenditure, were concealed 'in the totals, though plainly visible in the items.

A River and Harbor Bill of fourteen millions was lost in that total, as were also increases of five and a half millions for postal service, five millions of extra deficiencies, and seven millions of "miscellaneous." In other words, to use epithets instead of argument, the total shows thirty-six millions of retrenchment and reform, while the facts show thirty millions of extravagance and prodigality. All four epithets, however, are equally absurd. The increase was needed, was made, and ought to have been made.

When you examine the figures of the last two Houses—one Democratic and the other Republican—and charge off to each the rebates which belong to each, you will find that the last Democratic House voted the expenditure of $838,017,972, just $85,978,-813 more than its predecessor, also Democratic; that the last Republican House voted the expenditure of $948,800,734, an increase of $110,782,762 over the last Democratic House. The net increase, for which it had no Democratic precedent, was therefore $24,703,-949. Inasmuch as the United States was two years older and two years bigger, this would not be a bad showing on general principles; but the fact that the Fifty-first Congress appropriated two hundred and eighty-eight millions for pensions, against one hundred and seventy-seven millions appropriated by the Fiftieth, accounts for every cent of increase over the votes of the last Democratic House, and if there is any blame to be attributed to us for giving this large sum, it cannot be made by the party which has just made Judge Holman chairman of Appropriations, while on the records of Congress itself rests the proof that this chosen representative of retrenchment and reform voted to double the very increase about which there has been so much undisciplined outcry.

Undoubtedly some decreases are possible for the present House. They will find many honest debts of the United States paid and liquidated which will never have to be paid again. The navy will not have to ask as much as during the last two years, and perhaps the Sundry Civil Bill will bear reduction. But the legislative and judicial expenses are likely to increase, as well as the proper demands of the postal service.

Whatever course be pursued, if the country really cares about its expenditures, the people ought to be on the watch against the substitution of parsimony for economy, and against that legislative manœuvring which lessens the expenses of the year before election by thrusting them upon the year after election.

THOMAS B. REED.

II.—ECONOMY AND THE DEMOCRACY.

BY THE HON. W. S. HOLMAN.

THE growth of public expenditure during the last few years has arrested the attention of intelligent men in all sections of the Union. Statistical tables are wearisome, but a glance at the past and a few facts will illustrate how rapidly this government is drifting away from the policy of its founders. Their purpose was to establish a plain, frugal government that should treat its people with equal-handed fairness, opening up to all alike an equal chance in the struggle for life by protecting all, granting special favors to none,—a system in forcible contrast with the " splendid governments " which had filled all Europe for centuries with poverty and wretchedness.

The state of the republic in 1860, seventy-three years after the Federal Government was formed, expressed the masterly statesmanship that from the beginning had conducted its affairs. During that period it had passed through three wars, acquired its present imperial limits from ocean to ocean, and reached the first rank in the family of nations ; greatly excelling in the general equality and prosperous condition of its people all former experience in government, with taxation unfelt, and the annual expenditures reaching less than sixty-two millions of dollars—an increase, computed from the beginning, of less than a million dollars a year, embracing the long period it was exposed to the hostility of foreign powers. All the statesmen of that period knew that, occupying the most favored portion of the globe, the wealth of this nation must greatly surpass that of any other in any age of the world, but with the government standing impartial, the ever-growing wealth would be fairly diffused ; that wealth and luxury would abound, but as long as the government confined itself to the powers conferred on it by the constitution and remained impartial and frugal, the republic was secure. But the statesmen of that period understood as well as those of this do, that by artificial methods of developing the resources of the country, through favoritism in legislation, all this might be promptly changed, and that overgrown estates and favored classes and impoverished multitudes might, by a stroke of legislation, supplant the equality, happiness, and prosperity of the whole people equally protected and fostered by impartial laws.

All men know that excessive revenues in the treasury, drawn from the people, which scrimp every fireside of labor, mean lavish and corrupt expenditures, excessive salaries, unnecessary employments, subsidies, bounties, and contracts which crystallize into great estates. All statesmen have known that such expenditures cannot be indulged in by a republic without greatly imperilling its free institutions.

During the late war, of course, the conditions were, for the time, completely changed. There is no economy during a conflict of arms. When the war had terminated, it was practically impossible in matters of expenditure to reëstablish the government at once on the basis of a frugal civil service ; yet at an early moment progress to this end was visible. The old leaders of the Republican party still in some degree controlled its movements.

No party ever came into power whose leaders more sincerely sympathized with the people, their struggles and aspirations, than the Republican party. At its elementary convention in Pittsburg, Penn., when Hale and Julian were nominated for President and Vice-President, it announced principles so in harmony with the spirit of the earlier period of the republic as to reach the hearts of the people. With its demand for frugal government, it declared that the public lands—that then great heritage of the republic—should not be sold or granted to corporations, but should be held in sacred trust to secure homes for actual settlers—a grand declaration ! With these principles, and with a loud voice demanding retrenchment and purity in government, the Republican party came into power. While the counsels of its old leaders—such men as Washburn of Illinois, of the House, and Fessenden of Maine, of the Senate—controlled the party, the promises it had made were in the main, except as to the public lands, faithfully kept. At the close of the war the old views of the value and necessity of economy in government rapidly revived, and with manifest determination on the part of the people that economy should be restored.

In the Forty-third Congress, 1875–76, the whole appropriations, annual and permanent, were brought down to a fairly reasonable basis.

The current annual appropriations for the two sessions of that Congress were $362,851,212.06, while the permanent appropriations were $290,943,779.15; in all, current, annual, and permanent, $653,794,991.21.

Considering the magnitude of the permanent appropriations, which embraced interest on the public debt, sinking-fund, and the like, this result was reasonably satisfactory, and had it not been for the extravagance displayed by the Republican party in the second session of the Forty-second Congress, it is probable that the result of the congressional election of 1874 would have been a Republican triumph.

It will be remembered that, in the closing hours of the Forty-second Congress, and after the members were elected to the House of the Forty-third Congress, there was an unusual display of extravagance in salaries, including those of members of Congress. This the people promptly rebuked in the election of members to the House of the Forty-fourth Congress, in 1874.

The Democratic party, coming into power in the Forty-fourth Congress, reduced the annual appropriations (two sessions) to $299,145,788.88. The permanent appropriations had in the meantime increased, and yet the entire appropriations, annual and permanent, of the Forty-fourth Congress were but $595,597,-832.28—a reduction of $58,197,158.93, as compared with the appropriations of the preceding Congress.

This result was certainly satisfactory, for at that period the great body of the unfunded war debt was settled.

The Democrats came into the control of the House under a pledge of retrenchment in the expenses of the government, and the Senate was fully informed that the country demanded a restoration of the old-time economy.

Of course no one expected that a government that had recently passed through a great war, where lavish expenditure is inevitable, could return at once to severe frugality in expenditures, and the appropriations made for the years 1877–78 (Forty-fourth Congress) were reasonably satisfactory; but it seems that Congress had reached the limit of retrenchment, and in the Forty-fifth and Forty-sixth Congresses there was a material increase in the appropriations.

In the Forty-seventh Congress (1883–84) the permanent and annual appropriations had reached $777,435,948.54. During this Congress, both branches and the Executive were under the control of the Republican party, but in the Forty-eighth Congress, the Democrats controlling the House (1885–86), the appropriations, annual and permanent, were reduced to $655,269,402.33, about the same as those made by the Forty-third Congress; but in the meantime the permanent appropriations had been materially decreased.

In the Forty-ninth Congress (1887–88) the annual appropriations were very materially increased, and, with the permanent appropriations, amounted to $746,342,495.51.

In the Fiftieth Congress (1889–90) they had reached the indefensible sum of $817,963,859.80. This growth of expenditure no one could or even attempted to defend. It was displayed in the first session of that Congress as well as in the second. The only attempt ever made to excuse the excessive appropriations of that Congress was based on the persistency of the Senate in insisting on increased appropriations. The vigilance of the people was again expressed. The Democrats lost the House and the Republicans resumed the control of every department of the government.

With the members of the House of Representatives of the Fifty-first Congress coming fresh from the people, it was natural to expect that care in the public expenditures would be shown, but the rules adopted at the opening of the Fifty-first Congress created widespread apprehension among men who understood that rules "to do business" in Congress meant easy access to the treasury.

The appropriations made by the Fifty-first Congress reached the unexampled sum of $988,417,183.34, and with the money authorized to be refunded to the several States on account of the direct tax, and certain indefinite items, amounted to the sum of $1,007,930,183.84. But the sum of money actually appropriated by the Fifty-first Congress does not fully express the charges it imposed in the future on the public treasury. To illustrate : It created specifically 1,941 new offices, at an annual cost of $2,359,-215, and increased the salaries of 403 officials in the aggregate $245,108.12 ; a record in this particular not approached by any other Congress assembled prior to or since the war, with the possible exception of the Forty-seventh Congress. It authorized the construction of new public buildings to cost in the aggregate $17,046,639.54 ; it appropriated $28,087,495 for river and harbor work, and in addition thereto authorized contracts to be entered into in the case of a few specific places obligating the government in the further sum of $11,331,779, making a total of $39,419,274 authorized expenditures for rivers and harbors, or more than 75 per centum increase over what was ever voted for this purpose by any other Congress.; and, as if distrustful of its work being approved by the people, fastened its system of subsidies and bounties on the government for years to come, rendering the House of Representatives powerless to correct the abuse until the periods named shall have expired. From the very beginning of that Congress unsatisfactory results had been apprehended. The rules, while arbitrary on one hand, opened up on the other unjustifiable facilities for the appropriation of money.

The fruits of the new rules were a bitter disappointment to the members of the great party which elected that House, and filled them with indignation. An increase in the public expenditures in two years of $189,966,323.54 startled and exasperated all considerate men.

If the Congress of the United States sets the example of extravagance, the purity and integrity of the whole system are endangered. Hence the alarm that has been expressed time and time again by the people when any party has shown indifference to economy and purity in the government.

Excessive taxation, always inexcusable and unjust, impoverishes the citizen, creates countless charges upon the government, —a swarm of unnecessary officials who eat up the fruits of the labor of the people,—and in course of time inevitably consolidates the wealth of the country. Unnecessary taxation of itself is certainly a great evil, yet it is far less to be deplored than the inevitable result—lavish expenditures creating venal motives in every avenue and channel of administration.

The details of the appropriations of the Fifty-first Congress would be wearisome, but exceedingly instructive. But the policy of inexcusable expenditure by the Fifty-first Congress, declared in the rules it adopted, does not express fully the drift of the Republican party, as represented in Congress. It is more clearly expressed in its measures in favor of bounties and subsidies.

The country now fully understands the effects of the policy of the party in subsidizing corporations, during the late war and later, with lands west of the Mississippi equal in territory to seven great States of the Union ; those corporations promoting an unexampled immigration to occupy these lands and make their grants valuable, and reducing, by reason of over-production westward, the value of lands from the Atlantic to the Mississippi River and beyond. And the country understands that, while this policy greatly and injuriously affected the eastern section of the Union in interfering with the natural development of our country, the pecuniary benefits of these unexampled grants of lands, while inflicting irreparable injury on our landless people by increasing the price of the lands to them for homes, accrued largely to capitalists of Germany and England ; and the humiliation and dishonor brought upon the country by the Credit Mobilier through these subsidies should not be forgotten.

But still further to illustrate the effect of subsidies : A great corporation, near the close of the late war, obtained a subsidy of $500,000 a year for ten years for carrying the mails between San Francisco and China and Japan. Encouraged by the former success, in 1872 it applied to Congress, and obtained an additional subsidy of $500,000 for ten years. Soon afterward the fact was disclosed that the enactment of the law authorizing this last subsidy was obtained by the expenditure of large sums of money. In an investigation into the facts in the Forty-second Congress (a Republican Congress), Mr. Kasson, of Iowa, on behalf of a committee appointed to inquire into the facts, reported to the House of Representatives, February 25, 1875, that $703,100 was expended by that corporation in securing the enactment of the law authorizing this additional subsidy. With such fatal results of subsidies, bounties, and favoritism in legislation, can the American people, who hold the honor of their government as above price, look with favor on such policy ?

With this experience of the effects of the policy of granting subsidies in full view, this Fifty-first Congress entered upon a liberal system of subsidies to the owners of ships engaged in the foreign trade, carrying mails; and it now seems—a fact that was urged on the House in that Fifty-first Congress as likely to occur —that the same corporation which had expended in 1872 more than half a million dollars in carrying through an annual subsidy of $500,000 for ten years is now, and will be, the main recipient of this beneficent mail provision authorized by the Fifty-first Congress. It will be seen in the early future how many owners of ships are to be fostered by the treasury, and perhaps how many of the ships are owned in fact by capitalists of Great Britain.

That Fifty-first Congress, not content with subsidizing the owners of ships, generally gentlemen of wealth, granted bounties to the manufacturers of sugar. No particular industry had ever before been directly pensioned on the treasury. It is gratifying that this thoroughly un-American enactment, which gives special encouragement to a particular industry at the expense of all other industries of the United States, was promptly condemned by the people. Applications for bounties under this law furnish valuable information to the taxpayers of this country. Seven hundred and thirty cane-sugar producers are applicants, asking for more than eleven millions of dollars ; and the amount that will be paid them will reach from nine millions to eleven millions this year. Some astounding results are disclosed by the claims filed. Without going into detail, a few facts will illustrate the effects of this bounty law. It is said, and the report of the Commissioner of Internal Revenue seems to confirm it, that seventeen men in Louisiana will, if their claims for the production of sugar are verified, receive this year in the aggregate the sum of $2,356,720, an average for each person of $138,600 ; a sum which the average farmer might well consider an enormous fortune. It seems that even the sum that will be received from the treasury by the smallest sugar farmers in that State will reach $867, a bounty exceeding the entire earnings of the average farmer of the West. The tariff on sugar, while of course it increased the price, as the consumer paid the duty, was strictly a revenue measure, and gave no offence to the manly sentiment of equal fairness of men engaged in other industries. But will bounties paid to a favored class of producers animate the spirit of the great multitude of men engaged in other industries? Will not the patient toiler the products of whose fields command no bounty from the public treasury, embittered and discouraged, denounce as infamous the law that compels his labor to bear its part in the payment of bounties to enrich his fellow citizen engaged in an industry no more honorable nor in any degree more valuable to his country than his own? Will his indignation be diminished as he surveys his small estate, and remembers that these liberal bounties are paid to gentlemen of ample possessions? Will this increase his love for his country and his admiration of its even-handed justice? With such a record, is it surprising• that the Fifty-first Congress was condemned promptly by the people?

The two great parties which now struggle for supremacy are well illustrated by the views of two distinguished men of this present period, the late Mr. Randall, of Pennsylvania, and Mr. Reed, of Maine, both of whom were Speakers of the National House of Representatives and gentlemen of superior abilities.

From Mr. Randall's standpoint it was infinitely better that the government should be even penurious, with an overflowing treasury, than lavish and corrupt in its expenditures.

Mr. Reed's views are different. They were fully expressed in the rules of the Fifty-first Congress. The programme, fairly stated, was simple and direct : the majority should control the House ; obstructions and impediments should not be allowed ; the House should be organized "to do business." No one misapprehended the meaning of this—the excessive taxation of the people. Access to the treasury should not be obstructed by a discredited minority. Legislation should go on without hindrance. The result was natural enough—largely increased taxation of the people on the common necessaries of life, and a lavish expenditure of the people's money without any precedent in the history of our country.

Mr. Randall's views, as expressed in the rules he favored and their administration, meant restrictions on legislation, barriers against raids on the public treasury, a frugal and honest government that should not "take from the mouth of labor the bread it had earned."

WM. S. HOLMAN.

AN INTERNATIONAL MONETARY CONFERENCE.

BY THE HON. WILLIAM M. SPRINGER, CHAIRMAN OF THE WAYS
AND MEANS COMMITTEE OF THE HOUSE OF
REPRESENTATIVES.

COMMERCE between nations is increasing rapidly every year. The foreign commerce of the United States now amounts to nearly two billions of dollars annually, while that of Great Britain exceeds three billions five hundred millions of dollars. The prodigious number of transactions which comprise such enormous aggregates can hardly be realized. The increased facilities for transportation, the constant opening of new markets, the quick communication of intelligence by telegraphs, the publication of newspapers, trade reports, and commercial statistics, have brought all nations into one commercial family and established relations of mutual interest and profit.

The greatest hindrance at this time to international exchanges, next to restrictive legislation, is the want of uniformity in monetary systems and in weights and measures. The advantages of uniformity in these respects cannot be overestimated. In view of the intelligence which prevails in every part of the civilized world, and of the readiness with which all new inventions are adopted and employed, it is remarkable that there is at this time such a diversity as to coinage, weights, and measures between the various governments of the earth. Each nation seems to adhere to the systems of finance and domestic commercial exchanges which have prevailed heretofore, and which served every purpose of commerce in a state of isolation. If we consider the enormous volume of trade between all nations which has grown up in modern times, it is scarcely credible that so little advance should be made in the direction of securing uniformity of monetary systems and of weights and measures. The time is coming when the interests of business and of international exchanges will demand of the law-making powers of the respective nations the adoption of systems of uniformity in these respects.

The celebration of the four hundredth anniversary of the discovery of America is a most appropriate occasion for the assembling of an international congress in the city of Chicago during the World's Columbian Exposition, which should have for its object, and whose duty it should be, to formulate and submit for the approval of the governments sending representatives thereto, uniform systems and nomenclatures of coinage, of weights, and of measures. At this exposition will be exhibited the products of chief commercial importance of every civilized nation in the world. As one passes through the various buildings and beholds those products, he will find their value, their weight, and their measure expressed in different terms, so as to make comparisons almost impossible. The products in most cases will be familiar objects, but to compare them in price and quantity with the products of other countries will require a greater amount of intelligence than any one man will possess. There will be a perfect confusion of tongues, a modern commercial tower of Babel. This difficulty, however, must serve a useful purpose, and may perhaps result in the greatest advantage which will be secured by such an exposition of the products of the world. If out of this chaos of diversity should come complete systems of uniformity by which all commercial transactions could be expressed in the same terms, the exposition would prove the most important ever held, and the benefits to mankind would be as enduring as time itself. If an earnest effort shall be made on the part of the United States and all other governments whose products will be represented at this exposition, it is reasonable to hope, at least, that some good result will follow, if not the complete success of this much-needed reform.

The Congress of the United States should make proper provision for the assembling of such a congress. It should be in every sense a congress—a great, open, deliberative body, composed of the ablest citizens of the respective nations of the earth. Its proceedings should be published, the same as the proceedings of our Congress, and the press should be furnished with every facility for the reporting of the debates and proceedings. It should not be limited as to the time during which its deliberations are to take place. Ample time and opportunity should be afforded for the most thorough discussion of all the topics which may come before the body.

The President should be authorized, in behalf of the United States, to invite the governments with which we maintain diplomatic relations to send representatives to this international congress. The United States should be represented by at least twenty-one delegates, seven of whom should be appointed by the President and an equal number by the president of the Senate and by the Speaker of the House of Representatives. Not more than four to be appointed by each should be members of the same political party, and they should represent as far as possible all shades of opinion upon the subject of coinage. Those appointed by the president of the Senate and the Speaker of the House of Representatives should be members of this Congress who may be members of the Fifty-third Congress also.

The President of the United States should be instructed to inform the governments with which the United States maintains diplomatic relations that the government of the United States earnestly desires to secure uniform systems of coinage and of weights and measures, so as to facilitate as far as possible exchanges of commodities and to simplify monetary transactions; that this government especially desires an international agreement as to the relation which should be maintained between gold and silver, and uniformity in weight and fineness of the coins of each metal, and the adoption of a coin, or coins, that would be current at the same value in all countries of the world.

The President should be further instructed to call the attention of all such governments to the advantages which would accrue from the adoption of such uniform systems, and to say that the government of the United States would await with deepest concern the deliberations and conclusions that might be reached by this international congress, with the earnest hope that these efforts might be crowned with success. He should further inform such governments that, in the event that no conclusion is reached which would meet the approbation of this country, the law-making power of the United States will then be free to adopt such measures in reference to the subjects named as may be most conducive to the welfare of the people of this country.

The calling of such an international congress will not necessarily prevent the United States from legislating upon the subject of silver coinage in the meantime. It is universally conceded, however, that, owing to the present condition of the law-making power of the United States, no free-coinage bill can become a law during this Congress. It is possible that a bill having this object in view could pass the House of Representatives; it is barely possible that it might pass the Senate; but here the possibilities end. The President would undoubtedly return it with his veto to the house in which it originated, and there is no possibility of passing such a bill over executive disapproval by the necessary two-thirds' majority. Hence there will be no legislation on this subject by this Congress, which expires by limitation of law on the third day of March, 1893. The next Congress will not assemble in regular session until December of that year. This is the earliest period, then, at which it is possible to consider legislation which may thereafter be enacted into law in reference to the coinage of silver.

However desirable the free coinage of silver may be in the estimation of those in favor of legislation to secure that object, 'all efforts in that direction by this Congress will be futile. All legislative experience teaches that that which is most desirable cannot always be accomplished. Therefore that which is desirable, and which at the same time may be attained, ought to be the prime object of all legislators. What, therefore, is attainable by this Congress so far as silver coinage is concerned?

The calling of an international monetary congress and the discussion which such a congress would provoke would result in the greatest benefit possible to this country and to all other countries. Such a congress would not result in suppressing silver as a political issue, but would make it a great national and international question, to be settled at the earliest time practicable upon lines as broad as possible. All persons must concede that an international agreement upon this subject, which would secure uniformity of coinage throughout the world, is the object most to·be desired. With such an international agreement and uniformity, all apprehensions for the future would be dispelled, and there would be perfect security as to the value of each of the metals in all parts of the world and for all time to come. Those who favor the largest use possible of both metals will recognize at once the supreme importance of such an agreement as this. In view of the fact that this country cannot secure free coinage of silver for itself, even if that were desirable, prior to the time at which such a congress would assemble and conclude its labors, what objection can any bimetallist offer to making one last and determined effort to bring about a result which would be so beneficial to mankind ? But if such a congress should fail to reach a conclusion, or if the conclusion reached should not be acceptable to this country, the discussion which will have taken place will so enlighten the people of this country that when the Federal Congress assembles in December, 1893, it can enter upon the consideration of the subject with the light of the century thrown upon it. A campaign of education, as it were, will have been carried on, which must result in pointing the way to a proper solution of the question at that time.

There have been several international conferences held on the subject of coinage. There was one held at Paris in August, 1878. There were three commissioners on the part of the United States, Messrs. Reuben E. Fenton, William S. Groesbeck, and Francis A. Walker. Only nine governments were represented, namely, Austria-Hungary, Belgium, France, Italy, the Netherlands, Russia, Sweden and Norway, Switzerland, and the United States. The proceedings were conducted almost exclusively in the French language, but the secretary of the American commissioners obtained a stenographic report of the few English addresses, and these, with the journal of the conference, were transmitted to the Secretary of State of the United States. Congress has caused the report of the commission and the journal of the conference to be printed, together with an appendix which contains much useful information on the subject. Another international monetary conference was held in Paris in 1881. The same governments, with the exception of Russia and Italy, were represented in this conference, and also Denmark, Germany, Greece, Portugal, and Spain. The delegates on the part of the United States were William M. Evarts, Allen G. Thurman, and Timothy O. Howe. The journal of the conference and report of exhibits were printed by the Secretary of State.

The Pan-American Conference, which assembled in Washington in 1890, recommended the appointment of a commission, composed of one or more delegates from each nation represented in that conference, to consider the quality and kind of currency, the uses it shall have, and the value and proportion of the international silver coin or coins, and their relations to gold. The commission met in the early part of 1891. Three commissioners were appointed on behalf of the United States, namely, Nathaniel P. Hill, of Colorado, Lambert Tree, of Illinois, and William A. Russell, of Massachusetts. The delegates from the United States recommended that the governments represented unite in inviting a monetary conference of all the powers of the world, to be held in London or Paris, "to consider bimetallism and the equalization of gold and silver, to be fixed by international agreement, and the universal assimilation of monetary types both of gold and silver and their legal international circulation for all purposes." A committee representing the Spanish-American republics reported a similar recommendation.

Mr. Romero, the president of the commission and Mexican Minister at Washington, submitted an amendment to both propositions, to the effect that the government of the United States should be requested to " invite a universal conference of all civilized nations, to be held at the time it may deem desirable, to reach, if possible, an agreement upon a fixed ratio between gold and silver, and the adoption of a common coin for all of said nations." After a prolonged discussion of all these propositions, the commission adopted a series of resolutions setting forth the great benefit to the commerce of the world which such an agreement would secure, and expressing the opinion that the object could be accomplished by an international agreement; but, doubting whether the desired ends could be attained at present, the concluding resolution merely expressed "the wish that before long another commission may meet, which shall reach an agreement that will secure the adoption of a uniform monetary system between the nations of America advantageous to each and all."

It remains to be seen whether the United States will make any further effort in the direction indicated.

These conferences have not brought about the objects contemplated, but they were not without beneficial results. Much more important results, undoubtedly, would have followed if, instead of these small conferences, there had been a great international congress, composed of two or three hundred delegates, whose deliberations would have been conducted openly, where the representatives of the press would have been present, and where the widest publicity would have been given to the discussions and proceedings.

Objection to such an international congress has been made upon the ground that the great governments of Europe will oppose any agreement which will give silver a place in the coinage of the world, and that it will be impossible to attain success. It is possible that some countries may decline to send representatives to such a congress, or refuse to enter into any agreements upon the subject of coinage, of weights, or of measures. But that fact should not prevent other governments from sending such representatives, or from earnestly desiring to secure uniformity in these matters. If the Latin nations of this hemisphere and of Europe should reach a conclusion satisfactory to them, it would not be many years until all the other nations of the earth would adopt their system. In any event, success will never be attained unless great and earnest efforts are made in that direction. The time has arrived, the opportunity is offered, and the holding of such an international congress ought to be favored by all who desire to promote the commercial interests of the world.

If international agreements could be reached upon the subjects indicated in this article, and if such agreements should receive the approval of the great commercial nations, this achievement would be the crowning glory of the nineteenth century. But if no agreement should be reached, the education which would result from the holding of such a congress would be worth all the expense and effort that would be put forth, and would enable the representatives of our own country, when it is possible to secure results, to deal with the question of. coinage in such a manner as would best promote the welfare of our own people.

WILLIAM M. SPRINGER.

THE HIGHLANDS OF JAMAICA

BY LADY BLAKE.

WHAT most surprised me after a residence in Jamaica long enough to enable me to form an opinion of the climate all the year round, was its comparative coolness. In the West Indies the sweltering, stifling heat of the East Indies is unknown. The days are undeniably hot, the direct rays of a tropical sun being invariably too ardent to be desirable, but the nights are almost always cool and pleasant, and the evenings and early mornings are ideally delightful. All through the day, from about 9 A.M. to 6 P.M., a strong sea breeze, called by the early Spanish settlers "the doctor," blows almost continuously, and at night a deliciously cool and refreshing land breeze sets in, sweeping gently down from the Blue Mountains, and, as all things are judged by comparison, seeming downright chilly after the heat of the day, so as to render a blanket often a desirable adjunct to one's covering at night, even in the middle of summer.

The continuance, not the intensity, of the heat in the West Indies is what is trying to Europeans, accustomed to the bracing frosts and snows of more northern climes. After months and months of smiling summer, one begins to feel a little "run down," as the phrase is, and to realize that the winters of the stern and solemn North are a desirable tonic. But Jamaica, like Cleopatra, has the charm of "infinite variety." To be braced, there is no need to face the wearisomeness and discomforts of a long and tedious voyage, for above those hot dry plains tower the glorious Blue Mountains; "the eternal hills" will afford us just what we want. So we order a " buggy,"—as the light and convenient little hooded carriages in general use in Jamaica are termed, with that ugliness of diction that distinguishes most things coming from the United States,—and the pair of rat-like but well-bred and wiry little horses that draw it soon cause the scene to change from the untidy-looking cashaws, and dusty cacti, and penguins of the plains in this rainless month of July, to the nodding bamboos, the fluttering lilac plumes of the mountain-pride, the chocolate, coffee, and orange trees that form a luxuriant foreground to the romantic scenery of the picturesque gorge of Gordon Town, through which rushes and sparkles the Hope River, as if rejoicing to bring life and refreshment to the thirsty plain below.

High on either hand rise the grass-clad hills, now, alas ! denuded of the lofty forests that once drew down the blessing of rain in abundance. Here and there a tiny cottage is perched like a swallow's nest against some shoulder of the steep incline, surrounded by a field of pineapples and shaded by a bougainvillea, whose rich mantle of magenta blossoms proves that no color, in itself and in its proper place, is unpleasing.

Lower down, nearer the stream, stand more ambitious dwellings, with prettily carved and painted verandas, over which trail the great white blossoms of the peanmontia grandiflora, or the sweet-scented, wax-like flowers of the stephanotis. Geraniums, roses, heliotrope, and nasturtiums (exotics here) cluster in cherished beds in the garden, amidst a neglected tangle of tropical shrubs, where flame out the gorgeous crimson flowers of the hibiscus, or the pale-blue blossoms of the plumbago stretch gently upwards towards the light. A golden allamanda lolls over the fence, and, above, the huge dark-green, deeply-indented leaves of the bread-fruit (one of the most beautiful of trees), and the olive and ruddy brown leaves of the star-apple, " two-faced, like a woman," according to the negro proverb, form a delightful canopy, beneath which the owner of the miniature Eden may swing contentedly in his hammock and watch such passers as come by, principally files of women passing down to market, chattering volubly, their petticoats well drawn up over their stalwart hips, so as not to impede their steps. Bright-colored bandannas are twisted, turban-like, round their heads, on which are piled huge bunches of bananas, or gaily-painted baskets heaped high with green and brown avocado pears, bright yellow mangoes, yams, carrots, and scallions, all balanced with astonishing skill.

For miles and miles these women walk barefooted briskly and cheerily, though heavily laden with their wares for the market. When they draw near the town, some sit down and force their shrinking feet into the boots that were carried so much more conveniently on their heads, though the greater number reserve those uncomfortable impedimenta of an unwise civilization for the pleasing pain of their Sunday toilette. Unencumbered with the hideous high-heeled parodies known as " French boots " by the uninitiated, these women swing bravely along, sometimes traversing a distance of over twenty miles to Kingston, the mere distance in miles, not at all representing the endurance and exertion necessary to ascend and descend the steep and rugged mountain paths. It has been calculated that 10,000 people come in this manner every Saturday into Kingston market, sleeping the previous night (for markets in the tropics open with the dawn) in the piazzas of the town or in the bush by the wayside.

To return to our journey. For three miles through the beautiful gorge, it is all collar-work for the horses and a panorama of loveliness and interest for us ; then we reach the little hamlet that lends its name to the valley. Here the driving-road ends, and ponies await us for the ascent. They are small, but generally sure-footed and quiet, some of them, indeed, possessing powers of climbing that are positively cat-like. Riding in the hills is necessarily slow, as progression is very much like riding up and down the declivity of an exceedingly steep roof, with an occasional excursion along the extreme edge of the gutter for a change ; consequently distance is computed by the time taken to accomplish it, not by the number of miles traversed.

To reach our destination to-day will take about three hours. But what a glorious ride it is. The path winds along under mango and mahoe trees ; the lovely foliage of the wild tamarind makes a delicious shade , its long branches laden with bunches of twisted crimson pods, out of which hang rows of ebon-black seeds ; the bank beneath is a mass of gold and silver and maiden-hair ferns, through which peep the blue blossoms of the evil-eye, the yellow, trumpet-shaped bells of the gentian, or the brilliant scarlet flowers of the exquisite " dazzle."

Mocking-birds call from the thickets, and a minute, brilliant-green bird with a crimson spot on its throat, a creature that looks as if made of emeralds and one large ruby, is seated on a branch near the stream. It is the " Jamaica robin " or " tocty "; so small is it that formerly it was reckoned amongst the humming-birds and was so classed by no less a naturalist than Sir Hans Sloane. It belongs, in reality, to the kingfisher family, and, like the English kingfisher, nests in holes in banks. Humming-birds flash like jewels through the woods ; one tiny "bee humming-bird," the smallest of known birds, dashes almost into one's face in evident anger. Its nest must be close by. Here it is, oddly enough, perched at the top of a bunch of small unripe bananas ; a tiny, beautiful structure, hardly larger than a tailor's thimble, lined with down of the silk cotton-tree, and covered with traces of gray lichen, woven on to the nest in some marvellous fashion with the threads from a spider's web. In the nest nestle two little downy creatures hardly larger than good-sized honey-bees, with very long beaks in proportion to their size, which they open wide, clamoring vigorously at the sound of any chirp that seems to herald the approach of food. The parent bird hovers over them, and, undismayed by our curious presence, inserts her beak down each tiny throat in turn, pouring into it the welcome food.

Thirty or forty feet below the track gurgles along the mountain torrent, and over it hover numbers of butterflies ; and dragonflies, with iridescent bodies and what look like heavy black wings, flit about, seeking some quiet pool in which to lay their eggs. As we get higher the character of the vegetation changes. Tall wild ginger plants, with long, sword-like leaves, and white or orange-colored flowers that emit a strong sweet scent carried far by the air, so that the mountain side is almost heavy with perfume, grow by the acre. The sturdy silver fern still throws up its large fronds, but the gold fern and the maiden-hair ferns have disappeared ; in their place here and there a true fern rears its stately head ; the masses of pink begonias grow larger and denser, till in places the hillside is rosy with their shell-like blossoms. Juniper cedars become larger and more frequent, and diffuse an aromatic, delicious odor all around.

But our brain is growing regularly weary by the succession of beauties, and it is a steep, long, and tiresome climb up the last hill. Our poor pony has no light task ; an old man has begged for the "loan of a tail" (a very usual request in the hills) and is hanging on to that portion of our steed, more to the man's satisfaction than to that of the quadruped. It seems as if the top of the hill receded the further we go. It takes a whole hour crawling up it. The evening is beginning to close in, and now come the fireflies ; the whole mountain side is alive with them.

They dance and sparkle everywhere, in the bamboos overshadow-ing the path, in the grass at our feet. Once or twice we mistake them for shooting stars. One poor wretch is caught in a spider's web in that white flowering yucca, and glitters to the last as it writhes in torment, while the spider, with human relentlessness, drives its fangs into its beautiful victim. But our journey is over ; at last we reach our destination, the government cinchona plantation.

The plantation was made in 1868 by the direction of Sir John Peter Grant, governor of Jamaica, with the object of propagating cinchona and extending its cultivation in the island. The fall in the price of quinine, consequent on the spread of cinchona-plant-ing in Ceylon and India, has prevented the Jamaica cinchona from proving the gold mine it was once fondly hoped it might turn out. Still, even at the reduced price, it pays its way fairly well, and a war would render the profits large. For two centu-ries the Jesuit's bark, as it was popularly called from having been first used and distributed by the far-seeing and untiring Jesuit fathers, was the jealously-guarded monopoly of Peru. Its valua-ble properties are said to have been discovered by the following accident : A party of men, worn and weary, were making their way through one of the vast forests of South America. One of them was sick with fever, nigh unto death ; his companions were unable to carry him through the thick jungle, and, coming to a small pool of water, the sick man there lay down, as he supposed, to die. The others went forward to seek assistance, if it could be found. After a few days, having come to some habitations and obtained relief, the men returned to where they had left their comrade, with the intention of burying his body, when to their as-tonishment the man was not only alive, but the fever had left him and he was recovering. Lying by the little pool, the sick man had assuaged his burning thirst by drinking of the water, bitter as it was, no doubt, from the trunk of a tree that had fallen and lay rotting in it. Before long the fever left him, and he began to mend.

This circumstance is said to have first led to the discovery of the value of Peruvian bark. Not long afterwards a great lady, wife of the viceroy of Peru, was cured at Lima of a dangerous fever by the administration of a decoction of the bark ; on her return to Spain she introduced its use in her own country, and

Linnæus immortalized the Countess of Chinchon by bestowing her name on the genus. It was not till 1860, after a long, laborious journey through the Andes, that Clements Markham succeeded, not without running some risk, in obtaining a supply of young cinchona plants, every obstacle being opposed by the people to their being carried out of the country. From these plants the cinchona cultivations of India, Jamaica, and other British possessions had their origin, and throve so well as rapidly to bring down the price of quinine. The cinchona, with its oval deeply-veined leaves, is a pretty tree, especially when in blossom, and the bunches of delicate fluffy pink-and-white flowers emit a delicious fragrance. The branches are often gray with lichens, and the richer the growth of lichens, the more valuable the bark.

The climate of these uplands is perfect, resembling the most lovely English summer weather, with a fresh, exhilarating feeling in the air that recalls Switzerland and the Alps. The evenings, however, are cooler than those of our English summer, so that when the day closes it is pleasant to have a fire of fragrant cedar logs in the sitting-room. The scenery all around is strikingly fine. Blue Mountain Peak, the highest mountain in the West Indies, on whose summit, as is related with pride, ice has more than once been found, rises on one hand ; John Crow Peak on the other, beyond which rises range upon range of mountains, melting away in a blue haze on the horizon. Below glistens the placid sea ; through it the palisades writhe like a dark serpent with Port Royal for its head, guarding the magnificent harbor, while "distance lends enchantment to the view" of hot, dusty Kingston, with the Liguanea plain brightened here and there by the green gleam of cane fields.

The rides through the high mountain district are most beautiful, but one must have a steady head to venture on some of the paths, which, in places, are barely a couple of feet wide, the mountain rising sheer at one side, with a precipice at the other, down which a single false step on the part of one's pony would send one spinning a couple of thousand feet. On many of these paths it is dangerous to stop for a single moment, and impossible to turn round or pass man or beast. In one instance a lady dropped her handkerchief and had to proceed without it, as the track was so narrow that no one would dismount to pick it up.

The hills are thickly covered with masses of the largest and most juicy wild strawberries to be procured anywhere; in places they grow as if planted in regular beds. Cape gooseberries and blackberries abound, and there are bilberries in quantities, but the lowly shrub from which we were wont at home to pluck the latter has here sprung into a regular tree, in whose shade we sit and rest when wearied with strawberry-picking.

Enjoyable expeditions may be made in all directions. A ride to the top of the peak and a night in the hut near the summit for the enterprising, or a tramp to the top of cloud-capped John Crow, clearing the way as we go with machetes; the shrill whistle of the unseen "solitaire" ringing all round us; every now and then the presence of a wild hog hidden in the bush telling how much he is disturbed by the unwonted intrusion. So invigorating is the air that one may walk for miles without feeling fatigue.

To the lover of botany or the collector of ferns, the highlands of Jamaica are simply paradise. Flowers of the most brilliant hues and graceful forms, from the homely gorse and modest pansy, which have "gone wild" in the island, to true denizens of the tropics abound everywhere. The pink, velvety maurandia grandeus hangs its festoons over rock and bush; the crimson petals of the blakia triverirs show star-like amid the dark foliage, and the little heath-like crephea decandria, so common in English green-houses, fringes the path. It is a pity that most of the tropical flowers have no popular names, but have to be distinguished by their stiff, pedantic, scientific nomenclature lacking all the poetry and charm attaching to names such as the shepherd's weather-glass, the heart's-ease, the forget-me-not of English meadows. Trails of large, white, sweet-scented dog-roses fling themselves over the bushes, and clusters of passion-flowers delight the eye, while their fruits, known as sweet-cups, are juicy and agreeable to thirsty palates.

But perhaps the most delightful of all these expeditions is a day spent in the tree-fern forests. The largest and most magnificent hot-house gives but a faint idea of the grandeur and beauty of tropical vegetation in its native home, and one there enjoys it in the cool shade, free from the stifling atmosphere so oppressive in hot-houses. Huge tree-ferns tower five-and-twenty and thirty feet high. On seeing similar ones in the mountains of Hispaniola, "the Spaniards argued the richness of the soil, making ferns grow to such a vast bigness, which in Europe were so inconsiderable."

The stems of the tree-ferns give shelter to myriads of filmy ferns of fairy-like delicacy and loveliness. They climb over the rocks, cling to every branch, and embrace each fallen stem. Selaginellas and mosses lend their aid to enhance the beauty of the scene, and even in this greensward shade flowers are not wanting. The small dark-blue flowers of the manettia lygistum peep out from amongst the shrubs over which they twine, while, above, the rich bells of the merianea bullifera (which takes its name from the well-known artist and naturalist Mme. de Merian) hang blushing at their own beauty.

Transparent-winged butterflies, curious as beautiful, and countless moths flutter up from moss and tree as one forces a way through the intertwining boughs, and it is just possible that an æsthetic spider with formidable fangs has made its funnel-shaped nest and covered the trap-door with translucent films in that luxuriant mass of ferns; so it is as well not too rashly to thrust one's hands into hidden neighborhoods. However, one of the many advantages of Jamaica is that the dangers of venomous reptiles and insects are few. Poisonous snakes there are none, and such harmless kinds as it once possessed have become so scarce that to find one is a rare prize.

Scorpions there are, but, unless molested, one never hears of their stinging. In the mountains they are seldom seen. I once found one, when breaking off a piece of rock to watch a community of ants. Comfortably ensconced on a ledge of rock in the midst of the ants was a small, light-colored scorpion with a young family of six or seven on her back, and some "children of a larger growth" squatting around her. Probably the scorpions had chosen the spot in order to feed on the ants and their eggs, but the ants apparently had no fear of the intruders, as, had they turned on the scorpions, the latter would have fared no better than did Gulliver among the Lilliputs. It is singular to watch a maternal scorpion carrying her family on her back. I have counted as many as seventy young ones so carried. As they grew larger, the little creatures sometimes descended and ran about, and when alarmed scuttled back to their point of vantage, using their parent's legs as a scaling-ladder. The mother is said to feed her young with her saliva. It was formerly supposed that the infant scorpions preyed upon their mother, sucking out her body till she was left a dry skeleton. This is certainly not the case, and the idea probably arose from the old scorpion sloughing her coat after the departure of the brood. For the reputation of the scorpion's amiability, I regret to say that sometimes the parents devour their offspring. I kept a scorpion and its young for some days securely papered up in a box from which nothing could have escaped ; having procured a bottle that seémed a more desirable abode for the family, I opened the box ; the mother scorpion was there, but its offspring were gone.

Mosquitoes, as everywhere in the tropics, do their best, like some higher beings, to render themselves obnoxious. In the woods they are of a peculiarly fierce temperament, but they are not as numerous in Jamaica as in other islands of the West Indies, and during the winter months there is almost complete immunity from them even in the plains. Ticks are the chief pest of the island, but they, again, only appear during a few months of the year, and scarcely make their way to the high hills.

But, to make amends for the unpleasing qualities of some insects (if it is permissible in a slight paper like this, for unscientific convenience, to class ticks in that category), there are others that afford one nothing but delight. A beautiful sight is to watch a flight of emperor-moths (*Urania Sloanus*), which sometimes appear soaring and wheeling in the air in hundreds, flying up and up till they are lost to sight. Though so numerous, these lovely moths are difficult to capture, their flight being so high and strong as more to resemble that of a lark than that of an insect; indeed, I have more than once mistaken an emperor-moth for a small bird. The groundwork of the wings is black, with iridescent stripes and patches of blue, green, and rose-color. Whence they come is a mystery. I believe the caterpillars are unknown to science, though somewhere in the mountains they must exist in thousands. The moths appear to come down from the higher mountains, flying down sometimes as far as the plains. The easiest way of obtaining specimens is by shooting them with a small collecting-gun charged with sand.

The mountains of Jamaica, even to the natives, have been *terra incognita* till very recent days. When the Spaniards discovered Xamayca, though the seacoasts were thickly populated by Indians, the "inland parts were unpeopled solitudes." The Spanish settlers only inhabited the plains, and the early English settlers seem to have followed the example, for, after the great earthquake of 1692, an eye-witness thus speaks of the Blue Mountains : " But those wild desert places being rarely or never visited by anybody, not by negroes themselves, we are yet ignorant of what happened there." The introduction of the coffee-tree probably first led to the opening-up and settlement of the uplands. Numerous comfortable little houses with their coffee works and barbecues, around which flourish rich European and tropical flowers in a delightful medley, are now dotted about the former desolate mountain solitudes ; negro huts cluster here and there beneath clumps of bananas, and their cultivations are creeping up and invading even the higher hills ; but much remains to be done. Narrow and precipitous bridle-paths are at present the only means of access to those regions of wondrous beauty and healthfulness, and are ill adapted for carrying down the rich produce to which the extended cultivation is giving rise, and impossible to be attempted by invalids in search of renewed life and health.

If, as we hope, Jamaica may ere long become a health resort and playground, not only for the West Indies and America, but for Europe, a driving-road to the sanatorium that must then arise amidst the mountains is an absolute necessity, for many invalids who now throng the Mediterranean Riviera will then acknowledge that the Jamaican mountains, which restored their vanished strength, are not only one of the loveliest but one of the healthiest spots in God's creation.

EDITH BLAKE.

SHALL WE HAVE FREE SHIPS?

BY CAPTAIN JOHN CODMAN.

In the January number of THE NORTH AMERICAN REVIEW Mr. Cramp essays a reply to your question as to the cost of ships. Leaving out of consideration what he says of contracts for national vessels as irrelevant to the purpose, his answer, condensed, is this: "Do you mean tramps? Well, it is beneath the dignity of an American mechanic to build vessels of that class. We would not duplicate them at any cost. Do you mean such ships as the 'ocean greyhounds'? I have to say that every shipyard has methods, systems, and practices peculiarly its own. I would not build ships just like them, but I would build ships equally good for the same price."

It is very common to sneer after this manner at the great fleet of independent steamships, which, notwithstanding the large number and tonnage of the regular lines, far exceed them, and are actually doing the principal business upon the ocean, many of them owned and commanded by American citizens. It is true that they are roughly finished, for fine brass and joiner work is not required for freighting; but the plea that they are unseaworthy is negatived by the fact that underwriters insure them and the cargoes they carry. Shippers and underwriters may be supposed to understand their own affairs, and captains and officers to set a value upon their own lives. At all events, it is undeniable that, when an American desires to have an independent steamship (call her a "tramp" if you please) or an iron sailing ship to be employed exclusively in foreign trade, he invariably has her built in England or Scotland, registers her in the name of a British subject, and takes a mortgage upon her for her full value—a round-about course that he is forced by our absurd navigation laws to pursue, and one that he would certainly avoid if he could be equally well served at home.

In considering what Mr. Cramp has elsewhere said, I shall treat him, I trust, with courtesy ; while, as a Free-Trader, looking upon protection as an injustice, I cannot regard subsidies and bounties for the promotion of shipbuilding otherwise than as unjust extortions, or, at the best, needless charities, and those who ask for them as suppliants at our hands. Mr. Cramp has voluntarily placed himself in that attitude. Somewhat analogous to the subject under consideration is a most valuable and comprehensive paper written for *Scribner's Magazine* of November, 1891, by Mr. John H. Gould, on "The Ocean Steamship as a Freight Carrier." Both writers agree in what is patent to all others as well as to them, that the American foreign carrying trade is rapidly becoming annihilated. Mr. Gould observes :

"Every nation is interested in the extension of its ocean freight-carrying business. The welfare of the farmer, the artisan, and the merchant is inter-woven with that of men who live on the sea. Commerce and the industries go hand in hand, and the magnificent showing that the former makes is only an indication of the prosperity of the latter. No more apt illustration of the growth of the American nation in the last quarter of a century can be pointed out than the development of her ocean traffic."

Now, the magnificent showing of commerce here presented applies to the United States ; but the prosperity of the "ocean freight-carrying business," with which he would connect it, applies to almost every other civilized nation under the sun, which we have protected in the transportation of our commerce to the exclusion of our own people, as Mr. Gould himself has shown. The facts he has adduced in proof of this are in direct opposition to Mr. Cramp's theory that our commerce can only be successful if carried on in American-built vessels, which cannot be built unless "the farmer, the artisan, the merchant," and every-body else, including the poor laundresses and shop-girls, contrib-ute their money to confer bounties and subsidies upon Mr. Cramp and his fellow shipbuilders.

One would think that the testimony before the shipping com-mittee, and the subsequent debate in Congress that defeated the monstrous Bounty Bill, of which Mr. Cramp was one of the chief engineers, had disposed of the "historic lie" that Great Britain grants subsidies for the promotion of shipbuilding, or that she subsidizes the infinitesimal part of her immense steam fleet for any purposes whatever other than those of postal necessity and those for adaptation to naval requirements. The results of the Subsidy

Bill passed by the last Congress should effectually dispel the illusion that legislation of this kind will promote shipbuilding or the carrying trade. It was a direct and needless bonus to already existing steamship companies, who will not be induced by it to build a single vessel that they would not have built in the course of their regular business, and who will not reduce their rate of freight or passage one penny for the benefit of the people who have bestowed this bounty upon them. And yet the president of the New York Chamber of Commerce, in the otherwise exceedingly able article contributed to THE NORTH AMERICAN REVIEW of October last, is still so infatuated with the idea that the Pacific Mail Steamship Company ought to be in some way hired to carry all American goods, that he introduces this paragraph into his discussion of " Our Business Prospects ":

" It is a humiliating fact that every bale of New England-made goods destined for China is shipped by the Canadian Pacific Railway to Vancouver, and from thence to its destination by English steamers, and this large traffic has been diverted from the American railways and from the Pacific Mail steamers because that line of steamers has not heretofore been able to compete with the English government subsidy."

A part of this is quite true, notwithstanding that a considerable subsidy was given to the Pacific Mail Steamship Company, and, large as that subsidy is, this state of things is likely to continue. But it is not because the steamers of that line are unable to compete with the English lines. The ships of the latter are all built so that they may serve as men-of-war if required, as are the " City of Paris " and other steamers of like class on the Atlantic. Consequently a great deal of weight is added and a great deal of room thrown out in order to adapt them to this purpose. Moreover, the speed required necessitates heavy machinery and an enormous consumption of coal. Therefore, with all the subsidy they receive on this account, they cannot carry freight any cheaper than the Pacific Mail Company's ships.

Senator Edmunds, who is quite as much of a Protectionist as Mr. Smith, hit upon the cause which the latter does not apprehend, when he said that " we cannot fight the laws of nature with congressional enactments." The Senator had studied geography in his youth, and Mr. Smith seemingly had not. Mr. Edmunds knew that degrees of longitude are shorter as we advance to the pole ; Mr. Smith, perhaps, had not yet made that discovery.

Now, a Lowell mill-owner, however much he may talk of the

"patriotism of home industry," has an eye to the main chance,
and does not care a button under what flag his merchandise is
shipped if he can get it speedily to market. The shortest way
from Lowell to China is by the Canadian Pacific Railway and
the British steamers from Vancouver. It may be a "humiliating fact" to Mr. Smith, but if he has any fault to find it should
be with the Creator, who flattened the earth, instead of bulging
it out, at the poles.

Mr. Cramp is careful to mention the British lines that are
subsidized, but he had not sufficient space to mention the vast
majority of the lines and the almost innumerable "tramps" that
receive no subsidy or bounty whatever. Fortunately for his purpose, Germany does subsidize a single steamship line plying
to the East Indies, and from this he draws the inference that
Germany subsidizes all her steamships "indirectly."

It is the boast of Mr. Cramp that he can build for the same
money a steamship equal in all respects to any that are built upon
the Clyde ; and yet he has never built one. Why not ? The
Inman and the Red Star lines, some of whose ships are subsidized
and some not, are owned chiefly by American citizens, who would
be glad to see their own flag fly at their peaks, did our laws permit. But if, as is the case at present, they must fly a foreign flag,
they would obtain the same subsidy from England or from Belgium that is now accorded them, did Mr. Cramp build the ships
for them. Messrs. Peter Wright & Co., being Philadelphians,
would naturally give him the preference over a British shipbuilder, were he able to fulfil the conditions. Moreover, these
gentlemen have signified their willingness to avail themselves of
the subsidy offered by Congress to American-built ships, of $4 per
ton per mile, for the sake of having some of their steamships under
their own flag, if an American shipbuilder will build them as
cheaply and in as satisfactory a manner as they are built upon
the other side of the Atlantic. But thus far we have heard of no
such proposition on the shipbuilders' part. Mr. Cramp complains that this subsidy of $4 per mile does not afford sufficient
"encouragement" for the American shipbuilder to compete with
the English subsidized lines. Then why does he not, with or
without this bonus, try his hand against the unsubsidized
ships ? The reply to this will doubtless be the stereotyped one
that "the difficulty lies in the cost of sailing the ships, and not

in the cost of building them. American captains, officers, and sailors would not be content with the pay and food accorded to foreigners. We want a bounty for them and not for ourselves." But American captains and officers do sail in these foreign ships ; and in the great ocean carrying trade there are more of them thus employed than under their own flag. As for the sailors, there is but the smallest proportion of them in our navy and merchant marine who are Americans. The sailor is still, as he has been, to my knowledge and in my experience, for the last half-century, a merchantable commodity, purchased at the land- lord's price without the slightest regard to the ensign that flies at the peak of the ship.

Crossing lately in a steamship of the Red Star Line, sailing under the Belgian flag, but owned almost exclusively by our countrymen, I asked the American captain what would be the difference in the cost of running his ship if her nationality were transferred. "No difference whatever," he replied, "excepting in the cost of the bunting made in General Butler's protected mill."

Mr. Gould furnishes a list, which, however, is not complete, of trans-Atlantic steamship lines running from the port of New York, numbering 29 and aggregating 236 ships, with a tonnage of 969,573. Although Americans own the majority of the stock in some of them, they are all under foreign flags, as Americans are forbidden to hoist their own national colors over their own property.

At the head of the list stand the four lines largest in ships and tonnage, neither of which has ever received a shilling from its gov- ernment beyond mere letter postage, and the first and greatest not even that. The Wilson and Anchor line ships are all built in Great Britain. Some of the North German Lloyd and Hamburg-American are still built there, as all of them were until by the policy of free ships the Germans learned to build their ships at home—that disastrous policy which Mr. Cramp says would cause "the destruction of American shipbuilding." It would, indeed, be most singular if it should cause the destruc- tion of shipbuilding in the United States, when it has promoted it in all other countries. At the outset, when the iron steamship superseded the wooden sailing ship, the people of all nations, excepting our own, who were forbidden to do so, went to Eng- land for their ships ; and now, not only Germany, but France,

Italy, Russia, Spain, Brazil, and even Japan and China, are building ships for themselves. And from that era the carrying trade of all these nations has greatly increased, while ours has dwindled to almost nothing. If any of them have given "encouragement," as Mr. Cramp asserts, in the way of subsidies, it has been for postal and not for shipbuilding purposes, as is instanced by the fact that the subsidies have been paid to Eng-. lish-built ships as well as to their own.

Mr. Cramp still hopes to see his favorite policy of a general bounty "adopted at no distant day." In the meantime he will do all in his power, as he has done heretofore, to discourage any kind of American shipowning that does not bring money to the pockets of the domestic shipbuilders.

Ten years ago Mr. John Roach, who entertained similar ideas to those of Mr. Cramp, estimated that the money paid to foreigners for doing our carrying trade amounted to $140,000,000 annually. Since that time it has vastly increased, until it will certainly be much more than $200,000,000 this present year. Were we permitted to own ships, we might not only appropriate a great part of this immense sum to ourselves, but we should have a source for our navy to draw upon in time of war, instead of leaving it to depend for the manning of its ships on men picked up from all the nationalities of the earth—men who have not one patriotic American instinct in their breasts. But we must forego all these advantages, forsooth, until that "no distant day" anticipated by Mr. Cramp when we shall all contribute to the eleemosynary fund that he demands. His anticipation was not realized by the legislation of the last Congress, which was largely Republican in all its branches. It certainly will not be realized in the present Congress, where the majority of the House of Representatives is so largely Democratic. On the contrary, a free-ship bill will most assuredly be there introduced and passed. It is even possible that the Senate may accept it, with some modifications, and that the President may attach his signature to it. At all events, it will be the beginning of the end. The power of obstruction will fall from the hands of the Maine and Delaware shipbuilders, and they will be forced to the conclusion that the best thing they can do is to get up from their knees and go to work in the endeavor to rival and perhaps surpass the ships of the Clyde. –

JOHN CODMAN.

OUR COMMERCIAL RELATIONS WITH CHILI.

BY WILLIAM E. CURTIS, CHIEF OF THE BUREAU OF AMERICAN REPUBLICS.

THE foreign commerce of Chili averages annually about $125,-000,000 ; and it is the only one of the nineteen American republics, with the exception of the United States, whose balance of trade is regularly upon the right side of the ledger. The statistics of the commerce of the other Latin-American nations have usually shown an excess of imports, and the balance has been paid in coin borrowed in Great Britain and the money markets of the European continent to promote internal improvements and private enterprises.

The commercial prosperity of Chili is largely due to the possession of vast deposits of precious metals, and the almost unlimited beds of nitrate of soda which underlie the sands of the desert which stretches for more than a thousand miles between the Andes and the ocean. These nitrate beds are owned by corporations or individuals, who pay a large export tax to the government upon the saltpetre and other products into which nitrate is converted. The government receives from this export tax an income reaching annually to the sum of $20,000,000 or $25,000,000, which has been used in extending the comprehensive system of internal improvements that has contributed so much to the rapid development of the natural resources of the country. In addition to the nitrate beds owned by corporations or individuals, there is a large tract remaining in possession of the government. This has been surveyed with the intention of selling it at auction to the public, but as the production of nitrate is now fully equal to the demand, it has been decided a better policy to defer the sale for the present.

The population of Chili by the last census was 2,665,926, but these figures are believed to be much below the actual number of inhabitants, because of the reluctance of the common people to be enumerated. An accurate and complete census would doubtless show a total population of at least three millions, and probably more, without including the savage and half-civilized tribes in the southern provinces.

The foreign debt amounts to about $45,000,000 in United States currency, which was contracted chiefly for the construction of railways and other public improvements ; and the bonds of the country bearing 4½ per cent. interest have, until the recent revolution, been held above par. There are about 2,400 miles of railway in operation, a considerable portion belonging to the government, and there were about seven hundred additional miles under construction when the trouble between the late President and the Congress occurred last spring. Now that peace has been restored, work upon these lines will doubtless be promptly resumed.

The most important road under construction is that which is intended to connect the railway system of the country and its Pacific ports with the line that has already been opened across the continent from Buenos Ayres to the western boundary of the Argentine Republic, and give the commerce of Chili an outlet to the Atlantic, thus avoiding the long voyage through the Straits of Magellan. The rails are already laid to the mountain wall that separates the two republics, and through that an English company is now engaged in piercing a tunnel about three miles in length that will cost many millions of dollars.

Of the exports of Chili about three-fourths are annually purchased by Great Britain, and the greater part of the remainder by France and Germany, although in 1890 the official returns showed a direct commerce with thirty-one nations. These exports consist of mineral products, silver, copper, and nitrate of soda,—which compose about 75 per cent. of the whole,—and agricultural products, wheat, wool, flour, hides, and skins. About one-half the wheat goes to Europe. The rest is divided between Peru, Ecuador, and Panama. In early times—the days of the Argonauts—Chili supplied California with flour and other breadstuffs. Then during the war between Chili and Spain California introduced and retained the trade upon the west coast, but the agricultural resources of Chili were rapidly developed a few years since, and now she claims all the markets for breadstuffs on the Pacific south of Panama, and with her present population will be able to supply them, although her capacity for production has been restricted by nature.

The commerce of Chili with the United States is very limited, and varies annually from five to six millions of dollars, which is very nearly equally divided between imports and exports. She sends us a few cargoes of nitrates and saltpetre, a little carpet wool, and a few hides and skins. The duties collected upon our imports from Chili during the last year amounted to less than $200,000. She buys of us annually cotton goods to the value of half a million dollars; a similar amount of lumber and furniture; nearly as much refined petroleum; a little more than that value in manufactures of iron and steel, including railway supplies; about $100,000 worth of agricultural implements; the same amount of mining machinery and electrical supplies; a small amount of provisions, a little refined sugar, and a few other articles which her merchants cannot elsewhere obtain. The business is almost entirely conducted by three houses, one in Boston and two in New York. These firms have sailing vessels, which make regular voyages around Cape Horn, carrying selected merchandise to their agents in Valparaiso, and bringing return cargoes of wool and nitrates of soda which are used in the manufacture of fertilizers. There is a small business done also with San Francisco, chiefly through the same houses.

It is very seldom that an ordinary merchant in Chili comes to the United States to purchase goods. It is quite as infrequent that the people of that country come here as tourists, although the fine steamers that sail between Valparaiso and Europe are usually crowded with passengers. The social and commercial relations between the two countries have never been more intimate. High tide in trade was reached in 1890, when our imports from Chili were valued at $3,183,249, and our exports at $3,236,945.

The foreign commerce of Chili is controlled and almost monopolized by Great Britain, and many of the great commercial houses in England have branches in Valparaiso and other ports. During the last few years a great deal of German capital has been introduced into Chili, and some of the largest commercial houses are now controlled by merchants of that nationality. The banking capital is mostly held by natives, but Englishmen and Germans are found among the directors of the financial institutions.

British subjects are numerous and prominent in the membership of her boards of trade, stock exchanges, and other commercial organizations, and in Valparaiso the English language is spoken almost as commonly as the Spanish. There are a few American families in Chili, and the Protestant missionary work and Protestant schools are largely sustained by the religious organizations which have their headquarters in New York, but in social as well as in commercial circles their influence is small compared with that exercised by the large English colony. The cities along the coast, from Valparaiso northward for more than a thousand miles, are largely populated by English subjects, and should they be attacked in case of war, England would suffer more than Chili.

In 1889, the latest year for which complete statistics are obtainable, Great Britain purchased $48,000,000 of the $66,000,000 of produce exported by Chili. In 1888 Great Britain purchased $57,000,000 of the $73,000,000 exported. In 1889 Great Britain furnished $28,000,000 of the $65,000,000 imported by Chili, and in 1888 she furnished $26,000,000 of the $60,000,000 imported. These imports consisted entirely of manufactured merchandise, the largest item being cotton goods and other forms of wearing apparel. Wines and fancy articles, the finer qualities of wearing apparel, and other luxuries are purchased from France and Germany.

It is not probable that there will ever be any considerable amount of commerce between Chili and the United States. The natural conditions forbid it, and the lines of trade are so thoroughly established that unless her commercial relations with Great Britain and Germany should be entirely cut off, the business of the country will still be conducted through the branch houses which the manufacturers and merchants of London, Liverpool, Birmingham, Manchester, and Hamburg have had long and firmly established at Valparaiso and other ports of the republic. The trade relations between England and Chili are as fixed as they are with Calcutta and Bombay, and the younger sons of the British merchants find their commercial career in Valparaiso as naturally as they do in Sydney or any other of the colonies of that empire upon which the sun never sets.

We do not need the nitrates of Chili as they are required by the impoverished soil of Europe, nor her copper or silver, and there is very little of her products, except wool, that we could use. If a reciprocity treaty could be negotiated under which her wools should be admitted free into our ports in exchange for equivalent concessions in favor of our cotton goods, machinery, agricultural implements, and other manufactured articles, the trade between the two nations might be increased to the amount of a few millions of dollars annually. But such an arrangement is impossible. There is no reason or inducement for Chili to make tariff concessions in favor of the United States. She is not seeking new markets, and it is not necessary for her to seek them. Her wool finds favor and ready sale in England and Belgium to the extent of her capacity for production; her import duties are the lowest imposed by any American nation, and the greater part of those derived from the United States are already on the free list. To discriminate in favor of a country with which she has comparatively no commercial relations, and which could not increase her commerce or her prosperity, would be a preposterous proposition. Aside from the influence of foreign tradesmen, which would be united against it, no ambitious politician in Chili would advocate or defend so unpopular and unprofitable a negotiation.

The United States can reach the markets of Brazil and the other republics of America by the negotiation of reciprocity treaties and the intelligent enlistment of private enterprise ; but in Chili there is little hope of extending our export trade beyond what can be accomplished by offering her people merchandise of a superior quality to that which can be furnished by Europe.

The people of that republic are intelligent, highly educated, and luxurious in their tastes. In the shops of Valparaiso and Santiago may be purchased everything that can be found in Paris or London. The residences of the rich are as sumptuously furnished as any of the palaces on Fifth Avenue, New York. The schools and universities of the country are equal to those of any other on the globe, and the educated classes surpass those of the United States in linguistic accomplishments. It is very seldom that you find a lady in Chili who cannot converse fluently in at least one foreign language, and some can speak two or three languages besides their own. The fashions of Paris reach Santiago as soon as they reach New York, and the Alameda and parks of Santiago are as brilliant of an afternoon as Rotten Row or Central Park. The highest degree of luxury is demanded by all who can afford it, and they will buy the best they can obtain, no matter where it comes from.

Therefore the manufacturers of the United States can expect to sell merchandise in Chili only by sending there articles of a quality superior to those their rivals in Europe produce. The telephone, the electric light, and all other modern inventions intended to promote the comfort and convenience of life, are more readily accepted there than in almost any other country ; and the mining and milling interests demand and procure the most improved and economical machinery that can be furnished them.

The agricultural resources of Chili are limited. They will never enable that country to compete with the United States, the Argentine Republic, Australasia, and other great producers of breadstuffs, and all the cereals raised in Chili will be required for domestic consumption as the population increases. Nor are the present conditions such as to encourage great agricultural immigration, as in the countries named. The public domain in the northern provinces consists mainly of a desert covered with sand, and rugged ranges of mountains that shelter vast mineral wealth.

The fertile valleys in the populated districts are held in great estates by families who reside at Santiago and in other cities, and cultivate them upon the same system that prevails in England and Ireland. Towards the south there are agricultural lands of considerable extent, and the government is now constructing a - railway to encourage their development.

The mercantile element of the country are generally foreigners. The professional men, the politicians, the officers of the army and navy, the directors of large institutions and establishments, the managers of estates, and the owners of mines are natives. The national pride and patriotism are intense, and are found to an even greater degree among the women than among the men. No one who has not studied the social and political conditions of the country upon the ground can appreciate the ardor with which a citizen of Chili will maintain what he conceives to be the honor and integrity of his nation ; and in a contest with a foreign power the people would sacrifice everything rather than submit to interference or subjugation. The native race of Chili was never overcome, and it has been strengthened rather than diluted by mixing with the best stock of Spain.

WILLIAM E. CURTIS.

THE OLYMPIAN RELIGION.

I.—ITS SOURCES AND AUTHORSHIP (Continued).

BY THE RIGHT HONORABLE WILLIAM EWART GLADSTONE.

The actual position of Homer, as a transcendent workman, in relation to the materials of his work, ought, in order to come at the truth of the case, to be comprehensively considered.

It was evidently a position very different from that of Buddha, of Zoroaster, or of Mahomet. Yet, in the result of his life and thought, it has some important, though diversified, approximations to theirs. For, like them, he constructed, or adjusted, a public religion, which also, in adjusting, he reformed; though unlike them in this, that his product was more a work of art, and less a work of religion, properly so called. We have actually before our eyes, in the "Iliad" and "Odyssey," a religious system, which distinctively belongs to the Poems, and of this system, as it stands there, he, if he composed the Poems, was unquestionably the immediate artificer. For surely no one who has drunk deep into the spirit of these great works can say that he was only a faithful copyist, who noted down with care the particulars of an established national cult, such as only required to be diligently transferred from usage into song. For if we examine the theurgy of the Poems, we find that it is as warm, as instinct with vitality, and as dramatic as any part of the human or terrestrial action. And more. Those admitted into the studio of a painter, when he has his work in progress, and who are permitted to gaze at it, readily enough find that it has not yet attained its finished or normal state : a limb, a hand, a vestment, tells us that it is not a thing formed, but only forming. Just so it is with the Olympian religion in Homer, as compared with the picture offered us by the classic times. In this later picture everything has been in a manner stereotyped, and so remains.

But observe for a moment such relations as are exhibited to us in the Theomachy among the divinities themselves ; or, in the fifth " Iliad," as between certain gods and human warriors ; or in respect of deities like Dionusos and Aphroditè, who have only, as it were, an embyronic relation to the Achaian nation. We cannot do otherwise than at once refer phenomena so peculiar to ethnical and circumstantial causes which had not yet exhausted their motive force : we see that the system was still in a condition of flux, and that the materials had not yet everywhere coagulated. The composite character of the half-formed nation, Greek or Achaian, whichever it be called, which causes, also explains, this remarkable phenomenon. I have already adverted to the fact that there were several factors of the community, indigenous or immigrant, and that they could not but have their several religious traditions. Both the ethnical and the religious elements would take time to settle down into their several locations. Great poems produced in such a state of facts would bear the marks of what is termed in trade a "going" concern, of mobile material and an advancing process. Nay, such poems, the rarest productions of man, might—perhaps it ought to be said they would—themselves become part and parcel of the motive force for pushing that process onwards, and for determining its eventual conditions. And the brain of the man who made the poems could not but be, in an indefinable but possibly not inconsiderable degree, the maker also of the religion. To some extent we may have the means of ascertaining what were the aims with which he wrought; for example, whether the combinations and adjustments of the Poems, both in Olympian and in terrestrial respects, are such as to show that the Poet was evidently a worker in the interest of, or with a view to bringing about, a full-formed national unity. For, if that purpose were in his serious contemplation, then, among the means of attaining it, he would not overlook the consolidation and proper construction of the religious traditions which had to travel from a state more or less chaotic or promiscuous to a state of unity and order.

We have, then, to contemplate Homer in his workshop. It is the great workshop of his brain, and all around him lies the material on which he has to operate. It has been drawn mainly from the men of Pelasgian and Achaian birth, or from those Phœnician by extraction, who had coalesced into a whole, but whose several contributions to that whole were still, at the points of juncture, made sufficiently distinct. These men had their several traditions, and their leanings or habits in a variety of matters; in social relations, in polity, and in religion. On the first two of these great subjects he has not presented to us an elaborated pattern. It was enough for him to record particular facts and ideas, without any strict coördination into a uniform and normal system. With regard to religion the case is different. Here, and here only, he has framed and transmitted to us an artfully-compacted scheme.

It would be ridiculous to suppose that even his mental force was sufficient to mould the ideas, and, above all, the usages, of a community far from homogeneous, into positive uniformity. In truth, they never were so manipulated at all, at any period of their history. The varied testimonies of classical antiquity, the work of Strabo in its notices of things sacred, above all, the remarkable itinerary, so to call it, of Pausanias, which, in mapping out the country, exhibits the immensely various worships of Greece, so far as they were worships carried on by each local community, all these show us distinctly that in practice the Olympian system included an aggregate of local cults sufficiently numerous to exhibit large diversities of distribution, and still to bear testimony to considerable differences of origin. Even this is not all. The evidence thus conveyed is only such as had a basis in visible remains, in structures more or less permanent. Could we in Greece, as at Pompeii, examine private interiors, we should probably open a new chapter of knowledge in the particulars of domestic worships. When Eumaios* dedicated two portions of his meal as first fruits, the one to Hermes, the other to the Nymphs, it is possible that his house was not without visible symbols of the personages thus represented in the abstract. Or, at any rate, we may assume the likelihood of such domestic decorations in houses of a certain social plane, and in the historic times, when the resources of art had come to be more fully developed and more widely applicable.†

---

*Od., XIV., 435.

†In January, 1890, through the kind courtesy of the authorities, I witnessed at Pompeii a *scavo*, or excavation, of a portion of a painter's house. On the wall, at a certain level, there were painted figures, apparently of his Penates, in very small dimensions. Beneath them, on another level, was the figure of a serpent, in very large dimensions: the more noteworthy as being found at that centre of an advanced and luxurious civilization.

But no emblems of this interesting class survive to enlarge and integrate our knowledge of Achaian religion.

It is important to bear in mind that, whatever devastation may thus have been brought about by time, it did not in all likelihood operate with the same force on the several component parts of the religion of the country. Phœnician and Achaian influences were all associated with political power and with property. The religious ideas belonging to these sources probably shaped for themselves at an early date the temples and shrines which supplied the records of Pausanias. But if the elements of the Pelasgian or popular creed were different, and differently compounded, it is probable that they remain comparatively destitute of representation of that kind. We have, indeed, abundant traces in the Poems of a system of Nature-worship which had been, or was being, thrown into the shade by the more imposing hierarchy of Olympos. This the Poet himself everywhere labors to depress as far as the nature of his office permitted; a limitation of his power necessary to be observed, for as that office was essentially popular, so it required him to keep his verse in sympathy with the entire people. This old Pelasgian system crops out incessantly in the Poems ; and from the permanence of popular traditions in such matters, we may conjecture that it subsisted largely in the ideas and dwellings of the masses, while it appears but slightly in the architecture, the art, the public institutions, and likewise finds little place in the literature, of the country. In these great departments Olympianism has reigned supreme.

The local and domestic Nature-worships, on which we may suppose that the people fed, had no effectual centre of unity. We do not know how far they may have been kept alive in the Mysteries, to which no certain key seems yet to have been found. Some provision was probably made for the unity of national religion by the developed institution of the Olympian games in the eighth century B. C., and by a paramount worship of Zeus in connection with them. We seem thus to obtain a glimpse of the open space which it may have remained for Homer to fill. He could not pass an act of uniformity, nor fuse into one working scheme for daily life all the several cults that prevailed in the several neighborhoods, or among races which might long retain at least a portion of their distinctive characteristics. But, on the literary side at least, there was nothing to prevent the initiation of a great unifying process in religion. This for himself, and in the main for his successors, the Poet seems to have accomplished. Doubtless, even in the literary aspect of the case, all the main lines were already drawn, the chief objects of worship ready to hand, the limits of his freedom as an artist fixed. Within those limits he worked genially, richly, and to the utmost of his vast power as a creative intellect. Study the Iris of Homer, whose delicate tints and gracious outline can hardly be said to have lived into the classical mythology. Study the Leto of Homer, so glorious,* so mysterious, and so pure, who outside the " Iliad " passes almost wholly out of sight. Observe the Apollo, who out of reverence will not fight Poseidon ; † the Athenè, who refrains from visible action when on her uncle's special ground in Scheriè ; ‡ the incessant adjustments effected between the local and the central power. In these and in a multitude of other points we are almost forced to see how, if in the matter of the Achaian religion it was not given to Homer to create, yet it was given him to develop, to harmonize, and to modify. There was one power, of itself a vast power, of which poets then had a monopoly among men, and Homer among poets ; the power of record. Within proper limits, with a fine discernment of the capacities and the yearnings of his race, he could affix the stamp of perpetuity, perhaps could even sometimes pass the decree of oblivion ; and could by the exercise of his gift impart to his Olympian scheme interest, beauty, dignity, that were to last throughout all time, even when he did not minister directly to the religious wants of his own and the following generations.

Through long and obstinate neglect of the Homeric Poems as a subject of independent inquiry, an idea requiring large correction has obtained superficial but wide acceptance in this if not in other countries ; that the religion exhibited in the Homeric Poems subsisted without material change through the historic age of Greece, and also corresponded, in all that was material, with that which prevailed in the Italy of the Romans, and which was finally, after a long struggle, overthrown by the slowly-victorious advance of Christianity.

Now, in truth, the religion which was professed from the days of Homer, and which dominated the entire Greek and Roman periods, if taken at its inception and at its ending, was and was

---

* ἐρικυδής : Il., XIV., 327.   † Il., XXI., 461.   ‡ Od. VI., 329.

not the same religion. It was the same religion, in this respect—
that at no epoch during that course of over fifteen hundred years
was there a general or palpable breach in the continuity of its
traditions ; while the names and individualities of its deities
were reputed to be maintained. But it was not the same in so
far that its ethical tone had, not indeed uniformly, but on the
whole seriously, declined ; that the traces visible in it of any
primitive monotheism had nearly disappeared ; that a mass of new
and heterogeneous matter had overlaid it, and had altered the
more delicate lines of its features ; that both the personal characters and the relative positions of the several members of the
thearchy were materially tampered with ; and that it had become
impossible definitely to trace home to their several birthplaces,
by historical derivation, the multitudinous elements of which it
was compounded.

But the Homeric religion, taken as a whole, exhibits all the
notes of a fresh formation. The ingredients of which it is composed, modified perhaps by Homer's genius, and each allotted to
its proper place in his system, bear upon them to a very large extent the stamp of the race, the country, the line of tradition,
from which they were severally derived. We can thus follow
them, at the least, one stage nearer to their first form by treating
them according to what may be termed their ethnographic mark.

And this process is aided, as well as certified, by the large and
varied illustrations which the religions of Troas, and of the lands
comprised within the outer geography of the " Odyssey," supply
for clearing our ideas of the great Homeric theanthropy both by
comparison and by contrast.

It may properly be asked how the present inquiry stands related
to the great science termed that of comparative religion. The
answer is that it is strictly an investigation belonging to the domain
of comparative religion ; not, however, of comparative religion
at large, but with reference first to Homer and secondly to
the sources from which he drew. First, noting the places of the
several divinities in the Olympian thearchy, we inquire how they
come by those places ; and we perceive that the niches in the
Homeric temple were in all likelihood obtained in virtue of their
actual recognition in some branch or other of the popular worship ; of their relation to one or other of the factors from which
the Greek nation was constructed. In referring, then, to these

ethnical factors, we at once work out an important chapter of comparative religion. We have to undertake a further process in the same branch of science so soon as we follow any of these divinities, in time, up to the preëxistent worships of the Greek peninsula; or, in both time and place, as in cases like those of Poseidon, Artemis, or Aphroditè, beyond the territorial limit of the lands under the sway of Agamemnon. But this is only when we can trace them upwards to their older homes in virtue of suggestions furnished by the materials of the text.

Within these limits, so far as I can discern, is confined the primary mission of the Homeric student. To examine the points of resemblance between the Homeric divinities and those of other ancient systems without limit would be a work of great interest, but of wider scope, and one that could hardly be undertaken with advantage until inquirers shall have more nearly arrived at common conclusions upon the religion as it is exhibited in the Homeric Poems, and when considered as a substantive and independent sphere of study. The natural limit of our subject will thus be found in the material supplied by the Poems, combined with that which was anterior to but associated with them.

I have here spoken of comparative religion, not of comparative mythology. The use of this latter phrase, if it be strictly taken, involves ideas which appear to me not wholly true, and possibly mischievous with reference to the present investigation. If mythology may be defined as the science which deals with fable, it implies that in ancient religion all is fabulous. I do not say that the word religion implies the contradictory proposition : for, so far as the term goes, the bond between earth and heaven which it declares may have been a bond of purely human manufacture. On the other hand, it may have been one framed, as the races of civilized man have hitherto believed, not without some special dispensation of the Deity. So that the phrase I use leaves entirely open an important question, which ought not to be prejudged, but held in reserve for consideration upon the evidence, so far as it may be relevant. If we find that, so far as the proposed inquiry goes, it presents to us signs that, like the mechanical arts, religion was for the Greek race progressive, and tended, under the action of our human powers as they now exist, gradually to shake off its impurities, to consolidate its principles, to elevate its aims, and to establish its command over sentiment and life, then our inquiry supplies us with no reason to refer it, upon internal evidence, to a superhuman origin. But if, on the contrary, we should perceive in it a proneness to assimilate corrupt admixture, and to decline in simplicity of structure and therewith of moral power ; if it is found to be from the past that the rays of light proceed, and if the spiritual atmosphere, on the whole, appears to darken as we advance, then we shall have found in human experience some grounds for believing that the fountain-head of religion is divine ; as it seems plain that man never could have been able to create that which he would then be proved, by the evidence of facts, to have been unable duly to conserve.

It may be well to give further explanations on the inception of the religion represented in Homer. It seems to be plain that, in dealing with the religion which is found in Homer, we deal with a scheme as yet in the first stage of its existence. The materials are old, but the combination is new. The worship of Dionusos, afterwards so largely developed in Greece, and a manifest element of its practical system, is mentioned by Homer with the use of terms which show that it had not as yet established itself in the popular affections.* The worship of Aphroditè is described as appertaining especially to Cyprus, with Paphos† for its centre, and it had evidently advanced to Cytherè ;‡ but there is no mention of it within the Achaian borders. The transactions in the island of Ithaca, as they are detailed in the " Odyssey," appear to show us the religion of the place in a state of actual transition from an older system to that embodied in the Poems. The Hellenic families or tribes, as distinguished from the Pelasgian or other prior inhabitants, were of recent arrival ; and even the families associated with the Phœnician name, which had come in all likelihood from the southeast, cannot be traced back beyond four or five generations ; so that there had not been a very long time for religious varieties to accommodate themselves to new positions. The splendid presentation of them, in an elaborately-constructed scheme, could not be otherwise than novel. The exterior edges, so to speak, of the original factors of the system are still in the main discernible ; while the Olympian summits supply its working centre, and its acknowledged home.

Because it is so associated with Mount Olympos, and because it is desirable to give a name to the present subject which may

* Il., VI., 132.   † Od., VIII., 363.   ‡ Od., VIII., 288 ; XVIII., 192.

sufficiently distinguish it from the unreduced and irreducible mass of traditions afterwards accumulated during a long and shifting history, I have called it the Olympian religion. My account, however, of the religion of the Poems will naturally include the important illustrations which it receives from beyond the Hellenic borders in such portions of them as have their scene laid in foreign lands, and as are consequently in natural contact with the traditions of other races and nations.

For it holds good universally, I believe, in early times, that each differing nation, or race, or combination of men having a standing community of pursuit, interest, or existence, had also its own distinct religious traditions. If so, there is an indissoluble connection between ethnography and comparative religion. And this union is most of all important in such a case as that before us. For here we are happy in being able both to note the principal component parts of the aggregate, and to mark them by particulars of time and place: as in astronomy distances are measured away from the surface of the earth by ascertaining a plurality of points, so these schemes of religion may, by the light they throw on one another, assist us in establishing their common principles, or in fixing their points of divergence, or in tracing them upwards in the direction of a common origin.

Although ethnography supplies in a considerable degree the basis of the Achaian religion, it necessarily forms in itself the subject of a separate inquiry, dependent upon the collation of a multitude of particulars taken from the text of the poems. At present we can only adopt and apply the main conclusion to which such an examination leads. It establishes, I conceive, by conclusive evidence, that the nation which, according to the "Iliad," made war upon Troy, was not of one blood like the descendants of Abraham, but was essentially composite. Of this compound there were three principal ingredients.

First, there was the race, doubtless including varieties, which formed the mass and groundwork of the nation, and which, in the general tradition of Greece, passes under the Pelasgian name.* This race we may trace through the "Iliad" by its subordinate position; by the strength of the distinctions drawn between the aristocracy and the mass of the army; by the significant use of personal names associated with industrial pursuits;

* *e. g.*, Æsch., "Hiketides," 265, seqq.

and by the association of this name in particular with that one of
the three established national designations which is neither archaic
and military like the Danaan, nor aristocratic like the Achaian
name.   I mean the Argeian name, which, in the "Iliad," has a
certain affinity, so to speak, with the πλη𝔰ι' ,* or rank and file, of
the army, and which by etymological derivation probably points
to occupations purely agricultural.

Next to this in date we have to place the Phœnician element ;
numerically small, but socially and intellectually powerful.   There
is even some reason to suppose that the Poet recognized this element as one of the twin sources from which he drew the commanding characters of his protagonists ;† and that, if Achilles
was his authentic model of the Hellenic hero, Odysseus represented
for him that form of the heroic character which has a Phœnician
basis.   The notes of Phœnician association supplied by him are
numerous ; and they extend to several of the worships indicated
in the Poems ; to those in particular of Poseidon, Hermes, and
Aphroditè.   It must, however, be carefully borne in mind that the
Phœnician name in Homer includes all that came into the peninsula with and through the Phœnician navigators.

The third great ethnical ingredient which may have supplied
the poet with materials for his Olympian system was furnished by
that higher race which supervened upon the older inhabitants of
the Greek peninsula.   Of this race, at the period of the Poems,
the main seat is in a part of Thessaly.   Its type is enlarged into
a colossal image in the character of Achilles ; and it seems to be
especially associated by Homer with the Hellenic name.‡   The
materials of detailed proof, in this third department of the case,
are more scanty than in the two which have previously been
mentioned.   They may be said to be almost confined to the solemn
prayer of Achilles in Book XVI. of the "Iliad."   But while the
particulars, as to religion at least, are meagre, the presence of this
higher factor is undeniable, and arguments of high probability

---

* Il., II., 488 ; XV., 295.

† See "Phœnician Affinities of Ithaca," in *Nineteenth Century* for August, 1889.

‡ Il., II., 681-685. The geographical and ethnological particulars, which throw
so much light on the religious indications of the Poems, can only in this paper be
given summarily as results.   The grounds for my conclusions in these departments
have been stated by me more largely in former works : "Studies on Homer and his
Age" (1858), Vol. I. (but the statements of this earlier work require considerable correction); "Juventus Mundi" (1869), chapters III.-VI., and "Homeric Primer"
(1878), chapter VII.

indicate its important share in the office of supplying the mate
rials for the Olympian fabric. For there is, as we shall find, a
mass of evidence in the Poems which absolutely refuses association either with the Pelasgian or the Phœnician systems of religion. The most remarkable portion of it is connected with the
characters of Athenè and Apollo ; but it embraces a number of
varied points, and the whole of it concurs in admitting only one
rational explanation. Like a relationship established by likeness
of feature, these particulars, unlike anything that we find either
in the indigenous religions or in those imported by or through
the Phœnicians, require us to search for their parentage elsewhere.
They, indeed, bear a strong intrinsic resemblance to a portion
of the Hebrew traditions, as they are recorded in the Book of
Genesis, as well as to other occasional portions of the old tradi-
tionary religions.

It follows from what has been already said that we shall have
to inquire, at the proper stage of our inquiry, how far and in
what particulars the grounds can now be traced for the opinion of
Herodotos that the religion of the Greeks, as connected with the
names of the divinities, was largely derived from that of Egypt.
A field more abundantly fruitful is offered by the Assyrian monuments, which record matter not within the compass of the inquiries
effected by the father of history, and establish at a large number
of points a probable or almost certain connection between Olympian ideas and Assyrian or Babylonian originals.

We have also indications, in various degrees of distinctness, as
to not less than three forms of the religions outside of Greece,
and contemporary with the Poems. · These are :

1. The religion of Troas.

2. The Poseidon worship, in a portion of the outer zone of the
" Odyssey."

3.. The Helios worship, in another portion of the outer zone.

But it is necessary all along to carry with us the recollection
of the intense nationalism of Homer, which was the probable
cause of his universal silence on the derivation from abroad of
whatever in his time was or had become Achaian, whether in arts
or institutions, in descent or in religion. We need not, however,
suppose him to have been embarrassed by this consideration in
his references to worships contemporary and avowedly situated in
a foreign land. But with reference to whatever he gives us as a

portion of Greek life or history, we find ourselves placed by him in a sort of *cul de sac,* which leads us to a certain point, and then furnishes no further passage.   When we find that his great families had only been on the ground for a limited time, and that certain Olympian worships had also a modern character, we have to look elsewhere for their origin.   But we have either to extract from Homer, as it were by cross-examination, what he probably had no intention to tell us, or else to rely upon similitudes established by foreign archæology and history for so much of knowledge as we can authentically obtain of the exotic sources of the Olympian religion.

W. E. GLADSTONE.

[TO BE CONTINUED.]

NOTES AND COMMENTS.

CONSUMPTION AT HEALTH RESORTS.

DURING a recent visit to the hotels in the Adirondacks and many other health resorts in this country, I was greatly impressed with the slight attention paid to the prevention of the communicability of consumption, which physicians now consider an established fact. Many of my friends and patients have told me that while visiting these resorts they could not help feeling nervous about catching consumption when they saw so many persons around them suffering from this disease.

For this reason I think the time is opportune for the public to be placed in possession of some definite information on this subject, which will give them an opportunity to judge intelligently of the possibilities of infection, and by their influence to insure that the proper precautions are taken to make it quite safe to inhabit the buildings and occupy the rooms their unfortunate consumptive brethren have used.

It is now generally believed by the medical profession that consumption is caused by a specific agent, which if implanted in suitable soil will multiply, develop, and produce the condition known as consumption. This agent is called the bacillus of consumption, and is a minute rod-shaped body belonging to one of the numerous families of bacteria. It is a recent discovery of the microscope. Its development and entire life-history have been carefully studied and are well known. It has been proved by many observers that the bacilli, if injected into animals, will produce consumption; a like result will be produced if they are allowed to inhale air or take food containing the bacilli. No direct experiments could, of course, be made to prove that this communicability extended to the human race; nevertheless, a wonderful combination of circumstances has arisen which makes it almost a certainty that this is the case, and that it is effected in the same ways.

It is only a few months since the entire civilized world was filled with anticipation and wonder by Dr. Koch's discovery for the cure of consumption. Nothing in medicine or surgery ever created so much excitement, and hope was entertained that at last the disease which causes about one-fifth of the deaths of the human race had found its master, and in future would be robbed of all its terrors. In the early days of this "craze" the celebrated German physician, Professor Virchow, warned the profession against the indiscriminate use of this remedy, as he believed that, in place of curing the sufferers from consumption, it disseminated the disease through the body and hastened its course. He was immediately accused of jealousy of Koch, and the craze and injection went on. At this time the composition of the Koch remedy was known only to a few physicians in Germany, and the physicians in other countries depended entirely on their faith in Koch, who had an established reputation for reliability and truth. As soon as Virchow's opinion became known, a few observers endeavored to prove the truth or fallacy of his statement, and it was not long before they added their warnings to that of Virchow. There was an immediate reaction when this was announced ; for every physician began to have fears, when he learned that Koch's remedy was the product of the bacillus of consumption, that possibly he was only adding fuel to the fire in resorting to its use. Subsequent events have proved the truth of this to a great extent, and there are few physicians who believe in the efficacy of this cure for consumption; but its discovery and use have suggested strongly the possibility of inoculating consumption.

That consumption can be communicated to the lower animals by causing them to inhale air impregnated with bacilli, I have already said, has been proved by experience. To repeat these experiments on the human subject is impracticable, but one case is on record in which the disease was unquestionably taken by inhalation. Tappenier was making some experiments on the possibility of communicating consumption to dogs by causing them to inhale the atmosphere of a room impregnated with its bacilli. His servant, a man forty years old, and free from all hereditary or personal taint, had been cautioned against entering this impregnated room. But in a spirit of bravado he did so many times. He was taken sick, and after an illness of fourteen weeks died; on post-mortem examination it was found that he had the same form of consumption as the dogs that died from exposure in the chamber.

Another remarkable instance is the case of the Fugeans, amongst whom consumption was unknown until a missionary and his wife went to reside there. The latter was suffering from consumption. She took some of the children from their savage state and clothed them and did all she could to educate them. After a short time acute consumption developed amongst these children and many died ; but not a single case occurred amongst the children who remained in their savage surroundings.

Many similar instances could be reported from medical literature, were this the proper place to do it. The accumulation of such evidence is becoming so great that every physician of experience feels forced to share the belief in the communicability of consumption. There are also few physicians who have not had one or more cases that for years they have thought had been contracted in this way. One reason why this fact of communication from one to another cannot be more closely followed up by physicians is that patients change their places of residence and their physicians so frequently that it is impossible to obtain that detail of the life-histories which will connect them together.

How else than by communication are we to account for the rapid spread of consumption amongst savage nations, where this disease was unknown before civilized people began to visit them? This is true of our own American Indians, the inhabitants of Central Africa, and many other people. Intermarrying, or any other condition which might make hereditary transmission a possible cause, certainly could not account for its rapid progress. Besides, some of the best observers and investigators believe that consumption is not hereditary, and there is much evidence in favor of this view.

With such evidence of the possibility of inhaling the bacilli, the question would naturally be asked, How do the bacilli get into the atmosphere, when they are not found in the breath of sufferers from this disease? We know positively that in these cases bacilli are present in the mucus which is raised after coughing. In its moist condition it is impossible for it to be inhaled, but when it dries and becomes dust, it is blown about, and it is in this form that it becomes dangerous.

That this is true can easily be proved by examining the dust or scrapings from the walls or furniture of a room which has been occupied by a consumptive. They will contain the bacilli, and if inoculated into animals, or if animals are made to inhale them, they will produce consumption. Some idea of the number of bacilli which each sufferer must dispose of can be formed from an observation made by Heller. He estimated on a slide under the microscope 1,000,000 germs in a cubic millimetre of the sputa of a consumptive; and from this he further estimated that 300,000,000 bacilli were thrown out at each expectoration. This I think rather high; but it is certain that the number thrown out at each successful cough is very great.

Why some people contract consumption while others subjected to the same exposure escape, we are at present unable to say definitely. We only know that consumption follows the law of all diseases, and that it has a power of selection and needs a suitable soil in which to implant itself.

I think it has been shown that the evidence of the communicability of consumption from one person to another is very strong. The conditions necessary for this communication have also been shown. It should, therefore, not be difficult to answer the query so often made, How can consumption be avoided by those who are susceptible to its bacilli?

First—Every physician who has patients suffering from consumption should instruct them wherein the danger lies to others as well as themselves; for it is not impossible for a consumptive to reinfect himself by uncleanly habits. Consumptives should be impressed with the importance of a proper disposal of the sputa, and effectual means should be employed to prevent its conversion into dust.

Second—The proprietors of hotels in health resorts for these guests should add two or three rules to the ones they have already posted in their bedrooms, and I can safely leave them to the imagination. Suitable cuspidors should also be provided, which should contain a non-smelling disinfectant, and they should be emptied and cleansed morning and evening regularly. It should be made imperative and stand as an unwritten law that cuspidors should always be used. The bedding or any other linen about the room should be removed and cleansed before any sputa on it could become dry. When a guest leaves the hotel, the walls, floor or carpet, and furniture of the room he occupied should be wiped off with a damp cloth. This would be little more trouble than the present method of dusting and cleaning the room, and would take really no more time. Most of the bacilli would in this way be removed from the room, and a new guest would enter it without danger.

Free ventilation should also be amply provided for. All such precautions are carried out in hospitals and places where consumptives reside which are under medical supervision, and this accounts in a great measure for the remarkable escape from consumption of the nurses and attendants in these institutions. The best Adirondack hotels at the present time do carry out some of these suggestions, but still there is room for improvement. The part the general public should take in this matter of precaution is, by the force of their opinion to make it absolutely imperative that proprietors of hotels in health resorts for consumptives should take the precautions referred to, so as to meet the prevailing belief in the communicability of consumption.

This article is not intended to unduly alarm the public, but simply to bring to their appreciation the position they occupy towards this interesting and important subject. Their position is clearly this: that while the great majority can expose themselves with perfect safety to the possibility of inhaling the bacilli of consumption, there are others who would be running some risk. With this knowledge in our possession and the means in our power of reducing the danger to a minimum, it is plainly the duty of everybody to assist in making these suggestions operative. When this is done, there can be no doubt that the number of consumptive cases will be very materially lessened.

WALTER F. CHAPPELL, M. D.

HENRY CLAY ON NATIONALIZING THE TELEGRAPH.

THE correspondence, note-books, and private papers of Alfred Vail have lately been deposited in the National Museum at Washington. Mr. Vail was the inventor, in connection with Professor S. F. B. Morse, of the electric telegraph, and it was his mechanical knowledge and inventive genius that gave practical shape to Professor Morse's ideas. Vail was associated with Morse as his partner, and his money constructed the first available Morse instrument and brought about its exhibition before Congress.

These Vail papers show that Vail was a partner of Morse in inventive brain and push, as well as in money. They exhibit hundreds of his own drawings designed for the improvement of the telegraph, and his note-books sparkle with suggestions. It was he who exhibited the machine before Congress in connection with Morse in 1838, and it was he who received the first message over the wires after they were built from Washington to Baltimore. In his papers may be read the whole history of the origin of the telegraph, and the correspondence includes many letters from noted men as to its use and its probable effect upon business and the country. Some of these deal with the question of the government control of the telegraph and show that the sentiments both of the inventors and of the greater statesmen of the time were in favor of the United States Government owning and operating the new invention. This opinion was generally expressed at the time the telegraph was first shown to the Congressional Committee on Commerce in the Capitol at Washington. Mr. Vail's letter describing this exhibition has never been published. It is written to his father and is as follows:

" WASHINGTON, D. C., CAPITOL, ROOM COMMITTEE ON COMMERCE, }
February 13, 1838. }

" MESSRS. S. VAIL & SON :

" The Committee on Commerce have just witnessed the operation of the machine with entire satisfaction, and the effect which it produced, I think, is the forerunner of success in our object. They have just left the room after giving Professor M. instructions how to proceed, and they speak of it as a serious thing whether the government take it under their control, or corporations. Mr. Smith, the chairman, said it would do immense mischief if it were not under the government. They advised Professor M. to invite all of the members of Congress and heads of departments to witness the operation of the machine prior to introducing the subject before the House. This course will be taken by us. I have prevailed upon Professor M. to use the dictionary which he has done with complete success. But had he used the alphabet, it would have been a different story. I could not induce him to give up the alphabet until the last hour, so reluctant was he. The proposition will be to try a circuit from Philadelphia to New York. The members of the committee think that would be best, and Professor M. is to give his proposals written. From all I can now see I fear I will not be able to leave this week—perhaps not the next. I am looking every day for a letter from you with means. I have only about ten dollars, half of which is specie and which I do not wish to part with. The House was in an uproar all day yesterday upon a resolution which Mr. Wise offered on

account of a letter in the *C. and En.* of New York, charging one of the members
with taking compensation for pulling the strings with the government. It is now
generally understood to be a member of the Senate from Maine. I will write again
as soon as there is anything happens which will interest you. Now you must act
and now you must enable me to act. If it is necessary for me to stay two weeks, I
must stay, although I would rather return as soon as possible. Give my love to
Mother, Mary, Sarah. Dr., and the children. I remain,
"Yours affectionately, "ALFRED VAIL."

Six years after this letter was written a telegraph line between Washington and Baltimore had been completed. It worked well, surprising
every one in Washington by announcing Henry Clay as nominated for the
Presidency by the Whig convention in Baltimore, hours before the news arrived in the ordinary way, and on May 24, in the chamber of the United
States Supreme Court, the famous first public despatch, "What hath God
wrought," was penned by Miss Annie Ellsworth, the daughter of the then
Commissioner of Patents, and was sent over the wires to Baltimore, where
Mr. Vail received it.

At this time the inventors still hoped that the government would purchase and assume the control of the telegraph, but no movement was made
by Congress to that effect. A few months later the owners of the invention
received an offer of $200,000 for it, and the acceptance of this offer was con-
ditional on the consent of Alfred Vail. When Vail received notice of this
fact in August, 1844, he wrote a letter to Henry Clay telling him of this
offer and asking his advice. After stating that he believed that the general
government should have the refusal of the telegraph, he says that the whole
question of the sale has been left with him and he is at a loss what to do.
He then goes on as follows:

"Having been personally and daily engaged in experimenting, and my mind
with every day's experience expanding with the progress and the development of
the telegraph, I have taken a broader view of the subject and its results than mere
dollars and cents, and the more I reflect upon it the more I am led to believe that
the electro-magnetic telegraph is destined to have and to exert a greater amount of
moral influence upon the community, if under proper guidance, than any discovery
in this or any other past age of the world. If, on the other hand, it should be controlled by vicious and designing men, possessed, so to speak, of the attribute, or,
rather, of the faculty of ubiquity, what amount of evil may they not inflict upon
that same community in a political, moral, and in fact in every point of view that
can be conceived of ! The questions upon which I ask advice are : Whether or not
the government should have the refusal ; and the probability of the government's
taking it. I do not pretend to more patriotism than my neighbors, and I believe I
look to my own interests closely, as every man should do, and I profess to have an
innate and abiding sense of duty and care for the prosperity of my country and the
perpetuity of the liberties we enjoy, which every man should possess whose privilege
it is to live under such a government as ours.

" The questions are propounded and the opinion solicited for myself alone, for
my own satisfaction before I act in the premises, subject to any suggestion you may
be pleased to communicate. Should I have transcended the bounds of propriety in
making the appeal, I trust you will pardon the humble individual whose observation of passing events has led him to esteem you as a public benefactor, and ascribe
it to the profound respect of
" Your obedient and very humble servant,
"ALFRED VAIL."

To this Henry Clay replied in an autograph letter, in which he expresses
himself in favor of the government owning the telegraph, but insinuates

the difficulty of getting Congress to make any appropriation for it. I copy Mr. Clay's letter. It reads:

" ASHLAND, 10 Sept., 1844.
" DEAR SIR :

" Absence from home and the pressure of a most burdensome correspond-ence have delayed the acknowledgment of the receipt of your favor of the 15th ultimo. I should be most happy to give you a satisfactory response to your inquiries respecting the electro-magnetic telegraph, but I fear I can say nothing that will in the least benefit you. Assuming the success of your ex-periments, it is quite manifest that i. is destined to exert great influence on the business affairs of society. In the hands of private individuals they will be able to monopolize intelligence and to perform the greatest operations in commerce and other departments of business. I think such an engine ought to be exclusively under the control of the government, but that object can-not be accomplished without an appropriation of Congress to purchase the right of the invention. With respect to the practicability of procuring such an appropriation from a body governed by such various views, both of con-stitutional power and expediency, you are quite as competent to judge as I am. As the session of that body is now nigh at hand, I submit to you whether it would not be advisable to offer your right to it before you dispose of it to a private company or to individuals. If I understand the progress of your experiment, it has been attended with further and satisfactory demon-strations since the adjournment of Congress. I am,

" Respectfully, your friend and obedient servant,
" To ALFRED VAIL, *Esq.*   " H. CLAY."

These letters are only a few of a large number of all kinds and from many eminent people. The whole correspondence is full of strange and interesting matter. It shows in a beautiful light the character of Alfred Vail, and demonstrates, in the words of Amos Kendall, who knew both in-ventors intimately, that when justice is done the name of Alfred Vail will stand associated with that of Samuel F. B. Morse in the history and intro-duction into public use of the electro-magnetic telegraph.

FRANK G. CARPENTER.

VALUES AND WAGES IN MEXICO.

THE *Norte,* a newspaper of the city of Chihuahua, referring to my arti-cle on " Wages in Mexico," which appeared in THE NORTH AMERICAN RE-VIEW for January, in which I stated that the wages of field laborers range in Chihuahua from 18¾ cents to 25 cents maximum, says that they are not so low, and that, on the contrary, that state is perhaps one of those in Mexico where field hands and workmen in general are better paid. The wages of field laborers there, the *Norte* says, vary from 37½ cents minimum to $2, the latter being the sum paid to cowboys who furnish their mounts.

Since the construction of the railroads, it is said, wages in general, and especially those paid to the poorest classes of laborers, have had a remark-able advance, which has been maintained, with a tendency to a further rise rather than a fall. For instance, bricklayers get at least $1.25 per day, while a foreman bricklayer gets $3 per day. It is difficult to get a servant for less than $10 a month, besides board, and other laborers are paid on the same scale. The data I published were furnished to me by the officials of the Mexican Government, who had taken great pains to obtain correct information on the subject, and represented the average wages in the different counties of the state; but if wages are higher in Chihuahua than stated, it will only strengthen the substance of my article.

In confirmation of the data contained in the article I will quote from the list of current prices of Mexican products which appears in the *Official Journal* of the Federal Government of Mexico, of December 15, 1891, the price of a *fanega* of corn, equivalent to about two bushels, in different parts of that country:

At Tepic (Territory of Tepic)......	$1.87	At Allende (Chihuahua)........ ..	$4.50
At Guadalajara (Jalisco)	$2.25 to 2.50	At Alamos (Sonora)................	6.50
At Cuatxingo (Mexico).............	3.50	At Culiacan (Sinaloa)...............	11.00

This remarkable difference in prices is noticed on some other grains and produce, such as beans, chickpeas, wheat, and barley, and is due to the different conditions of each locality, and especially to the abundance or scarcity of rain, which naturally affects the crops, and also to the difficulty of communication and the consequent high freights. Prices would find their level if grain could, for instance, be carried profitably from the places where it is abundant to those where the crops have failed or been poor. This state of affairs, however, shows the great chances which Mexico offers to business men.

M. Romero.

FLYING-MACHINES.

" Does the leetle, chatterin', sassy wren,
No bigger'n my thumb, know more than men ?"—Trowbridge.

There is nothing to prevent man from flying, like the eagle of the Alps or the condor of the Andes, except his want of inventive skill; and if the signs be true, this will not very much longer prevent the desired consummation. Nature has not given man wings; neither has she given him fins, yet he outstrips the strongest of the finny tribes in traversing the deep; she has not given him weapons, yet he vanquishes the fiercest warriors of the forest and jungle; she does not protect him from cold or heat, yet he is neighbor both to the polar bear and the tropical elephant.

There is no miracle in the swallow's arrowy flight; it only applies the well-known laws of dynamics. Darius Green's logic was good so far as it went. The trouble was not that

" The bluebird and phœbe
Are smarter'n we be,"

or that

" the bat
Had got more brains than's in his hat,"

but that his brains did not work long and hard enough over the problem of flying.

Man may equal and even surpass the swallow in speed, but he can never possess the swallow's perfect command of his movements in the air, to curvet and turn at sharp angles like a ray of light from opposing mirrors. Three physical laws preclude such a possibility.

First—The time required for the production, change in direction, or overcoming of motion, is inversely as the mass moved.

Second—The relative strength of a body, whether to resist or to exert force, diminishes with its magnitude.

Third—The relative sustaining effect of moving air upon a body diminishes with the magnitude of the body.

The smallest material thing in existence is the ultimate atom. This has infinite strength—*i. e.*, it is capable of resisting an infinite stress, and is therefore capable of receiving and imparting, unchanged itself, any force brought to bear upon it. The next smallest thing is the molecule, which no power less than chemical affinity can disintegrate. A single pair of molecules, held together by the maximum power of cohesion, is the next strongest thing in existence. As the number of cohering molecules increases, the more easily does the mass yield to a disintegrating force. Thus, the little wooden bridge which will sustain a hundred times its weight, without bending perceptibly, if enlarged indefinitely will fall apart of its own weight, and the child's paper boat, which rides triumphantly on the miniature lake in a basin, if increased in all its dimensions would collapse in a shapeless mass. The only way in which we can conceive of Gulliver's Brobdingnags as possible is by supposing that the size of the atoms of which they were composed was great in proportion to their bodies. Under like conditions only could the roc of the "Arabian Nights" sail the air like the eagle of reality.

But even then the gigantic bird would have a harder task to perform than the eagle, just as the eagle has a harder task than the swallow, unless the aërial atoms themselves were enlarged, and their sustaining power, when in motion as wind, were thereby increased in the same proportion.

For these reasons, then, man will never poise himself in the air like the dragon-fly, nor zigzag through it like the swallow. Nevertheless, there appears to be no adequate reason why he should not, some fine Fourth of July, astonish

> " the nation
> An' all creation
> By flyin' over the celebration,"

if he can only devise a motor, with the necessary accessories, which will not add too much to his own weight. But even great additional weight will not be an insurmountable obstacle, provided a sufficiently rapid motion can be attained.

It takes time for the greatest power to move the smallest mass ; that is to say, if a force were applied for only an instant (*i. e.*, a point of time) to a mass, it would not move it in that instant. If, then, a great weight should press for only an instant against a small resistance—as that of the air—it would for that instant be sustained. Hence it is only necessary for the weight to move fast enough horizontally to rest for only an instant upon any given mass of air, in order to be sustained. As it moved from mass to mass it would not have time to fall through any one of them. Of course this condition can be reached only approximately ; but the closer the approximation, the less uplifting power would be required in the motor.

The principle is strikingly illustrated by Mr. Langley, of the Smithsonian Institution, by comparing such a mass to a skater moving rapidly over thin ice. The briefest pause or diminution in his speed, and his support would instantly yield ; but it is only necessary for him to move fast enough to glide over a film as thin as tissue paper.

Here, then, is the problem of aërial navigation theoretically solved. Given, a mass of any size or weight, spread laterally so as to rest upon a sufficiently large mass of air, and moving with sufficient speed horizontally, and your flying-machine, so long dreamed of and so ardently sought, is achieved !

Such is, or is to be, Professor Langley's *Aëroplane*, the realization of the magic carpet of the "Arabian Nights." May Fortune and his happy genius bring speedy success !

JULIEN ST. BOTOLPHE.

NORTH AMERICAN REVIEW.

No. CCCCXXV.

APRIL, 1892.

PATRIOTISM AND POLITICS.

BY HIS EMINENCE CARDINAL GIBBONS.

I HAVE no apology to make for offering some reflections on the political outlook of the nation ; for my rights as a citizen were not abdicated or abridged on becoming a Christian prelate, and the sacred character which I profess, far from lessening, rather increases, my obligations to my country.

In answer to those who affirm that a churchman is not qualified to discuss politics, by reason of his sacred calling, which removes him from the political arena, I would say that this statement may be true in the sense that a clergyman as such should not be a heated partisan of any political party ; but it is not true in the sense that he is unfitted by his sacred profession for discussing political principles. His very seclusion from popular agitation gives him a vantage-ground over those that are in the whirlpool of party strife, just as they who have never witnessed Shakespeare's plays performed on the stage are better qualified to judge of the genius of the author and the literary merit of his productions than they·who witness the plays amid the environment of stage scenery.

It is needless to say that I write not merely as a churchman, but as a citizen ; not in a partisan, but in a patriotic, spirit ; not in advocacy of any particular party, but in vindication of pure

VOL. CLIV.—NO. 425.   25

government. There is a moral side to most political questions ; and my purpose here is to consider the ethical aspect of politics, and the principles of justice by which they should be regulated. In view of the Presidential election coming on, the remarks I am about to offer are, it seems to me, specially opportune.

Every man in the Commonwealth leads a dual life,—a private life under the shadow of the home, and a public life under the ægis of the State. As a father, a husband, or a son, he owes certain duties to the family ; as a citizen, he owes certain obligations to his country. These civic virtues are all comprised under the generic name, patriotism.

Patriotism means love of country. Its root is the Latin word *patria*, a word not domesticated in English. The French have it in *patrie ;* the Anglo-Saxon and Teutonic races have it literally translated in Fatherland. " Fatherland," says Cicero, " is the common parent of us all : *Patria est communis omnium nostrum parens.*"* It is the paternal home extended, the family reaching out to the city, the province, the country. Hence, with us Fatherland and Country have come to be synonymous. Country in this sense comprises two elements, the soil itself and the men who live thereon. We love the soil in which our fathers sleep, *terra patrum, terra patria*, the land in which we were born. We love the men who as fellow dwellers share that land with us. The other day when Dom Pedro died in Paris, he was laid to his last sleep on Brazilian soil, which he had carried away with him for that very purpose. Let a citizen from Maine meet a citizen from California on the shores of the Bosphorus or on the banks of the Tiber, they will, at once, forget that at home they dwelt three thousand miles apart. State lines are obliterated, party differences are laid aside, religious animosities, if such had existed, are extinguished. They warmly clasp hands, they remember only that they are fellow American citizens, children of the same mother, fellow-dwellers in the same land over which floats the star-spangled banner.

Patriotism implies not only love of soil and of fellow citizens, but also, and principally, attachment to the laws, institutions, and government of one's country ; filial admiration of the heroes, statesmen, and men of genius, who have contributed to its renown by the valor of their arms, the wisdom of their counsel, or

* De Fin., III., 19,

their literary fame. It includes, also, an ardent zeal for the maintenance of those sacred principles that secure to the citizen freedom of conscience, and an earnest determination to consecrate his life, if necessary, *pro aris et focis,* in defence of altar and fireside, of God and Fatherland. Patriotism is a universal sentiment of the race :

> " Breathes there the man with soul so dead
> Who never to himself hath said,
> ' This is my own, my native land ! ' "

A certain philosophical school has taught that love of country has its origin in physical comfort. *Ibi patria ubi bene.* But is it not true that one's country becomes dear in proportion to the sufferings endured for it ? Have not the sacrifices of our wars developed the patriotism of the American ? In fact, it is the most suffering and persecuted races that are endowed with the deepest patriotism. We may even go so far as to say that the rougher the soil, the harsher the climate, the greater the material privations of a land, the more intense is the love of its inhabitants for it. Witness the Irish peasant. And are not the Swiss in their narrow valleys and on their steep mountain sides, the Scotch on their rugged Highlands, the classic models of patriotism ? Nay, the Esquimau, amid the perpetual snows that hide from his eyes every green spot of earth, loves his home, nor dreams of a fairer.

Patriotism is not a sentiment born of material and physical well-being; it is a sentiment that the poverty of country and the discomforts of climate do not diminish, that the inflictions of conquest and despotism do not augment. The truth is, it is a rational instinct placed by the Creator in the breast of man. When God made man a social being, He gave him a sentiment that urges him to sacrifice himself for his family and his country, which is, as it were, his larger family. "Dear are ancestors, dear are children, dear are relatives and friends; all these loves are contained in love of country." *

The Roman was singularly devoted to his country. *Civis Romanus sum* was his proudest boast. He justly gloried in being a citizen of a republic conspicuous for its centuries of endurance,

---

* Cari sunt parentes, cari liberi, propinqui, familiares, sed omnes omnium cari- tates patria una complexa est. (Cicero, De Off., I., 17.)

for the valor of its soldiers, for the wisdom of its statesmen, and the genius of its writers. One of its greatest poets has sung: "It is sweet and honorable to die for one's country."* So execrable was the crime of treason regarded that the traitor not only suffered extreme penalties in this life, but he is consigned after death by Virgil to the most gloomy regions of Tartarus.†

Love of country shows itself in the citizen by the observance• of law and the good use of political rights, and in those that, for the time being, govern, by justice and disinterestedness in their administration. Ministers of religion manifest their patriotism, not only as citizens, but also as spiritual teachers and leaders of the people, by inculcating the religious, moral, and civic virtues, and by prayer to the throne of God for the welfare of the land. "I desire, therefore," wrote St. Paul to his disciple Timothy, "first of all that supplications, prayers, intercessions, and thanksgivings be made for all men; for kings and for all that are in high station, that we may lead a quiet and peaceable life in all piety and chastity; for this is good and acceptable in the sight of God our Saviour."‡

The Catholic Church in our country is not unmindful of this duty. A prayer composed by Archbishop Carroll to beg Heaven's blessing on the land and its rulers, a masterpiece of liturgical literature, is recited every Sunday at the solemn service in some parts of the United States, and notably in the Cathedral at Baltimore, in which the custom has never ceased since it was introduced by Baltimore's first Archbishop over one hundred years ago.

To the soldier, patriotism has inspired the most heroic deeds of courage and self-sacrifice. The victories of Debora, Judith, and Gedeon, achieved for God and country, are recorded with praise in Sacred Scripture.

The stand of Leonidas in the pass of Thermopylæ with his three hundred Spartans against the million Persians of Xerxes; the boldness of his answer to the oriental monarch's summons to lay down arms, "Let him come and take them;" the recklessness of his reply to the threat, that so numerous were his foes that the very heavens would be darkened by their arrows, "'T is

---

* Dulce et decorum pro patria mori. (Horace, B. III., Ode II.)
  † Vendidit hic auro patriam, dominumque potentem
    imposuit. Fixit leges pretio atque refixit. (Æneid, B. VI.)
  ‡ I. Timothy, II., 1-3.

well. We shall fight in the shade ; " the fierce battle ; the fall of almost all the Grecian heroes ; the total defeat of the Persian host—are commonplaces of history, are themes of the schoolroom. That day ranks among the great days of the world. Had Xerxes triumphed, Europe had become Asiatic, and the trend of history had been changed.

The three calls of Cincinnatus to the Dictatorship from the solitude and cultivation of his Sabine farm, his three triumphs over the enemies of the Republic, kindled not in his breast the fire of political ambition. When the foe was repelled and his country needed him no longer, he laid down the sword of command for the plow, left "the pomp and circumstance" of the camp for the quiet of his rural homestead, like him whose grave hallows the hillside of Mount Vernon—two notable instances of patriotism, making men great in peace no less than in war. Need I recall to the readers of THE NORTH AMERICAN REVIEW Regulus, Horatius Cocles, Brutus, the first consul, whose heroic and patriotic deeds have been the exultant theme of the classic authors of Rome ?

Patriotism finds outward and, so to say, material expression, in respect for the flag that symbolizes the country, and for the chief magistrate who represents it. Perhaps, it is only when an American travels abroad that he fully realizes how deep-rooted is his love for his native country. The sentiment of patriotism, which may be dormant at home, is aroused and quickened in foreign lands.

The sight of an American flag flying from the mast of a ship in mid-ocean or in some foreign port, awakes unwonted emotion and enthusiasm.

The interest which an American feels in a presidential election or in any other important domestic event, is intensified when he is abroad. When I was travelling through the Tyrol, in 1880, I had a natural desire to find out who had been nominated for the Presidency ; but in that country news travels slowly. On reaching Innspruck, I learned that Mr. Garfield was the nominee. I got my information from an American student buried in the cloisters of a seminary, to whom the outside world was apparently dead. I never discovered and I dare say his professors never knew how he obtained his information. But the news was correct.

Americans are in the habit of visiting Rome every year in

large numbers. The greater part of them on their arrival instinctively repair to the American College. Perhaps, the name of the college attracts them; perhaps, also, the consciousness that they will hear their mother-tongue. And when they enter its portals, where they are always sure to find a warm welcome from the genial rector, their eyes are gladdened by the familiar features of the " Father of his Country."

Love of country, as I have described it, which is fundamentally an ethical sentiment, and which was such in all nations, even before Christian Revelation was given to the world, and which is such to-day among nations that have not heard the Christian message, is elevated, ennobled, and perfected by the religion of Christ. Patriotism in non-Christian times and races has inspired heroism even unto death. We do not pretend that Christian patriotism can do more. But we do say that Christianity has given to patriotism and to the sacrifices it demands, nobler motives and higher ideals.

If the virtue of patriotism was held in such esteem by pagan Greece and Rome, guided only by. the light of reason, how much more should it be cherished by Christians, instructed as they are by the voice of Revelation! The Founder of the Christian religion has ennobled and sanctified loyalty to country by the influence of His example and the force of His teaching.

When St. Peter was asked by the tax-collector whether his Master should pay the tribute money or not, he replied in the affirmative, and the penniless Master wrought a miracle to secure the payment of the money, though He was exempt from the obligation by reason of His poverty and His divine origin; for if the sons of kings are free from taxation, as Christ Himself re-. marked on that occasion, the Son of the King of kings had certainly a higher claim to exemption.

The Herodians questioned Jesus whether or not it was lawful to pay tribute to Cæsar. By this question they sought to ensnare Him in His words. If He admitted the obligation, He would have aroused the indignation of the Jews, who deemed it unlawful to pay tribute to a Gentile and idolatrous ruler. If, on the other hand, He denied the obligation, He would have incurred the vengeance of Rome. He made this memorable reply, which silenced His adversaries: " Render to Cæsar the things which are Cæsar's, and to God the things which are God's."

The Apostles echo the voice of their Master. "Let every soul be subject to higher powers; for there is no power but from God. Therefore, he who resisteth the power, resisteth the ordinance of God; and they who resist, purchase for themselves damnation. Render, therefore, to all their dues: tribute to whom tribute is due; custom to whom custom; fear to whom fear; honor to whom honor."* "Be ye subject to every authority for God's sake, whether to the king as excelling, or to governors as sent by him for the punishment of evil-doers, and for the praise of those who do well."† This short sentence, "There is no authority but from God," has contributed more effectually to the stability of nations and to the peace and order of society than standing armies and all the volumes ever written on the principles of government. It ennobles obedience to constituted authority by representing it, not as an act of servility to man, but of homage to God. It sheds a halo around rulers and magistrates by holding them up to us as the representatives of God. It invests all legitimate laws with a divine sanction by an appeal to our conscience.

If the Apostles and the primitive Christians had so much reverence for the civil magistrates in whose election they certainly had no voice; and if they were so conscientious in observing the laws of the Roman Empire, which often inflicted on them odious pains and disabilities, how much more respect should the American citizen entertain for the civil rulers in whose election he actively participates! With what alacrity should he fulfil the laws which are framed solely for his peace and protection and for the welfare of the Commonwealth!

The deification of the State in pagan times rested on a principle contrary to reason, and exacted sacrifices destructive of the moral worth of the citizen. The State absorbed the individual. It was held to be the proprietor and master of the citizen, who was only an instrument in its hand, to be used, cast aside, or broken at will. Christianity knows how to conciliate patriotism with the exigencies of man's personal dignity. Social perfection, or civilization, is in that form of government that secures to its members the greater facility for pursuing and attaining their end in life. That is the Christian notion of the State, and the American also, as laid

* Romans, xiii.   † I. Peter, ii.

down in the Declaration of Independence. It is stated therein that government is for the citizen, to secure to him his inalienable rights—that is to say, rights that are his and are inalienable by virtue of the supreme end marked out for him by the Creator.

Again, unlike pagan civilization, which despised the foreigner as a barbarian and a foe, Christian and American civilization sees its ideal in that universal charity revealed to the world by Christ, who came to teach the brotherhood of all men in the Fatherhood of the One God. Patriotism and cosmopolitism are not incompatible in the Christian. They find a model in the religious order, in the Catholicity and unity of the Church. And even in the political order, the United States offers a miniature picture of the brotherly federation of nations—forty-four sovereign States, sovereign and independent as to their internal existence, yet presenting to the rest of the world a national unity in the federal government.

And, indeed, when we reflect on the happiness and manifold temporal blessings which our political institutions have already conferred, and are destined in the future to confer, on millions of people, we are not surprised that the American citizen is proud of his country, her history, and the record of her statesmen.

Therefore, next to God, our country should hold the strongest place in our affections. Impressed, as we ought to be, with a profound sense of the blessings which our system of government continues to bestow on us, we shall have a corresponding dread lest these blessings should be withdrawn from us. It is a sacred duty for every American to do all in his power to perpetuate our civil institutions and to avert the dangers that threaten them.

The system of government which obtains in the United States is tersely described in the well-known sentence: " A government of the people, by the people, for the people ;" which may be paraphrased thus: Ours is a government in which the people are ruled by the representatives of their own choice, and for the benefit of the people themselves.

Our rulers are called the servants of the people, since they are appointed to fulfil the people's wishes ; and the people are called the sovereign people, because it is by their sovereign voice that their rulers are elected.

The method by which the supreme will of the people is registered is the ballot-box. This is the oracle that proclaims their choice. This is the balance in which the merits of the candidates are weighed. The heavier scale determines at once the decision of the majority and the selection of the candidate.

And what spectacle is more sublime than the sight of ten millions of citizens determining, not by the bullet, but by the ballot, the ruler that is to preside over the nation's destinies for four years!

> " A weapon that comes down as still
> As snowflakes fall upon the sod ;
> But executes a freeman's will,
> As lightning does the will of God :
> And from its force nor doors nor locks
> Can shield you, 'tis the ballot-box."

But the greatest blessings are liable to be perverted. Our Republic, while retaining its form and name, may degenerate into most odious tyranny ; and the irresponsible despotism of the multitude is more galling, because more difficult to be shaken off, than that of the autocrat.

History is philosophy teaching by example. A brief review of the Roman Republic and the causes of its downfall will teach us a useful lesson. The Republic prospered so long as the citizens practised simplicity of life and the civil magistrates administered even-handed justice. Avarice and ambition proved its ruin.* The avarice of the poor was gratified by the bribery of the rich ; and the ambition of the rich was fed by the votes of the poor.

In the latter days of the Republic bribery and corruption were shamefully practised. Marius was elected to the consulship by the purchase of votes and by collusion with the most notorious demagogues. Pompey and Crassus secured the consulship by intimidation, though neither of them was legally qualified for that office. The philosophy of Epicurus, introduced during the last years of the Republic, hastened the moral and mental corruption of Rome. The loss of the political autonomy of Greece, which preceded that of Rome, may be traced to the same cause. To the early Romans the oath was sacred, and perjury a detestable crime. We find in a letter of Cicero to Atticus a curious incident that shows how far the politicians of his day had departed from former standards.

---

* Primo pecuniæ, deinde imperii cupido crevit; ea quasi materies omnium malorum fuere. Sallust. Catalin. c. x.

" Memmius," he writes, " has just made known to the Senate an agreement between himself and an associate candidate for the consulship on the one hand, and the two consuls of the current year on the other." It appears that the two consuls agreed to favor the candidacy of the aspirants on the following terms: The two aspirants bound themselves to forfeit to the consuls four hundred thousand sesterces if they failed to produce in favor of the consuls three augurs who were to swear that in their sight and hearing the Plebs (though such was not the fact) had voted the law *Curiate,* a law that invested the consuls with full military powers; and also if they failed to produce two ex-consuls who were to swear that in their presence the Senate had passed and signed a certain decree regulating the provinces of each consul though such was not the fact.* What a crowding of dishonesty in this one transaction! Can the worst kind of American politics furnish the match of this slate gotten up regardless of truth and oath ?

Cato failed to be elected consul, although eminently worthy of that dignity, because he disdained to purchase the office by bribes.   Cæsar had so far debauched the populace with flattery and bribes and the soldiers with pensions, that his election to the office of chief pontiff and consul was easily obtained.

During the Empire elections were usually a mere formality. Bribery was open and unblushing.   Toward the end of the second century the Empire was publicly sold at auction to the highest bidder.   Didius Julianus, a rich senator, obtained the prize by the payment of $620 to each soldier of the Prætorian guard. But he was executed after a precarious and inglorious reign of sixty-six days.

The history of the Roman Republic and the Roman Empire should be a salutary warning to us.   Our Christian civilization gives us no immunity from political corruption and disaster.   The oft-repeated cry of election frauds should not be treated with indifference, though, in many instances, no doubt, it is the empty charge of defeated partisans against successful rivals, or the heated language of a party press.

But after all reasonable allowances are made, enough remains of a substantial character to be ominous.   In every possible way, by tickets insidiously printed, by "colonizing," "repeating," and

* Book IV., Letter XVIII.

"personation," frauds are attempted, and too often successfully, on the ballot. I am informed by a trustworthy gentleman that, in certain localities, the adherents of one party, while proof against bribes from their political opponents, will exact compensation before giving their votes even to their own party candidates. The evil would be great enough if it were restricted to examples of this kind, but it becomes much more serious when large bodies of men are debauched by the bribes or intimidated by the threats of wealthy corporations.

But when the very fountains of legislation are polluted by lobbying and other corrupt means ; when the hand of bribery is extended, and not always in vain, to our municipal, state, and national legislators ; when our law-makers become the pliant tools of some selfish and greedy capitalists, instead of subserving the interests of the people,—then, indeed, all patriotic citizens have reason to be alarmed about the future of our country.

The man who would poison the wells and springs of the land is justly regarded as a human monster, as an enemy of society, and no punishment could be too severe for him. Is he not as great a criminal who would poison and pollute the ballot-box, the unfailing fount and well-spring of our civil freedom and of our national life ?

The Ark of the Covenant was held in the highest veneration by the children of Israel. It was the oracle from which God communicated his will to the people. Two cherubim with outstretched wings were placed over it as sacred guardians. Oza was suddenly struck dead for profanely touching it. May we not, without irreverence, compare the ballot-box to the ancient Ark ? Is it not for us the oracle of God, because it is the oracle of the people ? God commands us to obey our rulers. It is through the ballot-box that our rulers are proclaimed to us ; therefore, its voice should be accepted as the voice of God. Let justice and truth, like twin cherubs, guard this sacred instrument. Let him who lays profane hands upon it be made to feel that he is guilty of a grievous offence against the stability of government, the peace of society, and the majesty of God.

Our Saviour, filled with righteous indignation, seizes a scourge and casts out of the Temple those that bought and sold in it, and overturns the tables of the money-changers, saying: " My house is a house of prayer, but you have made it a den of thieves." The polling booth is a temple, in which the angel of justice holds the scales with an even hand.   The political money-changer pollutes the temple by his iniquitous bargains.   The money-changer in Jerusalem's Temple trafficked in doves; the electioneering money-changer traffics in human beings.

Let the minister of justice arise, and, clothed with the panoply of authority, let him drive those impious men from the temple. Let the buyers and sellers of votes be declared infamous ; for they are trading in our American birthright.   Let them be cast forth from the pale of American citizenship and be treated as outlaws.

I do not think the punishment too severe when we consider the enormity and far-reaching consequences of their crime.   I hold that the man who undermines our elective system is only less criminal than the traitor who fights against his country with a foreign invader.   The one compasses his end by fraud, the other by force.

The privilege of voting is not an inherent or inalienable right.   It is a solemn and sacred trust, to be used in strict accordance with the intentions of the authority from which it emanates.

When a citizen exercises his honest judgment in casting his vote for the most acceptable candidate, he is making a legitimate use of the prerogatives confided to him.   But when he sells or barters his vote, when he disposes of it to the highest bidder, like a merchantable commodity, he is clearly violating his trust and degrading his citizenship.

The enormity of the offence will be readily perceived by pushing it to its logical consequences:

First, Once the purchase of votes is tolerated or condoned or connived at, the obvious result is that the right of suffrage becomes a solemn farce.   The sovereignty is no longer vested in the people, but in corrupt politicians or in wealthy corporations ; money instead of merit becomes the test of success ; the election is determined, not by the personal fitness and integrity of the candidate, but by the length of his own or his patron's purse ; and the aspirant for office owes his victory, not to the votes of his constituents, but to the grace of some political boss.

Second, The better class of citizens will lose heart and absent themselves from the polls, knowing that it is useless to engage in a contest which is already decided by irresponsible managers.

Third, Disappointment, vexation, and righteous indignation will burn in the breasts of upright citizens. These sentiments will be followed by apathy and despair of carrying out successfully a popular form of government. The enemies of the Republic will then take advantage of the existing scandals to decry our system and laud absolute monarchies. The last stage in the drama is political stagnation or revolution.

But, happily, the American people are not prone to despondency or to political stagnation, or to revolution outside of the lines of legitimate reform. They are cheerful and hopeful, because they are conscious of their strength ; and well they may be, when they reflect on the century of ordeals through which they have triumphantly passed. They are vigilant, because they are liberty-loving, and they know that " Eternal vigilance is the price of liberty." They are an enlightened and practical people ; therefore are they quick to detect and prompt to resist the first inroads of corruption. They know well how to apply the antidote to the political distemper of the hour. They have the elasticity of mind and heart to rise to the occasion. They will never suffer the stately temple of the Constitution to be overthrown, but will hasten to strengthen the foundation where it is undermined, to repair every breach, and to readjust every stone of the glorious edifice.

In conclusion, I shall presume to suggest, with all deference, a brief outline of what appear to me the most efficient means to preserve purity of elections and to perpetuate our political independence.

Many partial remedies may be named. The main purpose of these remedies is to foster and preserve what may be called a Public Conscience. In the individual man, conscience is that inner light which directs him in the knowledge and choice of good and evil, that practical judgment which pronounces over every one of his acts, that it is right or wrong, moral or immoral. Now, this light and judgment which directs man in the ordinary personal affairs of life, must be his guide also in the affairs of his political life; for he is answerable to God for his political, as well as his personal, life.

The individual conscience is an enlightenment and a guide; and it is itself illumined and directed by the great maxims of natural law and the conclusions which the mind is constantly deducing from those maxims. Now, is there not a set of maxims and opinions that fulfil the office of guides to the masses in their political life ?

The means which I propose are :

First, The enactment of strict and wholesome laws for preventing bribery and the corruption of the ballot-box, accompanied with condign punishment against the violators of the law. Let such protection and privacy be thrown around the polling booth that the humblest citizen may be able to record his vote without fear of pressure or of interference from those that might influence him. Such a remedy has already been attempted, with more or less success, in some States by the introduction of new systems of voting.

Second, A pure, enlightened, and independent judiciary to interpret and enforce the laws.

Third, A vigilant and fearless press that will reflect and create a healthy public opinion. Such a press, guided by the laws of justice and the spirit of American institutions, is the organ and the reflection of national thought, the outer bulwark of the rights and liberties of the citizen against the usurpations of authority and the injustice of parties, the speediest and most direct castigator of vice and dishonesty. It is a duty of the citizens of a free country not only to encourage the press, but to coöperate with it ; and it is a misfortune for any land when its leading men neglect to instruct their country and act on public opinion through this powerful instrument for good.

Fourth, The incorporation into our school system of familiar lessons embodying a history of our country, a brief sketch of her heroes, statesmen, and patriots, whose civic virtues the rising generation will thus be taught to emulate. The duties and rights of citizens along with reverence for our political institutions should likewise be inculcated, as Dr. Andrews, President of Brown University, recommends in a recent article. There is danger that the country whose history is not known and cherished will become to the masses only an abstraction, or, at best, that it will be in touch with them only on its less lovable side, the taxes and burdens it imposes. Men lost in an unnatural isolation, strangers to the past life of their nation, living on a soil to which they hold only by the passing interests of the present, as atoms without cohesion, are not able to realize and bring home to themselves the claims of a country that not only *is,* but that was before them, and that will be, as history alone can teach, long after them.

Fifth, A more hearty celebration of our national holidays.

The Hebrew people, as we learn from Sacred Scripture, were commanded to commemorate by an annual observance their liberation from the bondage of Pharaoh and their entrance into the Promised Land. In nearly all civilized countries there are certain days set apart to recall some great events in their national history, and to pay honor to the memory of the heroes who figured in them. The United States has already established three national holidays. The first is consecrated to the birth of the "Father of his Country"; the second, to the birth of the nation; and the third is observed as a day of Thanksgiving to God for his manifold blessings to the nation. On those days, when the usual occupations of life are suspended, every citizen has leisure to study and admire the political institutions of his country, and to thank God for the benedictions that He has poured out on us as a people. In contemplating these blessings, we may well repeat with the Royal Prophet: "He hath not done in like manner to every nation, and His judgments He hath not made manifest to them."

If holidays are useful to those that are to the manor born, they are still more imperatively demanded for the foreign population constantly flowing into our country, and which consists of persons who are strangers to our civil institutions. The annually recurring holidays will create and develop in their minds a knowledge of our history and admiration for our system of government. It will help, also, to mould our people into unity of political faith. By the young, especially, are holidays welcomed with keen delight; and as there is a natural, though unconscious, association in the mind between the civic festivity and the cause that gave it birth, their attachment to the day will extend to the patriotic event or to the men whose anniversary is celebrated.

Sixth, The maintenance of party lines is an indispensable means for preserving political purity. One party watches the other, takes note of its shortcomings, its blunders and defects; and it has at its disposal the means for rebuking any abuse of power on the part of the dominant side, by appealing to the country at the tribunal of the ballot-box. The healthiest periods of the Roman Republic were periods of fierce political strife. The citizens of Athens were not allowed to remain neutral. They were compelled to take sides on all questions of great public interest. Not only was every citizen obliged to vote, but the successful candidate was bound to accept the office to which he was called, and to subordinate his taste for private life to the public interests.

England owes much of her greatness and liberty to the active and aggressive vigilance of opposing political camps. Political parties are the outcome of political freedom. Parties are not to be confounded with factions. The former contend for a principle, the latter struggle for a master.

To jurists and statesmen these considerations may seem trite, elementary, and commonplace. But, like all elementary principles, they are of vital import. They should be kept prominently in view before the people, and not obscured in a maze of wordy technicalities. They are landmarks to guide men in the path of public duty, and they would vastly contribute to the good order and stability of the Commonwealth if they were indelibly stamped on the heart and memory of every American citizen.

JAMES CARDINAL GIBBONS.

A SOUTHERNER ON THE NEGRO QUESTION.

BY THOMAS NELSON PAGE, AUTHOR OF "MARSE CHAN," "MEH
LADY," "ELSKET," ETC.

A FEW months ago that Englishman who is perhaps the closest student among his people of our American institutions, Professor James Bryce, gave in THE NORTH AMERICAN REVIEW his views as to the Negro Problem.* He declared that the most serious problem which the people and the government of the United States have to deal with is the position of the colored population of the South.

No Southerner will gainsay Professor Bryce's declaration as to the gravity of this matter. It is true that a year ago—when the Lodge Bill was pending, and when the ratio of relative increase of the white and negro races was not yet known—the peril appeared to at least one part of the country more immediate than it has done since "the Force Bill," as the South termed it, failed and since the results of the census have become known. But the problem is serious enough now, and is the gravest one which we face to-day. What was thought of it at that time may be gathered from the attitude of the people of the South whilst the Lodge Bill was under discussion. Consideration of all other matters, whatever, practically ceased. The South alone understood what it meant.

Senator Hoar, of Massachusetts, speaking of the South on the floor of the Senate, on the 23d February, 1889, said : "The person hears the sound of my voice this moment who in his lifetime will see fifty million negroes dwelling in those States."

The proposition stated seems to us who know the negro to contain its own argument. We of the South who see them at short range are astonished that Senator Hoar and that great body

* "Thoughts on the Negro Problem," by Professor James Bryce, NORTH AMER-
ICAN REVIEW, December, 1891.

of people whose views he represents do not understand the perils of the situation. At one step more they confront the rest of the Anglo-American people ; for the only thing that stands between the negro race and the people of the North to-day is the people of the South.

The chief difficulty in the solution of the question is to be found in the different views held as to it by the two sections. They do not understand it alike.

Two propositions may be safely affirmed ; one, that there must be a grave error somewhere ; the other, that there must be a right position, and the sooner the American people find it and plant themselves on it, the better for us and for those that come after us ; the better for the negro race as well ; for the future of the negro depends upon the white.

Perhaps no clearer or more authoritative exposition of the views held by the North on this question can be found than that set forth in an address before the Massachusetts Club of Boston on the 22d of February, 1890. The favor with which it was received by the class to whom it was delivered testifies the extent to which the question is misunderstood at the North. After nega-tiving the Southern idea of the question, the speaker declares : " The problem is whether American citizens shall not enjoy equal rights in the choice of their rulers. It is not a question of the negroes' right to rule. It is simply a question of their right to choose rulers ; and as in reconstruction days they selected more white men for office than men of their own race, they would probably do so now."

The view which the South takes of this question is that it is a great race question, on the correct solution of which depends not only the present salvation of the South, but the future of the nation. That there exists a race question of some sort must be apparent to every person who passes through the South. Where six millions of people of one color and with a certain history live in contact with ten or twelve millions of another color and with a widely different history there must of necessity be a race question.

The negro began his career as a citizen under heavy disadvan-tages, his ignorance being only one of them. He has not be-haved unnaturally. Fresh from slavery he was enfranchised as a voter, and was drafted into the Union League under carpet-bag officers as an ally, through whom was to be secured the perpetual ascendency of "the party of the Union." With the same end in view the whites were disfranchised. It was a great mistake. Since then the real issue at the South has been the race issue. Other issues have arisen from time to time, but this has been the paramount issue.

The result is singularly anomalous. The feeling has not reached the point of personal hostility, at least, on the part of the whites ; but as the older generation which knew the ties between the races in the relation of master and servant passes away the race feeling is perhaps growing intenser. The negro becomes more and more assertive. The white steadily becomes impressed more and more deeply with the conviction that upon the continued domination of his race depends not only the present but the future greatness of this country. He is not left to mere theory as to this. The history of the negro race, unhappily, furnishes an unanswerable argument, that, whatever a sentimental philanthropy may assert, there underlies the whole matter the potent and mysterious principle of race quality. Slavery will not alone account for it. Bondage cannot enthrall the mind. In the recorded experience of mankind, slavery alone has not repressed intelligence.

The negro has not progressed, not because he was a slave, but because he does not possess the faculties to raise himself above slavery. He has not yet exhibited the qualities of any race which has advanced civilization or shown capacity to be greatly advanced. What the future may bring forth no man may certainly foretell ; it belongs to prophecy. We can only hope. But the past is fixed.

Where the negro has thriven it has invariably been under the influence and by the assistance of a stronger race. These wanting, he has inevitably and visibly reverted towards the original type.

Since the dawn of history the negro has been in one place or another—in Egypt, in Phœnicia, in Rome, and other countries—brought in contact with civilization. For over two hundred years he has been under the immediate influence of the most potent race of modern, if not of all, times, and within the sweep of the ripest period of the world's history. In New England he has not been a slave for a hundred years. The result there is instructive.

Dr. Henry M. Field is an extensive traveller, a close and wide observer, an honest recorder, and the friend of the whole human race. He is a member of a Northern family of which New England may be justly proud. Speaking of the negro's condition he says : *

"Here we are doomed to great disappointment. The black man has every right which has belonged to his white neighbor ; not only the natural rights which, according to the Declaration of Independence, belong to every human being—the right to life, liberty, and the pursuit of happiness ; but the right to vote and to have a part in making the laws. He could own his little home, and there sit under his own vine and fig tree, with none to molest or to make him afraid. His children could go to the same common schools and sit on the same benches, and learn the same lessons as white children. With such advantages a race that had natural genius ought to have made great progress in a hundred years. But where are the men that it should have produced to be the leaders of their people? We find not one who has taken rank as a man of action or a man of thought, as a thinker or a writer, as artist or poet, discoverer or inventor. The whole race has remained on a dead level of mediocrity. If any man ever proved himself a friend of the African race it was Theodore Parker, who endured all sorts of persecutions and social ostracism, who faced mobs and was hissed and hooted in public meetings for his bold championship of the rights of the negro race. But rights are one thing and capacity is another. And while he was ready to fight for them, he was very despondent as to their capacity for rising in the scale of civilization. Indeed, he said in so many words, 'In respect to the power of civilization, the African is at the bottom, the American Indian next.' In 1857 he wrote to a friend : 'There are inferior races which have always borne the same ignoble relation to the rest of men and always will. In two generations what a change will be in the condition and character of the Irish in New England. But in twenty generations the negro will stand just where he is now, that is, if he will not have disappeared.'

"That was more than thirty years ago," proceeds Dr. Field. "But to-day I look about me here in Massachusetts, and I see a few colored men. But what are they doing? They work in the fields, they hoe corn, they dig potatoes, the women take in washing. I find colored barbers and white-washers, shoe blacks and chimney sweeps ; but I do not know a single man who has grown to be a merchant or a banker, a judge or a lawyer, a member of the Legislature or a justice of the peace, or even a selectman of the town. In all these respects they remain where they were in the days of our fathers. The best friends of the colored race, of whom I am one, must confess that it is disappointing and discouraging to find that with all these opportunities they are little removed from where they were a hundred years ago !"

But suppose there have been a few lawyers and doctors, and even a judge or two, selected rather with a view to recognition of the complexion of their skins than the qualities of their minds, these are the exceptions which prove the rule, and not one has attained a point above mediocrity. ,

* "Sunny Skies and Dark Shadows," by Dr. Henry M. Field.

The history of the negro race in Liberia and Hayti has been even more disappointing to the hopes of his friends than elsewhere. In both of these countries a civilization was created for him. Liberia was founded for him by the Caucasian in as high hope as even was this Republic. Christendom gave its assistance and its prayers. How has the negro progressed there ? Mr. Charles H. J. Taylor, late U. S. Minister to Liberia, a colored man himself, wrote an account of that country which was published in the Kansas City *Times*, of April 22, 1888. Not a factory, mill, or workshop, of *any kind, he says, is to be found there. "They (the government) have no money or currency in circulation of any kind. They have no boats of any character, not even a canoe, the two gun-boats England gave them lying rotten on the beach." . . . . "Look from morn till night you will never see a horse, a mule, a donkey, or a broken-in ox. They have them not. There is not a buggy, a wagon, a cart, a slide, a wheelbarrow in the four counties. The natives carry everything on their heads." The whole picture presented is hopeless.

It is not better in Hayti. For nearly a hundred years the negro has been masquerading in governing Hayti, and a more fantastic mummery never degraded a land. Under negro rule San Domingo, once the queen of the Antilles, has sunk into a state of almost primeval barbarism. We have two recent pictures of Hayti, by Englishmen, both of whom assure us that they have no race antipathy; one James Anthony Froude, the historian, the other Sir Spencer St. John, for years British Resident at Hayti. They both agree. The picture presented in Sir Spencer St. John's work, "The Black Republic," is astounding, revolution succeeding revolution, and massacre succeeding massacre ; the country once teeming with wealth, covered with beautiful villas and plantations, and with a considerable foreign commerce, now in a state of decay and ruin, without trade or resources of any kind ; peculation and jobbery paramount in all public offices ; barbarism substituted for civilization ; voudoo worship springing up in place of Christianity, and human flesh oftener than once sold in the market place of Port-au-Prince, the capital. Sir Spencer St. John says that a Spanish colleague once said to him, " If we could return to Hayti fifty years hence, we should find the negresses cooking their bananas on the ruins of these warehouses." On which, he remarks, "It is more than probable, unless in the meantime influenced by some higher civilization, that this prophecy will come true. The negresses are in fact cooking their bananas amid the ruins of the best houses of the capital."

These examples seem to establish the fact that the negro does not possess the elements of character, the essential qualifications to conduct a government even for himself, and that if reins of government be intrusted to his unaided hands he will fling reason to the winds and drive to ruin.

Were this, however, true only of Liberia and Hayti we might bear it with such philosophic composure as our philanthropy admits of. But the South has had a personal experience of the negro's rule. For eight years a number of the Southern States were partly, and three of them were wholly, given up to the control of the negroes, directed by leaders, at least, of undoubted ability, and sustained by the influence of the entire North. The white was disfranchised. The negro and his chosen leaders were invested with absolute power; the entire weight of government was, under the misapprehension born of the excitement which then reigned, thrown blindly in his favor. Then was the occasion which Mr. Cable selects for his illustration. The negro selected his own rulers. What was the result? Such a riot of folly and extravagance, such a travesty of government as was never witnessed save in those countries in which he had himself furnished the illustration. Carpet-bag rule, with the negro as its facile and ignorant instrument, inaugurated a new system of debauchery and crime.

Space will not admit of a detailed description; but a few facts will be sufficient. A more complete picture will be found in the series of carefully prepared papers, which appeared a year or two since entitled, "Noted Men on the Solid South," to which I refer, and to which I am indebted for much of my material in this branch of the subject.

The Louisiana State Lottery was one offspring of a misrule which proved strong enough to defy for years even the Federal Government.

Soon after Warmouth came into office in Louisiana he stated in his message of January 4, 1868, to his legislature, "Our debt is smaller than that of almost any State in the Union, with a tax roll of $251,000,000, and a bonded debt that can and will be reduced to $6,000,000." Two years later, "the census of 1870 showed the debt of the State to have increased to $25,021,734, and that of the parishes and municipalities to $28,065,770. Within a year the State debt was increased over half, and the local indebtedness had doubled. Louisiana, according to the census, stood in the matter of debt at the head of the Union."* This was but the beginning. The total cost of four years and five months of carpet-bag rule amounted to $106,023,337, or $24,040,088 per year. Taxation mounted up in proportion in some places to 7 and 8 per cent. of the assessed value. Dr. Henry M. Field cites a case reported to him where it was as high as 16 per cent. The public printing had in previous years cost about $37,000 a year. During the first two years of Warmouth's régime the New Orleans *Republican,* in which he was a large stockholder, received for public printing $1,140,881.77.† Time and space fail to tell of the rapine, the profligacy which existed. The taxable values of New Orleans between Warmouth's advent and Kellogg's exit fell from $146,718,790 to $88,613,930, a net decline of $58,104,860 in eight years, whilst real estate in the country parishes shrank in value from $99,266,839.85 to $47,141,696. So much for Louisiana.

In Mississippi the corruption was almost as great and the result almost as disastrous. In South Carolina it was even worse. The General Assembly which convened in Columbia in 1868 consisted of 72 whites and 85 negroes. In the House were 14 Democrats and in the Senate 7; the remaining 136 were Republicans. One of the first acts passed was anomalous. After defending the rights of negroes on railroads, in theatres, etc., it provided that if the person whose rights under the act were claimed to be violated was colored, then the universal rule of law was changed, and the burden of proof was on the defendant to establish innocence.

The public printing was also swelled expenses. The total cost of the printing in South Carolina under negro rule exceeded in one year by $122,932.13 the cost of like work in Massachusetts, New York, Pennsylvania, Ohio, and Maryland together.‡

In 1860 the taxable values in the State amounted to $490,-000,000 and the tax a little less than $400,000. In 1871 the

---

* Hon. B. J. Sage, in "Noted Men on the Solid South," p. 404.
† Ib., p. 508.   ‡ Ib., p. 100.

taxable values had been reduced to $184,000,000, and the tax increased to $2,000,000. In nineteen counties, taken together, 93,293 acres of land were sold in one year for unpaid taxes. After four years of carpet-bag Republican rule, the debt of the State had increased from $5,407,306 to $18,515,033. There had been no public works of any importance, and the entire thirteen millions of dollars represented nothing but unnecessary and profligate expenditures.*

These are simply statistics. No account has been taken of the imposition practised throughout the South during the period of negro domination; of the vast, incredible and wanton degradation of the Southern people by the malefactors, who, with hordes of ignorant negroes just from the bonds of slavery as their instruments, trod down the once stately South at their will. No wonder that Governor Chamberlayne, Republican and carpet-bagger as he was, should have declared, as he did in writing to the New England Society : " The civilization of the Puritan and Cavalier, of the Roundhead and Huguenot, is in peril." A survey of the field and a careful consideration of the facts have convinced me that I am within the domain of truth when I say that the Southern States, with the exception perhaps of one or two of the Border States, were better off in 1868, when reconstruction went into force, than they were in 1876, when the carpet-bag governments were finally overthrown ; and that the eight years of negro domination cost the South more than the war, inclusive of the loss of values in slave property. I think if Mr. Cable and those who accept his theorem will study history, even as written only in statistics, taking no account, if they please, of the suffering and the degradation inflicted upon the white race during the period in which the South was under the dominion of the rulers selected by the negroes, they will find that there is not so much difference between the proposition which he formulates and that which the South states, when she declares that the pending question is one of race domination, on which depends the future salvation of the American people.

Twenty-seven years have rolled by since the negro was given his freedom ; more than twenty years have passed since he was given a part in the government, and was taken up to be educated. The laws were so adapted that there is not now a negro under

* Mr. Hemphill's paper on South Carolina in "Noted Men on the Solid South," p. 102.

forty years old who has not had the opportunity to receive a public school education. The South has viewed his political course with suspicion, and in this direction has opposed him with all her resources ; but she has not been mean or niggardly towards him. On the contrary, in every place, at all times, even while she was resisting and assailing him for his political action, she has displayed towards him in the expenditures for his education a liberality which in relation to her ability has amounted to lavishness.

The Rev. Dr. A. D. Mayo, eminent alike for his learning and philanthropy, and a Northern educator, declared not long ago : " No other people in human history have made an effort so remarkable as the people of the South in re-establishing their schools and colleges. Overwhelmed by war and bad government, they have done wonders, and with the interest and zeal now felt in public schools in the South, the hope for the future is brighter than ever." " Last year," he says, speaking in 1888, " these sixteen States paid nearly $1,000,000 each for educational purposes, a sum greater, according to their means, than ten times the amount now paid by most of the New England States." Virginia expended on her public schools from 1870–71 to 1890–91, according to the figures of Colonel F. G. Ruffin, Second Auditor of Virginia, taken from official sources, $22,759,249.38. Her negro schools, including school buildings and permanent improvements, cost her $5,380,513.65. For the year 1887–88 her negro schools cost her, by the same estimate, $400,000, of which the negroes paid about $60,000.

Governor Gordon, speaking of Georgia, in a recent address, said: " When her people secured possession of the State government, they found about six thousand colored pupils in the public schools, with the school exchequer bankrupt. To-day, instead of six thousand, we have over one hundred and sixty thousand colored pupils in the public schools, with the exchequer expanding and the schools multiplying year by year." He says further that the negroes pay one-thirtieth of the expense, and the other twenty-nine thirtieths are paid by the whites. The other Southern States have not been behind Virginia and Georgia in this matter.

Now, what has the negro accomplished in this quarter of a century ? They are barbers, and white-washers, shoe-blacks and chimney sweeps. Here and there we find a lawyer or two, unhappily

with their practice in inverse ratio to their principles, or now and
then there is a doctor. But almost invariably these are men with
a considerable infusion of white blood in their veins. And even
these have in no single instance attained a position which in a
white would be deemed above mediocrity. Fifteen years ago there
were in Richmond, where I live, a number of negro tobacco manufacturers and other negro dealers. Now there are hardly any
except undertakers. They have been losing ground as mechanics.
Before the war, on every plantation, there were first-class carpenters, blacksmiths, wheelwrights, etc. Half the houses in
Virginia were built by negro carpenters. Where are they now?
In Richmond there may be a few blacksmiths and a dozen or two
carpenters; but where are the others? A great strike occurred
last year in one of the large iron-works of the city of Richmond.
The president of the company told me afterwards that, although
the places at the machines were filled later on by volunteers, and
although there were many negroes employed in the works who
did not strike, it never occurred to either the management or to
the negroes that they could work at the machines, and not one
had ever suggested it.

The question naturally arises, Have they improved? Many
persons declare that they have not. My observation has led to a
somewhat different conclusion. Where they have been brought
into contact with the stronger race under conditions in which they
derived aid, as in cities, they have in certain directions improved;
where they have lacked this stimulating influence, as in sections
of the country where the association has steadily diminished, they
have failed to advance. In the cities, where they are in touch
with the whites they are, I think, becoming more dignified, more
self-respecting, more reasonable; in the country where they are
left to themselves I fail to see this improvement.

This improvement, however, such as it is, does not do away
with the race issue. So far from it, it rather intensifies the feeling, certainly on the part of the negro, and makes the relation
more strained. Yet it is our only hope. The white race, it is
reasonably certain, is not going to be ruled by the negro either
North or South. That day is far off, and neither Lodge bills nor
any other bills can bring it until they can reverse natural law,
enact that ignorance shall be above intelligence, and exalt feeble-
ness over strength. The history of that race is a guaranty that

this cannot be. It has been a conquering race from its first appearance, like the Scandinavians of old,

> "Firm to resolve and steadfast to endure."

The section of it which inhabits the United States is not yet degenerate. That part of it at the South is not. It is not necessary to recall its history. Let one who has not been generally regarded as unduly biassed in favor of the South speak for it. Senator Hoar, speaking of the people of the South on the floor of the Senate, in the speech already referred to, said :

> "They have some qualities which I cannot even presume to claim in an equal degree for the people among whom I, myself, dwell. They have an aptness for command which makes the Southern gentleman, wherever he goes, not a peer only, but a prince. They have a love for home; they have the best of them, and the most of them, inherited from the great race from which they come, the sense of duty and the instinct of honor as no other people on the face of the earth. They are lovers of home. They have not the mean traits which grow up somewhere in places where money-making is the chief end of life. They have above all, and giving value to all, that supreme and superb constancy which, without regard to personal ambition and without yielding to the temptation of wealth, without getting tired and without getting diverted, can pursue a great public object, in and out, year after year and generation after generation."

This is the race which the negro confronts. It is a race which, whatever perils have impended, has always faced them with a steadfast mind.

Professor Bryce arrives at the only reasonable conclusion : that the negro be let alone and the solution of the problem be left to the course of events. Friendship for the negro demands this. A single outbreak would settle the question. To us of the South it appears that a proper race pride is one of the strongest securities of our nation. No people can become great without it. Without it no people can remain great.

The question now remains : What is to become of the negro ? It is not likely that he will remain in his present status, if, indeed, it is possible for him to do so. Many schemes have been suggested, none of them alone answerable to the end proposed. The deportation plan does not seem practicable, at present. It is easy to suggest theories, but much more difficult to substantiate them. I hazard one based upon much reflection on the subject. It is, that the negro race in America will eventually disappear, not in a generation or a century,—it may take several

centuries. The means will be natural. Certain portions of the
Southern States will for a while, perhaps, be almost given up to
him ; but in time he will be crowded out even there. Africa
may take a part; Mexico and South America a part ; the rest
will, as the country fills up, as life grows harder and competition
fiercer, become diffused and will disappear, a portion by absorption into the stronger race, the residue by perishing under conditions of life unsuited to him.

Meantime he is here, and something must be done. In the
first place let us have all the light that can be thrown on the subject. Form an organization to consider and deal with the subject, not in the spirit of narrowness or temper, but in a spirit of
philosophic deliberation, such as becomes a great people discussing a great question which concerns not only their present, but
their future position among the nations. We shall then get at
the right of the matter.

Let us do our utmost to eliminate from the question the complication of its political features. Get politics out of it, and the
problem will be more than half solved. Senator Hampton stated
not long ago in a paper contributed by him, I think, to this
REVIEW, that, to get the negro out of politics, he would gladly
give up the representation based on his vote. Could anything
throw a stronger light ön the apprehension with which the negro
in politics is regarded at the South ?

There never was any question more befogged with demagog-
ism than that of manhood suffrage. Let us apply ourselves to
the securing some more reasonable and better basis for the suffrage. Let us establish such a proper qualification as a condition
to the possession of the elective franchise as shall leave the ballot
only to those who have intelligence enough to use it as an instrument to secure good government rather than to destroy it. In
taking this step we have to plant ourselves on a broader principle
than that of a race qualification. It is not merely the negro, it is
ignorance and venality which we want to disfranchise. If we can
disfranchise these we need not fear the voter, whatever the color.
At present it is not the negro who is disfranchised, but the
white. We dare not divide.

Having limited him in a franchise which he has not in a generation learned to use, continue to teach him. It is from the
educated negro, that is, the negro who is more enlightened than

the general body of his race, that order must come. The ignorance, venality, and superstition of the average negro are dangerous to us. Education will divide them and will uplift them. They may learn in time that if they wish to rise they must look to the essential qualities of good citizenship. In this way alone can the race or any part of the race look for ultimate salvation.

It has appeared to some that the South has not done its full duty by the negro. Perfection is, without doubt, a standard above humanity ; but, at least, we of the South can say that we have done much for him; if we have not admitted him to social equality, it has been under an instinct stronger than reason, and in obedience to a law higher than is on the statute books : the law of self-preservation. Slavery, whatever its demerits, was not in its time the unmitigated evil it is fancied to have been. Its time has passed. No power could compel the South to have it back. But to the negro it was salvation. It found him a savage and in two hundred years gave seven million of his race a civilization, the only civilization it has had since the dawn of history.

We have educated him ; we have aided him ; we have sustained him in all right directions. We are ready to continue our aid ; but we will not be dominated by him. When we shall be, it is our settled conviction that we shall deserve the degradation into which we shall have sunk.

THOMAS NELSON PAGE.

RECIPROCITY AND THE FARMER.

BY THE HON. HILARY A. HERBERT, CHAIRMAN OF THE COM-
MITTEE ON NAVAL AFFAIRS.

WHEN the McKinley Bill, with its free sugar and high rates on
manufactures, had gone over from the House and was pending in
the Senate Mr. Blaine made a furious assault upon it. The
ground of his attack was, that, while it raised the duties on many
things the farmers consumed, it did not "open a market for another bushel of wheat or another barrel of pork"; and he further said, that free sugar would not "sweeten the pill." The
remedy he suggested, and which he seemed to think would enable
the farmer to take "the pill" without making mouths, was
legislation by which "free sugar in the United States should be
accompanied by free breadstuffs and provisions in Spanish
America."

Congress did not in form accept Mr. Blaine's proposition. It
made a compromise between his views and those of Mr. McKinley.
It gave Mr. McKinley free sugar for the campaign of 1890. That
left sugar, coffee, tea, and hides, all free; but, going in Mr. Blaine's
direction, it required that the President, after January 1, 1892,
should, whenever in his opinion the tariff laws of any country
producing and exporting sugar, coffee, tea, or hides, were "reciprocally unequal and unreasonable," impose a tax of seven-
tenths of one cent per pound and upwards on sugar, three cents
per pound on coffee, ten cents per pound on tea, and one and one-
half cents per pound on hides, the product of such country.
Thus the essential basis on which these commercial arrangements
are to stand remains as Mr. Blaine suggested. The reciprocating
nations are to have over those not reciprocating the advantage of
seven-tenths of a cent per pound on sugar, three cents on coffee,
etc.

The difference is that Mr. Blaine proposed to retain the sugar tax, and release it only on the products of such countries as should grant us equivalents.

But Congress preferred to release duties on sugar and then arm the President with the threat to not only re-impose duties on this article, but also to tax the hides, tea, and coffee of such nations as should refuse to reciprocate. This was the scheme adopted, and the new markets to be sought were to be found, it was understood, chiefly in countries to the south of us. It was a complete programme : the home market for the manufacturer, new markets abroad for the farmer. Has the farmer reason to be satisfied with the bargain thus made in his name ?

· Germany does not appear to have been in the mind of Mr. Blaine when the scheme was inaugurated. Nevertheless, under it we have made an agreement with that Empire, which, it is hoped, may be of benefit to our farmers.

But it must not be supposed that the removal by Germany of her restrictions against the introduction of our pork products resulted from the McKinley Bill. The President in his annual message said :

"Germany, Denmark, Italy, Austria, and France, in the order named, have opened their ports to imported American pork products. The removal of these restrictions in every instance was asked for, and given, solely upon the ground that we have now provided a meat inspection that should be accepted as adequate to the complete removal of the dangers, real or fancied, which had been previously urged."

The arrangement with Germany which followed, and which, on its face, was made in consideration of the continued introduction of free sugar, gives us no exclusive privileges.

Germany had, like us, a system of high-tariff duties that weighed heavily on her people. The outcry for cheaper food supplies was irresistible. Yielding to this, she was arranging with Austria-Hungary, Italy and Belgium to lower her tariffs on breadstuffs, provisions, etc., and she simply consented to extend the same rates to us. We are allowed to compete in her markets on equal terms with these and, perhaps, other countries. This we get, and nothing more.

It appears, indeed, so far as the published papers show, that Germany herself made the first move towards this arrangement, and it is by no means certain that she would not have consented · to put us on the same footing with these other countries, even had no reciprocity law been adopted by us.

These commercial agreements, let it be understood, are not treaties; they are only arrangements that can be, at any time, repealed by law. How will they affect us while in operation ?

Fortunately for the purposes of this discussion, we have a reciprocity treaty with the Hawaiian Islands of many years' standing. It was made by, and has proven satisfactory to, the political party that is now negotiating these new treaties on like lines of policy.

The actual results of the Hawaiian treaty for thirteen years are before us, from 1877, when it took effect, to 1889 inclusive, carefully compiled by Mr. S. G. Brock, Government Statistician, in an official report, June 20, 1890. The figures used in discussing this treaty are from that report. The Hawaiian treaty admitted free of duty into the ports of the United States Hawaiian sugar, rice, etc. Sugar constituted the bulk of these importations. All agricultural and most manufactured articles from the United States were admitted free into the islands.

Under stimulus of the treaty our imports from these islands increased rapidly. In 1876, the year before it took effect, such imports were $1,376,681. In 1889 they amounted to $12,-847,740. Exports also increased. In 1876 our exports to these islands were $724,267. In 1889 they footed up $3,336,040. This is the bright side of the picture, and it is painted in glowing colors by Mr. Claus Spreckels in THE NORTH AMERICAN REVIEW for March, 1891, where he highly extols " the wise and far-seeing policy embodied in the Hawaiian treaty." No one knew better than Mr. Spreckels the cost at which the tax-payers of the United States had maintained that treaty, for much of that cost had gone into his own pockets as profits upon sugar. As to that side of the question he was industriously silent. But Mr. Brock gives us the information, page 9 of his report, thus :

" If the merchandise admitted free under the treaty had paid the duty levied upon the similar goods imported from other countries, the duty would have amounted to $5,452,311.97 for the fiscal year 1889, and to $43,898,978 for the thirteen years ending with that year, or since the reciprocity treaty has been in force."

This sum, $43,898,978, our consumers paid to the growers of Hawaiian sugar, rice, etc., as premiums on their products. To appreciate the exceptional fact that in this case the duty went to the foreigner, it must be borne in mind that these islands furnished only about one-tenth of our imported sugar. On the other nine-tenths we paid a tax averaging 2.06 cents per pound. The consumer of duty-paid sugar of course paid to the importer the price it had cost to bring the sugar to our ports, plus the tax. And this enabled the importers of these free sugars to add also to their article the price of the tax, although they had never paid it; this for the plain reason that the supply of free sugar not being equal to the demand, the owner of such free sugar would always withhold it from market till the market price of the tax-paid article was offered. The tables collated in Mr. Brock's report, page 37, corroborate this reasoning, and show that the people of the Pacific coast did not save a penny in the price of their sugar by reason of the treaty. Every dollar of the $43,000,000 of taxes released on Hawaiian sugar went into the pockets of the producers of that article, Mr. Claus Spreckels and others. And so it would have been if the sugar imported free of duty had amounted to nine-tenths instead of one-tenth of our total imports. This brings us to see clearly that if we impose an import tax on sugar and rely to any appreciable extent on taxed sugars to complete our supply, no exceptions in favor of particular countries, giving them free access to our markets, will avail to reduce the price of the product of these favored countries in the American market below the price of the tax-paid article.

It will be seen that we have not taken the trouble to ascertain the relatively pitiful sum of duties released to our people by the Hawaiians. We simply put against our actual losses, in release of duties, the full values of all our exports. Balancing the account for thirteen years, and counting in those exports that would have gone to the islands without any treaty, as well as those that went because of it, the sum total of all our exports for this period is $35,870,801. Deducting this sum from the $43,898,978 of duties released, we have $8,028,177, which we could have realized as clear profit by purchasing and destroying all our merchandise exported to the Hawaiian Islands during the period in question.

The treaty grew worse for us year by year. Our largesses stimulated the production of Hawaiian sugar and rice, and each year we released more and more of duties, which under a sounder policy would have gone into our treasury to pay Government expenses, thus enabling us to reduce taxation.   Our people at large would have profited immensely if the Protectionist, who once wished for a wall of fire around our country to keep out foreign trade, had been permitted in 1876 to erect and maintain his flaming structure between us and the Sandwich Islands.

The results grow worse still when looked at from the standpoint of the farmer.   Farm products constitute usually three-fourths of all exports from the United States ; yet of this Hawaiian market, opened up for him and paid for at such a fearful cost, the farmer has had less than one-fourth.   Out of the $3,336,040 exports from the United States in 1889, breadstuffs, provisions, and animals foot up only $759,653.   Is the farmer to fare any better in those new Central and South American markets we hear of ?   South America is a vast continent, with much the same climates as our own, and it has millions of square miles of cheap and fertile lands that, when brought into cultivation, bid fair not only to supply its own wants, but to rival the United States in the bread and meat markets of the world.

Mr. W. E. Curtis, chief of the Bureau of the American Republics, in an official report sent in to the last Congress, arguing then for subsidies, said : " Chili has already driven the flour of the United States off the west coast of South America, and now supplies Peru, Ecuador, and Bolivia.   The California millers are also beginning to feel the competition of Chili at Panama and along the west coast of Central America, and unless cheaper freights are offered from San Francisco southward we shall lose a large and lucrative market.   The Argentine Republic was an importer of breadstuffs a few years since, but the agricultural development of the pampas is so rapid and extensive that the present product not only supplies the local demand, but furnishes an annual surplus, valued at $14,000,000, for export.   The same is true of Uruguay, which has also become an exporter of wheat and flour within the last two or three years, and has an enormous productive capacity, now being rapidly developed by Italian emigrants.   The time is not far distant when these three countries will deprive the United States of the greater portion of its flour market in the West Indies and South America, and will enter into active competition with us in Europe."

The first arrangement we made was with Brazil, admittedly the most populous and wealthy of the countries to the south of us. Let us examine that agreement. We admit free of duty all sugar, molasses, coffee, and hides, the product of Brazil. Brazil admits from the United States, free of duty, certain articles ; and certain others with 25 per cent. off. Tables appended to the published copy of the agreement show the character and extent of our present, as well as of possible, markets in that country. The rates given enable us to calculate, upon a given hypothesis, exact results.

These tables show that if we should supply Brazil in full with everything she was annually importing from all countries when our commercial arrangement was made we should have a market there for products valued at $58,635,182. Deducting amount of our exports at that time we should then have a market for $53,-204,650. Of this new market our farmers would get $8,433,000; about seventeen per cent. of the whole. Will they secure even that ? The remissions of duty in our favor are all small. On agricultural products the range is from one and one-quarter per cent. on lard up to twenty cents on other products. The rate on cotton-seed oil is higher, but is unimportant, as this article is not, and never will be, largely imported into that cotton-growing country. The ad valorem advantage given us, averaged on all our exports to that country, as shown by the tables, is less than ten per cent.

When this arrangement with Brazil was proclaimed it was hailed with delight. Some of the farmers of the West, in the exuberance of their rejoicings, formed themselves into a new order called the Knights of Reciprocity. It might have been well if these gentlemen had waited for results.

The agreement had been in operation nine months on the 31st of December, 1891. Full and fair notice was given to shippers before it went into effect, and the results are that from April 1 to December 1, 1891, as compared with the like months of the preceding year, our exports to Brazil were :

	1890.	1891.
Total domestic	$10,071.871	$7,063,222
Total agricultural	5,208,001	4,682,546

Here was an actual falling off in our exports of farm products under the arrangement in nine months of $525,455. Mr. Hale, speaking on this question, said in the Senate on January 28, that Brazil had " been in a condition of uneasiness and ferment ever since the treaty went into effect, " etc.; but this excuse will not do. During the period in question she bought of us, as statistical figures show, $2,009,000 of other than farm products more than during the corresponding period of 1890. And she sold us of her products during that same time the enormous sum of $79,283,244. Instead of buying of us farm products she did not need, she sent this money to Europe to buy there the cheap manufactured goods she does need. Nor is it an answer that European countries took our last wheat crop. Europe every season draws alike from North and South America. If sufficient advantage had been given us, our provisions would have gone to South America to take the place of wheat going to Europe.

Brazil, if we except an insignificant portion of Guiana, is the only country on the whole continent to the south of us that has responded to our advances. Government figures have given us the results, and so we safely say that reciprocity, so far as South America is concerned, is to our farmers but a mirage in the desert. In Central America and the islands of the Caribbean Sea the outlook for the farmer is better, although extravagantly over-estimated.

The conventions covering Cuba, Puerto Rico and San Domingo went into operation September 1, 1891, and we have the statistics covering our trade with these countries under the agreements for the four months ending December 31 last. Grouping these three with Brazil, and aggregating the trade with them all under reciprocity, as compared with that of corresponding periods for the previous year when we had no commercial arrangements, we have the following results :

1891. Exports other than agricultural to reciprocating countries	$12,016,066
1890. " " " " " " "	7,892,531
1890. Increase under reciprocity	$4,123,535
1891. Export agricultural products to reciprocating countries	$7,832,531
1890. " " " " " "	7,321,057
Increase	$511,474

This shows a gain in the sale of farm products under reciprocity of seven per cent., whereas the increase in the exports of other products, principally manufactures, is a fraction over 39 per cent.—over five to one against the farmer.

The average annual gain in the export of agricultural products to all countries for four years back has been about seven per cent.

There is a maxim in equity that one is presumed to intend to do that which he does do. Applying this equitable rule and presuming that the statesmen who devised this scheme knew the economic conditions prevailing in these countries, the conclusion follows that instead of hunting new markets abroad for the farmer they were really seeking fresh fields for American manufactures.

Besides Germany and the four countries from which we have these returns, the President has made arrangements with Salvador and certain British West India Islands. Three other small states in Central America are expected to come in soon.

The first of January, when the President was directed to begin his tariff war on recusant nations, has passed. Countries to the south of us importing two hundred and forty-eight millions have treated with us. Others whose imports are three hundred and seventy-four millions still stand out. The President, by letter, has notified Venezuela, Hayti, Nicaragua, Guatemala and Colombia, besides Spain for the Philippine Islands, and Austria-Hungary that, on March 15 next, he will, unless they reciprocate, impose such duties on their products as the law requires. Why he should except any country, unless it be England and Belgium, is not apparent, for it is the boast of the Protectionists that all other countries have protective-tariff laws. Certainly the reciprocating countries will demand that all nations shall be treated alike. How else can they get what they bargained for, a better market than others who have made no contract ?

If the President shall take this view of the case we will soon have

On tea a tax of...$13,456,000
On coffee a tax of... 15,000,000
On hides (estimated) a tax of... 8,000,000.

Total...$36,456,000

This tax is estimated on the whole amount of our imports of these for the reason that our consumers must pay the tax on the taxed products and an increased price for the articles brought in free. The rule deduced from the Hawaiian treaty is, it will be remembered, that the cost price of the tax-paid article will regulate the market so long as the importations of the free article of like character are clearly insufficient to supply the demand. That rule will apply to tea, because we have arranged for no free tea; to hides, because we have arranged for only four million dollars of free hides and we import twenty-seven millions; to coffee, because we import ninety-six millions, whereas the reciprocating countries bring us only sixty-three millions. The increased price we pay to the favored people for their products is the consideration for their concessions.

And here it may be interesting to glance again at the arrangement with Brazil. The concessions she made to us, calculated according to the tables published with the commercial arrangement, amounted to $576,000 ; yet the tax which we will remit on coffee alone to Brazil, on the basis of last year's imports, will be $9,722,000. We have seen, too that the total market in that country for agricultural products not already occupied by us was $8,433,000; and we have seen also, that instead of gaining any portion of this we are losing even that which we had.

As to sugar, considering that reciprocating countries only lack now $10,000,000 of sending us what we need, it is probably true that they will eventually supply us fully, and by their competition keep down the price of sugar as now to the level of prices elsewhere. Then not a pound of sugar will come to us from peoples not reciprocating. They cannot afford to pay the tax. At this point it may be, too, that the reciprocating nations will, some of them, tire of their bargains ; and certain it is, that the inducement for outsiders to come inside our sugar ring will cease.

What is to be the effect of discriminating against the nations that refuse our terms ? The tea-growing countries have so far all refused. We will tax their tea, pay more for our breakfasts, and nobody will be hurt except ourselves. But besides the reciprocating countries there are 17 peoples sending us sugar, 31 sending us coffee, and 41 supplying us with hides. What will all these do but make agreements in self-defence to divert their trade into other channels ? Who can measure the friction, the ill-feeling, the disturbance of trade relations, and even of political amities that are to result from this scheme ? What can Nicaragua say if a proclamation is levelled at her products, and not against the coffee of Peru ; and what will the Argentines say if their hides are taxed, while the hides of Chili or Ecuador escape ?

The political enmity now existing between France and Italy, and which has caused the latter to join the Dreibund between herself, Austria, and Germany, has grown largely out of a reciprocity treaty. Spain and France are quarrelling over a similar question. Mr. Foster said recently in a speech in New York that no nation could make reciprocity treaties that had not a protective tariff. He ought to have said that no nation except one that has a protective tariff has need of such treaties. If he had said this he could have proven the truth of his remark by pointing to the difference between the trade of Great Britain and of the United States with the very countries we are seeking to capture. The United Kingdom buys from Latin America eighty-nine millions ; she sells there one hundred and seventy-seven millions, exporting two for one without making a threat or paying a dollar of bounty. We buy from the same countries two hundred and seven millions and sell them ninety millions ; more than two to one against us, and then when we enter the field to buy and threaten our way into these markets from which we have excluded ourselves by our own laws, we boast that no nation can tax its own people to pay bounties to foreign nations except one that has such laws as we have. Certainly not.

How different all this is from that just and fair and profitable reciprocity with all the world which Jefferson had in mind when he declared for " Peace, commerce, and honest friendship with all nations—entangling alliances with none l "

HILARY A. HERBERT.

OUR NATIONAL DUMPING-GROUND.

A STUDY OF IMMIGRATION.

BY THE HON. JOHN B. WEBER, UNITED STATES COMMISSIONER OF IMMIGRATION, AND CHARLES STEWART SMITH, PRESIDENT OF THE NEW YORK CHAMBER OF COMMERCE.

THE HON. JOHN B. WEBER:

THE subject of immigration is beginning to attract attention, but as we have not yet passed through the preliminary stage of public discussion, the drastic legislation manifested in the first impulse of the public mind is not likely to materialize this winter. Inquiry, I believe, will lead to the conclusion that the evils of immigration are purely imaginary in some features, greatly exaggerated in others, and susceptible of nearly complete remedy by the amendment of existing laws.

The immigration problem will eventually settle down to the consideration of the following points :

Is this country made the "dumping-ground" of the refuse material of the Old World, and, if so, to what extent do the authorities aid such movement? Do we wish to reject the bad without reference to its effect upon the good ?

What system, if any, can be devised which will enable us to sift the grades, accept the desirable, and reject the undesirable ?

Is it wise to stop all immigration or to diminish its volume by methods that do not materially affect the influx of the unproductive kind, and yet decrease that element which by reason of age and vigor is the most productive ?

The investigation of the subject by a Commission, of which I was a member, specially appointed by the Secretary of the Treasury to visit Europe for that purpose, demonstrates that at the present time in the countries which I visited, viz., France, Belgium, Holland, Germany and Austria, neither governments nor societies, directly or systematically, transport their paupers, criminals, or other defectives to this country. In Russia, which is another of the countries investigated, governmental persecution impoverishes and expels the Jewish people. The constitutional vagabond of Europe does not emigrate. The slums are sluggish, and are seldom so agitated that the filth is flung across the sea. Individual instances occur, but as compared with the grand total of immigration, the percentage is infinitesimally small, and these cases can, by additional legislation, be almost perfectly covered.

The general character of eligible immigrants arriving here is substantially the same as that of past years, the large percentage of "prepaids" furnishing on this point evidence of an unmistakable nature. Prepaid tickets are tickets purchased in the United States and sent to relatives and friends on the other side, who, it is fair to assume, being members of the same family, are in a manner vouched for as desirable. If they are in respect of general quality similar to the pioneers who have so materially aided in the development of our natural resources, why should it not be assumed that their coming will continue to add to the national wealth, unless a change of conditions has been reached? Has such a change occurred?

Our resources have hardly been touched, certainly the point of exhaustion has not been approached, so that development is feasible and desirable. We are told, however, that the cities are overcrowded and that a vast army willing to labor is unemployed. The precise or reasonably close approximation of this number is difficult of ascertainment. It is as easy to state it at two millions as at one million. That there should be any considerable number of unemployed is deplorable, but it is a condition which, in greater or less degree, has existed as far back as I can remember, and probably always will exist at certain periods, particularly in the large cities. Immigration contributes to the overcrowding of the city of course, although two-thirds of the arrivals continue to go West, most of them to farms. In point of fact, the chief immigration into the cities is due to the emigration from our own rural districts. This condition exists in Europe as well as here, and so alarming has it grown there that in Germany legislation to check and prevent it is talked of as probable this winter. There is something incongruous in the statements published in the same edition of an American newspaper, that farms are being abandoned in New England, that an army of men willing to work are unemployed in the cities, and that the grain crop is so bountiful in Dakota that farmers are offering from $2.50 to $3 per day for harvesters.   There is a faultiness in the distribution of labor, and this demands and should receive early attention and consideration.   I do not believe the conditions of prosperity in the rural districts have retrograded, but it is obvious that the city has marched faster in progress and improvement.   Their relative positions have changed.   Wealth has increased faster, attractions have grown greater, hours of labor have been reduced, living has become better, educational facilities have improved in a far greater degree in the city than in the country.   The fact is, we are moving so fast that the readjustments continually required cannot keep up with the changing conditions, and friction and individual suffering are unavoidable.   By means of organization labor has improved and elevated its status, thus widening the distance between its own position and that of the farmer.   The more labor advances in the cities, whether by reason of organization or by stopping immigration, the greater the exodus from country to city.

It is charged that foreigners furnish a larger percentage of paupers and criminals than the native element.   This is probably true, but it is hardly because they are foreigners, but because they are of the poorer half of society, and consequently less able to cope with misfortune or to withstand temptation.   It is not so creditable to a rich man to refrain from stealing a loaf of bread as it is to a hungry one.   Wealthy Americans would not be as numerous if it had not been for the immigration of so many Europeans.

About fifty years ago the American or "Know-nothing" party was formed in this country.   Many honest men joined it, sincerely believing that our interests were being jeopardized by the increasing arrival of foreigners ; that we were rushing headlong to destruction, and that the safety of our institutions rested solely upon the success of that organization.   The party did not succeed, however, but the republic still exists, and next year we expect to show to the world the marvellous progress of our country at an exposition held in a city, which at the time the Knownothing party existed was but little more than a barren prairie, but now numbers over a million of people, while the political organization which was so fearful of the destruction of our republican institutions has perished, leaving nothing as a monument of existence save the lesson of warning to posterity to avoid racial and religious bigotry in the formation and conduct of political parties.

The safety of this country respecting the influx of strangers to our shores lies in the supply being drawn from various countries, whereby nationalities are blended, the best characteristics of each being retained and a high type of physical strength produced, the most desirable foundation of mental quality. It would be unfortunate if the bulk of our immigrants came from one country. The best justification for the prohibition of the Chinese is that not only are they of a different race and in no wise beneficial to us in the assimilative process, but they are so numerous that if once the ball is set in motion they will pour in upon us in such vast numbers as to "China-ize" America. We are not so threatened by other countries. We are in no danger of being Germanized, Frenchified, Italianized or Europeanized. The sharp corners of the various nationalities coming to us are largely rounded off by contact with each other rather than with Americans. For a time their intimacies are with their own countrymen or other foreigners who preceded them and who have already become to some extent Americanized, but it does not take long to graft Americanism upon sound, vigorous European stock. We aim to absorb the best ideas of other lands, to reject the weaknesses and fallacies of the old world ; and actual contact with so many nationalities gives us the superior advantage to which, I believe, we are largely indebted for the splendid results of which we rightfully boast.

Consular inspection is regarded as a cure for many of the immigration evils which, as already stated, I believe are exaggerated and largely imaginary. The fundamental idea of such inspection is the personal examination in Europe of the intending emigrant by our consuls and the medical experts under their supervision, with the addition of certificates from the home authorities to establish character. The supporters of this plan may be divided into three classes :

First, Those who believe that such a system will better sift and exclude the undesirable, but who are in favor of the immigration of the good element.

Second, Those who believe that this country is in a greater or less degree made the dumping-ground of Europe, and who, to prevent this, would favor shutting off the whole stream because of the impure little rivulet which trickles into it.

Third, Those who fancy that closing the gates will reduce competition and increase demand in their class; that direct complete restriction will not secure legislative sanction, and who therefore favor that indirect method which promises to interpose the greatest obstacles and the most serious hindrances.

This article is entirely too brief to discuss in detail the feasibility and practicability of Consular inspection in Europe. The subject has been treated at length in the report of the Commission sent to Europe to investigate immigration, which was recently submitted to the Secretary of the Treasury. As one of that Commission, the conclusions I reached were unfavorable to Consular inspection; and these conclusions, briefly stated, are: that such inspection is not practicable or feasible, and will not effect a better sifting and rejection of defectives, but will facilitate the admission of the undesirable, and hinder and obstruct the desirable; that in districts where possible, because of the limited emigration, it is not necessary; that as regards the excluded classes, except as to convicts and paupers, detection is as easy here as abroad, and in some cases more so; that in regard to character the certificate of foreign local authorities must be the basis; that these officials cannot be compelled to certify, and, as their desire is to retain the good and facilitate the going of the defective, their certification may prove to be an expensive fiction; that it will create a brokerage in selling to objectionable persons certificates obtained by eligible ones; that the defects of local certification are already on exhibition in the case of the Italians, who in order to emigrate must have passports, which, under their laws, are not granted to criminals, many of whom, according to the statement of one of our consuls, have obtained certificates of clean character under assumed names, known to the authorities to be false; that the expense of $500,000 annually will be necessary to prove Consular inspection a failure; and that a better system is available, which will almost entirely, and more certainly, cure the real evils existing without imposing unnecessary burdens upon those who are believed to be valuable additions to our population.

The foregoing conclusions, as well as the following suggested system and additional legislation, are based upon the theory that the desire is to sift immigration, to admit the good and reject the bad. If the American people wish to restrict immigration without reference to quality, if the desire be to simply reduce the total number, I frankly admit that, in my opinion, Consular inspection will accomplish that object. But I assume that our people have no intention to shirk the question and by cumbersome and expensive machinery to do by indirection that which they can do by direct methods.

The suggestions referred to are as follows :

Perfect existing statutes where they are weak.

Continue a rigid inspection at our ports ; guard the frontiers, especially on the north, for the putting up of bars at our seaports will drive the current of undesirables to Canada only to come across the border.

Place the expense of all returned immigrants upon steamship companies, whom self-interest will force to look for reimbursement to their sub-agents, who have a personal knowledge of the qualifications of intending immigrants better than any one else, and who would have a direct pecuniary concern in the return of a defective ; make sub-agents in this country responsible for the sale of prepaid tickets, estimated to be nearly 60 per cent. of the whole ; then up to the time of their acquiring citizenship hold all aliens liable to compulsory return to the country to which they owe allegiance, or to the ports from whence they came ; expelling those convicted abroad of crime, upon discovery, those convicted here, after serving sentence, and paupers, as soon as they reach the implied condition ; this status to continue until the burdens of our citizenship have been assumed and its privileges obtained. At present an alien may enjoy about all the benefits and protection of our citizenship while avoiding its heaviest obligations.

Foreign governments would expel an American if he fell into a state of pauperism or were convicted of crime, and this is a kind of reciprocity upon which parties in this country would not be likely to divide. This suggested method would not place any obstacle in the way of those whom it is desirable to add to our population. It is feasible and practicable, which the other plan is not. It would relieve us of paupers, when they reached or disclosed the pauper state. It would rid us of convicts upon discovery, and of criminals as soon as they served sentence. We are under no moral obligation to provide shelter, furnish maintenance, or extend the protection of government to those not fitted to bear the burdens of citizenship, or who by their own misconduct have forfeited the acquirement of its privileges, and we can prescribe such legal obligations as seem necessary for self-protection. We try no visionary experiments, we follow no theoretical plan, but adopt that which nearly all Europe practises; we disturb no traditions of our fathers, nor assail the sentiment that this country is the home of the free and the asylum of the oppressed, for it was never intended to extend its privileges so as to embrace criminals and paupers.

For many years the tide of immigration has set this way, during which time our country has challenged admiration wherever our history was understood and our progress known. By reason of this incoming, our almost limitless resources have been partially developed, forests levelled, railroads built, and canals dug, while cities have sprung up, and the wilderness has been made to blossom, and fields to groan with the weight of grain to feed not only our own vast population, but to supply a large surplus to the toilers across the sea. It may be curious to some, but it is nevertheless true that the continued influx of foreigners has elevated rather than depressed the labor status of their predecessors. Americans, except in the early days, have done very little hard manual labor. When the foreigner came in, the native engineered the jobs, the former did the shovelling. The American in every walk and condition of life (politics, perhaps, occasionally excepted) has been "boss" ever since. The foreigner plows and sows, the native reaps; the one builds railroads, the other runs them and waters the stock ; one digs canals, the other manages the boats; one burrows in the mines, the other sells the product, and so on through all the various vocations. This is not, however, because one is a foreigner and the other an American, but because the latter is keener, brighter, and intellectually stronger, and these qualities keep him in the lead and—out of the almshouse.

First the German did the digging (going back to the time when I began to take notice of the evolution of nationalities in this country), then the Irishman crowded him out of the ditch, not downward, however, but upward to a higher level ; then came the Pole and the Hungarian

Slovak, and the Irishman was advanced. Following these came the Italian, elevating his predecessors, and, as we have drawn the line on the Chinaman, he (the Italian) promises to remain for a time the hewer of wood and the drawer of water. Stop this stream, and where will the supply come from to make good not only the waste by death, but the needs of the continued expansion and development of our still hardly touched natural resources? Stop the stream, and where will the new material come from which with a little training and experience develops into useful domestic help? At the Labor Bureau connected with the New York Immigration Station you will generally find three mistresses for every arriving servant girl, and every mail brings appeals from all over the country asking for female help. We must not be deceived into believing that we can continue to receive the women if we reject the men.

Consular inspection will prevent the emigration, from every country in Europe except Great Britain, of men within the military age, the most active and productive period of life, and send to us the quite young and the old. Immigrant girls may not be overwise ; natural instincts, however, prompt them to protect the young and respect the aged, but also to *marry* the men whom foreign powers desire and need for soldiers as props to sustain monarchical governments. We cannot have the women without the men, and before shutting off the most desirable, we had better consider where the future supply is to come from. Natural increase will not furnish it, for Americans do not raise families, and such is the remarkable influence of association, such the powerful effect of contact with American civilization, that foreigners soon learn that it is not the proper thing to be bothered with children. This is an evil destructive both of morals and health, and attention to it would have been forced upon us long before this, had it not been for the new blood that makes up the loss. France is at a standstill because of this evil, and her statesmen are justly alarmed. Deduct from the increase of population for the last decade, as shown by the recent census, the number of immigrants and their increase after landing during that period, and our boast over the growth of this country—for the statistics of population always figure in these claims—would be changed to a wail.

Congress will hardly amputate the foot to get rid of a corn.

JOHN B. WEBER.

CHARLES STEWART SMITH, ESQ :

IMMIGRATION, whether following the natural law of selection or forced by persecution, has been from earliest historic times the law and condition of human progress ; and this grand movement of the human race, starting from its cradle in the East, account for it as we may, has flowed uniformly westward by some impulse that has had the strength of the law of gravitation. Exceptional diversions from the westerly direction are observable, like the irruption of the northern hordes of barbarians who, attracted by plunder, assailed and finally overthrew the colossal power of Rome, and settled in her dismembered territories. Again, incidental currents are marked, such as the settlement and occupation of Australia, prompted at first by the discovery of gold, and afterwards sustained by the colonizing instincts of the English people.

The loss or gain to the countries sending forth the immigrants and the relative advantages or disadvantages to those receiving them is an interesting study. For example : The expulsion of the Moors from Spain under the penalty of death, prompted by a fanatical desire for religious unity, was successfully accomplished ; but the result was the ruin of that country, for the Moors were the principal skilled workers in manufactures, commerce, agriculture and architecture ; and the splendid monuments of Moorish genius alone remained to tell the story of national decay.

The present apparent determination of the Russian government to force the emigration of its Jewish subjects, with a savage intolerance which has excited the attention and protest of the civilized world, will be likely to produce disaster to the commercial and financial interests of that empire ; indeed, the circumstances attendant upon the late Russian loan point already to this result, for not only the purse but the press of Continental Europe is under Hebrew control. The revocation of the Edict of Nantes drove from France the flower of her population and the most accomplished of her artisans, and compelled them to find in Germany homes to which they were welcomed and where they founded industries which have since become national. The historic answer to this stupendous blunder and crime of Louis XIV. was made when the Germanized descendants of the French Huguenots marched with the victorious German army under the shadow of the Arc de Triomphe into the centre of the French capital.

The apparently insignificant and unnoticeable immigration of the Pilgrims from England to this country in the time of the Stuarts has proved to have been the beginning of the most important migratory movement of our race since the beginning of the Christian era, if not during all the world's history ; the emigration of one million Jewish slaves from Egypt, under Moses, can only be compared with it in historic importance and development.

In 1793 Washington expressed his disbelief in encouraging immigration on a large scale. On the contrary De Tocqueville in 1835, with a larger vision, wrote concerning America, "No power on earth can close upon the immigrant that fertile wilderness which offers resources to all industry and a refuge from all want."

My purpose is to inquire into the effect, during the present century, of the increasing stream of immigration upon the social and material interests of the United States, and the voluminous statistics prepared under the direction of the Treasury Department are partially repeated to give emphasis to the situation.

In the absence of records of immigration to this country prior to 1820, it has been estimated that 250,000 immigrants arrived from the close of the Revolutionary War to 1820; the number of alien passengers from 1820 to 1855, inclusive, was 4,212,624, and the number of immigrants from 1856 to 1890, inclusive, was 11,188,556, making (after allowance for sojourners) a grand total of 15,427,657 immigrants who arrived in the United States from the close of the Revolutionary War to 1890. The leading nationalities composing this number are shown by the following figures :

Germany	4,504,128	France	366,346
Ireland	3,481,074	Russia and Poland	324,892
England	2,430,380	Scotland	323,823
Sweden and Norway	925,031	Switzerland	171,269
Austria-Hungary	431,488	Denmark	142,517
Italy	388,558		

From 1881 to 1890, inclusive, the total number of immigrants was 5,246,613, which it will be observed was over 50 per cent. of the entire immigration from the close of the Revolutionary War to 1881. The largest immigration occurred in 1882, when 788,992 immigrants arrived at our ports ; the next largest volume was in the preceding year, when the number was 669,431.

The ages of the immigrants arriving from 1881 to 1890, inclusive, show that 21.4 per cent. of the total number were under

15 years of age, 68.1 per cent. were between 15 and 40 years of age, and 10.5 per cent. were over 40 years of age ; and the occupations of these immigrants were classified as follows:

	Males.	Females.	Total.
Professional	25,257	1,749	27,006
Skilled	514,552	25,859	540,411
Miscellaneous	1,833,325	245,810	2,079,135
Not stated	73,327	42,830	116,157
Without occupation	759,450	1,724,454	2,483,904
Total	3,205,911	2,040,702	5,246,613

The "professional" class embraces musicians, teachers, clergymen, artists, lawyers, physicians, etc.; the "skilled" includes those engaged in forty or more different occupations, trades, etc.; and the "miscellaneous" represents laborers, farmers, servants and merchants. If we add to the class "without occupation" the number of those whose occupation is not stated we arrive at a grand total of 2,600,061, or nearly 50 per cent. of the whole number of immigrants who arrived during the last decade. Of this total who were apparently without occupation 1,767,284 were females, of whom 537,007 were under 15 years of age ; and there were also in the class "without occupation" 579,715 males who were under 15 years of age.

The number of Japanese immigrants from 1861 to 1891, inclusive, was 3,672, but a very large proportion of them have returned ; the census of 1890 gives a total of 1,099 in the United States. No record exists of arrivals from Mexico and the British American possessions.

The total arrival of Chinese from 1821 to 1890 was 290,655. The largest number in any decade was from 1871 to 1880, inclusive, which amounted to 123,201. The census of 1880 gave the total number in the United States at 105,000, of which 75,000 were in California ; and it appears that arrivals since then have been more than offset by departures, as the census of 1890 gives the Chinese population of California as 3,318 less than in 1880, and it is estimated that the entire Chinese population in the United States to-day is about 100,000. In the year 1882 this insignificant number of so-called heathen frightened the then 52,000,000 of inhabitants into the passage of an act by Congress, under the influence of political clamor, excluding the Chinese laborers, and deprived the country of this moderate influx of patient and effective workers. The act was a disgrace to our boasted civilization, and an affront to a great and friendly nation of 450,000,000 of people, who have always made scholarship the road to power and preferment, and whose artistic productions have excited the wonder of the Western world and furnished models for Europe and America to copy. China knows how to bide her time, and her answer to our exclusion act, which was passed with slight diplomatic courtesy, will yet come in accordance with the dignity and self-respect of that nation.

By the census returns of 1880 our population was 50,155,783, of whom 6,679,943, or 13.32 per cent. of the whole population, were foreign born. The figures of the last census on this class are not yet available ; but estimating the foreign-born population at about 10,000,000 the percentage is about 16 per cent. of the total population of 62,622,250.

If I am correct, that the returns of the eleventh census will show that the foreign-born population of the United States now amounts to about 10,000,000, and if we assume that one-fifth of that number, or 2,000,000, are wage-earners at the rate of $1.00 per diem on the average, then the foreign-born of our population alone, without estimating the accumulations of their immediate descendants, add to the earnings of this country, on a very conservative estimate, at the rate of about $600,000,000 per year ; and, furthermore, without foreign labor the great public works of the United States would have been retarded for a quarter of a century. In addition to the pecuniary side of this question, no one will deny that foreigners are frequently among our best citizens, and that they have contributed largely to the artistic, literary, scientific, commercial and industrial advancement of the country. Alexander Hamilton was an emigrant boy, brought to this country by the first President of the Chamber of Commerce of New York. The first of the Agassizs, the Astors and the Girards were all foreign-born ; and a poor Scotch lad who came to this country forty years ago has donated millions of dollars to found institutions for the education and refinement of his adopted countrymen.*

Turning to the side of the immigration problem which excites the apprehension of thoughtful men and casts a shadow over the social aspect of this question, and which is now engaging the attention of Congress, we find that Frederick H. Wines, of Springfield, Ill., who is a special agent and expert employed by

* Andrew Carnegie, Esq.

the Census Bureau for the statistics of pauperism and crime, de-
duces the following results from the statistics of the eleventh
census:

" The foreign population of this country contributes, directly
or indirectly, in the persons of the foreign-born or of their immediate descendants, considerably more material for our State
prisons and penitentiaries than the entire native white population.   Of the 43,127 penitentiary convicts reported on June 1,
1890, whose birthplace and parentage are known, the foreign-born
element of the population furnished 14,725 convicts, the colored
population (including Chinese and Indians) 14,687 and the native
white population only 13,715 convicts.   In other words, each of
these elements furnished about one-third of all the inmates of our
State prisons and penitentiaries."

Regarding pauperism the same authority reports: "The total
number of paupers in the almshouses of the United States in
1890 was 73,045, of which 66,578 were white and 6,467 colored;"
and as the result of a careful analysis in detail of these figures Mr.
Wines states : "Very nearly three-fifths of all the paupers supported
in almshouses are contributed by the foreign-born element of
the population and their immediate descendants. The disproportion between the two elements (native white and foreign-
born) in respect of the burden of pauperism is even greater than
that in respect of crime. The foreign-born paupers alone out-
number all of the white native paupers whose parentage is known,
whether the parentage be native or foreign. They also equal
in number all of the white native paupers purely of native origin and the colored paupers taken together."

The following statistics and note are furnished by the Secretary of the Department of Public Charities and Correction of the
city of New York :

	Total prisoners rec'd.	Of Foreign Birth.	Percentage of Foreign Birth, to total.
Penitentiary..................	1,868	724	39 per cent.
City Prison (the Tombs).....	20,142	14,911	74 per cent.
Work House.......	21,710	12,896	59 per cent.

" Our records do not show the birthplace of parents of prison-
ers, but the Superintendent of the workhouse expresses the
opinion that it is safe to say that 90 per cent. of the native-born
committed are of foreign parents, and doubtless this is true of
other institutions."

It is contrary to the plain teaching of history and the experience of mankind for any nation either to force or prohibit natural and proper immigration within its own borders. And the United States, with the exception of the suspension of Chinese immigration, has heretofore confined such restrictive laws to the requirements of self-preservation from fraud or unjust burden upon its communities, and has done all in its power to encourage immigration by wise and liberal land-grants and like inducements to settlers.

In addition to the Act of 1882 suspending Chinese immigration, the laws of the United States prohibit the coolie trade, and exclude all persons who shall contract to labor in the United States before arrival therein. Convicts (excepting those convicted of political offences), lunatics, idiots, destitute immigrants, any person unable to take care of himself or herself without becoming a public charge, are not permitted to land ; and the expense of the return of the aforesaid persons not permitted to land must be borne by the owners of the vessels in which they come. There is also levied a tax of fifty cents, to be paid by the owners of the vessel, for each passenger not a citizen of the United States. This tax constitutes an immigrant fund, which is used to defray the cost of regulating immigration, and can be applied to the relief of immigrants in distress. Arrivals from Canada and Mexico are excepted from the fifty-cent passenger tax.

The danger to our institutions does not come from the anarchists and bomb-throwers. We can rely upon the operation of the law and police vigilance to protect society from these pestilent fellows, and Chicago justice has settled this question for some years to come ; there is, however, a real and permanent danger to this country in the continued influx of so large a proportion of ignorant masses, for, as stated by an ex-president of the Board of Education, of New York City : " Four-fifths of all our criminals are uneducated, and it costs $29.40 per annum to educate a child in a grammar school in this city, and $110 per annum to maintain a criminal in the penitentiary."[*]

It is impossible to make a character-standard for the immigrant a passport to the privilege of landing upon American soil; such an inquisition into the former life and occupation of the numbers who are flocking to this country would be impossible upon the part of American consuls ; but a simple test of intelli-

* J. Edward Simmons, Esq.

gence is practicable and could be enforced. An Act of Congress requiring all immigrants over fifteen years of age, as a condition before embarking for the United States, to appear before the American consul and receive from him a certificate, to be presented on arrival, that the party intending to emigrate to the United States could read and write his native language, would be in itself to some extent a guaranty of character. It would naturally restrict the number of immigrants, but it would improve their quality and furnish fewer inmates for our prisons and poorhouses.

I hold the opinion that existing laws, properly enforced, with an amendment embracing the reading and writing qualification above indicated, would protect society from the evils connected with immigration, and would insure to us the immense benefits arising from the enormous human stream which must continue to flow to this country.

CHARLES STEWART SMITH.

MICHIGAN'S PRESIDENTIAL ELECTORS.

BY THE HON. EDWIN B. WINANS, GOVERNOR OF MICHIGAN.

A GENERAL misconception or lack of information seems to prevail concerning the character and probable effect of the change directed by the present legislature of Michigan in the manner of choosing the State's Presidential electors. Press comment indicates an impression in other States that Michigan has violated precedent and introduced a dangerous innovation by providing a mode of appointing her electors different from that employed elsewhere. A glance at the early practice in the various States will remove this impression.

The Constitution of the United States provides that, " Each State shall appoint, in such manner as the legislature thereof may direct, a number of electors equal to the whole number of Senators and Representatives to which the State may be entitled in the Congress." Since 1860 it has been the practice * in all the States to select Presidential electors by vote of the people upon a general ticket, each elector being chosen by the vote of his whole State. Prior to 1860, however, the different State legislatures had, at different times, provided a variety of methods. At the first Presidential election in January, 1789, electors were chosen in ten States. In seven they were chosen by the legislatures and in three by popular elections. In 1796, the electors of six States were chosen by popular elections and in ten States by the legis-latures. In 1824, the legislatures of six States chose the electors, and in all the other States there were popular elections. In 1832, South Carolina was the only State whose legislature made the choice, and she alone continued the practice until 1860. Among the States in which the selection was made by popular vote two methods were in use ; one by general ticket, as is customary at present, the other by dividing the States into districts, the voters

* The Colorado electors were chosen by the legislature in 1876.

of each district choosing one or more electors. The States which preferred the district system, one after another adopted the general ticket, but as late as 1824 Maine, Massachusetts, Maryland, Kentucky, and Illinois elected by districts.

Different methods of division into districts were employed. In 1792, the legislature of North Carolina divided that State into four districts, and the members of the legislature residing in each district chose three electors. In 1828, electors were chosen by congressional districts in Maine and New York, and those thus chosen selected the two additional electors for each State. Maryland continued the district system until 1832. At one time, the State was divided into a number of districts corresponding to the number of electors. Later, the State was divided into nine districts, two of which chose two electors each, the remainder choosing one each. At another time, the division was into four districts, the first choosing four electors, the second and third choosing two each, and the fourth choosing three. The instances cited show that many of the older States were " Michiganized " from the beginning.

The recent act of the Michigan legislature directs, in effect, that the voters of each of the twelve congressional districts of Michigan shall choose one Presidential elector. The State is also divided into two electoral districts, an Eastern and a Western, each comprising six congressional districts, and the voters of each electoral district are to choose one of the two additional electors to which the State is entitled.

The change was made in the belief that the district system will enable the people of the State to give a much more definite and satisfactory expression of their choice for the Presidency. The most complete expression possible would be obtained by allowing the people to vote directly for the candidates of their choice, without the interposition of Presidential electors. This method was fully discussed in the constitutional convention of 1787, but was not then considered expedient. One of the arguments advanced was, that to submit the election of a President to direct vote of the people is to take this important power out of the hands of those best fitted for its exercise and bestow it upon those least capable of using it wisely. The system finally adopted was chosen as the best of the many plans proposed for the choice of a President by delegates chosen by the people. The object in view was the selection of a limited number of men, chosen from among their fellow citizens because of special fitness, who were to meet for deliberation upon the merits of public men, and, after careful consideration, exercise their own judgment in voting for a President.

Nominating conventions were then unknown, and the Presidential electors were not pledged to vote for particular candidates, but were left free to use their own discretion or to reflect the preference of the section they represented. Appeals to this discretion were often made after the electors were chosen. It was not contemplated, when the Constitution was adopted, that all the electoral votes of each State should necessarily be cast for the same candidate, and in the earlier elections it was common for different candidates to receive electoral votes from the same State. As late as 1824 the New York electors divided their votes among four candidates for President and two for Vice-President. Moreover, had it been the design of the framers of the Constitution that each State should cast its entire electoral vote as a unit, there would have been no occasion for the appointment of electors. The whole matter could have been arranged by allowing each State so many votes for President, instead of so many Presidential electors. The Presidential votes of a State could then have been cast by one officer as well as by twenty, or could have been certified to the President of the Senate by the executive officers of the State. The fact that each electoral vote was to be cast by an individual is proof that individual and independent action by the electors was contemplated. But the original intention has been so far lost sight of that in our day the electors have no discretion whatever. They simply meet and vote for the candidates previously nominated by their party conventions. The only essential qualification of a modern Presidential elector is fidelity to his party. He is merely the mouthpiece of the party who choose him, and any exercise of his individual judgment, contrary to the sentiment of his party, would be considered a crime. Our people can no longer be regarded as incompetent to exercise their own judgment, and if they were now incompetent, the electoral system would be no safeguard, for, in point of fact, it is the discretion of the people and not that of the electors to which effect is given.

While the electoral system seems destined to continue for a

time, it is within the power of each State legislature to give every section of its State a fair representation in the Electoral College. The most unsatisfactory result of choosing the electors by general ticket is that it practically compels the selection in each State of electors who are all pledged to one candidate, and nullifies the influence of large portions of the State where that candidate is unpopular. In any State there may be a large section, a congressional district, or several of them, in which a heavy majority of the voters are strongly opposed to the election of a particular candidate, yet, against their will, their influence is practically cast in favor of that candidate because a different sentiment prevails in the remainder of the State.

In many of the States parties are evenly divided, but by choosing the electors on a general ticket the principle of the odious unit rule is applied, which permits the majority of a delegation to dictate the votes of the minority, and which is no longer tolerated even in nominating conventions. Thus the entire electoral vote of a State may be cast for a candidate who is opposed by forty-nine per cent. of the voters. Wisconsin will have twelve votes in the next Electoral College. The political complexion of the State is fairly doubtful, and the vote will probably be a close one, yet one party or the other in that State will have absolutely no representation in the Electoral College. If the Electors were to be chosen by districts, can it be doubted that the result in any State would be a more exact expression of the preferences of her people?

Objection has been made to the district system on the ground that it will divide the electoral vote of a State and thus lessen her influence in the selection of a President. I answer, that if popular sentiment in a State is divided, her electoral vote ought to be divided, be the result what it may. The political minority help to make up the basis of population upon which the electors are apportioned to the States, and common fairness demands that they be given their proportionate share of the electors. In every State the people of limited districts decide who shall represent their interests in the National House of Representatives. There is no express provision in the Constitution that members of Congress shall be chosen by districts. They are to be chosen every second year "by the people of the several States," and the people of the States, through their legislatures, divide the States into congressional districts. That this method is fair and just, and secures to the people of the State a proper representation, is not denied even by those who insist upon choice of electors by general ticket. A proposition to elect by general ticket the congressional delegation of any State would be instantly resented in every district, yet the people of those districts are forced to turn over to the State at large the expression of their Presidential preferences. Surely the election of a President is as important an exercise of power, and should as fairly reflect the wishes of the voters, as a congressional election. The sacred principle of majority rule would be as faithfully applied in the districts as in the State, and the application would be far less vexatious and arbitrary. The people of each district would speak for themselves, and the result would be a far more accurate and detailed showing of preferences. Most of the districts would be doubtful and every voter would feel that his influence would have its weight in the selection of a chief magistrate.

The enactment of the Michigan statute has developed, among advocates of the general ticket, a theory that a choice of electors by districts is a violation of the Constitution, which directs that " Each State shall appoint " the electors. It is claimed that a State legislature has no authority to refer the choice to the people of sub-divisions of the State. But it seems idle to discuss a question which was settled by early practice and by the acquiescence of the men who framed the Constitution. It has been shown that by direction of different State legislatures the district system was in use for many years after the adoption of the Constitution. Is it to be assumed that the men who framed that instrument permitted a misconstruction of its language in so important a particular to pass unchallenged for more than forty years ? President Madison, in a letter to George Hay, dated August, 1823, said : " The district mode was mostly, if not exclusively, in view when the Constitution was framed and adopted, and was changed for the general ticket and legislative election as the only expedient for baffling the policy of particular States which had set the example." Here we have the explanation of the gradual change of method. As the people divided into parties, the majorities in certain States, having control of the legislatures, decided to shut the mouths of their opponents. Hence the adoption of the general ticket. Virginia ratified the Constitution in June, 1788, and in November her legislature directed. " That for the purpose of choosing twelve electors on behalf of this State to vote for a President in conformity to the Constitution of government for the United States, the several counties in this commonwealth shall be allotted into twelve districts, in manner following." One hundred and three years later it is announced that this action was unconstitutional. Judge Story, after reciting that the general ticket, the district method, and the legislative election had each been employed, remarks, "No question has ever arisen as to the constitutionality of either mode, except that of a direct choice by the legislature." ("Story on the Constitution," Sec. 1,472.) Even President Harrison, who has strongly expressed his disapprobation of the Michigan law, and who may be presumed to have fully stated the arguments against it, does not contend that it is a violation of the Constitution.

An advantage of the highest importance would be gained through the district system by destroying the commanding importance of pivotal States. A bare plurality of the popular vote in two States has decided several Presidential elections. As a general election approaches every man interested in the result can name the States in which the result is considered assured, and interest is practically withdrawn from those States and centred upon the few doubtful ones. In these, intense excitement is aroused, and the fight is waged with a bitterness and determination born of the conviction of their special importance. Indiana becomes a "bloody angle" and New York a "battlefield." Business comes to a standstill, men are crazed for the time by the intensity of their excitement, and general demoralization prevails. These decisive States must be carried at any cost, and enormous corruption funds are raised and poured into them from every quarter. Thousands of votes are bought and sold, and corruption and debauchery are openly carried on, because the perpetrators can rely upon party spirit to shield them from punishment. And when it is all over, one wonders what the result would have been in those States had the people been left in peace to vote their own preferences. If the electors were chosen by districts, this concentration of unhealthy effort in particular States would cease. The contest would be confined to the individual districts, and so many of these would be in doubt that political managers could not ascertain, as they now can, just what must be done to carry the day.

President Harrison in his last annual message to Congress used the following language : "The recent Michigan legislation provides for choosing what are popularly known as the congressional electors for President by congressional districts, and the two senatorial electors by districts created for that purpose. This legislation was, of course, accompanied by a new congressional apportionment, and the two statutes bring the electoral vote of the State under the influence of the gerrymander."

Without stopping to discuss the propriety of. this aspersion coming from one who is himself a probable candidate for the electoral votes of Michigan, let us inquire what is the chief evil of the gerrymander. The term is used to designate the practice of so dividing a State as to give one party an unfair advantage in a majority of the districts. The practice is an undoubted wrong, and has at times been indulged in by each of the great parties, but it is a practice which immediately affects the voters of every district, and experience has shown that public sentiment is quick to condemn its arbitrary use. Its injustice lies in the fact that it lessens the representation to which the political minority, by reason of their numbers, are justly entitled. But if we condemn the gerrymander because it lessens the representation of the minority, what is to be said of a system which excludes the minority from any representation whatever ? Yet this is the exact result attained by choosing Presidential electors on a general ticket.

In a recent article a distinguished ex-Senator of the United States discusses the gerrymander, and, referring to the apportionment of Alabama, says: "The district of smallest population has only 151,757 inhabitants, and another contiguous district has 253,891, a difference of upwards of 100,000 citizens." He adds: "Suggestion as to the motive for such geographical and numerical arrangement is quite superfluous."

At the last congressional election, the first district of Michigan had a population of 257,114, and another contiguous district, the second, had 153,655, a greater disparity than that shown in Alabama. Is comment here superfluous ? Since 1880 the difference between the most populous and least populous congressional districts of Michigan has been as follows : In 1880, 64,951 ; in 1884, 50,607 ; in 1890, 103,459, and under the new apportionment of 1891, 44,253. Three of the new districts, the first, second and seventh, may be considered safely Democratic.

Three others, the third, fourth and twelfth, are as safely Repub lican. The remainder are fairly doubtful districts, with the chances in favor of the Republicans in at·least two of them, and it may safely be asserted that Michigan was never more fairly apportioned.

Equally unwarranted with the claim that Michigan is gerrymandered is the assumption that the district system was adopted for a temporary party advantage. In the last State campaign the tariff ˙ issue was fully discussed, and although local considerations caused two of the Democratic candidates to run ahead of their ticket, the rest were elected by an average plurality of about 3,000. In the Congressional elections, upon national issues, the total Democratic vote for Congressmen exceeded the total Republican vote by 9,628. With these facts in view, there was strong reason for the belief that, without a change in the method of choosing electors, the entire electoral vote of Michigan would be cast for the Democratic candidate of 1892.

We divide our States into districts for the election of State Representatives, and into other districts for the choice of State Senators, in order that the people of all sections may be represented. We choose our Members of Congress from districts within the States, that the different views of our people may be represented in the national legislature. Every section of the State is heard in the selection of United States Senators. Only in the choice of Presidential electors is this local representation denied.

The legislature of Michigan, in the exercise of its constitutional power, and in the hope that all the States will join her in returning to the methods of the Constitution, has given the voters of every section of the State an opportunity to express their choice for the Presidency.

EDWIN B. WINANS.

FRENCH GIRLS.

BY MADAME ADAM.

ONE of the most curious and unexpected facts for mothers in France—one which has brought about within the last twenty-five years an actual revolution that is having its effect upon our customs—has been the emancipation of our young girls, caused by the intercourse of young women in France with American and English girls. What is most surprising and strange in it all is that education has not brought about this change. Convents and schools have the same rules and teach the same principles, without modifications of any kind. The religious faith of young women has remained the same, and the peculiar result is that those who are generally the most independent affect, or really feel, the necessity of practising their religious duties in the most scrupulous manner. French girls have all along observed religious conventions more closely as they assumed a more independent bearing. Formerly, a young woman did assume a slight independence of spirit, or become a little more skeptical and filled with a little more of the Voltaire school, as soon as she became a married woman, because of the contact with the more untrammelled mind of her husband. To-day, she places herself in touch with ideas which she believes to be of a better *ton*, just as fast as her opinion of the old French manners and customs decreases.

Do not imagine that these deep seated changes in the make-up of the character of young French women have come about in a single class of society or in Paris alone. The same modifications have appeared in the provinces, in the smallest towns and in the most retired castles, in exactly the same proportion as where they had the largest path to make. You see, for instance, young women escorting each other, riding horseback alone, going out with a maid or a governess, without their mothers ; and they go out with their brothers, too. They are to be found at receptions, where they are announced, where young men come to seek them, though their mothers do not appear. They even go out with an unmarried escort no older than themselves. One of the causes that have brought about this change is the life-at watering-places, at the seaside resorts and especially at places along the Mediterranean. I well remember the first time my little daughter—she was then ten years old, and was playing near me with a little French friend no older than herself—saw, from the balcony of the house in which we lived in the English Quarter at Cannes, a young English girl pass by in the direction of the Esterel escorted by a young man. My daughter said to her little companion :

" There goes an English girl out walking with her bròther." And the other with an inimitable air answered :

" No, dear, perhaps it is n't her brother. Perhaps it's only her friend."

" What ! Her friend ! Not even her father ? "

" Not even her father."

" But," cried my daughter, as much scandalized as one so young could be, " do her mamma and papa allow her to go out alone at her age on the mountain with a young man ? She cannot be a well-bred young lady."

" She is the daughter of a lord," replied the little friend, quickly, " I am sure ; I know her."

" Mamma, is what Lunette says true ? " demanded my child of me. " Do you think that proper—you, who are grown up ? "

" No, no," I replied, " and I hope that the fashion will never be adopted in France."

To-day my daughter's daughters have the manners and customs which have undergone these new changes, and they are Anglicized and Americanized like their friends. Nothing can give an idea—and I speak with knowledge, as one who has suffered—of the revulsion of feeling which a mother experienced twenty-five years ago at Nice, at Hyères, at Mentone, at Cannes, when she saw English girls go out alone with a " friend," as Lunette said, or, dividing into couples, go off in large numbers on excursions from which they did not return until evening. It was almost anguish, this feeling that one could not avoid ; to think that these young girls, who, after all, had mothers, should run such danger ! Although, indeed, when one looked more carefully and saw the great boobies whose awkward style and long steps the English girls copied, and who seemed to have taken away from the girls all the French modesty and much-scorned exclusiveness, one could reassure oneself.

Our children, as they grew up, were still shocked beyond all expression at what they called the want of style and the want of manners of the English. In social circles the camp of young French girls was never allowed to mix under any circumstances with the camp of American and English girls. There were whisperings of mockery on one side and the other, ironical pity for the slavery of the one, scandal at the " boyish " manners of the other. There was something like a state of warfare between them, and the young men of both parties rarely took the risk of inviting a girl from the other clan. Some Frenchmen, friends of young Englishmen, had themselves introduced especially to American girls, but they compromised themselves in the minds of their sisters and friends. Our girls rather exaggerated their reserve, and it seemed as if they affected the plan of shielding themselves under our wing. In vain would a young man propose a walk on his arm in the drawing-room to a young French girl. Her indignation would break forth in, " Ah, Monsieur, am I an American or English woman ? " Our girls, for instance, who were well-bred never looked their partner in the face while dancing, and would reply with modesty to his compliments, or blush at each word that seemed to them unfit for their womanly ears. They would stop the conversation with, " Monsieur, I beg of you not to continue. I have heard too much already that was not meant for me to hear." Indeed, our young girls had a respect for their own innocence that made them reject all knowledge, all comprehension of anything that might disturb their purity or make them lose in the least what they guarded with so much jealousy. They would have suffered, if they had guessed anything their parents hid from them, and would have considered that they were guilty in understanding it.

Their minds were shielded by their parents and their friends, and the latter were careful in their presence. A word was sufficient to make them pass quickly over a dangerous subject. " Do not forget that there are some young girls here "—and the story would be stopped short. Everything, as I say, was done to keep the thoughts of young girls on poetic, gay, and juvenile subjects.

Facts about nature and science were only revealed to them when they had to be initiated into certain mysteries of life. A young woman who studied botany became a curiosity the moment when she pronounced certain words. Ornithology was the most accepted science, because it was useful to mothers at the time of marriage for certain necessary revelations. The nests and the little birds gave a poetic turn to talks that were necessary on the wedding day or the day before. But how many girls have been frightened and unnerved at these revelations, and how they would have fled to the far ends of the earth if they had dared, rather than contract a marriage, as Monsieur le Maire says! Our young women, whether of the higher or the lower nobility, of the peasantry or the tradespeople, lived in a complete and ethereal ignorance. They did not know evil. It is quite true that they were not armed to guard or defend themselves, and they were often thrown into marriage unprepared, because of scruples and hesitations only too common on the part of mothers, who have not the slightest suspicions of the consequences; and they were as often indignant and disgusted by the exigencies. On the other hand, a young girl who opposed her family in a reasonable marriage with no other pretext than that the aspirant did not please her was unanimously censured. " Mademoiselle wishes to choose, herself, to marry, herself," they would repeat with severity. How could such a thing be permitted ! " Do not her parents know better than she what will suit her ? She is a girl who will come to no good."

Then, a young girl never read any papers but fashion papers. Her educational books were examined, carefully looked over and expurgated. Even her dreams were classic ; they must have been ideal in the extreme, and nothing material could have been imagined by her, nothing but a platonic husband promised her in life. It was not proper to have too good health, either, or too much appetite, if she would be a really aristocratic young woman.

And we brought up this child so pure, to be wedded to a French husband who was already beginning to bite at all kinds of sports, to think only of amusing himself in every way, growing more and more jeering and sceptical, respecting very few things in life, loving pleasure above all, good living and an outdoor life ! How many of our young girls have returned, forever unhappy, to cower on the breast of a mother, to confide their sad disillusions to a friend married even as they were ! How many have sought refuge for their wounded spirits with a priest, who counselled them to guard their souls for God, and not to yield them to a husband who had not tried in any way to conquer them ! The masculine nature became odious to certain too innocent wives ; marriage remains in their minds as a sort of ambush into which they had been thrown without warning.

It was, therefore, necessary to prepare our daughters better for our sons, to give them better instruction in the materialistic and prosaic sides of life, to initiate them into the sciences which should show how all beings must submit to general laws ; but it was distinctly not necessary to make them become acquainted with young Frenchmen in a way that would cause these latter to lose the little respect they had for women.

An English or American youth sees in a woman a superior creature or a sister or a wife. A young Frenchman sees a woman, and immediately suspects one who is either distinguished by a vigorous mind or individual character. Not much inclined for marriage, he finds too many female friends always at hand to be attracted by young women who are not bred up to be good mothers and wives, and who would simply be feminine companions, not friends. Without doubt, if marriage could be the association dreamed of by social philanthropists, it would be the state in which woman gave her husband help and advice in his outside work, and in which she was able to interest him in the affairs of the home, in the early education of her children, in the administration of the household. But a Frenchman has little taste for such equality with his wife, who though she has not his qualities has nevertheless their equivalents. He does not object to her using these faculties in society. He either wants a housekeeper who may be a little *bibête*, which, he says, " rests him," or he wants a brilliant woman of the world who amuses him.

The new English and American ways will make our French girls who are married more worldly, more passionately fond of outdoor sports like their husbands, and less praiseworthy housekeepers. They will be drawn away from their true purpose, which they might have attained by a little forethought on the part of their mothers. Had they become good housewives they would have been able to find a sphere for themselves in which they would have, little by little, formed themselves for public life also, and which would have made them useful to their husbands, just as the latter in carrying out their own affairs well have made themselves to-day capable of carrying on the affairs of their country.

The meeting of young French girls with American and English girls, always growing more frequent at winter resorts, baths, watering places, in educational institutions and in daily intercourse, has little by little melted the ice ; and our girls commenced by envying their sisters, and then gradually came to imitate them. The yoke they had to bear irritated them, and, among themselves, instead of blaming the independence of the foreigners' manners, they began to cry out for want of them.

This came about first at balls, where the imitation commenced in conversation and in a more deliberate carriage ; not as some think in flirtation, which has not been, and never will be, able to force itself into our customs, on account of the danger which this game of love would bring upon our girls—a danger which American and English girls do not run (I trust I can surely believe) with young Englishmen and Americans. The first young French women who conversed with their partners, who made a tour of the ball room, who rested in the interval between dances at some distance from their mothers, were very severely judged ; but, little by little, contagion affected the most timid, and three or four generations sufficed to bring about a total change. Certain things which appeared natural then, appear ridiculous to-day ; such as the action of the parents among the tradespeople who did not allow their daughters to waltz or to appear in décolleté dress.

There was an English game which helped these matters along in a singular manner. This was croquet. Every mother can recall the first astonishment she felt when she saw her daughter enter into a discussion with a young man who had just been presented to her, or carry a mallet over her shoulders with a little swaggering air as she stretched her figure back or gave jeering answers or laughed aloud. Certainly criticism was not lacking at the start, and when those young girls who astonished even themselves, scarcely recognizing themselves any longer, saw their parents and friends blaming them and some of their companions remaining faithful to the old customs, they began to accuse themselves and promised to be more careful.

The grandmothers lost their heads over the whole affair. They at first called their sons and daughters to task : "How can you tolerate manners like these ? Why, your daughter has the manners of a fishwoman!" In a little while you will only hear her speak when she stands with her hands on her hips ! Young girls with their noses in the air—why, they come from the street !" When they cried out so against this new abomination, these good grandmothers followed the dictates of an egoism that they failed to recognize. But as soon as these liberties had once been taken and the objections conquered their reign was at an end ; and at last all the little children, young girls, and later on young women only had liberty while in their hands, and they were consequently spoiled. They could put on that famous little swaggering air at their grandmother's. Their education and its severities devolved upon the mothers, and the grandmother might well say to her daughter, "you bring up your daughter very badly," but she herself would be indulgent. The lot of the grandmother was certainly the most delightful and enviable in the family.

Happiness, influence, confidence, all were lost on account of the grandmother. Peccadillos now could be counted by the hundred, and there was no more running to grandmother to sue for pardon. Youth absolved itself. The young people met their cousins at grandmother's house ; they became a little freer with them ; they got better acquainted, and showed a little of their hearts, of their thoughts and sensibilities, without appearing to parade them before the world or in the house of their parents, which would have been a sign of very bad taste. They played little city and country games at their grandmother's house. At certain times of the day the old lady had a knowing way of telling them, "Go and amuse yourselves, children ; youth passes quickly enough." All this took place within the family precincts, with brothers, cousins or friends of one or another—friends of childhood, whose parents had themselves been friends of their parents. But later on, they permitted these things to go on with young men who had been introduced to them within a day or a week, and they occasionally allowed it also with strangers who came from no one knew where, introduced by an introduced friend—and you can see the seriousness of the guarantee ! Was there not indeed a reason for the older heads to imagine that the ruin of the family was at hand !

Ah! that croquet that occupied young girls' minds in the country, at the seaside or at watering places the whole day, instead of which they used to have moments for reading, music, and embroidery! And those skirts which were suddenly raised high on the ankle to accomplish a certain stroke in the game, and the next moment carried short to be out of the way; what immodesty! what manners! Great Heavens! And then came the little boyish cap, the tight fitting jerseys—those flannel betrayers of the form ;—all this followed in the game of court tennis and lawn tennis. To give those heavy blows with a mallet to the balls, or those vigorous strokes with a racquet, interspersed with talk of biceps, of breast, of ankles—what joy, what elegance for the young girls of France! But how can we help regretting the old graceful movements and games. And the evening! Ah, the scandal of it! These young girls playing at roulette or *petits chevaux* in the Casinos, or dancing with the greatest roué—this time scarcely introduced! Or again in the country, as in the drawing room, young women scoffed at the idea of listening to people whom they used to listen to with such pleasure when they were permitted to talk with them; not to speak of the mixed troops of young boys and girls who play billiards, talk loudly, dispute, and drown the voices of their parents with distance!

In the city young people go out with a maid or a *trotteuse—* that is, with a person who is hired to walk an hour or two with your daughter; someone whom you do not know any better than a professor of languages; whom you can neither overhear nor oversee when they are out of doors; whose moral ideas, whose manners you do not know. And yet to this person you intrust your daughter, thinking of her physical health. Alas, it is a question what becomes of her moral health! What has become of the good precepts, the long talk with the mother and the grandmother, which formed the soul and elevated the thoughts, taking that pretty form traditional in our language? Where are the hours of reading together when analyses and comments were made as they proceeded? All that is confided to the professors now, who form the girls' minds mechanically and enlist them in regiments by the hundreds, to assist in promulgating the mechanical theories that are ordained by custom. After the convent and the pension come lectures; but, most important of all, the individual and original education within the family is quite abandoned. What young girl would to-day be willing to take her final lessons in literature and history from her mother and her grandmother ? She would think it unfashionable.

A mother who is not rich turns herself into a *trotteuse.* She runs to the lecture room also There are few individual lessons, for these young girls detest them as they detest solitude and home. They must be out of doors and with their friends. Formerly, the mother directed after a fashion the education of the daughters even in the convent. To-day, she yields to them and has no supervision of their studies. Mademoiselle wishes now to take everything, to know everything, drawing, music, languages, algebra, dancing,—and it is ruinous.

Still, if the custom of the dowry had disappeared with these manners of the past, it might have been better ; but that has remained, adding to the expenses of education, expenses that increase as boys and girls demand more and more and give less and less in return. English and Americans, when they gave these manners and customs, would have done well to help the girls find husbands for themselves and to teach them to go into marriage without new responsibilities and without drawing on the fortune or the comfort of their parents, acquired with such difficulty and sacrifice. All these new fashions would have been, and should be, accepted with resignation by the parents, if the rupture in the question of family property, involving rights therein that are dear to the French, did not threaten to make the opposition still stronger before long. How often one sees parents smile sadly at each other and say with deep regret, "I have no children. My daughters take no more interest in their mother's life. My sons do not trouble themselves about any of my affairs." And what a void, what bitterness all this makes for the older members of the family !

These poor old people cannot live up to the standards of their daughters, who only a few years ago talked with them as comrades, and who treat them to-day as inferiors. These young people discuss and judge after their own manner, they form their minds more and more personally and independently, opposing the ideas of the family with an avidity that corresponds with their youthful activity. And taking their dreams for intellectual power, they become infatuated and look upon their parents as old and superannuated. They still go occasionally to their brothers and fathers for counsel, for they are bureaus of news from the dear outside world. But they desert their mothers when it is not necessary for the latter to accompany them to lectures. They abandon their grandmothers, who do not interest them at all, who are no longer even amusing. Amusing! To be amusing—that is the touchstone of the generation which is succeeding the pessimists !

The family has already split in two, one part being the younger members, who simply amuse themselves ; the other, the mature and the aged—the mature fretting over these changes and digging deeper the abyss of separation, the aged trying to make themselves young again by any and all means, so as not to be thrown aside ; and they succeed in giving themselves at least the appearance of youth. The sight of the first is heartrending, that of the second lamentable—painted men and women with red and blonde hair, trying to retain complexion or ward off white hairs, who, seeing that they are being finally abandoned, wish to be young again and to amuse and be amused.

The vacation, which formerly united the most divided families, now sees them scattered. Those who make a supreme effort to gather together see at such time that the estrangement of the young people and the middle aged has only increased. Jealous of their independence they wish to make their own lives and to lead them by themselves. The error is growing more and more serious, caused by the impatience felt at any restraint. A young girl once married, *fin de siècle*, as they say in Paris, that is, having to a greater or less degree these faults or good qualities,—it is immaterial which,—will not allow her mother to give her advice in regard to the management of her household and in bringing up her children. It is quite true that by this she rids her household of the meddling interference of a typical mother-in-law. At any rate she prefers to the experience of her family, her own inexperience and the advice of a hired nurse or cook, which she is always free to follow or not as she wishes.

The children who remain at home do not interest the father now when he returns at night, except with the little accounts of their own plans and amusements for the day, if these happen to attract him. The home no longer has any attraction for him ; it is no longer a place of high interests, the means for the exchange of the highest ideas and of the best sentiments ; it is the place where he is free to don his dressing gown and to put on his slippers, and he cannot now teach good lessons by his example or his personal authority. It is useless for him to study his children, or to try to bring them up well, to watch them and retain their respect. It is the place for rest, and he gives himself up to that. There is no more advice, for it is seldom followed ; no more principles by which the minds of the children were formerly moulded according to the judgment of the entire family ; no more of the spirit which was always ready for the greatest sacrifices where one of the members needed the devotion of the rest and appealed to it. To-day each one is for himself. If the dowry did not exist in France, if the young girls did not still feel the material need of their families, they would be free like American girls before they were ten years old, and would later choose husbands for themselves. They must be interested in the fortunes of their parents, even though this is only for the sake of knowing who they can aspire to marry and who can pretend to marry them. In Paris young girls are constantly thrown together, and they escape from their families in this way. In the provinces and the country, being much more isolated and thoughtful, they are at times more or less open to some paternal restraint, but submission is with them only an exception ; they only think of marriage, which will set them free and give them the right to go out into the world alone at the age of twenty-five.

One can hear and see the changes which have taken place in twenty-five years when one hears them talking together. For the grandmothers and the mothers of the old school it is paralyzing. The questions, the confidences, exchange of ideas, projects for the future, judgments on what they call sentimentalities of life, criticism on young men whom they appreciate to a surprising degree—all this was formerly reserved for the family's ears alone, for the mother and the grandmother ; and now it has become the privilege of the friend, or of several friends, and more's the pity !

As we would weep over a world which is disintegrating and dying, so in France one has to weep over the family. But all that is torn from its bleeding heart is added to the individual. The young woman is making herself ; now she is only at the entrance of the new life which young men are leaving behind them. She will become, from day to day, in every sense more of a companion in marriage. At present she only sees before her the pleasure of escaping from a cage. She will understand in a little while the responsibilities of liberty. Better armed against social dangers, she will choose more intelligently those by whose side she will strive for the comforts of life. Already, among our girls who are free from their families, who have broken from a world too narrow for them, we can see rising a superior womanhood, and we must acknowledge it a strong one. They have lost, it is true, the poetry concealed under the old veiled existence, the emotions of their devout and silent sentiments—delicate and sweet as they were—but they have conquered much in exchange.

They are loyal and just, and being after all of one blood, they have the worship of the larger family, that of the French nation. Our grandmothers and mothers can think of one fact that will always be a great consolation for them—that is, that if our daughters belong less to us, they belong more to themselves, and if we have much more unhappy lives, perhaps they are becoming far happier.

JULIETTE ADAM.

THE FREE ZONE IN MEXICO.

BY M. ROMERO, MEXICAN MINISTER TO THE UNITED STATES.

IN THE northern part of Mexico, along its border line with the United States, there extends a strip of land which is governed by trade regulations wholly different from those of the rest of the republic. This strip is known as the Free Zone, or, in Spanish, *Zona Libre*, and it is, it seems to me, an institution wholly misunderstood in this country. The general opinion seems to be, first, that it was established by Mexico as an act of antagonism, if not of unfriendliness, towards the United States, and, second, that its main, if not its sole purpose was to encourage smuggling, to the prejudice of the fiscal interests of this country. I wish to show how unfounded such impressions are ; and, prompted as I am by a due regard for a fair understanding and harmony between the two countries, I believe it will not be considered presumptuous on my part to offer some statements concerning that subject. I will not be expected to write in defence of the Free Zone. The official records of Mexico show that, far from being its friend, I have ever been its most earnest opponent, and I am the only Mexican Secretary of the Treasury who has so far officially advised its abolition. I intend to consider the matter impartially and fairly, and to do this I will first state how the *Zona Libre* originated in Mexico, and then define what we mean by that term.

When, in pursuance of the treaty of February 2, 1848, the Rio Grande River, from El Paso del Norte to the point where it flows into the Gulf of Mexico, was accepted as the boundary line between Mexico and the United States, new settlements sprang up on both banks of the river, and things began to take their level under the new conditions. The two nations, which so far had been separated by a desert, were at once brought into close contact with one another, and it was found that the economical and commercial conditions on the north and south banks of the Rio

Grande were in striking contrast to each other. In the towns of the United States along the north bank no taxes were levied and no restrictions of any kind were imposed upon internal trade. The import duties on foreign goods brought into the United States were at that time relatively low, and this country was then at the beginning of its unexampled career of material progress and prosperity. On the opposite bank, in Mexico, the towns were loaded down with the onerous system of taxation which had come down to us from the Spaniards. The heavy taxes which were levied on internal commerce had largely increased the cost of foreign and domestic goods, and the collection of these taxes made a system of interior custom-houses, with all their attending evils, a necessary institution. There were many and very onerous restrictions both upon foreign and domestic trade, and the import duties on foreign goods were so high as to be, in many cases, practically prohibitory. Many commodities were actually excluded from the country under the plea of protection to our national industries, and among these were articles of prime necessity, such as grain and provisions. The result of this condition of things was that radically different prices prevailed in the towns on both sides of the river. At Brownsville, Tex., for instance, on the north bank of the Rio Grande, all sorts of domestic articles and the necessaries of life, such as provisions and clothing, were bought at a low price, while in Matamoras and other Mexican towns, on the south bank, the same articles of domestic production and often of an inferior quality cost twice and even four times as much as at the stores just across the river. A still greater disproportion existed in the price of foreign goods on either side of the river, and the cheapest commodities were always sold on the left bank of the Rio Grande.

This difference of taxation and consequently of prices on the frontier, necessarily brought about one of two results. It either caused the inhabitants of the Mexican towns to emigrate to the settlements on the other side of the river, in order to enjoy the advantages which were to be had in this country, or it induced them to purchase in the United States the goods which they needed and to smuggle them across the Rio Grande to their homes in Mexico.

In 1849, the year following the adoption of the new boundary line by the two countries, the situation on the Mexican frontier became so untenable and disquieting that our federal congress was obliged to pass, on the 14th of April of that year, a law authorizing for three years the importation through the frontier custom-houses of the state of Tamaulipas of such provisions as were needed for the use of the people of the frontier. Such goods had up to that time been prohibited by the existing tariff, or had been subject to almost prohibitory duties. This law did not meet the exigencies of the situation, because it was restricted to provisions, and these were not the only things that men require for their life and comfort.

On August 30, 1852, the United States Congress passed a law by which the contrast between the conditions of the two sides of the Rio Grande was made still greater, and the condition of things on the Mexican side became worse than ever. By that act foreign goods could be sent in bond to Mexico over certain routes specified in the law and others to be authorized by the Secretary of the Treasury. These goods could be held on the frontier in the United States until a favorable opportunity came for their exportation into Mexico, and they were free of all duties on the part of the United States. There was no similar privilege within the territory of Mexico, as all foreign goods, of whatever kind they might be, were there subject to the payment of duty upon their importation. The result was that the inhabitants of the Mexican side of the river were placed under such disadvantages that the public men of Tamaulipas, the only state which at that time had towns on the border facing the border villages of Texas, came to believe that they must have privileges similar to those existing in the United States, to enable them to live on the frontier. It was this belief that originated the Free Zone, and, in the unsettled condition of Mexico, such men soon found an opportunity to bring about what they desired.

This statement of facts shows that the Free Zone was not really an invention of the Mexican authorities of the state of Tamaulipas, but an imitation on a larger scale of a similar measure enacted more than five years previously by the United States Government for the benefit of that portion of its territory bordering on Mexico.

On February 5, 1857, we adopted our present constitution, which went into operation on the 16th of the following September. On the 1st of December of that year, General Don Ignacio

Comonfort, who had just been elected President under the new constitution, was inaugurated. Two weeks later he unfortunately issued a pronunciamento against the very constitution to which he owed his election and consequently the legality of his powers, and he thereupon dissolved the Federal Congress then in session. Almost all the Mexican States refused to consent to such a daring violation of the constitution, and many of them, specially those far removed from the capital, reassumed their sovereignty, and their legislatures granted extraordinary powers to the governors, in order to enable them to defend their institutions against those who had betrayed their trust in trying to overthrow the constitution, acting very much as some of the Brazilian States recently did when the president of that republic, Marshal Diodoro Da Fonseca, attempted to assume the Dictatorship.

By virtue of such powers the Governor of the State of Tamaulipas issued on March 17, 1858, a decree designed to afford a remedy for the hardships from which the frontier population of that State were then suffering. This decree established what has since that time been known in Mexico as the Free Zone. It permitted all foreign goods intended for the use of the frontier towns of that State, for the ranches in their jurisdiction, or for trade between those towns, to be exempt from all federal duties, but not from municipal or State taxes. Such goods could remain in bond in the same towns either at the house of the importer or at the public warehouse. The Federal Government not then having warehouses on the frontier, all packages had to go, of course, to the house of the importer. Thus, goods imported into the frontier towns could remain stored indefinitely without paying any storage or any other charges to the Federal Treasury, and they only paid import duties when they were taken from the frontier towns to the interior of Mexico.

Nothing could furnish a better idea of the true object of the ordinance issued by the Governor of Tamaulipas, if there were room for any well-founded doubt, than the grounds on which he based his action, which he stated in the preamble of his decree in the following words :

" The citizen Ramon Guerra, Governor *ad-interim* of the State of Tamaulipas : whereas, our towns on our northern frontier are in a state of actual decadence for the lack of laws to protect their commerce ; and, whereas, being situated in close proximity to a commercial nation which enjoys free trade they need equal advantages in order not to lose their population, which is constantly emigrating to the neighboring country ; now, therefore, desiring to put an end to so serious an evil by means of franchises which have so long been demanded by the frontier trade; favorably considering the petition of the inhabitants of Matamoras, and using the extraordinary faculties with which I am invested by the decree of December 23, of the Honorable Legislature of the State, with the advice and consent of the council, I have seen fit to decree as follows," etc.

The articles of the decree which I give below contain the main provisions about the Free Zone and show exactly how far it was intended to go :

ARTICLE 1.—Foreign goods designed for the consumption of the city of Matamoras and of the other towns on the bank of the Rio Bravo, Reynosa, Camargo, Mier, Guerrero, and Monterey Laredo, and for the trade which these towns carry on among themselves, shall be free from all duties, with the exception of municipal duties and such taxes as may be imposed, to the end that the burdens of the State may be borne. In like manner, goods deposited in government warehouses, or in warehouses belonging to private individuals, in the said towns, shall be free of duties so long as they are not conveyed inland to other towns of the State or of the Republic. The terms on which this trade is to be conducted are laid down in the following articles :

. . . .

ARTICLE 7.—Foreign goods leaving the privileged towns to be conveyed into the interior of the Republic shall, at the time of so doing, become subject to the duties laid upon them by the tariff, and they shall never be conveyed into the interior without having paid, at the custom-house of their place of departure, all duties which are required to be paid in the port, and without the observance of all the requirements and provisions of the laws in force, in order not to be molested or detained on their way.

The Governor of Tamaulipas foresaw that his decree would naturally facilitate smuggling, to the disadvantage of the Federal Treasury of Mexico ; but I am sure he little imagined that the Treasury of the United States would suffer in consequence thereof, and he earnestly recommended the citizens of the State to try and prevent such a result by all means in their power, as appears from the following article of his decree :

ARTICLE 8.—As the privilege granted by this decree ought not to cause any detriment to the national revenue, it is the duty of the inhabitants of the frontier to prevent, by all the means in their power, this privilege from being converted into a shameful smuggling traffic; it is, therefore, the duty of every inhabitant of the frontier voluntarily to become a sentinel, constantly on the watch to prevent smuggling; otherwise, the Government will be under the painful necessity of withdrawing this privilege, by revoking the present decree.

The Governor's decree ended with this article :

ARTICLE 9.—This decree shall be subject to the revision and approval of the legislature of the State at its next meeting in ordinary session and to that of the Federal Congress when constitutional order shall be restored, although it shall go into force as soon as published in the privileged towns.

Therefore, I order it to be printed, published, circulated, and duly enforced.

Done at Ciudad Victoria, March 17, 1858.

RAMON GUERRA.

JOSÉ MARIA OLVERA, *Chief Official.*

The foregoing decree was confirmed and amplified under the plea of establishing regulations for its execution by another decree of the Governor of Tamaulipas, bearing date of October 29, 1860. The former decree was submitted, in compliance with the provisions of its last article, to the legislature of the state, and also to the Federal Congress for its approval, and was sanctioned by the latter body July 30, 1861.

This brief statement will, I think, be sufficient to show that the establishment of the Free Zone was a step taken in fulfilment of the duty of self preservation, so to speak, and imitating similar measures adopted by the Congress of the United States, and that it was by no means a measure approved in a spirit of unfriendliness, much less of hostility, towards the United States, as has been generally believed in this country.

The second impression prevailing here in regard to the Free Zone is equally unfounded, as I will try to show. The events connected with the foreign intervention in Mexico did not permit the natural effects of the Free Zone to be felt in the country until the Republic returned to its normal condition, that is, until after the downfall of the French intervention and the so-called Empire of Maximilian, events which took place during the year of 1867. In January of 1868 I was called to the Treasury Department by President Juarez, and in my annual report to Congress, September 16 of that year, I stated that one of the causes of the then depleted condition of the Mexican Treasury was the large contraband trade that was carried on through the Free Zone and enjoyed by the frontier towns of Tamaulipas ; further remarking that the customhouses of those towns were scarcely able to meet their clerk and office expenses, and that this fact showed that the Free Zone had not made that region prosper ; and that, in my opinion, that institution was not the proper remedy for the evil which it was intended to cure.

It is true that the privilege granted by the Free Zone to the inhabitants of the northern portion of Tamaulipas to import and consume foreign goods without paying federal duties, to store them in their own houses, and to keep them in bond for an unlimited time,' was a powerful incentive to smuggling from the Free Zone either to Mexico or the United States ; and that Mexico, which has suffered greatly by that result, has been obliged, with a view to the repression of smuggling, to establish a costly, oppressive, and complicated system of inspection ; but protection to smuggling was not the object of the creators of the Free Zone, nor is it possible that smuggling should have been carried on to the prejudice of the United States, to the same extent to which it has been done to the disadvantage of Mexico.

As the duties levied by the Mexican tariff are much higher than those collected in the United States, it is evident that the most lucrative contraband trade, and the easier one to make, is that which is carried on to the detriment of the Mexican Treasury. Smuggling is more easily done in Mexico, because the Mexican frontier is very sparsely populated, and therefore the difficulty of guarding it is greatly increased, while the frontier of the United States is more thickly settled and better protected against illicit traffic.

It does not seem to me reasonable to imagine that the Free Zone was established for the purpose of encouraging smuggling, to the detriment of the United States Treasury, when in fact it harms Mexico to a much greater extent than it does this country, as, in order to injure the United States, the Mexicans would not be willing to injure themselves ten times as much ; and if the contraband carried on under the shadow of the Free Zone was a sufficient reason for its suppression, the interest of Mexico in this matter would long since have settled the question.

Any human institution can be abused by men. The goods stored in the frontier towns of the United States, in accordance with the act of August 30, 1882, were easily smuggled into Mexico, and yet when the United States Congress passed that law, they did not intend, of course, to encourage smuggling, to the detriment of Mexico, although such was practically its result. In the same manner the Governor of Tamaulipas at first, and the

Mexican Congress afterwards, did not intend, in establishing the Free Zone, to encourage smuggling, to the detriment of the United States. To prevent smuggling from the Free Zone, as far as this was possible, the Mexican Government has been obliged to duplicate its frontiers of inspection with the United States, at great expense and considerable inconvenience to bona-fide merchants, as it has, besides the custom-houses right on the boundary line with proper inspection between each of them, some distance further south, under the name of fiscal police, another system of custom-houses and inspection to prevent smuggling between the Free Zone and the rest of the country.

What would the people of the United States think if Mexico should charge that such provisions of the tariff of this country as are lower and more liberal than ours were enacted by the United States to encourage smuggling, or if they should demand that the tariff be changed because it did encourage smuggling ? What would the people of this country think if we should ask them to repeal the act of August 20, 1852, because it encouraged smuggling in Mexico ? The Mexican people feel exactly as the people of the United States would feel if the circumstances were reversed.

I think it will not be amiss to make a few remarks about the different phases that the Free Zone question has assumed in Mexico, since the restoration of the Republic in 1867. The Committee of Ways and Means of the Fifth Mexican Congress reported, in its session of 1870, a tariff bill which sanctioned the Free Zone, and this matter was fully discussed during the latter part of October and the beginning of November of that year. Members of the Cabinet have in Mexico, not only the privilege of the floor in both houses, as in the United States, but the right to participate in the debates and to express the views of the Executive. As Secretary of the Treasury of Mexico, I made a thorough study of this important and complicated subject, and I took part in that debate in the sessions of the House of the 28th and 29th of October, and 4th and 5th of November, 1870, making extended remarks against the Free Zone, and I recommended its abolition to Congress, in behalf of the Executive. The reasons which led me to this conclusion were mainly of a constitutional character, namely, that the Free Zone constituted a privilege in favor of a State, forbidden by our constitution ; and that although I was aware that the situation of the frontier towns of Mexico required the adoption of suitable remedies, I thought that one could be found of such nature as would embrace the whole country, and be divested of the odious character of a privilege. My efforts were in vain ; Congress voted in favor of the maintenance of the Free Zone ; and although that vote never became a law, the tariff then under discussion nevertheless exercised great influence upon the existing and other administrations, as it showed what was the opinion of the representatives of the people on that question.

The abolition of the Free Zone was agitated in Mexico after I left the Treasury Department in November, 1872. When four years later, in 1878, I was again at the head of that Department and saw that it was not possible then to abolish the Free Zone, because the frontier influences were then stronger than ever, I thought that we ought at least to make proper regulations, with a view to prevent, as far as possible, any abuses of its franchises, and the regulations of June 17, 1878, were then issued. After that there was a strong reaction in favor of the Free Zone, especially when General Gonzalez, a citizen of the State of Tamaulipas, became President from 1880 to 1884.

General Diaz succeeded General Gonzalez on December 1, 1884, and in a new tariff act issued by him, January 24, 1885, the Free Zone, which had been up to that time restricted to the State of Tamaulipas, was extended to the whole frontier, namely, to the States of Coahuila, Chihuahua, and Sonora and to the territory of the Lower California, for a distance of 20 kilometres from the boundary line, thereby placing it on a better footing than it was before, when it appeared as a privilege confined to a single State and denied to others which were exactly in the same condition. But the same tariff act, which so extended the Free Zone, limited considerably its franchises by the regulations contained in Chapter XII. of the tariff of January 24, 1885. The frontier towns and the representatives in Congress, however, exerted such pressure in the Federal Congress that by an act dated June 19, 1885, the limitations established in that tariff were suspended, and very liberal regulations were again adopted in the succeeding tariff of March 1, 1887, which remained in force until the present one of June 12, 1891, was issued. This act marked a new era, in so far as the Free Zone is concerned, as article 676 of the same subjects all foreign goods coming to the Free Zone, which heretofore had been free of all import duties, to a duty of ten per centum upon the import duties in the other Mexican ports, excepting cattle of all kinds, which will pay full duties.   I consider this provision as the beginning of a new system which will finally result in doing away with that institution.

As I have already remarked, the opinion of Mexican statesmen on the Free Zone question has been divided, some entertaining the belief that it should be abolished because it grants to one section of the country privileges which are not authorized by the constitution, and others, by far the largest number, holding that, under the circumstances, it was an imperative necessity, as its abolition would be equivalent to the destruction of the frontier.   The friends of the Free Zone represented that the frontier towns of Mexico owed their prosperity to that institution, and that they could not exist without it.   There was a coincidence, which is one of the causes that induced a great many Mexicans to attribute to the Free Zone more beneficial results than it has really produced, and this circumstance, to which I shall refer, has had a great influence in its maintenance and extension.

The situation of the Mexican frontier up to the beginning of the Civil War in the United States was, as I have already remarked, one of poverty and even of misery, and formed a striking contrast with the one existing on the other side of the Rio Grande. That war broke out almost simultaneously with the establishment of the Free Zone, and the situation of the Mexican frontier changed very materially as a consequence of the war, during which, and for some time afterwards, welfare and prosperity crossed from the left to the right bank of the Rio Grande, on account of the general prostration then prevailing in the South.   Superficial observers attributed that prosperity not to its true cause, which, in my opinion, was the war, but to the Free Zone ; and feeling convinced that it had been productive of extraordinarily favorable results, they naturally considered it as a panacea for all evils, and its extension as one of the country's most imperative necessities.   The latter opinion finally prevailed in the councils of the Mexican Government from 1877 to 1885, and this led to the extension of the Free Zone to all the boundary States.

There is another point of view of this question, which, in my judgment, has so far passed entirely unnoticed.   The Free

Zone is really an advantage to the United States, since, as I have already stated, the Mexican system of legislation concerning customs and excise duties has generally been restrictive and even prohibitory, both by reason of the high import duties and of the existence of inferior custom-houses, and also of State and municipal taxes on foreign goods, which require vigilance and restrictions that cannot but hamper business transactions. Any relaxation of such a system of restriction cannot but be favorable to foreign nations trading with Mexico, and specially to a neighboring country like the United States, whose manufactures are mainly, if not exclusively, consumed on the Mexican frontier.

If the Free Zone has inconveniences for this country much less serious than those which it has for Mexico, it possesses, in my judgment, another decided advantage which has also remained hitherto unnoticed. It practically makes of a portion of Mexico a free market for all products and manufactures of the United States, since merchandise of all kinds from this country may be imported into and consumed on Mexican territory duty free, and be warehoused in the region of the zone for an unlimited time. No greater privileges can be asked for the commerce of a nation, and the only drawback in this respect that I see to the Free Zone is that it does not embrace the whole of Mexico. Supposing its privileges were extended to the whole of Mexico, would the United States consider the free admission of their products in my country as prejudicial to their interests? How strange it appears under this view of the question—the idea prevailing here that the Free Zone brings only harm to the United States and has been established to the advantage of only European goods, when the largest amount of goods imported there under its franchises are from the United States !

The Government of the United States has been recently trying in a very earnest manner to obtain from foreign countries, and specially from the American republics, the free entry, or the admission at a reduced rate of duties, of a limited number of its products and manufactures, and they naturally feel pleased when a new agreement is made. And yet the liberal terms provided by Mexico in favor of the free admission of all the products and manufactures of this country into our Free Zone, has been taken here as an unfriendly act on our part towards this country.

There can be no doubt as to the right of the Government of

Mexico to establish such duties and regulations on the foreign trade of the country, even in case they would harm in any manner the mercantile interests of any other foreign nations, and I therefore think it unnecessary to establish the right of Mexico to adopt and maintain the Free Zone.

I think it proper on this occasion to state that the misunderstanding which has prevailed here with regard to the object and tendencies of the Free Zone and the manner in which that misunderstanding has been expressed by certain Federal and State officials, has really served as a powerful argument to the Mexican defenders of the Free Zone who accuse their opponents of subserviency to this country, attributing to them a design to sacrifice the interests of Mexico to the demands of the United States. It may not be out of place for me to quote here certain views regarding this aspect of the question that I expressed as Secretary of the Treasury of Mexico, in my annual report submitted to the Federal Congress under date of September 16, 1870, and which are as follows :

" The friendly representations made by the United States Government to that of the Republic in relation to the injury accruing to the United States from the Free Zone are also worthy of being taken into consideration by Congress not that it may seek to please the neighboring nation in a spirit of servility, at the expense of the rights and interests of the Republic, which it is under obligations to care for and uphold above everything else (which spirit would be unworthy of our national representatives); but as a neighborly act, and in order to have a right to be heard and treated with consideration in case that in the process of time some difficulty may arise on our northern frontier of such a nature as to possess, regarding Mexico, the character which the Free Zone possesses as regards our neighboring nation; in order, moreover, that Mexico may acquire a new title to be heard and considered in a cordial and friendly, as well as just and equitable, manner when she may have occasion to offer remonstrances with a view to the protection of her interests. A nation's dignity is not so well upheld by refusing to consider the moderate and amicable remonstrances of a neighboring nation, as it is by hearing and considering such remonstrances and then acting according to the requirements of justice."

For more detailed information on this subject, and especially for the English translation of some of the official documents bearing on the same, I refer the reader to a message which the President of the United States sent to the Senate on March 16, 1888 (Senate Exec. Doc. No. 130, Fiftieth Congress, 1st Session), and to the report and accompanying documents of the Comm on Foreign Affairs of the House of Representatives, on the relations of the United States with Mexico, presented by Mr. Schleicher on the 25th of April, 1878 (House Report, No. 701, House of Representatives, Forty-fifth Congress, 2d Session).

I sincerely hope that the foregoing remarks will in some measure contribute to dispel the wrong impressions prevailing in the United States as to the Mexican Free Zone, and that thereby, when the agitation on this subject shall have completely disappeared, it will be then easier to adjust this matter in such a manner as will be honorable and satisfactory to all concerned.

M. ROMERO.

THE MODERN CART OF THESPIS.

BY W. H. CRANE.

THESPIS, the encyclopædias tell us, was born about 540 B. C., and is the earliest playwright mentioned in history. None of his works has descended to posterity, and probably posterity ought to be grateful. He was a Greek, and, if we may believe the scholarly opinion of Miss Clara Morris, who contributed a clever monograph on the drama to a popular magazine last autumn, the fewer we have of Greek plays the better. But the only relevancy of Thespis to the topic of this paper consists in this, that we actors are to this day universally styled Thespians, and that while the players of his dramas roamed over the country in carts, carrying their stage with them wherever they went, and were confined to a pretty peninsula jutting out from a lost corner of Europe, we Thespians of to day cover in our journeys an immense empire, thousands of miles in extent and inhabited by the most restlessly intellectual and critically exacting people on the face of the earth.

There are now in the United States between twenty-five and twenty-eight hundred theatres and opera houses, of which the great majority are open to date-engagements, extending over various periods of time, from one night to a week, and, in some cases, a series of weeks. Such theatres exist in New York City, notably the " Grand Opera House " and the " People's," on whose boards plays run one week each, and no more. But when we leave the large cities, we find that every theatre is open to dates, and that very few towns support stock companies which can satisfy audiences through a season of forty weeks. In fact, the stock-company theatres in the great city of New York can be numbered on the fingers of one hand ; and in the other large cities of the United States they are hardly a factor in the composition of our dramatic entertainment. The American stage has become essentially peripatetic, as much so as the petty stage that delighted the rustics of Bœotia or Attica who stood with gaping mouths and attent ears about the carts of Thespis.

This fact is a natural result of an evolution which could have been foretold by any one who had made a proper estimate of the American character at the time when the urban population of the United States began to take on its extraordinary growth. Political economists tell us that the ratio of town dwellers to farm dwellers in the United States has greatly changed during the last three or four decades, and is still changing, and in the same direction, so that, whereas it might have been at one time as one to seven, it is now more like three to seven. One-half of the inhabitants of the State of New York live in cities, or in towns that are ambitious to become cities. These urban communities cannot support well-drilled stock companies, but they crave the service of good actors and the production of the best plays of the period ; and it is a necessary consequence of our social scheme that what is wanted by any community that is able to pay for the satisfaction of its wants is certain to arrive. The mountain cannot come to Mahomet, therefore Mahomet goes to the mountain. Chicago cannot go to Paris to shudder with, and at, Bernhardt, therefore Bernhardt goes to Chicago, and "Fedora" and " Camille " become as real in some edifice built on what was recently an Illinois prairie as on the stage of the Théâtre Français. This illustration serves for the entire phenomenon. We may say of the American people, as Juvenal said of the Greeks of the time of Nero, "The whole nation is a travelling actor." At all hours of the twenty-four, railway trains are carrying companies of actors from one town to another, and new bills are being posted for each one of twenty-five hundred theatres.

The stars of the modern American stage do not, indeed, "shoot madly from their spheres," but their orbits are as varied, as constant, and nearly as rapid, as those of the cometic stars that, from time to time, adorn the skies. For them there is neither fixity nor rest, except during the languorous days of summer among the mountains or on the seashore. From September to June they shoot hither and thither, not as Goethe sings, "without haste, yet without rest," but (in sober verity) with great and anxious haste, and with no thought of present rest.

The members of a company must be collected at stated times, which wait for no man and hardly for a leading lady; railway trains must be boarded on the minute, nor will conductors cause a "lightning express" to tarry even to suit the tardy convenience of a Booth or a Bernhardt. It is these exigencies and anxieties, we say to one another, that wear us out before our time; and yet somehow we do not, as a matter of fact, wear out much sooner than others of our fellow beings, and many of our excellent actors whose lives are passed upon the road are in sound health and activity well up into the sixties.

The make-up of the numerous theatrical companies that annually take the road is not in the slightest degree that "fortuitous concourse of atoms" to which certain materialistic philosophers are wise enough to attribute the composition of the Universe. Every large city has dramatic agencies, on whose books actors of both sexes are entered and classified. From June to September, while the artists rest, the agencies are busy in mapping out the routes for the coming season. If an inexperienced person with some money, less knowledge, and a vast ambition to reap a harvest of fame and United States currency, visits an agency, he finds himself in possession of an option on talent of all descriptions, tragic, comic, farcical, musical, emotional, saltatory,—in a profusion surpassing his wildest dreams.

When he is brought face to face with the possessors of these gifts, the prospective manager is delighted to find that he has at command absolutely the best representatives of the modern drama. The moment is a golden one; a fortunate combination of circumstances has placed in his grasp an opportunity which could not have been foreseen, and may never occur again. An unequalled leading juvenile, whose press-notices are spread before him in quantities sufficient to fill a Saratoga trunk, happens at this precise moment to be disengaged. His usual salary has been three hundred a week, but, in consideration of the esteem in which he holds the prospective manager, he is willing to contract with this gentleman for the season on the basis of one hundred, of which four weeks are to be paid in advance, and charged to the last month of the season. The most brilliant lady in America (see her press-notices); the most talented second lady; the wittiest soubrette (press-notices again); the most accomplished all-round versatile (see press-notices as to his renditions, whether of *Bob Acres* or the heavy father in "Hazel Kirke"); all these, together with the customary component parts of such a company as is required to make the proposed route an unqualified and unprecedented success, are bubbling over with the same esteem for the new manager, the same willingness to accept scaled-down salaries, and to receive four weeks pay in advance. There are absolutely no limits to their genius, their enthusiasm, and to their well-founded expectations touching the drafts which they will enable their fortunate director to make on the purses of the expectant public.

The reader can foretell with tolerable accuracy the destinies of such undertakings, so managed. If they were to succeed, it would compel a revision of all current theories of probabilities and, perhaps, of possibilities. It is computed by experienced theatrical managers and speculators that about one-half of the travelling dramatic companies lose money during each season. More than one-half of these companies are conducted over their routes by practised managers, who have been in the business long enough to know what to do and what to avoid doing ; what leaks to stop ; what means to take of "working the press"; to bill towns in advance ; to enlist the good words of prominent people ;— yet some of these experienced men fail to make money. And we may therefore assert that every beginner who forms a company out of the material in the dramatic market and starts out on the road with it is sure to lose all that he invests. It is quite on the cards also that after he has lost all his money, he will continue to play the desperate game on credit, and wind up with the sheriff in the box office and the wardrobes of his company held for board. Such exhibitions of human folly occur every year in large number and with monotonous regularity, and each one has a humorous as well as a melancholy side. We are compelled to smile at the simplicity of the man who puts faith in rural press-clippings from which all unfavorable criticisms are carefully excluded, and in the self-laudations of artists out of a job ; while we lament that the earnings of years in some obscure but useful employment should be dissipated in a few weeks devoted to a vain search for renown and money. A philosopher who neither laughs nor weeps, but who observes human affairs calmly, notices with satisfaction that the funds thus scattered are not wasted ; they swell the revenues of useful railways and local hotels ; and there are worse methods of spending money than in lining the pockets of unapplauded actors, since these are not wholly depraved, and may come in time to praise themselves less, and to deserve that the public should praise them more.

Unsuccessful ventures imply that successful ventures exist, and they therefore are the results of imitation attempted with insufficient or unsuitable material. Their fatal no-logic consists in this, that, whereas good dramatic companies are well compensated, therefore bad ones will be. Thrown into the form of a syllogism, the argument would read as follows:

A. B., the manager of the celebrated star, Mr. Blank, cleared forty thousand dollars on the road last season with a trained company whose capacities were well known to him.—I propose to start out this season without a celebrated star, and with a company hastily put together, touching whose capacities I am experimentally ignorant. *Therefore,* I expect to clear forty thousand dollars.

The absurdity of this conclusion is so obvious that we are compelled to believe one of two things : either that the unlucky speculators do not reason over the matter at all ; or that they proceed on the supposition that the inhabitants of our interior towns are so greedy for entertainment that they will readily accept whatever shows travelling managers choose to bring them. And perhaps the motive power behind all these dramatic failures is a combination of the stupidity and the false hypothesis which we have depicted.

"Against stupidity even the gods themselves fight in vain," says the German poet, and if the gods give it up, we certainly must. But as to this hypothesis that the audiences of the American inland are not good judges of dramatic performances, we may be pardoned a few words that may not be wholly useless.

A thousand people, from the age of sixteen upwards, in an interior town, of the class that can afford good seats at the theatre, are, in the aggregate, better read in dramatic and general literature, and have more clearly defined theories of intellectual enjoyment, than a thousand people taken in mass from the parquette and balcony of a New York theatre on any given evening. This is assertion, but it is based on sound reason. People in the interior do not work so hard, they think more, they read more, they discuss current and literary topics more thoroughly. Life with them is not a constant excitement ; not a round of excesses, both in pleasure and business, as the case is with the wealthier portions of the population of a metropolis. Magazine editors tell us that rural readers are not only the mainstay of these periodicals, but that they are the most critical and appreciative. People in great cities are too busy to criticise dramatic performances ; they go to the theatre to be amused, and their subsequent comments amount to nothing more than vague expressions of superficial opinion. The writers of the dramatic columns in the morning journals are paid to criticise plays and players, and it is easier to echo these practised scribes than to frame new theories.

Charles Dickens illustrates this condition in "Nicholas Nickleby." Nicholas, during his career as an actor, visits sundry citizens of Portsmouth in order to sell tickets for a benefit. One of the Portsmouth *bourgeoisie* buys tickets in order to encourage the Drama, of whose decadence he speaks in melancholy terms, just as many people do to-day, and earnestly begs the young actor to do all in his power to restore that veneration and regard for the "Unities of the Drama," whose welfare ought to be dear to all playgoers. Here is a rural shop-keeper who knew what the "Unities" are. If you were to take your note-book to-night and interview all the people in the parquette of "Palmer's," "Daly's," or the "Star," what sort of answers would you write down as to what the "Unities" are ? And yet whole folios have been written to enunciate the principle that adherence to the "Unities" is the first law of a symmetrical play.

All over the United States the people of the towns know what good acting is, and they know who the good actors are, and what the good plays of the period are, and they expect to get the good plays represented by the good actors, and staged and acted in the best manner, and nothing short of this triple combination will satisfy them. And when this combination is accomplished, there is no talk among the members of the company about attachments at the box-office or counting the railway ties on the journey home. Success is mapped out as an accomplished fact, as clearly as the proposed route ; and the manager may count with certitude on the expected profits of the season. This certitude obtains in the case of numerous companies whom it would be invidious to name, although we may say that in each of these cases the play is of distinguished merit and the star is famous. In short, the interior public demands renowned stars in renowned plays.

The star-system has been much criticised and often condemned, but it is worth while to pause before we criticise and condemn established facts that are the product of natural evolution. Certainly, when we go to see and hear "Hamlet," we wish to have the exhibition as good as it is possible to make it. But whoever represents *Hamlet* to us with fidelity and genius is entitled to the name of a star. This designation is not one that is affixed at will to an artist; it attaches itself to him from the nature of the case ; he is a star, therefore he is styled one.

That people should wish to see a distinguished artist in a play of undoubted merit and attractiveness, in the rendition of the principal character in which he has shown himself to be specially qualified, is perfectly natural and proper ; and this wish is the basis of the success of the star-system, which is now so firmly incorporated with our dramatic destinies, that our great actors have come to look upon New York city as a mere incident in a season of forty weeks, and as entitled to receive its proportion of time relatively to the other towns of the United States,—say one-twentieth, and not much more.

The better-class audiences of the towns of the United States will not tolerate inferior plays by inferior actors ; and those who believe that they will, and who act on that belief, will soon discover their mistake. Nor does it ever answer for the best companies to cut out vital portions of plays in order to shorten the hours, or to introduce gags, whether local or not. The path of safety and success lies in the direction of scrupulous respect to an approved text of the play, and an earnest endeavor all through the performance to do and say with the utmost care and artistic finish all that is to be done and said.

That the travelling-star system magnifies the personal qualities of the actor at the expense of the literary quality of the drama is an unfounded conclusion. Dramatic composition follows fashions, and those fashions are the product of their times. The Shakesperian drama is conspicuous by its illustrations of great passions, such as jealousy, in "Othello," and reckless ambition, as in "Macbeth ;" and in no plays that have since been written has there been greater room for the display of genius in the prominent rôles, that is, for the star actor. In the drama of the Restoration and that of the last century in England, when all good English acting was confined to the stock companies of London, and all provincial troupes were mere gaugs of barn-stormers, the interest and plot depend upon the combination of character, not upon the relations of any single one to the rest. In the "School for Scandal" nearly every one of the characters is required to be impersonated by a fairly good artist, and the comedy goes off well even when none of the artists rises above that level. Such is not the fashion of the present day. In the great majority of the plays which command success throughout the United States, one conspicuously good, and therefore celebrated, artist is the pivotal figure ; the drama centres in him or her, and the execution must be commensurate. What would be said of a fairly good *Camille,* a fairly good *Fedora,* a fairly good *Hamlet ?* These are the *Camilles, Fedoras,* and *Hamlets* that fail ; but a fairly good *Charles Surface* is not a failure, because, even if he "come tardy off," we still have left the glitter and blaze and wit of the other characters, the sophisms of *Joseph,* the baleful advocacies of *Mrs. Candor,* the sneers of the *Backbites.* But the "School for Scandal" is not a play to take on the road ; nor is any play fit for this purpose if it has been originally constructed for a stock company.

We are not forecasting in this paper the future of our Drama, but we think we are safe in saying that stock companies will be during a long period (in the United States) the exception rather than the rule ; that the best and most popular plays will be, like the works of Sardou, written with reference to star-acting of an emotional or humorous type, and of the highest attainable degree of excellence. In many of our American towns audiences may not become more critical and exacting, but the number of towns in which audiences shall be critical and exacting will during many years constantly increase. The system of travelling companies will become more solidified, and, in the true acceptation of the word, scientific ; since science is only another term for the prevision of events, and the wise manager has it in his power to be in touch at all times with the dramatic taste and requirements of every town in the country, and to regulate his operations accordingly. By so doing, he elevates them from the grade of ventures to that of comparative certainties.

WILLIAM H. CRANE.

MONEY AND USURY.

BY HENRY CLEWS.

WE HAVE no record in any period of the social history of our planet when men were not in the habit of paying for the use of the property of other men. Such compensation marks the dawn of civilization—a time when it was discovered to be better to hire another man's goods or lands than to kill him for the sake of becoming their owner. An equivalent for the use of lands or buildings we style rent; for the use of chattels, hire; for the use of money, interest. One of the most noticeable facts about the last-named equivalent is that in almost all communities its amount, as related to the material for the use of which it is paid, has been made the subject of legislation. Laws have never been enacted regulating the prices of rents or of the hire of chattels, but statutes regulating the interest of money are beyond computation as to number; and their existence dates back to epochs beyond which public record and the memory of mankind run not to the contrary.

Since this is an undeniable fact, there must be a reason for its origin and its persistent vitality. May not this be the reason ?— that money not being a commodity, but the representative of all commodities, capable of passing through all metamorphoses of lands, houses, cattle, grain,—in short, of all transferable things whatsoever,—may be said to have an unchangeable value, whereas every commodity is constantly undergoing changes of value : *therefore*, while the owner of any commodity may lawfully demand any price he pleases for the use of such property, and take all he can get, the owner of money must not demand or take more than a certain price, which price shall be stated by the lawmakers of the community. This is, we think, if it be granted that money is not a commodity, the logical basis of usury laws. We do not assert that usury laws are enacted solely in order to assert a principle. As a matter of fact, they are placed on the statute-books in deference to a sentiment which is supposed to pervade the public mind, that poor people must be protected from the rapacity of money-lenders.

It will not be difficult to show that the alleged principle on which usury laws are based is illogical ; and, further, that, as a matter of fact, these laws do not prevent poor borrowers, or borrowers upon hazardous pledges, from paying high prices for the use of money. That money is not a commodity because it is the representative and summary and equivalent of all commodities is a conclusion which is not only open to doubt, but may be with reason flatly denied. That the greater includes the less is an axiom; and if money includes all commodities, it must itself be the greatest of commodities. The advocates of usury laws assert that money is merely a measure of values, and is, in fact, a yard-stick. But this definition fails to explain how it is that the amount of cloth set off by this yard-stick changes from day to day ; whereas the first essential of a measure is that it shall be uniform and unchanging. In fact, it is impossible to demonstrate that money is in any respect a " measure of value." This phrase, although much used and abused by writers on political economy, has no real meaning. There is, indeed, no measure of value except it be the general average resulting in society from the continually varying relations which commodities bear to each other in respect of prices. To-day a bushel of No. 1 winter wheat shall be exchangeable for a barrel of crude petroleum, or ten yards of sheeting, or one gold dollar ; to-morrow the same bushel of wheat shall be exchangeable for two barrels of crude petroleum, or fifteen yards of sheeting, or one gold dollar and a half. Where do we find the " measure of value " here ? And if we are baffled by this problem of four bodies, how are we to solve the problem of the four thousand bodies that compose the system of commercial products ?

We venture the opinion that money is not only an admitted equivalent for all commodities, but is itself a commodity and the greatest of commodities in this respect—that it is the most strongly desired, the most widely known, and the most universally possessed. It cannot be a measure of values, because there is no measure of values ; and the nearest approach to such a phenome-

non is the opinion of those who possess exchangeable commodities and who wish to exchange them.   And if it is not a measure of values it must be a commodity, because it is continually
made the subject of exchange all over the world.

Some writers have asserted that money is not a commodity,
because it is neither produced nor consumed.   The objection to
this statement is that the statement is not true.   Money is both
produced and consumed.   It is first dug out of the earth, and
afterward it undergoes a constant consumption by abrasion and
by being used in the arts.   It is estimated that the production
of gold keeps but slightly in advance of its consumption year by
year, while in the last twenty years the production of silver has
been much in excess of the consumption.   Therefore the relations
of gold and silver have changed.   Gold is dearer and silver is
cheapèr.   This one fact shows that the precious metals, which
by the common consent of mankind are money, are in truth commodities.   If they fail to be measures of value each of the other,
much more must either or both of them fail to be measures of
value of all other commodities.

We have dwelt at such perhaps needless length on this question of the real nature of money in order to determine the problem whether laws enacted to fix the price of the use of money
have a basis of reason, and have any more right to exist than
laws enacted to fix the price of wheat, cotton, and sugar.   Laws
of the latter class are not wholly unknown.   The ignorant and
cruel men who got into temporary power in France in 1793 enacted various statutes of this character.   There had been a bad
season, and grain and beef were scarce.   Domiciliary visits, and
the pressing attentions of numerous patriots who were anxious to
furnish a hundred heads of other people to the guillotine daily,
had made Paris an undesirable place of residence.   Consequently
such butchers and bakers as were courageous enough to do business in Paris considered themselves entitled to charge such a
profit on beef and bread as would reimburse costs of purchase
and compensate the risks of so dangerous a place of abode.   But
the Dantons and the Robespierres saw in this reasonable course
of dealing a heinous crime against the republic.   They therefore
enacted that the butchers and bakers of the municipality should
furnish so many pounds of beef and bread for so much, and no
more, in francs or assignats ; and, further, that paper assignats

should be as good as silver francs. A good many butchers and bakers went to the scaffold for disobeying these laws ; many more closed their shops or left Paris ; and the capital was on the brink of starvation when of their own accord the ruling demagogues suffered the laws to become a dead-letter. In fact, there was no alternative, since no community can thrive under laws that conflict with nature ; and if the penalty for the infraction of such laws is death, the community would soon cease to exist at all.

We thus arrive at the conclusion that the traffic in money should be free, as it is in all lawful commodities between citizens of the same commonwealth. In other words, no reason worth the name exists why a person having money which he is able to spare to the uses of others should not receive from them such compensation for its use as he and they may by contract agree upon. And all reasons urged against usury will be found to be either wholly sentimental or based upon misconceptions of the true functions of money.

Possibly if there were an inherent quality in lent money by virtue of which loans would invariably return to their owners at certain definite times, there might be a semblance of justice in limiting the rent for use, although there would then be a departure from the true principle of unfettered dealings between citizens. And in such a case there would be no occasion for usury statutes, since now in all the markets of the world the interest of loans made on absolutely the best securities is below the limit set by law. But the tendency of lent money, except upon such securities, is not to return to its owners ; on the contrary, its tendency is to remain in the hands of the borrowers, or to be dissipated by them and lost to the lenders. As securities become weaker, this tendency becomes stronger ; and where there is no security or pledge at all, loans are rarely repaid. The probabilities, therefore, on all loans, excepting those made on collaterals that are absolutely as valuable as money itself, are an infinite series of variations ; and the scale of compensation, from its own nature, is correspondingly flexible.

The rent of money in all such cases ceases to be rent pure and simple ; it is to a definite extent rent ; then to a much larger extent, insurance, since there must be losses, and the good debtors must pay for the bad ones ; then to a still larger extent, compensation for the opprobrium that an absurd sentimentalism attaches to the title of usurer, and also for the risks that the lender runs in some States of the United States, noticeably New York, of not only forfeiting the loan, but of being arrested and criminally punished for usury. In the State of New York a few years ago it was lawful to lend money at 7 per cent. and criminal to lend it at 8; it is now in the same State lawful to lend it at 6 and criminal to lend it at 7. A movement is now on foot to make it lawful to lend it at 5 and criminal to lend it at 6. If there is any reason or justice in such legislation as this, there will be just as much in finally enacting that no one shall receive any rent at all for the use of money. In fact, such a statute as this would be best for the community, since it would be wholly and universally disregarded, and would lead to practically free dealings in money.

That usury statutes do not prevent borrowers on dubious securities from accepting loans at all sorts of rates above those fixed by law may be deduced from the nature of the case itself, and may be illustrated by continually recurring facts. In the State of New York, where usury statutes are more vigorous than in other States of the Union, not only imposing forfeitures of loans, but also fine or imprisonment or both, all loans on second mortgages, chattel mortgages, unlisted stocks, and the thousand other insecurities which are constantly made the pretext for borrowing money, are negotiated at from 10 to 150 per cent. per annum. Pawnbrokers are permitted to charge 36 per cent.; and the license which the State thus grants them for a consideration shows that our legislators do not regard usury as a crime *per se,* but that it is a technical villany which one may practise to any extent so long as one pays the State for the privilege: and yet the pawnbroker can much better afford to content himself with a small percentage than the lender on unlisted stocks or on chattel mortgages. In fact, hardly any percentage is a fair equivalent for the risks run by the latter classes. Unlisted stocks are, as a whole, no more available than waste paper if the lender wishes to recoup from any other person than the borrower; and chattel mortgages are not a security at all, since the borrower retains the basis or subject of the loan in his own possession, and, although he gives, over his seal and signature, the right to the lender to enter his premises and take the alleged pledge in default of payment, yet the courts hold that it is trespass to make such an entry if the borrower chooses to shut his doors; and hardly a month passes in which holders of chattel mortgages are not arrested and locked up or held to bail, in the city of New York, for this species of trespass. Such conditions are powerful factors in determining the prices which borrowers on chattel mortgages are required to pay for the use of money. The customary practice is that the borrower agrees to repay for each ten dollars which he receives twelve dollars and a half within two or three months, or at the rate of 100 to 150 per cent. per annum.

This is not interest : it is insurance against the dishonesty of the borrower (and borrowers on such insecurities are frequently dishonest) and against arrest and criminal prosecution, since such things are of constant occurrence. People who do not want to return borrowed money find no difficulty in procuring warrants from police justices against their creditors who have agreed with them to commit usury. In fact, under the Penal Code the magistrate has no option. The statute is perfectly clear :—"A person who directly or indirectly receives any interest, discount, or consideration, upon the loan or forbearance of money, goods, or things in action, greater than is allowed by statute, is guilty of a misdemeanor." All misdemeanors are criminal, and are punishable by fine or imprisonment, or both. Hence, if a citizen swears to such a misdemeanor, the magistrate must issue a summons or warrant against the trespasser. If the majority of borrowers were base enough to avail themselves of this absurd statute, all transactions in money except on choice securities "on call" would cease ; but since only a small minority resort to the police courts to evade payment, the statute accomplishes this result : that lenders who might otherwise content themselves with 30 per cent. demand and receive 100 or 150.

People who want to borrow money on securities more or less inferior to those regarding which there is no question, have such a thorny road to travel that legislatures can do them no greater injustice than to compel them to be parties to an unlawful act, while they are simply striving to accomplish a lawful purpose. Any human being has a right to ask any other human being for a loan of money : getting it is quite another thing. One ought not, as a rule, to get it unless he offers an equivalent. All the harmonlous operations of nature result from the action of equivalents ; but the possessor of money *may* be willing to exchange its use for something that is not as good as itself, provided the risks are fairly compensated. What these risks are can never be absolutely or definitely ascertained, even by diligent research into each particular case ; but surely no persons are so well fitted to investigate and settle them as the two parties who are negotiating. Certainly there is more risk in lending money on a chattel mortgage, or a second real-estate mortgage, or a trader's note; than in lending on bar silver or government bonds ; and unreasonable borrowers are satisfied to compensate lenders for such increased risks, and lenders are not foolish enough to part with money unless they are thus compensated ; but the legislature enacts that no such difference exists, and that all parties to transactions in money must disobey the mandates of reason in order to obey the mandates of the statute-book. The statute is on a par with one which should enact that the sun must rise at the same hour every day in the year. There are inconveniences in being in dubious credit, and there are inconveniences in having short days in December ; but since both are the results of natural causes, which have always operated and will always go on operating, we submit that statutes in either case are not particularly valuable.

The path ought to be made smoother for really deserving borrowers whose securities happen to be not of a high order ; but usury statutes prevent any such amelioration, and, on the other hand, add to the natural difficulties. The lender says, with justice, to the would-be borrower : " You approach me with something which is not the equivalent of what you want to obtain from me ; further, you invite me to become an accessory to a misdemeanor that is criminally punishable in my person, but not in yours ; so that the law virtually punishes me, and pardons you, for an offence of which we are equally guilty, and thus commits a great injustice ; and, finally, you get all the benefit of the crime, and are absolved from paying what you owe, if you see fit to lodge a complaint against me in a criminal court or defend a suit in a civil court. Under such circumstances my price for the use of my money is 100 per cent. per annum." The borrower answers : " I am not the kind of person to treat any one who lends me money in the manner you mention, and my intention is to repay the loan." " Very well," replies the lender ; " it is quite possible that you are not that kind of person, and then again it is possible that you may be; at any rate, the law puts it in your power to be, and you voluntarily place yourself in a class of lawbreakers whom a wise legislature has licensed to break laws with impunity. I refuse to take chances except at the rate mentioned."

Such a borrower may be compared to an honest sailor who has been pressed into service on a pirate ship—he is voyaging in bad company, and need expect no mercy. And yet the statutes that place him in such a position are the very ones that have been enacted to improve his condition and his facilities for commerce with his fellow men !

That bodies of men chosen by their communities at home should hold sessions professedly in the interests of the people, and enact usury statutes, would be a remarkable phenomenon did we not know that nothing is remarkable in the annals of lawmaking, and that collective folly is as natural to legislative assemblies as to breathe or walk about. Said Oxenstiern : "Go forth, my son, and see with how little wisdom the world is governed." Said Napoleon : "The lawmakers of the convention of '93 were a set of idiots." History has already passed upon Napoleon's Berlin decrees and his other laws against the use of and traffic in English merchandise. The witchcraft laws of New England have died ; Quakers are no longer persecuted in Massachusetts and Connecticut ; Great Britain has abolished all usury statutes ; Connecticut has done the same, as well as many of her sister States ; they never have disfigured the statute-books of California ; but in New York, the greatest of the States, the most commercial, the richest, the State *par excellence*, where the fullest play should be given to the traffic in useful commodities, it is a crime to lend money on time at 7 per cent. per annum !

Usury statutes undoubtedly date from the days of Moses and the departure from Egypt. Exodus XXII., verses 25 and 26, enacts as follows : "If thou lend money to any of my people that is poor by thee, thou shalt not be to him as an usurer, neither shalt thou lay upon him usury. If thou at all take thy neighbor's raiment to pledge, thou shalt deliver it unto him by that the sun goeth down." This statute, however, did not forbid usury in its entirety ; it permitted the Jew to demand any rate that might suit him from the Canaanites and the Philistines. And it is an inferior justification of any unnatural law at the present age of the world that it was once in authority among the members of a tribe of ignorant people, who had just escaped from a prolonged season of servitude, and were the subjects of a sumptuary and inquisitorial legislation such as has never been equalled on this planet.

Laws that regulate the rate of interest in cases where no contract is made, or on sums that have become overdue, are natural and reasonable ; but no legislation can be seriously defended that attempts to prohibit one citizen from making any contract with another, touching useful commodities or services, which both agree to ; still less where it brands one of the contracting parties with guilt and enables the other party to rob him with impunity, and even to procure his incarceration. If we are wrong in this way of thinking, we prefer to be wrong in company with the enlightened sense of Great Britain, Connecticut, and California— to mention no others—rather than to be right in company with the antiquated sense of New York, and of the Israelites of some thousands of years ago, just escaped from servitude under the Egyptians.

HENRY CLEWS.

THE OLYMPIAN RELIGION.

II.—OUTLINE OF ITS PARTICULARS.

BY THE RIGHT HONORABLE WILLIAM EWART GLADSTONE

I HAVE already referred in the two previous articles to the sources and authorship of the Olympian religion. In this and the succeeding article I shall examine its particulars, with only one preliminary observation. For the present purpose it should be viewed apart from the forms which it had assumed in the historic period, and from the religion of the Italian peninsula.

What, we have to ask, was the substance of this Olympian religion? what was its pervading character? and what were its leading and governing details? It seems, at first sight, as if it could be principally described by negatives. For example: in the Achaian army before Troy, and in the Greek peninsula at the period of the "Troica," we have no sign of the great institution of Priesthood. Nor did priests, in the historic period, ever become a real power in Greek society, although the office continued to be one of dignity. Again: as there was no priestly order, so there were no sacred Books. If we consider how in the two great divisions of Latin Christendom, respectively, the priesthood and the Bible supply the most powerful of all living forms, we shall be able to see how much this double negation means. There was not, indeed, any collective organization; or any provision for unity; or any moral code; or any standing office of instruction for those who professed the religion, either in their youth or in mature age. There were sacrifices, greater and smaller, which were offered originally by the king, or in private by the head of the house. These we may consider, on one side, as a kind of bribe to the gods; but, on the other hand, and for the better minds, they had in them an element of reverence and piety. There were prayers, limited indeed and jejune as compared with the prayers of the gospel, but yet, in Homer's time, of frequent practice, and of some disciplinary and educative power. Certain points of natural morality were very strongly recognized by men : the care of the supreme god* for the suppliant and the supplicant, which thus far made weakness a sacred thing ; the tenderness and regard† which every man had for his wife ; the strong and even fastidious sense of personal decency ; the stringent law of incest and an utter estrangement from all offences contrary to nature.

In truth, and without exaggeration, the extreme forms of sin, some of them still rampant even in Christian countries, may be said to have been unknown among the Achaian Greeks, as they are represented in the Homeric Poems. All these points, here summarily stated, deserve a careful examination. There were also the sacredness of the oath, the inviolability of marriage, the respect paid to age ; which were, each in its degree, props to religion. But over and above all these, it is plain, when we contemplate the Achaian mind and life, that religion was, at the Homeric period, a present, familiar, and active idea in the common life of the common man. It came spontaneously to the front in every serious occasion of existence. The religious man was also the man socially and morally good. Humanity, in its youth, had not licensed the odious art of setting up abstract opinions, or professions of belief, as substitutes for right conduct, or apologies for its absence. The idea of a divine power, whether conceived in the singular or the plural, and although subsisting in a most imperfect shape, was, I think, nearer to the still childlike mind of the Achaian Greek than it is under the rule of a far purer creed, when life has become so much more complex and artificial. Of course I make an exception of those who have made the things unseen a matter of serious personal concern for themselves, to live and to die by. The Olympian scheme may have become for the Romans, in the main, an instrument of civil government ; for the average educated Greek of the classical period little better than a shadow ; but there still lingered something of an archaic sincerity about the Homeric system. As a religion it was indeed weak, narrow, and inadequate ; from some points of view even dangerous because seductive ; yet, after all, it was a religion.

In two important points the religion was particularly weak. One of these was its relation to a future life. The delineation of the Under-world in the " Odyssey," though it rises high at times in

* Il., XIII., 624; XXI., 75. Od., IX., 270; XVI., 422.   † Il., IX., 341.

poetical excellence, and abounds in characteristic touches, appears to be based entirely upon foreign, and perhaps principally Egyptian, traditions, which it enfeebles in their most essential points. It is gloomy and dreary, hopeless and helpless ; but it does not present to us any picture of actual retribution except in the cases of two persons, Tantalos and Sisuphos, of foreign extraction and probably foreign birth.* Tituos and Orion are also here, but neither of them is to be considered as akin to the Achaians. Minos † administers justice among the dead (*themist-euei*) apparently as a judge would in a human community. Heracles appears in sorry plight, but it is his Shade only, and he himself is among the Immortals. Upon the whole, there is not given, for the Achaians, any connection between general conduct and future happiness or misery ; and when Menelaos ‡ receives the promise of a state of bliss, it is not for his virtues, which seem to have been great, but because he is the husband of Helen, and the son-in-law of Zeus.

This doctrine of a future life, feeble in Homer, and without effective sanction, becomes wholly ineffective in historic Greece. But there is one marked exception supplied by the Poet in the case of what may be termed political perjury. For here the Powers that ruled below are invited to inflict the vengeance ; and on this occasion only are Nature-powers invoked by the Achaians, because their general residence, according to the poet, is in the Under-world. Tartaros itself appears to have been a place for the punishment of gods guilty of rebellion, in conjunction with whom it is particularly named. But although in the case of political perjury the tie between the two worlds is recognized,§ the Poet does not anywhere venture upon applying the doctrine by specifying any person as having suffered, or as being about to suffer, the punishment.

Upon the whole, in respect to the doctrine of a future life, the Olympian system takes its place far beneath older religions, especially those exhibited in the Zendavesta and the Egyptian monuments. It can hardly be affirmed, as respects the second point I have to name, that the comparison with Asia, even including the Hebrews, or with Egypt, is similarly disadvantageous to Achaian religion. It is the profoundly important point of sexual morality. In the " Iliad " monogamy is geographically separated from polygamy by the Hellespont ; and I

* Od., XI., 582-600. † Od., XI., 563. ‡ Od., IV., 563-569. § Il., III., 278 ; XIX., 259.

suppose it is to be assumed that under this head a monogamous people probably stood higher, in conception and in practice, than one which had polygamy practically exhibited before its eyes as a recognized institution. It is, however, obvious that among the Achaian Greeks there was no fixed restraint upon licentiousness of the ordinary kind, unless it were within the bond of marriage. The concubines of many chieftains before Troy are named in the "Iliad"; and when Briseïs (herself a substitute for the daughter of Chruses) is taken away from Achilles, another substitute is supplied for his bed.* But Agamemnon does not rest upon the plea of long-continued absence from home when he announces his intention to install the daughter of Chruses as a mistress at his palace in Argos, despite the claims of Klutaimnestra.† Further, we learn that, when Eurucleia was purchased by Laertes, there was no unlawful connection between them, because, and as it seems only "because, he eschewed the resentment of his wife." ‡ On the other hand, the illicit relations between a portion of the women servants in the palace of Odysseus and the Suitors are mentioned among the justifying causes for putting them all to an ignominious death.§ Speaking more generally, it cannot be doubted that the common idea of marriage in the Poems, probably in harmony with the general practice, is elevated and pure. Except where an idea of that description was prevalent, such a scene as the sixth "Iliad" gives us between Hector and Andromachè could hardly have been conceived; and much less could the wonderful history and character of Penelopè.

It may, however, be said that, viewing the licentiousness of many among the divinities, we can give no credit to the religion for any actual or relative chastity found among the Achaians. Undoubtedly the moral law had less application, under the Olympian system, to those divinities than to men. But we must always bear in mind not only that there were models of strict purity among them, but that we must distinguish between the mythological incidents of the scheme and a true religious heart, quite out of keeping with those incidents, which had not yet ceased to beat within it. It may still remain a question whether the superiority over the Trojans in regard to sexual license, which is traceable

---

* Il., IX., 663-665.   † Il., I., 29-31; 109-115.   ‡ Od., I., 430-433.   § Od., XXII., 440-445; 462-644.

in the Poems, may have been largely due to that principle of self-command, or *sophrosunè*, which was so deeply imbedded in the Grecian character.

There are, in effect, three characteristics to which I attach especial weight as proving of themselves that the Olympian scheme of Homer exhibits a real and practical, though an imperfect, and not only an imperfect, but at certain points a contaminated, religion.

Firstly, it embodies the doctrine of Providence, or an actual divine government in human affairs ; not only as worked by the gods, but also as recognized by and familiar to the minds of men.

Secondly, it exhibits a constant resort to prayer in present emergencies. This practice does not extend to a concern with remote events ; and the prayer is in most cases limited to the needs or aims of the person who offers it. If it be a public prayer, then, of course, it embraces collectively the case of all those whom the person offering it may represent.

Beyond this, it seems clear that there was an act of worship not only in the sacrificial feasts, but at every meal or entertainment, at the least where animal food was used.*

Thirdly, it appears that worship and moral conduct were regarded as having some real connection one with the other. The virtue specially religious was the care of the suppliant and the stranger ; but the *theoudès*, the devout or pious man, is never a man of wicked life, and the case of Hector may be taken as one which exhibits liberality to the gods in sacrifice as suitably associated with affectionate, upright, and warmly patriotic character.

If we look beneath the surface, the affairs of this world are, in truth, governed, according to the poems, by the interplay of three agencies. These are : (*a*) the gods ; (*b*) destiny ; (*c*) human will. And the acts of men and events of life are the resultant, to use the phrase of mechanics, from these competing forces, each of which is real, and acts upon, and is limited by, the others.

The limit on the power of gods is exhibited by Telemachos, when Nestor has suggested that, with Athenè's aid, he might be able to give the Suitors something else to think about than wedding or wooing Penelopè. " Ah, no," replies † the rather feeble-minded youth, " that is indeed a great affair, and not within the compass of my hope ; no, not though the gods should will it."

* Il., IX., 206-221, and Od., XIV., 435.   † Od., III., 225—228.

Here he manifestly is not thinking of any obstacle which destiny might offer, but of the strength of the Suitors, which gods could not overcome, or else of the lack of strength in himself, which they could not sufficiently supply. For this Athenè (as Mentor) rebukes him, and holds that the thing can be done ; but immediately proceeds to bring into view that other limitation : " impartial, all-sweeping death cannot be warded away by gods, even from their favorites, when the hour has sounded for the destiny of natural dissolution to take effect." * Again, Telemachos replies : " Think not of saving Odysseus ; already the Immortals have designed death and dark fate for him." † Here we have the three powers shown in separate action, and finally one of them overcome by the action of the other two.

Destiny may overcome man ; or, again, man may overcome destiny.‡ Destiny may be too strong § even for god and man united. Again, gods or a god may overcome man ; but nowhere do we find that man overcomes a recognized Achaian god. Especially the combination of god and destiny, the *moira theou*, can bring about the strangest falls, such as that of Queen Klutaimnestra, who was good before she yielded to the great temptation, enhanced, probably, by her resentment. ‖

Again, the very highest divine power, represented in Zeus, may set destiny aside and overrule it ;¶ but it is an extreme exercise of prerogative, and will not be approved by the Court of the Olympian heaven.

Great advantage has been obtained, in the study of prehistoric religions, from tracing the roots of the names given to the several divinities. While the Homeric poems offer remarkable facilities for establishing the connection of religion with ethnography, it must be admitted that, with regard to the significations of names, they furnish us with little assistance by well-established conclusions as regards the principal or properly-Olympian deities, if we except the single case of Zeus, on account of his affinity with Dyæus. According to the accounts given by Herodotos, most of the names were derived from Egypt ; the remainder from the Pelasgians, excepting that of Poseidon, which he conceives to be Libyan.** He perhaps had in view the names of Phta for Hephaistos, and that of Neith for Athenè, which seem, how-

* Od., 230-238.   † Ibid., 240-242.   ‡ Il., XVI., 730.   § Od., III., 227-228.   ‖ I'd.,
III., 265, 266.   ¶ Il., XVI., 441.   ** Herod., II., 50.

ever, to be disputed. What others he meant to indicate it is hard to say. Among the names he excepts is that of Themis. But Themis appears to have been Themsi, the Egyptian goddess of justice.* He seems to be right in saying that some of those names were derived from the Pelasgians, whom we may presume to be largely represented by the Albanians of the present day ;† a race never Hellenized like their congeners farther south in the peninsula. Hahn, in his " Albanesische Studien," traces etymologically to the primitive tongue of the country the names of Zeus, Demeter, Okeanos, Thetis, Helios, Rhea, Kronos. Not one of these, except the first, belongs to the grand living and working thearchy of Homer. Hahn also gives a root for Themis,‡ which means saying or speaking, but this is far less probable than Wilkinson's suggestion drawn from an Egyptian source.§

If we find a root for Zeus both in Indian and in Albanian speech, this, as far as it goes, tends to show that the deity was worshipped over wide spaces, and among nations which had long lost all connection one with another ; and even suggests, that his name may have been the representation of a deity single and supreme.

We have seen that Hahn gives the names of six other deities mentioned in Homer.‖ It is remarkable that here he confirms the evidence of the Poems, for every one of them appears there in connection, not with the Olympian system, but with the dynasties of what Mr. Grote has called the foretime.

Who, then, were the individual deities, that inhabited the palaces constructed for them by the skill of Hephaistos within the folds of Olympos ? ¶

We must discard, in answering this question, all regard to the number twelve, which, if warranted by Latin traditions, has no place in the scheme of Homer. The only numerical indication he has given us is that Thetis, on her visit to Hephaistos, finds that deity engaged in constructing twenty automatic chairs or

---

*Wilkinson, in Rawlinson's " Herodotos," II., 92.

† Hahn, p. 234.

‡ Rawlinson's " Ancient Religions," p. 98. Max Müller's "Science of Religion," Lecture III., pp. 171, seqq.

§ Rawlinson, pp. 136, 137. Also Max Müller.

‖ Hahn deals with other names which do not appear in Homer, and refers to Athenè, but without any clear sign that the name is of Pelasgian derivation. Hahn, Alb. Stud. Hept I., Abschn. IV., p. 253,

¶ Il., I., 607,

stools for use by the gods in the Olympian court. But this limit,
although one of number, does not admit of a clear and deter-
minate verification.   Towards making out a list, however, I offer
the following observations :

1. The five really great gods, with whom there is no other
that can compare in ruling powers, are Zeus, Heré, Poseidon,
Apollo, and Athenè.

2. Next come the deities whom the Poet himself represents to
us as usually present in Olympos among the assembled Immortals.
These are Hephaistos,* Arès,† Hermes,‡ Iris,§ Leto,‖ Artemis,¶
Themis,** Aphroditè,†† Dionè,‡‡ Paieon,§§ Hebè.‖‖ Thus far
we have sixteen occupants for the twenty seats.

Helios also is introduced (Od., XII., 376) as addressing Zeus
and the body of the Immortals ; but this is in the outer Zone of
the " Odyssey," and even the name of Olympos is carefully
avoided in the passage.

We have thus far the number of sixteen. There are others with
claims more or less obscured : Demeter, Persephonè, Dionusos, and
Thetis, who is of low rank, but is a most important personage in
the " Iliad." Aidoneus, on account of his rank in the Triad, can
hardly be excluded, though he has not the active ruling powers of
Persephonè. And Heracles is said (Od., XI., 503) to join in the
banquets of the gods, and to be mated with Hebè, an undoubted
Olympian. Histiè might also be named, but her personality is
faint : she is only mentioned, I think, four times, and always, as
Ouranos is, by way of attestation.¶¶ On the whole, the number of
the Homeric Olympians seems to oscillate from a little below
to a little above the number twenty. And twenty was a small
number, compared with the crowds of those who ruled in the
various orders of the Assyrian and Egyptian systems, of either
of which it is very possible that Homer may have had some
inkling. But it is probable that he was not unwilling to be in
this matter somewhat indeterminate. Accommodation was of the
essence of his method, and accommodation involved much compromise. He was content to use his deities as the purpose of
his poems required, and he did not need to be prepared with an

---

* Il , I., 571.   † V., 368, 369 ; XIII., 523.   ‡ Il., XXIV., 334; Od., V., 3. 28.
§ Il., XXIV., 77, 144.   ‖ Il., V., 447.   ¶ Ibid.   ** Il., XV., 93.   †† Il., V., 421,
427.   ‡‡ Il., V., 370.   §§ Ibid., 899.   ‖‖ Il., IV., 2; V., 905.   ¶¶ Od., XIV., 159,
et alibi.

aye or no upon the exact rank of each in a system compounded of the materials supplied to his hand by heterogeneous nationalities. So much for the Olympian gods, properly to be so called. Partly in the background, partly in the lower levels of the scheme, partly upon the wings of purely poetic figure, the following preternatural entities fill up the scheme of Homer :

1. The Nature-powers, who, on great occasions are (except Okeanos) summoned to the great chapter, or general assembly, of the upper world.

2. Foreign deities wholly unassimilated, such as Kirkè, Calupso, Proteus, Amphitritè, the Seirenes, Ino Leucotheè, a damsel deified for Amphitritè's domain ; Atlas, Eidotheè.*

3. Ministers of justice or of doom : Erinues, Kères, Harpuiai.

4. Powers directive of human fortunes : Moira, Moros,† Aisa, Kèr (the singular being most commonly used in this connection), Kataclothes.

5. Purely figurative and poetical conceptions : Dream (Oneiros), Sleep (Hupnos), Death (Thanatos), Terror (Phobos), Panic (Deimos), Strife (Eris), Rumor (Ossa), and the like.

Some of these shadowy personages come nearer than others to full impersonation. Eris, for example, is the mistress and the sister of Arès (Il., IV., 440) ; and she is also despatched by Zeus (Il., XI., 2–12) to stir the army to battle by her shouting. And Hupnos (Sleep) not only joins with his brother Thanatos (Death) in transporting the dead Sarpedon to his home, but is bribed, by the promise of a wife from Herè, to undertake his hazardous operation upon Zeus (Il., XIV., 267, seqq., and XVI., 682). On the more gracious side of these subjects, we have the slightly-drawn figures of the Charites, and of the Muses, who bear the high title of daughters of Zeus (Il., II., 491) and officiate at Olympian banquets (Il., I., 604), but who perhaps derive their chief importance from the invocations of the poets.

6. Finally, we have, in dark shadow, the presentation of the rebel powers in the supernatural world. These are the Titans, who dwell in Tartaros, or under it, with Kronos for their companion and their chief (Il., XIV., 203, 274; XV., 225). And with them come the Giants ; about whom we only know that they were plunged into ruin, and that they were of the kindred of Poseidon

---

* Od., V., 335.

† Moros may perhaps be defined as Moira, less the element of personality.

(Od., VII., 59, 60; X., 205, 206). Most of these figures are faintly sketched upon a remote background, and it is hard to say whether we are to take them as persons or not.

Important distinctions of quality and prerogative are to be observed even among the Olympian divinities most properly so called. One chief line of cleavage is between the five great deities and the rest of the band. The preëminence of these five cannot be too carefully borne in mind.

1. They are (with differences among themselves) differently related to the conditions of time and space.

2. They are never subjected, in the Poems, to palpable defeat or disparagement.

3. They take part providentially, rather than corporally, in the direction of human affairs. But this rule has exceptions ; such, for example, as the action of Poseidon in the fourteenth and fifteenth books of the "Iliad."

4. They do not enter visibly into battles of men (Il., XIV., 386).

5. In the Theomachy, they have no conflict among themselves.

6. Their power is not absolutely limited to a particular function or department.

7. No one of them has individually any concern with food or drink, except as to their satisfaction in the reek of sacrifice. Consider, on the other hand, the case of Sleep in Il., XIV., 241, and more conspicuously that of Hermes, who enjoys, after his long flight, ambrosia and nectar in the grotto of Calupso. (See Od., III., 92–96.)

8. The deities below the line are not, as a rule, made the objects of special prayer from mortals. The case of Artemis, in Od., XX., 61, will require a separate discussion.

9. Among the common distinctions of the five, however, we cannot include a higher moral standard as belonging to the class.

But all the Olympian deities, above as well as below the line, are subject to the general conditions of theanthropism. Corporally they alike bear the human form. (See, for example, Il., II., 476–479, where this is given to Zeus, Arès, and Poseidon.) Mentally, they have a like equipment of human faculties and propensities, on a scale generally enlarged.

There are also distinctions of power, and otherwise, even among these five greater gods. In sheer power Zeus is manifestly superior to any other deity singly (Il., VIII., 208–211 ; XV., 136); while, as between him and the aggregate, or a powerful combination, the question may be said to rest in doubt. Upon the whole, however, the five are linked together by power more than any other single attribute. They differ very much both in moral and in intellectual characteristics. They differ also in point of ethnographical relations. Athenè' and Apollo may be said, in many important respects, to form a class apart.

The assembling of the gods constitutes a marked feature in the Homeric system.

The forms of this assembling were various. In a certain sense, they were perpetually in company one of another, by virtue of their habitual residence on Olympos. As, for example, the colloquy of Zeus and Thetis is followed by his going to his own palace (Il., I., 533); but all the gods rise up to receive him on his arrival, which implies that they were in some sense assembled. Then follows a spirited conversation, with a full-formed entertainment for its sequel. Again, in the seventh book, when the Achaians proceed to raise a bulwark for the ships, the proceeding is observed from Olympos and a conversation of gods takes place (VII., 443–464).*

Neither of these meetings was an *agorè* properly so called. But in Il., IV., 1, the gods appear as sitting in *agorè* (ἠγορόωντο), and in Il.,VIII., 2, Zeus constituted or appointed an *agorè* (ἀγορὴν ποιήσατο). This *agorè* of the gods is like the *boulè* or council among men. The numbers gathered are small, and under ordinary circumstances there is no formal summoning. But, on the great occasion preceding the Theomachy, a general assembly of Immortals of all classes is held, and the Nature-powers appear, down to the humblest. Okeanos alone receives no summons, and it seems that respect for his seniority, and a reverence due to him as the source of the whole divine order, saved him from being called to a meeting where there was no place vacant for his influence. Themis† is the agent employed by Zeus to call the deities together.

There is room for criticism on the mode in which this incident has been presented. The great Assembly, thus formally called together, when it is gathered does not deliberate, but fights. Further, its members do not all fight, but only a few.‡ Next,

---

* See also Il.· VIII., 36; XIV., 224; XV., 84.   † Il., XX., 4.   ‡ Il., XX., 31–40.

of those who are in the fight, one, namely Aphroditè, never makes an appearance in the embattled rank, but only leads the defeated Arès off the field.* Again, this Assembly has no influence whatever on the issue of the war ; for that issue had been determined and decreed long before. And, lastly, of the five divinities combatant on the Trojan side, there are two, Apollo and Leto, whom the poet never subjects to any disparagement : consequently, in these cases, pleas have to be found by which a contest is avoided. There remain three deities to be disposed of ; two of the partisans of Troy, namely, Arès, the opponent of Athenè in the war, and Artemis (who in Troas seems clearly to be the Earth-goddess afterwards worshipped at Ephesus), are ignominiously defeated. The River-god Xanthos is also worsted, but with more honor. In the Poems generally, Homer has represented only Olympian debates and differences. But here he seems to deal with the cults of the two countries as they are exhibited in the human sphere, and we see the earthy religion of Troas smitten to the ground before the more refined and intellectual scheme which the Poet has elaborated for his nation.

But this is an exceptional case. The regular *agorai* come to practical conclusions, though the concurrence of the Court is usually conveyed only by a tacit assent.

In the third Book of the " Iliad,"† Athenè carries from the divine Assembly the commission under which she suggests to Pandaros that he should break the solemn pact of the two nations. This proceeding no doubt ministers to the accomplishment of the grand plot such as it has been arranged with Thetis, but it is the only suggestion of an immoral act which ever grows out of the meeting of an Olympian council. In the eighth Book, the injunction of non-interference by Zeus is received with general acquiescence, only Athenè murmuring, and obtaining from him something which approaches to a mitigating clause.‡ In the first " Odyssey " the whole plan for the relief and return of Odysseus is stated and adopted ; Poseidon, who is the only god otherwise minded, absenting himself.§

From the simple fact that there were assemblies of the gods, it appears that they constituted a polity of some kind.

A monarchy, strictly so called, can hardly be regarded as a polity, so far as regards the relation between the monarch and the

---

* Il., XXI., 416.   † III., 68-73.   ‡ VIII., 10-12, 28-40.   § Od., I, 76-95.

other members of the community; although the monarch may establish a real polity as among those members themselves, and as between the classes which they may compose. But the Olympian scheme was no pure monarchy in the sense I have described.

We may test the position of Zeus principally in two ways. First, by the amount of his ultimate coercive power in relation to the other divinities. Secondly, by finding an answer to the question whether the plots of the two great Poems were accomplished conformably to his mind and will.

Both require examination in detail. As to the first, we have seen that no single deity could compete with him. He had actually inflicted corporal punishment upon Herè (Il., XV., 18–25); and Poseidon had to give way to his threat (*ibid.*, 205–211). But it remains doubtful whether, after the Olympian scheme was established, a powerful combination of deities could have dethroned him as it did before that great consummation (Il., I., 397–406). As to the second question, it may be truly said that the reëstablishment of Odysseus in his family and on his throne was agreeable to justice, of which he was all along the champion; and also that the fall of Troy was due to the perpetration of an atrocious outrage and the obstinate refusal of redress (Il., VII., 357–364). Yet, in the " Odyssey, " Zeus has to tolerate the cruel persecution of Odysseus by Poseidon, with which he could have had no sympathy; and in the " Iliad " he consents to the overthrow of Troy against his inclination (ἐκὼν ἀέκοντί γε θυμῷ, Il., IV., 43), and on the principle of give and take as announced by Herè, "We will cede to one another, I to you and you to me" (Il., IV., 62, 63); this, too, although Ilios was to Zeus the dearest of all cities on the habitable earth (*ibid.*, 44–49).

So that Zeus, at any rate, did not carry to a corporal issue the question of his power to overrule the rest of the deities collectively, and found it either necessary or prudent to allow in given cases a given scope to their adverse wills, as the condition on which his general supremacy in the affairs of men could be maintained.

Again, as to the form in which the Olympian government was carried on, it was what we may term constitutional. Affairs were largely discussed in council, and the will of Zeus is never set against the aggregate will of the rest. It is true that the plot of the " Iliad," considered as the μῆνις, or Wrath, and also its consequences, are determined by him at the suit of Thetis, and ratified by the nod (Il., I., 528), without other sanction or intervention. To this determination applies the declaration of Il., I., 5, that the design of Zeus was duly fulfilled. In lesser cases he allowed the self-assertion of others ; and this is the grand exhibition of his own. It is based on retribution for a gross and singularly ungrateful outrage.

In its idea and its practice the Olympian religion is a polytheism, but one reduced to order and method. It is kept within these lines mainly by the political influence of a presiding mind, although the resort to the strong hand is frequently brought into view ; and in both respects the Poet maintains a substantial analogy to the course of human affairs ; the main distinction, perhaps, being that Zeus has not, while Agamemnon has, his superior among his own powerful vassals. Self-will, and even caprice, are traceable in the special action of the deities singly ; but the collective government of the gods works for good.

W. E. GLADSTONE.

[TO BE CONTINUED.]

NOTES AND COMMENTS.

GEORGE ELIOT AND MRS. HUMPHRY WARD.

"MODERATE your transports, Marchioness," said Mr. Richard Swiveller to his titled friend upon a celebrated occasion, and the advice might be opportunely repeated to more than one critic and reader of the present day. Our danger is the opposite to that of the time in which Scotch reviewers were not only hard on English bards, but chary of praise to any newcomer. Every newspaper, every weekly review—with a few stern exceptions of both kinds—is a watch-tower for the discovery of genius.

One of the latest planets to swim into the ken of those who keep weather eyes on the literary sky, is the author of "Robert Elsmere" and "David Grieve." Not merely the professional discoverers have hailed the lady with acclamation, but in private life scores of the apparently judicious deem her a great novelist. A frequent means of praising Mrs. Humphry Ward, especially since the appearance of "David Grieve," is to compare her—for modern criticism is nothing if not comparative—to the author of "Adam Bede" and "Silas Marner." And there is undoubtedly a superficial likeness. Both women are learned to the verge of pedantry, both have a far-reaching interest in life and the problems of human conduct, both get their novels under way and keep them under way by elaborate and often cumbrous means.

But resemblance, partial even in these particulars, ceases altogether with these; and what seems to me the radical difference between George Eliot and Mrs. Ward—apart from the striking difference in native ability —is to be found in their respective manifestations of that moral purpose which appears to be their chief bond of union. In short, George Eliot began writing fiction as a novelist, and ended as a moralist: Mrs. Ward began as a moralist, and has she yet become a novelist? "Miss Bretherton," her first creative work, is an apparent exception to this crudely stated formula; but "Miss Bretherton," charming as it is, leaves the reader suspecting that the author may have undertaken it not from an impulse to represent character, but with a determination, highly laudable in itself, to talk about art and the theatre. The human spectacle, for its own sake, may fairly be called the inspiration of the "Scenes from Clerical Life," of "Adam Bede," of "Silas Marner," even of "The Mill on the Floss." But Mrs. Ward wishes in one case to defend natural religion as against revealed religion, in the other to prove the superiority of the most unsatisfactory marriage—thus David describes to Lucy their condition, without betraying any consciousness of a lack of gallantry either on his part or on that of his author—to an ideal *union libre*. In both instances she dresses her puppets suitably and moves them about in an ample and taste-fully colored scene. These dolls walk and talk; in contrast with the handi-work of inferior artists they seem to live and breathe—for never, it must be admitted, has the novel of sheer purpose been so deftly managed as by Mrs. Ward; but put them over against Dorothea, Rosamond, Gwendolen, or even against Grandcourt, Tito, and Lydgate, and they are only marionettes, skil-fully twitched through the moral show which Mrs. Ward is bent on exhibit-ing to a public that suffereth long and is kind.

The mention of these three men of "Middlemarch," "Romola," and "Deronda," is a reminder of Mr. Stevenson's assertion that women's men are never real men, and that Tito himself carries with him the suggestion of a comb at the back of his head. Mr. Henley is a degree less violent, and allows the "male principle" to Lydgate. These gentlemen are, after all, Scotch reviewers, and most men are disposed to welcome as brothers Lyd-gate, Tito, and the exquisitely brutal Grandcourt. But what man and brother would extend the right hand of fellowship in sex to David Grieve and the Reverend Mr. Elsmere? When they are mentioned, Tito yields the comb.

If George Eliot be superior to Mrs. Humphry Ward in holding to the novelist's true vocation and in the far deeper realization of her characters, her superiority is no less marked in drama, in passion, and above all in humor. Marner—to take but a single illustration—Marner finding the golden-haired child where the golden coin had been before, is not approached, at however great a distance, by any scene in Mrs. Ward's volumes; those cer-tain few pages of "The Mill on the Floss" have more passion in them than the whole of Mrs. Ward's painstaking description of the two weeks of unwedded bliss experienced by David and Elise; and, as for humor, Mrs. Poyser alone would be almost enough to rank George Eliot among the English humorists of the nineteenth century. Mrs. Ward, on the other hand, does not number this most saving grace among her many gifts. Or, rather, such sense of humor as she may have is limited and obscure. Her Derbyshire peasants wrestle grimly with a dialect that excludes thought of anything else on the reader's part, but the author of "Silas Marner" contrives so to surround her country folk with the atmosphere of Warwickshire taverns that they have had no rivals in rustic breadth and humor except Joseph Poorgrass and the other Shakespearian peasants of Thomas Hardy. In truth, the apparently judicious have scarce a leg to stand on when they liken Mrs. Ward to George Eliot. For if in substance she is no analogue, in manner the analogy holds still less, as anyone may see who will look at the English of "Mr. Gilfil's Love Story" and then at that of "Miss Bretherton," or make a similar examination of the diction of "The Mill on the Floss" and the diction of "David Grieve." Mrs. Humphry Ward writes ably and well, but she has no style, and at her best George Eliot is a master of style.

These few remarks protract themselves unduly. They were meant merely to point the moral of Mr. Swiveller's more important remarks to the Marchioness, but the briefest word about Mrs. Ward and her great predeces-sor would be incomplete without a reference to religion, in the treatment of which they are also conspicuously unlike. George Eliot sedulously keeps her religion out of her novels. With Mrs. Ward it is ever creeping monoto-nously into the view, although the result of her application of improved heat-ing apparatus to what Emerson calls somewhere "the Unitarian cold green-house"—memory, I own, is sole voucher for the quotation—is hardly more comforting than George Eliot's distant and invisible choir, "whose music is the sadness [it should read] of the world." But, religion apart, there is no good excuse for confounding ethics with genius, conscience with art, or—Mrs. Ward with George Eliot.

CHARLES TOWNSEND COPELAND.

TYPHUS FEVER.

ON FEBRUARY 11th of this year there came to my office in the morning mail four postal cards; each reported a separate case of typhoid fever in the house No. 42 East Twelfth Street, New York City. My attention was at once aroused by the exceedingly unusual fact of typhoid appearing in four persons in the same house on the same day. I asked Dr. F. H. Dillingham and Dr. Charles F. Roberts to go with me, and we together drove to the house indicated. Before we left it we had found not four, but fifteen well-developed cases of typhus fever, and in other houses, before the day had passed, forty-four additional cases were discovered. It was comparatively easy to trace these cases. The steamship "Massilia" had arrived in this port a few days before from Marseilles, France, having on board a number of Russian Hebrews, who, fleeing alike from the famine and the police of the Tsar, had sought refuge and liberty in this country. They had been helped on their way by the Hirsch Fund, and they were, for the most part, in charge, at the time we found the disease, of the officers of that charity.

The subsequent action of the Board of Health was that which experience has shown to be the best. Through the energy of President Charles G. Wilson of the Board ample accommodation for the patients we expected was secured at once on North Brother Island. Then came the work of fighting the disease. Additional inspectors were sworn in, and everything was made ready for a heavy siege. We did not dare to hope that the outbreak would stop there.

There are only two ways of fighting typhus fever. These are: 1st, Isolation of the sick and those exposed to the contagion; and, 2d, The destruction, or thorough disinfection, of all articles which may have come in contact with the sufferers.

It is not always necessary, however, to isolate those who have been merely exposed, but it is necessary to keep them under the strictest sanitary surveillance and to examine them daily. Persons who have a fixed habitation may be permitted to carry on their business provided the examination goes on. At the first symptom of the disease these people are of course isolated. Persons who live in lodging houses, taking their rooms by the night, here to-day and there to-morrow, should always be quarantined over the period of incubation. The importance to the Health Department of these periods of incubation in diseases may be understood by explaining them. The period of incubation is that time necessary after a person has contracted a disease before it shows itself actively. It is the time which the disease takes to hatch out, if I may so express myself. As it is believed that during the period of incubation a person suffering is not dangerous to others, and as towards the close of this period symptons begin to show themselves, it enables the Department to isolate the sufferers before they become centres of infection.

In typhus fever the medical authorities on the disease place the period of incubation between one and twenty-one days. The experience of this Department would indicate that from nine to sixteen days is much nearer the actual time. After the expiration of the longer period we consider the suspect to be safe, although "to make assurance doubly sure" we continue the isolation, or the surveillance, until twenty-one days be passed.

In the case of these Russian Hebrews we were so far fortunate in the fact that they were among the immigrants assisted by the Hirsch Fund. This carried with it the conclusion that they were kept together for the most part. The disease broke out when the agents of the fund were looking for places for the immigrants. The coöperation of the United Hebrew Charities has been a very valuable aid to the Health Department.

To date (March 4th) there have been found 130 cases in New York City. Of these 106 were passengers on the "Massilia" and 24 were residents who caught the fever from the former. The disease has appeared in this city, New-burgh, Providence, R. I., Kinderhook, Oakdale, Mass., Pittsburg, and St. Louis. In Providence and Newburgh the sufferers were Italians; but of the two hundred and odd Italian immigrants on the "Massilia," only three have been found to have developed typhus. This is owing to their isolation from the Russians on board the steamer.

The disease is well under control. To date there have been seven deaths, and, calculating on the number of adults affected, the mortality is about 18 per cent. Of the sufferers about thirty per cent. were children, and it is known that children rarely have the disease in a severe form.

The parent outbreak of the disease took place in the famine districts in Russia, and the patients in whom the disease showed itself here were of those unfortunates who have been weakened by want in the dominions of the Tsar. It is impossible for me to persuade myself that this outbreak is the measure of the danger to the people of the United States from the Rus-sian famine. The famine gives no sign as yet of abatement, nor so far as the published reports go may we believe that the Russian authorities have, up to the present time, perfected any adequate measures of relief. It is, in fact, a question whether relief can be afforded to sufferers so great in number and spread over such a vast extent of territory. If this be true, then the famine is destined to become greater, the sufferers more numerous, the misery more awful, and the resultant diseases of more terribly malignant type. If, once more, unrestricted immigration and imports be permitted to go on from a country under these conditions, then we are threatened by a very serious and real danger. "Near is my coat but nearer is my skin," runs the Spanish proverb, and while it may be our duty to welcome the oppressed, it is certainly true that our first duty is to our own people and our own homes.

We cannot say that the present danger is such that we should quaran-tine this country against Russian immigrants and articles of commerce. This extreme measure is not needed, with the knowledge we now have of guard-ing against the immigration of disease. But it is plainly necessary that we should class all Russians and Russian goods as suspects and should treat them accordingly. Articles of commerce coming from Russian ports should be thoroughly disinfected, and all immigrants from infected districts in that country should be isolated on their arrival and carefully watched until the period of incubation be passed.

There is no cause for alarm, much less for panic, but there is abundant cause for careful, thorough, and scientific supervision and watchfulness.

With these we shall be perfectly safe, for with disease as an immigrant it is true that forewarned is forearmed in this day and generation.

CYRUS EDSON.

THE FROST CURE.

IT HAS often been observed that great truths are not revealed till Time has prepared the way for their reception; still it is a curious fact that nearly all the most important steps in the progress of science were half-anticipated by men apparently unconscious of having approached the threshold of a world-changing discovery.

In the morning twilight of the Christian Middle Ages, America was visited twice, and, if we shall believe Professor Karsen, at least three times, by adventurous sea-rovers who hardly thought it worth while to report their skirmishes with the natives of a wild forest-land. Before the end of the eleventh century, printing-presses were used in China for the multiplication of pictures, though not of books; and about the same time the Mongol invaders of Eastern Europe increased the terror of their arms by means of machines described as "brass tubes, belching forth fire with great noise," but which were certainly not used to discharge balls. Pythagoras vaguely outlines all the essential principles of a system which only two thousand years later was rediscovered by Keppler and Copernicus.

In Turkey the inoculation cure of cutaneous diseases was occasionally practised two centuries before the time of Dr. Jenner, but future generations may consider it a much stranger fact that the nineteenth century more than once so closely approached the discovery of the *Frost Cure.* For medical statistics, read aright, might even now make it doubtful if smallpox, cholera, and yellow fever combined have proved half as destructive of human life as a delusion which a hygienic reformer describes as the "Cold Fallacy,"—the habit of ascribing all sorts of ailments to the influence of a low temperature. The air of the outdoor world, of the woods and hills, he says, is, *par excellence,* a product of nature, and, therefore, the presumptive cause of innumerable evils. Cold air has become the general scapegoat of sinners against nature. When Don Juan's knee-joints begin to weaken he suspects himself of having "taken cold." If an old glutton has a cramp in the stomach, he ascribes it to an incautious exposure on coming home from a late supper. Toothache is supposed to result from "draughts;" croup, neuralgia, mumps, etc., from the "raw March wind." When children have been forced to sleep in unventilated bedrooms till their lungs putrefy with their own exhalations, the *mater-familias* reproaches herself with the most sensible thing she has been doing for the last hundred nights—"opening the windows last August, when the air was so stifling."

Even old-school physicians begin to suspect that "the danger of cold air currents has been greatly overrated;" but what if the demon of popular delusion should turn out to be not only a harmless sprite, but a minister of mercy—the most harmless as well as the most powerful disinfectant, and Nature's panacea for the disorders of the human organism ?

Is Time "preparing the way" for that truth by half-way discoveries?

Priessnitz, the founder of hydropathy, managed to cure obstinate cases of dyspepsia by cold shower-baths; but it is highly probable that the same purpose could be attained, in a more natural and much less disagreeable manner, by the inhalation of fresh, cold air.

Mountaineers and the natives of high latitudes are almost indigestion-proof, but dyspeptics can save themselves the trouble of a trip to the Norwegian Highlands by the simple plan of sleeping, snugly covered, in the immediate neighborhood of a wide-open window, and imbibing large draughts of the cool night air. In cold weather a few hours will thus suffice to stimulate the torpid organism; but even in midsummer, each night can be made to undo the mischief of the preceding day. So far from being unpleasant, that method of refrigeration can become a positive luxury; each lung full of cool air revives the languid system, as cold water refreshes the parched palate. On the other hand, it might be questioned if the father of hydropathy ever really came to relish his own prescription. A Canadian bear will make a wide circuit, or pick his way over the ice-floes like the hegira heroine of "Uncle Tom's Cabin," rather than swim a lake in cold weather. Baptist missionaries do not report many revivals before June.

Ice has become a substitute for less harmless antiseptics in many hospitals, and a few months ago a Spanish physician, of Santiago de Cuba, proved by a series of triumphant experiments that yellow fever patients can be cured in ice-lined bedrooms. This *camera polar* ("polar chamber") was furnished with double walls and floors, the interspaces being filled with a mixture of sand and blocks of sea-ice, *i. e.*, common sea-water frozen by the usual evaporation process of our ice factories. Vessels with chloride of lime were put here and there to absorb moisture and noxious gases—a combination of artificial contrivances by which its inventor proposed to "reestablish the atmospheric conditions of the Arctic zone, where a dry, low temperature prevents the development of climatic fevers." That idea is an indisputable step in the right direction, but there is more than one reason to suspect that the effective element of the *camera polar* plan was cold air, pure and simple. Ordinary water, frozen in the usual way, would have answered the same purpose, and the dryness of frosty air is not an indispensable condition of its efficiency. In the humid bottom lands of the Mississippi Valley the first good night-frost puts a stop to climatic fevers, without the aid of sea-salt or chloride of lime.

Europe and North America have for years recorded the progress of a phenomenon, which a friend of mine calls the "Siberia mystery,"—the northward exodus of the more enterprising elements of population. During the last two thousand years the centres of civilization have moved at least eight hundred miles nearer the poles; the balance of political and intellectual power has been transferred from Rome and Athens to Berlin, London, St. Petersburg, Boston, and New York. Within the limits of our own national territory a similar current is setting towards the frozen tablelands of our northern border. The overpopulation of the sunnier latitudes cannot explain the enigma, for there is more elbowroom in the Elysian terrace lands of the southern Alleghanies than on many bleak prairies of the far Northwest. The key of the mystery may be found in the stimulating influence of a low temperature. Frost is an antidote, and greatly modifies the penalties of our manifold sins against the health laws of Nature. It enables gluttons to digest greasy-made dishes; it helps topers to survive excesses that would kill a native of the tropics in a few weeks. It also counteracts the chronic indolence of exhausted constitutions. In the uplands of the Black Hills a squatter is not apt to neglect his woodpile. In "Duluth, the solid" (lake often solidly frozen to a depth of eight feet), a business man can shift with a minimum of after-dinner rest. The efficacy of the plan is undeniable, but with open bedroom windows and less superheated tea, its benefits might be enjoyed nearer home.

The "mountain-cure,"American physicians call the last expedient in cases of far-gone consumption. The patient, wardrobe, library, and all, is transported to a tent-camp in the upper Adirondacks, where the temperature in October often sinks to fifteen degrees below zero. Blankets are allowed *ad libitum*, but no stove-fires at night, and even in daytime highland blizzards may oblige the convalescent to take refuge under his blankets. Few breeds of tubercle-microbes have been able to resist that prescription for more than a month, and in the course of a winter such remnants of pulmonary substance as the invalid may have saved from the influence of city life will get expurgated effectively enough to remain in fair working order for years to come.

Those remarkable results have been variously ascribed to the purity of mountain air, or to that mysterious "allotropic form of oxygen called ozone;" but again, there is a probability amounting to what lawyers would term a violent presumption, that they are simply due to the protracted influence of cold air. The prevalence of pulmonary diseases decreases with every mile further north on the road from the factory districts of the English border to the pastoral regions of sea-girt Scotland, and next to the natives of Senegambia, where indoor work is almost unknown, the Norwegians, Icelanders, and the Yakuts, of Northern Siberia, enjoy the most complete immunity from consumption. The severe frosts of the Arctic regions counteract even the filthy habits of the hovel-dwelling Esquimaux, and whalers in an atmosphere not specially distinguished for its purity or abundance of ozone manage to get the better of incipient tubercles by frequent exposure to icy gales.

The suggestiveness of those facts would, perhaps, have been less persistently ignored if the study of the symptoms and proximate causes of consumption had not tended to divert attention from its original causes and the means of its prevention. The description of " vermiform microbes " and the methods of coloring their semi-transparent tissue certainly attest the ingenuity of the Breslau experimenter, and his disciples are perhaps right in pronouncing him the first analytical pathologist of modern times, but their pompous demands upon the gratitude of consumptives often remind one of that speculative philosopher who tried to console a severely wounded soldier with the reflection that, "Pain, my friend, is really nothing but a reversion in the molecular action of the sympathetic nerves connecting the brain with the extra-cerebral nervous termini."

The Frost-cure doctrine is, indeed, a logical, and, practically, by far the most important, correlative of the "germ theory of disease." A few years ago the proprietor of a Hot Springs sanitarium advertised his establishment with the motto : " Warmth is life ; cold is death." In a modified form that aphorism may become the keystone-principle of sanitary philosophy : Warmth is life ; cold, even in a moderate degree, is death—not to man—but to myriads of disease-germs far more sensitive to changes of temperature.

FELIX L. OSWALD, M. D.

A PHASE OF PRACTICAL PHILANTHROPY.

MAHOMET set a tolerably good example when the mountain did not move, and charitable people who would help the workingman are beginning to follow it. They have come to feel that they can no longer walk about in an up-town cloud of benevolence with the hope that down-town suffering will be any the less. They are going out to meet the poorest classes on their own ground. From boys' clubs to University Extension there are a hundred signs of this new feeling, and by no means the least promising expression of it is the movement that goes by the name of University Settlements. Its spread to America from England, where it is still new, gives it now a special interest for Americans. Briefly, it may be said to consist of the occupancy of a house in city "slums" by college bred men or women banded together for doing all in their power for the moral, mental, and social good of the poor about them. The vast difference between University Settlements and previous plans lies in the residence of the workers in the very midst of the poor; they are no longer visitors, but neighbors.

How the entire movement commemorates the short life of Arnold Toynbee need not be told. A glance at the work of Toynbee Hall and the other Settlements at home and abroad will show better than any broad statements what the movement is.

At Toynbee Hall, opened seven years ago, fifteen to twenty Cambridge University men are always to be found in actual residence. Many "associates" and visitors for longer and shorter periods bring them aid. The building resembles a small English college, and, standing in the unsavory Whitechapel district of London, primarily creates an "atmosphere" purifying the air about it. Many of the residents have not independent means to free them from breadwinning through the day. At night these men return to the Hall, and give themselves to any service they can best perform for their unfortunate neighbors. Night classes in various studies, and entertainments of many sorts fill their evenings with usefulness.

Those who can give their entire time to the work enter more fully into the political and social life of the region. It is felt that new laws are not so much needed as the creation of a just sentiment in favor of those existing. The influence of competent leaders plays its part in all communities but the most degraded. In such places as Whitechapel there has often been nobody to see that public affairs are properly conducted. The Toynbee men supply this need. One of them is chairman of a branch of the Dockers' Union, the enormous labor organization which made itself so strongly felt in London not long ago; another works with the Charity Organization Society. In the schools, in the Children's Country Holiday Work, and in a score of other activities one or another of the residents does something. Through the lectures provided by Toynbee Hall it is said that the leading public and literary people of England are heard nowhere more frequently than in Whitechapel. The political, social and educational life of the region are all distinctly better for the Settlement.

But, some will ask, what do the people care? A single instance shows how they have joined in the work for their own uplifting. For years Mr. Barnett, the clergyman at the head of Toynbee Hall, has been trying to have a free library in Whitechapel. When the proposition first came up the people's vote defeated it heavily. Recently the subject was again brought forward, and the region was canvassed under Toynbee Hall direction. The vote in favor of the library was nearly four to one. Other elections have been influenced with equal success. The men's and boys' clubs, conducted by Toynbee men for sundry objects of improvement, are exceedingly popular. Without the favor of the people the Hall could not have become, as it has, the social centre of the neighborhood. They see disinterested, earnest work in their behalf by men whose daily lives are in no wise divided from their own, and heartily respond to what is doing for them.

Toynbee Hall is perhaps the most conspicuous of the London University Settlements, but in other parts of the vast city other organizations are carrying on a similar work. They are different, however, in that, for the most part, they represent each a school of thought or religious belief. Though no work could be more truly religious than Toynbee Hall's, it has no avowed religious aims, and men of all shades of belief join in its labors.

Oxford House, in "the squalid streets of Bethnal Green," stands for the young High Church party of Oxford. Its means may be more conspicuously religious, but its end differs in no important degree from that of Toynbee Hall. From seven to fifteen young Oxford men carry on the resident work. They are assisted by a great many undergraduate visitors. The University Club, begun in 1885 with twelve members, and now counting fifteen hundred workingmen on its rolls, is one of the chief undertakings of the House. With the Club are connected a large co-operative store for general merchandise and small co-operative societies in special branches of trade. A number of minor clubs for different objects are also managed from Oxford House. In outdoor preaching, hospital visiting, houses of shelter, and especially in sanitary work for the neighborhood, great good is accomplished. The Oxford House Papers, two volumes of collected lectures delivered at the House by Oxford scholars, are highly valuable contributions to the literature of popular religion. The personal influence of the men of this Settlement is closely akin to that of the Toynbee residents.

On a smaller scale than either of these Settlements, several other groups of cultivated men and women are doing a like work in London. Mrs. Humphry Ward's University Hall works upon lines which readers of "Robert Elsmere" will readily imagine. The spread of radical Bible criticism is not the least noticeable of its aims. The Wesleyans and Jews have each their Settlement. One of the most efficient of them all is the Women's University Settlement, where graduates of Girton, Newnham and other women's colleges do an excellent work, under Mrs. Barnett's guidance and largely through charities already organized, for children and women. It is impossible to enumerate the other phases of the Settlement work even in London. In Birmingham, Glasgow and Edinburgh, missions and Settlements of college men are equally active.

The first attempt in the direction of Settlement work in New York was made by the Neighborhood Guild nearly five years ago. Like the English Settlements it has been conducted by college graduates, though few in number, living in the midst of the people they have tried to reach. Personal influence, mainly through men's, girls' and boys' clubs for social and other purposes, has been the chief means towards the Guild's achievements. The Neighborhood Guild has not yet realized its ambition to become the Toynbee Hall of New York, but though its activity has not been so constantly great as its founders hoped, it has done a steady, good work. Its extension into a University Settlement adequate to the city's needs is now apparently near at hand.

The Women's College Settlement, of New York, has for the past few years been doing excellent things in its Rivington Street House. Seven or more graduates of Smith, Wellesley, Vassar, and Bryn Mawr, one of them a physician, living at their own expense within its walls and helped by frequent visitors, have carried on their quiet work for the neighboring women and children. The region is inhabited largely by Russian Jews, though many other races are represented. Clubs and classes teach the boys and girls of the district many things, from physical culture to political science, besides the good manners they learn by example alone. A military drill appeals strongly to the boys. The girls are instructed in hygiene and household arts of the highest value to women of all classes. The Settlement's free library of fifteen hundred volumes has had within the past year the astonishing circulation of ten thousand. The baths in the basement do their share of civilizing, and are most heartily appreciated. On thirsty days the neighboring saloons are said to find a formidable rival in the free ice-water fountain in front of the Settlement. A Summer Home maintained by the Settlement gives children in groups of about twenty a series of fortnight outings in the country. There are too many good things about the work for one to relate here, and publicity is rather shunned than sought.

A similar Settlement of women is about to be formed in Philadelphia. In Chicago, Hull House, more distinctly due to one woman of wealth and less a *College* Settlement, is conducted on a kindred plan. Andover House, Boston's University Settlement, has just begun its labors. It is too early to say exactly what lines will be followed and what results attained. At its head is a man thoroughly familiar with the London Settlements, the author of the book from which much that is said of English matters in this sketch is drawn. There is little danger, therefore, of groundless experiments, and the best of good things may be expected.

Indeed, the time for looking upon University Settlements as experiments has passed. To the clear examples of London and New York, common sense adds the assurance that every new element of the plan is a good one. The poor are inevitably better for close association with whole-souled men and women working for them in methods that do not permit a suspicion of sham. And through re-action upon the Settlers—so to call them—and the half of society into which they are born, the benefits cannot be confined to the poor alone. No one device of men is going to "solve the social problem," but University Settlements bid fair to do a larger share of the good work than some more noisy projects.

M. A. DE WOLFE HOWE, JR.

NORTH AMERICAN REVIEW.

No. CCCCXXVI.

MAY, 1892.

THE MAN, OR THE PLATFORM?

BY SENATOR M. S. QUAY, OF PENNSYLVANIA ; SENATOR G. G.
VEST, OF MISSOURI ; REPRESENTATIVE C. A. BOUTELLE, OF
MAINE ; REPRESENTATIVE J. C. BURROWS, OF MICHIGAN ;
REPRESENTATIVE W. L. WILSON, OF WEST VIRGINIA ; AND
REPRESENTATIVE C. D. KILGORE, OF TEXAS.

SENATOR QUAY :

THE Man, or the Platform ? Personality, or Principle—which
is more potent in national politics ? Should party fealty depend
upon the character of the candidate rather than upon the issue he
is put forward to represent ? \

These are the questions suggested by the topic you furnish.
They are broad, historically considered, but as they concern the
politics of the United States to-day they may be briefly and
readily answered.

The conventions of the great political parties at Minneapolis
and Chicago next month will present to the electors two candidates
for the Presidency. They will also place before the people their
statements of belief and opposing theories of legislation and administration. The candidate successful at the election will be
charged with the duty of administering the office of Chief Executive so as to carry out, wherever practicable, the principles
enunciated by his party simultaneously with his nomination.

VOL. CLIV.—NO. 426.   33

Thus, once in four years is presented to our people a choice not only between men, but between policies of government. The relative importance of either varies with the year, almost with the hour. It is affected by domestic industrial conditions, by commercial affairs and prospects, and by foreign relations. Practically then the relative value of the Man and the Platform fluctuates with the changing political conditions. The battle of 1884 was a contest of personality. Issues were obscured by flights of missiles aimed at the character of the candidates, and the result was believed by many to have been determined neither by the strength of the batteries of abuse nor the accuracy of the artillerists, but by skilful jugglery with the ballot-boxes of a limited and thickly populated portion of a single State.

The campaign of 1888 was preëminently one of issues rather than of candidates. Abuse was practically eliminated, and the preference of voters for either candidate was a far less important factor than was the sense of voters upon the question of protection to American industry. Upon this the Republican party won, though the Democratic candidate was weighted by the fact that his campaign was an effort to make him his own successor. Somewhat in line with the anti-third-term idea is a theory—plastic as yet, but tough and indurating to conviction—of the impolicy of attempting a Presidential reëlection. Owing to the enormity and the antagonisms of the corporate and material interests of the country, the clash of disappointments and resentments in personal ambitions, and the almost exact equipoise of parties, the retention of a President, no matter how wisely and impartially and skilfully (politically speaking) he may have discharged the duties of his high office, is difficult, and the Democratic candidate would certainly have been much stronger in 1888 had he not been elected in 1884. If there was any perversion of the ballot in 1884 there was none at the pivotal points in 1888. Personal factors in this campaign were the unassailable character of the Republican candidate and his marvellous faculty for discussing, day after day, great and varying public questions in speeches all differing in form and without an error of treatment or blunder of expression.

The campaign of 1892 will again be conducted upon principle rather than personality. This is demonstrated in advance of the conventions by the varying prospects of at least two of the aspirants for the Democratic nomination, which rise and fall as.

the financial issue promises to become more or less prominent in the platform of that party. The Republican candidate will represent a definite industrial policy already framed in law, and a currency of stable value in domestic and foreign transactions.

The other question, that of party fealty, ought never to arise, because the party organizations ought to be so sensitive to public opinion, and so wisely led by those influential in council, as never to evolve a candidate unworthy of his cause. When the question is raised it is always unfortunate, not merely as affecting practical results, but as diverting the attention of the masses from policies to persons. Such a campaign is one of prejudice rather than education. However, as party organizations have wrought since Presidential nominations have been made by national conventions, there has been no occasion when voters ought not fairly to base their choice of parties upon platforms rather than upon candidates.

M. S. QUAY.

SENATOR VEST:

IT WOULD be an ideal republic in which parties, candidates, and voters were influenced entirely by a desire for the general good.

It is not pessimistic, however, to admit that the time will never come in a country controlled by popular suffrage when platforms will not be framed and candidates selected with the leading purpose of carrying elections. Nor will higher civilization, with increased wealth and luxury, bring a change for the better. More expensive methods in private life and growing governmental patronage will furnish greater temptations to sacrifice convictions and principles upon the altar of expediency.

The art of constructing a political platform so as to suit many interests and opinions, exposing as little surface as possible to the fire of an enemy, is with conventions an important feature of partisan management; but the public generally has come to regard these quadrennial manifestoes much as it does railway notices to the effect that " Passengers will not stand on the platform when the train is moving;" or, in other words, it believes that the party will pay little attention to its platform after the canvass.

This statement may seem harsh and exaggerated, but it must be confessed that the facility with which parties have constructed and disregarded platforms in the past justifies the opinion that political exigencies will be equally potent in the future.

It does not follow, however, that in every instance where a party has disregarded its platform the motive has been vicious or corrupt, for in a new and rapidly developing country where conditions and issues are changing constantly, there can be no fixed and immutable policy declared by any organization that should certainly govern its action in every contingency. This is especially true in a large degree as to economic questions and the details of administration ; for what might be demanded by the highest patriotism in certain environments would with changed conditions become "midsummer madness."

It is easy to understand, for instance, that in our early history patriotism may have advocated the encouragement by Congress of infant industries ; but when these infants have become not only full grown, but exacting and oppressive veterans in their demands for governmental partnership, the system of encouragement once necessary must be regarded as unjust and wicked discrimination.

Modified and qualified as just stated, the fact yet remains that political platforms have steadily deteriorated in their influence upon voters until the platitudes of which they are usually composed must be looked upon as the traditional accompaniment of a convention, occupying in public estimation the same relation to a canvass as the brass bands and torchlight processions which are expected to attract the citizens' attention, although they may not affect his judgment.

Parties, however, and their machinery are absolutely necessary to popular government. They elicit free discussion and insure vigilant inquiry, with legitimate criticism as to public measures and men. To denounce party organization as an unmixed evil is like decrying fire and water because they often cause disaster.

Nor is it true that parties are divided only upon the question of controlling official patronage.

Between the Democratic party and its opponents have always existed, and will always exist, radical and fundamental differences in regard to the constitutional grants of power, especially those affecting taxation and revenue, which must always align the mass of intelligent voters on one side or the other. No platform is necessary to this result.

The fundamental and irreconcilable disagreement between those who insist that the constitution embodies certain specific grants of power from the States to the federal government, the limitations of which, fairly construed, must apply to all public questions, and those who believe that the general-welfare clause of the constitution permits the federal authorities to do anything which they believe necessary, began with the convention which framed the federal constitution and will continue to the end.

It may be safely assumed from the nature of the controversy and the history of past political contests, that heredity of opinion, sectional feeling, or deliberate investigation and honest conviction, will cause a majority of voters to act constantly with one of the two great parties.

Between the opposing forces stands that large body of voters known as Independents and Mugwumps, who profess allegiance to neither party, and whose action must decide the evenly balanced contest.

With them, platforms and political history amount to little, or they would be found acting with those who are regular soldiers under a party flag.

It is useless to deny that party bonds are more easily broken than they were, and that the personality of candidates is becoming more potent. The number is fast increasing of voters who prefer in the candidate courage and honesty to high-sounding declamation in the platform. Of course when the platform announces principles and policies which commend themselves to the judgment and conscience, and the candidate's character gives assurance that he will adhere to these principles and policies, the path of duty is plain. When, however, the platform is acceptable, but the candidate lacks the essential attributes of honesty, courage, or ability, a very different question is presented .to the voter.

It is impossible to avoid the conclusion that the party which offers an unworthy candidate must pay the penalty by losing popular respect and confidence.

The strength of republican government is in the honest instincts of the people, and it is impossible to convince an honest voter that it is his duty to support a man for office whom he believes to be dishonest or incompetent. The trickster may for a time deceive his constituency, but the man who deals fairly, sincerely, and courageously with public questions will always in the end command popular respect and confidence. He may be often mistaken as to his duty, and be sometimes called upon to oppose heresies which have many adherents, but the people by intuition will at last reject the demagogue and cling to one whom they believe to be candid and courageous.

It is also worthy of remark that no platform can embrace all the questions which may arise in the rapid development of a great country but fairly beginning its career as a nation, and the people are justified in believing that the best guaranty of safety to the ship of state is having at the helm a brave and honest pilot.

The political history of our country shows that the idols of the people have not been our most accomplished statesmen, but men whose courage and patriotism were questioned only by party rage. Jackson and Lincoln had neither the majestic character of Washington, the varied knowledge and culture of Jefferson, nor the eloquence of Clay and Webster, but the people, with that unerring instinct which is better than the learning of all the schools, trusted them implicitly.

G. G. Vest.

THE HON. C. A. BOUTELLE:

As the object of elections under our form of government is to secure the most satisfactory representation of the wishes of the people in the administration of public affairs, it seems natural that more importance should be attached to the declarations of principle and policy in behalf of which appeals are made to popular support than to the individuality of candidates who are put forward as the exponents of the doctrines or ideas of the supporters, and who may often be comparatively little known by the great mass of voters.

The fundamental fact that our political system is based upon the competition of parties representing distinct theories or practices of government, and not upon the contests of factions devoted to the fortunes of individual chiefs or leaders, seems to render it inevitable that, under ordinary circumstances, the average voter should be governed more by the declarations of public policy to be inaugurated or maintained than by his impressions as to the personal characteristics of the candidates.

I think this tendency is clearly shown in the history of our most important Presidential elections. In 1860 the name of Abraham Lincoln had become hardly more familiar to the country at large than his homely features, the likenesses of which were so curiously scanned after his defeat of the famous William H. Seward in the Republican national convention. It was the clarion cry of " Free soil for free men !" that aroused the marching legions of that victorious campaign, and the enthusiasm of the liberty-loving people identified the standard-bearer with the inspiring challenge of the platform : " *We deny the authority of Congress, of a territorial legislature, or of any individual to give legal existence to slavery in any territory of the United States !*"

Who can doubt that four years later, when the great President had become better known, but when the spirit of faction was strongly aroused against him, the victory at the polls was far more largely influenced by the issue joined between the parties than by all that was said or thought of the personal qualities of the candidates. The loyal sentiment of the nation rallied to the support of the President, *because* his party declared against any basis of peace except unconditional surrender, and had called upon the Government " to prosecute the war with the utmost possible vigor to the complete suppression of the Rebellion." Not even the candidacy of the distinguished soldier who had but recently been the idolized chief of the Union armies, and who vainly sought to throw his military prestige into the scale as an assurance of patriotism, could save the Democratic party from the popular rebuke which overwhelmed the authors of a platform that pronounced the war a " failure," and demanded immediate overtures for peace, three weeks after Farragut had thundered through the gates of Mobile Bay, almost at the very hour when Tecumseh Sherman was marching into Atlanta to split the Confederacy wide open, and when Grant and Sheridan were tightening their death-grip on the throat of the Rebellion, in Virginia.

With principles so vital and momentous at stake, the most conspicuous personalities were dwarfed in comparison, and the people followed not a leader, but the gleaming banner of a beloved and imperilled country, to the defence of which they were summoned by the dauntless proclamation of the Republican party.

So, in 1868, while the renown of the foremost military hero

of the war was undoubtedly an important aid to the party that nominated General Grant, the Republican success was still more largely due to public approval of the demand for "equal suffrage for all loyal men in the South," and the pledge that "the national honor requires the payment of the public indebtedness in the uttermost good faith to all creditors." The denunciation "of all forms of repudiation as a national crime" struck the popular chord of integrity, and met with quick response from a people who had shed their blood as freely as they had contributed their money to uphold the national honor.

In 1872 the unexpected nomination of the famous Protectionist, Horace Greeley, by a convention of "revenue-reformers," followed by a reluctant indorsement by a Democratic national convention, involved such incongruity that the framing of a distinctive party platform was impossible, and a disastrous defeat resulted from the attempt to secure the election of one of the ablest, and in many respects one of the most excellent, men in public life, as the Presidential candidate of a party whose doctrines and policies he had for many years mercilessly ridiculed and denounced.

In 1876 and 1880, it will be remembered, after making all allowance for the popular interest in the candidates, that the serious contentions of the two campaigns were over the planks of the respective platforms. In the former year the Republicans insisted upon redemption of United States notes in coin and a tariff in the interest of American labor, while the Democrats denounced the protective tariff and demanded the repeal of the Resumption act. In 1880 the Republicans won again on a platform reaffirming the principle of protection and declaring the "complete protection of all citizens in all their privileges and immunities the first duty of the Nation." The Democrats declared for "a tariff for revenue only," and denounced as "the fraud of 1876-7" the very tribunal which they had so earnestly invoked.

In 1884 the nomination of Mr. Blaine brought into the foreground of a Presidential canvass the most brilliant and powerful individuality in American politics, and there can be no doubt of the remarkable enthusiasm created by his famous tour of the Northern States, in which his unequalled versatility and personal magnetism were so potently employed in behalf of his party. But Mr. Blaine's fame and his marvellous hold upon the Republicans of the country were based upon the fact that he had become so widely recognized as the most fearless and trenchant champion of the cherished principles of Republicanism, and he was supported as the embodiment of the platform on which he stood. I have my own opinion as to the result of that Presidential canvass and the methods by which it was reached, but, without going into that collateral discussion, I think I may safely assume that no one will claim that popular interest in the personality of Mr. Cleveland was a principal factor in the Democratic success in 1884.

In 1888 Mr. Cleveland's renomination gave his party the benefit of such prestige as attached to the first Democratic administration since 1861, and the selection of General Harrison by the Republicans gave them a candidate from an illustrious family, who had rendered gallant service in the field and made an excellent reputation during his term in the United States Senate, but no campaign was ever fought more directly upon the principles of the party platforms than that in which the Democratic President was defeated in his own State and beaten by sixty-five majority of the electoral votes, in spite of the suppression of popular suffrage in the solid South. No stronger evidence of the popular interest in the party creeds could be found than is furnished by the discussions of the last Presidential campaign, in which the Mills Tariff Bill was made a leading issue by its indorsement in the Democratic, and denunciation in the Republican, platform. The same feature is conspicuously demonstrated by the fact that the publication of Mr. Blaine's famous interview, in which he criticised President Cleveland's message and expounded the Republican doctrine just prior to the 1888 campaign, exercised a greater influence upon the canvass than the personality of either of the distinguished Presidential candidates. I may add that the declaration of the Republican national platform in favor of temperance undoubtedly saved to that party many thousands of votes that it would otherwise have lost.

My conclusion is, that the declarations of the principles and policies of the parties will, in this year's campaign, as in the past, have greater influence with the voters than the individuality of candidates. Of course this view is predicated upon the condition that the candidates shall be fairly acceptable and representative men ; for, while I believe the American people have more regard for principles than for individuals, I am equally sure that the nomination of an unmistakably bad man for the great office of President of the United States is a dangerous experiment for any party. The people may be deceived, but they will not knowingly elevate to the chair of Washington and Lincoln any man unworthy of the respect of his countrymen.

In this age of telegraphs and fast mails the people think, and know what they want, and will declare in their respective platforms the policies they desire to have carried out. The Republican party will confidently make its appeal for an honest ballot, an honest currency, and a tariff that will protect American labor and develop all the resources of our magnificent country. On that platform it will not fail to place a candidate worthy of the public confidence. On all these doctrines the Democrats must join issue unequivocally ; or the evasion will condemn them. No party can dodge or straddle the leading issues this year, and while the silver question has found Mr. Cleveland tongue-tied in Rhode Island and Mr. Hill dumb in the Senate, the party platform must speak out as the Democratic House has spoken, and the candidate will be judged by the party and the platform.

Believing that the avowed principles of the Republican party furnish the soundest basis for the prosperity of the American people, and having faith in their intelligence and patriotism, I look forward with confidence to the rendering of their judgment between the two great parties, wherever that judgment can be freely and fairly expressed.

C. A. BOUTELLE.

THE HON. J. C. BURROWS :

IN A government like ours, resting on free and popular suffrage, it is not only the right, but the duty of the citizen to vote. His ballot is his voice, and the ballot-box the only medium through which he can make it effective on questions of public policy, and secure their crystallization into law. Even this, however, must be done by indirection. This is from necessity a representative government. At stated intervals public servants are chosen by the whole body of the people to speak and act for them in the conduct of governmental affairs. The candidates for these official positions both in the State and in the nation are usually selected through the instrumentality of party organization, and so become the representatives and exponents of party principles and purposes.

When party candidates have been selected and political creeds promulgated, the intelligent and honest voter will identify himself with that political organization which most nearly represents his views on questions of governmental policy. Of course the first duty of the voter, who has a just conception of the obligation he owes to society and the State, is to thoroughly and conscientiously examine every question upon which he is called to pass judgment, wholly free from all partisan bias, and reach a conclusion with sole regard to the public weal. Too many voters, especially young men, determine, or rather drift into, party allegiance first, and settle their political convictions afterwards. A necessary prerequisite to intelligent partisanship is intelligent investigation and well-grounded judgment touching matters of public concern.

Parties never make issues—issues form parties and so crystallize individual thought into political action.

The voter having previously determined and settled his creed of political faith, it becomes his duty to identify himself with that party which stands committed to the policy he approves. In no other way can he hope to give effect to his views on public questions.

This is a government by parties springing from the people, and the individual citizen must speak through party organization, or not at all. To this end the body of the people composing political organizations select delegates to a national convention, empowering them to promulgate the party's platform and nominate the party candidate to be supported thereon. This platform is supposed to embody the dominant views of the adherents of the party, and the opinions of the candidate selected are presumed to be in harmony with the party's declaration of principles. If the platform contains a clear and unequivocal declaration of party faith and purposes touching all matters of political controversy, and the candidate in his letter of acceptance, or otherwise, fully indorses the principles of the party as therein set forth, the voter, if his views are in harmony with the candidate and the platform, can give to such a party conscientious and vigorous support.

But it may sometimes happen that a large and respectable

minority of the party are not in accord with the party platform in some of its material declarations, and the party nominee is known to hold opinions contrary to those embodied in the party platform. In other words, the platform may represent the controlling thought and policy of the party, while the candidate is known to be in harmony with the views of the minority. In such case the voter may be at a loss to determine his political action.

Party managers, however, usually contrive, when great and serious differences divide the rank and file of the party, to construct a platform in such doubtful phrase as to make it susceptible of an interpretation to suit either faction of the party, and thus hold the party adherents in line. If, however, a serious difference exists between the adherents of a party and its candidate, both party and candidate will, in their desire for success, seek to cover up that difference by obscurity of language. The absence of clear statement, either by the party in its platform or the candidate in his letter of acceptance, is conclusive evidence of intentional deception. In such a case, neither the party nor the candidate can have the slightest claim upon the allegiance of the voter. Language of doubtful meaning in a party declaration or by a candidate upon a question sharply at issue is not to be tolerated by a self-respecting people. Obscurity of language on important questions of public policy is conclusive evidence of dishonest purpose, and is of itself sufficient reason for distrust of a party or its candidate or both. The clearest possible statement of party faith is due from a party and its candidate, and only such avowal can command the respect and support of the honest voter.

But let it be supposed that the party in its platform makes unequivocal declaration touching vital issues of national concern, and the nominee is known to hold views opposed to such declaration, the question arises, Which should exert a controlling influence over the voter in determining his political action—the platform, or the candidate? In the first place it is difficult to conceive of any party, actuated by an honest purpose, nominating a candidate known to be opposed to its declaration of principle in any material part as embodied in its platform ; and it is equally incomprehensible that a candidate can be found so lost to all sense of personal honor as to accept a nomination on a platform with which he is not in full accord. But, if such a condition were possible, it would carry on its face such an expression of duplicity as ought to drive the honest voter from all affiliation with that political organization. It would justly forfeit the confidence of the voter both in the party and its candidate. Somebody is to be deceived. If the principles of the party as announced in its platform are to be carried out in contradistinction to the views of the candidate, those who voted for the candidate rather than for the platform are to be betrayed; while, on the contrary, if the views of the candidate are to control, then the voter who sustains the party by reason of its platform is to be deceived. Thus, in either event, a portion of the voters will surely be betrayed. Under such circumstances, if there is a party having a platform and candidate in harmony, and they are both in accord with the views of the voter on the vital questions at issue, the intelligent and honest citizen will identify himself with such a political organization, whatever its name or his own previous political affiliation.

If, however, the voter lacks the moral courage to wholly sever his connection with such a party, then it becomes material to inquire which should determine his vote—the platform, or the candidate. Unquestionably the platform. Party principles as expressed in party platforms, and supplemented by party power, are stronger than the convictions and purposes of any one man, and in the end will surely prevail. The candidate, whatever his personal judgment, will not be able to withstand the solicitations of his party, upon whose support he must depend for future political preferment. He may be ever so determined, party and personal considerations will prompt him to find a way to his party's support and the abandonment of individual purposes. The platform of a party, representing the convictions and judgment of the majority of the party adherents, will certainly prevail over the convictions of the candidate who is under the strongest possible temptation to come to and agree with the controlling element of his party. Under these conditions, the voter should look alone to the platform in determining his political action.

J. C. BURROWS.

THE HON. WILLIAM L. WILSON:

It took fifty years of party contests in the United States to develop the existing machinery of national conventions for nomi-

nating candidates for the Presidency, and for setting forth, by
way of formal platform, the principles, professions, and promises
of the party.

This does not imply that previous campaigns were lacking in
definite issues or were devoid of partisan heat and bitterness. It is
doubtful if we ever had more rancor in our politics than in the
Jacksonian era, when, in addition to the burning issues that
excited and divided the people, the strong personal antagonism*
of candidates aroused like feelings among their supporters.

Mr. Van Buren was the first Democratic candidate nominated
by a national convention, but not until his second candidacy, in
1840, was a platform of party principles also made part of the
work of the convention. As we read this first official statement
of principles made by representatives of the party thus assembled,
we find it a clear, honest, and reasonably explicit statement of
fundamental Democratic faith, and of the attitude of the party to
the great controversies of the day.

But the first Democratic candidate with a platform was inglo-
riously routed by a candidate who ran without the aid or incum-
brance of any platform, and whose supporters, although kindled
with an enthusiasm never equalled in any of our national campaigns, could not have united on any common ground, except
that of hostility to the administrations of Jackson and of his successor and political heir, Van Buren.

It is clear then, from a review of our Presidential canvasses,
both before and since 1840, that a party platform is not a necessary equipment for a political battle, and that great issues may
be clearly understood and vigorously fought over without being
put into any definite and official formula.

But as long as our system of national conventions continues,
we shall have both a candidate and a platform from every great
party, and it will not be easy to say whether the one or the other
should be most regarded by the patriotic voter in determining
his political action.

It may be laid down as a rule that no voter ought to support
a party whose programme as to great questions he does not approve, or to vote for a Presidential candidate whose personal and
political integrity he does not believe to be above reproach.

When, however, one reviews the platforms issued during the
past twenty-five years by national conventions and finds them

so full of boastful rhetoric and insincere profession, so untrue and sweeping in condemnation of political opponents, and, in the light of experience, so little trustworthy as to promise and pledge, he is obliged to conclude that party platforms alone are unsafe guides for determining his political action at the polls.

The position of our great historical parties on almost all main issues is determined for them, not so much by their resolutions in national convention, as by their past history, their traditions and the general beliefs and feelings of their members, so that these quadrennial platforms are often of no special significance, except as they amuse us by their artful dodging on inconvenient temporary issues, and their efforts, by virtuous protestation, "to pander to the better element." Nevertheless, there are times when party platforms become matters of vital controversy, which bring on heavy battles within the party ranks, or even result, as with the Democratic party in 1860, in their temporary disruption. It is precisely at these times that both the platform and the candidate become exceedingly important. Whenever the people are in dead earnest as to important public questions they will not tolerate any juggling with them in platforms, and they choose leaders more for their merits than for reasons of expediency. In less earnest times, the "dark horse," or the unknown candidate, who has few party antagonisms and a brief or colorless public record, is often taken as a stronger runner before the people than a real party leader.

Yet the preference for such a candidate in itself shows the desire to escape the criticism upon the man which a better-known personality or more conspicuous public record might bring into the canvass. Conceding, however, on the basis of these general and obvious remarks, the importance of a party platform, and the duty of every party to deal in frank and sincere utterance, I believe that the man is, in the long run, more important than the platform: first, because the great parties, as a rule, occupy well known positions on public issues, and, secondly, because in the character and ability of the candidate, we find the best pledge of the party's sincerity and professions.

No rarer good fortune can befall a political party than to find or develop a truly great leader. By such a great leader I mean a man who, to the capacity of leadership, adds the sincerity and intelligence to lead in the path of patriotic and party duty. It is not possible to exaggerate the worth of such a man to his party and to his country when important questions arise that cannot safely be committed to universal suffrage for immediate, off-hand decision. It is at just such dangerous crises that ordinary politicians and ordinary leaders refuse to tell the people disagreeable truths, are eager to flatter their ignorance, and are only anxious to find out where the people want to go, regardless of the ultimate effect on party or country.

The most thoughtful student of politics in our day has truly said, that the danger to democratic institutions comes when vital questions are submitted to popular decision that it requires tension of thought to understand and some self denial to submit to their correct decision.

Any long divergence between "democratic opinion and scientific truth as applied to human societies" involves serious disaster.

If, at such vital time, some leader who has a strong hold on the respect and confidence of his party uses that respect and confidence to save it from temporary delusion and serious error, he does it a service that a myriad of mere party managers could never accomplish. Moreover, a true leader has an influence on the *morale* of a party that can come from no other source. "How quickly," says Mr. Bagehot, in his "Physics and Politics," "a leading statesman can change the tone of a community. We are most of us earnest with Mr. Gladstone; we were most of us *not* so earnest in the time of Lord Palmerston. The change is what every one feels, though no one can define it. Each predominant mind calls out a corresponding sentiment in the country; most feel it a little. Those who feel it excessively, express it excessively; those who dissent are silent or unheard."

It becomes patriotism to strengthen the respect of the masses for such a leader, and to encourage their confidence in his faithfulness to their true interests, because it is chiefly when they are prone to go wrong, or are most exposed to error in their decisions, that this confidence comes to their rescue, and saves them from the penalties that invariably follow political as other misdoing.

If it be said that I am giving undemocratic prominence to mere leadership, I answer that even under universal suffrage we must take men as they are and with the training which they bring out of the past. The Democratic party to-day, and henceforward, has no more urgent political duty than the education of the people to the honest and capable performance of the work of self-government, and I am but repeating a truth as old as Christianity, and even older, when I say that, in the education of the masses, the life of the teacher is more catching than his tenets.

In the ages and countries of the past, military heroism was the prime virtue of citizenship, as the chief duty of the citizen was to defend the life and liberty of his country from foreign enemies. In our own land, and under free institutions, the prime virtue of citizenship is the civic heroism that, in the defence of true political principles, makes light of personal sacrifices, and does not hesitate to withstand the clamors of the people, the *ardor civium prava jubentium*, when it is necessary to save the life or liberty, good name or prosperity, of the country from the vital mistakes of its own people.

Let us do what we can to develop this type of heroism, and, wherever we find it in robust existence, to clothe it with such popular confidence and official trust that it need not waste itself in vain sacrifice, but inure to the safety and permanent good of the country.

WILLIAM L. WILSON.

THE HON. C. D. KILGORE:

A POLITICAL party, according to Edmund Burke, is " an association of men united for the purpose of promoting by their joint efforts the public welfare upon principles about which they agree." Political parties do not exist except among a free people, and they are essential to the preservation of free government and constitutional liberty.

The principles professed by a party, and upon which it seeks public favor, by modern usage find expression in party platforms. Such platforms declare boldly on such principles and policy as have the united and enlightened sanction of the party—cautiously on such as are not yet baptized fully into party fellowship.

In the year 1800 a congressional caucus gave to the world the first party platform known to American politics. It was an able and forceful presentation of the political creed of Mr. Jefferson, luminously defining the rights of the citizen, and accurately interpreting the delegated powers of the Federal Government and the reserved powers of the State Government. He was chosen

President of the United States as the great exponent of the principles of the party he had founded. From 1800 to 1844 contests for political supremacy were conducted without any formal promulgation in party platforms of the political principles upon which the battle was fought, though the canvass was in each case made, and candidates were elected, on issues clearly defined and well understood by the people. The successful candidates of that period were each an issue in himself more potent than all the platforms that could have been devised.

Party conventions do not create, but merely advance, policies and principles. These are greater than men and parties and platforms,—are immutable and ever-living. They are as well understood by the people before as after a convention has named its candidate and announced its platform. The candidate is in many instances predetermined by public expression, and the convention only ratifies the popular choice, and avows his opinions as to the polity of the government and the policy and principles upon which it should be administered. If either Mr. Sherman, or Mr. McKinley, or Mr. Cleveland, or Mr. Carlisle should be nominated, without any announced platform, and be elected President, there would be no doubt in the minds of the people as to the principles and policy which would prevail, and no man would have to inquire of his neighbor, or "read it out of a book," in order to be enlightened on the subject.

Public men and public measures are so closely identified that any representative man of high character, strong intellectuality, and pronounced convictions on great public questions, with the inspiration of a courageous statesmanship, stands before the country as the embodiment of the well-known fundamental principles of the party to which he belongs. Such a man, as a candidate, combines all the elements of strength, and he can command the zealous and enthusiastic support of his own party and of many conservative men of all parties—platform or no platform.

A political party may be united on well-understood vital principles, and may be, and frequently is, wide apart on important questions of policy. In such cases it is slow to pronounce on a specific policy which has not secured the sanction of the great body of the party, and the failure to declare satisfactorily on some such question will not repel voters who are mainly in accord with the principles expressed in the platform and represented by an acceptable candidate. They are won by the great governing principles to which they yield assent, partially or entirely, and if a clean, brave, able, patriotic man and statesman leads the fight, the people will stand by him though the platform be not acceptable in all things.

The people are strongly wedded to a pure and aggressive policy vitalized by a lofty regard for principle and clean methods. They are, as a mass, loyal to that leadership which tends to elevate and purify the politics of the country. They believe that principle ought to be placed high above spoils ; that a political party ought to be conducted so as to advance the principles which it professes and which give it life ; that the government ought to be administered in the interest of the public welfare and in accord with the principles and policy about which they agree. They have an idea that a party has a higher and nobler mission than the mere achieving of success, that it may distribute public plunder to those who have public favor.

No platform, however binding, can impose any restraint on the cunning, corrupt politician or the meandering, unscrupulous spoilsman. He employs methods which have a tendency to debauch the people, and perpetually menace liberty and good government.

The history of Presidential contests demonstrates, with fairly conclusive force, that the personality of the candidate has more to do with success than any declaration of principles contained in the platform. The people will support with enthusiasm a candidate for President whose character and standing command their admiration, though the platform does not meet the sanction of their judgment.

Nominate a man well and widely known to be the exponent of the purer and better principles of free government, the embodiment of all the elements of a progressive, enlightened, and courageous statesmanship, able and upright, of clean, direct, and honorable methods, and whose greatness stands confessed in the confidence of the people, and a vast army of patriotic voters will flock to our ranks, and success will unfailingly reward our fidelity to principle.

C. D. KILGORE.

THE POET OF DEMOCRACY.

BY JOHN BURROUGHS.

"To PUT the true praise" of an original and first-class man, especially if he be one's contemporary, "and set it on foot in the world," is not always an easy matter. Sir Wm. Petty, who used the words I have quoted in conversation with Pepys, said in the same connection that good writers were not admired in their own age because there were so few persons at any time that did mind the "abstruse and the curious." But there is one class of good writers who are always admired in their own day, and the true praise of whom is quickly set on foot. I mean those writers who use the language and speak the thought of their time.

But there is another class of writers who do not speak the language and the thought of their time, but of a time to come or a time just dawning, whose true praise is slow in getting under way. It is an old story and need not be dwelt upon in connection with our Poet of Democracy, Walt Whitman, whose just appreciation is so tardy in getting ahead among current readers. Probably, however, it is no more tardy than he himself anticipated, as he declared at the outset of his career that he was willing to wait to be understood for the growth of the taste of himself, and that the proof of the poet was to be sternly deferred till his country had absorbed him as affectionately as he had absorbed it. The absorption by a people like ours, so thoroughly under the illusion of the refined and the conventional, of a poet like Whitman must be a slow process, if it ever thoroughly takes place.

It has been the aim of Whitman not only to speak in the democratic spirit, but to exemplify it in his own person, and he has done so with a frankness that has shocked and repelled current readers. The penalty has been that his true praise has been delayed, and false praise and false censure have vied with each other in misleading the public with regard to him.

The false praise has come from those who simply welcomed him as a great rebel against the current literary mode, or a bold defier of prevailing social conventions. Much as I cherish the memory of the eloquent and chivalrous Wm. D. O'Connor, and great as was his service in màny ways to Whitman, I cannot but feel that when he praised him for his outspokenness on matters of sex, because the great masters of the past had been outspoken, his praise was false and misleading. Whitman's friends have no right to appeal in his behalf to a court whose jurisdiction he has denied. "Leaves of Grass" is not modelled upon the past ; it makes a bid for the suffrage of the future, and if it speaks out freely upon matters of sex, the author must show a deeper reason than the precedents of other times.

His false censure has come mainly from those who had not the wit or the patience to understand him (which is true of the most of his adverse critics), and who, because he was not like other poets, denied that he was a poet at all.

His true praise must be sought in his faithfulness to his own standards, in the degree in which he has spoken in the spirit of democracy, of science, and the modern ; not only spoken, but lifted and suffused these things with poetic emotion, his results bearing upon the problems of life in a helpful and stimulating way.

"Leaves of Grass" requires a large perspective ; you must not get your face too near the book. You must bring to it a magnanimity of spirit, a charity and faith equal to its own. Looked at too closely it often seems incoherent and meaningless ; draw off a little and let the figure come out. The book is from first to last a most determined attempt on the part of a large, reflective, magnetic, rather primitive, thoroughly imaginative personality to descend upon the materialism of the nineteenth century, and especially upon a new democratic nation, now in full career upon this continent, with such poetic fervor and enthusiasm as to lift and fill it with the deepest meanings of the spirit and disclose the order of universal nature. The poet has taken shelter behind no precedent, or criticism, or partiality whatever, but has squarely and lovingly faced the oceanic amplitude and movement of the life of his times and land, and fused them in his fervid humanity, and imbued them with deepest poetic meanings. One of the most striking features of the book is the adequacy and composure, even joyousness and elation, of the poet in the presence of the huge materialism and prosaic conditions of our democratic era. He spreads himself over it all, he accepts and absorbs it all, he rejects no part; and his quality, his individuality, shines through it all, as the sun through vapors. The least line, or fragment of a line, is redolent of Walt Whitman. Whether he makes poetry of it all may be questioned, but he never ceases to rule it and master it.

The thought that is ever fermenting in him, tingeing everything he ever wrote in prose or verse, revolving, taking new forms, ramifying through his whole moral and intellectual nature, and drawing all his energies in its train, was the thought of his country, its present needs, its future prospects. We find him thinking, desiring, loving nothing else, planning, planting, watering for nothing else, writing his poems with the sole purpose to fuse and compact his country. He has touched no theme, named no man not related in some way to America. The thought of it possessed him as thoroughly as the thought of Israel possessed the old Hebrew prophets. Indeed it is the same passion, and flames up with the same vitality and power; the same passion for race and nativity enlightened by science and suffused with the modern humanitarian spirit. Israel was exclusive and cruel. Democracy, as exemplified in Walt Whitman, is compassionate and all-inclusive :

"My spirit has passed in compassion and determination around the whole
   earth;
I have looked for equals and lovers and found them ready for me in all
   lands;
I think some divine rapport has equalized me with them.
You vapors, I think I have risen with you, moved away to distant conti-
   nents, and fallen down then, for reasons.
I think I have blown with you, you winds;
You waters, I have finger'd every shore with you."

Whitman is of the people undoubtedly, but it is not the conscious America that he speaks for and expresses so much as it is the unconscious, the America of destiny and of history, the America that Europe fears and loves and is interested in, and comes here to see and looks in our literature to find, but fails to see or find, or at least only in hints and fragments. The conscious America, the America that has so far expressed itself in our poetry and art and criticism is quite a different thing. Certain traits and aspirations of our people are much clearer-voiced in the New England poets than in Whitman—in Lowell and Longfellow and Whittier, the aspiration for culture and refinement—for the well-bred, the well-dressed, the well-schooled, the well-churched. The college, the church, the club, the lyceum—the influences and currents they set going—a career of honor and distinction, or of usefulness and respectability—all these things are voiced in our standard poets. What Whitman has expressed, or aimed to express, is more latent and dynamical—more like the climate, the geology and geography, and the brawn and fecundity, of a new continental race. He would not be the schoolmaster of the people, he would be their prophet and savior.

What the modern spirit, the spirit of democracy, means when carried into the sphere of art and poetic utterance may be a question. Whitman has given us his view of its meaning—namely, to effuse the atmospheres of actual concrete life and nature, and not at all the housed and perfumed atmosphere of the accepted poets. This makes his undertaking new and distasteful to current readers.

The lesson of this poet is not merely one in philanthropy or benevolence, it is one in practical democracy, in the value and sacredness of the common, the near, the universal; it is that the quality of common humanity—workingmen, farmers, mechanics, soldiers, sailors, hunters, etc.—is the quality with which a literature for our age and country is to be saturated and filled. The spirit in which our poet writes is that spirit of universal humanity which it shares with all natural open-air objects and processes—the only spirit in which man's concrete life on this globe can be carried forward. We do not live and breathe and grow and multiply, we do not have health and sanity and wholeness and proportion, we do not subdue and improve and possess the earth, in the spirit of something exclusive, exceptional, far-away, aristocratic, but in the spirit of the common and universal. The only demand is that the common or universal shall be vitalized with poetic thought and enthusiasm, or imbued with the ideal of a rare and high excellence. Whitman's poetry is ever looking to superior persons or invoking them, is ever pointing to the grandeur and significance of the common and the near. He lifts things out of a corner, out of a class, and shows their universal relationships—shows that all things are beautiful to him who brings the spirit of beauty, that all things are divine to him or her who brings the thought of the divine, that all things are great, every one without exception, if you take enough of the picture within vision.

The poems, I say, are bathed and flooded with the quality of the common people ; not their crudeness and vulgarity, their half-culture, but with the commonness and nearness which they share with real things and with all open-air nature, with hunters, travellers, soldiers, workers in all fields, and with rocks, trees, and woods. It is only in the spirit of these things that a man himself can have health, sweetness and proportion ; and only in their spirit that he can give an essentially sound judgment of a work of art, no matter what the subject of it may be. This is the meaning of Burke's remark that "The true standards of the arts are in every man's power, and an easy observance of the most common, sometimes the meanest, things in nature, will give the truest lights."

"What is commonest, cheapest, nearest, easiest, is Me,"

says our poet,

> " Me going in for my chances, spending for most returns,
> Adorning myself to bestow myself on the first that will take me,
> Not asking the sky to come down to my good will,
> Scattering it freely forever."

If Whitman's poetry is not also bathed and saturated with a lofty and determined spirituality, if it does not give out the qualities of the noblest thoughts, the most chivalrous behavior, the most stern self-denial, the most uncompromising rectitude, it falls far short of the standards which must be held up to us in this country.

Most of the hostile criticism of Whitman has been aimed at a man of straw. Heine made a vital distinction when he said : "The critic's great error lies in asking ' What ought the artist to do ?' instead of asking ' What does the artist intend ?'" Very few critics of Whitman have taken the trouble to ask what does the poet intend ? what are his aims ? what are his methods ? They have chosen rather to say, he fails to do this or to do that, he fails to make artistic poems, he fails in the principles of good taste, he fails to observe all the proprieties, he fails to bring us only the pleasing and the beautiful.

Suppose he did not work with this end in view. Suppose that, instead of elaborating a theme, his aim was to exhibit a man. Suppose that, instead of a book of highly-wrought poetic verse, polished and finished to the last degree—the interest always centering in the theme, never in the man—his purpose was to make a book full of vista and suggestion, full of escapes and outlets, with flowing but incomplete lines, starting thoughts but never elaborating them, begetting beauty, but never courting it, producing the impression of something fluid, protean, generating, like nature herself; with no more outside art than have the clouds in the sky, or the grass in the fields, or the leaves upon the trees, seeing to it only that life and power pulse through it all. We are not troubled about the arrangement of the clouds, or the grass, or the leaves. May not poetic thoughts, images, and concrete objects be so embosomed in a great personality, so charged and vitalized by spiritual emotion, and borne along by such a tide of living power, that we shall rather welcome the escape from conscious art than lament the want of it? It is so in nature; why may it not in a measure be so in poetry? It seems to me the only question is, "Are you man enough?" My own conviction is that Walt Whitman has shown himself man enough. The man-element in his work overtops all others, and gives unity and cohesion to all others. To exploit this man-element, to saturate the land with it, his poems are written. He may well say:

> " This is no book;
> Who touches this, touches a man."

We here come upon a marked feature of the poems considered as literary performances, upon which too much stress cannot be laid. It is never so much the theme treated, as it is the man exploited and illustrated. Walt Whitman does not write poems strictly speaking, does not take a bit of nature or life or character and chisel and carve it into a beautiful image or object, or polish and elaborate a thought, embodying it in pleasing tropes and pictures. His purpose is rather to show a towering, loving, composite personality moving amid all sorts of materials, taking them up but for a moment, disclosing new meanings and suggestions in them, passing on, bestowing himself upon whoever or whatever will accept him, tossing hints and clews right and left, provoking and stimulating the thought and imagination of his reader, but finishing nothing for him, leaving much to be desired, much to be completed by him in his turn.

Our interest and profit are always in the poet more than in the theme. See him moving through life, absorbing and transmuting its elements, drawing out their meaning and value and passing on, identifying himself with all forms and conditions of our national existence and situation, and putting on experience after experience like a garment. See him in the war poems, the tender nurse and father ; see him in " Calamus " the loving comrade, the type of manly affection ; in " Salute au Monde " behold him raising high the hand of fellowship towards the whole world ; in the " Song of the Open Road " and in " Crossing Brooklyn Ferry " see his large and subtle philosophy and his robust faith and charity :

> " Now I reëxamine philosophies and religions,
> They may prove well in lecture rooms, yet not prove at all under the
>   spacious clouds, and along the landscape and flowing currents."

*   *   *   *   *   *   *   *   *   *   *   *

> " Only the kernel of every object nourishes;
> Where is he who tears off the husks for you and me,
> Where is he that undoes stratagems and envelops for you and me ? "

In " Whispers of Heavenly Death " behold him pensive and yearning before the inscrutable mysteries ; in " Sea Drift " see the poet in him trying to syllable the language of the unresting sea ; in the poem of " Myself " see him revelling in the whole universe, giving free rein to every faculty and attribute he possesses, and abandoning himself to a play of power unrivalled in modern poetry. Always, as I have said, it is the man exploited rather than the theme treated—it is action, power, personality ; it is me, it is you ; it is our privileges and opportunities ; it is faith, hope, charity ; it is the body, the soul, immortality ; it is our mastery over the facts of nature and destiny. He gives scenes, pictures, momentary glances as in nature, but no architectonics, no finished verbal structure—nothing apart from his personality.

We have the poet's own word that the main *motif* of his book is the treatment of man as he is in himself, in his own rights :—

> "Pressing the pulse of the life that has seldom exhibited itself (the great
>   pride of man in himself) "—

in contradistinction to the bards of the past—who have treated man as the "creature of politics, aggregates, rulers, and priests."

The poets of English literature have no doubt treated human nature more or less relatively, or as showing itself in particular conditions facing this or that problem or circumstance, rather than unloosed and confronting them all.

Our poet's aim is to outline a typical democratic man and to treat him absolutely as he is in himself, to speak out of the facts of the human body, the human passions, and the moral and spiritual nature *per se*, without any reference to precedents or conventions, or to schools or creeds; to unfold and exploit the natural abysmal man, stripped of all artificial trappings, freed from many of the distinctions imposed upon him in civilized society and exulting in that freedom.

If this looks like a return to the savage—to the barbarian—the reader has only to refer to the poems themselves to see that this is not what is meant. It is the highly developed man—the man atop of the science and the humanity of the nineteenth century—that is stripped and exploited, stripped of all ecclesiasticism, but imbued with a profound religious spirit ; stripped of poetic traditions, but charged with poetic insight and emotion ; stripped of political prejudices and preferences, but filled with the most determined patriotism ; freed from artificial checks and restraints, but quickly responsive to all generous instincts and impulses ; upholding temperance, chastity, spirituality ; cherishing the old, the poor, the deformed, the despised ; bringing the woman flush with the man ; exulting in the purity and sacredness of every organ and attribute of the human body, and speaking out of that conviction with absolute freedom and directness.

It was no part of the poet's plan to exhibit man as a member of society, or the club, or the church, or the family, or the state, but absolutely as a member of the universal brotherhood of man, acted upon and swayed by forces that make for the longevity and perpetuity of the race. Had his purpose been to show him as subject to laws and conventions, to family ties and to worldly prudence, the outcome had been different. We should have had no " Children of Adam," no exposures of what social usage covers up, no exhibition of " that pride which refuses every lesson but its own."

Everywhere the poet identifies himself with this typical, composite, democratic man, measuring himself by the largest standards, matching his spirit against the cosmic forces, and appropriating to himself all the sins, sufferings, joys, heroism of mankind :

" I match my spirit against yours, your orbs, growths, mountains, brutes,
Copious as you are, I absorb you all in myself and become the master myself.

This same composite, all-embracing character is seen in the poet whom he outlines and illustrates:

" Whichever the sex, whatever the season or place, he may go freshly, and
        gently, and safely, by day or by night,
He has the pass-key of hearts—to him the responses of the prying of hands
        on the knobs,
His welcome is universal—the flow of beauty is not more welcome or uni-
        versal than he is."   •

" The mechanics take him for a mechanic,
And the soldiers suppose him to be a captain, and the sailors that he has
        followed the sea,
And the authors take him for an author, and the artists for an artist,
And the laborers perceive he could labor with them and love them,
No matter what the work is, that he is one to follow it, or has followed it,
No matter what the nation, that he might find his brothers and sisters
        there."

        .   .   .   .

" The gentleman of perfect blood acknowledges his perfect blood,
The insulter, the prostitute, the angry person, the beggar see themselves
        in the ways of him—he strangely transmutes them,
They are not vile any more—they hardly know themselves, they are so
        grown."

Whitman averages up the race, but the whole push and stress of his work is to raise the average.

" I announce a man or woman coming—perhaps you are the one.
I announce a great individual, fluid as nature, chaste, affectionate, com-
        passionate, fully armed.
I announce a life that shall be copious, vehement, spiritual, bold.
And I announce an old age that shall lightly and joyfully meet its transla-
        tion."

Since the above pages were written the subject of them has passed from this life. Serenely, expectantly, almost joyously, did he meet his translation. Blessed release from the bondage of disease and pain ! As we performed the last solemn rites over his remains that March day in a Camden cemetery, the sun shone, the birds warbled, the waters glinted, and a great spirit of con-tentment and triumph seemed to brood over the earth,—all typical of the "large, sweet soul that has gone." Huge granite blocks, dear Master and friend, guard the portals of thy tomb, but the symbols of thee in our hearts will always be the sunshine, the tender and budding growths, and the flowing currents of the world.

JOHN BURROUGHS.

THE FAMINE IN RUSSIA.

BY THE HON. CHARLES EMORY SMITH, UNITED STATES MINISTER
AT ST. PETERSBURG.

THE present famine in Russia is one of those stupendous catastrophes which almost baffle comprehension. The general figures are sufficiently appalling ; but it is only when we picture the individual distress in its grim details and then multiply it by millions that we gain an adequate conception of the real gravity of this calamity. It is my province to deal only with the facts as they are. That involves statements and not opinions. It concerns economics and not politics. There are phases of the subject which for obvious reasons cannot here be touched upon. Whether the visitation of Providence has or has not been aggravated by administrative faults, whether there are wrongs which ought to be righted, whether the Russian Government is or is not rich and strong enough to deal with the emergency, are not questions to be discussed here. When famine afflicted Ireland, the American people did not stop to ask whether the opulent and powerful British Government could take care of it. If there are things to be said on other points this is not the place to say them. If there are representations to be made in other directions they will not be weakened by showing just, generous, and sympathetic friendship. The present question is simply one of fact and humanity. But even the salient outlines have been given only in fragmentary, disconnected, and sometimes contradictory forms, and an authentic statement will not be without interest, and possibly not without value.

It is hard to realize that in the very heart of one of the great powers of Europe there are from fourteen to sixteen millions of people in absolute want of the necessaries of life, and dependent upon measures of relief for continued existence. Yet this is the simple truth. The area over which the famine prevails is ten times as large as the State of New York. It contains a population of more than thirty millions. To say that one half of this vast population are in utter, helpless destitution, without food and without means of getting it, and that they must have perished if continuous succor had not for months been provided from other sources, seems incredible, but it is a moderate estimate. Even this statement does not present the full magnitude of the scourge. Besides the millions who may be described as completely dependent, there are other millions who are reduced to abject penury, and who can sustain themselves to the next harvest only in the most precarious way. And when to this reign of gaunt hunger we add the ravages of disease, the epidemic of typhus, the suffering from the severities of an exceptionally rigorous winter, the decimation of stock and destruction of material, and the consequent difficulties of recuperation, we have a picture of widespread distress which can hardly be overdrawn.

The first inquiry which naturally suggests itself is, whence comes so dire a disaster ? Is it possible that a single drought has produced a famine of this sweeping character ? Is it possible that there was a general failure of the crops throughout such an immense area of the richest soil in Russia ? Is it possible that such utter destitution, which reads more like ancient or remote oriental visitations, can come within the range of the modern European system ? An examination of a few crucial facts serves to explain what is at first almost incomprehensible. The region covered by the famine embraces what was, indeed, only a short time ago the most fertile and productive part of Russia. But for several years past the crops have been steadily diminishing. In 1886 the distressed provinces produced 140,914,948 chetverts of grain, or 845,489,688 bushels. In 1887 the product was three million chetverts less ; in 1888, thirteen millions less ; in 1889, thirty-five millions less ; until in 1891 it sank to 71,371,900 chetverts, or only about one-half that of 1886. A comparison with the total crops of the Empire shows the important relation which these provinces bear in the general production. Leaving the Caucasus and Poland out of the calculation, in 1886 the product of the distressed provinces was 54.87 per cent., or more than one-half the total product of the fifty governments of European Russia. In 1891 the ratio fell to 39.17 per cent.

The exports were not reduced in the same proportion. In 1888, the highest year, they amounted to 484,891,000 poods, or 17,456,076,000 English pounds. In 1890 they were 371,000,000 poods; and in 1891, the year of the famine, they still summed up 310,000,000 poods. The exports of 1891 were not, of course, from the crops of the year, but from the reserves of previous years, and they were made before the Imperial prohibition of exports came into effect. Considering the production, the consumption, and the exports together, we reach a significant result. The great staple of Russia is rye, and rye bread is the staff of life for the peasant. According to the best calculations that are available, the reserve of rye at the end of 1888 was about 338,-000,000 poods. In 1889 the consumption and exports exceeded the production by 202,000,000 poods; in 1890 the excess was 41,000,000 poods; and in 1891 it was 283,250,000 poods. Thus, despite the draft upon the reserves during the preceding years, there was still a diminishing surplus until the fatal blight of 1891 came; but that brought a deficit of 188,000,000 poods, or 6,768,000,000 pounds. As the amount annually consumed per capita is reckoned at 14½ poods, or 522 pounds, this deficiency of rye— which, be it remembered, is almost the exclusive food of the peasant—is equal to the quantity of food needed for the sustenance of 12,965,517 persons for a year! There follows but one of two alternatives—either starvation or summoning other supplies. The total harvest of 1891 of all cereals and potatoes for the sixty governments of European Russia and Poland, deducting the exports of that year, was about 14 poods per head, or a deficit of about half a pood as compared with the requirement. With the quantity on hand at the beginning there was probably enough within the Empire, if rightly distributed, to sustain the population. But while there was a surplus in some parts, there was a large deficit in others, and with the limited means of communication it was impossible to establish an equilibrium.

The primary explanation of this complete or partial failure of the crops in twenty provinces was the terrible drought in 1891. Over a large part of the afflicted territory five months passed without a drop of rain. During a portion of this time a burning sun blistered the parched soil and withered every vestige of veg-

etation. But there were other and concurrent causes. Through
the spring the fierce winds from the East swept over the un-
sheltered steppes and blasted the early promise. The winter
of 1890-1891 was one of little snow, and the unprotected frozen
soil drank less than the usual moisture from that source. Ordinarily, with the melting snow and spring floods, the overflowing
Volga spreads, like the Nile, over the plains along some parts of
its border, and nurtures a coarse grass which serves as fodder.
But even this failed last year. There was, indeed, an accumulation of all the plagues. Millions of súroks or Siberian marmots
—a species of prairie-rat—made their appearance in some provinces and, having lost their usual granaries, committed great
ravages. What the peasants call blight-clouds—myriads of
insects darkening the skies—hovered over the land, and wherever they rested they left a desert. And, finally, in estimating
the causes, something must be attributed to the primitive and un-
thrifty methods of cultivation. The famous black soil of Russia is
rich and deep, and, ordinarily, when " tickled with a hoe, it laughs
with a harvest." The rude wooden ploughs of most of the peasants penetrate but little below the surface, and with them the
drought was fatal. But, within the domain of the same drought,
on other farms where improved implements were used, where a
greater depth was reached, where irrigation existed, and where
the suroks were guarded against, there was a fair yield.

These diverse facts from different localities will explain the
diverse reports. There were spots even in the famine provinces
where the crops were good. There were districts which showed
fair harvests, side by side with others where not a blade of grass
or a sheaf of grain was reaped. How complete the failure was in
many sections may be judged from one of many illustrations
within my personal knowledge. Prince W. owns a large estate in
Tamboff. He has a valuable stud of blooded animals, which
naturally receives the best care. Yet so utter was the blight in
all his region that he was reduced for fodder to the refuse of the
sunflower plant. In such districts the besom of destruction
swept everything before it. The garden of vegetables was left as
desolate as the field of grain. Through wide districts no potatoes
were grown, and this must be remembered in reckoning the short
supply of food. In former days there were magazines within
each district kept constantly full of reserves of grain to meet

emergencies. But with the extension of the means of communication, and with the decline of direct proprietary interest through the abolition of serfdom, these safeguards have been neglected. When the reserves were called upon they were found to be missing. The magazines had crumbled and disappeared, and practically the only stores were those in the hands of the speculators. The drought came and the famine followed, with no hope of succor except from beyond the hapless region thus smitten.

When we pass from the causes to the consequences we touch a depth which no plummet can fully sound. The distress within the fated section is something beyond description. Without attempting to picture the pathetic scenes which are reported by every observer, it may be possible to indicate something of the nature and degree of the suffering. To the Russian peasant the yearly crop is everything. He saves little or nothing, but one harvest carries him to the next. The crop means not merely food but clothing, fuel, fodder, taxes, farm necessities, and all the requirements of his simple life. When it fails everything fails with it. It is terrible enough to think of fourteen millions of people on the brink of starvation and saved only by outside relief. But this is only one element of the misery. To the pangs of hunger have been added the hardships of a bitter winter. The season has been the coldest for many years, and it has been difficult to procure material even for the scanty fire that serves to keep the peasant warm. The house of the Russian peasant is a rude structure, generally of a single room, of which the most conspicuous object is the great brick stove or oven in the centre. Little fire is sufficient to heat the pile of bricks, and the shivering inmates gather around it and lie on the loft above it. But this year there is a famine of fuel as well as of food. The steppes are barren of trees, broad regions are remote from forests, and the ordinary fuel is straw. The drought was equally fatal to this supply, and in many cases the peasants were compelled to huddle together, several families in a single cottage, and to tear up the thatched roofs of abandoned homes, to cut up the planks of empty barns, to seize even upon the wooden ploughs and everything that would burn, in order to keep from freezing.

Then there is besides a famine of clothing. The garments of the peasant are of home-spun flax with a sheepskin overcoat. But the crop of flax failed like every other, and through the long

winter nights there has been none to spin. In many instances
the sheepskin was sacrificed in the early autumn for bread ; the
frail, coarse-woven suits were thin and worn ; and thus most of the
family were compelled to remain within doors, while from the
meagre and battered wardrobe of all a variegated costume was
improvised, so that one of the number could sally forth for food.
It was not an uncommon spectacle to see a wan, pale, hollow-
cheeked girl presenting herself at the soup-kitchen in the ragged·
coat of her father, in the ancient boots of her mother, and with
some sort of coarse sacking for her only dress. Anything more
pitiable could hardly be imagined than these woful sufferers,
without food, without fuel, without clothing, without work,
almost without hope, but never without patience.

Yet, unhappily, there is more to be added. Where there was
no bread it was necessary to find a substitute. The "hunger-
food," used especially in some of the remote sections, is a compound which is altogether revolting. It is variously made up of
wild arroch, straw, leaves, bark, ground acorns, a bit of potato,
sometimes with a little rye flour and sometimes without it. The
constituents differ in different places. Visitors to the famine
region have brought specimens of this "hunger-bread " to St.
Petersburg, and it has touched every heart that fellow-men could
be reduced to such extreme necessity. The use of such a diet
and the scantiness of all food could not fail to induce disease. In
some of the famine provinces there has been no typhus, but in
others it rages as an epidemic. In Tamboff there are only sporadic
cases, while in parts of Samara and Kazan the inmates of every
other house are prostrate. The Buguluk district, where the situation is at the worst, has 80,000 inhabitants and only one doctor.
In several sections the death-rate has been fifty per cent. higher
than the normal, and there are localities where the mortality has
increased several fold.

Without considering the various provinces in detail, that of
Samara may be taken as essentially typical of all. Samara is half
the size of Prussia. One of its seven districts is alone as large as
Holland. The total population of the province by the census of
1888 was 2,264,384. The official reports show that 1,368,000, or
nearly two-thirds of all, are in absolute destitution and wholly dependent on relief. Of this number only 964,500 are in receipt of
relief from the zemstvos or district councils. The remainder,

more than 400,000, have no resource except private charity. Even for the sufferers on the lists of the zemstvos the aid is scanty and insufficient. The following table gives the number of persons in each district of Samara who receive relief, the quantity in poods of grain or flour allotted to them, and the period for which this allowance is made:

District.	No. of Sufferers.	Period, Months.	Allowance.
Samara	114,450	6	603,700
Stavropol	52,830	6	159,700
Buguluk	189,630	9	1,181,900
Buguruslan	73,600	7	346,600
Bugulma	79,850	6	302,200
Nicholaresk	250,000	10	1,852,000
Novozenisk	204,140	9	1,111,500
Total	964,500		5,557,600

Reduced to simple terms, this is equivalent to five and a half poods, or 198 pounds, per capita for an average of about eight months. But the quantity ordinarily consumed per capita for that period, including children, is 348 pounds. The regular ration for the soldier in the ranks is three pounds a day. The allowance, therefore, is but little more than half the requirement, and from even that restricted allowance nearly one-third of the necessitous are altogether excluded. In the presence of this overwhelming destitution the zemstvos have found themselves unable to provide for all, and any principle of distribution involving discrimination would have worked hardships. Under their rules peasants between the ages of eighteen and fifty-five capable of work, whether they have work or not, are excluded. Children under two years of age are likewise ruled out. These classes are saved only by sharing with those who are included. In the Nicholaeevsk district alone 114,000 workers were left without relief. The zemstvos seem to have proceeded on the theory that the peasants who owned one, two, or three horses were not destitute, because they could realize on this stock. A horse was reckoned at not less than 20 roubles, and two horses if sold at 40 roubles would furnish ample support for the winter. Unfortunately this calculation, which was made in the early autumn as the basis of the regulations, turned out to be entirely fallacious. Hunger pressed, fodder was as scarce as bread; money was still more rare; so that peasants were compelled to let their horses perish for lack of provender, or to sell them for two or three roubles, oftentimes for less, and still more often to slaughter them for the paltry value of the hide. Under the overpowering distress and necessities all calculations completely broke down.

Indeed, nothing more signally illustrates the gravity of the calamity than the terrible decimation of farm animals, and this is one of the most serious factors of the problem for the future. In Samara out of 1,160,300 horses enumerated in the early autumn, more than 600,000 have been killed or have perished. Out of a total of 460,000 cattle only about 180,000 are left, and of the two and a quarter million sheep scarcely any remain. The details of a few villages, which have been specially gathered and furnished to the writer by an observer on the ground, will bring this awful havoc still closer home. In the village of Antonoffka only 40 horses remain out of 319 ; in Irschoffka, only 23 out of 227 ; in Soloffka, only 20 out of 240 ; in Gallgoffka, only 23 out of 400 ; in Patroffka, out of 500 families that had horses in the autumn only 200 have any left; and in Aleneffka 300 out of 700 farmsteads have no horses for the spring farming. In the province of Saratoff only one-third of the horses remain, and one-eighth of the cattle. In Tamboff more than half have been sacrificed. Official reports state that in Voronezh 100,000 horses out of 400,000 had perished up to the first of January. Thus the total destruction through all the famine provinces amounts to millions, and years will be required to recover from the blow. Measure this loss, consider the lean and haggard animals that remain, think of the peasants pinched and enfeebled by a long winter of hunger, remember that even the seed-grain has been consumed in many cases under the terrible stress of the hour, and we can form some idea of the difficulties under which the spring farming opens.

Many seeking to escape from these dread conditions have emigrated even as far as Tomsk in Siberia, perhaps never to return ; many have wandered forth only to fall into a worse situation. Some have perished on the road, some have found their way back, and some have met a more cruel fate. Early in the autumn a number of German colonists left their homes in Samara in the hope of finding a better state of affairs, and moved eastward into Orenburg. But they were yet within the domain of the famine, and, to make matters still worse, the early winter overtook them before provision could be made for houses. In this exigency they were compelled to dig holes in the earth for dwelling places. Disease and death inevitably followed, and the informant of the writer related how he saw in some of these caves seventeen or eighteen inmates with two or three dead among them. As soon as intelligence of this appalling situation reached St. Petersburg Sisters of Mercy were hastened to the scene, but the best they can do is simply to alleviate the distress. It is not to be understood that this is a picture of what exists everywhere, but it is one of the many incidents of an · almost immeasurable calamity which is full of pathos and pity.

In the presence of this national disaster the Russian Government has not been passive. Without reviewing the administrative system, it must be said that it has sought to grapple in liberal measure with the tremendous problem. Before the first of March it had appropriated 150,000,000 roubles, or $75,000,000, for this purpose, and the · direct outlay before June can hardly be less than 200,000,000 roubles. Besides this, taxes have been remitted, and work has been furnished where practicable. Vast quantities of grain have been bought and brought from the rich fields of the Caucasus, though, with the limited means of communication and the loss of horses, it has been difficult to convey it to the regions remote from the railroads. Large public works under the direction of the famous General Annenkoff of the Trans-Caspian railroad, and employing hundreds of thousands of men, have been undertaken. The forests of the imperial domain have been opened to the peasants for fuel. The direct appropriations by the Government to the zemstvos are nominally advances or loans, but it is hard to see how they are to be repaid. A large proportion of the peasantry are already in debt. Even in 1888 the peasants of Samara had to borrow 1,056,000 roubles, and the grasping Koolaks or usurers multiply the burden. With this load of indebtedness, and with the sweeping destruction of stock, it seems impossible to repay the present advances of the Government, and the enormous sum may doubtless be treated as a gift.

But, regarded for the present nominally as a relief loan, it is limited in its application to the members of the local communes. The allowance is thirty pounds of grain a month per capita. This, as already seen, is less than half the normal requirements of healthy men ; but small as it is, when the peasant has paid the cost of milling and transport, his thirty pounds are reduced to twenty. But, on the other hand, small as it is in the individual item, it becomes colossal in the aggregate, and at the famine prices involves colossal expenditure. So little suffices for the Russian peasant that a sum equivalent to seventy cents will sustain life for a month. But when it becomes a question of a million lives for which the government must care, as in Samara alone, and when this support must be continued for a period of ten months, the cost rises to seven millions of dollars. As has been shown in the case of Samara, the proportion of sufferers relieved by the zemstvos is two-thirds, leaving one-third wholly dependent upon private benevolence; and, taking all the famine provinces, even this one-third mounts up to the millions. This appeal to personal philanthropy has brought out noble examples of generosity and devotion. The proprietary class have, as a rule, in this emergency, proved worthy of their position and responsibilities. There are single families taking care of as many as twenty thousand people. The women especially have come forward with a consecration and self-sacrifice which commands admiration. If it were not invidious or indelicate, many cases might be cited of ladies of gentle birth who have left their homes, braved the dangers of disease, faced the hardships of an unaccustomed and trying life, and given up weeks and months to the work of feeding the hungry and ministering to the sick. With much that has been deplorable, there have been also in this work many exhibitions of true nobility. One other thing ought in fairness to be said. The Emperor has been published abroad as indifferent. It is only just to remark that this peculiar kind of indifference has been manifested not merely in a vigorous direction of the later governmental operations of relief, even to the summary dismissal of inefficient agents, but in gifts from his private purse, which, if the belief of St. Petersburg can be accepted, amount to fifteen or twenty times all the contributions of all the world outside of Russia.

A word respecting the large and generous contributions from America may be of interest. The dispatch of three ships, as thus far known—the "Indiana," the "Missouri," the "Conemaugh," and perhaps a fourth—laden with flour and other breadstuffs, has made a deep impression in Russia. Besides these ample cargoes very considerable sums of money have been forwarded. Independently of those which have been sent through private channels and of which there is no account, the amount received at the present writing is more than one hundred and twenty-five thousand roubles. The spirit which prompts these liberal offerings is most warmly appreciated by the Russian Government and people. The knowledge of it has extended even to the remote interior, and the name of America is gratefully cherished. Such arrangements have been made at St. Petersburg for faithful and efficient distribution through responsible and trustworthy channels that assurance may confidently be given of the judicious and conscientious application of all the American donations to the object to which they are consecrated. It seems clear that, including the cargoes, these donations will aggregate a million roubles in value. That is equivalent to supporting more than 21,000,000 of people a day, or more than 700,000 a month, and the American contributors may accept that result as their practical work of humanity.

And, finally, what of the future? The famine is a severe temporary blow to Russia, but not irreparable. In actual losses, in increased prices, in direct and indirect consequences, it costs the Russian people more than a thousand million roubles. With their indebtedness and the devastation of their stock, the unfortunate sufferers in the afflicted provinces are plunged in a condition from which, at the best, it will take years to recover. But the Empire as a whole, with its boundless resources, has great recuperative force. The chief thought now is turned to the next harvest in the famine region. If it shall be fair, the skies will brighten; but if there shall be another failure, the clouds will settle down blacker than ever. The immediate problems, aside from sustaining life, are to provide seed for the spring sowing, and to make up the loss of farm animals. It is difficult to judge how far the first has been successful, and it is certain that the second is a work of time. Worn and emaciated with long struggle, and stripped of their material, the peasants face the requirements of a new harvest year under a load which would crush almost any other people. But their patience and endurance are without limit, and whatever their destiny, they accept it with a grim stoicism.

CHARLES EMORY SMITH.

THE RULE OF THE GOLD KINGS.

BY THE THE HON. WM. M. STEWART, CHAIRMAN OF THE SENATE COMMITTEE ON MINES AND MINING.

THE leading nations of the commercial world, France excepted, refuse to use silver coin as money of ultimate payment. Some of them, notably England, do so in pursuance of law ; but the United States treats silver coin as credit money, depending for its value upon a promise of redemption in gold, in violation of law. The law makes no discrimination between the coins of gold and silver, but all administrations of the Treasury Department since 1873 have discriminated against silver coin and in favor of gold coin in the payment of national obligations.

No political party has openly defied public opinion by a declaration that silver ought to be treated as a commodity and gold coin alone used in the payment of national obligations. On the contrary, the Democratic party, previous to the election of Mr. Cleveland in 1884, uniformly declared in its national platforms that silver was honest money equally with gold. In 1880 the platform of the national Democratic party contained the following :

"We pledge ourselves anew to honest money, consisting of gold and silver, and paper, convertible into coin on demand."

In 1884 the national platform of the Democratic party contained more explicit language, as follows :

"We believe in honest money, the gold and silver coinage of the Constitution, and a circulating medium convertible into such money without loss."

After Mr. Cleveland's election, and before he took the oath of office (on February 24, 1885) he attempted to induce the Democratic party to suspend the purchase and coinage of silver under the Bland act, and alleged, as a reason, that gold coin was the standard, and that a silver dollar was worth less than 85 cents. He disregarded the fact that he was elected on a platform which declared that silver coin was honest money, and that silver as well as gold was the money of the constitution. He said :

"Silver and silver certificates have displaced and are now displacing gold, and the sum of gold in the Federal Treasury now available for the payment of the gold obligations of the United States and for the redemption of the United States notes called 'greenbacks,' if not already encroached upon, is perilously near such encroachment." (Letter to Hon. A. J. Warner and others, Members of the Forty-eighth Congress.)

Contempt for the Democratic platform and the laws of Congress could not have been more strongly expressed. There were no " gold obligations of the United States." All such obliga- tions were then and are now payable in coin of either gold or silver, at the option of the Government. He could not have been ignorant of the great debate in Congress, in 1878, imme- diately preceding the passage of the Bland act, or of the resolu- tion which followed as a result of that debate. That resolution, after reciting the various acts of Congress relating to the subject, declared :

"That all the bonds of the United States issued or authorized to be is- sued under the said acts of Congress hereinbefore recited are payable, prin- cipal and interest, at the option of the Government of the United States, in silver dollars, of the coinage of the United States, containing 412½ grains each of standard silver; and that to restore to its coinage such silver coins as a legal tender in payment of said bonds, principal and interest, is not in violation of the public faith, nor in derogation of the rights of the public creditor." (*Cong. Record*, Forty-fifth Congress, second session, Vol- ume 7, part 1, page 627.)

Mr. Cleveland was untiring in his efforts to stop the coinage of silver. In August, 1885, he instructed Mr. Walker, our Consul-General at Paris, to inform the Monetary Conference, then in session, that the United States was almost prepared to discontinue the coinage of silver. After the receipt of this infor- mation the Conference entered into an agreement to dissolve the Latin Union. In his messages to Congress in December, 1885, and 1886, he strenuously urged the repeal of the Bland act and the utter demonetization of silver.

During the Fiftieth Congress the Senate amended the Bond Purchasing Bill, as it was called, which came to it from the House, by adding thereto a provision requiring the purchase of enough silver, in addition to the amount required to be purchased under the Bland act, to take the place of national bank notes retired. This bill was smothered in the Committee of the House through the influence of the Executive.

The Convention in 1888, which nominated Mr. Cleveland, was, through his influence, silent on the silver question. The Republican party was then out of power, and it became its turn to make promises, to regain control of the government. It declared that—

"The Republican party is in favor of the use of both gold and silver as money, and condemns the policy of the Democratic administration in its efforts to demonetize silver."

After the election the country was very soon made to understand that the gold association of London and New York was doing business at the old stand, corner of Fifteenth Street and Pennsylvania Avenue, Washington, D. C. But the friends of honest money, the gold and silver coin of the constitution, renewed their efforts to restore silver to the place it occupied as the money of the people previous to the mysterious and disastrous legislation of 1873.

The Administration marshalled its forces to defeat the coinage of silver on the terms and conditions applicable to the coinage of gold. It was a drawn battle between the representatives of the people and the representatives of Lombard and Wall Streets, headed by the Republican Administration, which acquired power under the promise to use silver as money and not as a commodity.

A compromise was finally effected. An act was passed in July, 1890, requiring the purchase of four and a half million ounces of silver bullion per month at the market price, and the issuance of legal-tender treasury notes thereon. This act would have been a step towards free coinage if it could have been administered according to its manifest purpose and intent. But it fell into unfriendly hands. The act declares that it is the established policy of the United States to maintain the parity of the two metals (gold and silver, not the two coins) according to the present legal ratio.

Such parity would make $412\frac{1}{2}$ grains of standard silver worth one dollar, and $25\frac{8}{10}$ grains of standard gold also worth a dollar. Silver would be worth, if such parity were maintained, $1.2929 per ounce. The President set the key-note for the depression of the price of silver by assuming that silver is not honest money. He declared in numerous speeches in his campaign "around the circle" that he would exert all the power of his administration to make each dollar equal to every other dollar. He did not say, in so many words, that the United States had issued and put in circulation about $500,000,000 of silver coin, or its paper representatives, which was not good money, and that there was a law on the statute-book providing for the issuance of about $50,000,000 annually of the same kind of depreciated money, but he indorsed the argument of his gold associates that the silver dollar is a seventy-cent dollar.

I am aware that it has been erroneously stated that the treasury notes issued under the act of 1890 are secured by bullion at its market price, dollar for dollar. This is not true. Treasury notes have no security except the promise of the Government to redeem them in gold or silver coin, at the option of the United States. The bullion purchased by the issuance of these notes is held in the Treasury for coinage, and when coined the United States will make the difference between the market price at which the bullion was bought and its coinage value. The holder of treasury notes cannot demand bullion in exchange for or in redemption of the note he holds. By the express language of the law it is the right and duty of the Government to pay these notes in silver coin, dollar for dollar. They are, in fact, representatives of so many silver dollars, unless the government finds it convenient or profitable to pay them in gold.

Is it possible that the President of the United States means to say that the Government has put in circulation between $400,-000,000 and $500,000,000 of fraudulent seventy-cent dollars, and is continuing to issue such dollars at the rate of $50,000,000 a year ? If not, what does he mean, and what has the Administration done to remedy this evil and sustain the parity between the two metals ?

The law provides a method of advancing the price of silver by increasing the demand for its use. The silver purchased by the issuance of treasury notes is required to be coined and used for the redemption of such notes. Has the President made any attempt to extend the use of silver by coining and using it or having it ready for use as required by law ? On the contrary, has he not sanctioned the action of the Secretary of the Treasury in denying to silver the use provided for it by the act of 1890 ? The act provides that the treasury notes issued for the purchase of silver bullion shall be redeemed in either gold or silver coin, at the option of the United States, not at the option of the holders of such notes. The act declares that the Secretary of the Treasury "shall (not "may") coin of the silver bullion purchased under the provisions of this act as much as may be necessary to provide for the redemption of the treasury notes herein provided for."

This the Secretary has refused to do, and he has also refused to require the redemption of such Treasury notes in silver coin under any circumstances. On the contrary, he declares that rather than pay out silver as required by law, he will sell bonds, buy gold, and increase the national debt for the purpose of redeeming treasury notes, and let the silver bullion purchased for that purpose lie idle in the vaults of the Treasury.

On the 17th of November, 1891, when the Secretary made his customary visit to New York to ascertain the wishes of the gold association or trust, he faithfully promised to violate the law. He said that—

" The resumption act confers authority upon the Secretary of the Treasury to issue bonds to any extent he may feel called upon to do to increase or maintain the gold reserve. The act of July 14, 1890, commands him to preserve the parity between gold and silver. It has always been the custom of this country to pay its obligations in gold. (Applause.) Therefore, should there be any trouble about this, and the present hundred millions of gold or reserve fund, as we call it, be intrenched upon, it was in his power under the law to issue bonds for gold paying 5 per cent., and replace or increase the reserve fund."

The resumption act confers no such authority. It simply authorized the Secretary of the Treasury to sell bonds to obtain gold to redeem any legal-tender treasury notes which might be outstanding on the 1st day of January, 1879, but did not authorize the sale of bonds to buy gold for any other purpose. The act of 1890 provided for a different class of treasury notes, which were not outstanding on the 1st day of January, 1879, and also provided for the coinage of silver with which to redeem them. The promise which the Secretary of the Treasury made to his gold associates at Delmonico's on the 17th of November last was approved by the President in his message of December last, in the following words :

" Under existing legislation it is in the power of the Treasury Department to maintain that essential condition of national finance as well as of commercial prosperity—the parity in use of the coin dollars and their paper representatives. The assurance that these powers would be freely and unhesitatingly used has done much to produce and sustain the present favorable business conditions."

Was the refusal of the Secretary of the Treasury, with the approval of the President, to obey the law and provide for the redemption of treasury notes by the coinage of silver treating silver coin as money ? Was it not a manifest violation of law ? Was it not a violation of the party pledge to use both gold and silver as money ?

France, in 1875, ceased to coin silver, but she did not attempt to disparage the silver which had already been coined. On the contrary she has always kept her reserves of gold and silver about equal and paid her public creditors in either gold or silver, whichever was most beneficial or convenient for the government. The contrast between the administration of France in obeying the law, and the action of the Treasury Department in disregarding the statutes of the United States by discriminating against silver, is most remarkable.

The United States contracted an enormous war debt, payable in greenbacks. In March, 1869, an act was passed declaring that the public debt was payable in gold or silver coin. The act of July 14, 1870, authorizing the refunding of the national debt under which all outstanding United States bonds were issued, provides for their redemption in coin of the standard value of that date, to wit, a dollar composed of $25\frac{8}{10}$-grains of standard gold or $412\frac{1}{2}$ grains of standard silver.

From 1873 until the present time every obligation of the United States has been payable in silver. No Secretary of the Treasury has exercised the option to pay in silver, but in violation of law every Secretary has given the bondholder the option to require payment in gold, and finally the present Secretary, with the indorsement of the President, has made a solemn promise, without the authority of law, to issue bonds to redeem treasury notes which, by the act of 1890, are redeemable in silver. The repudiation of silver by the Administration, and the assumption that it is not good money for the payment of debts, are, in effect, a declaration that silver coin and its representatives in treasury notes and silver certificates are not good money. It is a declaration that one-half of the money of the

United States in actual circulation, exclusive of the reserves in the Treasury and in national banks, is not good money, but is a depreciated and fraudulent currency palmed off by the Government of the United States upon the people.

Whither does the assertion that the silver dollar and its paper representatives are only seventy-cent dollars lead ? More than one-half, as before stated, of the money in actual circulation in the United States is of this character ; and under the act of 1890 • $50,000,000 more of the same kind of money is annually added to the circulation of the country. What is to be done with it ? Shall it be repudiated and retired, and the actual circulation be contracted one-half, or shall it be made good by appropriate legislation ?

The United States cannot afford further to depreciate and degrade silver and deny to it its money function. The legislation has gone too far. Silver bullion must be maintained at a parity with gold bullion at the ratio established by law. Free coinage will do this, and nothing short of free coinage will accomplish the purpose ; for whenever the Government at the mint discriminates against either of the metals, the people will do the same. If silver is not to be restored to the place it occupied previous to 1873, why did the Democratic party, while it was out of power, declare that silver was honest money equally with gold ? Why did the Republican party, when it sought to regain power, declare that it was in favor of the use of both gold and silver as money, and why did it condemn the administration of President Cleveland for its efforts in demonetizing silver ?

The value of all articles desired by man, when the quantity is limited, is determined by the law of supply and demand. Until the unfortunate legislation of 1873 there was an unlimited demand at the mint for both gold and silver at the ratio established by law. That unlimited demand, so far as gold is concerned, still remains, but the demand for silver for coinage has been destroyed by law. The market value of both gold and silver always has been and always will be the mint price, because no man would sell either gold or silver for a less price than he can obtain at the mint. Free coinage maintained the parity of the two metals from the foundation of the Government until the right of coinage was denied to silver. Who can say that free coinage would not now have a like effect in restoring and maintaining such parity ? Free

coinage would make the demand for silver equal to the demand
for gold, and the mint price would determine the market price as
it did from the foundation of the Government until the conspiracy
was formed to reject silver.

What must be the inevitable result upon the civilized world of
the single gold standard ? Eighteen years ago there were about
$7,500,000,000 of gold and silver coin in the world, which, in the
language of the Royal Commission of England, was one money.
To-day all the gold coin in the world does not exceed $3,700,000,-
000. If the basis of circulation and credit is confined to gold
alone, the danger line is already passed. Never in the history of
the world did there exist as large a volume of credit as we now
have, resting upon so narrow a basis.

Since silver was demonetized there have been purchased, and are
now held as government and bank reserves, not less than a thousand millions of gold coin, besides many thousands of millions that
have been daily purchased to liquidate obligations contracted to
be paid in silver or paper. The United States has purchased
several thousand millions to pay interest and maturing obligations,
and now holds for reserves (for little or none of it is in circulation) nearly $600,000,000 of gold. Germany has followed the
example of the United States in the purchase of gold. Egypt
and Italy have been compelled to do the same. These purchases
were compelled by law, because the right to use silver was denied
by legislation.

The gold contractionists are not satisfied. They are attempting to compel Austria (and she has begun the deadly work) to buy
some $200,000,000 of gold to hold in her treasury as a basis for
gold resumption. This will require about 5 per cent. of all the
gold in the world. They further threaten that England will
require India to replace her $900,000,000 of silver with gold,
which would require 25 per cent. of the gold in the world. The
gold advocates even contend that France must ultimately join the
gold trust and dispose of her $650,000,000 of silver and replace
the same with gold.

It must be borne in mind that the nation or the people who
succeed in this fierce competition in accumulating gold must pay
the highest price, which means that they must sell their labor
and their products cheapest. The competition in purchasing
gold to discharge obligations payable in silver has already reduced

the price of farm products in this country fully 50 per cent., and if the process which the gold men advocate is continued until the gold standard is reached throughout the world, prices must fall more than 50 per cent. below their present level. The obligations to pay money already existing will require sacrifices such as no generation of men have ever made.

The Secretary of the Treasury, in his celebrated speech of November 17, 1891, admitted that there was not gold enough for use as money. He said :

"It is now agreed on all sides that gold alone furnishes too narrow a basis upon which to conduct the money affairs of the world."

A more patent truth was never uttered. In the face of this admitted fact he proposed to treat the $500,000,000 of silver coin, silver certificates and treasury notes as merely credit money depending upon the narrow basis—gold—and pledged himself to the gold syndicate that he would not sell bonds and buy gold to redeem treasury notes as provided by the act of 1890, for the purpose of avoiding the use of silver as money.

What more daring and audacious proposition could be suggested for the purpose of enhancing the price of gold and depressing the price of property than to sell bonds and buy gold to redeem all the treasury notes which may be issued under the act of 1890 ? The execution of such a project, if successful, would destroy the reserves of gold of every country in Europe, enormously advance the price of gold, and increase the disparity between gold and silver bullion. Is not this a strange way of executing a statute, the declared intention of which is to maintain the parity between the two metals ?

The advocates of gold express great anxiety to make each dollar as good as every other dollar. This may be done, it is true, by a promise to redeem one dollar in another dollar. The Government may promise to redeem its paper money and its silver money in gold coin. While such a promise can be maintained, the paper money and the silver money are as good as the gold money, but the silver money in such a case is merely credit money, depending upon the promise to redeem in gold for its value, and is no better than paper money.

The only possible way to make a silver dollar as good as a gold dollar, in the full sense of the expression, is to restore silver to the place it occupied previous to 1873. Give it the money function ; treat it as the money of the constitution ; open the mints to its free coinage ; make an unlimited demand for it at a fixed price, and the price so fixed at the mint will be the market price of the bullion ; for no one will sell 412½ grains of silver for less than a dollar if he can have it exchanged at the mint for a dollar. This method has been tried and never failed. It is the mode prescribed by the constitution, indorsed by the Democratic party in 1880 and 1884, and by the Republican party in 1888, but now repudiated by a Republican administration.

The fact that the Executive Department has prevented the use of silver as money for eighteen years, by obstructing the passage of a free-coinage law and by refusing to recognize silver coin as money for the purpose of paying national obligations, is a warning which the people cannot afford to disregard. Is it probable that the gold trust will select different candidates in the future from those whom it has selected in the past ? Is it probable, so long as the gold trust is allowed to designate candidates for the Presidency, that the people will obtain relief from the calamity of contraction, falling prices, stagnation in business, and hard times ?

Free coinage of silver is no experiment. It was practised from the foundation of the Government until 1873. At that time there was not too much coin of gold and silver for use as money. There has not been too much of both gold and silver produced since that time to supply the growing demands of business. The entire production of both metals has not been enough to keep pace with the growth of population. There has not been half enough gold produced for that purpose. There is no probability of an increased supply of gold. On the contrary, the demand for gold for ornaments and use in the arts is increasing. The amount of gold coin must decrease rather than increase. All the gold in the world is either owned or controlled by a very few men. The question for the people to decide is, Shall the rule of the gold kings be perpetual ?

WM. M. STEWART.

THE BEHRING SEA CONTROVERSY.

BY GEN. B. F. BUTLER AND THE MARQUIS OF LORNE.

GEN. B. F. BUTLER:

It is not a misfortune that, in examining this subject of difference between Great Britain and the United States, we are
relieved from going into the musty learning which might be
necessary to determine our national rights and our title to property that we claim. For all present use those questions are passed
by.

All claims to the lands and waters on this continent have
been obtained through the right of discovery and occupation.
Through these, more than a hundred years ago, Russia
came into possession of the Aleutian Islands and the territory now called Alaska, and exercised exclusive jurisdiction, un-
questioned, against all the world, until she transferred her said
possessions and appertaining rights thereto, to the United States.
Since then and until within the last five years this government
has exercised over said possessions jurisdiction substantially the
same as that which had been previously exercised and claimed by
Russia.

Now, one nation only, Great Britain, sets up an adverse claim,
insisting that her subjects under her flag may appropriate, at all
seasons of the year, the fur-bearing seals and sea otters, which
have their homes on the islands and shores, wherever they may
be found while swimming in the sea—not forbearing also to
slaughter them on shore. To such action of the Canadian English
subjects our government protested and took measures to protect
these animals from being thus hunted to their possible extinc-

tion and to our injury. Whereupon her government suggested to our government that these opposing claims of the two nations be submitted to arbitrament to determine the rights of each, by which both nations should abide ; proposing that until those rights were so established both nations should cease hunting the seals, and should send ships to guard the waters in dispute from all vessels violating the claimed rights of either party. They, consequently, entered into an agreement known in diplomacy as a *"modus vivendi,"* i. e., a manner of conduct of subjects of both nations in that regard while the contentions were being decided, so that the seals might not be destroyed ; and that *modus* has existed for one sealing season. It now appears beyond dispute that under that *modus,* while United States vessels and English vessels were guarding the waters, many thousand seals were destroyed, more than were ever taken in a single season before ; so that so far as the seals were concerned the *modus* was a misnomer, being in fact a *modus exterminandi.* Our vessels seized four of the poaching schooners, two under the American flag and two under the British flag, and took them to San Francisco, and had them condemned by the courts. The enormous navy of England, which is her pride and her boast, during that year seized two British poaching vessels and took them into her ports, but history does not record any other trouble that happened to them.

The submission by treaty of the rights of the parties to arbitration is a mutual acknowledgment as regards each other to the full extent of the rights claimed by each while the arbitration is pending. And both are bound not to do anything to disturb the claimed rights of either until a decision is reached.

After delays in relation to the details of the arbitration, of which neither party complains, the treaty establishing it was concluded in due form by England, was signed by President Harrison and was by him submitted to the Senate.

Supposing that nothing stood in the way of the ratification of the treaty, the President addressed a note to Lord Salisbury, asking that the *modus vivendi* should be continued during the pendency of the arbitration, and stating the necessity of both nations very early taking the seals in charge, because some forty-seven vessels had sailed from Canadian ports for the purpose of catching the seals at an earlier day and in a larger number than ever before ; so that, in his belief, there was danger of the destruction of the seals, as the larger portion of the catch was of the female seal in the water on its way to our islands and shores to its breeding haunts.

To that note the British premier made answer, that he did not propose to renew the *modus vivendi* during the time of the arbitration, because that time was likely to cover the sealing season of 1893, and as the Canadian poachers had expended a great deal of capital in fitting out their vessels, if they failed to catch seals enough to make the enterprise profitable, they would be damaged. His Lordship was apparently unmindful of the fact that, if the arbitration went on long enough, all the seals might be destroyed, and that when the arbitrators found in favor of the United States there would be no property on which the award could operate, and so the trouble and expense of the arbitration would be thrown away.

Let us illustrate his Lordship's proposition. It may, perhaps, be well done in this way : A had a fine and profitable piece of timber land, inherited from his ancestors, to which nobody had made any claim within the memory of man. Suddenly his neighbor B claims the right to cut the wood and timber off that land, and makes that claim in the form of chopping it down and taking it away. A tries to stop him in this unneighborly work of devastation. B, asserting his rights, says, " I will submit our respective rights to this property to arbitration," B being a litigious fellow. A, not wanting a lawsuit, says, " Agreed ; let us arbitrate, but in the meantime let us so arrange it that nobody shall cut any of the trees during the arbitration." While the formalities of making out the form of arbitrament are going on, both mutually agree to help watch the woodchoppers so that the trees may be spared. The arbitration being concluded upon, A says to B : "Let us continue to watch the woodchoppers until the award is made." " Oh, no ! " says B, " my woodchoppers have put themselves to great expense in providing the tools with which to cut down the timber, and teams to haul it away, and they will lose their investment of capital if they do not go on cutting and taking the timber. Therefore, I am going to aid them all I can in their operations."

What would be said of such a transaction in ordinary life and such conduct between man and man ?

But Lord Salisbury's proposition does not stop there even.

He says : "Let my choppers go on and cut all the wood they can ; you find out the names of those who do it, if you can, and take the bond of each of them, so that they may pay the damage." Now, then, if such action was taken by B against A, and he should go to his friends and say, "What ought to be done to a man who has treated me like that ?" would not the reply of his friends be, "If he does not apologize for his insulting proposition, and behave himself, whip him like a dog, if you can ; whether you can or not, it is due to your manhood and self-respect to try ?" Would not the just judgment of all men sanction such a course ?

Leaving our illustration and returning to the case under consideration :

What President Harrison did do was, to reply to Lord Salisbury, in proper phrase, that he should maintain the dignity and honor of his country and her national rights by protecting those and her property with all the resources within his power. *Nothing more.*

For that he has been severely and wantonly criticised by all the anglophobists and anglophilists in the country. Their cry is : "Such language will bring on a war with England. Would he have a war for a few seals ?" No, nor many, nor for almost any amount of money that could be named, but we should have a war, if our wrongs can be rectified in no other way, for one seal or for one dollar, if the attempt is to force it from the United States by insult, contumely, and disregard of our honor and high place among the nations of the earth. And the united press of England added to these cries the aspersions on our President that he was compelled to this proposition, to sustain the honor and dignity of our country, by his desire to be re-elected to his high office, and that he acted upon that ignoble and selfish motive only. Such accusations as to the motives of our highest officer and of our ruler in foreign affairs are a gross, national insult of the vilest sort, and are indeed more provocative of war than could be the loss of the largest sum of money. This is not the first time we have suffered such insults from Great Britain, and that in the person of her high officer ; it was duly resented then, as I hope may ever be the case.

Because of similar accusations made by Mr. West, the British Minister, in a private letter, that President Cleveland was actuated by such political motives in some of his official acts, which letter was published by the recipient without the knowledge of Minister West,. President Cleveland, deeming it a British insult, made representations of the matter to the British Government and asked that West be recalled, and that Government advised President Cleveland to send him home. This the President did, " without standing on the order of his going."

Before going farther, let me declare my opinion and most firm belief that a war between this country and Great Britain is impossible, because England could not be well provoked by anything that our sense of justice, our honor as a nation, and the high position we hold, would permit us to do, or allow to be done, towards any nation.

Let us see what is England's condition as regards a war with us. I admit she has a large and powerful navy on which she relies to threaten us with the piratical warfare of bombarding our cities, destroying our property, and murdering our women and children. No other nation in the world threatens to carry on a war in that way except against barbarians.

England knows that she could not land men on this continent who could stay here seven days. She did manage in the War of 1812 to land a flying party near Baltimore, which marched to Washington and destroyed our public ouildings.

During all the wars of Europe, even under Napoleon, wherein quite all its capitals were occupied by invading armies, no such act of vandalism was done, and as soon as the English had done it in our case the incendiaries fled to their ships. Even Moscow was set on fire by the Russians themselves to prevent its falling into the hands of Napoleon and affording him the additional prestige that he would gain by occupying it as his winter quarters.

Great Britain is not a warlike people. She never had more than twenty-five thousand soldiers from her own islands between the four seas on any battlefield. and those were at Waterloo, while we had in our late war more than that number to starve or die of wounds or sickness in a single prison. Does any one believe that England will ever forget that at the close of our war we disbanded quite two millions of soldiers, and that half a million of them are yet alive to take a hand in any war in which the honor of our country is assailed by Great Britain ? I have said, and perhaps may be criticised for it, that she is not a warlike nation. Her government is continually making war on small nations and hiring someone else to do the fighting.

If there is anything on which England can pride herself for prowess in war it is her navy. But she cannot forget that, until almost within this generation, that navy could only be supplied with sailors sufficient to man it by dragging them from their homes by press gangs. The Marquis of Salisbury seems to have faith in bonds in settling difficulties between England and this country. Be it so. England has given this country bonds in untold millions that she will keep the peace and be of good behavior. The first gun fired in the Behring Sea by one of her war vessels against one of our war vessels would be war, as much as the first gun fired at Fort Sumter or as the Battle of Gettysburg. War abrogates all treaties of amity and commerce. War permits the confiscation of all property of one belligerent found on the shores or within the jurisdiction of the other. Every debt, demand, certificate of stock, due from an American would be at once forfeited and confiscated. Every rood of our land owned by English syndicates or subjects would be lost to her. It would seem as if we could find the means to carry on the war by selling her property in open market, and using the proceeds ; and when we hear the shells from her fleet, if we should do so, breaking the plate glass in Broadway, we should be comfortably remembering that a great deal of it belongs to English people.

Stopping the export of cotton for three months would starve Manchester and its workmen, and be of advantage to us, as cotton is very low in price and we could use it.

Let us look at some other foreign complications which are to be taken into account by England in case of war with us. Russia still has her eye on Constantinople, and might think it a good time, when England was thus crippled, to carry out her dream of empire so long and steadily maintained by her Czars. She might be deterred from entering on her purpose lest she should disturb the peace of Europe. But India lies at Russia's very door with every road opening into it, and the possession of her wheat fields would give her command of the sustenance of the Eastern Hemisphere, at a time when the superabundance of corn and wheat from the valleys of the Red River of the North and the fields of Manitoba, which now fill fifteen thousand freight cars yearly, and which pass over the Canadian railways, would be blocked by

the American forces.   England, indeed, would not doubt that
upon land we are her superiors.

In a war by sea she must suffer far more than we.   She
has substantially the carrying-trade of the world, reckoning
what she robbed from us during the War of the Rebellion by the
aid of the rebel cruisers which she sent from her ports, and for the
doing of which she humbly expressed her regrets in the most
formal manner in the treaty at Washington as a preliminary to
be allowed to treat with us, as follows :

> "And whereas Her Britannic Majesty has authorized her high commis-
> sioners and plenipotentiaries to express, in a friendly spirit, the regret felt
> by Her Majesty's Government for the escape, under whatever circum-
> stances, of the " Alabama " and other vessels from British ports, and for the
> depredations committed by those vessels:
> "Now, in order to remove and adjust all complaints and claims on the
> part of the United States," etc.

Our letters of marque and reprisal (for we did not agree to
the treaty of Paris, which England pressed us to adopt at the
beginning of our Civil War and which put privateering under the
ban of international law) would swarm out of every port, and sweep
her commerce from the ocean.   One thing is certain : If our
ships are not as heavy as hers, they are swifter and lighter heeled,
which her commercial marine would find out to its cost.

These are a few of the reasons why I cannot conceive that we
can ever have a war with England ; and because, also, we shall
never demand anything of her but what we believe to be right,
nor submit to anything from her which we believe to be
wrong.

Much criticism has been expended upon President Harrison
because of the honest, manly, firm, and unflinching declaration
that no interference with our rights would be permitted while our
case was being tried.   This was called " Jingoism," and it was
said that it was only done by him for selfish political purposes.
The change of a single word in all that makes it high praise.   It
was manfully done for the *politic* purpose to maintain the honor
and dignity of the country.   And it has succeeded, as in the history of our diplomacy such manful presentation of our rights has
always done.   Let us recall to the mind of this generation that
when we have had great men for Presidents, our rights have always
been thus presented to every nation which has undertaken to baffle

us by neglect, or through adroit diplomacy to postpone a fulfilment of treaty engagements.

Let us call to mind the French Spoliation claims, which had
been recognized by France for more than twenty-five years before
she would make a treaty to pay them, whereby those of our citizens who had been despoiled by her continuous neglect went
down to their graves in poverty and distress. By treaty the
French nation had promised to pay the money in yearly instalments, but neglected to answer the draft of President Jackson's
Secretary of the Treasury when presented on the 23d of March,
1834, to the French Minister of Finance, who declared that no
money had been appropriated for the American indemnity, and
that it could not be paid.

What said President Jackson, without further diplomacy, in his
message to Congress on this state of affairs? He sent a message
to Congress which gave no uncertain sound. He said : " It is
a principle of international law that when one nation refuses to
pay a just debt, the aggrieved nation may ' seize on the property ' belonging to the citizens of the defaulting nation. If,
therefore, France does not pay the money at the next session of
the Chambers, the United States ought to delay no longer to take
by force what it can not get by negotiation." Nay, more.
" Since France," said the President, "in violation of the pledges
given through her minister here, has delayed her final action so
long that her decision will not probably be known in time to be
communicated to this Congress, I recommend that a law be
passed authorizing reprisals upon French property in case provisions shall not be made for the payment of the debt at the approaching session of the French Chambers."

How was this received by the French newspapers?

" With one voice, the French newspapers, ministerial, opposition, and neutral, denounced the message as an insult to France,
so gross that it would be infamy not to resent it."

The French Minister at Washington was recalled, and our
Minister at Paris, Mr. Livingston, was informed that his passports were at his disposal. The President wrote to Mr. Livingston to demand his passports and come home if the Chamber of
Deputies, then in session, did not appropriate the money. Congress did not sustain President Jackson. There were cowards
in Congress at that day, especially in the Senate, as there have

been since. On the 14th of January the Senate resolved, without one dissenting vote : " That it is inexpedient, at present, to adopt any legislative measures in regard to the state of affairs between the United States and France."

Similar resolutions were introduced in the House, but their passage was prevented only because of technical objections. This action of Congress encouraged the Chamber of Deputies, so that it passed a bill appropriating the money to pay the instalments due, but added a condition which forbade the ministry to pay the instalment until the President had apologized for the language which he had used theretofore, and the minister drew up a form of apology for Jackson to sign. Our Congress adjourned without giving the President any money to protect the honor of the country. The President demanded of the French Government its *final* determination; and if the instalments were not paid the *chargé d'affaires* was to close the office of the legation.

After the answer was received, France prepared its army and a navy to act against the United States. Jackson sent his message to Congress, in which he said : " If this array of military force be really designed to affect the action of the government and people of the United States on the questions now pending between the two nations, then indeed would it be dishonorable to pause a moment on the alternative which such a state of affairs should present to us. Come what may, the explanation which France demands can never be accorded ; and no armament however powerful and imposing at a distance or on our coast, will, I trust, deter us from discharging the high duties we owe to our constituents, to our national character, and to the world."

After this message the people rallied around Jackson. They had stood by him from the first. He was only deserted by the sneaks and the politicians. We had one statesman—and he became a President of the United States—in the House of Representatives ; and he made a speech which carried that House in support of the honor of the nation. "Sir," exclaimed Mr. Adams, "this treaty has been ratified on both sides of the ocean ; it has received the sign manual of the Sovereign of France, through his Imperial Majesty's principal Minister of State ; it has been ratified by the Senate of this republic ; it has been sanctioned by Almighty God ; and still we are told in a voice potential, in the other wing of this Capitol, that the arrogance of France—nay, sir, not of France, but of her Chamber of Deputies—the insolence of the French Chambers, must be submitted to, and we must come down to the lower degradation of reopening negotiations to attain that which has already been acknowledged to be our due. Sir, is this a specimen of your boasted chivalry? Is this an evidence of the existence of that heroic valor which has so often led our army on to glory and immortality? Reopen negotiations, sir, with France? Do it, and soon you will find your flag insulted, dishonored, and trodden in the dust by the pigmy States of Asia and Africa—by the very banditti of the earth."

From France came a proposition three weeks later. The President informed Congress that the government of Great Britain had offered its mediation, and that he had accepted its offer. But at the same time he notified the mediating power that *" the apology demanded by France was totally out of the question."* On May 10 he sent the following communication to the Capitol : *"* Information has been received at the Treasury Department that the four instalments under our treaty with France *have been vaid to the agents of the United States."* And when this was done Jackson was applauded with the same unanimity as that with which he had been attacked for his conduct in the French affair. This is one specimen of American *"* Jingoism. *It has always been successful.*

We may be replied to by some gentlemen who wear whiskers of a particular pattern that this demand was not on England ; that the country opposed to us was France.

Let me give another instance. During our War of the Rebellion, in the summer of 1863, when the English shipyards were building armed vessels, and the English Government allowing them to escape from their ports, to destroy our commerce and burn our whaling fleet in the far-off oceans, this Government remonstrated with England on such conduct for more than two years as a breach of neutrality and as wilfully affording aid and comfort to our enemy. Our minister was instructed to present in the strongest language this unfriendliness and injustice to us. Meanwhile two ironclad rams were being built at the Laird shipyards, under pretence that one was for Egypt and the other for France. But it was known to our government that they were intended to come on to our coast to destroy our blockading fleet, or to raise the siege of Charleston. If that were done the English blockade runners would carry on British trade at a profit, just as the Canadian poachers can now steal seals at a profit.

At last, after our minister had exhausted all power of reasoning and remonstrance with Lord John Russell, the British premier, to have these rams interdicted by Britain from leaving the port of Liverpool, and Mr. Adams had reported that he could do nothing to have these rams kept in England, it was currently reported here that at a cabinet consultation President Lincoln took his pencil and wrote on a visiting card directed to Mr. Adams: "Tell Lord John Russell that another 'Alabama' is war." On September 5, 1863, although Mr. Adams had never before even hinted anything about the acts of England being war, in accordance with Mr. Seward's despatch of July 11, 1863, Mr. Adams says to Lord John Russell, after calling his lordship's attention to what was proposed to be done by these rams so escaping: "It would be superfluous to point out to Your Lordship that *this is war.*" Three days afterwards he received the following despatch: "Lord Russell presents his compliments to Mr. Adams, and has the honor to inform him that instructions have been issued which will prevent the departure of the two iron-clad vessels from Liverpool." *So no more "Alabamas."*

Manly diplomacy once more succeeds, and against England, too, when she was stronger and we were weaker than either will ever happen to be again. It destroyed her favorite project of sweeping our commerce from the seas by means of rebel privateers sailing from her ports, which she had schemed for since May, 1861, when she had offered to Jeff. Davis to adopt the treaty of Paris. She urged our Government also to accept this measure, which forbade privateering, pledging to Davis that it should not apply to his rebel privateers, concealing from our Government and its diplomatic corps that she was in diplomatic correspondence with the rebel chief as a belligerent, before we had acknowledged such belligerency.

It has been difficult to deal in this paper with the status of the Behring Sea controversy, because, as I have been writing, the two governments were acting upon it by telegraph. One day war seemed to threaten, and almost the next the treaty was to be ratified. On one day Earl Salisbury is in an aggressive attitude;

he receives the bold presentation of our ultimatum ; he replies to it at first adversely and defiantly, and, to speak plainly, insultingly, because he proposes to change the negotiation on our part to one with Canadian seal poachers to get their bonds to pay the damages for which we hold England responsible. The President's answer to that, is to reiterate his ultimatum that the *modus vivendi* must be maintained during the arbitration, or we will defend and protect ourselves at all hazards and with all our resources. The next day the Earl Salisbury sends a note receding from his position, which he discloses to Parliament and receives cheers for so doing. The Senate of the United States at once, as well they might have done before, ratified the treaty unanimously, and the arbitration is to go on, the seals are to be guarded by both nations, and the Canadian seal poachers are to be arrested, and all things are to remain *in statu quo* until the award of the arbitrators. The views of our contentions change as suddenly as the scenes of a kaleidoscope ; not, however, with any of their beauty.

The treaty providing for the arbitration ought to have been ratified because our government had agreed so to do. Nations as well as individuals should fully and thoroughly carry out every contract, however informally concluded. I have not said and do not say, because I do not believe, that the arbitration should have ever been originally agreed upon.

In almost every instance where we have had an arbitration with Great Britain we have got the worst of it. Space will only allow me to give one or two instances of this fact. In the matter of our "national losses" because of the misconduct of England in our Civil War an arbitrament established by the treaty of Washington was held at Geneva. When we presented our case before the arbitrators, England refused to go on with the hearing until we would abandon all our claims to national losses (such as having our commerce destroyed, our war prolonged, and its expenses largely increased), and demanded that they should be withdrawn from the consideration of that tribunal, and that the United States confine its case to claims of its private citizens for injuries done to them, and we were not allowed to present even our claim for the sinking of the public warship "Hatteras" by the pirate "Alabama," for whose escape from England, under whatever circumstances, England had expressed her regret, as we have seen. Our government was weak enough to agree to withdraw our national

claims, "and present only the losses suffered by our citizens" as
national losses. It is true the arbitration gave us some fifteen
and a half millions without interest for all that this nation
suffered at the hands of England during the war. Who got the
worst of it by this arbitration ?

There was another arbitration provided for in the treaty of
Washington. England made claims against us for the value of
the fish our fishermen on the northeast coast had caught, certain'
mackerel swimming in the sea within three miles of the Canadian
shores. We agreed to arbitrate that claim with England, to be
submitted to three men, one appointed by us, one by England,
and one to be agreed on by the parties, or else appointed by some
foreign power, the award of whom, that is, all three agreeing to it,
was to be binding on the parties. England chose a very able gentleman from Canada ; we appointed a gentleman from Massachusetts, a country lawyer who had probably never seen a mackerel
until it was boiled ; and England proposed the name of Del
Fosse, who represented Belgium here. But Mr. Fish would not
agree to him because Belgium was substantially only a province
of England. Whereupon the appointment had to be submitted
to the representative of Austria at London, and he very promptly
nominated Del Fosse. The arbitrators met, the case was heard ;
Del Fosse and the Canadian arbitrator being a majority awarded
the sum of five million five hundred thousand dollars, something
like one-third of all that had been awarded us by the Geneva tribunal
for all the losses we had suffered through the misconduct of England during the war. And although the award was not agreed
to or signed by our arbitrator, through the performances of our
Secretary of State under Johnson this money was paid for a few
fish swimming in the sea in the northern waters of Canada, the
right to catch which we had enjoyed as Colonists ; and in the treaty
of peace of 1783 these rights were secured to us by the War of
the Revolution, by the manly courage of John Adams, who declared that he would allow the war to go on rather than surrender the right, which was clearly ours, to fish in the seas.

Now, by this arbitration, a majority of the arbitrators of our
rights in the Behring Sea are to be chosen by England and other
European powers (she has been careful this time), and the treaty
provides that the award of the majority is to be binding. The
English newspapers are early in discussing as to whom the Euro-

pean countries (who, with England, are to appoint such majority of arbitrators) will appoint, and they congratulate themselves that England is safe. I agree with them. *She is safe.* And I therefore say that the arbitration ought not to have been made. The arbitrament was proposed by England.

B. F. BUTLER.

THE MARQUIS OF LORNE:

A STRANGE North land, a weird North water is that Alaskan region, that part of the Pacific called the Behring Sea, on the American side ; a main land rising into vast plateaux and cones, and furrowed for the passage of streams, great even when measured by the wide scale of America ; a giant limit of the mountain chains that wall off the Pacific along all its Eastern side, save in the low-lying centre part near Panama, and here, in the far north, broken away into hundreds of islands, large and small, from the great breakwater of Vancouver, to the lonely rock inhabited only by puffins and gulls. Wide as is the Archipelago along the British Columbian shore, it still sows the Alaskan water with all imaginable shapes in a still formidable multitude of isles, and then threads away into the long string which shows that in other days a chain of hills ran out towards Asia. Now only the broken fragments show like a ruined and submerged rampart, and in front of them is a mighty force—a deep trench in the ocean flow, as though it had been dug to make unscaleable the rocky walls of the primeval ruin. It is these far-away retreats which are the best loved by hunted seals, about whom so much is now written. If we could only persuade American and British ladies to let these seals have a *modus vivendi*, or chance of life, for a few years, how grateful they would be; but as this involves the buying of no new seal jackets for at least two or three years, what hope is there for them? Yes; if President and Prime Minister are now discussing with earnestness how to preserve the existence of the seals, it is a case again of *" cherchez la femme ; "* for the pursuit of these seals is a profitable business, and nobody likes to drop it.

The company which has the sole right of killing seals on land has its men ever ready to watch them as they land, and to cut off their retreat to the sea as they are comfortably dozing on the rocks, and drive them inland to the slaughter ground, where they club them to death.

The so-called "pelajee," or ocean hunter, intercepts the seals on their way to the islands, and in fog and wet kills them in the water. Dreary-looking places the breeding grounds are, for there is not a single tree to be seen on these rocky masses lifted out of the gray sea. A white fog constantly broods around them, and the air is so moist that in the winter, when there is any frost, each rock face on a hillside is seamed like a comb with icicles. This dampness produces the only beauty in their coloring, for the grass is often long and very green. The Indians are an ugly race, but have skill in fishing, and have long ago learned the value of furs, and the use of guns and nets.

One of the ablest of American statesmen is said to have remarked to an English friend: "Sir, whenever the British government has had any difference with foreign countries, it has been observed that opinion here at Washington is on the British side. Yes, sir, we are always with you, except, curiously enough, in the event of any dispute between ourselves and you!" It may be doubted, in the matter of the Behring Sea contention, whether even this exception holds good. There can be very little doubt that the vast majority of American citizens believe, and, we may add, every distinguished lawyer in the United States backs the opinion, that there can be no warrant for the barring of the open sea, and for the exclusive power of fishing or of hunting therein.

When Russia made over to the American government her territory opposite Siberia, Uncle Sam made an investment which a Scotsman would have called "buying a pig in a poke." Something was bought with something else inside of it, and that was about all that was accurately known of the transaction.

To be sure there were maps, with a bewildering number of islands and "shadowy promontories" marked upon them, and it was also obvious that these studded a sea giving access to that mysterious Arctic Ocean, which each nation in turn burns to enter with a view of reaching the North Pole. But it was not, it is believed, with a view to the exclusive possession of the highway to that magnetic attraction that the United States invested its dollars. Information was rather vague as to the region purchased. It was painted to the imagination as most interesting. Its fogs were very clearly described, and it was known to have a fair amount of winter, snow, and frost, although these advantages failed when compared with the rival attractions in the same line enjoyed by New England. But volcanoes formed an entirely novel acquisition for Uncle Sam. He had never enjoyed the possession of a real live mountain before. He, therefore, now put several into his pocket, with a sensation that the Monroe doctrine had at last led to something real. Then there were glaciers also, and this rather roused the spirit of local protection among the producers and consumers of Wenham ice. But it was agreed that, although the purchase of so much waste land and water, peopled only by a few Indians and a selection of Russian half-breeds, would not return any dividends, the acquisition was interesting. And it has, at all events, produced one of those small but irritating contentions which will always arise where commercial companies employ their fishermen or hunters in the chase.

Scientific interest as well as commercial gain has stimulated the attention paid to the hunting in the North Pacific—for the sea otter, the sea lion, and the fur seal are creatures only found to-day in large numbers in these regions.

On the Atlantic there has been for many years so indiscriminate and imprudent a slaughter of walrus, seal, and salmon, as well as of other fish, that all hope of re-stocking the walrus and seal haunts near the coasts has disappeared ; and the efforts of scientists are busily occupied with attempts to re-stock the rivers with salmon and even the sea banks with valuable sea fish.

It is probably this fact which has led American scientists to lay in some instances an undue stress on the chances that the fur seal may be exterminated. Certainly the fur seals have disappeared from the shores of the Southern Hemisphere, where they were formerly to be found in abundance. In the Southern Pacific there was no " catch " of seals taken at sea. They were slaughtered only on the islands and shores where they formed their " rookeries." It was the slaughter made in these places, where they were comparatively helpless, that caused them to disappear. The experience of the South will certainly be repeated in the North were the same tactics to be employed. Indeed, the ease with which the animals can be taken on land has induced Russians and Americans to endeavor to monopolize the profits by allowing the seals to be caught on the islands only. The fishing proper has been done by schooners, the number of which has only this year reached fifty, in which the seal is pursued in the open sea, that is, more than three miles from shore when off the American coasts. It is obvious that the means of destruction used on this limited scale are wholly insufficient to work much damage to the herds on their way to the islands. Once on the islands and their immediate neighborhood, the preservation or destruction of the herds depends solely on the regulations under which the American Company, the lessee of the islands from the Government, conducts its operations.

It is natural that, with the lessons of destruction of life seen on the Atlantic side, the scientists should be inclined to support the interested representations of the monopolists connected with the American Company in deprecating any chase of the seal at sea. But it will be apparent that, whereas on the Atlantic the instruments of destruction have been used for generations, the machinery for fishing and for the chase is so feeble on the Pacific side that this fear is groundless and cannot apply to the case.

It is the interest and desire of all parties having, or likely to have, a share in valuable animal life to preserve it according to the light of scientific knowledge,—for, as the farmer says, the amount of "cropping must depend on the quality of the soil."

Dr. Dawson, who, with Sir George Baden Powell, examined the Behring Sea, and all the fishermen who could give pertinent evidence, declare in the strongest terms that the present sealer outfit is not sufficient to hurt the herds for another year, at all events. They have come to this conclusion after much trouble and much travel, and Dr. Dawson's testimony is evidence that will be held in respect by all American scientists.

But what was not expected has happened in that the fisheries turn out to be likely of infinitely greater value than the most hopeful imagined. The codfish appear to be the same as our old friends of the Atlantic ; although the salmon are all widely different in look from their Atlantic cousin, and, as most people think, very inferior in flavor. There seems, however, to be no inferiority in the cod, and the banks on which they are found are nearly equal in extent to those around Newfoundland. They may be larger, for they are not yet fully surveyed, but it is computed that there are 100,000 square miles of fishing ground.

Of course, if the sea were not an open sea, all this cod fishery might also be given off to some one company with monopoly rights. Nobody doubts that seals landing on islands or mainland shores, or swimming in water within the three-mile limit of the coast, are the property of the landowners, but away at sea there can be no more property in them than in the salmon which come regularly to certain rivers and then become landowners' property, but are anybody's game when on their way to the rivers and out at sea. This has been on other occasions insisted on by American jurists.

Mr. Adams, of the United States, in 1822 wrote: "The pretensions of the Russian (Imperial) Government extend to an exclusive territorial jurisdiction from the 45th degree of north latitude on the Asiatic coast to the latitude of 51 north on the west coast of the American continent, and they assume the right of interdicting the navigation and the fishing of all other nations to the extent of one hundred miles from the whole of the coast. *The United States can admit no part of these claims.*"

A little later Mr. Adams again said : "The right of navigation and of fishing in the Pacific Ocean, even upon the Asiatic coast north of latitude 45 degrees, can as little be interdicted to the United States as that of traffic with the natives of North America." President Angell, a great American authority, says: " On what grounds, and after what modern precedent, we (the United States) could set up a claim to hold this great sea, with its wide approaches, as a ' mare clausum,' it is not easy to see." Again he says : "Our government has never formally set up the claim that it is a closed sea. Governor Boutwell in 1872 said : ' I do not see that the United States could have the jurisdiction or power to drive off parties going up there for that purpose, unless they made such attempt within a marine league of the shore.' " He rightly concludes in reference to the preservation of the seals: "It cannot be difficult to make some satisfactory adjustment of this question." Professor Geffcken, of Germany, a most able and impartial critic, takes precisely the same view.

British seamen in the last century hunted and fished in Behring Sea. The right was insisted on by Great Britain in the convention made with Russia in 1825 in connection with matters affecting this very sea. The first article declared : " It is agreed that the respective subjects of the high contracting parties shall not be troubled or molested in any part of the ocean called the

Pacific Ocean, either in navigating the same, in fishing therein, or in landing at such parts of the coast as shall not have been already occupied." Great Britain always declared that the Pacific Ocean embraced Behring Sea, and that Russia could not close it. And in 1887, an American Government official, in contending that the seizure by Russia of an American vessel was illegal, notes that "the Russian code of prize law of 1869 limits the jurisdictional waters of Russia to three miles from the shore."

Neither Britain nor any other maritime nation could have recognized any monopoly in any sea beyond the three-mile limit. The Russian company's monopoly could only extend to the land and its immediate neighborhood, and that was quite sufficiently valuable, specially as to the seal-fur trade, to make the highest in Russia, whether by rank or fortune, eager to become shareholders in so lucrative an enterprise. In early days, too, the competition there was not keen, and the mere absence of fishing and sealing vessels cannot, of course, be held to imply that they came not because they were forbidden to do so. They came not, because they knew not of the value of the harvest they might gather. The way was long to the field, and there were no ready markets at hand.

Wide salt water has always been open to all keels, and no imaginary claims of exclusion, derived from half barbarous times, can invalidate this world-wide freedom, which it is equally to the advantage of all maritime nations to enjoy.

Likewise good regulations as to close times should be mutually arranged, so that the supply of fish or sea animals be not exhausted. Now it is absolutely denied on the strongest evidence that any "rookery" or seal colony has ever been destroyed, depleted, or even injured, by the killing of seals at sea only, whereas it is proved that the heavy slaughter on the land where the seals congregate has caused the seals to vanish from several places where they formerly were to be found in thousands. It stands to reason that a moderate use of both methods of hunting is what ought to be enforced. Just as the oyster supply dredged up by the fishermen is regulated at the ancient British Burgh of Whitstable by the state of the market, so ought international arrangements to be made to check any over-heavy draft on the vitality of the seal herds, as observed from year to year.

During last year eye-witnesses of the highest character have

declared that the seals are abundant, and that there is no necessity that a fair number should not be taken, both from the islands
and from the ocean. The arbitration of this year will enable the
governments concerned to make regulations for future years,
which shall put each neighbor on the Pacific in a position to use
wisely and with a view to future profit the annual migration of
the seal herds.

It is well to remember that the only debatable point which
delayed the ratification of the Arbitration Treaty by the Senate is a very small one, and refers only to the single season's
hunting by no great number of vessels. While men of indubitable
probity declare that this cannot injure a property, the value of
which consists chiefly in a right, which cannot be assailed, to catch
the seals on shore, it seems unnecessary to have any further delay
in concluding the reference to arbitration. This arbitration will
decide the more important matter of the right of a maritime power
to close any portion of the ocean to the citizens of other nations.
Some complaints of delay have arisen on both sides, but it is
certain that the British have expedited the correspondence as far
as practicable, and it is, indeed, only natural that both sides
should desire the settlement of a question which cannot be said to
involve the permanent national interests of either party. The
United States believes that it purchased certain rights from the
Russians. These are only in part questioned by those who fully
admit all rights as to land ownership, but object only to be deprived of that which not only the British, but all other maritime people, claim as common property, namely, the right to
hunt at will over the unenclosed length and breadth of the
ocean itself.

When the arbitration has done its work the seal-fishing industry must be protected by a sensible close time, giving the
subjects of the United States and Britain each the power to use
and not to abuse the advantages given by the northern migration
of the fur seal. It is incompatible with any international comity
that one power alone can patrol the open sea. Other nations—
Russia, France, Germany, or any that may be named—have a
right to the navigation of these waters, and it is primarily in the
interest of the powers having harbors in the more immediate
neighborhood that provision should be mutually made for the
preservation of the seal species, not by the dragging in of ancient

alleged Russian exclusive privileges, but by the sensible delimitation of seasons for hunting, based on scientific investigation, which shall be impartial and founded on painstaking observation and practical experience. The fair solution of this matter is the extension of the principle of arbitration already agreed on, so that compensation shall be given for any property taken in contrariety to the ultimate award of the arbitrators on either side, and the future determination to avoid that waste which would injure alike the subjects of the London and the Washington governments.

LORNE.

PARTY GOVERNMENT ON ITS TRIAL.

BY GOLDWIN SMITH, D. C. L.

A STRANGER visiting Washington at this time is told, and would soon learn for himself, that there is little thought or prospect in Congress of national legislation during the present session. The soul of the legislature is absorbed by the coming party fight for the Presidency. The two parties lie watching each other's movements like two hostile armies, manœuvering each of them for any coigne of vantage, and looking out anxiously for opportunities of discrediting its rival. Of the national interest every one admits that there is little care. Even such questions as that of commercial relations with Canada, which involve no party issue, are at a standstill, because the joint action for which they call is impossible, neither of the parties being able to trust the good faith of the other. The constitution has been practically suspended by the party machines, and the party machines are at a dead-lock. It is doubly a dead-lock, because the House being in the hands of one party and the Senate in those of the other, what one branch of the legislature passes the other is sure, on party grounds, to reject. Thanks to a strong intervention of national good sense outside Congress, finding its organs in the press, the country appears to have come safe through the crisis of the Silver Bill, and to have escaped those well-known results of a decayed and depreciated currency, an experience of which led Tom Paine, no strait-laced economist, seriously to propose that the penalty for any attempt to repeat the experiment should be death.

But it is on party spirit probably that the main responsibility rests for the existence of the peril, and for any loss or inconvenience that it may already have brought on industry and trade. The silver men and the silver States had an intelligible motive of their own, but it is not likely that of men so shrewd as the mem-

bers of the American legislature many were the victims of the
silver fallacy. Most, we are told and may well believe, were
simply yielding to an apparent party exigency in voting with the
silver States. The Executive is almost as completely paralyzed
as the legislature. It can hardly move in any direction for fear
of estranging from the party some sectional or local vote. Even
in the diplomatic field, where if anywhere patriotism ought to
prevail over party, the Executive, while it is struggling against a
foreign power for the rights of the country, is embarrassed in its
action by party opposition and traduced before its foreign adversaries and the world at large by party animosity. At a crisis
which seems to threaten war experts declare that the country
is defenceless, and if you ask how it comes to pass that the
United States are without a navy, that their coasts lie exposed
to assault and their wealthy cities to devastation, while a sum
larger than the entire military expenditure of first-rate war
powers is spent in army pensions, the answer is that ships of war
cannot turn the party scale by their votes. Amidst the dis-
tractions and fluctuations of party anything like a steady and
farsighted policy in external affairs becomes almost impossible.
The treatment of the Canadian question, for instance, is a history
of vacillation and irresolution, of policies adopted in the national
interest, and vetoed by some local or personal interest which
party courts or fears. There is reason to apprehend that the
question may remain unsolved, and that a power antagonistic to
the American Republic may thus be allowed to form itself under
the auspices of European Toryism in the north of this Continent,
though by that result a stain would be brought on American
statesmanship deeper even than that which was brought on it by
its failure to solve the question of slavery, since the question of
slavery was not certainly capable of satisfactory solution, whereas
the Canadian question certainly is. A railway company which
derives a great part of its earnings from trade carried on within
American territory, from American connections and from privileges enjoyed under American jurisdiction over its American
competitors, is allowed with impunity to make itself an engine of
estrangement between Canada and the United States and of Tory
designs against American institutions, because party demands the
support of certain localities or commercial circles which prefer
their own interest to the interest and honor of the country.

A distinguished member of the Republican party has been heard to say that he was against the admission of Canada into the Union because he believed she would "vote Democratic." He might as well have said that she would vote Guelph or Ghibelin. But the avowal proved that in his breast, and probably not in his breast alone, party had triumphed over national aspiration, and over the plain dictates of American statesmanship, of which the highest objects must be the unity, independence, and security of this continent.

Not to the people of the United States alone come these loud warnings. Disclosures in Canada have revealed and and are still revealing the political condition to which the same system has brought us there. By nature no people are worthier than the yeomen, merchants, and artisans of Canada ; nor could there have been a more promising basis for free institutions than their character affords. Their social and commercial morality is still grand, though it can hardly remain forever unaffected by the example of immorality in the government. Confederation brought with it a vast extension of the party system, and all that it draws in its train. The result, as we see, is a domination of knavery and corruption. The machine has been worked unsparingly and by first-rate hands. One of Sir John Macdonald's merry sayings was that the best cabinet would be one consisting of twelve mediocrities, each of whom you could, if you liked, put in the penitentiary. He made, as we see, and Canada finds to her sorrow, progress towards the realization of his ideal. The natural effects have been produced upon the political character of the people. Direct bribery prevails to a lamentable extent, and has been largely employed by the government in the recent elections. Government candidates hold out, with the coarsest effrontery, promises of jobs to the constituencies, and by those promises they prevail. Conviction of public theft has almost ceased to be a political disqualification. A member branded with it by a resolution of the House of Commons, returns to his constituents, avows his act, pleads that he is no worse than the rest, and is re-elected. A member of the Cabinet, about whose guilt there is no moral doubt, receives not only a whitewashing but an ovation. If Mr. Mercier had not opposed the Dominion Government in an election there would have been no inquiry into his malversations, and, as it was, his overthrow was probably due not more to his being corrupt than to his having lost the means of corruption. His censor and assailants were at the same time practising corruption on the largest scale. All this is party.

But the grand example is England. Let those who believe in party government as the best of all systems, or as our inevitable destiny to the end of political time, look across the Atlantic to the classical land of party and see what it is doing there.

Whether Home Rule for Ireland be good or not, nobody can doubt that it is a measure of tremendous import. If it led to separation, as probably it would, and as Mr. Parnell manifestly intended that it should, the ultimate result would be either the fall of the British power, or the re-conquest of Ireland, and a fresh cycle of woes ; its immediate consequence would be the delivery of Ireland to the priests and the overthrow of national education. It apparently involves a dishonorable desertion of the Irish Protestants, who are stretching out their hands to England in protest. A more momentous step it would be impossible for British statesmen to take. Yet party is willing to take it for the sake of ousting hated opponents and regaining power. Bright truly said that there were not among Mr. Gladstone's followers, outside of the Irish section, twenty men who approved his bill. The rest were voting for party, and at the bidding of its caucus, a few months before, they had been Unionists supporting a Coercion Act more stringent than those which they afterwards denounced as tyranny, applauding the arrest of Mr. Parnell and of scores of his followers, and cheering when he was branded as a conspirator wading through dismemberment to rapine. Such they had been, and so they had continued to act till the result of a general election made it clear that without the Parnellite vote their party could not regain power. Not only their views of policy but their views of history were changed when party gave the word, and Pitt's great achievement, the Union, lauded by them before as equal in beneficence to his fiscal reforms, suddenly became an injury, while admiration was transferred from its author to the patriots of Vinegar Hill. Even British respect for law was thrown aside ; agrarian outrage was palliated if not encouraged, and a peasantry highly excitable, and very bloodthirsty when excited, was exhorted to remember scenes of blood.

Party it is which is ready and eager to throw the United Kingdom into the smelting pot, to cover its past with dishonor, and expose it to mortal peril in the future, for the sake of a victory over rivals and restoration to power. Home Rule, with the manifest possibility of dismemberment or civil war in its train, is the price offered for the Irish vote. Even the aid of foreign enemies, as the American Fenians proved themselves to be, is not disdained by party maddened with the strife for power. Little cause have British statesmen to point the finger of scorn at the fishers for that same vote in the political waters of the United States.

But of the price which party in England offers for return to office Home Rule is now but one item. It offers church dis-establishment, though its leader has been, throughout his life, of all upholders of church establishment the most eminent, and the one who defended it on the highest ground of principle. It offers measures of economic change, socialistic in their tendency, of indefinite extent, and holds out to the proletariat a hope of something like legislative confiscation of the property of the rich. When an arch wire-puller like Mr. Schnadhorst calls a convention of agricultural laborers, appeals to their discontent, stirs up their class feeling against the landowner, and promises them in effect a redivision of the land, can it be supposed that his real object is economical justice ? His real object, manifestly, is to gain for his party the agricultural laborer's vote. If he can do this, he is ready to set rural society in a flame. The other party understands his move, and feebly attempts to outflank him by holding an agricultural convention of its own. On all sides, men who have hitherto posed as sound economists and political philosophers, now carried away by the frenzy of the strife, are dangling before an enfranchised proletariat hopes of a redistribution of wealth by socialistic legislation, which they must know to be deceptive, and, if entertained by the masses, pregnant with the danger of social war. Party is at the bottom of it all.

Sweeping measures of political change are tendered at the same time and with the same object. The House of Lords is to be . abolished or reduced to impotence, while no constitutional check or balance in the nature of a Senate is proposed in its room. The last limitations of the franchise are to be swept away. Any minor safeguards which wealth or intelligence still retain in the electoral field are to be destroyed. The Septennial Act is to be repealed. Parliaments are to be made triennial or perhaps annual, and thus the House of Commons, in which now whatever is left of authority resides, and which is practically not only the legislature but the government of the country, is to be reduced to a mere slave and organ of the popular will. This result has indeed been to a great extent brought about already by the operation of the local caucus for elections introduced by Mr. Joseph Chamberlain, but the repeal of the Septennial Act would complete the work. There would thenceforth be no authority but that of the local caucus, or of the collective local caucuses under a general organization managed by some national boss like Mr. Schnadhorst.

The last bid of party for power, however, is perhaps the most desperate of all. It is the payment of Members of Parliament, coupled with the assumption by the State, of all the expenses of elections. The conservative portions of the British Constitution generally have become names and shadows, though they still impose to a surprising and fatal extent on the imagination of British statesmen, luring them into sweeping measures of suffrage extension and other concessions to democracy, which they fancy are safe because there is legally a crown with a royal veto, and an Upper House of Parliament ; as though the veto of the crown had not long been practically extinct, or the House of Lords were like the American Senate, a really coördinate branch of the legislature. But two conservative institutions of a practical character have hitherto survived, and have been real barriers against democracy, which otherwise would have come in like a flood, bridled by no limitations such as are imposed on it by the written constitution of the United States. These two institutions are the non-payment of members of the House of Commons and the liability of the candidate for the expense of election. Living in London being costly, and involving the abandonment in the case of country members of their business or calling, has confined the representation generally to men of independent means. The few representatives of labor who have found seats in the House are maintained, sometimes rather grudgingly, out of the trade fund, while the Irish members are maintained out of a political fund which has been apparently on the point of failing. Election expenditure also, though reduced, is still considerable. The two barriers together have hitherto sufficed to exclude generally from the House of Commons those whose object in entering public life is to eat a piece of bread. But now the Gladstonians are promising payment of members and the assumption of election expenses by the State. Among the Gladstonians in Parliament not a few are rich members for manufacturing districts, whose radicalism may be not uncharitably suspected to be partly donned for the sake of the seats which are objects of their social ambition. It must be with secret bitterness of heart that these men consent to the payment of members, knowing, as they do, that they sign the warrant for their own deposition in favor of the demagogues who will make politics their trade. But party gives the word, and they must obey. Apart from the interest of their own ambition, such men can scarcely fail to feel a pang at the thought of the hands into which they are delivering the country and the Empire. The agricultural laborer is a worthy man in his way, and by his sturdy toil has made English fields bear unrivalled harvests ; but he is as ignorant of all political questions as the team he drives, and his only idea is voting for the party which will give him three acres and a cow. The factory hands, who predominate in the electorate of the north of England, are far superior to the farm laborer in intelligence, but for the most part citizens of the labor market rather than of their own country, caring for little but increase of their wages and the material enjoyments which it will bring to solace lives of dull, monotonous toil ; impregnated moreover with socialistic sentiment, open in their state of half education to economical fallacies, and animated by class feeling against the capitalist, who lives apart from them in his suburban villa, and whom they are taught by labor journalists and orators to regard as the "spoiler" of their "toil." The Irish peasantry and the populace of Irish cities are thoroughly disaffected, and they have eighty seats in their hands. To a sovereign people composed of such political elements, or to the demagogues who can get control over it, payment of members and assumption of election expenses by the State will consign the direct rule not only of the British Islands, but of the two hundred and fifty millions of British India and all the other dependencies of the Empire. Political madness, it would seem, could scarcely go further. But what is so mad as faction at a crisis for the struggle for power ! The excitement of ordinary gambling is individual, that of faction is intensified by contagion. A strange sight it is, that of a highly-civilized, wealthy, refined, and luxurious community thus calling in the barbarians, and plucking a social revolution on its own head, to satisfy the desperate ambition or the party animosity of a small number of its members.

Nothing short of a revolution, political, religious, social, and economical, is the price now bid by a party in England for a change of government. Nor is this all. Violent efforts have been made to wreck the House of Commons itself or force on its dissolution by the practice of obstruction, and in this an active part has been played by men who have all their lives figured as scientific publicists and calm speculators in politics, but have lost their self-control and philosophy in the fury of the faction fight. That House, which was once the model and the guiding light of deliberative assemblies throughout the world, has thus been reduced to a state in which deliberation is hopeless and even the common decencies of debate can no longer be upheld. If the minority will not let the majority govern, there is an end of parliamentary government. It is no longer a contest of party; it is morally a civil war. Had Lord Salisbury been the man for the situation, he would have taken up the gauntlet thus thrown down by the recklessnesses of the opposition. Having a great majority behind him and the public force in his hands, he would have passed, if necessary, by the application of the cloture, such measures as might have redressed the balance of the constitution, restored the authority of the House of Commons, taken legislation and government from under the feet of Mr. Schnadhorst, and effectually shut the door against revolution. But Lord Salisbury, though a man of the highest reputation for ability, was not the man for the situation. He is a diplomatist, rather than a statesman. To the great political problems which he was called upon to solve, he seems never to have seriously given his mind. His one political aim seems to be the preservation of the House of Lords. For this he is ready to pay by concessions to Socialism, which only serve to whet its appetite while they compromise the principles and shake the nerve of his own party.

It is right to say that one side has sinned almost as much as the other. Obstruction was first practised by Lord Randolph Churchill, who, in his essay on " Elijah's Mantle " proving himself indisputably the heir of Disraeli, avowed with astonishing frankness that, in party warfare, he thought of nothing but success, leaving moralists to say what they pleased. The present series of disasters began with the unprincipled coalition brought on by

Lord Randolph between the Tories and the Parnellites for the overthrow of the Gladstone government. Nothing in the whole of this disgraceful history is more disgraceful than the abandonment of the Crimes Act by the Tories, in requital for Parnellite support, and the language of their leaders in the Commons in what was called the Mamtrasna debate.

Another liability of the party system displayed in a strong light by these events is the growing power of sectionalism. Any selfish or fanatical section which will devote itself exclusively to its own interest or its own fancy, regardless of the general good, can by playing on the balance of parties lay both parties and the national government at its feet. The Home Rulers have only eighty votes out of six hundred and sixty in the House of Commons. Yet, by sectional action they made themselves masters of the situation, and are now in a fair way to carry a measure, fraught with tremendous consequences to the country, which has not one-sixth of the House, themselves included, really in its favor.

Assemblies still styled deliberative have entirely ceased to deliberate. They have become mere battlefields on which the missiles of party argument and invective are interchanged between the two hostile hosts. If a semblance of the deliberative character anywhere remains it is perhaps in the American Senate.

The great sponsor for the morality and the necessity of party is Burke, whose words in "Thoughts on the Present Discontents" have been cited a thousand times. Burke is a magnificent writer, but unless read with reference to time and circumstance he is very apt to mislead. He is the Prince of Pamphleteers, but he is a pamphleteer, and, like all pamphleteers, to some extent makes his philosophy for the occasion. "Thoughts on the Present Discontents" is the manifesto of the Rockingham connection of Whigs against the cabal of "King's Friends," who were striving to put an end to constitutional government and instal the personal government of George III. in its place by backstairs intrigue, jobbery and corruption. To vindicate any connection of constitutional statesmen against backstairs intrigue, jobbery, corruption, and the personal government of George III. was not difficult. But as a general vindication of the party system, if it was so intended, this renowned passage will not bear examination. "Party," says Burke, "is a body of men united for promoting by their joint endeavors the national interest upon some particular principle in which they are all agreed." The particular principle apparently can be nothing but their joint opinion on the great question or questions of the day. But the great question or questions of the day will in time be settled. When they shall have been settled, what will there be to render the bond of party moral or rational; what will there be left to hold the connection together but the common desire of political power and pelf? The party will then become a machine, and its cohesion will be maintained either by mere personal association or by motives and influences more or less corrupt. By the philosophy which is always forthcoming in defence of existing arrangements, particularly those arrangements in which many persons have an active interest, it has been alleged that men are naturally and almost providentially divided from their birth into conservatives and liberals. But this bi-section of humanity is a politician's dream. Temperaments vary through an infinite series of gradations, and the same man is conservative on one subject and liberal on another. Youth as a rule, perhaps, is prone to innovation, while age is reactionary. Yet nobody is so violently reactionary as a young aristocrat. Is the community then to be artificially divided into two sections, at perpetual war with each other, for the purpose of carrying on the system? How is the apportionment to be made, and why, if the existence of the two parties is necessary, should each of them be always traducing and striving to annihilate the other? Burke's glowing language about a generous contention for power on manly and honorable maxims, and without proscription of opponents, sounds like a satire on party politics as they are. The reality is that which he would exclude by contrast,—" delusion of the ignorant by professions incompatible with human practice and followed by practices below the level of vulgar rectitude." If he could only have seen the machine and the bosses! If he could only have looked into the office of Mr. Schnadhorst! If he could only have been present at a nominating convention for the Presidency or witnessed a general election in the England of these days! A convention of Whig magnates gathered round the dinner table of the Marquis of Rockingham to settle the policy of the connection, and distribute the pocket-boroughs at its command, was the only sort of convention that he had ever seen. Party, unless there is some great question, such as parliamentary reform or slavery, to justify its existence, can be nothing but a fine name for faction, of which the ties are passion and corruption, and which always must be in the end, as it always has been, the ruin of the commonwealth.

. Yet how under the representative and elective system are we to dispense with the party machine ? There is the problem. How are the individual votes to be combined and directed so as to elect the representatives and form the basis for the government ? It is clear they cannot combine or direct themselves. The electors in any but the smallest constituency know nothing of each other, nor have they any opportunity of conference or communication of any sort. There is in them no organ of spontaneous initiation, no faculty of collective choice or action. The theory is that they lay their heads together to choose the best man. The fact is that they can do nothing of the kind. In England, which all the world has fancied itself to be copying, the members for counties were originally elected in the county court and the members for boroughs in the town hall. There was a conference and a real election, though the influence of the leading men no doubt determined the choice. A semblance of the original institution remains in the nomination at the hustings, which is followed by the demand for a poll. When the poll had become the real election in England the nomination was long made in some conclave of municipal or local grandees. Now there is nothing to nominate the candidates and to organize the votes, but the machine ; and without something to nominate the candidates and to organize the votes how can an election be made ? Take away the machine, and the electorate will be so many grains of political sand without power of self determination or cohesion. The "Mugwumps" cannot nominate or elect, because they have no machine. They can do nothing but flit backwards and forwards from one machine to the other, to the great discontent of the managers of both. It is curious that so simple a point should never have presented itself to any of the framers of elective institutions. British statesmen have just given an elective council to London, as though it were possible for those five millions of citizens to lay their heads together and elect. The election will inevitably fall into the hands of the ward politicians and the wire-puller.

This opens a still deeper question. The framers of the American Constitution erred plainly enough in taking the legal and Blackstonian version of their British model as practically true, assuming that the King was the real executive, and that the House of Lords was a branch of the legislature coördinate with the House of Commons. They erred in fancying, with Montesquieu, that the executive, legislative and judicial powers under the British Constitution were really independent of each other. Their imitation is impressed with these misconceptions. But a still more serious question is whether they did not err in taking the House of Commons for an elective assembly, and in imagining that the qualities in it which they approved and wished to reproduce depended on its elective character. Elective in theory the House of Commons no doubt was ; but, in fact, only a very small part of it was at that period elective, while the larger part by far consisted either of actual nominees of the crown or the proprietors of rotten boroughs, of members for constituencies so close that the election was a farce, or of men who owed their seats to the fiat of great landowners, or to some local influence not of a popular kind. Of the 558 members, 90 were returned by 46 places, in none of which the number of voters exceeded 50 ; 37 were returned by 19 places, in none of which the number of voters exceeded 100 ; and 52 were returned by 26 places, in none of which the number of voters exceeded 200. The majority of the 558 members was elected by 15,000 voters, not the two hundredth part of the male adults in the kingdom. The owners of the nomination boroughs were generally, from interested motives, constant supporters of the government. The really elective element was no doubt influential out of proportion to its numbers because it was the only index of national feeling, as the intense interest attached to Westminster elections shows. But it was far from being the predominant or even the characteristic element of the House. As Erskine said : " The House of Commons from being a control upon the crown had become the greatest engine of its power." Of this there was proof enough in the affair of Wilkes, and afterwards in the quarrel with the American Colonists. Contested elections were comparatively rare. In 1780 there were contests in only three counties in the whole of England, and only in fifty-nine boroughs. In 1790, though the ferment created by the French Revolution had begun, there were only six contests in the counties and fifty-one in boroughs. It was urged also with truth by the opponents of parliamentary reform that of the leading men most had owed their entrance into the

House of Commons, not to election but to nomination. Lord Liverpool's Cabinet in 1818 consisted of fourteen members, eight of whom were peers. Of the six Commoners two sat for a treasury borough, one for a pocket-borough, and two for what were virtually nomination counties in Ireland; so that of a government supposed to be founded on the elective principle one member alone really owed his place to election.* Yet the House of Commons and the government, as dependent on its vote, were assumed by all the world to be elective, and imitation proceeded on that hypothesis. The elective element was taken to be not only the normal element, but the source of all that other nations admired as specially excellent in British institutions. The limitations of that element, such as the treasury, or nomination, boroughs and the influence of great landowners in county elections were taken to be corruptions and superfetations which had only to be removed in order to allow the elective principle to show forth its full beneficence, and make government entirely wise and the nations perfectly happy. But in face of the actual results we are constrained to ask ourselves whether it may not have been in part the limitations, equivocal as their character was, that made the institution workable. Alexander Hamilton, who from antecedents as well as temperament, had an advantage over the more enthusiastic children of the Revolution, was not without an inkling of the truth. He shrewdly suspected that what were called elective institutions in England were in fact made workable by those restrictions of the elective principle which were called corruption.

What a dance, if Hamilton was right, has the political world been led by its supposed imitation of British institutions! The world might be excused, since the British themselves did not know what their institutions really were, and, indeed, hardly know what they are at this hour.

Party government, many of the people who are not politicians are beginning to admit, is on its trial. But we must ask whether elective government is not on its trial also ; or, rather, whether elective government, properly so-called, has ever in the case of nations or large constituencies really existed, or can be made really to exist ?

GOLDWIN SMITH.

*See Jephson on "The Platform," I., 339.

THE CHINESE QUESTION AGAIN.

BY THE HON. JOHN RUSSELL YOUNG.

THE *Congressional Record* of April 4 gives a complete report of the famous debate on the question of Chinese exclusion. It is worthy of study by those who would know how our rulers determine the gravest questions. Representative Geary, of California, almost immediately after prayers, called up the bill. The rules were suspended and " under the rule, fifteen minutes were allowed for debate." That is to say, fifteen minutes were all that the nation's representatives could give to one of the most important propositions of the time. Mr. Hooker, of Mississippi, made a plea for "two hours." Surely two hours would be little enough for what would practically be the determination of commercial and diplomatic relations between two great nations. The House was inexorable. There was a free-wool debate impending, and for wool hours and hours could be given, not one hour for China. Then Mr. Hooker craved "half an hour"; a half hour, at least, for a momentous issue. Mr. Blount, of Georgia, however, would have the " regular order." This, as the Speaker explained, was a "fatal objection" to the entreaty for a half hour, and fifteen minutes were all that could be conceded.

Then came the "debate!" The report covers three pages of the *Record*. This is not all that will appear on the subject, as we observe that Representative Hooker asked from the House "unanimous consent to extend his remarks in the *Record*." This was granted to the debaters, and, as the outcome, one may expect a pamphlet of essays called " speeches." A credulous constituency will accept them, and they will live in legislative history as the "debate on the Chinese question."

The "debate" was confined to five speeches of from " three to five minutes each," hurriedly panted out by the members, as we may well believe, under the Speaker's imminent gavel. They were terse, nervous little addresses, and read as if they had been delivered with a bullet-like directness. Mr. Geary favored the exclusion of the Chinese "in the interest of American labor," and because China "lived in constant violation of the treaty." Mr. Hermann wanted "our gate-ways double-locked and barred" against "the degraded beings," while Mr. Cutting had read something from Bayard Taylor about the Chinese being "the most debased people on the face of the earth," "whose touch was pollution." Although the observations of Mr. Taylor, as I remember them, were written at a time when China was a sealed land and were based upon a trip through the unsavory quarters of the teeming port of Shanghai, still they had a value in the "debate." Mr. Hooker, speaking from the South, made a plea for the integrity of treaties, commending to our example the fidelity of China in that respect. Mr. Hitt, of Illinois, whose experience in diplomacy gave his words special authority, made an eloquent protest against "the savage exclusion and extreme punishment of all strangers" as a "revival of the darkest features of the darkest ages in the history of man." It was in vain ! Fifteen minutes closed the "debate," and 222 representatives voted—179 for and 43 against the bill. There were no political lines in the voting. Bingham and Reyburn and Harmer voted with Cummings and Breckinridge and Timothy Campbell, and, as far as the House could speak, Chinese expulsion became a law.

Immigration should never be a burning question with China. I have always found the Chinese rulers indifferent to it. I recall but one conversation with Li Hung Chang, the Premier of China, during the time I was accredited to his government, in which the subject was even mentioned. And yet for a long time I was in constant intercourse with that distinguished statesman. This one allusion was made rather as a comment upon some action proposed by our government, and was in the nature of a question as to whether I could point out that special paragraph in "Wheaton's International Law" wherein it was provided that a Hottentot was more desirable as a resident than a Chinaman. My reply was that as the question was one in which His Excellency had no interest, it would be a waste of time to discuss it. The opinion I formed during my intercourse with Li Hung Chang was confirmed by a study of the causes which led to the fall of the American house of

Oliphant & Co., once a noted factor in the Eastern commercial world. The Oliphants were ruined by the British Governor of Hong Kong, who, at the request of the Chinese Viceroy at Canton; suppressed the cooley trade with Peru. The action of the Cantonese official, the merciless manner in which the Oliphants were pursued, even to their bankruptcy, form the one object-lesson which statesmen should consider, in endeavoring to understand the Chinese question. Whether the house of Oliphant would have been ruined by Sir John Pope Hennessy and the Canton Viceroy had it been an English and not an American establishment, I have never been quite able to determine.

While the Chinese authorities, and especially the Prime Minister, were indifferent to emigration, they were sensitive as to our manner of treating it. We have not really been severer than the English in India and the Imperial Colonies. We have never gone so far as to force opium on the people or to refuse to the Chinese government consular representation at our ports. But with our generous impulses towards the Chinese, we have managed by ignorance and indifference to drift into the appearance of injustice. The mind of China has in a sense been poisoned. Small things are magnified and idle debates distorted. Every hard phrase has been hurried to Peking, and with due garnishment and exaggeration spread before the rulers. We have few if any interests in China in common with Western powers. If anything, our interests are antagonistic, and there is a constant war upon them. With a liberal policy towards China I am persuaded that this war would have had barren consequences. But, to use the language of the sporting field, we seem to have ignored our true interests and to have been playing the hand of Russia and England. Such a transaction as the passage of the Scott Bill four years ago, and such a debate as this in the House on April 4 could have only the gravest consequence in Peking.

We might have expected such a debate from a Senate composed of Greeks of the lower Empire, but not in a free intrepid American assembly. Here were national and international interests of the gravest importance—interests which no legislature could usefully consider without the directing mind of the executive authority. I know of no government within the range of observation or study which would have allowed a question so important to flounder in the eddies of ignorant and partisan debate.

Yet, so far as current events can be read, the administration permitted the debate to go by default. The question required careful inquiry and ample information as to present and prospective trade relations and special knowledge as to the development of our empire on the Pacific and our ultimate territorial rights in Australasia. There was likewise the nation's honor as affected by treaties. No debate, no statement of hypothetical cases, could throw light upon it. That light could alone come from the government. Without it, Congress has stumbled in darkness to dangerous and imperfect conclusions.

Nor can the administration be released from a certain responsibility for this unsatisfactory turn in the Chinese business. I say this with the utmost respect for the President, grateful as I am, in common with my countrymen, for a beneficent, conscientious, and able administration. When the President came into office, there were hopes that he would take up the question and deal with it to a wise result. These hopes were based upon his action as a Senator, when China was concerned, as well as upon those engaging traits of manly, independent action which have made him first among statesmen. I know that those high in authority in China looked upon his advent as a restoration of the relations between the two countries, which we owed to the genius of Mr. Burlingame. Nor shall I ever cease to regret that these hopes were doomed to disappointment.

What has been our policy towards China? To describe it roughly,—such a policy as we might observe towards the rulers of Madagascar or the African kings who reign in Stanley's Nyanza regions. I read the other day that an elaborate dispatch addressed to our government some months ago by the Chinese Minister had received no attention. It had, I presume, been put aside in the hurry of department work until living issues arising out of the hog trade or duties on sugar had been determined. We should probably treat a dispatch from a Congo sovereign in the same way. But while a neglected Congo sovereign could be soothed by a hamper of gaudy cloth or a casket of beads, the rulers of China are gifted, courteous, and punctilious. We know the history of the Abyssinian war, how a foolish letter from the Abyssinian King Theodore to the Queen was tossed into a pigeon-hole by some heedless Foreign Office subordinate, how royal anger flamed into evil deeds of retaliation, and how, before peace could be maintained, an English expedition costing millions was compelled to carry the heights of Magdala. I have no such fear in our relations with China. There will be no Chinese retaliation to invite military interference. It will come in a silent, effective way—in the atrophy of trade, the gradual diminishing of influence, the American lowering the flag which for a generation held the first place in China, the keen Englishman and the persistent German taking his place. This retaliation has already come in the refusal of Mr. Blair as a Minister, under circumstances which amounted to an affront, and which was probably so intended by the authorities in Peking.

Recent legislation can, in our charity, be deemed a consequence of ignorance and indifference. With the administration silent on Chinese affairs, how can legislators hope for useful knowledge? Congressmen represent feelings of local vexation, and look upon the Chinese question as a quarantine business, and imagine that we should deal with it as with yellow fever or leprosy. The vital features are ignored. Haste and prejudice and sloth pervade our discussions. We make treaties, but we do not enforce them. The Chinese are blamed for what is our own fault. We denounce the Chinese government for the immigration of Chinese, and overlook the fact that this immigration is from an English port and under the English flag, and that China has no more control over it than over the immigration of Irishmen from Londonderry. We interfere in the internal economy of China by abetting a Russian intrigue for the possession of Corea. When China makes a treaty under the pressure of a Presidential canvass, we inform her that unless within a few hours she ratifies certain amendments the action will be tantamount to rejection. We know that in this manner Bismarck treated Paris when under the German guns. We know that it is the tone of war, and not that of friendly diplomacy. Unhappily, unlike the Congo chiefs, hungry for cloths and beads, the astute rulers of China know it likewise, and resent it in their sure, silent, Oriental way.

Of that Corean incident little is known in the United States, and yet it is a potent cause of Chinese grievance. It was never other than a bit of diplomatic wantonness, the outcome of an eager naval officer's experiments in Oriental diplomacy. It will be understood more clearly when I say that China looked upon our negotiations with Corea for a kind of mock autonomy as we should regard negotiations of England with the State of Maine for a Maine embassy in London and an English embassy in Augusta. If we have an understanding with Russia looking towards the progress of the Russian Empire in Asia, then Corea becomes an intelligible proposition. But of what value is such an understanding, except to satisfy some pitiful Jingo sentiment towards Great Britain? And for this questionable advantage we keep Peking, so far as our interests are concerned, in a state of irritation and suspicion. Corea is not and never has been our affair. Its recognition is a menace to Chinese self-respect and is ever a shadow upon our relations. China may say with truth and bitterness : "You claim to be a fair nation ! Yet when the heavy hand falls upon us, America aids in striking the blow ! You interfere with our suzerain rights over a province, and pilot the Russian into our dominions. You pay your own people four or five per cent. for money and ask China for ten or twelve per cent. You compel us to pay tael for tael for every loss to the missions from local disturbances—you tell the Chinese that you are not responsible for losses to our people. Your Congress may toss us indemnity as an act of grace, but you compel indemnity from us as a right. You make treaties which we gladly accept ! Your people break them, and upon us you devolve the blame. You hold China responsible because Chinese laborers leave Hong Kong, forgetting that Hong Kong is as English as Cardiff or Melbourne. You compel us to surround your missions with troops, and yet in the United States the Chinese are abandoned to the mob. You eliminate from our treaties by act of Congress whatever is of advantage to our people—you carefully reserve whatever helps your own. The rights you deny us in America you enforce for Americans in China. You ask protection and hospitality. You give us fines, imprisonment, and deportation."

American policy towards China should be based upon the same lines as American policy towards England and France. Out of the fulness of our diplomacy what have we not done for the American hog in Paris and Vienna and Berlin ? For that, praise now and always ! But what might we not also have done for the American man in Peking and Tokio ? These Eastern nations lean towards us, and would rest upon our strong arm. American genius under Perry opened Japan — American genius under Burlingame brought China into the diplomatic family of nations.

Where now is the power bequeathed to us by Perry and Burlingame? We are the neighbors of these empires. The richest markets in the world are nearer to us than were Liverpool or Queenstown twenty years ago. The development of our Pacific empire, now in its infancy, rests upon the commercial relations that should exist with Asia. This commercial empire of the East, if I may so call it, belongs to us by the ties of geography, enterprise and sympathy. We have no interests that jar with those of these vast and venerable empires. We do not menace their independence like Russia, nor seek the profits of shame like those reaped from the opium sin by England. Emigration or immigration in whatever form should be the merest accident. It could be arranged whenever we take it seriously in hand. There is no reason why American statesmanship should not direct the over-flowing tides of Chinese life towards Borneo, New Guinea and the Congo. There is every reason why we should be the ally and not the enemy of China. The youngest nation of the world could well give the hand of strength and courage and joyful, sincere endeavor to the oldest nation of the world, and assist her towards the solution of the gravest problem that ever taxed the wisdom of statesmen. It will never be done until we realize that the laws of justice are immutable even among nations—that strength can never come from wrong, and that issues reaching down into the very heart of our national honor and prosperity are not settled by a fifteen minutes brawl, called a "debate," in the House of Representatives.

JOHN RUSSELL YOUNG.

LONDON SOCIETY.

BY LADY JEUNE.

IT WOULD be very difficult exactly to point out when and where the change began which has been gradually transforming London society, but the death of the Prince Consort and the withdrawal of the Queen from public life marks a distinct epoch. The long mourning and seclusion of the Court was the commencement of the Queen's abdication of her position as head of society, and though from time to time she has appeared, it has been at too long intervals and in too fragmentary a manner to have any perceptible influence. During that period the social revolution has been advancing, and the few gatherings which the Queen honors by her presence and the guests invited to meet her, present in the most vivid manner the change that has come over society since she became a widow. No one is brought into personal contact with the Sovereign except those she knows or expresses a desire to see, but the gathering is cosmopolitan.

In a democratic country like England, the personnel of any Government, whether Whig or Tory, is largely composed of self-made men, who, with their families and belongings, gratify the keenest of English ambitions, that of getting into society, with a facility that was impossible fifty years ago, in the days before the passing of the Reform Bill. When the government was entirely in the hands of the two aristocratic parties, Whigs and Tories, society, political though it was, was essentially aristocratic and exclusive, the members of each ministry and their subordinates being men of birth, who belonged naturally to the society in which they moved ; but with the extension of the franchise, the wealthy, well-educated middle classes took their share in the political arena, and, as the logical consequence, claimed their right to some of the social advantages of their leaders. Such social recognition was a prize highly valued and dearly bought, and the price of the much-coveted invitation often meant a

wavering vote.   The wives of the leaders of political parties were
very sparing and very cautious in their hospitality, and the fate
of a government has often hung on the sending out of an invitation for an "At Home" at the house of the Prime Minister.

During the time that Lord Palmerston was in office, Lady
Palmerston wielded a political power very little less potent than
that of her husband, and an invitation to her Saturday parties
at Cambridge House was as eagerly sought for as any political
reward, and no one was a more efficient political aide-de-camp
than she.   She was a strong party woman, and never bestowed her
hospitality outside the circle of her personal friends or on any save
warm adherents or wavering opponents.   She and Lady Derby
divided the task of party entertainments, but with so many years
of Whig ascendancy, to Lady Palmerston fell the lion's share of
dispensing social favors—and the Tory leader's wife had a less
arduous task.   These reunions were exclusively political, and very
rarely were outsiders admitted, while members of the medical
profession, the bar, the stage, and even of literature itself, were
seldom seen.

Lady Waldegrave was the first woman in a political position
who opened her house to everyone, without distinction of party,
and though she scandalized the more exclusive of her friends,
she helped more than anyone to bring about the cosmopolitanism
which is now the prevailing characteristic of English society.   In
her house everyone rubbed shoulders with his opposites.   Tories
and Whigs, Home-Rulers, doctors, barristers, actors and actresses—all found a welcome under her hospitable roof and in
her warm and kindly sympathy.   Since her death no one has
taken her place, for party feeling has run so strongly that no one
else probably could have accomplished anything like bringing the
antagonistic elements of Gladstonian, Conservative and Liberal-
Unionist society into harmony between four walls.   With the
disruption of the Liberal party and the desertion of its great
Whig supporters, all society, in a political sense, in that party
has ceased ; and the task of gathering together the fragments has
been taken up in a very perfunctory manner by the wives of
aspiring future politicians, leaving to the wife of the Prime
Minister that of entertaining the House of Commons and their
families, and we may fairly say that political society, as a distinct
feature in England, for the moment, has passed away.

London is so much larger and richer, the number of people who receive has so enormously increased, and the facilities for going into society are so very much more numerous, that the invitations to the house of a great party-leader are no longer sought after and intrigued for. The centre of society has, in fact, changed ; a large portion of it remains where it always has been, and its members have opened fresh fields of enterprise for themselves. Literature, art, and science have advanced to positions new to them, and a small section, but a very important one, has formed a society of its own, all the more important because it has the acknowledged leader of society at its head—and is exercising an influence on English life and morals, the effects of which we can as yet hardly estimate.

The tendency of society in England is to grow large ; indeed, to become unwieldy. London has become the centre of the civilized world, and everyone gravitates there ; and as it is the fashion to know everyone and go everywhere, the struggle to accomplish this feat inevitably expands society. People have not the leisure to see their friends in a quiet, simple way as formerly, where real intellectual pleasure was always to be found in a certain number of small coteries which existed. Life is too full and too busy, and anyone with any pretence to social smartness finds his engagements so numerous that his only way of seeing acquaintances is by inviting them to the house, where, packed together in a hot room, much too small for half their number, a surging crowd of people comprised of the most opposite elements rub against each other, and try to find enjoyment in the fact that they are in a room with a large number of people more or less interesting and distinguished, none of whom they know by sight, and in whose existence they never interested themselves till it became the fashion to invite the lions and make them roar. To the hostess of the nineteenth century such hospitality is a pain and not a pleasure ; for, assuming that she is a person of some appreciation of the great qualities of her guests, it cannot be aught to her but an annoyance that she is unable to give everyone of her friends the proper position and attention which he merits ; but she has no alternative, for her large acquaintance and many engagements preclude her showing them hospitality in any other way.

The French salon has never found a counterpart in England. The inclination of the English as regards society is to eat, and not

to talk. An English man or woman's idea of hospitality and
society is a dinner and a dress coat, and that in conjunction with
as much formality and state as possible ; and the simplicity of
French society in this regard, which meant dropping in during a
given evening one day a week to a well-known house where neither
meat nor drink was provided, and where intellectual nourishment
was the only food, never recommended itself to the English ways
of life. It found some adherents in the days of Miss Berry,
whose house in Wimpole Street was for many years the rendezvous
of all the most distinguished people of her time.   Lady William
Russell, the mother of the late Duke of Bedford, one of the most
accomplished women of the day, surrounded herself with a society
as pleasant as it was small, and, to the last day of her life, was
always to be found in the evening in her house in Audley Square.
Lady Jersey, Lady Sandwich, Lady Granville, and Lady Ashbur-
ton were the only *grandes dames* who in English society ever tried
to imitate the salon, and their *entourage* was very small. · Their
aristocratic prejudices were too strong to admit anyone outside
the charmed circle, and many of the most distinguished men of
their time lived and died unknown to them.

Whatever may be the reproach of the end of the nineteenth
century, a want of appreciation of distinction in any form is not
one.   There never was an age where fame of any kind was
more of a cult, or where notoriety was a surer passport to social
eminence.   Whether the greater intellectual qualities of mankind
are recognized in proportion may be doubted, but society now
runs mad after anyone who can get himself talked of, and that
not in the sole direction of great ability or distinction.   To have
a good cook ; to be the smartest-dressed woman ; to give the
most magnificent entertainments, where a fortune is spent on
flowers and decorations ; to be the last favored guest of royalty ;
or to have sailed as near to the wind of social disaster as is com-
patible with not being shipwrecked ;—are a few of the features
which characterize some of the smartest people in London society.
It must be admitted that these qualifications are not high or difficult to attain to, while the training ground is large and well-
studded with instructors.

Luxury, ease, comfort, are the watchwords of a large part of
society in London, and they are undermining our society as surely
and as certainly as they did that of ancient Rome.   We have

grown very rich, and we have a large leisured class whose only aim and occupation is amusement, and where such exists it must demoralize and relax all social restraints.

Men and women who only live for pleasure, and who have no sense of the obligations of life and its duties, are becoming the parents of the young England around us, and to a serious degree the example of their lives is being impressed on the boys and girls who are their children, and who ought to carry on the traditions of which we in all time have been so proud. The influences of which we speak are perhaps less felt among boys than girls. School-life still develops the manhood and courage of Englishmen, and though the luxury of early preparatory schools is increasing to a very evil extent, the rough and tumble life of our public schools counteracts its influence, and gives all boys the knocking about which we still believe is so important for the development of the hardier qualities of a man's character. The battle of life—the struggle in all professions—is so keen that it brings out a man's strongest qualities, and the competition which he has to meet, and which is becoming harder every year, renders him more impervious to the enervating influences of the day. But society, as well as the tone of society, is not governed or instituted by men, their rôle in society being a very secondary one ; for society in its tone and composition is created by women, and as women are virtuous or the reverse, so is their *entourage.*

It would be idle to deny that recent scandals in London society, which have been the talk of the world, and the existence of which surprised and shocked the moral sense of England, are only the outcome and logical result of the easy-going manner in which women of the highest rank and culture have allowed the old-fashioned rules and restraints which governed society to be relaxed. The decay of these restraints has been in many ways almost imperceptible, but the spirit of freedom and liberalism in every matter of life, whether social, political or religious, has impregnated every condition of life, and has gradually swept away the reserve and illusions of our forefathers.

Nowhere is this more conspicuous than among girls, whose lives are as different from those of their grandmothers as light from darkness. The respect for parents, the self-denial and self-abnegation, the modest reserve which used to be the character-

istic of the "English miss," have disappeared, and in her place
we have a creature no doubt attractive and original, but not the
girl of the past. Parents and children now meet nearly on an
equality, but where there is any inferiority it is on the parental
side. The young lady of to-day reads the newspapers, what books
she chooses, and discusses with equal frankness the last scandal
and the latest French mode ; she rides in the park unattended by a
groom, but always with a cavalier ; she drives unattended in hansoms ; she dances with partners who do not care to be presented
to her mother, and she leaves her chaperon not to dance, with the
real enjoyment of girlhood, but to retire to some leafy corner of
the ball-room, where she can, to use the modern phrase, "sit
out," instead of dancing. She spends her own money, and dresses
as she likes, and more often than not spends more than she can
afford. Her stay in London is one round of pleasure from morning to night, varied during the autumn and winter by country
visits, which are only a repetition of London on a small scale ;
and in her life there is no question of aught but pleasure ; and
no more curious change is to be observed than that, while
some years ago girls would go anywhere for a dance, now they
only desire to go to the best balls and to be with the smartest
people.

The reason for the change which has come over the English
girls is no doubt to be found in the fact that for many years past
they have not had, as far as regards society, a "good time." The
young married woman has been as formidable a competitor to
them as she is also said to be to another and an entirely different
class of female society. Hence in dress, conduct, conversation,
and often in knowledge, they copy their envied rival, or, by attaching themselves to some smart young married woman,
they profit by what she squanders in the prodigality of her
success.

However great the difficulties girls find in England in entering the social lists, they are much more hardly handicapped in
the matter of dancing, and still more in that of marrying. Nothing
is more comical, nay, even sad, than to see the devices to which
ball-givers resort, to get men to come to their houses and when
there to dance. Everything is done to tempt them. Balls begin
at midnight, because the *jeunesse dorée* of England will not dance
early ; the *recherché* supper and the best of wines are provided ;

and long before midnight patient rows of sleepy chaperons and anxious girls await the arrival of the young Adonis, who, after surveying the serried ranks scornfully through his eyeglass from the end of the ball-room, retires below to partake of the hospitality provided by his thoughtful host, and having thus done his duty goes back to his club. And what is true of dancing is even more so as regards marrying. Men who are poor are afraid to marry, knowing the life of ease and comfort which is the lot of most girls and that marriage will entail an amount of denial and self-sacrifice they are not willing to undertake. When great passion or affection are concerned, the case alters, and hand in hand a man and woman face the struggle together. But the nineteenth century has taken away much of the poetry and romance which gild the pathway of life when the gold is not of a sufficiently substantial kind to provide more than bread and butter.

Parents also feel naturally that when a man has no profession or prospects which will ultimately increase the income he can offer their daughter, that marriage would not only be unwise but wrong, and the effect is that girls marry later and, often, with a better prospect of happiness. But girls do not marry as easily or as well as formerly, and the confidant of fashionable London mothers will bear me out in saying that the universal cry is, " The men won't marry."

The increased expense of living and the difficulty that men with small incomes have in marrying, affect other classes in England; but in the middle and professional classes the improved education which women receive opens other careers to them besides the domestic one, and the choice of husbands is more varied and wider. It is the expense of living, and of living up to a certain position, that has driven so many of the daughters of the aristocracy to make marriages among men in business, and it is one of the principal causes of the democratization that is going on so rapidly in England. Money is the idol of to-day; without it life is ugly, hard, and wearisome ; and if with it the romance and poetry of existence fly away, it helps to grease the wheels of the coach, and rubs and softens down many excrescences. It has been said, everything can be bought but health, and it is nearly true; wealth is a great power, either in its use or abuse; it is the keystone of success in the smartest London society, and

no truer words were ever written than those of the Poet Laureate
of our nineteenth century life:

> " Every door is barred with gold,
> And opens but with golden keys."

If we take up a society paper which chronicles the fashionable
doings of the week, the list of the smartest and most magnificent
entertainments are not those given by the *haute noblesse* of
England, but by a host of people, many of whose names are
foreign, and who thirty years ago would not have been heard of
outside their provincial homes ; and to their houses flock princes
and princesses, and the acknowledged leaders of what was once,
and that not long ago, the most exclusive society in Europe. The
atmosphere heavy with the perfume of flowers ; the spoils of the
Riviera ; the bewitching sounds of the voice of the last fashionable prima donna, brought there at a fabulous price ; the delica-
cies of the supper room, and the banquet with its priceless wines—
are the temptations which the crowd of magnificently dressed
and beautiful women and blasé men cannot resist, and such is the
nightly spectacle offered to any observer of what we term the
" smart set " of London society.   Shades of the former leaders of
society and patronesses of Almacks, do you not turn in your
graves at the sight of your grandchildren and their children
associating on terms of intimacy and equality with a crowd whose
sole recommendation is that it panders and ministers to the most
demoralizing influence of an age already bad enough !

When all that is needed to insure an entrance into the highest
society in England is unlimited wealth, where morality is unnecessary, and where it is patronized by the highest in the land—
is it to be wondered at that the deterioration which is going
on is much more complete, and will be more disastrous in its
effects, than any one likes to admit.   To those who feel seriously and deplore the effect that the recognition of the new elements which now compose society in England must have, the
position becomes one of great difficulty.   There is a great difference between an affectation of being shocked and a real manly
protest at much that is going on around us.   But neither is of
any avail to stop a condition of things which, bad as it is, is condoned and accepted by those whose position and weight should
make them raise up their voice in protest.   This is an age of
charity, and where there is no open scandal, no breaking of the

new and most important addition to the moral law, "thou shalt not be found out," it is much more convenient to shut your eyes, and not incur the displeasure of the great ones of the world by crying in the wilderness.

The agricultural depression, and the necessity for retrenchment enforced on all the smaller landed proprietary, by obliging them to shut up their houses and live in a much reduced state, or to come to London, where in spite of its luxury it is easy to be poor, have destroyed a strong counteracting influence ; and, like an engine over which its driver has lost control, society goes tearing wildly on unchecked in its career.

It must not, however, be supposed that there is no society in England save that which we have described, for there still exists a larger and more important one in many ways, where we find happy homes and families, and where the sense of duty and the responsibilities of life are the keystones on which their existence is built ; where in a faithful way its members still discharge the responsibilities which great rank, birth, and vast possessions, entail, and whose existence is the backbone of English life. In some way there has never been a time in England when there was so strong a feeling of charity and of the obligations to their poor brethren which riches entail on their possessors, or when that charity was more nobly and generously bestowed. For their existence we are thankful, for they represent the power of resistance which alone can withstand the pressure of example and influence from the other strata of society.

It is not only from the widespread and general luxury, extravagance, and freedom, of the richer class of England that the evil which we deplore arises, though they are large and serious enough, but because the influence and example of the upper classes spread below and spread insensibly. How can we chide and condemn the vices of the poor in England when the example set them is what we see ? Surely we must feel infinite pity for the poor outcast women of the world who sin because they must live, while there can be nothing but a feeling of horror for women who set their virtue so low as to make it the price of dresses which will " cut out " the toilettes of their women friends in society ; nor can we have any but a feeling of contempt for the men who, marrying on small means, suddenly find their whole *entourage* changed by the addition of horses and carriages, French cooks, and all the modern luxuries of a fashionable *ménage,* and who shut their eyes and accept the gifts of the fairy godfather who has wrought all these miracles. In all societies there are men and women low enough to accept these positions ; but in England thirty years ago such a position would have been impossible, and no man or woman occupying it would have dared to appear in society. *Autres temps autres moeurs,* and with so many examples of the charity of the world and the complaisance of husbands, no wonder the " smartest set " in London society has created a condition of things that respectable English opinion considers a reproach and a danger to the country.

The decay of strong religious belief in some sections of English society is at last beginning to have effect in sweeping away some of the strongest restraints to which human nature can be subjected. We do not maintain that, in the great waves of passion which sweep across the lives of men and women, religion has always been an unfailing protector, but insensibly its influence controls actions and inclinations which would have been calamitous in their effect. Modern thought is changing the aspect of life and, with it, the relations of men and women, and that not in a repressive direction. The spread of education among women, and the emancipation which is its natural corollary, will work still greater changes, all in the direction we deplore ; and unless some unforeseen event occurs which will change the direction in which society is moving, public opinion will insist on its reconstruction on a firmer and entirely different basis, and the lines of demarcation which now divide society will become more clearly defined. The " smart set " will follow its natural inclination, which has for its object the gratification of every pleasure and whim which are the fashions of the moment. The other, with certain ideals of duty, will, as now, endeavor to realize the responsibilities these impose, and, being composed of the strength and backbone of the country, will always be the power to adjust the baneful influence of its competitor. Fortunately for England the mass, and the most important mass, of opinion will be on the side of the latter ; but, unfortunately, owing to the glamour shed over the former by the rank and position of its leaders, it will always be the smarter, and, therefore, the fashionable set.

M. JEUNE.

THE OLYMPIAN RELIGION.

II.—OUTLINE OF ITS PARTICULARS (Concluded).

BY THE RIGHT HONORABLE WILLIAM EWART GLADSTONE.

PASSING on from the personal equipment of Homer's preternatural world, we have next to consider what were the distinctive qualities of its inhabitants as an order of deities.

The first answer must be that they were immensely varied; so varied, indeed, that they cannot receive any adequate description in a slight outline such as this. Their singularly differentiated characters require to be set forth one by one; and in their individual diversities we find one of the most important and fruitful provinces of the present inquiry. Still there are distinctive properties which the gods possess in common, and by which they are differenced from men.

The first of these qualities is that they are immortal. This is a property so essentially theirs that they are signified by it as a class. They, and they only, are the Immortals; and to name the Immortals is to speak of the gods. It appears, indeed, that the gift could be imparted to man. This is suggested in Tithonos, the partner of the couch of Eos;* and it seems in Homer to be an elementary part of the movement towards deification. If it be asked whether an Immortal could be deprived of the privilege, the answer seems to be, first, that, as a rule, penalty in no way interfered with immortality; and, secondly, we learn from the language of Arès† that, though the gods could not die, the heart of their life might possibly be beaten out of them by a penal infliction.

The next universal characteristic of the gods is, that they are incorporated in human form. Wherever this is at all doubtful,

* Il., XI., 1, and Od.,V., 1.   † Il., V., 885–887.

it is because the image presented to us is so slight that it hovers between a person and a metaphor. The human form is presupposed even in the case of the Nature-powers; as when a wood-nymph has offspring by a man, or a river-god by a woman. So thorough and well rooted is this conception in the Poet's mind that, in a passage intended to glorify Agamemnon, he sets off, as we have seen, the personal appearance of the supreme chief by reference to the corporal excellences of various divinities; he was like Zeus in eye and head; his waist like Arès (the nimble god); his chest like Poseidon.*

The third common characteristic of deity as such is a large excess of power beyond any possessed by mortals. This power is exhibited in various forms : in superiority to limitation; in the performance of acts not within the scope of natural law; and, in the cases of a very few higher deities, by direct and immediate action on the mind of man. It is to be observed, as a general rule, that there is always a peculiar amount of power possessed in the peculiar province to which each divinity is attached. So it is that even Aphroditè can master the mind and inclination of Helen,† and that Hephaistos gives life to the metallic figures he has made, apparently even in the case where they are set upon the shield of Achilles.‡ But it is only to his greater gods that Homer assigns important prerogatives outside a particular sphere of action. Of this divine power the maximum must be said to reside in Zeus: yet he can be beguiled and deceived in being sent to sleep (as it appears, but the process is not described) against or without his will.§

But, fourthly, there is also by the side of this power an universal characteristic of limitation. This is indefinitely large and stringent in its application outside the provinces of specialty. So severe is it in the case of Aphroditè that, when she ventures upon the battle-field to carry off her smitten son Aineias, she is attacked by Diomed and wounded in the hand, so that she lets her burden fall, and repairs to Olympos with the aid of the chariot of Arès.‖ Thus in her case we are obliged to confine by conditions even the general proposition that the power of deities exceeds that of mortals. It holds, however, so generally that Achilles, whose might borders on the superhuman, is baffled and

* Il., II., 478, 479. † Il., III., 383, seqq. ‡ Il., XVIII., 535-540; 546-549. Od., VII., 91-94. § Il., XIV., 252, 262, 280, 359. ‖ Il., V., 318, 330-339, 363-367.

foiled by the Nature-power Scamandros when acting in his own right as a river-flood.*

At the other end of the scale, Zeus himself is not free from limitation in other cases besides the peculiar case of preternatural stratagem. He did not know, because he did not see, what Poseidon was doing on the battle-field in Troas; and he did not see, because he was looking in another direction, over the line of the Balkan mountains.† Again, after he woke, he accepted with a smile the assurance of Herè, confirmed by an oath, that she had not incited Poseidon against the Trojans. But he remained‡ unaware of the device by which she had contrived that the activity of Poseidon should be prolonged, through an exhortation which Hupnos delivered to him, apparently as her messenger.§ Aphroditè, Arès, Helios, and others make their complaints to him, and thereby show that he had not previous cognizance of the facts. I need not prolong the list of his limitations in this place. But it may be observed that they are limitations in the sphere of mind, not in that of external nature. The different deities of Homer stand differently related to locomotion; but there are no stages in the movements of Zeus as he passes from point to point. I have dwelt upon the case of Zeus, because, as he is at the summit, and as the Olympian system exhibits to us divinity in many conditions of inferiority to his, it will be readily understood that, as we move through the list of deities on a descending scale, limitation is progressively increased.

This proposition, however, has one most conspicuous exception. Although the mere power of Zeus is greater than that of Athenè, and is sometimes used in order even to coerce her, she, apart from these interferences, is exempt from all limiting conditions, whether material or mental. She is never ignorant, never deceived, never baffled. The case of Apollo closely, but less conspicuously, approximates to hers.

Fifthly, next to limitation, we must consider the case of actual wants. It cannot be said that the Olympian gods are wholly free from what we consider as corporal wants, for example, from what Aischulos calls the γάστρος ἀνάγκη. What can be truly said is that a large provision is made for the enjoyment which is

* Il., XXI., 263-274.   † Il., XIII, 1-7.   ‡ Il., XV., 42-47.
§ Il., XIV., 356.

associated with the supply of wants, by the banquets which, though not uniformly in one place, are˙ understood to be habitual with the gods. But, behind this curtain of luxury, something also of necessity remains. Not only Aphrodité and Arès, but Aidoneus, and even Herè, had at different junctures been wounded by the hand of man; and, though it is not recorded of the goddesses, the two gods* had to be cured of their wounds by Paieon. Again, as to food. Neither Athenè nor Apollo ever adverts to sacrifices as giving by their savor a physical satisfaction. But Zeus twice very unequivocally describes this reek of the victims, together with the libation, as the share or privilege of the gods ;† the same words being put into his mouth on both occasions. Actual eating and drinking are, as we have seen, ascribed individually to deities less exalted. Calupso provides nectar and ambrosia for Hermes,‡ which he drank and ate to the satisfaction of his soul ; and when Thetis visits Hephaistos, his bride and housewife Charis proposes to furnish *xeinia* forthwith, evidently meaning food. To this there is no parallel in the case of the higher gods. And, when Poseidon is on the field of battle before Troy, it is laid down that it is not allowed (οὐ ϑέμις ἐστὶ) to them to take part in the battles of men,§ although Arès, a deity of lower rank, had previously done it to his cost.

Zeus is the most human in his affections of all the gods, and sometimes regards with a strong natural compassion the sorrows of men, which at other times he is heartily delighted to behold ; ‖ but it cannot be said that other deities are as much given to emotion. The sympathies of Herè with particular persons, and especially with the Greeks at large, seem to dwell entirely in the region of the intellect, and in their operation are purely national and political. All the credit that can be given to the Olympian order, in the region of the affections, is that they are not devoid of sympathy with their own offspring. Aphrodité exerts herself for the relief of Aincias.¶ Arès is violently excited to revenge on learning the death of his son Ascalaphos ;** and Poseidon repeatedly protects or rescues not his sons only but more remote descendants.†† All this, however, indicates much more of animal or instinctive, and perhaps of racial, than of

---

* Il., V., 401, 899.   † Il., IV., 43; XXIV., 70.   ‡ Od., V., 92.   § Il., XIV., 386.
‖ Il., VIII., 51, 52.   ¶ Il., V., 311, seqq.   ** Il., XV., 113.   †† e. g., Il., XI., 750-752.

moral sentiment. For Poseidon betrays the quality of his paternal affection by bitterly persecuting Odysseus for measures of pure self-defence taken against the savage Poluphemos; the one monster of the Poems, whose passions and vices are unredeemed by a single virtue. Much higher in rank stand the affection and pain of Zeus on the extinction of his noble son Sarpedon.*

It would be improper to pass without particular notice the libertinism of the gods. They exhibit a prevailing laxity in sexual relations. On this topic it is to be observed, in the first place, that there is no such taint in the Homeric pictures of Athenè or (as I think) of Apollo; a fact which is only here noticed as a mark of Homer's profound reverence for those two divinities, without examining into its cause. Artemis also is wholly untainted; and, in the Hellenic image, is seemingly intended to be the representation of maiden and of matronly chastity. Passing from the exceptions to what is more nearly the rule, I deal here with the conspicuous case of Zeus in the fourteenth "Iliad."† He enumerates in series the human connections which produced respectively Peirithoos, Perseus, and Minos with his brother Rhadamanthos, Heracles, and Dionusos: the last of these undoubtedly divine, though from a human parent. He then passes to Demeter and Leto. And all these amatory affairs are paraded by the offender himself, at the meeting with Herè; a poetical impropriety which may be compared with the protracted speeches in the battle-field, or with the relation by Achilles to Thetis of a lengthened story in a great part of which she herself had borne a principal part. The impropriety is perhaps to be explained on similar grounds in all the cases: it seems to be a vehicle for imparting to the Poet's hearers what he desires that they should know with a view to the purposes, ethnographical or historical, which he had in his mind. We are, I think, to consider Zeus as describing in this passage, to an extent which in some degree we can trace, the formation of the Achaian nationality and religion. The connection with Danaè, for example, perhaps is meant to indicate the introduction of the Phœnician element into the Greek peninsula; that with Demeter, the reconciliation, so to call it, of the newer ideas with the old Nature-worship of the country; and that with Leto, the very special features which Apollo contributes to the Olympian scheme.

*Il., XVI., 459.   † 315-328.

This view, I think, is supported by the case of Poseidon. There are assigned to him, in the two Poems, a number of important filiations in the Peloponnesos and in Scheriè, which obviously bear an ethnographical character ; helping to attach, for example, the Phaiakes to the Phœnician connection, and Nestor to the same stock. It is possible that the Poet may have been governed by some similar consideration in assigning to Hermes and Arès respectively the paternity of some personages mentioned in the "Iliad." But, at the least, all these ascriptions have a moral aspect. Take them as we will, they clearly imply that there was nothing in Homer's conception of these several divinities to interpose a moral bar in the way of his imputing to them acts which in the case of men would carry with them more or less of stigma. I say more or less, for while in the "Iliad" spurious offspring is broadly distinguished from legitimate, the distinction does not always carry with it social consequences. In certain cases the innocent bearer of the stigma is admitted to equality in rearing.

Chastity may be called the outermost barrier of morality, and is the first, accordingly, to give way. The indulgence of sexual passion is general with the gods, unless there be a single exception in Apollo—a question requiring a separate discussion. It subsists among the goddesses also ; and though not universally, yet most grossly of all in Aphroditè, who is simply its impersonation, and represents no other power whatever. Besides Aphroditè, we may notice the cases of Demeter and of Eos.*

Let us turn to a more general view of the quality of Olympian god-head.

Subject to certain reservations, which will be more properly considered in connection with the delineations of the Homeric deities individually, it must be confessed that their characters are self-centred and are based upon Hedonism, or the Epicurean system in its fullest development. They appear not to incur any responsibility ; not to be subject to the moral law, which does not exist for them, because they have no superior, by whom its sanctions could be applied. They are exempted from its sway by the possession of exceptional power. The case of these imposing conceptions shows as if superiority in power, which ought always to be accompanied by a higher acknowledgement of duty, operated

* Od., V., 121-124 ; XV., 250—251.

in a manner directly the reverse, and aggravated the derangement not only of human nature, but of every nature modelled, like that of the Olympian gods, on corresponding lines. True, we must 'distinguish between the pictures of deities still non-Hellenic, and therefore not entitled, in the Poet's eyes, to religious homage, and the representation of deities such as Herè, Poseidon, or Hermes. The first conception, which deals with non-Hellenic deity, amounts in certain respects almost to caricature. The second exhibits to us the genuine tendencies of a highly intellectual people in the process of moulding their religion ; and they go far to prove that religion itself was on the road to become not a regenerating power, but rather, in important particulars, an instrument for aggravating the moral disorders of the world.

We have thus far treated of the qualities and powers of the Homeric gods in their several personalities. Let us now turn to consider more at large the general characteristics of the combination into which they were formed, and which I have named the Olympian religion.

When we come to contemplate this Olympian scheme as it is in itself, we cannot fail to be struck by the marked, systematic, and pervading character of its general characteristics, in which it so greatly differs from formations such as those of the Babylonian, Assyrian, and Egyptian religions. Let us enumerate some of these notes.

In the first place, the Olympian scheme of Homer is a highly scientific formation. Its numerous parts or ranks are placed in defined, and for the most part well-defined, relations to each other, and, notwithstanding their large range and diversified aspects, all are made to work together for a common end.

Without attempting here to define the degree in which the great undertaking of Homer partook of the elements of moral reform, thus much at least appears to be certain, and, if certain, peculiar. He first, and he only, in the history of ancient religions, brought order out of chaos, and unity out of diversities which might well have seemed irreconcilable. What were the materials with which he had to work ? There was, first, the comparative purity which we seem justified in ascribing to the Achaian or Hellenic ideas. There was the Pelasgian cult of Nature-powers, a system little capable of lifting itself, or of being lifted, above the surface of the earth. Lastly, we have the more developed forms of religion which had come over sea in Phœnician company, and which evidently drew after them a flood of moral corruptions. These offered to the Poet's eye an assemblage of materials anything rather than tractable. But, almost in despite of themselves, they were wrought into a poetical and literary unity. The task which he undertook and performed was one wholly without parallel in any other country. But it was essential to his nation-making work that he should constitute an Olympian unity, and without it the historic Hellas never could have existed.

In the next place, the scheme is highly national and political. Political, inasmuch as the divinities are members of an organization methodically ordered for a common purpose, so that in speaking of an Olympian hierarchy we speak, in the main, of an Olympian State. And it is national in more than one respect. In the first place, because its leading powers are charged with a strongly Achaian coloring. In the Trojan war the really great and powerful deities are all on the Achaian side, subject only to this qualification—that for a temporary purpose Zeus holds them back, and in so doing has in all cases Apollo for his obedient minister. The Olympian scheme, as Homer sets it forth, is variously national. Poseidon is attached to his Hellenized descendants; Herè is absolutely unremitting in her vigilance for the army at large, as well as for its leaders. It is the more special office of Athenè to keep watch and ward over the greatest of the national heroes personally; and Apollo, in the " Odyssey," presides over the crowning exploit of Odysseus. But it is also national in a still higher sense. The subject of the Iliad is not the war of Troy, but the wrath of Achilles exhibited during and in connection with the war of Troy. The plot results from an Olympian consultation, and is adjusted principally with a view to the glorification of Achilles; and it is in the figure of Achilles that we have the Poet's crowning exhibition of Hellenism. But though care and effort are concentrated upon this point, they are also distributed over the whole field of the nation. To every considerable chief there are awarded, in one part or another of the " Iliad," space and opportunity enough for a rich harvest of exploit and of fame; and even secondary personages, such as Meriones and Automedon, are not left wholly without their share of martial honor.

The Christian religion stands in contrast with the paganism which it destroyed and replaced in this, among other particulars, that its main business has been the government of individuals and not that of states, although the government of states is doubtless a portion of its work, and ought to be directed in all things by its principles.

The Olympian system, on the other hand, as it stands in Homer, is more concerned with public affairs than with private character. Of private rights, indeed, it may have taken some cognizance, and when Odysseus recites the means of repairing his wasted fortunes, and among them contemplates the acquisition of much booty,* it is probable, though there is nothing distinctly specified, that this booty is to be prize of war. But the religion is very slightly charged with the formation of private character, beyond this, that the good man is devout and regular in the worship of the gods, like Eumaios in the "Odyssey";† and that misconduct cannot be covered by the mere tribute of sacrifice.‡ But the inner schooling of the individual, the expression of religion in devout affection, or in the control of appetite, or as a renewing process which is to cover the whole field of human nature, is unknown to this Olympian scheme ; and piety hardly counts, though justice may, in the prospect or retrospect of life. It is predicted that Odysseus shall live and die in a happy old age, with his people prospering around him ; § but there is in this remarkable prophecy no reference to his relations with the gods. We hear of them in certain forms of duty ; they are the guardians of nature's fundamental laws ; and they are sought out in great emergencies ; but beyond this they have no concern with human life in the private sphere. Indeed, in some cases, they are charged with its offences and miscarriages. On the other hand, they care for the general tranquillity, and resent the infraction of public right.

Whatever be the relaxations in the moral code of the divinities,—and they are undeniable,—their general government of the world not only "makes for righteousness" on the whole, but is directly and systematically addressed to the great end of rendering it triumphant. And this is claimed by Zeus in the Olympian Assembly.‖ The terms which he employs are remarkable : "Men complain of us the gods, and say that we are the source from whence ills ($\kappa \acute{a} \kappa a$) proceed, but they likewise themselves suffer woes outside the course of destiny ($\dot{v}\pi\acute{\epsilon}\rho\mu o\rho o\nu$), through their

---

* Od., XXIII., 357.   † Od., XIV., 435, 446.   ‡ Il., I., 93, seqq.   § Od., XI., 136; XXIII., 284.   ‖ Od., I., 32-34.

own perverse offending" This offending is indicated by the term ἀτασθαλίη, used by Homer to designate the kind of wrong-doing which is the result, not of temptation working upon us through passion or infirmity (these are described as ἄται), but which is spontaneous, wilful, and unrestrained by regard to God or man. The word comes near to the full idea of sin; and is deeper and more expressive, in regard to the moral law, than any phrase, so far as I know, to be found in the literature of historic Greece. Then Zeus goes on to illustrate by example what he has said : " for Aigisthos has committed his great crimes in spite of the express warning which we sent him from the gods through Hermes ; but these outrages of his shall be punished by the hand of Orestes, when he comes to his full age."

And this claim of Zeus is a fair one. For nothing can be clearer than that each of the two Poems is constructed and ad-justed with a view, in the main, to the triumph of right and the punishment of wrong. Troy is to fall, notwithstanding the strong personal attachment which Zeus felt for it on account of the liberal sacrificial system by which his altar profited; and the design of this retribution is the design which Zeus has either devised or at least accepted. On the other hand, not only do the troubles of Odysseus end in his restoration, but his return is gilded with the prophecy of a prosperous old age.*

Beyond this, there is very little to be said in abatement of the general proposition that, whatever be their collective conduct, the common speech of the gods is below the human level in point of morality. A debate in Olympos is far inferior in tone to a debate in the Achaian Assembly. The superlative quality of nobleness is to be found in the speeches and conduct of heroes. The speech of Sarpedon to Glaukos,† the rebuke of Odysseus to Eurualos in Scheriè,‡ can hardly be surpassed. We look in vain for such discourses among the gods. The Olympian council of the last Book meets to perform an act of humanity in the conser-vation and redemption of the body of Hector. The thing done is right; but the whole process is made to turn on procuring the acceptance of the gifts of Priam by Achilles ; undoubtedly a good working method, but one not uplifted by any sentiment more lofty than the expression by Zeus of the love which the gods en-tertained for Hector by reason of his constant offerings.

* Od.. XI , 134-137; XXIII., 281-284.   † Il., XII., 310.   ‡ Od., VIII., 166.

Nor is it easy to conceive a worse transaction than that of the fourth Book where it is arranged between Zeus, Herè, and Athenè that Pandaros shall be incited to break the truce so solemnly made for the settlement of the whole quarrel by single combat. On the suggestion of Herè, this mission is enjoined by Zeus upon Athenè; but it was a command that Athenè herself was eager to receive.* She at once rushed away to fulfil it, assuming a human personality for the purpose.† Without doubt it was necessary for the plot as decreed by Zeus on the prayer of Thetis that the truce should be broken. I think it is also true that Zeus does not act upon the minds of men in specific instances without some intermediate agency or manifestation, as Athenè acts upon the minds of the Suitors. Still it is singular and highly significant that Homer should thus employ the direct agency of the highest among his deities to secure the perpetration of what is among the very grossest of all moral offences, to wit, the deliberate breach of a most solemn engagement.

With this case before us, we cannot be surprised that Athenè, in the " Odyssey," should boast to Odysseus of her skill in guile,‡ and pay him the compliment of saying that he is her counterpart on earth. Yet more striking, from some points of view, is the case of Autolukos in the " Odyssey," who was instructed in the arts of fraud by Hermes himself; § an incident appertaining in great measure to the peculiar attributes of that divinity.

The third and the most remarkable among the characteristics of the Olympian religion is that which has been more commonly than happily termed anthropomorphism. The phrase is misleading, because it signifies no more than that the Homeric divinities are associated with the human form. But there is a far wider and deeper incorporation than this of the human with the divine element, which I venture to express by a term which, at any rate, is capable of conveying it in its full breadth—the term theanthropy. It is not the form only, but the mind, the character, the appetites, the modes of thought and speech, and both of acting and of suffering, which, subject to a reservation that is presently to be made, are pervadingly and intensely human. Nor is this humanism in the divinities confined to the individual : it marks the polity as a whole, not less than the single member of it ; and the government of the world by the Olympian

* Il., IV., 64-73. † Ibid, 36-38. ‡ Od., XIII., 295-301. § Od., XIX., 396.

gods, with circumstantial differences, is. essentially modelled upon the basis of human action. This theanthropic spirit is, more than any other particular, the *natura naturans* of the Olympian scheme. But besides the exhibition of theanthropic conditions in affirmative forms, we observe the determined theanthropism of the Poet in a multitude of arrangements, by which he throws into the background those forms of religion which are not in harmony with the spirit of the Olympian scheme, or contrives some compromise with them under which they are tolerated, but not allowed to retain an inconvenient form. It is not possible to go through, in this place, the mass of details from which alone these assertions can be made good. But by way of sample I will specify a very few of them.

The solar attributes of Apollo, derived from a nature-cult, are permitted to survive in decorative epithets, but so as nowhere to disguise his Olympian character or embarrass his action. Helios, the solar deity, possibly the working chief of Troic religion, is thrust almost, though not altogether, out of view in the " Iliad "; probably because he could not be exhibited on the same stage as the Olympian Apollo without confusion. But in the Outer geography of the " Odyssey" his full figure is shown, because on foreign ground he is not in competition with the Achaian and Olympian conception. The exquisitely beautiful Artemis of the "Odyssey" has a far inferior reflection in the " Iliad," evidently because she was associated in Troas with the system of earth-worship. Again, considering what we know of the widely-diffused practice of serpent-worship, we might be surprised at not finding it in the Poems. Animal-worship, however, in any form was obviously in deadly hostility to theanthropy. Therefore the serpent is carefully shut out from receiving homage ; yet subject to this accommodation, that it keeps its place as a vehicle of presage, and that a position of great dignity is allowed to it, not, however, as a power, but as an emblem, on the breastplate and belt of Agamemnon.*

In all these characteristic points, the Olympian scheme is widely different from every other religion of the ancient heathen world. Nor is the record of distinctions yet exhausted. It has, as compared with any other among those religions, less in its aggregate of an abstract or didactic, and more of a

* Il., XI., 26, 33.

literary, as well as a patriotic, character. I do not say that it represents more accurately the beliefs of the people among whom it sprang into existence than may be the case with some of the rest. Possibly, nay probably, it offers a less faithful picture. We do not here find ourselves in contact with a philosopher like Confucius or Zoroaster, or a reformer like Buddha. The motley group of gods to whom we are introduced do not, like the systems of Babylon, Assyria, and Egypt, convey to us an undigested and almost chaotic record of popular worships. Those are disjointed stones; these are an elaborate and magnificent structure. Those are raw material in its earliest stage; these are coördinated, and in coördination modified, by the hand of a master. A great and commanding genius takes in hand a reconciling work. What sovereigns have during these later centuries sometimes attempted in combining by compromise the varying beliefs of their people, was in this case endeavored, and in great measure achieved, by a Poet. It is no wonder if, in such a case, we can trace the mark of the chisel upon the marble, and even find ourselves admitted to a shadowy view of the great artificer in his workshop.

W. E. GLADSTONE.

NOTES AND COMMENTS.

MEXICAN TRADE.

THE Statistical Bureau of the Treasury Department of Mexico has just issued a statistical abstract of the exports from that country for the fiscal year ending June 30, 1891. It appears therefrom that the United States are fast absorbing the Mexican trade. The total exports for that year amounted to $63,276,395.34, and the share therein of this country was $44,983,086.37, or 71.09 per cent. of the whole. Next comes England, whose share of Mexican products is valued at $10,882,728.33, or 17.20 per cent.; in the third place is France, with the sum of $3,653,551.33, or 5.77 per cent.; in the fourth place comes Germany, with $2,785,874.86, or 4.40 per cent., and Spain, with $515,193.74, or 0.81 per cent.; then Holland, Russia, and Italy, the three with only $192,851.65, or 0.30 per cent.; and finally Guatemala, Colombia, Nicaragua, Salvador, and China, all with $262,264.06, or 0.43 per cent.

Notwithstanding the restrictive measures recently adopted in the United States against the importation of Mexican lead ores and live animals, the increase of trade with Mexico has been steady since the building of railroads which connect both countries, as is shown by the following table:

MEXICAN EXPORTS TO THE UNITED STATES DURING THE LAST SIX YEARS.

1885-86.	1886-87.	1887-88.	1888-89.	1889-90.	1890 91.
$25,429,594.56	$21,728,714.79	$31,059,626.66	$40,853,362.74	$43,022,440.67	$44,983,086,37
58.26 per ct.	56.37	63.54	67.91	68.84	71.09

The export trade with the leading European commercial nations during the last six fiscal years is as follows:

	1885-86.	1886-87.	1887-88.	1888-89.	1889 90.	1890-91.
England	$11,600,067.74	$13,362,186.57	$10,540,965.23	$12,535,534.99	$13,722,122.52	$10,882,728.33
	26.57 per ct.	27.17	21.56	20.84	21.96	17.20
France..	3,936,276.78	5,112,521.14	4,474,723.31	3,196,038.33	3,159,259.50	3,653,551.33
	9.01 per ct.	10.89	9.15	5.81	5.05	5.77
Germany.	1,571,399.20	2,175,770.11	2,177,106.09	2,061,563.09	1,593,773 15	2,785,874.86
	3.60 per ct.	4.42	4.45	3.43	2.71	4.40
Spain...	913,523.78	625,293.84	457,842.02	659.3,30.96	534,057.27	515,193.74
	2.09 per ct.	1.27	0.94	1.10	0.85	0.81

Of the total exports for the fiscal year 1890-91, $36,256,372.16 were in precious metals and $27,020,023.13 in other commodities. The United States received of the former $23,400,832.94, which is equivalent to 64.54 per cent., and of the latter $21,582,253.43, or 79.88 per cent.

The articles exported from Mexico during the last year were as follows:

Precious metals	$6 256,372.16	Lead	$1,125,468.64
Heniquen	7,048,556.76	Tobacco	1,105,446.73
Coffee	6,150,458.72	Other articles	8,058,836.56
Hides and skins	1,804,828.69		
Sundry woods	1,726,527.08	Total	$63,276,395 34

The preceding tables show that while the Mexican export trade with the leading commercial nations of Europe remains, in some cases, stationary, in others increases in a small degree, and in some diminishes, that trade with the United States marks a very rapid and decided growth, due, specially, no doubt, to the contiguity of territory, and the different nature of the products of each. I think it very likely that the participation of the United States in the Mexican commerce will grow larger every year in proportion to the development of the country, and keep pace with the results shown during the last year, unless it be checked by restrictive legislation on the part of either government, which I hope will not be the case.

Referring to the export trade of the United States with Mexico, I am sure that a similar increase will substantially appear during the fiscal year of 1890 to 1891. The last published report of the Statistical Bureau of Mexico corresponds to the year ending June 30, 1889, and shows a discrepancy with that of the Treasury Department of the United States for the same year, arising from the fact that in the latter only such articles as go to Mexico by sea are considered, no notice being taken of those going by rail over the border, and most of the commodities imported into Mexico from the United States go now through the frontier, transported by the railways which connect the two countries. In the United States Statistical report for that year, for instance, the total imports into Mexico, amount to $11,486,896, while in the Mexican report they foot up to $22,669,421. The former bureau fixes the exports to Mexico for the last fiscal year (1890–1891) at $14,969,620, but I am sure this amount is hardly one half of the real exports, as the exports by rail are not considered at all. In comparing the exports and imports of this country to and from Mexico, the fact must not be overlooked that the exports from Mexico are given in the Mexican report in Mexican silver, while the imports from this country into Mexico are stated in United States money, or gold, and the difference between these metals is now at about 35 to 40% in favor of gold.

The Statistical Bureau of the Treasury Department of the United States has always acknowledged these facts and earnestly tried, although so far unsuccessfully, to mend them. The Chief of that Bureau in his annual report on the foreign commerce of the United States for the year ending June 30, 1891, says (page 13):

"6. The statistics of exports of domestic commodities to Mexico and to Canada by land are defective, owing to the fact that there is no law requiring railway companies to furnish to collectors of customs statistics of domestic merchandise transported over their roads to these foreign countries."

The same official says in a foot note (page 111) in his quarterly report of the imports and exports of the United States for the three months ending September 30, 1891:

"In the absence of law providing for the collection of statistics of exports to adjacent foreign territory, over railways, the values of exports to Mexico are considerably understated. The official Mexican statistics state the value of the imports of merchandise from the United States in 1888 as $19,226,311, and for 1889 as $22,632,693. Statistics of their imports for later years have not been received. Substituting for our imperfect exports the imports from the United States as reported by the Mexican Government, it will appear that the value of our exports to Mexico about equals the value of our imports from that country."

M, ROMERO.

TWENTY-FIVE YEARS OF ALASKA.

A QUARTER of a century has elapsed since the treaty was signed which transferred the possessions of Russia on the American Continent to the United States. In other parts of the Union the same twenty-five years have witnessed the birth of territories and their development into states, but Alaska is still in an undefined and experimental stage of its existence—an outlying province, a territory without autonomy or representation, a district with a Governor who does not govern. As a business transaction the purchase of Alaska was a great success, but as a political innovation and experiment its acquisition has not thus far produced any gratifying results.

Secretary Seward and Senator Sumner, the advocates and promoters of the Alaska purchase, have often been praised and extolled for their far-seeing policy in pushing the measure, but whether they saw far enough may well be questioned. At the time of the negotiations between the United States and Russia for the sale of the latter's province, which England had refused to buy, British Columbia was a poverty stricken and neglected colony—the Cinderella among Great Britain's outposts. The fur trade was still in the hands of the Hudson Bay monopoly; the few inhabitants were dissatisfied; the trade of its only seaport, Victoria, was largely in the hands of Americans. Overland railways were still a dream of the future, and communication with the mother country was kept up by annual sailing vessels.

There was an opportunity for far-seeing statesmen. The acquisition of that strip of coast, which would have made United States territory continuous, could and should have been accomplished then, even if the price had been five times that of Alaska. Had the step been taken we should now command the North Pacific beyond dispute, and beyond all possibility of complications such as have now befallen us. There would have been no Behring Sea trouble, no boundary question to stir up strife among kindred nations.

So much for the "might-have-been"; let us now consider what *is*. England's statesmen have long since recognized the possibilities hidden beneath the shabby plumage of their ugly duckling on the North Pacific, and to-day she rejoices in the possession of a transcontinental road over her own soil; by which she can send troops in transit to any part of Asia, and at the end of it she has a flourishing province, rich in fish and timber, a strongly fortified naval depot, and two growing cities with magnificent steamships plying to the Orient. And all this lies in the very path to our outlying province—cut-off, isolated Alaska. Our mail steamers, our surveying vessels, and other Government ships pass to and fro through British waters and through a British province which England will not relinquish under any circumstances now conceivable.

Turning from the birds in the bush to the one in our hand, the question arises, " What have we done with Alaska in these twenty-five years?"

At a comparatively insignificant expense to the Government we have learned more of Alaska's geography and topography, its people and its resources, in twenty-five years than Russia learned or tried to learn in one hundred and twenty-six years of possession. Our people have drawn more money and products out of the country than the Russian people did, and our Government has received more revenue from the country than the Czar's treasury ever derived from the same source. (On the last named point we shall probably not be able to boast in the future, since England, on the strength of her position in British Columbia, is striving to prevent us from deriving any revenue hereafter.)

For the twenty years preceding the year 1860 the gross receipts of the Russian-American Company from all sources in Alaska were about $11,000,-000, out of which dividends were paid amounting to $1,500,000, and $2,250,-000 to the Imperial Government in the shape of import duties on Chinese teas purchased with Alaskan furs. During the twenty years, from 1870 to 1890, we drew from Alaska products of various kinds to the value of over $60,000,000, while the United States Government received a cash revenue of over $6,000,000.

We have inaugurated the industries of cod fishing, whaling, salmon canning, and gold mining, and to-day the native population, whose number the Russians never ascertained, but who have certainly not increased, consume in one year more flour and soap than they did in half a century under the Russian régime.

Russia left the people of Alaska to the iron rule of a trading monopoly invested with judicial powers, while the courts of appeal were so far away that they were out of reach of anybody but the all-powerful company. This company could flog the people or transport them at will, but could not settle the smallest account without reference to the home office, involving years of delay. We have given the people liberty of action and freedom of movement, and we have established at least one court of final resort in the country.

The Russian Company maintained schools only for training its own employees and their offspring, who were obliged to render not less than fifteen years' service in return. We have established free schools at all points where they are wanted, and in some places where they are not wanted. Instead of the dormant missions of the Russian Orthodox Church which dotted a narrow fringe of coast lands, we have now, in addition, the stations and schools of seven denominations scattered broadcast over Alaska.

Russia jealously barred out all visitors from her shores. We have opened the more accessible part of the country to thousands of tourists who view from the deck of palatial steamers the grandest scenery on the continent.

Russia, or, rather, the Russian-American Company, conducted costly explorations for minerals, and officially proclaimed that no precious metals existed in paying quantities. Our prospectors, unaided, have searched, and continue to search, every valley and gulch in Alaska, and, as a result of their labors and ventures, Alaska now boasts of the largest quartz mill in the world, and has become an exporter of bullion.

On the shores of the inside channels, which the Russians twenty-five years ago dared not navigate without an armed guard, shotted guns, and boarding nettings, we are met to-day by the busy hum of thriving mining towns, with sidewalked streets, enlivened by rumble of wheels and clatter of hoofs, with hotels and boarding-houses, large stores, steam laundries, saloons and churches, steam ferries puffing from shore to shore, the muffled roar of blasts and the glare of electric lights.

All these are changes we have wrought in twenty-five years, and which Russia failed to bring about in one hundred and twenty-six, which proves that for the brief time of American occupation we have made in Alaska a commercial, industrial, and educational record, of which we may justly be proud, even though politically we have left the territory very much where it was, and have not brought it into any intimate relation with the mother (may we say step-mother ?) country.

To a great extent this has been due to the difficulty of dealing with abnormal situations to which our common legislative and administrative methods do not apply. Mail service and all other functions of the Government in Alaska cause an expenditure out of all proportion to the service required and performed, and consequently Congress has been unwilling to provide the usual territorial machinery. In other parts of the Union the pioneers of new sections of the country have always taken themselves the first steps towards organization, camps have grown into towns, and townships into counties, but in Alaska the circumstances are entirely different. Its population now foots up 32,052, divided as follows :

Whites	4,294	Mongolians	2,287
Mixed (Russian and natives)	1,829	All others	112
Natives	23,530		

Total...32,052

Though in the summer the canning and whaling industries swell the number of white people in Alaska to four thousand, the resident American citizens do not number much over one-fourth that number, and even these are much scattered, affording but an unsatisfactory basis upon which to build even the most primitive political structure.

Upon the whole it would appear that until the country gives proof of further development, and until it shall have been decided whether any further revenue will flow from Alaska as an offset to expenditures, we have granted enough, and we can complacently face the question: "What have we done with Alaska in twenty-five years of possession ?"

IVAN PETROFF.

CONTRACTS AND THE CURRENCY.

IN DISCUSSING the financial problem as affected by the silver coinage, the friends of an honest currency are too prone to overlook the fact that gold fluctuates in value, as well as silver. Debtors have been cheated with the rise of gold, and very sadly cheated, too, just as with silver coming to the front creditors will likewise be cheated. When silver was demonetized the creditors gained, and by the rise in gold values our national debt, while it was nominally being paid off at a tremendous rate, actually increased—measured as commodities, which is the true method of estimating it—from the time of the close of the war until well along into the eighties.

If stability of value is the quality that gives character to an "honest dollar," then a gold dollar cannot lay claim to the title any more than a silver one can. It is only somewhat less dishonest. Just now one robs Peter to pay Paul, and the other endeavors to rob Paul, at a somewhat heavier rate, to pay Peter. The silver men say in effect to the "sound money" men: You fixed the law once so that we had to pay you more than we owed you. We intend to fix it now so that we shall pay you less than we owe you.

It is a sorry game, that of cheating by law. All will suffer in the long run, both debtor and creditor. Ought there not to be enough fair-minded, honest-hearted men in Congress to agree upon some measure that should assure the equitable fulfilment of contracts? If not; if the American people are to be divided into two opposing factions on the question of the currency, each endeavoring to see which can get the advantage of the other in a "skin game," then the outlook does not seem very encouraging for the future of America.

Would not the desired end be secured by a simple enactment to the effect that, in the fulfilment of all contracts involving the payment of money, payment should be made of an amount representing the pu[,]asing power of the sum agreed upon at the time the contract was made. The purchasing power would be determined by the market value of certain staples at a given date. To enable the easy and accurate computation of this, the Secretary of the Treasury might be instructed to have monthly lists of the prices of these staples prepared and posted in all public places throughout the country. It would thus be shown that, upon such a date, one dollar was good for so much corn, so much wheat, so much cotton, so much wool, so much pig iron, so much flour, so much coal, etc. By striking an average the abstract purchasing power of a dollar on the date in question would be shown. If in the next month's statement any fluctuations of a marked character should be manifest, and these were not counterbalanced by other fluctuations, then the dollar's abstract purchasing power would be represented by a different average.

For instance, if on June 6, 1891, Smithson agrees to pay Johnson $1,000 six months from date in return for merchandise bought of the latter, then under this rule the $1,000 to be paid on January 6, 1892, would mean a sum corresponding to the purchasing power of $1,000 six months before. If the purchasing power had diminished, then more than $1,000 would be required in payment; if it had increased, less than $1,000 would be needed.

For instance, if the purchasing power of a dollar were represented by 98 on June 6, and on January 6 it had increased to 102, then, a dollar being worth more, it would not take so many of them to pay the debt, and $980 would satisfy it, for it would purchase just as much value in goods as $1,000 did then.

In practice, of course, under ordinary circumstances the fluctuation would not be likely to be anywhere near so great as in the example given, for the changes in the values of so many staples would largely counteract each other, and the average that would represent the abstract purchasing power of the dollar would probably change but little in so short a space of time.

In the same way, stability in the value of wages would be secured by such a plan, for the workman would be paid an amount corresponding to the purchasing power of his wages at the time he was hired.

Under such a system it is conceivable that the standard of the currency might be lead, or pig iron, as well as gold or silver. However the currency might fluctuate, the standard for the payment of contracts would remain the same—the purchasing power of the sum agreed upon at the date of contract. Neither debtor nor creditor could then be cheated, and, with a stable standard of payment assured, there then would be no motive for maintaining an unstable currency.

SYLVESTER BAXTER.

CAN WE HAVE CHEAP CABS?

IN THE sense in which the term applies to all the great cities of Europe, there is no cab system in this country.

London and Paris, the two greatest cities of Europe, will best illustrate the conditions under which a system of cheap cabs has been developed, and a brief review of the system, as it exists in those cities, discloses the only reasons why similar enterprises have not thriven in America.

In the city of London there are about twelve thousand licensed cabs, which earn an average of one pound each per day. The average fare for each trip is not more than two shillings, and it therefore follows that London cabs are used at least one hundred and twenty-five thousand times every day. In Paris the use of cabs is still more universal. In that city there are thirty thousand licensed public carriages, but, as many open carriages are used in summer, replacing closed cabs, laid up for the time being, not more than twenty thousand are in use at one time. Their average earnings amount to twenty-five francs a day, based on an average fare not exceeding two francs per trip. In order to yield this amount, the cabs must be used two hundred and fifty thousand times within twenty-four hours.

On the other hand, if New York is taken as an example in this country, a very different state of affairs is found to exist. The municipal records of New York show that there are in that city fifteen hundred public carriages of all classes. These include hansoms, cabs, coupés and carriages. The best estimate of their daily earnings is $7 per day for each vehicle, with an average fare of $1. These figures are based on the authorized charges, and are liberal; if the revenue derived exceeded this per diem amount, the profit from the business would tend to increase the number of conveyances offered for hire. It would appear, therefore, that the people of New York use carriages about ten thousand times every day. The purposes for which they are used, however, vary greatly in this country and abroad. In London the cab is used by almost every one who has occasion to move about the city,—the government official, the professional man or merchant and his clerk, his wife and daughters on their social or shopping tours, the tourists on their rounds among the various places of interest, and, in fact, every person whose object is to be transferred from point to point cheaply and ex- peditiously. One can hail a cab in nearly any part of the city at any time, and at a trifling expense be set down at any destination with a reasonable dispatch.

The Parisians go even further than this. The large number of cabs available, and the regular and low rates of fare, serve to make the use of them a part of the every-day life of the citizen of every class. The Paris cab is ubiquitous. There is a choice of them always at the beck and call of the pedestrian. They are engaged and used by every class and condition of people. Not only do the wealthier people and the middle classes call them into requisition for short as well as long trips, but the fare is so cheap, and the movement so prompt, that clerks and shop girls, mechanics and laborers, are numbered among their patrons. Washer-women with their baskets employ them, and they may frequently be seen laden with a family and their household goods in process of moving from flat to flat.

In New York, on the other hand, no such conditions are found. The number of public cabs which can be taken on a moment's notice is too small for consideration. They are to be procured only at a few specified stands, unless accidentally caught on the streets without a passenger, and they are not used habitually by any class of citizens, but exceptionally, and because an emergency makes it necessary. The large percentage of conveyances, with the exception of those plying between the railroad stations and steamship landings and the hotels, can only be secured from the livery-stables by tele- phone, and are only ordered for specific occasions. The vast difference in the use of public carriages in the United States and Europe is, however, easily accounted for by the physical and other conditions existing in Ameri- can cities. It is well known that both London and Paris are excellently paved, and, therefore, the wear and tear on both horse and carriage is re- duced to the minimum, while the maximum of comfort is secured to the pas- senger by the smoothness of the streets. This is demonstrated by the fact that the average amount required for repairs in London is $85 per annum for hansoms and $50 for four-wheelers, while the sum expended for the same purpose here amounts to $125 for hansoms and $75 for four-wheeled cabs. Abroad the cab horse will perform the service for five years; in this country his usefulness is ended in three. The streets of our American cities are noteworthy for their bad paving. Cobble-stones and Belgian blocks, inter- sected and bisected with car tracks, are the most serious obstructions to the successful maintenance of cheap cabs, and when to this is added the com- plete system of street railways, which every one of our prominent cities pos- sesses, and the exorbitant charges exacted for cab service, the small use of public cabs is sufficiently accounted for.

Several attempts have been made to introduce so-called cheap cabs in our cities, but in every instance failure has resulted,—from the simple reason, in my opinion, that the rates of fare have not been made cheap enough. Our street-car system is comprehensive in each of the large cities, and affords a ready and cheap means of transit for the masses, with more or less rapidity of movement, yet street cars do not, and cannot, fill the place of cabs. Public convenience demands cheap cabs, and the movement in this direction is growing each year, but in order that they may prove remunerative, it is necessary that the charges shall be cheap enough to bring them into general use, and the number of cabs available large enough to lead the people to depend upon the service.

Most of the items of expense entering into the cost of providing cabs are as low in this country as in Europe, some of them lower. The cabs and har- ness can be had as cheaply, horses cost less, provender is cheaper, and the only advantages which the foreign cab-owner possesses are the lower wages and the reduced expenses for wear and tear by reason of better pavements.

The best proof that a cheap cab system will be supported, provided the rates are low, is shown by the experiment made in Philadelphia. In 1882 the Pennsylvania Railroad Company placed in service in that city forty hansoms and ten four-wheeled one-horse cabs, charging for hansoms about the same rates that prevail in London, *i. e.*, for hansoms, 25 cents for a mile and a half for one or more passengers, and 15 cents for each additional mile, or, if hired by the hour, 65 cents. For four-wheelers a somewhat higher tariff was fixed, viz., 40 cents for a mile and a half for one or two persons, and 10 cents for each additional passenger, or, if hired by the hour, 75 cents for one or more persons. After the London custom these cabs are hired to the drivers at a certain sum per day, varying, according to the season, from $3.50 to $4.50 for the use of a cab and two horses. They are constantly in service, and the venture has paid a good return on the investment. In the meantime the original plant has been increased, and the present equipment consists of 50 hansoms, 25 four-wheelers and 3 victorias, with 128 horses in the stables.

This experiment, it is true, is on a small scale, but it has demonstrated beyond a doubt that moderate charges will popularize cabs, and that they will pay as an investment. This result is accomplished in the face of the fact that Philadelphia is the most unfavorable city in the country for such an experiment, since it has the worst-paved streets and a system of street-cars so complete as to include every important street in its service.

In view of the reasons given for their success abroad and their failure here, the question of maintaining a profitable system of cheap cabs in New York and other large cities hardly admits of a doubt, provided that the principles which underlie the foreign system be applied as far as changed conditions will admit. The fixing of fares that will place them within the means of persons in every condition of life is paramount to all other consid-erations. The rates so fixed must be adhered to, so that a person may en-gage a cab with the same confidence that the public charge will be exacted, and no more, that he would feel on entering a street-car. In order to accom-plish the result, the enterprise must be upon a scale sufficiently large to make the cabs common and to give to the public the assurance that they may depend upon them when needed. If these conditions are fully met, despite the apparent competition of street-cars and the disadvantages of inferior pavements, I can see no good reason why such an undertaking should not be successful.

As it would probably be difficult to raise the amount of capital required for trying the experiment on so large a scale as would be requisite to provide a complete system for a city like New York, a beginning might be made in the manner that has proven so successful in Philadelphia. A well-regulated service of cheap cabs at the railway stations and ferry landings would un-doubtedly meet with as much favor and yield as fair a revenue in New York as a similar institution now in prosperous existence in its less populous neighbor. This would be but the entering wedge to a system that would eventually serve the entire city.

A. J. CASSATT.

GROWTH OF CITIES.

THE growth in urban population and wealth is one of the most marked and interesting of the social phenomena of the time. In each particular, and in every great state in Christendom, with the single exception of Russia, the expansion in the towns is much greater than in the rural communities. We see little of this tendency of things in Russia, because that country has not yet reached the stage of social and industrial development which brings it about, and which is present in a greater or less degree in all the nations of Central and Western Europe, and in the United States. France, which grows only to a trifling extent in inhabitants in the country, as a whole, grows rapidly and continuously in its business centres. Outside of the cities its population is steadily shrinking, and has been for years past. In Great Brit-ain and Germany the aggregate increase is more marked than in France, as well as more widely diffused, but outside of the towns it is not at all striking or important. The same is true of Austria, though in a smaller degree.

The drift of population and wealth to the cities finds its most conspicuous manifestation, however, in the United States. Here, too, the data which reveal it, and by which it can be measured, are most abundant and accessible. The following figures show the percentage of increase in inhabitants in the twenty-six leading cities of the country between 1880 and 1890, and in the States in which these cities are situated, as well as the per capita amount of the assesed value of real and personal property which they contained in each of these years. The figures of population are from census bulletins. Those which relate to wealth have been kindly furnished me by the officials of the Census Office, and have not hitherto been made public :

	Percentage of Growth in Population.		Assessed Values of Property in Cities, Per Capita.	
	In the City.	In the State.	In 1880.	In 1890.
New York....................	25.62	18.00	$906.96	$1,119.90
Chicago.	118.58	24.32	234.45	199.44
Philadelphia............ ...	23.58	22.77	686.67	1,022.36
Brooklyn.............	42.30	18.00	411.04	561.50
St. Louis...............	28.89	23.56	471.55	544.37
Boston.....................	23.60	25.57	1,762.39	1,832.96
Baltimore......	30.73	11.49	734.38	640.48
San Francisco.	27.80	39.72	1,044.96	1,043.70
Cincinnati.................	16.37	14.83	663.58	598.75
Cleveland..	63.20	14.83	440.52	381.15
Buffalo.....................	64.80	18.00	540.89	635.05
New Orleans...............	12.01	19.01	424.80	545.02
Pittsburg.....	52.58	22.77	599.33	863.31
Washington, D C.........	29.71	.....	508.95	665.42
Detroit.....................	76.96	27.92	715.13	786.05
Milwaukee...............	76.90	28.23	483.41	515.90
Newark, N. J.....	33.20	27.74	610.69	626 93
Minneapolis................	251.35	66.74	499.41	831.29
Jersey City.................	35.02	27.74	483.86	484.39
Louisville.............	30.20	12.73	531.76	504.61
Omaha....................	360.23	134.06	246.17	142.62
Rochester.............	49.83	18.00	471.33	746.47
St. Paul	221.07	66.74	578.69	917.84
Kansas City................	137.91	23.56	189.61	621.52
Providence..................	26.02	24.94	1,102.28	1,064.10
Denver........	199.51	112.12	454.52	621.34

It will be noticed that in nearly every instance the city here presented has grown faster in population than its State. But the showing can be made much more favorable to the cities. Only the larger or representative ones are given here. If all those of 8,000 inhabitants and upwards were cited it would be seen that the rural element is being distanced rapidly in the race. Out of every 100 of the aggregate population 3.35 people were in towns of 8,000 inhabitants and upwards in 1790, 4.93 in 1810, 6.72 in 1830, 12.49 in 1850, 16.13 in 1860, 20.93 in 1870, 22.57 in 1880, and 29.12 in 1890. In 1790 there were 6 cities in the country which touched and passed the 8,000 mark; there were 286 in 1880, and 443 in 1890. A hundred years ago a little more than 1 in every 30 of the aggregate inhabitants of the country resided in towns of the limit indicated, while now the towns contain almost 1 in every 3. There were but 14 cities in the country in 1870 of over 100,000 in population; there were 20 in 1880, and

28 in 1890. In 1880 there was only one town (New York) in excess of 1,000,000 in population; in 1890 there were three—New York, Chicago and Philadel phia. The drift citywards, which was tolerably uniform in volume in the decades from the beginning of the Government onward to 1880, has been unusually large in the past ten years.

As the valuation of property given here is that shown by the assessors' books, the figures do not in all cases reveal the relative standing of the cities in point of wealth, the basis on which taxes are levied not being the same in all cities. On the whole, however, the figures present, with a tolerable degree of accuracy, the standing of each town in 1880 and 1890 in this respect. The apparent falling off in the per capita wealth which is shown in a few of the towns named is undoubtedly due, to some extent at least in the case of Chicago and of Baltimore, to the absorption, within the decade, of outlying districts in which the holdings of property were not so great as in the parent towns. Property, in the aggregate, expanded in assessed value, in round figures, $101,000,000 in Chicago, and $34,000,000 in Baltimore, in the ten years; but this growth, for the reason named, perhaps, did not keep pace with that of population. Louisville's seeming per capita shrinkage, as I am informed by a fiscal official of that town, is due to a change in the basis of taxation since 1880. One or other of these causes will probably be found to hold good as to the two or three other cities in the list in which the proportionate wealth was apparently smaller in 1890 than in 1880. The true value of the property of the country has not yet been fully ascertained by the census officials, but they estimate that it is about $1,000 for each man, woman, and child of the population. It amounted to $780 in 1870, and to $870 in 1880. We know that by far the greater part of this expansion in wealth has been made in the cities.

But this exhibit still fails to do entire justice to the cities, and for these reasons :

1. The assessed valuation of all property, as shown by census figures for thirty or forty years past, bears a steadily decreasing ratio to the actual value.

2. It is a notorious fact that personal property, to a steadily and rapidly increasing degree, eludes the vigilance of the assessor. Obviously these circumstances, especially the latter fact, have a much more marked effect on values in cities than in thinly-settled districts. We know this to be true, because the census report of 1880 showed that, while the cities of 7,500 population and upwards held only 22 per cent. of the country's population in 1880, they contained 40 per cent. of its personal property, and because in the ten years ending in 1880, while, as shown by the assessors' books, real estate throughout the country augmented about 31 per cent., personal property shrunk about 10 per cent. Of course, every person who is qualified to speak with intelligence on these subjects is convinced that personal property, instead of decreasing in those ten years, must have increased in value in a much higher ratio than real estate. The census figures for 1890 on this point have not been given to the public at the present writing.

As the drift of population towards the cities is seen in all the nations which are advanced in the elements of civilization, the forces which produce it must of necessity be equally extended in the field of their operation. These are, chiefly, the increase in education, which gives rise to new aspirations and predilections ; and the instinct of association which has always been potent in the human breast, but which in this age, far more than was the case at any period in the past, has both the opportunity and the incentive to assert itself. The first of these forces renders men dissatisfied with the old conditions, and furnishes the spur which impels them to seek or create means to improve their circumstances. The second force draws men together for mutual assistance and puts them in harmonious coöpera tion. Division of employment takes place and individual tastes and apti tudes are developed. As a result, labor-economizing appliances are continu ally being devised, and the task of each person is gradually lightened, while the aggregate product or wealth of all and the proportionate share of each are steadily and rapidly increased. Ethnological and political influences also operate in this direction, though, perhaps, with less potency and per sistency than the social and economic forces. Racial vigor tells in the struggle for national development, and that country grows most rapidly and symmetrically in which Government interferes least with the legitimate activities of the people. These conditions are more fully and fairly met in the United States and Great Britain than in any other nations, and in these countries the growth in population and wealth is greatest.

The resultant of the operation of these forces finds its natural and inevi table expression in the creation of cities. Thus in cities, while labor for each individual is simplified and lightened, its rewards are largely increased and the conveniences and comforts of life are multiplied.

How long will this drain of population from the thinly to the thickly settled communities continue? Perhaps reason may suggest an answer to this query. The basis of all wealth is agriculture, and the highest material and moral advancement of a people is dependent on the harmonious devel opment of their agricultural, manufacturing, and commercial interests. The free interchange of commodities between the nations, which is likely to come in the not remote future, may lessen the rigidity of this requirement, so far as concerns the leading nations, but it cannot safely be disregarded altogether. A time must come under existing tendencies when farm arti cles will command, with respect to other commodities, a price sufficiently high to render their production more profitable than at present. Then the drift from farm to factory and mercantile house will slowly subside, and a general readjustment of employments and interests will gradually be brought about.

Charles M. Harvey.

THE NEW YORK TRADE SCHOOLS.*

The charge has often been made that the higher education given in the public schools unfits young men for manual labor, that the pub lic school graduate, to use a common expression, is "lost to the trades." The advocates of a high standard of public education have not been able to contradict this charge. They have seen that the youths who entered the trades usually left school at fourteen or fifteen years of age, and they have also seen that the young men who have had the benefit of a liberal educa tion looked for clerkships or employment in what are known as genteel callings, where perhaps the pay was low and the chances of promotion small,

* Mr. J. Pierpont Morgan has recently given $500,000 to the endowment of these schools.—ED.

instead·of endeavoring to unite skill of hand with a well trained mind, and so avail themselves of the present high wages and the future openings which skilled labor in this country commands. Manual training was grasped at as a solution of the difficulty, and although it has proved of great value in developing observation as well as dexterity, and thereby aiding in ordinary educational work, yet those who entered the ranks of skilled labor continued to leave school at just the age they should be there, and those who graduated did not become mechanics.

If a system of education carried on at the public expense swelled the ranks of the non-producers, and rendered young men unfit to earn a living by the labor of their hands, the result would be a sufficient reason for its con demnation. The reason, however, why a good education and manual labor are regarded as incompatible, is not because the well-educated youth is unwilling to become a mechanic, but because he is not wanted in the workshop, and until recently there has been no way of learning a trade except in a workshop. To learn a trade in a workshop requires a considerable length of time, from four to five years being the customary term. For the first two years of his apprenticeship the youth is expected to make himself useful by doing an errand boy's work and by attending to such odd jobs as may be required of him by his employer, by the foreman, or the journeymen. Then, when he begins to learn his trade, the temptation is strong to keep him at what he can do best, lest he may spoil material and waste the time for which he is paid. Systematic instruction is rarely attempted, and in many workshops, owing to the subdivision of labor, is impossible. It is not surprising that four or five years are considered necessary to learn a trade in this way; it is, on the contrary, remarkable that it can be learned at all. A youth who remained at school until he was eighteen would be too old for the lad's work required of the beginner, and he would be twenty-two years of age before he could earn a man's wages. Shortening the school term is therefore a necessity under this system of trade instruction.

The question might reasonably be asked, Why should so long a time be spent in acquiring a trade; why, if so much time is wasted in work not connected with learning a trade, could not the apprenticeship be made two instead of four or more years? This reduction would enable a youth to get a good education, and yet give him the opportunity during his minority to become a skilled workman. Here the power of organized labor has to be met. The trade-unions say that an apprenticeship must be at least four years long. How that time is passed is a matter of indifference. The policy of the trade-unions, or rather of the foreign-born labor leaders who control them, is not to make good workmen, but to keep our young countrymen out of the trades. To carry out this policy, not only is a narrow limit put upon the number of young men who shall be allowed to learn a trade, but their apprenticeship is made as unprofitable and, consequently, as discouraging as possible.

During the last few years attempts have been made by the unions, and in some cases with the approval of the associations of master-mechanics, to require those young men who are permitted to learn a trade to be indentured, that is, to be bound to serve and obey their masters for a term of years. Such was the custom until the commencement of this century. But the old-time apprentice was practically an adopted son, living with his master, working under his supervision, and associating on equal terms with his children. This patriarchal system is not now possible, as the master no longer works with his men, and can give very little care to his apprentice ; neither does he want the lad in his home. Respectable parents are seldom willing to surrender the control of their sons, and no spirited lad can rest contented in a position which differs only in name from slavery. He either seeks to have the indenture set aside, or, if he remains, he is likely to attempt to "get even" with his master by loafing or indifference. No surer way can be found of making manual labor appear contemptible than by depriving the youthful mechanic of his liberty.

Eleven years ago the New York Trade Schools were established, to enable young men to learn certain trades, and to give young men already in these trades an opportunity to improve themselves. Trade instruction was then almost unknown in this country, and it was some years later that the report of the Royal Commission on Technical Education gave the first clear idea of what was being done in Europe. This effort to introduce in this country a new system of trade instruction encountered the hostility of the trade-unions. It, however, received the hearty support of many master-mechanics, while the approbation of the newspapers caused the trade schools to become widely known. The attendance, beginning at thirty, soon ran into the hundreds, until now each winter between five and six hundred young men fill the workrooms. At first the attendance was drawn from the workshops where the young men felt they were learning but little, and from that large class of young men who are earning a living at what are known as boy occupations, which have no future for the man. For their accommodation evening instruction was given. Then another class of young men saw the advantages that might be derived from trade-school instruction ; young men who had remained at public or private schools until eighteen or over, and who were supposed to have been educated above working with their hands. These young men, who were too old, or unfitted by their bringing up, for a long apprenticeship with its drudgery and waste of time, were quick to see that not only as skilled workmen could they earn higher pay than can easily be obtained in other callings, but that there were openings for them as master-mechanics more promising than could be found in stores and offices. They wanted more thorough instruction than could be given to the evening classes, and they were able and willing to pay for it. For them day instruction was provided, and in many cases, in their eagerness to learn, the same young men joined both the day and evening classes. This desire to acquire a trade on the part of well-educated young men is not merely a local one. Young men come to the New York Trade Schools each year from all parts of the Union and from Canada. Young men from Maine and California, from Nova Scotia and Florida, meet in the trade-school workshops.

The multiplication of trade schools will give our young countrymen the opportunity to become skilled workmen now denied them in many trades by the unions, and the thoroughness of trade-school instruction will make American mechanics the best in the world. Bringing well-educated young men into the trades, as trade schools will do, means the elevation of labor. It means that a portion at least of the gulf that separates those who work with their brains from those who work with their hands will be bridged over. A calling is judged by the education of those who follow it. The clerk earning perhaps five dollars a week is shown into the rich man's drawing room, while the mechanic who receives four dollars per day is left standing in the hall. Coarse hands and soiled clothing are not inseparable from a mechanic's work ; the athlete often does rougher, the sportsman and surgeon less tidy work.

A man whose name is honored throughout this country, an overseer of Harvard College, looking at a photographic group of graduates of the New York Trade Schools, remarked that it would be difficult to distinguish the young mechanics from a group of Harvard students. The fact that such young men wish to be mechanics, and that this desire exists all over the United States, would seem to prove that young Americans are not disqualified by education from working with their hands.

RICHARD T. AUCHMUTY.

NORTH AMERICAN REVIEW.

No. CCCCXXVII.

JUNE, 1892.

THE HARRISON ADMINISTRATION.

BY SENATOR DAWES, OF MASSACHUSETTS ; SENATOR DOLPH, OF OREGON ; AND SENATOR COLQUITT, OF GEORGIA.

SENATOR DAWES :

THE administration of President Harrison must be judged by its character, its capacity, its work, and its purpose. By these tests let it stand or fall. The character of an administration is its personnel and its methods, its instruments and its instrumentalities. It is not enough that the head of an administration be clean and his purposes above reproach. Those through whom he acts must be clean also. An administration cannot long remain healthy if the atmosphere it breathes is impure. There have been lamentable failures of men in high places who in character were stainless, and whose aims were upright, but who lacked the ability to discern between good and evil in the agents necessary to the discharge of their official functions. How is it with the present administration ? Succeeding a Democratic one, which had all the agencies of the government filled with those devoted to the propagation and maintenance of the doctrines and policies he had been summoned to reverse, it was incumbent on President Harrison, at the outset, so to change the personnel of the government that the agencies for carrying it on should be in accord with the principles and purposes he had been chosen to maintain and pursue. In what manner has he met these conditions ? He called into his Cabinet, as his advisers, men who commanded at once the fullest confidence of the country; some of them already so tried in the public service that they had been designated by common consent for the places they filled. Some of them were new men in public life, but brilliant service has in each case proved the sagacity and wisdom of the selection. Subordinate offices have been filled with able and clean men ; commendation of this administration does not demand or claim that there has been no exception. In the vast machinery of this government in operation at a thousand points, many of them thousands of miles beyond the eye of the Executive, it never has been and never can be the case that men who operate it will in every instance prove themselves fit and faithful. But one who has witnessed the successes and mistakes of administration in this particular during nine of these quadrennial periods, challenges, without fear for the present administration, a comparison with any or all of the others.

It has fallen to the lot of President Harrison during the years already elapsed to appoint more judges in the higher courts than any other President has done in a like period since the organization of our judiciary system. There can be no doubt that the general public judgment, with singular unanimity, is that the judiciary is to-day stronger in its own character and ability and in the public confidence by reason of these appointments.

It is an open and a frank administration. There is no deceit in its make-up or its practices. If there have been disappointments, they have grown out of differences of opinion and not from concealments. It has avowed its opinions and policies in open day, and with a clearness of statement that admits of no doubt. And it has that courage of its convictions that does not hesitate to announce before, and not after, election, its attitude towards any question, however disturbing, that may agitate the public mind.

What this administration has done in these three years of its existence tests its capacity. And here its record will carry it triumphantly through any ordeal to which it can be subjected by a scrutinizing public. The foreign intercourse of the nation has during that period encountered an unusual number of delicate and difficult questions, all of which have been treated with signal ability and wisdom. And there remains, as far as is known, no unsettled question that can disturb our peaceful relations with any of the nations of the earth. Our diplomacy was never in abler hands. Its achievements, from the Samoan complication bequeathed by its predecessor, to the Behring Sea arbitration, its greatest triumph, with which this its third year closes, form an unbroken series of signal successes. Treaties with Germany, with France, and with Spain, the Italian imbroglio at New Orleans, the Chilian complication, and a series of commercial treaties to be considered in another connection, have lodged in the State Department imperishable proof of diplomatic ability unequalled in recent history. The nation is stronger in its foreign relations, and its rights on the high seas and in foreign jurisdictions are more strictly enforced and more cordially respected, than when the portfolio of State came under its present control.

If the Treasury, from the nature of the duties devolving upon it, furnishes a less brilliant record than the State Department, it has yet been no less safe in the management of our finances. No wild experiments with our monetary system have shaken public confidence or disturbed values. Business throughout the country has reposed on the faith it has placed in the methods and movements of those who have had in their keeping the keys of the Treasury vaults. No concealments of purpose, nor sudden and fickle manipulations of the public funds, have bred distrust or made capital timid. No scandal has touched the name of its officials, but with clean hands it has closed its books each year, and pointed to its balances as proof of its health and vigor. Its Secretaries have treated with those engaged in the great business enterprises of the country not as enemies, but as promoters, helpers, stimulators of lawful business. They have never tampered with the currency, nor sought by any legerdemain to make seventy cents count a hundred and gain the difference; but they have met all honest demands with honest dollars.

The other Departments have been in equally able hands. The Navy Department has sprung into a new life ; and with the vigor of a strong man has taken hold of itself, and has shaken the accumulated dust of years out of its seams. Rehabilitation has already so far advanced that confidence and national pride have joined hands with necessity in pushing forward the work, and a new navy worthy of our national power and prowess is now well nigh assured. Failure can only come from loss of national control by the Republican party. Each of the other Departments has corrected abuses where they existed, has improved methods, and transacted the public business with a fidelity and dispatch unusual and commendable. Desertions from the army, hitherto deplorably frequent, have almost entirely ceased, and the tone and pride of the whole body of the soldiery has been elevated. The ever increasing and multiplied duties of the Post-office Department have been discharged in a business-like manner, never so satisfactorily to the public as now. Its revenues were never so great, nor have its expenditures, large as they are, ever yielded such gratifying results. So it has been with the Interior Department, with a wider range of duties than any other, increasing and becoming more complicated and perplexing daily. It has met them all with an ability equal to all its difficulties. In the Land Office chaos has given place to order, and the settler on the public domain, no longer regarded as a public enemy, is building his home in peace. In the management of the Indian Bureau the rights of the Indian have come to be as secure as those of the white man, and from the unoccupied lands of the reservations more than twenty millions of acres have been opened for settlement and divided into homesteads for the pioneer. The new Agricultural Department has taken such hold of the country under the present management, that nothing but political revolution can unloose its grasp. Each one of these Secretaries can open his portfolio to public scrutiny without fear, and can safely challenge criticism upon what has been accomplished as well as upon the methods of accomplishment.

There have been six new States, with a territory in all larger than that of the original thirteen, added to the Union since the election of Harrison. Four of them had been knocking at the door for years and were resisted under the last administration as long as it had life to resist. But for that election all of them would have been territories still.

The Pan-American Congress has vindicated its right to be, in the closer commercial relations it has established with Mexico and the South American republics. Knowledge of the character and needs of their markets has stimulated our producers to supply their demands. Our commerce with them is in consequence daily increasing, and that increase gives larger employment to home capital and labor. The Bureau of American Republics has become an intelligence office of incalculable value in every trade and manufacturing centre and at every depot of agricultural products in the land.

The "McKinley Tariff" is a measure of this administration enacted in fulfilment of its pledge so to revise the tariff that while the aggregate revenue should be diminished, protection to American labor and capital should not be impaired. While not perfect (no law ever yet was), and while it may in some respects require modification, as every tariff law before it has done, it still has accomplished both these ends. It has so enlarged the free list that for the first time in the history of the country the value of goods imported free of duty exceeds that of dutiable goods. It has, at the same time, so readjusted the duties on the dutiable goods, after this greatest addition in value to the free list ever made, that the duties paid on the goods still dutiable do not now exceed in per cent. those paid under the old law, including duties then paid on those goods now added to the free list, being forty-seven and one-half per cent., both before and since the passage of the McKinley Bill ; while the percentage of the whole duty on the value of the entire imports has been reduced from thirty-two per cent. before, to twenty-one and one-half per cent. since the passage of that law. At the same time that this reduction has been accomplished, protection to the home producer and the home market, home capital and home labor, has been made more effective. Nothing in this law has contributed so much to the double purpose in view, that of reducing by enlargement of the free list the aggregate of duties imposed and of making protection to the American producer more effective, as the provision regulating by law commercial treaties with nations producing raw material and other products which are necessary for our consumption but cannot be profitably produced at home. Under this provision we obtain an exchange of equivalents of the highest value to our national prosperity. For the admission, free of duty, of raw material and other products not producible here at profit and in quantities needed, we in turn are admitted into the markets of other nations, free of duty, with articles we make and they need. No other method could be devised so effective to make production at home cheap, and to multiply it by enlarging our market. This increases our export trade, already reaching the enormous sum of $1,100,000,000 in a single year, and, with that will increase our carrying trade, our shipping interest, and our commerce.

The space allotted to this article will not permit of further detail, however inviting. Much must necessarily be omitted that would well justify discussion in a review of the three years of the work of an administration conspicuous for the many important questions with which it has had to deal, in both our foreign and our domestic relations. But what has already been said is enough for a just judgment. Nothing has been here withheld, from an honest criticism of which its supporters have occasion to shrink. Of this conduct of public affairs the President has been not only the official head but the guiding spirit. Able as have been his advisers, and visible as their hand has been in this work, yet it has been at all times under the direction and control of the President himself, and in furtherance of his own aims and purposes. In it he has firmly and justly maintained the honor and rights of his country before all nations, as well as the rights of his countrymen at all times and in all places. With frankness and without hesitancy he has on all proper occasions declared the principles upon which the government is administered, with a clearness and force of diction seldom equalled. He has borne himself in all things as becomes the Chief Magistrate of a great nation.

HENRY L. DAWES.

SENATOR DOLPH:

It HAS been apparent for some time that President Harrison will be renominated. Undoubtedly, the popularity of Mr. Blaine, were he a candidate, would render him a formidable competitor for the nomination ; but with Mr. Blaine out of the race,—and he is out, as evidenced by his recent letter,—there is no candidate likely to create any considerable opposition to Mr. Harrison. If ever a President deserved the indorsement of his party by a renomination on account of fidelity to party principles and an able administration, it is President Harrison ; but principles are of more importance than men, and success should not be jeopardized in order to promote the political fortunes of any man, however deserving. Mr. Harrison's loyalty to the principles of his party is such that he would not jeopardize its success for a moment to promote his personal ambition. Can a stronger man than Mr. Harrison be nominated ? Whatever opposition there is to his renomination is not based upon any objection to his administration ;

that has been clean, strong, and patriotic, and any candidate who could be nominated would have to run upon the record he has made. Neither is it based upon any alleged lack of ability, capacity, or courage. He has not acted as if he regarded the declarations contained in the national platform, upon which he was elected, as meaningless platitudes, but as if he regarded them as controlling statements of the principles of the party, entitled to receive his careful consideration and earnest support.

Upon the great issues of the day he has held no uncertain position. He has, to the extent of his legitimate influence, aided the party in its efforts to redeem its pledges to the people, and sought to promote its principles. His appointments, made only after due inquiry and deliberation, have, in the main, been highly creditable. His judicial appointments, which have been more numerous than those of any other President, have been especially commendable, and highly satisfactory to the bar and the general public. As was to be expected from a man so conspicuous for patriotism and distinguished services during the War of the Rebellion, his administration has been liberal toward the veteran soldiers, who, when the life of the nation was in peril, endured the hardships and dangers of the march and the battle to preserve the Union. The liberal legislation of the last Congress, which redeemed the party pledges to this deserving class of citizens, secured his willing approval ; and where, owing to legal technicalities, an applicant has been unable to secure a pension under general laws, and Congress has declared by special enactment that a disabled soldier or his widow was entitled to relief, he has not interposed his judgment or the veto power to thwart its will.

Under the present administration the United States has had a vigorous, well-defined foreign policy—a policy under which the rights of the United States have been fearlessly and ably asserted whenever the occasion required it. The prompt action of the administration in our controversy with Germany preserved the autonomy of the Samoan Islands; the considerate, but firm and dignified, position of the administration secured suitable acknowledgment and apology from the Chilian government for the assault in Valparaiso upon American sailors. By the recent treaty with Great Britain a peaceful solution of the Behring Sea controversy, which at one time threatened to involve us in war, has been happily provided for, and the cause of international arbitration promoted. It should be stated that President Harrison is entitled to full credit for these triumphs of diplomacy ; and, while the President and the Secretary of State have been in full accord, the dispatch (owing to the illness of Mr. Blaine, which has at times prevented his close application to business) conveying our ultimatum to the Chilian government, and the dispatch to Lord Salisbury so admirably and forcibly stating our just claims to some arrangement for the protection of seal life until the convention had decided our claims in the Behring Sea controversy, were both written by the President.

Both of these State papers are models of terse English and vigorous reasoning, are clear and concise statements of international law, and are highly creditable, not only to the administration, but to the nation. The predictions that President Harrison's administration would lack personality, and that he would be overshadowed by members of his Cabinet, have proved false. His administration has been intensely personal. The President may have failed to satisfy radical reformers by the progress made in civil service reform, but it is a fact that the Civil Service Commission has been active, aggressive, and impartial in enforcing the civil service laws and regulations ; that the President has been in full sympathy with the Commission, and has done much—by the extension of civil service rules to the appointment of some seven hundred employees in the Indian Service, and to the employees in the Fish Commission ; by the elimination of politics from the administration of the navy yards ; and by providing for the promotion of clerks and other employees in the Departments for merit—to advance civil service reform and check the spoils-system. By his influence and active coöperation, the pledge of the party to revise the tariff and maintain the protective system was redeemed by Congress in the enactment of the McKinley tariff law. The influence of the administration has been unmistakably in favor of a stable currency —a currency every dollar of which is as good as a gold dollar, and the President's well-known opinions and public utterances on questions of finance have done much to preserve public confidence and promote business prosperity. The objection made in some sections to Mr. Harrison's renomination on account of his opposition to the free coinage of silver in this country without an international agreement fixing the ratio between gold and silver, and at the same time opening the mints of the principal commercial countries of the world to free coinage of silver at the agreed ratio, is one that could be made to any candidate who could possibly be nominated. There is no probability that the Minneapolis convention will declare in favor of free coinage of silver. No candidate for the Presidency could avoid declaring his position on the silver question. Neither is it probable that the Democratic convention will declare for free coinage of silver, and in such case there will be no choice between candidates on account of their views on this question.

Mr. Harrison has offended some prominent Republicans by his appointments. With the independence possessed by him it is not to be wondered at that in some cases the recommendations of his political friends have been disregarded and he has acted in accordance with his own judgment. Probably this has been done in cases where a more politic course would have been better for him and his party and as well for the public service. In such cases he appears to have acted according to his convictions of right and without regard to the question as to how his course would affect his personal popularity or his political advancement.

The charge that he is cold and unsympathetic is a charge that was made against Washington and other public men. That he is a Christian gentleman of irreproachable personal character, in favor of all political reforms and interested in all movements for the elevation of the race, cannot be denied, and no one questions his fidelity to his friends. When the man who, of all Republican leaders, is nearest to the popular heart had been defeated by Mr. Cleveland, Mr. Harrison defeated Mr. Cleveland in turn, although the latter had the power of the administration on his side. It is true that by the tariff message of President Cleveland and the action of the Democratic House the tariff question had been forced to the front and made the issue of the campaign ; but this shows that the verdict of the people in a Presidential election is for principles and not for men. No man will be elected President on account of his gracious manner, but whoever is elected will be chosen because he represents certain great principles, and is believed to possess the ability, courage, and honesty that will insure his fidelity to them. Mr. Harrison is an earnest, honest man, who aims to walk with firm step the path of duty, and who regards politics not as a means of personal aggrandizement, but as a means of securing the greatest prosperity for the

country and the greatest happiness for the people.   No one can
question his ability.   His messages and public writings are not
excelled for clear and forcible presentation of public questions,
for fearless advocacy of the doctrines of his party, and for lofty
patriotism.   His speeches during the campaign, and since his
election, show a critical knowledge of public questions, a wide
range of information, great versatility and power of expression,
and have never been equalled by similar addresses by any man upon
like occasions.   Upon the whole, the present administration has
been as able, conscientious, and beneficial to the country as any
which has preceded it.

J. N. DOLPH.

SENATOR COLQUITT :

IN THESE comments upon President Harrison and his administration, it is proper to say that they are in no respect dictated
by any feeling of party prejudice or personal animosity.   I readily
admit his ability, his integrity, and his many worthy traits of
character.   But I may, within the limits of the strictest decorum,
scrutinize the conduct, the character, and the tendencies of his
administration and the policies of the party he represents.

When he became President he found his party in undisputed possession of the government for the first time in fourteen
years.   The Republicans had controlled the Presidency, the
Senate, and the House, but not the three at any one time, from
March 4, 1875, to March 4, 1889.   For the four years last preceding there had been a Democratic President and a Democratic
House of Representatives, so that the Republicans were merely
a party of opposition and protest, easily made effectual by their
majority in the Senate.

The campaign of 1888 was fought by the Republicans, for the
first time since 1860, upon another's record rather than their own,
and upon their promise, in the event of success, to legislate for
what should be the best interest of the country.

Given by that election unlimited power, the new administration assumed from the start the complete responsibility which
belonged to it, suggested such policies as seemed desirable and
expedient, and proceeded to carry them out, as far as possible, by
legislative enactments.   What a grand opportunity !   There was

distress, there was calamity, there were clamors everywhere. The people, searching for the source of their calamities and a remedy for them, naturally turned their eyes to the incoming administration. They found in that administration neither sympathy nor relief.

President Harrison had been in office twenty months and the new Congress had finished a session of ten months when the first general election occurred. The Republican party experienced the worst defeat in its history; it lost half its membership in the House of Representatives, and retained control of the Senate only by the admission of six new States, let in, some of them, with less than the necessary population, in order that the political complexion of that body should not be changed. The administration party profess to believe that later elections have materially altered the situation and their prospects. This is disputed, and nothing but the election in November will settle the matter.

If I were asked to give my opinion of the causes of this decidedly adverse, and, in my judgment, entirely justifiable popular verdict, I should say that they are all comprehended in the administrative policy of governing the country for the particular benefit of certain classes and interests, and using, directly and indirectly, all legislative and executive powers to that end ; these classes and interests forming a narrow oligarchy in opposition to the needs of the multitude.

One of the most signal and unquestionable characteristics of the present day is the struggle of labor against capital, of the weak against the strong, of the undisciplined many against the organized few—a struggle of those who would enjoy the fruits of their own labor with those who would enjoy the fruits of the labor of others ; between money and the masses, between those who create wealth and those made wealthy by partial legislation, by the mystery of banking and the regulation of coinage.

In this struggle Republican policy and administration have yielded to the demands of the strong and encroached upon the rights of the feeble. By special opportunities afforded by law, by unfair taxation, by bounties for the few, by burdens for the many, by legalized iniquities, they pursue the cruel task of squeezing money from the pockets of an impoverished people, from the toil, the sweat and the drudgery of the hardworking poor. The government is no longer regarded as intended to protect the rights of all, but by class legislation to elevate the few. The boast that there has been an aggregate increase of wealth is not a worthy boast, unless there has been a proportionate increase of the means of happiness. It is not a worthy boast when that wealth is attained at a sacrifice of the real interests of the people. There are signs of increased luxury among the rich. The increase of wealth has added to the gratification of the few, but this has been followed by a falling off of the means of the many. The aim of all just and economical policy should be not merely to stimulate the greatest production of wealth, but to distribute among the greatest number—not an equal but an equitable distribution. The reverse of this has been the policy of the Republican party in its unjust discriminations. The result of this policy has been to torture industry, to turn it from its natural channel, to beget antagonism of class against class, each trying to gain advantage by legislative favor. Hence private wealth and public want abound, and we have the anomaly of increased wealth and no diminution of poverty.

The Democratic party in its platform of 1856 declared in favor of "progressive free trade throughout the world," and the Republican party, though nominating its first Presidential candidate that year, and seeking popular and available issues, declined to accept the Democratic challenge. With the exception of a casual reference in 1860 no mention was made of the tariff in a Republican national convention until 1872, and then the only doctrine advanced was a tariff for revenue with incidental protection. Adherence to this policy was announced in succeeding years, but it was not until 1888 that the party openly avowed itself in favor of a tariff for protection only—a tariff which not only would not raise revenue, but would reduce it, or cut it off altogether, as imports were checked or entirely prevented. This illustrates the active and constant advance of the money power.

The McKinley Bill was a complete exponent of this new, unfair, and un-American policy. It sought to reduce revenue by raising duties, and permitted the home manufacturer to fix the amount of his profits by allowing him to determine the rate of duty to be paid on the foreign product, or to destroy competition, if it so pleased him, by duties that forbade it. To sustain the false pretence that this was a farmers' tariff the duty was raised on corn, oats, oatmeal, wheat, wheat flour, cheese, butter, and hay, though we export more than we import of each of these articles, and the price of wheat, whether sold here or abroad, is fixed by the price in London.

. The reciprocity features of the bill simply intensify the favoritism displayed by its promoters and advocates. They are designed to create a market for our manufactured goods, which are to displace so much of our agricultural products. At least seventy-five per cent. of our exports go to Europe while not five per cent. go to South America. Over fifty per cent. find a market in Great Britain, chiefly products of agriculture. Our coffee from Brazil is mostly paid for in wheat and cotton sold in London. Reciprocity of this kind is intended to encourage trade with South America and discourage trade with Europe ; to assist our manufacturers in disposing of their wares to the south of us and to lessen the opportunities of our farmers to sell their products to the east of us. Our farmers want the best market for their wheat and cotton, with the privilege of cheap manufactured goods—it is denied them. Manufacturers desire the best market for their goods and cheap agricultural products in return—it is accorded to them.

Our manufacturers contend for cheap freights, subsidized fleets, and free trade with South America. They have their way ; reciprocity is for them. Our farmers would like the same privileges in Great Britain and all Europe that manufacturers seek in Brazil and other South American countries, but they can't get it.

Free trade for our manufacturers in South America is reciprocity, and all right ; reciprocity for our farmers in Europe would be free trade, and, of course, is all wrong.

The same spirit of favoritism and close adherence to special interests has all along characterized the financial policy of the administration. The entire weight of its powerful influence has been thrown on the side of the advocates of the single gold standard, who, successful in demonetizing silver in 1873, have ever since been earnestly aggressive in their endeavors to make money, which they control, dear, and everything that money buys, cheap. In spite of the law of 1878 which declares standard silver dollars a legal tender for all debts, public and private, the administration has continued to treat the more than 400,000,000 of these dollars since coined as mere token money, redeemable like paper money in gold, and it refused, with plenty of them in the treasury, to discharge a part of our bonded debt, preferring to continue it rather than pay it in silver. And this, too, in the face of a resolution of Congress adopted fourteen years ago by a two-thirds majority in each House that payment of the public debt in silver was in violation of no contract and in derogation of no creditor's right.

The " Force Bill "—happily never enacted into law—was directly in line with this policy of a popular government by a part of the people for their own benefit. The Southern States are opposed to special privileges arising from either a protective tariff or the single gold standard. Without Federal interference they will continue to send representatives in favor of constitutional money and constitutional revenue laws. Their determined opposition to a Republican tariff and financial legislation is reason enough, in the opinion of these specialists, why their elections should be controlled from the Federal capital and by the Republican party.

The limitations of this article will not admit further discussion. The errors of this administration and its policy may be summed up as follows : First, restrictions on commerce ; second, burdens on agriculture; third, bounties to manufacturers ; fourth, excessive taxation ; fifth, profligate expenditure of the people's money ; sixth, contraction of the currency ; seventh, Federal interference with State elections.

These are enough to defeat the claim of the present administration and the Republican party to a continuance in power.

A. H. COLQUITT.

MODERN REVOLUTIONS AND THEIR RESULTS.

BY KARL BLIND.

You ask me to give an article "showing the result of the labors of great revolutionists in our times, and the acquiescence of the European world in projects which were regarded as wholly destructive and inherently evil." It is a vast subject on which a great deal might be said. Still, in accordance with your wish, I will dash off a brief sketch, adding those anecdotal points and reminiscences which you suggest. Let me begin with a republic! When we were young, the Swiss Confederacy was an ill-assorted conglomerate of aristocratically-governed or priest-ridden cantons, each of which maintained its own sovereignty, to the detriment of all political cohesion. An ultramontane Separatist League (*Sonderbund*) was eating into its vitals. Neighboring monarchical powers, jealous of the progress of popular freedom, or aiming at the dismemberment of the Alpine Commonwealth (this was the design of the French Government), did their utmost, in order to tear off some slice of Swiss territory, to favor the schemes of the Jesuitic Secessionists, and to prevent the reform of Switzerland at large. The political helplessness and disgrace of that loosely-knit Confederacy was looked upon by royalist reactionaries as a mainstay of European order.

I vividly remember the breathless interest with which we followed for years the attempts made by the revolutionary free corps of "Young Switzerland," as it was called, to unseat the priestlings and the haughty patricians in various cantons. I recollect the delight with which the successful barricade fight and democratic revolution of Geneva was hailed. That local revolution was the harbinger of the final triumph of the Liberals over the "Sonder-

bund " which took place in 1847.   The first token of German sympathy was sent in that year to the Tagsatzung—that is, to the representatives of the Swiss people—from Mannheim, then one of the
headquarters of Radicalism.   The address was drawn up by the
writer of these recollections, and passed for being a bold step indeed,
so oppressive and so tyrannically Argus-eyed was the rule of the
princely Diet at Frankfort.   Switzerland, regenerated by the
overthrow of the Separatist League in a series of battles, gained
immensely in freedom and national unity as well as in military
effectiveness.   In most cantons an excellent system of popular
instruction has since been introduced.   A citizen army of over
200,000, with an additional landsturm or last levy of 262,000,
guards the independence of the country.   No power at present
thinks of encroaching upon Swiss sovereignty or territorial integrity.   In some ways the constitution of the mountain republic has
latterly even served as a model for France ; namely, as regards
the election of the executive, including its president, by the combined two legislatures (*Stände-Rath* and *National-Rath*).   Had
this been done in France as far back as 1848 instead of appealing
to the ignorant masses for the election of a president, Louis
Napoleon would never have had a chance of rising to supreme
power, and twenty years of vile despotism might have been spared
to that country.

I do not wish to dwell too much on what has been achieved in
Germany.   Time was when her prisons were filled with thousands
of men, young and old, whose crime consisted in having aspired
to the restoration of our unity as a nation and to the convocation of a parliament.   The flower of our university youth were
kept for years in dungeons.   A " Central Commission of Political
Inquisition," established at Mayence, extended its ramifications
everywhere.   The national tricolor, secretly worn by students under
the shirt, was treated as a symbol of high treason.   Eminent
patriots, like Jahn and Arndt, who had powerfully aided in the
overthrow of the Napoleonic yoke, were subjected to the meanest
persecution, although their political moderation, their adherence
to kingly government, was beyond a doubt.

All this occurred soon after the wars of Liberation, when the
German people had sacrificed their blood and their treasure in a
tremendous struggle.   The princes, restored to power, broke in
many cases all faith and promises made in the hour of danger.   The

Prussian king, Frederick William III., was foremost in this perfidy. No parliament was granted by him, in spite of his solemn promise. The same in Austria. In both countries it required an armed rising, a fight on the barricades, in 1848, before the people's wishes were fulfilled and their rights acknowledged.

The French Revolution of July, 1830, and the Polish rising which came in its wake, had for some time given a fresh spur to the hopes of German Liberals. Curiously enough, however, shortly before 1848, some of the best men, weary of waiting, seemed to lose much of their confidence in a near future of deliverance. This strain of melancholy feeling I detected in several of the chief leaders of the Liberal cause, who then honored me with their fullest trust, in spite of the great dissimilarity in our ages. I remember such conversations with Adam von Itzstein and Welcker, the prominent champions of the Constitutional movement, and with Professor Kapp, the philosopher, all members of the Baden Chamber. Kapp imagined "a hundred years might elapse before a fresh great Revolution would come." Even Frederick Hecker, who, with Gustav von Struve, afterwards bravely led the Republican rising of 1848, had a few years before, in a fit of despair, resolved upon pitching his tent in Algeria, never to see Germany again. Hecker was then in the prime of life, not far advanced beyond thirty, but in his temperament given to sudden ups and downs. I do not know how it was that some of us, much younger than he, foresaw with certainty, as in a bright vision, what was inevitably coming. J seemed a thousand pities that a force like Hecker should be lost. An address of Heidelberg citizens, suggested and drawn up by me and sent to him, recalled Hecker from his Algerian roamings and projects to serve in the Baden Chamber. All over Germany, in the early part of the Revolution, which broke out a few years later, there was no name more popular among the masses than his.

I pass over the dynastic Reign of Terror which came after the defeat of the popular upheaval, as well as over the "fratricidal war" of 1866 and the truly glorious war of 1870-71. Looking at the present German Empire, I confess I am one of those who do not regard our national unity as complete without our former federal provinces of Austria, which we lost in 1866. Nor do I, considering what even Italy has achieved, admire the complicated system of the existing German constitution, let alone parliamentary government in the true popular sense. Still, thinking of the days when we had, ever and anon, to go to prison under a charge of high treason—a fate once shared even by my wife—when, for the sake of a united and free Germany, we fought, with arms in hand, were court-martialled, and loaded with chains day and night in underground casemates ; remembering all this tumultuous strife and those sufferings in solitary confinement within fortress walls, it is impossible not to feel that some success has been achieved, in spite of that temporary terrible reaction which in 1849 swept hundreds of thousands into a gory grave or into exile in distant lands. Germany has now a central parliament of her own. The censorship of the press is abolished. No longer are criminal charges before her courts of justice dealt with in secret by Government-appointed judges ; but juries decide now, in accordance with our oldest national custom. Communal self-administration also has become a reality. A uniform criminal code and a common code of civil procedure have been introduced. There is uniformity of coin, weight, and measure now ; whereas, formerly, each State, large or small, maintained, in all these things, a system of its own, to the almost incredible disadvantage of trade and commerce. No man can buy himself free any more, by money, from the duty of defending the Fatherland, as was once the case in some German States. Schleswig-Holstein, which rose heroically in 1848–50, but was betrayed by princely governments, is now an integral part of Germany. So is Alsace-Lorraine, thanks to a war frivolously forced upon us by France. Again, a navy has been created, and thus the glorious traditions of our Hanseatic League have been revived, only with a wider national scope. More recently, the German flag has been planted in colonies beyond sea. All these results are in accordance with the aims of the revolutionary movement of 1848–49 ; and we can but hope that, by and by, there will be some further progress in the same direction.·

Was not Italy once "a mere geographical idea"? Prince Metternich satirically said so, and he wanted to keep her in that condition. Even when, in the days of the Revolution, more than forty years ago, republics were founded at Rome, in Tuscany, and in Venice, the outlook soon became gloomy again for the Italian nation. French and Austrian troops overthrew these commonwealths. A belief gained ground amongst but too many that long political subjection had rendered the people of the peninsula unfit for a sustained strenuous effort.

Here, a little personal fact may be mentioned. When at Paris, in 1849, as a member of a diplomatic mission from revolutionized southwestern Germany, I found the French capital in complete turmoil, owing to the attack made by the army of Louis Bonaparte upon the Roman Republic, which was then governed by Mazzini, Saffi, and Armellini. Under the leadership of Ledru-Rollin and other chiefs of the " Mountain " party, an unsuccessful attempt was made to overthrow Napoleon. The great demonstration in the streets which marched along the Boulevards to the National Assembly was dispersed by General Changarnier. I happened to be at the very point—the Rue de la Paix, close to the Madeleine Church—where the cavalry rode into the mass of men. By the merest chance I narrowly escaped the sword thrust of one of the police, who, preceding the troops for the seeming purpose of a legal dissolution of the manifestation, sprang with tiger-like agility into the crowd with drawn weapons.

Being some days afterwards—quite without reference to this event—arrested, in violation of the laws of nations, as one implicated in the attempt to bring succor to the Roman Republic, I used the involuntary leisure afforded me in the prison of La Force for beginning the study of Italian. I did so in a doubly curious way—namely, first, by taking up Silvio Pellico's book, "My Prison Life," which had a French translation at the bottom of each page ; and by not using any grammar or even dictionary, but going straight into the language, with the aid of French as well as Latin lore. Later on I filled up the gaps by a more systematic application. What I thus had learned in prison, from the work of one who had suffered cruelly in dungeons for the cause of his own fatherland, stood me afterwards in good stead, when coöperating for many years with men like Mazzini, Garibaldi, and Saffi.

What dreary years of apparent hopelessness they, like other exiles, had to go through ! I had known Felice Orsini, and I remember the shudder that went through the popular parties of Europe when, at Paris, on a gray winter morning, amidst snowflakes thickly falling, his head rolled into the basket of the guillotine. Again, I remember the confidential preparatory meetings held in Mazzini's little room for that Sicilian rising of 1860, into the planning of which Garibaldi—for reasons I cannot here explain—was at first not initiated. Yet, after the insurrection had been kept fully alive for six weeks under Rosolino Pilo, it was by the landing of the Thousand that the leader of the Red Shirts brought that revolution to a triumphant issue. I remember the special message Garibaldi sent to me through a trusty person before he started for the heroic expedition which failed at Aspromonte. He wished to inform me of the urgent reasons which compelled him to act, so as to prevent a dark plot hatched between Napoleon III. and Ratazzi—a plot directed both against Mexican independence and against Germany on the Rhine. I remember the confidential conversation I had with Garibaldi at the Isle of Wight in 1864, before his triumphant entry into London, when, as the appointed speaker of the London Germans, I presented to him, in company with Freiligrath, Kinkel, and a number of prominent compatriots, an address of welcome. Venice was then not gained yet for Italy, nor was her natural capital, Rome.

The dreams of Italian patriots, at least as regards the unity of their nation, are now realized. No longer is the peninsula a mere " geographical idea." Though not a republic, the country is at any rate not troubled by any complication of different dynastic interests. Much has yet to be done for the material welfare of the peasant and artisan classes. Proper stress is laid upon this—as I find from private intercourse—by that eminent historian and statesman, Professor Villari, now a member of the Cabinet, who came last year to London as one of the delegates to the Inter-Parliamentary Conference of deputies from various countries. If France and Russia were not possible causes of disturbance to the peace of Europe ; if Italy, happily bound in alliance with Germany and Austria-Hungary for mutual defence, were not compelled, by the dangers lurking in the West and the East, to keep up costly armaments on land and on sea, the bettering of the lot of her working classes would certainly be an easier task. " But expensive as these armaments are, it would cost Italy much more," as the *Riforma* has rightly said, " if she were to lay herself open to the risk of an attack."

This is the third French Republic since 1792. With what enthusiasm was its second proclamation hailed, in 1848, throughout Europe ! Unfortunately the peasant masses—two-thirds, or more, of the population at that time—were still sunk in ignorance ; thanks to the outrageous state of popular instruction, which had been neglected in spite of the many revolutions the country had gone through. In many departments, in 1848, more than seventy-five per cent. were unable to read and write. Even so late as 1865, there were departments with 60, 65, 69, 72, and 75½ per cent. similarly situated. I recollect that in 1848 there were peasants who believed Napoleon I. to be still alive, and that the Bonapartean Pretender, who was a candidate for the Presidency, was this identical *petit caporal*. Other peasants were made to believe by reactionary agents that King Louis Philippe had been driven from power by a palace revolution, in which Duke Rollin (*le Duc Rollin*, that is, Ledru-Rollin) and his courtesan, La Martine (Lamartine), were the chief actors ! When Napoleon III., in 1854, paid a visit at the English Court, he, with cynical amusement, told the Prince Consort that on his way with the Empress Eugénie to Biarritz the people through a large portion of the South of France cried : *" Vive Marie Louise ! "* (The consort of Napoleon I.). Napoleon III. also told Prince Albert that on a former journey he had heard cries of : *"Enfin viôlà le vieux revenu !"* (" At last the old one has come back !")

With so backward an agricultural population, great care ought to have been taken as regards the system of political suffrage. The whole class of electors under Louis Philippe had not comprised more than about 200,000, an absurdly small number among about 35,000,000 people ; that is, something like 10,000,000 males. Yet it was no less a mistake to extend the suffrage the day after the Revolution of February to the whole male population. At all events, the knowledge of reading and writing ought to have been made a condition to the exercise of the vote. And, furthermore, electoral districts might have been so arranged for a while as to give to the more cultured cities a proportionately larger representation than to the benighted country districts; all this, it need not be said, only as protective measures for the time being, until the rural males should become better educated.

This is a question on which I have had many an earnest discussion, during long years of proscription, with Ledru-Rollin (" the Father of Universal Suffrage "), Louis Blanc, and other French friends. Ledru-Rollin certainly would never hear of such restrictions. His name was too much historically bound up with the introduction of unlimited universal suffrage. Louis Blanc, privately, readily acknowledged the force of arguments which had the maintenance of the Republican cause for their object. Still, he, like some others, always ended by saying that he dared not move in the matter. It is difficult, indeed, to go back upon a measure of that kind, if once it is passed. Looking at the course of events no one can deny that universal and equal suffrage, without any modification, has given France twenty years of political serfdom under Napoleon, and finally brought about for her a great downfall as regards European standing.

Very few French Republicans—to this, too, I must testify, however reluctantly—foresaw the full danger involved in Louis Bonaparte's election as President. How often we were at issue with them between 1849 and 1851, in pointing out the probability of the success of a *coup d'état*, unless they were able to forestall it by timely action! Our friends uniformly underrated the capabilities of "Badinguet" or of that gang of needy adventurers who surrounded him. "Even if he attempted a *coup d'état*," they often said, "he would fall under the weight of universal derision!" They were badly awakened from their optimistic dream in the night of December 2. I may add that I was startled, a few years ago, on finding that the Boulanger danger was equally underrated by my French Republican friends—not only by the younger ones who had not had the experience of the gradual coming up of Napoleon III., but even by some of the older generation, who had themselves gone through imprisonment, transportation, and exile under Louis Bonaparte. This want of judgment in men otherwise distinguished as writers or scientists, and even prominent in political affairs, impressed me most painfully. I wrote to them letter after letter full of warning. It is true, when the danger had at last come to a head, and a few more days of hesitation might again have decided the fate of the Republic in the Cæsarean sense, all these friends at last saw clearly into the matter; each of them, by letter, then acknowledged to me, with a degree of contrition, that he had been wofully in error as to the character, the aims, and objects of Boulanger.

The neglected intellectual condition of the peasant population had been a main cause of the destruction of the French Republic of 1848. Another cause was the impracticable communistic theory which had gained hold on a numerically small but ardently active group of Democrats, whose propaganda culminated at Paris in the terrible street battles of June, 1848. It is now a

well-established historical fact that Bonapartist and Royalist
agents had helped to fan the flame of this insurrection for purposes of their own. Victor Schoelcher, the veteran French
Senator, proved this years ago ; and Louis Blanc, too, Socialist
as he was, acknowledged it. When the alienated brothers
of the Republican party, the Moderates and the Socialists,
had grasped each other by the throat, and thousands had
been killed or transported, the prospects of the Napoleonic Pretender became brighter : for he posed on the one hand as a "Savior
of Society" and " Restorer of Order," and yet, on the other, tried
to keep in touch with advanced Socialists.

Add to this that, unhappily, the Republican party, in a great
many of its members, was tainted then with the policy of conquest
in the direction of the Rhine. From such policy to Cæsarism is
but a step. Republicans and Bonapartists had often been mixed
up in a common conspiracy, both under the Bourbon Restoration and under Louis Philippe. " To tear up the Treaty of
1815 "—by which Germany, after all, had simply reacquired a
portion of her own, and the Netherlands had been restored to her
independence—was a common expression of French Democrats and
Imperialists for many years. I have had bitter personal experience of this state of feeling among my French friends. Whilst
upholding their Republican cause in public I had many a private
encounter with them on this hankering after the Rhine frontier
all along the river. With frequent entreaty I urged the better-
minded among them, shortly before the war of 1870, to do all in
their power towards preventing an outbreak of hostilities, " as it
could only entail a signal defeat, and a well-merited one, upon
their country." None of them believed in this latter possibility.

It was in 1869 that one of those aggressive Chauvinists, suddenly losing all control over himself, said, in my own house, before
compatriots of mine : " When France shall be a Republic again,
we shall march on the Rhine, even if we get the whole of Germany
upon our back ! (*même si nous aurions toute l'Allemagne sur le
dos*)." I replied: " Take care ; for if once you have her on your
back, you will not get rid of her very soon ! (*Prenez garde! Si,
une fois, vous l'aurez sur le dos, vous ne vous débarrasserez pas
d'elle si vite!*) " I then rose, as a sign that further conversation
on this subject was not desirable. Our fire-eating French friend,
whom I had never before suspected of such sentiments, and with

whom I had coöperated until then in the heartiest manner in the cause of Mexican independence and of President Juarez against the usurper Maximilian, soon afterwards made his exit.

The German victories practically gave France the Republic. Much has been done within the last few years to found a thorough system of popular instruction; and that is one of the most promising features of the present commonwealth—let priestlings rave as much as they like against a " Godless Republic." In the interest of European freedom in general we must hope that that which has been regained through defeat on the battlefield will not be jeopardized anew through senseless military adventures. A French victory—the most unlikely thing in such a case— would saddle France with the rule of the successful general, when once more the Republic would go down. A renewed overthrow of French arms—which may be predicted with safety—would be the overthrow also of the system of government under which the defeat had taken place. Napoleon I., when beaten, was followed by a Bourbon restoration. Napoleon III., when beaten, was followed by the Republic. The Republic, if beaten, would have to make way for a Royalist régime. All sensible wellwishers of progress anxiously desire, therefore, the maintenance of peace, rejoicing meanwhile in the continued existence of the third Republic, which has already outlived the usual span of life of the various forms of government in France since her great Revolution.

When a number of the most eminent generals and statesmen of Hungary were strung upon the gallows at Arad, in 1849, there were but few who believed in the future resurrection of the self-government of that country. How thankful Magyar exiles were for anything which a few men of other nationalities did, during dreary years of oppression, in the way of an advocacy of the claims of their nation ! By the persistent labor of Francis Deak, and through the victory, first of the Italian cause on the fields of Lombardy, and then of Prussian arms against Austria, Hungary regained her autonomy to the fullest extent conformable with her safety against Russian and Panslavic designs. She is one of the oldest Parliamentary countries of Europe, and her Parliament now reigns supreme. Those once prosecuted as guilty of high treason occupy the foremost positions in the land. Kossuth himself is only a voluntary exile. Hungary has a perfectly free press, and the largest amount of self-administration in town, village, and country. She has also a national militia of her own, as a safeguard of her institutions. In short, the Hapsburg dynasty has had to bow down before the vanquished. Sometimes I think of the evening when Count Teleki, after a friendly dinner at which General Klapka, the German poets Freiligrath and Kinkel, and the writer of this article, were present, left London to go back to his native land, where soon afterwards he mysteriously ended his life by a revolver shot. When I compare the condition in which Hungary was even then with what it is now, the transformation is only a degree less wonderful than the one effected in Italy, where a monument is being raised in honor of Mazzini by the Government and the Parliament of Italy, the king himself contributing 100,000 lire.

Shall I speak, in conclusion, of Poland? I have seen General Skrczynecki, one of the leaders of the war of Independence of 1830–31 ; Lelewel, the historian ; and Worczell, the ex-Senator, all men of that famous and heroic rising which ended with the "restoration of order at Warsaw." In 1849 I aided, in France, in the negotiation with General Mieroslawski for bringing him over to a command during the German Revolution. I have known General Langiewicz, the Dictator of the Revolution of 1863–64. Through the envoy of the secret National Government at Warsaw, Mazzini, Ledru-Rollin, and I had been informed, many weeks beforehand, of the very day when that rising would begin, which took the whole of Europe by surprise. The case of Poland has, therefore, always been present to my mind. But though Switzerland has been reformed in our time ; though Germany has been reconstructed ; though Italy is now made into a nation ; though France has regained her republican institutions ; and though Hungary also has achieved an extraordinary success, Poland still awaits her re-embodiment. To most men that may seem well-nigh an impossiblity now. Yet, if the Russian Government were heedless enough to venture upon an aggression in Europe which would bring upon her a retribution by a coalition of Powers, even Poland might get her chance. In that case, the present generation would, in all likelihood, see a notable reconstruction, tantamount to the building up of a protecting wall against the inroad of a political barbarism which aims at "making Europe Cossack."

Karl Blind.

A SILVER SENATOR REVIEWED.

BY MURAT HALSTEAD.

THE Hon. Wm. M. Stewart of Nevada, Chairman of the Senate Committee on Mines and Mining, opens his interesting paper on " The Rule of the Gold Kings " by excepting France from his general denunciation of the leading nations of the commercial world upon the accusation of refusing to receive silver coin as money of ultimate payment. Then the United States is set apart as " treating silver coin as credit money " depending for its value upon a promise of payment of gold ; and all administrations of the Treasury Department are charged with discriminating against silver and in favor of gold in the payment of national obligations.

France values silver, under the ratio, three per cent. higher than we do, and maintains silver legal-tender coin, precisely as we do, by refusing to silver the liberty of the mint, or equality with gold at the mint, and by providing, as we do, for the redemption of " silver as credit money," by covering the margin—by which, under the coinage ratio, it is of less market value than gold—with the more steady and precious metal. The maintenance of bimetallism in France is by the limitation of the coinage of the cheaper metal. Senator Voorhees, in THE NORTH AMERICAN REVIEW, making a plea for silver, held that the French mint was, as it had been for generations, free to silver as to gold ; but Senator Stewart mentions that " France, in 1875, ceased to coin silver." The Senator does not undertake to say why France so long ago " ceased to coin " the metal he holds in such high estimation. She did so because she had as much of it as she could safely undertake to redeem with gold, knowing perfectly that the value of the silver coin as a basis was the market value, and that all above that, on the face of the coin, was artificial, and must be made good, on demand, in gold. There is no one in France who does not know, or seem to know, that free silver coinage would mean the silver standard, and that this relegation of gold to the condition of merchandise, and its consequent banishment, would be a misfortune of the first magnitude ; and the degradation of the public credit of France is not a thing possible with the knowledge, consent, and advocacy of the French people.

The Senator from Nevada says our administrations of the Treasury Department have since 1873 discriminated against silver coin and in favor of gold coin in the payment of national obligations, and that France pays the public creditors in gold and silver, " whichever is most beneficial or convenient for the Government ;" and here the Senator ventures to contrast the administrations of France and the United States, stating that the French have obeyed and the United States disregarded the law. The Senator from Nevada is as completely in error in this as the Senator from Indiana was in his presumption that free silver coinage prevailed in France, and had done so for seventy-five years.

There is a true distinction in the management of coin by the French and ourselves that should be carefully noted, that false assumptions may be better defined. The French are a specie-handling people. Enormous amounts of gold, silver, and copper coin are in the pockets of the French, preferred to paper. We prefer paper. There is more silver in circulation in France than in the United States, because the French would rather have it than paper representatives of money. Americans prefer the silver certificates to the silver coin, or to gold as we coin it. If there is a fault in the Government in this association it is because we coin gold in pieces too large to circulate freely, and issue paper in notes too small—in the one case providing gold in shape for reserves, and in the other consulting the popular convenience. It is perhaps an American preference that it is better to wear out the paper than the gold or the silver.

It should be taken into consideration also that the United States is a silver-producing country and France is not, and we, therefore, have favored silver by forcing its coinage and purchasing it in great quantities as a basis for notes. The Senator from Nevada is not as specific as he should be when he charges that hostility to silver has been the policy of all administrations since 1873. It was in that year that what the Senator regards as the crime of the century was committed. This he styles the demonetization of silver. The awful event was the dropping of the coinage of the standard silver dollar, during a time of profound suspension of specie payments, and the temporary substitution of the "trade dollar." There was no silver or gold in circulation. Before reaching specie payments, the argument prevailed that debts made when "gold and silver" always meant "coin" should not be payable in one metal only; and the coinage of silver in legal tender form was resumed. In the eighty years before the "demonetization of silver" we had coined eight millions of silver dollars; in the eighteen years following this frightful "crime" we coined four hundred millions of silver dollars. When half dollars were unlimited lawful money we coined in that form eighty-two millions of dollars. In the eighty years before the awful crime of the century, discrimination against silver, was perpetrated, we coined ninety millions of lawful money in all amounts, in silver, and, in less than one-fourth that number of years since, we have coined more than four times that sum of the standard silver dollar. This is surely the most startling form that hostility to a money metal ever took.

As one Senator recently remarked to another on the floor of the Senate, "gold coin" mortgages in California being under discussion, "Do not let it occur again." The honorable Senator, who is Chairman of the Committee on Mines and Mining, says the Government discriminates against its own money, if it happens to be silver. Is it then the duty of the Government to force the money metal that is the cheaper upon its creditors? How should Congressmen be paid their wages? How are they paid? They can take gold, silver, or paper, as they please, and their preference is paper, and that nine times out of ten is of silver certificates. Should they be forced to take the silver coin itself! Would there be propriety and public beneficence in refusing the honorable Senator from Nevada "gold coin" if he should call for it? The Senator is mistaken in assuming that public obligations are paid exclusively in gold. Public and private debts are paid all over this country in silver paper. The gold and gold certificates are held in reserve. The attempt to force the silver standard has been marked by the men who do business in money, and they propose in that event to make a profit on the premium on gold and are prepared to do it.

Meanwhile, debts are paid in silver certificates. Only abroad is the question raised that a silver certificate may not be worth as much as a gold certificate; and here the silver agitation merely causes a reserve of gold. It is, of course, the depreciated money that runs first through the channels of commerce. The Senator from Nevada denounces those who hold, as he says, that silver money is not honest money, and he includes in the sweep of his wrath both the political parties, and quotes, to assail, ex-President Cleveland and President Harrison. The Senator is not delicately choice and accurate in his language. Silver money is as honest as any other money, so long as it is as good as the best in purchasing power. It possesses an intrinsic value measured by the world's standard—gold, that has rendered it at the lowest point worth 66⅔ cents on the dollar more in itself than the paper dollar. In redeeming paper, gold has to make good one hundred cents on the dollar, but the margin on silver that has to be made up is only 33⅓ cents. The dishonesty would be in dropping from the gold to the silver standard, reducing in ability to buy in market all salaries, pensions, life-insurance policies, building-association certificates, wages, and bank accounts at least one-third. This would be equivalent to debasing the coinage, and repudiation to the extent of thirty-three per cent. The fact is so, and it is no abuse to state it. Behind this stalks the ancient and hideous spectre of fiat money.

Clearly the free coinage of silver would not increase the value of the metal in market. The silver miners themselves, if they could escape from the obscurations of the lingo of the devotees and the demagogues of silver and the speculators in its variations, would comprehend that free coinage or the silver standard would yield no profit to them. Swapping silver with themselves could not enrich them any more than swapping pocket-knives enriched the boys. The conditions of the silver question demand radical and decisive action by the Government. There ought to be free coinage of silver, but not at the present ratio. The ratio surely is no sacred thing. It has been often changed, and there never was so great a demand for change as now. Of course it would be well if the required change could be made through a common understanding among the nations.

We shall never have that, however, while our silver agitators give to the European money centres the hope that they can exchange European silver for American gold. They will come to our terms in dealing with silver when they know it is our fixed, unassailable policy to keep the gold standard.

With our productions of gold and silver, iron and copper, cotton, corn, wheat, and oil, we have but to find out our strength, and issue our commands, to be obeyed. We are in possession of the potentialities. We have but to know ourselves to sit at the head of the table of the nations and execute our will.

In his dying words Secretary Windom told us if we adopted the free-coinage policy the greyhounds of the Atlantic would bear to our shores the surplus silver of Europe, and gold would be drawn in exchange for it. Our Government has been encouraging the production of silver by the purchase of sixty-three tons of it per month, and we are holding a vast store of silver bullion. Senator Stewart wants it coined. But we have seven times as much coined silver as the people care to handle. Why go on working the mints ?

The bullion is more convenient than the coin for public purposes, and there is sevenfold more coin than is wanted for private transactions. This bullion is a weapon, and we should strike with it boldly. There is needed, that · we may put a handle to it, an amendment of the Sherman–Jones silver law. Congress should authorize the Secretary of the Treasury to sell the bullion we have in store, and to ship the whole mass of it to the London market and draw the gold for it. That is the way to bring about an international silver conference. It is the aggressive way of defending ourselves. We are the great producers of silver. Instead of inviting it from Europe, let us send there for sale our superfluous accumulation. Let the greyhounds of the ocean be employed in transporting our silver product to Europe and bringing back the gold. We have been buying silver : why not sell it ? That is the change of policy wanted to fetch the conference that we have so long and mistakenly and vainly solicited. The conference should have but one object—that of the readjustment of the ratio between silver and gold, so that the relation might be according to the market price. Perhaps 18 to 1 would be about right, but the matter should be studied carefully.

Let the conference find the correct figures. Then we should have free coinage of gold and silver on the same terms. Indeed, it would follow as a matter of course. There would be no strain, for the ratio of the market could not cause friction. There would be no preference then in money metals, save as to the convenience of handling or as to taste for the beautiful. If other nations do not come to terms we should fix a ratio for ourselves and have free coinage. Others would be constrained to go with us and so establish our leadership. As for the trouble of recoining the silver, mechanical facilities are great, and it could be rapidly and might be tastefully done. It should be done, anyhow, for the improvement of the coin, in the artistic sense, and to correspond to the conditions of change. Gold should be reminted also, the double eagles converted into five-dollar pieces ; and so we would and should assert, and achieve—maintain the parity of the two precious metals, and make sure forever an abundant supply of sound, hard, ringing, lustrous money.

MURAT HALSTEAD.

PREHISTORIC TIMES IN EGYPT AND PALESTINE.

BY SIR J. WILLIAM DAWSON.

I.

It may be as well to confess at the outset that the subject of this paper is one which ordinary readers regard with suspicion. It raises many hard questions, is beset with difficulties and controversies, and trenches on the domain of those biblical and historical critics and archæologists whose work is apt to repel alike by its difficulty and uncertainty. I believe, however, that by a judicious mixture of geology, archæology, and history, sacred and secular, it may be possible to arrive at some certainty as to leading points. The greatest difficulty, perhaps, is in the choice of materials ; for when we recall the huge mass of literature with which the subject has been illuminated or darkened, from the great folios of Bochart down to the very modern labors of Delitzch, Maspero, Lenormant, Sayce, Wilson, Naville, Petrie, Conder, Tomkins, Pinches, Schrader, and a host of others, along with the large amount of geological, archæological, and topographical work added within recent years, the prospect is somewhat appalling. Still, by piling the whole together, we may hope with our modern " kodak " and magnesium flash to produce a little cabinet picture, which, if somewhat shaded in parts, may bring out the salient features of the oldest conditions of these old lands. I should, however, scarcely have ventured to attempt such a sketch but for the opportunity to apply personally the test of geological investigation to some of the crucial points, and thus to secure some elements of certainty, and for the further reason that I have just finished the revision, for a second edition, of a work in which these observations are recorded.*

*" Modern Science in Bible Lands," London, 1888 and 1891.

The term prehistoric was first used by my friend Sir Daniel Wilson in his " Prehistoric Annals of Scotland." It was intended to express " the whole period disclosed to us by archæological evidence as distinguished from what is known by written records." As Wilson himself reminds us, the term has no definite chronological significance, since historic records, properly so called, extend back in different places to very different times. With reference, for example, to the Chaldean and Hebrew peoples, if we take their written records as history, this extends back to the Deluge at least. Written history in Egypt reaches to 3,000 years before Christ, while in Britain it extends no farther than to the landing of Julius Cæsar, and in America to the first voyage of Columbus. In Palestine we possess written records back to the time of Abraham, but these relate mainly to the Hebrew people. Of the populations which preceded the Abrahamic immigration, those " Canaanites who were already in the land," we can scarcely be said to have history before the Exodus. In Egypt we have very early records of the dwellers on the Nile, but of the Arabian and African peoples whom they called Pun and Kesh, and the Asiatic peoples whom they knew as Cheta and Hyksos, we have till lately known little more than their names and the representations of them on Egyptian monuments. In both countries there may be unsounded depths of unwritten history before the first Egyptian dynasty, and before the Abrahamic clan crossed the Jordan.

What then in Egypt and Palestine may be regarded as prehistoric ? I would answer : (1) The geographical and other conditions of these countries immediately before the advent of man. (2) The evidence which they afford of the existence, habits, and history of man in periods altogether antecedent to any written history, except such notes as we have in the Bible and elsewhere as to the so-called antediluvian world. (3) The facts gleaned by archæological evidence as to tribes known to us by no records of their own, but only by occasional notices in the history or monuments of other peoples. In Egypt and Palestine such peoples as the Hyksos, the Anakim, the Amalekites, the Hittites, and Amorites are of this kind, though contemporary with historic peoples.

Prehistoric annals may thus, in these countries, embrace a wide scope, and may introduce us to unexpected facts and questions respecting primitive humanity. I propose in the present paper to direct attention to some points which may be regarded as definitely ascertained in so far as archæological evidence can give any certainty, though I cannot pretend in so limited a space to enter into details as to their evidence.

Before proceeding, I may refer by way of illustration to another instance brought into very prominent relief by the publication of Schuchardt's work on " Schliemann's Excavations."

We all know how shadowy and unreal to our youthful minds were the Homeric stories of the heroic age of Greece, and our faith and certainty were not increased when we read in the works of learned German critics that the Homeric poems were composite productions of an age much later than that to which they were supposed to belong, and that their events were rather myths than history. How completely has all this been changed by the discoveries of Schliemann and his followers. Now we can stand on the very threshold over which Priam and Hector walked. We can see the jewels that may have adorned Helen or Andromache. We can see and handle the very double cap of Nestor, and can recognize the inlaid work of the shield of Achilles, and can walk in the halls of Agamemnon. Thus the old Homeric heroes become real men as those of our time, and we can understand their political and commercial relations with other old peoples before quite as shadowy. Recent discoveries in Egypt take us still further back. We now find that the " Hanebu," who invaded Egypt in the days of the Hebrew patriarchs, were prehistoric Greeks, already civilized, and probably possessing letters ages before the date of the Trojan War. So it is with the Bible history, when we see the contemporary pictures of the Egyptian slaves toiling at their bricks, or when we stand in the presence of the mummy of Rameses II. and know that we look on the face of the Pharaoh who enslaved the Hebrews and from whose presence Moses fled.

Such discoveries give reality to history, and similar discoveries are daily carrying us back to old events, and to nations of whom there was no history whatever, and are making them like our daily friends and companions. A notable case is that of the children of Cheth, known to us only incidentally by a few members of the nation who came in contact with the early Hebrews. Suddenly we found that these people were the great and formidable Kheta or Khatti, who contended on equal terms with the Egyptians and Assyrians for the empire of Western Asia; and when we began to look for their remains, there appeared, one after another, stone monuments, seals and engraved objects, recording their form and their greatness, till the tables have quite been turned, and there is danger that we may attach too much importance to their agency in times of which we have scarcely any written history. Thus, just as the quarry and the mine reveal to us the fossil remains of animals and plants great in their time, but long since passed away, so do the spade and pick of the excavator constantly turn up for us the bones and the works of a fossil and prehistoric humanity.

Egypt may be said to have no prehistoric period, and our task with it will be limited to showing that its written history scarcely goes back as far as many Egyptologists suppose and confidently affirm, and that beyond this it has as yet afforded nothing. Egypt, in short, old though it seems, is really a new country. When its priests, according to Plato, taunted Solon with the newness of the Greeks and referred to the old western empire of Atlantis, they were probably trading on traditions of antediluvian times, which had no more relation to the actual history of the Egyptian people than to that of the Greeks.

The limestones and sandstones which bound the Nile Valley, sometimes rising in precipitous cliffs from the bank of the stream, sometimes receding for many miles beyond the edge of the green alluvial plain, are rocks formed in cretaceous and early tertiary times under the sea, when all Northern Africa and Western Asia were beneath the ocean. When raised from the sea-bed to form land, they were variously bent and fractured, and the Nile Valley occupies a rift or fault, which, lying between the bard ridges of the Arabian hills on the east and the more gentle elevations of the Nubian desert on the west, afforded an outlet for the waters of interior Africa and for the great floods which in the rainy season pour down from the mountains of Abyssinia.

This outlet has been available and has been in process of erosion by running water from a period long anterior to the advent of man, and with this early prehuman history belonging to the Miocene and Pliocene periods of geology we have no need to meddle, except to state that it was closed by a great subsidence, that of the Pleistocene or glacial period, when the land of North Africa and Western Asia was depressed several hundred feet, when Africa was separated from Asia, when the Nile Valley was an arm of the sea, and when seashells were deposited on the rising grounds of Lower Egypt at a height of two hundred feet or more.* Such raised beaches are found not only in the Nile Valley but on the shores of the Red Sea, and, as we shall see, along the coast of Palestine; but, so far as known, no remains of man have been found in connection with them. This great depression must, however, geologically speaking, have been not much earlier than the advent of man, since in many parts of the world we find human remains in deposits of the next succeeding era.

This next period, that known to geologists as the Post-Glacial or early modern, was characterized by an entire change of physical conditions. The continents of the northern hemisphere were higher and wider than now. Great Britain was a part of the continent of Europe, the European land probably reaching out into the Atlantic to the 100-fathom line. The Mediterranean was divided into two basins, and a broad fringe of low land, now submerged, lay around its eastern end. This was the age of those early Palæolithic or Palæocosmic men whose remains are found in the caverns and gravels of Europe and Asia. What was the condition of Egypt at this time? The Nile must have been flowing in its valley; but there was probably a waterfall or cataract at Silsilis in Upper Egypt, and rapids lower down, and the alluvial plain was much less extensive than now and forest-clad, while the river seems to have been unable to reach the Mediterranean and to have turned abruptly eastward, discharging into a lake where the Isthmus of Suez now is, and probably running thence into the Red Sea, so that at this time the waters of the Nile approached very near to those of the Jordan, a fact which accounts for that similarity of their modern fauna which has been remarked by so many naturalists. I have myself collected in the deposits of this old lake near Ismailia fresh-water shells of kinds now living in the Upper Nile. If at this time men visited the Nile Valley, they must have been only a few bold hunters in search of game, and having their permanent homes on the Mediterranean plains now submerged.

If they left any remains we should find these in caverns or

* Hull, "Geology of Palestine and adjacent Districts." Palestine Exploration Fund. Dawson, "Modern Science in Bible Lands," p. 311 and Appendix. References will be found in these works to the labors of Fraas, Schweinfurth and others.

rock shelters, or in the old gravels belonging to this period which here and there project through the alluvial plain. At one of these places, Jebel Assart near Thebes, General Pitt Rivers has satisfied himself of the occurrence of flint chips which may have been of human workmanship; * but after a day's collecting at the spot, I failed to convince myself that the numerous flint flakes in the gravel were other than accidental fragments. If they really are flint knives they are older than the period we are now considering, and must be much older than the first dynasty of the Egyptian historic kings. † These gravels were indeed, in early Egyptian times, so consolidated that tombs were excavated in them. Independently of this case, I know of no trustworthy evidence of the residence of the earliest men in Egypt. Yet we know that at this time rude hunting tribes had spread themselves over Western Asia, and over Europe as far as the Atlantic, and were slaying the mammoth, the hairy rhinoceros, the wild horse, and other animals now extinct. They were the so-called " Palæolithic" or historically antediluvian men, belonging, like the animals they hunted, to extinct races, quite dissimilar physically from the historical Egyptians. I see, however, that in a recent review of Miss Edwards's charming work, " Pharaohs, Fellahs, and Explorers," she is taken to task by an eminent Egyptologist for statements similar to the above. On the evidence of two additional finds of flint implements *on the surface,* he affirms the existence of man in Egypt at a time when " the Arabian deserts were covered with verdure and intersected by numerous streams," that is, geologically speaking, in the early Pleistocene or Pliocene period, or even in the Miocene !

Singularly enough, therefore, Egypt is to the prehistoric annalist not an old country—less old indeed than France and England, in both of which we find evidence of the residence of the Palæolithic cave men of the mammoth age. Thus, when we go beyond local history into the prehistoric past, our judgment as to the relative age of countries may be strangely reversed.

It is true that in Egypt, as in most other countries, flint flakes, or other worked flints, are common on the surface and in the superficial soil; but there is no good evidence that they did not

* " Journal of Archæological Society," 1881. Haynes' "Journal of the American Academy of Sciences."

† Dawson, "Egypt and Syria," p. 149.

belong to historic times.   A vivid light has been thrown on this point by Petrie's discovery in débris attributed to the age of the twelfth dynasty, or approximately that of the Hebrew patriarchs, of a wooden sickle of the ordinary shape, but armed with flint flakes serrated at their edges,* though the handle is beautifully curved in such a manner as to give a better and more convenient hold than with those now in use.   This primitive implement presents to us the Egyptian farmer of that age reaping his fields of wheat and barley with implements similar to those of the Palæolithic men.   No doubt at the same time he used a harrow armed with rude flints, and may have used flint flakes for cutting wood or for pointing his arrows.   Yet he was a member of a civilized and highly-organized nation, which could execute great works of canalization and embankment, and could construct tombs and temples that have not since been surpassed.   Can we doubt that the common people in Palestine and other neighboring countries were equally in the flint age, or be surprised that, somewhat later, Joshua used flint knives to circumcise the Israelites ?†

In accordance with all this, when we examine the tenants of the oldest Egyptian tombs, who are known to us by their sculptured statues and their carved and painted portraits, we find them to be the same with the Egyptians of historic times, and not very dissimilar from the modern Copts, and we also find that their arts and civilization were not very unlike those of comparatively late date.

There are, however, some points in which the early condition of even historic Egypt was different from the present or from anything recorded in written history.

- I have elsewhere endeavored, with the aid of my friend Dr. Schweinfurth, to restore the appearance of the Nile Valley when first visited by man in the post-diluvial period.   It was then probably densely wooded with forests similar to those in the modern Soudan, and must have swarmed with animal life in the air, on the land, and in the water, including many formidable and dangerous beasts.   On the other hand, to a people derived from the Euphratean plains and accustomed to irrigation, it must have seemed a very Garden of the Lord in its fertility and resources.

There is good reason to credit the Egyptian traditions that the

---

* Kahem and Garoh, Egyptian Exploration Fund publications.
† Joshua, V., 2, marginal reading.

first colonists crossed over from the Red Sea and settled in the neighborhood of Abydos, and that they made their way thence to the northward, at a time when the Delta was yet a mere swamp,* and when they had slowly to extend their cultivation in Lower Egypt by diking and canals. If we ask when the first immigrants arrived, we are met by the most extravagantly varied estimates, derived mainly from attempts to deduce a chronology from the dynastic lists of Egyptian kings. That these are very uncertain, and in part duplicated, is now generally understood, but still there is a tendency to ask for a time far exceeding that for which we have any good warrant in authentic history elsewhere. Herodotus estimated the time necessary for the deposition of the mud of the Delta at 20,000 years; but if we assume that this deposit has been formed since the land approximately attained to its present level, allowing for some subsidence in the Delta in consequence of the weight of sediment, and estimating the average rate of deposition at one-fifteenth of an inch per annum, which is as low an amount as can probably be assumed, we shall have numbers ranging from 5,300 to about 7,000 years for the lapse of time since the Delta was a bay of the Mediterranean.

It is true that the recent borings in the Delta, under the officers of the British Engineers, have shown a great depth in some places without reaching the original bottom of the old bay. Some geologists have accordingly inferred from this a much greater age for the deposit than that above stated,* and in this they are in one respect justified; but they have to bear in mind that only the upper part of the material belongs to the modern period. A vast thickness is due to the Pleistocene and Pliocene ages when the Nile was cutting out its valley and depositing the excavated material in the sea at its mouth. A careful examination of the borings proves by their composition that this is actually the case.† Geologists who have been guided by these facts in their estimates of time have been taunted as affirming that a great diluvial catastrophe occurred while quiet government and civilized life were going on in Egypt. The evidence for this early date of Egyptian colonization of the Nile Valley is, as every one knows,

---

* "Herodotus," Book II., Ch. 15.

† Judd, " Report to Royal Society," 1886.

‡ "Modern Science in Bible Lands," where evidence of similar dates in other countries is stated.

doubtful, and it might be retorted that archæologists represent the Egyptian government as dating from a period when the Nile Valley was an inland district, and when the centres of human population must have been, principally at least, on lands now submerged.

As an example of the fanciful way in which this subject is sometimes treated, I may cite the fabulous antiquity attributed to the great sphinx of Gizeh. We are told that it is the most ancient monument in Egypt, antedating the pyramids, and belonging to the time of the mystic " Horshesu," or people of Horus, of Egyptian tradition. In one sense this is true, since the sphinx is merely an undisturbed mass of the Eocene limestone of the plateau. But its form must have been given to it after the surrounding limestone was quarried away by the builders of the pyramids, and consequently long after the founding of Memphis by the first Egyptian King Mena. The sphinx is, in short, a block of stone left by the quarrymen, and probably shaped by them as an appropriate monument to the workmen who died while the neighboring pyramids were being built. A similar monument of immensely greater antiquity, from a geological point of view, exists near Montreal in a huge bowlder of Laurentian gneiss, placed on a pedestal by the workmen employed on the Victoria Bridge, in memory of immigrants who died of ship fever in the years when the bridge was being built.

It follows from all this that the monumental history of Egypt, extending to about 3,000 years before Christ, gives us the whole story of the country, unless some chance memorial of a population belonging to the post-glacial age should in future be found. There are, however, things in Egypt which illustrate prehistoric times in other countries, and some of these have lately thrown a new and strange light on the early history of Palestine and especially on the Bible history.

One of the kings of the eighteenth dynasty whose historical position was probably between the time of Joseph and that of Moses, Amunoph III., is believed to have married an Asiatic wife, and under her influence he and his successor, Amunoph IV. or Khu-en-Aten, seem to have swerved from the old polytheism of Egypt and introduced a new worship, that of Aten, a God visibly represented by the disk of the sun, and therefore in some sense identical with Ra, the chief god of Egypt; but there was something in this new worship offensive to the priests of Ra.

Perhaps it was regarded as a Semitic or Asiatic innovation, or led to the introduction of unpopular Semitic priests and officers. Amunoph IV. consequently abandoned the royal residence at Thebes, and established a new capital at a place now called Tel-el-Amarna, almost at the boundary of Upper and Lower Egypt, and from this place he ruled not only Egypt but a vast region in Western Asia which had been subjected to the Egyptian government in the reign of the third Amunoph. From these subject districts, extending from the frontiers of Egypt to Asia Minor on the north, and to the Euphrates on the east, came great numbers of despatches to the Pharaoh, and these were written not on papyrus or skin, but on tablets of clay hardened by baking, and the writing was not that of Egypt, but the arrow-head script of Chaldea, which seems at this time to have been the current writing throughout Western Asia.*

The scribes of the Egyptian king read these documents, answered them as directed by their master, docketed them and laid them up for reference ; and, strange to say, a few years ago Arabs digging in the old mounds brought them to light, and we have before us, translated into English, a great number of letters written from cities of Palestine and its vicinity about a hundred years before the Exodus, and giving us word-pictures of the politics and conflicts of the Canaanites and Hittites and other peoples long before Joshua came in contact with them. Among other things in this correspondence we find remarkable confirmation of the sacred and political influence of Jerusalem, which the Bible presents to us in the widely separated stories of Melchisedec, King of Salem, in the time of Abraham, and of the suzerainty of Adonizedec, King of Jerusalem, in the time of Joshua.

At the time in question Jerusalem was ruled by a king or chief, subject to Egypt, but, as in the times of Abraham and Joshua, exercising some headship over neighboring cities. He complains of certain hostile peoples called *chabiri*, a name supposed by Zimmei† to be equivalent to Ibrim or Hebrews, which to some may seem strange, as the Israelites were at this time in

---

* It is possible, however, that it may really have been a language of diplomacy merely, and may have been used by the Semitic agents of Amunoph as a cipher to communicate with the Egyptian court, and which could not be read by messengers or enemies acquainted only with Hittite or Egyptian hieroglyphics or with the Phœnician characters. For a similar case see II. Kings, xviii., 26.

† Inaugural Lecture, Halle, 1891.

Egypt. We must bear in mind, however, that according to the Bible the Israelites were not the only "children of Eber." The Edomites, Moabites, Ammonites, Ishmaelites, and Midianites were equally entitled to this name; and we know, from the second chapter of Deuteronomy, that these were warlike and intrusive peoples, who had, before the Exodus, dispossessed several native tribes, so that we do not wonder at the fact that the King. of Jerusalem was suffering from their aggressions. It may be noted incidentally here, that this wide application of the term Hebrew accords with the one of the name *Aperiu* for Semitic peoples other than Israelites in Egypt.

We have here also a note on an obscure passage in the life of Moses, namely, his apparent want of acquaintance with the name Jehovah until revealed to him at Horeb.* Now, as reported in Exodus, Moses in that interview addressed God as "Adon," which is supposed to be the Hebrew equivalent of "Aten," the meaning being Lord. This is a curious incidental agreement with the prevalence of the Aten worship in Egypt, and shows that this name may have been currently used by the Israelites, whose God Moses himself calls Adon, till commanded to use the name Jehovah.

A second point of contact of Egypt and Palestine is in the painting and sculptures of hostile and conquered nations in Egyptian temples and tombs. These were evidently intended to be portraits, and an admirable series of them has been published by Mr. Petrie under a commission from the British Association for the Advancement of Science. By means of these excellent photographs, now before me, we can see for ourselves the physiognomy, and form of head, of the Amorite, Philistine, Hittite, and many other peoples previously known to us only by name and a few historical facts; and thus with their correspondence, as preserved in the Tel-el-Amarna tablets, and their pictures as given by Petrie, we have them before us much as we have the speeches and portraits of our contemporaries in the illustrated newspapers, and can venture to express some opinion as to their ethnic affinities and appearance, and can judge more accurately as to the familiar statements of the Bible respecting them. Lastly, Maspero and Tomkins have,

---

* Exodus III., 16 et seqq. This passage has been often misunderstood, but it certainly shows that the name Jehovah had become nearly obsolete among the Hebrews in Egypt, and that the name usually given to God was Adon or Aten.

with the aid of the names fixed by the survey of Western Palestina, revised the lists given by Thothmes III., in the temple of Karnak, of the places which this Egyptian Alexander had conquered ; and they have thus verified the Hebrew geography of the books of Joshua and Judges.

Another unexpected acquisition is the solution of the mystery which has enshrouded that mysterious people known as Hyksos or Shepherd kings, who invaded Egypt about the time of the Hebrew patriarchs, and, after keeping the Egyptians in subjection for centuries, were finally expelled by the predecessors of the Amunoph already referred to. They constitute a great feature in early Egyptian history, but disappear mysteriously, leaving no trace but a few sculptured heads, Turanian in aspect and markedly contrasting with those of the native Egyptians. It now appears that a people of Northern Syria and Mesopotamia, known to the Egyptians at a later time as Mitanni, and who were neighbors of and associated with the Northern Hittites, have the features of the Hyksos. It also seems from a letter in the Tel-el-Amarna tablets that they spoke a non-Semitic or Turanian language akin to that of the Hittites. Thus we have traced the Shepherd kings to their origin, and, curiously enough, Cushan-rish-athaim, who oppressed the Israelites in the days of Othniel, seems to represent a later inroad of the same people.

Such "restitutions of decayed intelligence" now meet us on every hand as the results of modern exploration ; and we must reserve for a second article some additional examples, as well as some further consideration of their bearing on biblical history.

J. WILLIAM DAWSON.

THE NEW YORK CLEARING HOUSE.

BY WILLIAM A. CAMP, MANAGER OF THE NEW YORK CLEARING HOUSE.

ABOUT the year 1773 the bankers of London began a system of exchanging their checks and securities at one place, for the purpose of reducing the amount of real money necessary in the settlement of the transactions represented by them.

The clearing-house method thus introduced met with a great opposition from many of the large bankers in that city, which was gradually overcome : the present system was introduced, and is now practically the same in its methods as that of over one hundred years ago. Little is now known of the amount of its operations, nor are authentic records to be found, as indeed they do not exist.

It was not until after the organization of the New York Clearing House, which instituted the custom of keeping a complete record of its transactions (reported daily) and also a weekly report to the public of the average condition of each bank member of the Association (an arrangement that proved most desirable to the general public and the business community), that a similar system, although considerably abbreviated, was adopted and is continued to the present day in London.

It is a matter of surprise to many that London's average daily transactions (with the exception of one or two years) have been less than those of New York, but that is accounted for, in the opinion of the writer, by the different methods of business.

The certified check system in use here, and the general use of checks for payments in all kinds of settlement, large or small, largely increases the aggregate of clearings and constitutes an element of safety.

The percentage of actual money used by the banks of this city is very small, while in London the Bank of England notes are the principal medium.

Previous to October 11, 1853 (the date of the organization of the New York Clearing House Association), the banks doing business in the city of New York were subject to great risk, inconvenience, and loss of time in effecting their settlements with one another under the methods then prevailing.

Each bank was obliged to keep a ledger account with every other bank, involving a large number of entries daily, the settlements between them being made by cashiers' drafts every Friday; while the distance between some of them was also a serious difficulty.

As the number of banks and the amount of their business increased, it became apparent to all that some plan or system should be devised which would remedy the evil, and avert not only the delay but the risk involved in daily transactions. After much study by leading spirits among the bank officers the present clearing-house system was adopted, and put into operation as an experiment, with the result of marked success, and it has since proved so valuable as to be recognized as a necessity.

When organized, its object was simply (as the constitution states) "to be the effecting at one place of the daily exchanges between the several associated banks, and the payment at the same place and day of the balances resulting from such exchanges." But it was destined to develop into a tower of strength in times of financial distress, and a source of mutual protection to its members at all times.

Even the most sanguine and enthusiastic of its projectors could not foresee how soon the crucial test of its usefulness was to be applied, nor how well it would bear the strain. Within a very few years after its conception and formation it even became a powerful factor in the financial administration of the Government. Upon the breaking out of the Civil War in 1861, the banks of New York, by combination and equalization of their resources, were enabled, through the facilities afforded by the Clearing House, to unite in advancing to the United States Government $150,000,000, which at once restored its declining credit and enabled it to equip and arm its newly-formed military forces and provide for its other immediate requirements. Independently of the great advantages such a system affords the banks in their dealings with each other, experience has proved it to be, in times of emergency, a power for the suppression and avoidance of financial panics, unequalled in the history of this country or in that of the world, as instanced notably in 1873, 1886, and 1890, and on several other occasions.

It was asserted by a prominent bank president, at a meeting of the Association, during the panic of 1884, that the influence of the New York Clearing House in this country was greater than that of the Bank of England in Great Britain, and those experienced in its history accord with that opinion. That the methods employed are perfect is evidenced by the rapidity with which its enormous transactions are performed and the absolute correctness of its results. Hence, it has become proverbial that the Clearing House is in its results always correct ; for while of course it can, and does, make errors, they are, through its perfect system, always discovered in time to prevent delay or loss.

Every bank, not later than half-past ten o'clock each morning, can know its exact condition for the day, and consequently regulate its business accordingly. The balances resulting from the morning exchanges are settled daily, at half past one o'clock, in specie or legal tender notes, thus completing the settlement of each bank for the day.

The records and statistics of the office are voluminous and complete, and any information pertaining to its business or transactions, for the past thirty-eight years, can be obtained from these records by any bank entitled to such information.

A committee of five, selected from our ablest and most experienced bank officers, compose what is styled the Clearing House Committee, who are empowered by the Association, in case of necessity, to take prompt action in any or all matters affecting its interests.

The average daily Clearing House exchanges per year, for the past ten years, have been $115,218,234.79 ; the highest daily average for any one year during that period, being in 1881, amounted to $159,232,190.86. The annexed table, showing the yearly transactions, forcibly illustrates the effects upon the business of the country of the expansion and contraction of the currency and the effects of panics and speculations.

TABLE.

THE EXCHANGES, BALANCES, WITH AVERAGE DAILY EXCHANGES AND BALANCES OF THE ASSOCIATED BANKS OF THE CITY OF NEW YORK FROM 1854 TO 1891.

Year ending Sept. 30.	No. of Banks.	EXCHANGES. Amnt. brought to C. H.	BALANCES. Paid in money.	Average daily exchange.	Average daily balances.
1854	50	$5,750,455,987.06	$297,411,493.69	$19,104,504.94	$988,078.06
1855	48	5,362,912,098.38	289,694,137.14	17,412,052.27	940,565.38
1856	50	6,906,213,328.47	334,714,489.33	22,278,107.51	1,079,724.16
1857	50	8,333,226,718.06	365,313,901.69	26,968,371.26	1,182,245.64
1858	46	4,756,664,386.09	314,238,910.60	15,393,735.88	1,016,954.40
1859	47	6,448,005,956.01	363,984,682.56	20,867,333.19	1,177,943.96
1860	50	7,231,143,056.69	380,693,438.37	23,401,757.47	1,232,017.60
1861	50	5,915,742,758.05	353,383,944.41	19,269,520.38	1,151,087.77
1862	50	6,871,443,591.20	415,530,331.46	22,237,681.53	1,344,758.35
1863	50	14,867,597,848.60	677,626,482.61	48,428,657.49	2,207,252.39
1864	49	24,097,196,655.92	885,719,204.93	77,984,455.20	2,866,405.19
1865	55	26,037,384,341.89	1,035,765,107.68	84,796,040.20	3,373,827.71
1866	58	28,717,146,914.09	1,066,135,106.35	93,541,195.16	3,472,752.79
1867	58	28,675,159,472.20	1,144,963,451.15	93,101,167.11	3,717,413.80
1868	59	28,484,288,636.92	1,125,455,236.68	92,182,163.87	3,642,249.95
1869	59	37,407,028,986.55	1,120,318,307.87	121,451,392.81	3,637,397.10
1870	61	27,804,539,405.75	1,036,484,821.79	90,274,478.59	3,365,210.46
1871	62	29,300,986,682.21	1,209,721,029.47	95,133,073.64	3,927,665.68
1872	61	33,844,369,568.39	1,428,582,707.53	109,884,316.78	4,638,255.54
1873	59	35,461,052,825.70	1,474,508,024.95	115,885,793.58	4,818,653.67
1874	59	22,855,927,636.26	1,286,753,176.12	74,692,573.97	4,205,015.73
1875	59	25,061,237,902.09	1,408,608,776 68	81,899,470.26	4,603,296.65
1876	59	21,597,274,247.04	1,295,042,028.82	70,349,427.51	4,218,377.94
1877	58	23,289,243,701.09	1,373,996,301.68	76,358,176.06	4,504,905.90
1878	57	22,508,438,441.75	1,307,843,857.24	73,785,746.54	4,273,909.53
1879	59	25,178,770,690.50	1,400,111,062.86	82,015,539.70	4,560,622.35
1880	57	37,182,128,621.09	1,516,538,631.29	121,510,224.25	4,956,008.60
1881	60	48,565,818,212.31	1,776,018,161.58	159,232,190.86	5,823,010.36
1882	61	46,552,846,161.34	1,595,000.245.27	151,637,935.38	5,195,440.54
1883	63	40,293,165,257.65	1,568,983,196.15	132,543,306.76	5,161,128.93
1884	61	34,092,037,337.78	1,524,930,993.93	111,048,981.55	4,967,201.93
1885	64	25,250,791,439.90	1,295,355,251.89	82,789,480.38	4,247,069.39
1886	64	33,374,682,216.48	1,519,565,385.22	109,067,588.94	4,965,899.95
1887	64	34,872,848,785.90	1,569,636.324.77	114,377,209.13	5,146,315 82
1888	64	30,863,686,609.21	1,570,198,527.78	101,192,415.11	5,148,191.89
1889	64	34,796,465,528.87	1,757,637,473.47	114,839,820.23	5,800,783.74
1890	65	37,660,686,571.76	1,753,040,145.23	123,074,139.12	5,728,889.36
1891	64	34,053,698,770.04	1,584,635,499.88	111,651,471.39	5,195,526.21

Total Exchanges since organization, October 11, 1853......... $950,317,307,349.29
  "   Balances since organization, October 11, 1853.......... 42,424,129,850.12
  "   Transactions for 38 years............................... 992,741,437,199.41

The Clearing House, when organized in October, 1853, included every bank in the city, in all at that time fifty-two.

The conservative requirements of the system soon revealed weakness in the management of eight banks and these were obliged to liquidate in consequence of their inability to meet the immediate demand upon them for their daily settlements; a demonstration that their methods of business were unsound, and consequently unsafe. The result was, as shown in the table, a reduction of the total business of the Clearing House for the second year, but this gradually increased until the panic of 1857 caused a reduction in the following year of nearly fifty per cent. in the aggregate transactions, the volume of which was about restored the following year.

The excitement over the Presidential election of 1860 again caused a large falling off in the amount of business. The passage by Congress of the National Currency Act the year after immediately expanding the circulation, increased the volume of business in proportion to the issue of National Bank currency until 1873, when the financial panic of that year (the result of overtrading, especially in railroad enterprises) again showed its effects in an enormous reduction of business, from which it did not recover until the resumption of specie payments by the United States Government on the 1st of January, 1879, which increased the business from $22,500,000,000 in 1878 to $48,565,-000,000 in 1881.

The effect of the failure of two or three banks in 1884 from bad or criminal management, notably the Metropolitan and the Marine National, also seriously reduced the amount of transactions through the Clearing House ; but a rapid recovery of the financial condition of the banks, by prompt action of the Association, demonstrated its wisdom and the power of concerted action. Surely, never was the truth of the motto that " In union there is strength " more aptly illustrated than in the history of this great financial brotherhood.

Its strength lies principally in the plan known as the Loan Committee system, devised originally by able men, members of the Association, and improved upon from time to time by experience, until now it seems, when put into operation, a power so strong as to at once by the restoration of confidence avert the disaster of a financial panic. This plan consists in the issuance to banks requiring them of certificates of the Loan Committee (who are selected for their judgment and experience), based upon stocks, bonds, or bills receivable approved by the committee, with a margin of not less than 25 per cent., and the bank's obligation in addition. These certificates, bearing interest, and having the guarantee of the Association, and available for the settlement of balances at the Clearing House, make a perfectly safe as well as profitable security for the members of the Association, at the same time removing pressure upon such banks as need only temporary relief, by converting their collateral and bills receivable into an equivalent to a cash asset.

They have invariably accomplished the object of their issue, and in a brief period have always been retired and cancelled without loss. It is only when banks are actually solvent that such relief is extended. This was instanced in November, 1890, when three banks suddenly found themselves unable to meet promptly, as required by the Association, their Clearing-House balances. They were assisted by individual banks to the extent required for that day ; their condition was then examined by the committee, and two of them being found perfectly solvent were afforded the aid requisite for a continuance of business ; but the condition of the other, the North River Bank, not being satisfactory, further assistance was refused it, whereby the public was assured that if a solvent bank should suffer temporary stringency it would be aided and protected by the Association, while only scant courtesy could be expected for one whose methods and condition should be proved upon examination to be unsound.

To demonstrate how effective is the safeguard which this system affords as a means of mutual protection it is only necessary to call attention to an attempt recently made upon the securities and resources of a certain bank in good standing and credit by a party of unscrupulous bank-wreckers. Every business man in New York must remember with what marvellous celerity their schemes were brought to an abrupt termination and they themselves summoned before the bar of justice. So long as they were contented to devote their attention to outside banks their plans prospered, but almost the very day they presumed to trifle with a bank connected with the Clearing House Association their plans were frustrated.

Before any of the conspirators were aware that they were even suspected, the committee was sitting in special session and probing their actions to the bottom. The conservatism of the New York Clearing House is especially manifested in the fact that, while most of the clearing houses in the United States resort to transfers of balances in their settlements, this Association has never, except in the matter of loan certificates, accepted any other medium than legitimate gold coin or legal tender money.

This brief description of an institution whose operations and influences are only thoroughly understood or appreciated by those familiar with banking and finance may convey to the uninitiated some idea of its value and importance as associated with the banking interests of this city and of the whole country, to the proper administration of which it has become almost indispensable.

Great credit is due, as is justly recognized by the members of the Association, to those bank officers who have so ably served from time to time upon the loan committees, and also upon the Clearing House committees, for the performance of their arduous and responsible duties without compensation of any kind, and purely from a devotion to the interests of the Association, which was necessarily for the public good. The value of their labors is beyond estimate ; panics have been averted by their judgment and prompt action ; an enormous depreciation in values of all kinds prevented to an amount which cannot be calculated ; and many banks which are now prosperous have been saved from failure or liquidation.

WILLIAM A. CAMP.

THE PERILS OF REËLECTING PRESIDENTS.

BY THE HON. DORMAN B. EATON, EX-PRESIDENT OF THE UNITED
STATES CIVIL-SERVICE COMMISSION.

A PRESIDENT with no strong party or personal interest in the election of his successor can approach it with calm fidelity to his great trust. If he be more a partisan than a patriot, he will use his vast powers more for his party than his country. If the candidate of the President's party be the President's favorite, the public interests are quite sure to suffer. Make the President himself the candidate of his party for the succession, and the two most powerful of all human motives—that of personal selfishness and that of party zeal and hate—are combined against fidelity to the public interests. Only the most saintly of men and the noblest of patriots, when thus contemplating their own reëlection, can have the sense of duty needed for controlling the selection and conduct of more than a hundred thousand officers—subordinate to the President—in the interest of the public rather than in that of their own reëlection. In theory, nothing seems wiser than to make a second Presidential term dependent upon the people's judgment of the first. In practice, nothing is more dangerous than to make the hope of such a term a temptation to Presidents to fill all these places with electioneering politicians in aid of such reëlections.

When political parties combine the great forces of a nation for the election of worthy candidates or the support of a wise policy, they are as salutary as they are powerful. But when a party uses its powers for coercing appointments to parts of the public service in which no party principles are involved, and especially when such powers are united with those of the President for compelling the vast numbers in the civil service to become electioneerers for a second term for a President, then, surely, the party has transcended its sphere, has prostituted its functions, and has become a source both of demoralization and of peril.

Though no political party existed when the national constitution was framed, yet its authors, fearing evil from such party passions as have caused this prostitution, provided for presidential electors, to be selected in each State separately, who, by an independent vote, were to elect the President. It is a familiar fact that this system of electors has failed—has been made almost useless—by the influence of great parties. It is the one great failure of our constitutional system. Yet so completely have party theories dominated political thought, so blinding have the passions of party become, that rarely can we find a proper comprehension of the disastrous consequences of this failure, or of the changes it makes necessary in order to accomplish the purposes of the constitution in regard to the presidential office. Every suggestion of a remedy is likely, in the minds of perhaps the vast majority, to raise only these questions : How will it benefit my party ? Can it be made to injure the other party ? But this intrusion of party, where the interests of the country alone should be considered, makes the need of a remedy only the more manifest and imperative.

In the subordinate offices, the length of the official term and the matter of reëligibility are not, intrinsically, of prime importance. But when we come to the President, at the centre and summit of all official life, at the head of a great host of officers and employees of many kinds and grades, civil, naval, and military, whose services extend to every part of the Union and to foreign seas and nations, whose numbers exceed a hundred and fifty thousand, and most of whom, directly or indirectly, hold their places at the pleasure of the President,—that President having, besides his vast executive powers, a legislative power equal to one-sixth of that of Congress for making and repealing laws,— then, indeed, we have an office the fixing of the term of which and the filling of which not only involve this vast official force and the counterpoise of the constitution itself, but raise the most vital issues of party strife and national safety.

So important is the mere length of the President's term of office that to increase it fourfold,—to sixteen years,—we may well believe, would make executive power too great and corrupting for

Congress or the courts to withstand ; and that to reduce it to a fourth of its length, requiring Presidential elections annually, would soon make the people sigh for an aristocracy or an emperor.

The framers of our constitution carefully considered the fit length of the President's term and all the bearings of his eligibility for reëlection, so far as history or their experience afforded any light. But there had never been anywhere in the world such an office as that of our President, nor a country in which a political party could freely elect the chief executive. When the constitution was framed, there was no political party, nor for a long time after was there any like the parties of our time. After national parties had arisen, they were for a long time based on principle, and did not rely on patronage—that is, on subordinate offices—for gaining power or rewarding party henchmen. For a long time Presidents were nominated in congressional caucuses. There were hardly more than a hundred removals for party reasons from 1789 until Jackson's administration.

The elaborate organization, the stupendous power, the greed for office, of our parties, like their control of presidential and other elections, were unimagined by our early statesmen. They were acquainted only with little local parties or rather " factions " —as they fitly called them—based on the interests of slavery, of large or small States, of Northern or Southern States, of manufacturing or agricultural States; and these factions were almost without organization. A national party convention, a presidential election, the electioneering activity of more than a hundred thousand official subordinates of a President for his reëlection, the awarding of tens of thousands of places as prizes to the victors, potentially, by a President thus elected,—these workings of our political system were as much beyond the imagination of its authors as some of them are repugnant to the constitution itself and to the purposes of its creation.

Yet there was great fear of an increase of such factions, of the spirit of party, of the intrigue and corruption which presidential elections might involve. The system of presidential electors, as we shall soon see, was the trusted precaution of those statesmen, and their remedy against such evils.

The sessions of the Constitutional Convention began in May and continued until the middle of September. The questions of the reëligibility of the President and of the fit length of his term

—in their nature dependent—were always considered together ; and first early in June. It was then decided that his term should be seven years, and that he should not be eligible for reëlection ; only one State favoring reëligibility. The system of presidential electors had not then been devised. The questions of term and reëligibility were again discussed about the middle of July, when there were extreme opinions, ranging from a term of less than seven years to one of good behavior. Six States against four expressed a preference for reëligibility, provided a satisfactory mode of electing the President could be devised. Still, however, the opinion was unanimous that, if he was to be selected by Congress, he ought not to be eligible for reëlection. An important argument against reëligibility was the danger that, Congress being a continuous body, its members would be bargained with and corrupted,—an argument which, in the main, applies to great national parties also, because they are permanent, with a continuous series of officers ready to make corrupt bargains. The debate shows that there was no anticipation of such party supremacy and evils from partisan removals and office-seeking as our times have seen.

Those who favored reëligibility were to devise some new and safe scheme for electing the President. The scheme devised was the election by each State of a number of electors equal to her Senators and Representatives counted together ; and the body of electors thus secured was to elect the President, whereupon their official existence was to cease. In this matter each State was expected to act freely and independently. No Senator, Representative, or person holding any office of profit or trust under the United States could be an elector. Each presidential elector was expected to cast his vote for President according to his judgment. The thought that these electors would become a servile agency of party, taking no independent action of their own, so that the party election would determine absolutely who should be president, seems to have occurred to no one; a striking evidence that the despotic power of our parties was then inconceivable. Hamilton and Madison, Franklin and Washington, were unable to imagine that state of public opinion—rather, of party despotism—which, a few years ago, censured the alleged purpose of James Russell Lowell to cast his vote, as a presidential elector, irrespective of party and according to his conscience; the very thing which they intended, which the constitution provided for, and which the reëligibility of the President required.

Mr. Bancroft tells us that the convention was so converted by this electoral device that, on the faith of it, the reëligibility of the President was approved in July, and his term was reduced from seven years to six. Nevertheless, at the end of the month the convention again voted that the President's term should be seven years, and that he should be ineligible for reëlection. The subject was further debated in August, and it was referred to a committee from all the States, from which came a report, in September, limiting the term to four years. The subject had become complicated with questions between large States and small States ; and in the meantime theoretical confidence in the electoral scheme had greatly increased. A term of four years was finally adopted for the President, and he was left eligible for reëlection.

Thus we see that not only the original conviction of the convention, but its deliberate vote at the end of thorough discussion, was for a single term of six or seven years, without eligibility for reëlection ; and that a four years' term—a sudden suggestion— and the allowance of reëligibility were first approved near the end of the session ; after the convention, to use Mr. Bancroft's words, had fallen into " an anarchy of opinion," and had come to trust the saving virtues of a device which has utterly failed.

It is an instructive fact that Brazil, the latest republic to imitate our constitution, recognizing that failure, has reaffirmed the most careful judgment of our convention, by giving her President a term of six years and forbidding his reëlection.

The Federalist defends what was done on the basis of the assumed sufficiency of the electoral scheme. It declares it to have been " a desideratum that the executive should be independent, for his continuance in office, of all but the people themselves"; and so he would have been had presidential electors remained independent. But when party became supreme, they became servile. Public officers became an efficient force for reëlecting a President—almost a controlling force for his renomination. A President seeking a reëlection found as much reason, perhaps, to consider them as to consider the people.

The electoral system began to break down when party, led by Jefferson, began to be excessive ; and that experienced party leader—as the first President Harrison tells us in a message in which he condemns a second term—lamented the mistake made in allowing a President an opportunity for grasping a second term through prostitution of his subordinates. Jackson first made party an irresistible power; and, knowing well both presidential frailty and party passions, he comprehended the dangerous consequences of that opportunity. If one of the fiercest of partisans, he was yet honest, fearless, and patriotic. In his first message he advised that the President be made ineligible, and that his term be six years—the best advice Jackson ever gave his party. Twice afterwards, in messages, and with deeper earnestness as he saw the dangers increasing, he repeated this advice, and urged a constitutional amendment to make it effective. But the interests of his party, its officials and leaders, in existing methods had become irresistible. The mighty influence of Jackson was as inadequate as that of Jefferson to arrest the growing evil.

When a constitutional amendment allowing only one term to a President was pending in 1829, Buchanan opposed it with the characteristic servility to party which enabled that lamentable politician, thirty years later, to be effective for the degradation of his country. The partisan admirers of Jefferson and Jackson have never risen to the level of their principles or their patriotic courage. Shouting for these patriots, they are blind to the evils those men deplored. The virtue of any party must be rare indeed which will waive its advantage in having tens of thousands of its adherents in office at the opening of a presidential canvass. Reform can only come at the hands of a new party, or must not take effect until some years after its adoption.

From Jackson's time it was regarded as infidelity to party to repeat his advice. Polk required a pledge from the members of his cabinet not to use their position to affect the Presidency—of course against himself. He wanted no rivals. Mr. Curtis has recorded Buchanan's declaration that he found Pierce and his cabinet intent upon building up, through his appointments, a Pierce party for his own reëlection. There had been a revolution in presidential elections. The party interests in controlling them through the aid of the office-holders seem to have overawed as well as debauched Presidents. Tyler, who began with deprecating the vicious influence of office-holders on elections, ended by accepting a nomination for a second term from a convention promoted by himself, and mainly composed of officials depending on his favor.

Fillmore, a more kindly President, was opposed to a second term, but, yielding to the solicitation of friends, mainly his subordinates in office, he stood for reëlection.

Politicians who have worked rather for the President and the party than for the country deny him any right to refuse them the chances of extending their official life by renewing his. A party which has made a politician a President claims a right to his services, and to those of the vast army of officials he commands, for carrying the next election. The first President Harrison's profound sense of the evils of a second-term candidacy would probably have prevented his accepting a renomination, had he not died too soon.

Aside from Mr. Harrison, Mr. Cleveland is the only President since 1837, when the spoils system had become supreme, who has officially repeated the warnings of Jefferson and Jackson. In his letter accepting his first nomination, Mr. Cleveland used these words :

" When we consider the allurements of power, the temptation to retain places, and, more than all, the availability the party finds in an incumbent and a horde of office-holders, . . . we recognize, in the eligibility of the President for reëlection, a most serious danger."

Clay, Webster, and Sumner expressed a deep sense of the dangers of a President's seeking a second term ; and De Tocqueville, two generations ago, declared, in substance, that the practice puts the government itself into the scales against every candidate, except that one who alone commands the vast army of its officials. As the reform sentiment has gained strength, there has been more courage to oppose second terms. The labor-reform platform of 1872, and that of the Liberal Republicans of the same year, condemned them ; and so did President Hayes. Mr. Tilden expressed " the conviction that no reform of the civil service . . . will be complete and permanent ' until ' the President is constitutionally disqualified for reëlection."

We have space for only the most meagre treatment of other parts of the subject. The reëligibility which the constitution allows is not for a second term only, but for an indefinite series ot terms. The plausible argument which was then and is now, with a class of reasoners, its principle support, is this : that well-doing in the presidential office should be rewarded with reëlections, and that such a practice would inspire noble endeavors. This argument, which has some real strength, as well as great plausibility, applies with increased force to a President who has done well for two terms. Yet an unwritten law of practical wisdom, sweeping high over all constitutional and theoretical reasons, early forbade any man to be more than twice elected President. And if no term longer than four years shall be provided, we may perhaps in our day see an amendment of this law which shall forbid a single reëlection of a President. Is it certain that even now the party cry, "No reëlection of Presidents and a six years' term," would not be effective ?

A nation's gratitude to its favorite general in our day did not save him from defeat and humiliation when party interests and the greed of office-holders—for we can assume no controlling ambition on the part of President Grant—forced him into conflict with this salutary custom. Thus fell the greater part of presidential reëligibility and of the arguments in its favor.

To the extent that the hope of a reëlection does or can elevate the action of a President, that hope must, therefore, be utterly lost during his second term ; and this term, to that same extent, should in character be inferior to the first—a very distinct argument against a reëlection. The fact is that the hope of a reëlection is, in its very nature, a motive and an elevating force—if such at all—far inferior to a patriotic spirit, a sense of duty, or a recognized commitment to great principles before the people. The most unscrupulously ambitious of Presidents will most vigorously seek a second term. A man of noble nature, indeed, desires to be honored in the future; but knows that not seldom he can be, only at the cost of popularity in the present.

The most difficult step in gaining a second term is that of securing a renomination ; in which the public servants and the mercenary politicians are but too sure to be the most effective force. This is the great reason against renominations. When a President is a candidate,—and thus under a powerful temptation to coerce his subordinates, to pander to party leaders, to cause vast sums of money to be extorted from the public servants for election expenses,—these vicious elements will be far more powerful than when all candidates stand on a common level—no one having an army of office-holders at his bidding.

To make a President a candidate for reëlection is to set him upon the conflicting purposes of serving, at the same time, his country, his party, and, above all, himself. From the moment he is thought to aim at a second term, his motives, especially in conňection with all appointments and removals, are generally—if not justly—distrusted. His great office sinks in public estimation. Suspicion embitters party hate. Plausible distrust and misrepresentation fill the whole realm of politics, and rapidly enfeeble confidence in the President and respect for his motives. This in itself is a great misfortune ; for next to the evil of a corrupt use of the appointing power is a belief that it is so used. How many can be convinced that a President seeking a reëlection will not, in selecting postmasters, collectors, and all other officers, prefer an efficient electioneerer to a quiet, competent public servant ? A President may have that ideal sense of duty and that almost superhuman patriotism which are unaffected when the selfish exercise of his power can give him 65,000 postmasters—150,000 employees altogether in the Post-Office Department alone— who may become servile agents in his behalf in every city, village, and hamlet of the Union, but who, if that power is exercised patriotically, will attend only to their official duties. The experience of the last decade, in which more than once within the space of two years, or less, tens of thousands of postmasters, whose politics under good administrations are unimportant, have been removed to gain places for active partisans, compels us to think that such virtues are not common. Well-regulated post-offices should have (as English post-offices do have) no more politics than the Adams Express Company, a regiment of the army, or a ship of war. The great carriers of packages could transport and deliver the mails, as telegraph companies deliver messages, without the least embarrassment from the lack of politics, whatever peculiar objections might prevail against their so doing.

It is doubtless possible for the vast numbers in the public service appointed for party reasons—as anxious as a President to continue in office, and well knowing how highly he would appreciate an electioneering prostitution of their influence in his behalf—to nevertheless continue faithful to their duties, doing nothing to aggravate that excessive partisan activity which every patriot deplores ; but most people may think that few things contribute so much to these evils as a President standing for a second election.

We are sometimes told that the people are the best judges of the fittest person to be President, and that to restrict their choice by declaring any one ineligible is to distrust their' judgment and to contradict our republican theory. The constitution of the United States defines republican government for us, and mainly for the world. It condemns and excludes such reasoning. Though there should be a citizen preëminent in fitness for the presidential office, and from every quarter of the Union and every class of the people a preference for him should be declared, nevertheless he could not be elected President if (1) not thirty-five years of age; or (2) not for fourteen years a resident within the United States; or (3) not a native-born citizen—not having been a citizen when the constitution was adopted ; nor (4) can the electors of any State vote for two persons for President and Vice-President both of whom are inhabitants of the same State as themselves. Thus the people have no absolute right of choice.

Many of the reasons affecting the proper length of a President's term are too profound to be considered here. Yet we may glance at some of them. The framers of our constitution comprehended the need of a term of considerable length to give steadiness to policy, and experience, vigor, and consistency to administration. The need of a longer term increases with the vastness of territory, the numbers of the people, the complexity of affairs. Since parties have become the ruling forces, the only chance for doing justice to the policy of a party which has triumphed by electing a President is to allow him a term long enough to fairly test that policy in practice. This also the public interest requires.

It is mere usurpation and despotism for a party or a President to use the subordinate officers to keep itself or himself in power. These officers have a right to that reasonable independence to which such party despotism is fatal. It is one of the best features of the party system that a President is placed conspicuously before the people as under a moral obligation to be true to the principles approved in his election. The whole theory of party rule, and every element of justice involved in it, require that each party shall enter the presidential election on equal terms,—save as made unequal by different principles and candidates,—and forbid either party to have the advantage of a horde of public servants at its bidding. No one may hope to secure ideal equality. Yet a single term for a President, long enough to fairly test a policy,—say a term of six years,—would seem to be most fit. It would not too much restrain the freedom of the people or the chances of a new experiment in policy. It can hardly be claimed that through a six years' term political life would lose more than some part of its excessive activity. This period of service is midway between the shortest ever proposed and the longest ever tolerated for our Presidents. The average length of service for each person elected as President,—before the one in office,—had no death prevented, would have been five years and eight months.

May we not well believe that nearly all persons, save the politicians and venal voters, think our presidential elections are too frequent? Who would think such elections once in two years endurable? If we now had a presidential term of six years, who, except party managers, office-seekers, the buyers and sellers of votes, and the storm-birds of partisan politics, would wish to see the quadrennial term restored? Indeed, are we not justified in believing that, if the members of the convention of 1787—the leaders of a generation which saw no removals for party ends and no interference by officials with elections—could return here and be their own revisers, in the light of our experience, they would provide for a presidential term of six or seven years,—a term which they twice approved, and never abandoned until their confidence had been won by a device of presidential electors, the failure of which would be their great disappointment in contemplating their glorious creation?

Some patriot may suggest that a term of six years would have shortened the administration of Washington. But the great principles he represented were established during the first six years of his Presidency. And may we not believe that he would have advised a single term of six or seven years, had he lived to see the failure of the electoral system, as Jefferson and Jackson lived to see it, and so advised?

Some Republican may tell us that a single term of six years would have prevented the reëlection of Lincoln; but such a term would have been long enough for the work of reconstruction; and it might, perhaps, have prevented the excitement incident to his reëlection, which possibly developed the partisan hate of his assassin into a murderous frenzy. Many Democrats will doubtless suggest that such a provision would prevent the renomination of Mr. Cleveland. But it would have added two years to his administration, by which his policy and that of his party would have been adequately tested. Besides, we have cited his words which condemn a second term and answer the suggestion. In fact, all mere personal arguments, applying as they do with force only twice or thrice in a century, are shallow and inconclusive when weighed against the constant and powerful temptation and tendency to selfishness and corruption which the reëlection of Presidents involves. What all worthy and noble Presidents most desire—what an Aristides, a Marcus Aurelius, or a Washington, in the presidential office, would most seek—would be freedom to appoint and remove all officers and to discharge every function under conditions which, to the utmost, exclude every reason for suspicion and all justification for imputing selfish motives,—conditions as favorable to the general welfare as they are to the honor and glory of Presidents.

Such a President would feel that six years of such opportunity, at the head of a mighty nation, in which to lead a wise policy, to be faithful to great principles, to freely exercise his judgment in reference to the highest interests of his country, alike in the present and in the future, with no personal interests in the future but that it should gratefully preserve the record of his official life,—such a President would feel that an opportunity like this is enough to satisfy the noblest ambition ; and that to fill the measure of its duties would require him to be governed by the highest motives and to fitly discharge the most exalted functions of human life.

If a President holding office on such conditions should not have independence and patriotism enough to reappoint a worthy postmaster because he was worthy, he would at least be without a selfish interest to tempt him from his duty. If it would be possible, under such a single-term system, for the worthy head of the greatest customs office of the Union to be forced from his place when an election was near at hand, without being so much as charged with a fault, the President would at least be without the strongest of temptations to appoint the most expert of politicians and the least experienced of administrators as his successor. He might, perhaps, upon plain business principles—as has been the practice in England—promote to the vacancy some customs officer of adequate experience,—apparently a plain duty. Let it be certain that a President can serve but one term, and he will feel far more independent for doing his duty.

Justice to patriotic and unselfish Presidents requires that they be relieved of the tormenting solicitation and effrontery with which they are assailed, and their energies overtaxed, in filling offices as they are now filled. The question under existing practice, "Who will make the most efficient officer for the President's reëlection and for the party?" it may be safely said, is generally quite as much considered as the simple inquiry as to fitness for official duties, and is more harassing near a presiden- · tial election. Who can picture the all-pervading demoralization which comes from this source, the disgust and humiliation inexpressible with which a truly worthy President is compelled, in regard to thousands of offices every year, to consider all the vicious interests and rivalries of local and partisan politics—to say nothing of those affecting his own renomination, as to which the party hardly allows him freedom? They revolted even the stern nature of Andrew Jackson. A report by a committee of the national Senate in May, 1882, declares that " every chief magistrate, since the evil has grown to its present proportions, has cried out for deliverance."

It has been one of the evil effects of the second-term system to cause the interested appointees of a President to insist that his honor needs to be vindicated by a renomination—as if what they can do for him could give him a more honorable fame than what he has done for the people!

No well-informed person will assume that the denial of second terms would remove all the evils with which they are connected; for of some of them they are not the cause, but only the aggravation. But such a denial would certainly prevent the very methods of filling the presidential office from being a needless temptation of presidential virtue.

If appeals to reason alone shall fail to bring about the needed changes, the practical impossibility of much longer carrying on the government in the spirit of partisan removals and second-term nominations may perhaps force the making of them. In the lifetime of persons now living we shall have 500,000 postmasters, and it will require the removal of more than 375 every day for the President's whole term of four years—to say nothing of, perhaps, two million post-office clerks, carriers, and employees, or of as many more officers and employees of divers kinds—in order to fill all the places in the postal service with those partisans and expert manipulators of elections who, scattered through every city, village, town, and hamlet of the Union, constitute the vast horde of electioneerers most effective for the reëlection of Presidents. Happily, so many appointments and removals would be a physical impossibility. Happily, in politics, as elsewhere, the disastrous results of evil ways may reënforce the lessons of reason and the promptings of patriotism.

DORMAN B. EATON.

THE FUTURE OF WESTMINSTER ABBEY.

BY THE VENERABLE ARCHDEACON FARRAR.

I NEED hardly apologize for writing, as the editor of THE NORTH AMERICAN REVIEW requests me to do, on the subject of the future of Westminster Abbey. Americans are at least as fully alive as Englishmen to the unique interest and preciousness of our national Walhalla. Almost the first thing that an American does, on visiting England, is to make his pilgrimage to the Abbey ; but there are many Englishmen, even in London, who have never entered it. I was once baptizing the child of a noble-man in Henry the Seventh's Chapel, and one of the godfathers was another nobleman, who had just succeeded to a marquisate, and had been, for nearly fifty years, a member of the House of Commons. He had spent a great part of his life under the shadow of the Abbey, and was a man of ability and culture—yet he told me that, during that half century, he had scarcely once so much as entered the building, and knew nothing about it !

Down to the days of the Declaration of Independence the Abbey and its history is as much the inheritance of Americans as of Englishmen. Many of the graves and monuments in it—such as those of Earl Howe, and Sir Peter Warren, and Major André, and Sir J. Burgoyne, are almost more interesting to them than to Englishmen. It contains, in the window given by Mr. G. W. Childs to the memory of the two sacred poets, George Herbert and William Cowper, the *only* free gift, other than a bust or statue, that has been bestowed upon it in living memory. The bust of Longfellow, occupying so prominent a place in the south transept, is a beautiful sign that the two great nations, which are in truth but one nation, regard the literature of each as a common heritage ; and though I have no right to speak in any name but my own, I, for one, should heartily rejoice, if it were possible to have memorials also for such reformers as William Lloyd Garrison, such rulers as Washington, General Grant, and Abraham Lincoln, and such writers as Nathaniel Hawthorne and James Russell Lowell. Twice within the last six years we have had funeral services to commemorate the deaths of two of those eminent Americans whom I have mentioned, General Grant and Mr. Lowell ; and I esteem it no small honor that, on both occasions, the privilege of delivering the funeral discourse was mine.

I have said that, " *if it were possible,*" England would rejoice to place in her great and sacred mausoleum the monuments of the most famous Americans. But it is no longer possible, or can only be so, at the utmost, for a few years more. This fact renders it necessary to raise the question as to " the *future* of Westminster Abbey." The question has just occupied the attention of a Royal Commission, of which I shall speak further on.

The present state of things is this : If there be but one burial every year, the use of the Abbey as a place of *interment* for the illustrious dead might last for a century longer. But in that case any *monument* will be out of the question. The Abbey is already desperately overcrowded with tombs and cenotaphs. In the last century an enormous space was allotted to not a few whose reputations have proved to be only ephemeral, and to some who were, even in their own day, unknown to fame. At the present moment there is room for only two statues more ; and it is not difficult to name the two world-famous Englishmen—the great poet and the great statesman—for whom those two last places would be unanimously reserved. But even for the much humbler memorial of a bust, or a tablet, there is scarcely an inch of space. On November 2 the bust of Matthew Arnold was unveiled, and it is placed in the dark baptistery, where it is scarcely observed. I doubt whether the utmost ingenuity of the Dean and Chapter could find any space at all—even the most inappropriate and out of sight—for a dozen more busts of great men.

And already the want of space has led to unfortunate results. Mr. Gilbert's beautiful monument to Henry Fawcett in the baptistery is but half discernible in the darkness ; and the busts of Lords Lansdowne and Lord Russell have, of necessity, been thrust into obscure and unnoticed corners. The character of monumental records has thus been distinctly deteriorated.

"*To-morrow, victory or Westminster Abbey,*" said Nelson, on the eve of the battle of the Nile. But long before Nelson, in the days of the Commonwealth, Clarendon tells us that the body of the great Admiral Blake was brought all the way from Plymouth and, " with all solemnity possible, interred in Henry the Seventh's Chapel, among the monuments of the kings," because Cromwell wished "to *encourage his officers to venture their lives.*"

It would be idle to maintain that the prospect of such a posthumous honor is a matter of indifference to noble-hearted men. The Athenian felt- that it was no small reward to a hero if they painted his portrait in the Poecile ; and though, as Pericles said, "of illustrious men, the whole earth is a tomb," yet illustrious men, and those who love and follow them, have felt that there is a strong incentive in the desire to earn the memorial of national gratitude. " *Well then, Westminster Abbey let it be !*" said the dying Grattan, not without satisfaction. A Roman writer esteemed it the highest honor if he could look forward to the day when his bust should have a place in the Palatine Library founded by Augustus. George Eliot knew that she could hardly, as yet, have a tablet in the Abbey, but she did not shrink from showing by a sigh her regret.

Every man and woman who rises but an inch or two above that dead level of mediocrity, "in which every molehill is a mountain and every thistle a forest tree," has much to endure in life from the stupidity, the calumnies, the envy, and the misrepresentations of contemporaries. Browning, in answer to one of those misguided persons who had sent him an abusive article on his books, with the simple question, " *Is this poetry ?*" replied, that " he had too much experience that the human goose cackles when it is pleased, and hisses when it is malignant, ever to lift heel against what waddles behind it." But it is some consolation even to the greatest of the dead to hope that, when Death hath silenced " the chatter of irresponsible frivolity "—the sounds which, as someone has said, are the emptiest, and which therefore Echo loves—" those unknown voices which bellow in the shade, and swell the language of falsehood and of hate "—then the national gratitude of all who judge just judgment will accord them such recognition as they have honorably won.

Hitherto the memorials of the greater number of our most famous dead have been gathered in one great shrine for all men to

see. The dust of kings and rulers has mingled with the dust of
men born in the humblest ranks of life and ennobled by genius
alone. Poets, some of whom in life lacked bread, have here at least
found a stone ; * and philanthropists, whose lives were endangered by the fury of banded interests and appetites, find
that there is posthumous honor for those who have striven to
undo the heavy burden and let the oppressed go free. Thus the
Abbey furnishes a multitude of lessons. There is scarcely a
single point at which it does not touch the great interests of
English history. The kings of France, as Dean Stanley loved to
point out, lie almost alone at St. Denis, and the popes of Rome
at St. Peter's ; the kings of Spain lie alone at the Escorial; the
emperors of Austria at Vienna ; the czars of Russia at Moscow
and St. Petersburg; but at Westminster, the humblest, who were
great by goodness, repose in death by the side of their sovereigns.
Again there are churches like SS. Giovannie Paolo at Venice, and
Santa Maria Novella at Florence, which contain the memorials of
some of the famous dead. But there is no other building in
the whole world where the visitor can trace the traditions, or study
the records, or stand over the mortal remains of men who represent nearly all that is greatest in the national story of nearly
nine centuries. Under one roof lie not only

" The painful warrior, famoused for fight,"

but also the statesmen, the teachers, the divines, the orators, the
musicians, the actors, the novelists, the explorers, the discoverers,
the men of science, and the sweet singers—often sculptured as
they stood in life with their garlands and singing robes about
them. Of painters, we have only one—Sir Godfrey Kneller.

Crowded sources of interest make a visit to Westminster Abbey memorable to multitudes, of very different gifts. The student
of Catholicism rightly recognizes in its minutest details a subtle
and profound symbolism, intended to impress upon the soul the
great doctrines of the Trinity, the Incarnation and the Atonement.
The great architect sees in its exquisite proportions an epic poem
in stone. For the man of poetic sensibility,

" Bubbles burst. and folly's raging foam
Melts, if he cross the threshold."

---

* On the tomb of Samuel Butler, author of " Hudibras," the elder Wesley wrote:
" See him when starved to death and turned to dust
Rewarded with a monumental bust :
The poet's fate is here in semblance shown.
He asked for bread, and he received—a stone !"

The sculptor sees in it the most extensive and wonderful of all schools of statuary, showing every phase of varying influence which affected the plastic arts from their beginning. The herald may study in it the rise, the decline, and the obliteration of the art of emblazonment. The student of religious development reads in the changing forms of the tombs the thoughts respecting life and death which prevailed in the ages of faith, of reform, of insincerity and compromise. The man of letters feels himself nearer to his most eminent predecessors as he recalls a hundred anecdotes which connect the story of their lives with this or that spot in the venerable building. The historian finds inspiration for great themes in its endless suggestiveness. To the archæologist it is a storehouse of authentic records illustrative of customs and costumes long obsolete. Even the man who is profoundly ignorant, and has no tincture of any science, must be less than human if he does not feel its awe-inspiring impressiveness. And yet nearly all these manifold interests are beside and subsidiary to the main purpose of the Church—as a place of great and solemn assemblages and functions ; as a place where, in the rendering of the masterpieces of sacred music, we may hear

> " the pealing organ blow
> To the full-voiced choir below,
> In music high and anthems clear,
> As may with sweetness through mine ear
> Dissolve me into ecstasies
> And bring all heaven before mine eyes ; "

as a place, above all, where, day by day and year by year, through the long centuries, with sincere and loving devotion, though with very diverse opinions, men have listened to God's word, and uplifted their hearts in humble prayer.

The question, then, has arisen, in the minds of those who love their country, Whether this precious possession shall—so far as its most unique men are concerned—belong wholly to the past, and, by a sudden and grievous discontinuity, the memorials of the present and the future be severed from it ?—or whether it shall be so extended as still to concentrate within its sacred precints the grandest associations of England's fame ? Can any man, other than some worldly cynic, give any but one answer ?

When Cyrus wanted to tame the pride of the great river Gyndes he diverted the current into a multitude of channels. Will

England gain if the memorials of her history are henceforth scattered in a multitude of different churches and cemeteries ? If this would involve a national loss, can it be averted ? This was practically the question which had to be considered by the " Royal Commission appointed to inquire into the present want of space for monuments in Westminster Abbey," of which the first report, presented to both houses of Parliament by command of the Queen, in 1890, lies before me.

The Commissioners were unfortunately only six in number. The result was an even vote for two different proposals. The Commissioners were the Right Honorable D. Plunket, Sir Henry Layard, Sir F. Leighton, Dean Bradley, Mr. Jennings, M. P., and Mr. Waterhouse, the President of the Royal Institute of British Architects.

Much interesting evidence was elicited in their report. That some extension of, or addition to, the Abbey was needed, all were agreed. All were also agreed as to the desirability of pulling down the houses in Old Palace Yard. These houses are not only unsightly and obtrusive, but they threaten the Abbey with chances of destruction by fire. A much larger scheme of clearance was approved by the Embankment Commission in 1863. A clear view of the ancient buildings would thus be thrown open in the midst of a street, which, if the embankment were completed, would be the most magnificent in London, and perhaps in the world.

Many plans have been suggested, some of which I will mention: The scheme proposed in 1863 by Sir Gilbert Scott and approved (it is said) by the Prince Consort, was to sweep away a large number of houses and build a large cloister. To this scheme there would be the double objection of (1) enormous costliness, and (2) the remoteness of the new memorials from the Abbey Church, which, as it were, lends to them their consecration.

It has been suggested:

1. To utilize the immense Triforium, by removing thither some of the unsuitable and unsightly monuments. Access to the Triforium might be given by a spiral staircase. This plan would, at the best, be a makeshift. It has met with no favor. It would make of the Triforium, as Sir F. Leighton says, a *salon des refusés*.

2. To utilize the green strip of land which runs along St. Margaret's churchyard, by building a chapel and cloister.* This

* Suggested by Mr. Pearson, R. A.

is practically impossible. Public opinion would not permit the partial concealment of the present north side of the Abbey.

3. To utilize the site of the large ancient refectory of the monks, which runs along the side of the south cloister, and is now included in the garden of Ashburnham House. The house and garden had been, from time immemorial, in the possession of the Abbey, but were taken from it in 1881, in accordance with a clause introduced into an Act of Parliament with very little discussion in 1868. I shall always think that this was a high-handed and unwarranted procedure ; but the mischief is done, and as there is very little chance that it will now be undone, this scheme of re-building the old refectory as a mortuary chapel is not likely to be carried out.

4. To utilize the existing cloisters and the garth which they surround. But the garth already contains the mortal relics of generations of Benedictine monks ; the cloister walls are so crowded with monuments, that, unless these were removed,— which would be hardly fair,—only a few irregular spaces are left ; and under the cloister stones, during six centuries, no fewer than 1,757 persons, at least, have been interred. Apart from the fact that the cloisters are already thronged with memorials, this suggestion was almost universally condemned as inadequate.

5. To build " a wreath of chapels " between the buttresses of the Chapter-House. Such chapels, however, would be comparatively insignificant in themselves, and the public sentiment would never be brought to connect them with the great shrine. Nor would they admit of the solemn and stately services at the burial of great men which are now felt to be intensely impressive.

6. The sixth plan, with various minor modifications, is to build out from the Abbey a splendid memorial chapel, facing the Houses of Parliament, and connected with the Abbey itself by a wide cloister under the buttresses of the Chapter House. This plan was approved by the eminent architect, Mr. Fergusson ; and is also approved by the present distinguished architect of the Abbey, Mr. J. L. Pearson. It is identified with the name of the Right Hon. Shaw Lefevre, who, not only as First Commissioner of Works in 1880–1884, but ever since, has shown an enlightened and patriotic interest in this great question. The plan could have been accomplished in the year of the Queen's Jubilee, and would have provided for the English-speaking race, not only a

splendid monument of the long reign of Queen Victoria, but also a resource which would have lasted for centuries. First and last, indeed, involving, as it does, the purchase of sites and the demolition of houses, it would have cost at least £150,000. During the rejoicings of the Jubilee year this sum could have been raised by subscription with the aid of a government grant. It has the Queen's approval and sympathy, but Her Majesty "did not wish it to interfere with the scheme for the erection of an Imperial Institute, to which her consent had already been given as the principal monument of her Jubilee." Nothing, therefore, has yet been attempted in this direction,—but in spite of the dissent of three of the Commissioners, it may safely be prognosticated that this scheme alone will be regarded as possible, desirable, and adequate.

It remains to be seen whether the enthusiasm for England and her history is sufficient to stimulate the requisite energy and munificence. If not, if the memorials of the dead are henceforth scattered in various churches, and Westminster Abbey, so long the pride and glory of England, loses its splendid continuity of associations—I cannot but think that the omen will be disastrous. When, in the great church of San Paolo Fuori le Mura, at Rome, it was found that, after Pio Nono, there would be no room for the likeness of another Pope, the incident was thought to foreshadow an eclipse of Papal power. It would be not only an omen but a disaster, if, for lack of generosity, of public spirit, or of sense of our national duty to the past and the future, Westminster Abbey should cease to maintain its ancient influence. It would prove that we were degenerate sons of the fathers who have not only bequeathed to us the example of so many noble deeds, but who also enshrined the memory of those who wrought them in a church meant to be like the temple of Solomon, "exceeding magnifical, of fame, and of glory throughout all countries."

May the influence and public opinion of America help to convince England of the necessity for taking early steps to build, in closest connection with the Abbey, some grand memorial chapel which shall enable generations yet unborn to pay worthy honor to the famous dead, alike of the old home and of the Western world !

F. W. FARRAR.

WHAT I EXPECT TO DO IN AFRICA.

BY PROF. R. L. GARNER.

THE prime purpose of my visit to the wilds of West Africa is to study the speech and habits of those great anthropoid apes which inhabit the jungle of that low, marshy country lying under the equator, some three hundred miles north of the mouth of the Congo River. In order to do this, it is necessary for one to take up his abode in the deep forest, that he may become familiar with the domestic life and conditions of those man-like creatures and study them in a state of nature untouched by the influences of captivity or changed conditions.

To make sure of certain results, I shall call to my aid all the engines of human invention which may conduce to my success, and my outfit will embrace a phonograph, a photo-camera, telephones, electric battery, etc., the uses of which are quite evident; but the peculiar manner of applying them will be of interest to all. The most important feature of my outfit, however, is a cage which I have designed for the trip, and without which the use of some of my implements would be impossible. The cage is made of steel wire woven into a diamond-shaped lattice, with a two-inch mesh, and framed in strong steel frames. Each panel of the cage is three feet six inches square, and there are in all twenty-four panels, each one interchangeable with all the rest, so that they can be united with ease into a cube of seven feet square, and any side will serve for top or bottom, and any panel can be used as a door.

The uses of my cage will be very numerous. It can be erected as easily as a tent, and will be used at night to camp in. It will serve me as a house while I may be detained in making terms with the natives or studying their speech ; and it will be a fortress in the jungle, where I must spend much of my time in trying to find the secret which I seek.   But the use of my cage will not be limited to a mere place of safety from the wild beasts that prowl through the forests at night; it will serve also as a depot for my supplies, and thus save me the trouble and expense of having to find a place of safety for them in case of delay or absence.   This structure will be locked securely to the adjacent trees by three strong chains attached to a Y-shaped iron bolted through the top of the cage.   It will be provided with a canvas top and gum-cloth sides, mounted on rollers like window curtains, and easily managed.   It will be provided with a soft rubber mat or carpet, which will serve as an insulator when the cage is charged with electricity, and will also prevent the moisture from rising from the ground beneath the cage, in which I shall have to sleep a great part of the time.   It will contain hammock and camp chair.   Besides these it will be occupied by my phonograph, photographic instruments, telephones, and electric battery with which to operate them.   A single charge of this electric battery will last for about 300 consecutive hours.   By the use of a small switchboard I shall be able to fire my flash light at night, or to snap my kodak in the daytime, and to operate my telephones if necessary. In case of danger or unexpected attack, by the use of my switchboard and by means of an induction coil, I can charge the entire cage with electricity, developing an alternating current of about 300 volts.   In leaving my cage with its contents for any length of time, I shall simply charge it in this manner with electricity, in order that in my absence my meddlesome neighbors may be induced to let it alone.

A unique and marvellous experiment among the many which I expect to be able to perform, is that of phonographing the sounds of the apes at a distance from my cage, where my phonograph will be located at times.   I shall accomplish this by means of the telephones which I am having constructed for the purpose with a water-proof cable wire connected at one end with the diaphragm of the phonograph, and at the other end (which may be carried any distance, even a mile or more through the forest) connected with a small telephone concealed in a tin horn; all of which will be painted a dingy green in order that it may be concealed in the leaves or hidden in the moss or undergrowth of the forest.   In front of this horn will be placed decoys, baits, effigies, mirrors, or such other means as may be found necessary to induce the chimpanzees and gorillas to utter their sounds there, which sounds, of course, will be immediately transmitted to and recorded on the phonograph cylinder, which will be operated by electricity.

I shall be provided with some globes for incandescent light. They will be connected with the battery and placed in such positions that in case of alarm during the night the cause may be easily ascertained by simply switching on the light for a few seconds. If it is found that anything within the field of my kodak shall be worth photographing, the flash light will be fired and the picture taken, including the cage and its surroundings. Amid the deep silence of the forest, I shall take a photograph at night-fall, one at midnight, and one at dawn, thus preserving a vivid idea of the approach of darkness, the appearance of the forest by artificial light in the dead, still hours of night, and the awakening of life in the early dawn, when the first rays of sunlight glance through the foliage wet with tropical dew.

I expect to be able to secure photographic views of the home life of these great apes, as also of the natives of the same regions. I hope to secure photographs of their mouths in the act of talking, and at the same time the phonographic records showing the sounds they utter. With the aid of my phonograph I shall record and bring home the sounds of all the creatures of those deep forests that utter speech ; and with my camera shall preserve for civilized man a faithful panorama of the royal families, of the warriors armed with their simple instruments of death, the beaux and belles of royal society in evening dress, the peasantry, slaves and social parasites, the wild beasts, the tropical birds, and even the slimy serpents that infest the Eden of tropical Africa. I shall secure the social and religious songs, the rites and ceremonies, the music and speech of the people. I shall take photographs of their homes, which will afford a vivid idea of the domestic life and habits of this curious people, as they may be found worshipping their deities or dancing in their sins. We may thus ascertain how much bondage and civilization have respectively wrought for this race, by comparing their condition with that of their kinsmen in America, who have grown up under the influences of civilization. This will be an important ethnological fact to determine.

Of course my outfit will include some deadly weapons,—a rifle and a revolver, with 2,000 rounds of ammunition. In addition I shall use a silent and, for certain purposes, far more deadly weapon.   To fire a gun in the forest would, of course, alarm the animals within a radius of half a mile, and repeated firing would eventually drive them from the locality.   I have therefore devised a gun and missile suited to my special use.   The gun barrel is simply a straight reed about four feet long, bored out smooth and uniform, and the missile is driven by the force imparted by two strong rubber bands and two steel springs.   The weapon is charged with an arrow or dart having a steel head of peculiar de. sign, which is forced open on entering its quarry, the contents of the arrow-head being thereby discharged.   This arrow-head will contain fifteen drops of prussic acid.   In case I shall see an animal or a group of animals which I may desire to secure, by the use of this instrument I can secure either one or all of them, without unnecessary injury or alarm.   The effect of this acid discharged in the blood is almost instantaneous and painless death.   The dart, however, may be used to carry other kinds of poison, or used without any ; or the gun itself may be used with other missiles.

My masked battery consists of a rubber canteen of my own device, to which is attached a hose about two feet long, on the end of which is a metallic nozzle, provided with a ring to fit the fourth finger, and a valve opening and closing like a flute key. The canteen will be worn buckled under the arm, while the ring on the nozzle will be worn on the fourth finger of the right hand, so that it may be used on the instant in case of surprise.   This battery will be charged with concentrated ammonia, a douche of which in close quarters will set the most ferocious beast to think- ing.   When free from action the valve is shut tight ; on closing any part of the hand it opens, and the weight of the arm dis- charges the pungent contents of the battery.   I shall also use this battery in the capture of such small game or insects as I may wish to procure without maiming.   Having stifled them with the am- monia, I can administer chloroform, if I wish, so as to extinguish life without giving pain.   I shall carry with me also such utensils and chemicals as taxidermists use for preparing skins and skeletons of animals for mounting.   As our acquaintance with the *fauna* of this part of the world is so limited, it is quite possible that I may obtain some specimens hitherto unknown.   The same may be said of the *flora.*

I shall carry with me the usual camp and medical outfit.   My medical case, presented to me by Mrs. M. French Sheldon, whose recent journey through East Africa has been the wonder of modern travel, is a duplicate of that used by herself, with some additions made by experienced physicians. My camp equipment will embrace the lightest possible utensils. I shall go alone, with the exception of a cook and body servant, and from time to time twenty-five carriers, all natives. My travels will be necessarily slow, impeded by heavy burdens and long stops at the end of short stages, as the purpose is to study as thoroughly as possible the topography and geography of the country and its native products, as well as the speech of its inhabitants. Encouraged by the success of my experiments with monkeys and other lower animals, I have faith enough in my own ability to believe that I will find a means of communicating intelligently with the anthropoid apes which I am now about to visit. If I succeed in establishing the possibility of this communication, I shall accomplish for science what all the efforts of mankind have failed to do heretofore. If I fail to establish it and instead should prove the negative of the proposition I shall not have deprived science of any part of its acquired knowledge, but shall settle forever the controversy among men on that subject. I do not expect to find in those animals a high type of speech, but only one in keeping with their mental and domestic state and their surroundings, capable of expressing their passions and emotions, and the simple wants incident to such a state of life. Whatever may be the nature or value of their sounds, I shall at least record them on the phonograph and preserve them for science. So strong is my conviction of my ability to learn their language, that I undertake this journey at my own expense, with my life in one hand and my equipment in the other. Impelled by an honest zeal, and attended by the prayers of earnest friends, I shall seek the depths of the unbroken forests, and wrest the secret from those man-like creatures upon the threshold of their own abode.

I am aware of the fact that such a journey is beset with dangers, many of which are unforeseen. Without any desire to be sentimental or romantic, I do assert in candor that I would rather make this journey and succeed and die in poverty, than to forego it and fail, worth the wealth of India. I am not a fanatic upon whom the thought has suddenly dawned, for I have persistently sought for years that one great secret—the first form of speech. My labors in this field have been fairly successful, notwithstanding every conceivable disadvantage of working with the lower creatures of the simian type hampered by the surroundings of zoological gardens. If it was possible to accomplish so much with such odds against me, am I not justified in the most exalted hopes for the result of my expedition? And when I return in triumph, which I shall do, those who now deride and ridicule so wild an undertaking, may yet bow their uncovered heads to the truth.

While I have given here some details of my trip as I contemplate it, I must not be held as pledged to adhere to any special mode or means. If the plans I have laid shall fail, new ones will be thought out and put to the test. I feel adequate to the task of meeting these animals on their own grounds, believing that my intelligence will be equal to their brute strength. I am willing to forego the comforts of civilized life, the endearments of home, and the blessings of health and plenty, and take upon myself the hardships, the privations and the toil of such a journey, that I may give to the world the secret with which to pass the gates of speech. I ask no reward but success, I seek no end but truth, and to accomplish this I stake all there is in life.

If the good wishes and benedictions which are daily showered upon me could be realized, my journey through the jungle would be a triumphal march, over a pathway of flowers, but, alas! they cannot change the grim aspect of those solitudes nor banish the ghosts of disease which lurk in the marshes of that torrid coast; but it will lighten the burden and lessen the toil of the march to know that true hearts are measuring my absence, and kind lips are pleading for my safety.

RICHARD L. GARNER.

A MODERN FORM OF INSANITY.

BY DR. HENRY SMITH WILLIAMS, MEDICAL SUPERINTENDENT
OF THE RANDALL'S ISLAND HOSPITALS.

A CONSIDERABLE section of the annals of modern crime is
devoted to the misdeeds of a class of individuals who in common
parlance are termed "cranks." In the courts, the sanity of these
persons is often in question. It is commonly assumed that only
by hair-splitting refinements of analysis can criminals of this
class be brought within the pale of that charity which is everywhere accorded to the unsound mind. Yet the fact is that the
great majority of these unfortunates are the victims of a definite
disease of the brain and mind. This disease is called Paranoia.

Before studying the development of this disease, let us glance
at a few illustrative cases. That of the man Roth, who attempted
to shoot Dr. Hall, is typical. His belief, as noted in the daily
press, was that he had for years been persistently persecuted by
persons of eminence. The agents used were electricity, poison
in his food, etc. He believed Dr. Hall and his congregation to
be responsible for most of his sufferings. As threatening letters
failed to frighten the conspirators, he called attention to the
matter in a more emphatic way. He does not doubt that what
he did was perfectly right. Another notorious case is that of
Dougherty, who shot Dr. Lloyd at the Flatbush Asylum. He
believed that a prominent actress loved him, but that she was
prevented from seeing him by a league of enemies, who not only
thwarted him in his love affair, but persecuted him in every way.
The asylum authorities, who had detained him for a time, were
in his mind parties to the crime, so he thought himself justified
in going back after his escape and shooting Dr. Lloyd.

The following case, which barely escaped notoriety, is of
interest. A minister regularly occupying a pulpit had for years
devoted his spare hours to researches in philology. At last he
came to believe that he had discovered the origin of language,

and that his secret was known to the Hebrew people, who wished to keep it from the world. He based his belief on imagined cryptograms in the ancient Jewish writings. Later, he discovered similar cross-readings in the daily papers, and, strangely enough, these always made personal reference to himself. He was forced to believe that the foreman of every printing-office in the world was a Hebrew, placed there for the purpose of so juggling the types as to convey messages by a cipher system to all other Hebrews. Some of these messages, being interpreted, directed that he should be killed. He took measures to protect himself, especially at night, when he slept with an axe at his bedside ; and, finally, he determined to retaliate by killing certain of the offending foremen. Fortunately, he was restrained before he could execute this design. This man, while brooding over such thoughts, preached weekly from his own pulpit. Similar cases might be cited indefinitely. The details vary, but the essential symptoms are the same,—the presence of systematized delusions of persecution.

Thus much foreshadowed, let us consider the disease from its incipiency. Paranoia, more than any other form of insanity, is the result of inherited mental instability. Insanity, like most other diseases, is not directly transmissible as such. What is transmitted is an unstable nervous system, and this may be the heritage of a person in whose family there has never been a case of insanity,—if such a family exists. Perhaps a progenitor has been a drunkard or the victim of some wasting disease. His descendant may be merely nervous ; he may have chorea or epilepsy; he may become insane. At the best, he may usually, if properly educated, learn to understand himself and to live a sane and useful life. We have here to do, however, only with the cases in which a wrong environing influence aids in the development of a particular form of insanity. It is possible to outline pretty definitely the mental attributes. One may even point out in the child what might be termed the paranoiac temperament. Its characteristics are morbid sensitiveness and great egotism.

Unfortunately the parents of such a child usually take pride in the egoism that leads to eccentric acts ; while the extreme precocity of many of these subjects causes their egotism to be fostered by ill-adjudged praise. Usually the child of paranoiac temperament is the genius of his family and the show pupil at school. Pampered and praised, even though the entire household becomes subordinated to his sovereign will, he is not satisfied, believing that he does not receive his dues. With that idea, the germs of paranoia are planted in his mind. Whether or not these germs will develop into the pathological condition that we are discussing, will depend largely upon the influences that are brought to bear upon them during adolescence and early manhood. Perhaps the most unfavorable environment is one in which the mind is developed at the expense of the body. And, of course, the brilliant child is the one whose mental training will be forced. The other children of the family may stay at home, but this one must be sent to college and fitted for one of the learned professions. Usually he seems to justify this discrimination. Often he is an " honor " man at college, and he starts out into the world with every seeming prospect of an eminently prosperous career.

But all this time he has become more and more eccentric. He has associated little with his fellows. Often he has shown himself possessed of extraordinary energy and capacity for application. A peculiarity often noted is a tendency to make elaborate written records of trivial subjects. I knew one person who had literally kept a record as to every minute of his time since boyhood. Day after day, and year after year, such records as this would occur : "Arose at six ; five minutes for exercise ; ten minutes bathing ; twelve dressing. Read Shakespeare thirty-three minutes. Breakfast one minute late ; at table till 7:20. Walked to the office in twenty-seven minutes "—and so on throughout the day. Stupendous indeed must be the egotism that could imagine any possible future value in such wearisome details of a commonplace existence.

Occasionally the young person of paranoiac temperament breaks down under the unbalancing influences of overstudy while still at school. But usually the critical stress comes after he has gone out into the world. He is usually not yet insane. He may never become so. If his business or professional ventures succeed, he may become distinguished, and contact with the world may gradually correct the morbid tendencies. But if adverse circumstances arise and refuse to be put down, especially if the individual's vanity is wounded by failure to rise to the heights pictured by ambition, morbid brooding may develop out of vanity, selfishness, and suspicion, the delusion of persecution.

But it must not be supposed that the mature condition is merely egotism and egoism run riot. That it has come to be something more than this is proved by the appearance, sooner or later, of hallucinations of one or more of the senses. These do not necessarily coincide at first with delusions. The incipient paranoiac may hear voices about him and for a time be able to convince himself of their unreality. But, sooner or later, these , sounds become so tangible that they have the full force and import of actual voices. At first he hears them only when people are actually speaking, his mind merely misinterpreting what it hears. This perversion is technically termed an illusion. But at last he hears words and sentences when no real sound comes to his ears : these are true hallucinations. Perversions of other senses usually precede or follow this one. Illusions of touch and smell are common. The former lead to a belief in invisible spirits that touch the body ; and the latter convince the patient that attempts are being made to poison him with noxious gases. When to this cluster of perverted sensations hallucinations of sight are added, the galaxy is complete, and the victim moves and has his being in an ideal world peopled with odors, tastes, sounds and sights that are shut out from the common herd. A patient who had reached this stage outlines his own feelings as follows : "I have gradually come to a positive assurance that the thoughts of my mind are shared by others, and that they act from that knowledge with a view of influencing me and directing my actions ; that the appearances of animate and inanimate nature also correspond to my thoughts in such a way as to check and direct them ; that ordinary speech and language are so perverted as to have a double meaning, the secondary sense relating to my actions or thoughts. All is so constituted as to form a distinct and new and strange world, in which, however, most objects remain familiar."

The last clause is of especial significance. The patient lives a dual existence. For a time he is able to treat the actual world in the old familiar way—that is, sanely ; meanwhile keeping the new and strange world hidden. But gradually he comes to confound the two existences. If, for example, on going out to mail a letter, he finds a group of men on the first corner discussing this very letter and repeating its contents, the incident has practical bearings that cannot be overlooked. If, now, such experiences multiply until he is followed wherever he goes by voices that discuss his most intimate secrets, it is not strange that he is dominated by the delusions. He comes to believe that hosts of people are leagued against him, and all sane interests give way to a desire to thwart those imagined foes.

At this stage of his morbid career the patient becomes very dangerous, though he may still seem to be the most peaceable of men. Murders are often committed by patients in this condition. But many more intended murders that are carefully planned are never executed because of the irresolution of the would-be murderer. A typical illustration from actual experience will best emphasize this point. A very intelligent young man, who had given up his position as principal of a school because of the machinations of imagined enemies, secured a position in the New York Post-Office. Before starting out on the first morning, he said, casually, to his wife, "I mean to interfere with no one, and to try to do my whole duty." No sooner had he begun work than first one and then another of his fellow employees began nodding toward him, saying sneeringly, "Oh, he's doing his whole duty ; of course we are not doing ours," and so on. Presently they began to repeat other sayings of his, and to tell of all manner of things connected with his private life. One man in particular made such outrageous insinuations that he felt called upon to retaliate. He never spoke in response, but procured a revolver, and resolved to shoot the most insolent of his tormentors. But, fortunately, this dangerous resolve was combated by another delusion. As soon as he entered the room he became certain that all the employees knew of the weapon, and that several were watching him, prepared to spring upon him when he attempted to use it. Finding his plans for personal revenge thus thwarted, he made complaint to an official. A detective was sent to investigate. Puzzled at first, he at last solved the problem and averted a tragedy.

All this time the insane man had gone on with his work, to all appearances as sane a man as could be found in the department. Similar cases come to the notice of every alienist. The secretiveness of these patients makes it impossible to predict as to when they will act. Suspecting everyone they usually make a confidant of no one ; and, as shown in the case just cited, they will quietly brook all manner of imagined insults while plotting a terrible revenge. Their victims are usually altogether unconscious of their purpose. The man who so narrowly escaped being shot in the instance just cited does not to this day suspect that he worked beside an insane man, much less that he had offended him, and that his life was hourly in jeopardy.

The next stage in the development of the paranoiac mind is, anomalous as it may seem, a perfectly logical one. A patient with the delusions just outlined naturally broods long and earnestly over the situation in which he is placed. Wherever he goes his enemies pursue him, and he may for a time be greatly depressed by the troubles that are no less real to him because they originate, and exist, only in his imagination. At times he may question whether the fault does not lie with himself. But this doubting stage is not of long duration. Gradually it dawns upon the patient that Goliath would not gird his loins against a dwarf, and that he who can be of such interest to so many classes of men must really be a person of importance. The native egotism with which paranoiacs are so largely endowed fosters and develops this idea. At first it is a vague and faltering belief, but in time it comes to be a firm and unwavering conviction. According to the native bent of the individual the grandiose ideas will take a political, a social, or a religious direction. Among the most typical cases are those in which the patient comes ultimately to think himself the inspired messenger of God,—the new Messiah. With such a fixed belief as this, and with the hallucinations of sight and hearing so developed that the patient sees visions and receives divine communications constantly, the disease Paranoia may be said to have reached its culmination. The patient still believes himself to be persecuted, but he now has courage to bear up against his enemies, with the assurance of ultimate victory.

It will be understood that in giving this sketch of the development of paranoia I am attempting nothing beyond the most general outline. I have called attention to what I consider the fundamental properties of the disease. I should consider no case entitled to rank as paranoia in which there did not appear at one time or another, (1) Delusions of persecution ; (2) Hallucinations; (3) Delusions of grandeur. But the relative importance of these typical conditions may vary greatly in different cases. Individual temperament and experience may so change the aspect of a case that these broad outlines are obscured. In a certain case, for example, the grandiose ideas may seem to be the first development of the disease. The patient goes to bed seemingly sane, and awakens with the idea that he is a president, king, or Deity. His delusions were masked, perhaps not more than vaguely outlined even in his own mind, and the excitement of a political campaign or religious revival, or some domestic or business catastrophe, has produced, at a bound, mental changes that otherwise might have been effected only after years of insane brooding. Usually in such cases there occurs a temporary recession of the disease when excitement has subsided.

In another case, the hallucinations may for a long time be masked and difficult of detection. In yet another, the grandiose ideas are of slow development or are concealed with great subtlety. The germ of the grandiose idea is present from the first, in the form of egotism and its outgrowth, great ambition ; but modesty or secretiveness—two traits often confounded—may keep the patient from divulging his hopes either before or after their culmination in delusions of grandeur. The grandiose idea is, after all, only a day-dream come to seem an actuality ; and the most visionary of day-dreamers are not usually the most free to express their aspirations in words. Moreover, grandiose ideas, like all other things, are relative. Here is one patient whose highest flight of grandiosity makes him only a police captain; while beside him is another, not one whit more insane, who is the Pope and the secular king of the world as well. The one when sane was of little education and low position ; the other, a man of culture and position.

Again, all cases of paranoia are subject to periodic vacillations. There are periods of stress and strain, times of excitation when the manifestations of disease are vivid and pronounced. Then there may be long periods of remission when the insane ideas seem dormant. But back of all variation there is, as it were, an undercurrent of remorseless fate driving the victim on and on through channels of delusion and hallucination towards the paranoiac ultimatum, the delusion of grandeur. And when once this paranoiac seal is set upon a victim its stamp is ineffaceable. The characteristics of the disease, already outlined, sufficiently explain why this is so. On the physical side, it appears that there is going on a steady degeneration of a brain that was at best ill-developed. This degeneration, however, does not become sufficient to endanger the patient's life ; nor even to produce the very marked general dementia which is the goal of every other chronic form of insanity. Year after year, and decade after decade, the paranoiac may go on his erratic way, nursing an ever-multiplying host of delusions, building castles of sand, and wildly pursuing *ignes fatui.* If he has artistic or literary tastes he may produce, spasmodically, brilliant works, but his efforts are seldom long sustained in one direction.

Usually from time to time it suits his fancy to devote his energies to the cause of some reform league for revolutionizing society or the government. If his native temperament be amiable he will be simply a fanatic, perhaps a socialist; if vicious, he will probably become an anarchist. He is usually nothing if not progressive, and a new fad, especially if it be an occult one, is meat and drink to him. Revivalism, spiritualism, faith cure, Christian science, theosophy are his pastimes. In short, everything that is vague, visionary, occult, finds a following—often the originator—among the paranoiac ranks. They will propagandize these ideas from the house tops, but their own personal delusions are usually kept sacredly locked in their own bosoms. But their eccentricities of manner and speech usually cause their sanity to be called in question from time to time. If because of outrageous conduct they are placed in an asylum, often some acquaintance, regarding them as sane, stands ready with a writ of habeas corpus. And when brought before the sheriff's jury, they are usually discharged as perfectly sane. There are numbers of them at large in the community to-day, planning and from time to time executing such crimes as have already been cited, who have been released from one asylum or another by juries who believed that they did their duty. No doubt the average juror judges honestly in these cases according to his light, but his light is very dim.

It is, in fact, no easy matter to fathom some of these cases. The patient may understand fully what are regarded as his delusions, and may be able to discuss the psychological aspects of his case with acumen and brilliancy. If he is disposed to be candid, his peculiar interpretations will give the clue to his disease. But, quite as often, he intentionally hides all delusional ideas, and scornfully repudiates them if they are suggested. In some cases, dissembling is carried on to an extent that renders detection almost impossible. I have known a patient, influenced by delusions, to drive his wife from the house with furious threats against

her life ; and a minute later to meet the neighbors, who were summoned, with a smiling face, a manner of surprised benignity, and
with a scriptural quotation on his lips.   To decide on such a case
as that requires something more than casual observation and a
surface knowledge of psychology.

·Many people suppose that an insane man can be known as
such at a glance.   Such should be informed that many paranoiacs have pleasant, benignant faces, altogether unsuggestive of
their disease.   The "maniac eye" is largely a device of fiction.
But imagination is a wondrous perverter of our senses, and of
course everyone can see a wild glare in the eye of a "madman"
who has committed a murder, though the glare would have been
undiscovered had the same man come before a jury on a writ of
habeas corpus instead.   Looking upon the head of the bomb-
thrower, Norcross, a reporter wrote : "The face is one of those
which once seen can never be forgotten.   Meeting the owner of
the face for the first time, the casual observer would instinctively
associate him with revolution, anarchy, socialism, dynamite, and
feverish unrest."   But a man who had known him in life,
viewing this same "anarchistic" face said : "Norcross was
about the last person I would suspect of throwing a bomb
to take any one's life, or of contemplating suicide.   He
was mild-mannered and prepossessing in appearance.   In other
words, he was a fine, respectable, gentlemanly-looking fellow."
Comment in this relation is unnecessary.

Throughout this discussion I have, for the sake of convenience,
used the masculine gender.   It perhaps hardly needs to be
said that women are equally subject to the disease.   Its broad
outlines are the same in both sexes, but among females certain
minor modifications are noted.   Female paranoiacs less frequently
commit murders or other atrocities, but they do what perhaps is
worse, they blast the reputation of many innocent men,—ministers perhaps more often than any other class.   About the commonest of delusions, especially with spinster paranoiacs, is that
of being drugged and assaulted at night.   Auditory and olfactory
hallucinations furnish the foundation for these beliefs.   An es-
timable woman of this class has recently published a book in
which she gravely narrates delusions of this kind in detail.   Fortunately the context affords a key to her accusations.   Similar
works have been published from time to time, each one in sub-

stance like its fellows; all breathing earnestness, honesty, and delusion on every page. They illustrate the fulness of faith with which the paranoiac contemplates the air castles of his perverted mind.

The reader of the foregoing pages will doubtless feel that Paranoia has been made to seem a very dreadful and very hopeless condition. In truth, it is all that it seems. The paranoiac is the curse of his friends, the despair of his neighbors, a menace to society. And yet he has his place in the social organism. He is in the evolution of society what the "sport" is in the Darwinian scheme. Differing in mental conformation from his fellows, he must needs move in different channels from the generality of mankind. In other words, he must be the originator of new ideas, new methods, new actions. In the vast majority of cases his line of departure is not a useful one to humanity, so, according to the law of the survival of the fittest, he and his methods are weeded out. Occasionally his line of departure is in a beneficial direction. His methods then survive, his reforms are promulgated; he becomes a great prophet, a great genius; he is immortalized. Here, and here only, lies the point of contact between genius and insanity. Not all geniuses are insane, and few indeed are the insane who have a spark of genius. The rare exceptions are the paranoiacs whose perverted energies have chanced to carry them to useful fields not hitherto explored.

I have adverted to this phase of the subject because I wish to point a moral which I would that every parent and every director of the forming mind could take to heart. It is this : Whenever there comes under your care one of those eccentric, brilliant, precocious children whom you are prone to regard as a budding genius, learn to believe that you have probably to do with incipient paranoia instead, and govern yourself accordingly. By restraining the energies and checking the eccentricities of such a child you may do something towards moulding an aberrant mind back towards normality ; by stimulating the energies and fostering the germs of "genius" you may help to prepare a victim for an asylum or a prison. There is some hope that you may develop a sane man out of a child of paranoiac temperament; there is little fear that you will clip the wings of genius.

HENRY SMITH WILLIAMS.

THE SERVANT-GIRL'S POINT OF VIEW.

BY MRS. AMELIA E. BARR, AUTHOR OF "JAN VEDDER'S WIFE," "FRIEND OLIVIA," ETC.

A GREAT deal has been said lately on the servant-girl question, always from the mistresses' point of view ; and as no *ex-parte* evidence is conclusive, I offer for the servant-girl side some points that may help to a better understanding of the whole subject.

It is said, on all hands, that servants every year grow more idle, showy, impudent, and independent. The last charge is emphatically true, and it accounts for and includes the others. But then this independence is the necessary result of the world's progress, in which all classes share. Steam has made it easy for families to travel, who, without cheap locomotion, would never go one hundred miles from home. It has also made it easy for servants to go from city to city. When wages are low and service is plenty in one place, a few dollars will carry them to where they are in request.

Fifty years ago very few servants read, or cared to read. They are now the best patrons of a certain class of newspapers ; they see the " Want columns " as well as other people; and they are quite capable of appreciating the lessons they teach and the advantages they offer. The national increase of wealth has also affected the position of servants. People keep more servants than they used to keep ; and servants have less work to do. People live better than they used to live, and servants, as well as others, feel the mental uplifting that comes from rich and plentiful food.

But one of the main causes of trouble is, that a mistress even yet hires her servant with some ancient ideas about her inferiority. She forgets that servants read novels, and do fancy work, and

write lots of letters ; and that service can no longer be considered
the humble labor of a lower for a superior being. Mistresses must
now dismiss from their minds the idea of the old family servant
they have learned to meet in novels ; they must cease to look upon
service as in any way a family tie ; they must realize and practically acknowledge the fact that the relation between mistress and
servant is now on a purely commercial basis—the modern servant
being a person who takes a certain sum of money for the performance of certain duties. Indeed the condition has undergone
just the same change as that which has taken place in the relation
between the manufacturer and his artisans or between the contractor and his carpenters and masons.

It is true enough that servants take the money and do not perform the duties, or else perform them very badly. The manufacturer, the contractor, the merchant, all make the same complaint ; for independence and social freedom always step *before*
fitness for these conditions, because the condition is necessary for
the results, and the results are not the product of one generation.
Surely Americans may bear their domestic grievances without
much outcry, since they are altogether the consequences of education and progress, and are the circumstances which make possible
much higher and better circumstances.

For just as soon as domestic service is authoritatively and publicly made a commercial bargain, and all other ideas eliminated
from it, service will attract a much higher grade of women. The
independent, fairly well-read American girl will not sell her labor
to women who insist on her giving any part of her personality
but the work of her hands. She feels interference in her private
affairs to be an impertinence on any employer's part. She does
not wish any mistress to take an interest in her, to advise, to
teach, or reprove her. She objects to her employer being even
what is called "friendly." All she asks is to know her duties and
her hours, and to have a clear understanding as to her work and
its payment. And when service is put upon this basis openly, it
will draw to it many who now prefer the harder work, poorer
pay, but larger independence, of factories.

Servants are a part of our social system, but our social system
is being constantly changed and uplifted, and servants rise with
it. I remember a time in England when servants who did not
fulfil their year's contract were subject to legal punishment ;

when a certain quality of dress was worn by them, and those who over-dressed did so at the expense of their good name ; when they seldom moved to any situation beyond walking distance from their birthplace ; when, in fact, they were more slaves than servants. Would any good woman wish to restore service to this condition?

On the servant's part the root of all difficulty is her want of respect for her work ; and this, solely because her work has not yet been openly and universally put upon a commercial basis. When domestic service is put on the same plane as mechanical service, when it is looked upon as a mere business bargain, then the servant will not feel it necessary to be insolent and to do her work badly, simply to let her employer know how much she is above it. Much has been done to degrade service by actors, newspapers, and writers of all kinds giving to the domestic servant names of contempt as " flunkies," " menials," etc., etc. If such terms were habitually used regarding mechanics, we might learn to regard masons and carpenters with disdain. Yet domestic service is as honorable as mechanical service, and the woman who can cook a good dinner is quite as important to society as the man who makes the table on which it is served.

Yet, whether mistresses will recognize the change or not, service has in a great measure emancipated itself from feudal bonds. Servants have now a social world of their own, of which their mistresses know nothing at all. In it they meet their equals, make their friends, and talk as they desire. Without unions, without speeches, and without striking—because they can get what they want without striking—they have raised their wages, shortened their hours, and obtained many privileges. And the natural result is an independence,—which for lack of proper expression asserts itself by the impertinence and self-conceit of ignorance,— that has won more in tangible rights than in intangible respect.

Mistresses who have memories or traditions are shocked because servants do not acknowledge their superiority, or in any way reverence their " betters." But reverence for any earthly thing is the most un-American of attitudes. Reverence is out of date and offensively opposed to free inquiry. Parents do not exact it, and preachers do not expect it—the very title of " Rev." is now a verbal antiquity. Do we not even put our rulers through a course of hand-shaking in order to divest them of any respect the office might bring ? Why then expect a virtue from servants which we do not practise in our own stations ?

It is said, truly enough, that servants think of nothing but dress. Alas, mistresses are in the same transgression ! This is the fault of machinery. When servants wore mob-caps and ginghams, mistresses wore muslins and merinos, and were passing fine with one good silk dress. Machinery has made it possible for mistresses to get lots of dresses, and if servants are now fine and tawdry, it is because there is a general leaning that way. Servants were neat when every one else was neat.

To blame servants for faults we all share is really not reasonable. It must be remembered that women of all classes dress to make themselves attractive, and attractive mainly to the opposite sex. What the young ladies in the parlor do to make themselves beautiful to their lovers, the servants in the kitchen imitate. Both classes of young women are anxious to marry. There is no harm in this desire in either case. With the hopes of the young ladies we do not meddle ; why then interfere about nurse and the policeman : service is not an elysium under the most favorable circumstances. No girl gets fond of it, and a desire to be mistress of her own house—however small it may be —is not a very shameful kicking against Providence.

The carrying out of three points would probably revolutionize the whole condition of service :

First, The relation should be put upon an absolutely commercial basis ; and made as honorable as mechanical, or factory, or store service.

Second, Duties and hours should be clearly defined. There should be no interference in personal matters. There should be no more personal interest expected, or shown, than is the rule between any other employer and employee.

Third, If it were possible to induce yearly engagements, they should be the rule ; for when people know they have to put up with each other for twelve months, they are more inclined to be patient and forbearing ; they learn to make the best of each other's ways ; and bearing becomes liking, and habit strengthens liking, and so they go on, and on, and are pretty well satisfied.

AMELIA E. BARR.

THE PENALTIES OF A WELL-KNOWN NAME.

BY OUIDA.

WHEN in childhood, if we be made of the stuff which dreams ambitious dreams, we see the allegorical figure of Fame blowing her long trumpet down the billowy clouds, we think how delightful and glorious it must be to have a name which echoes from that golden clarion. Nothing seems to us worth the having, except a share in that echoing windy blast. To be famous : it is the vision of all poetic youth, of all ambitious energies, of all strúggling and unrecognized talent. To be picked out by the capricious goddess and lifted up from the crowd to sit beside her on her throne of cloud, seems to the fancy of youth the loftiest and loveliest of destinies.

In truth, celebrity has its pleasant side. To possess a name which is an open sesame wherever it is pronounced is not only agreeable, but is often useful. It opens doors easily, whether they be of palaces or of railway stations ; it saves you from arrest if you be sketching fortifications ; it obtains *kudos* for you from every one, from ministers to inn-keepers ; in a word, it marks you as something out of the common, not lightly to be meddled with, or neglected with impunity. It has its practical uses and its daily advantages, if it have also this prosaic drawback, that, like other conspicuous personages, you pay fifty per cent. dearer than ordinary people for everything which you consume. "Nobody would sell a wretched ambassador a cauliflower for two pence!" said a friend of mine, who is an ambassador himself, standing before the stalls of a foreign market place where this useful vegetable was being sold at four sous apiece. But he forgot that before the cauliflower could appear on his own table it would have to dress itself up with many condiments and become a choice dish with a long name, and he forgot also the old true saying, *il faut souffrir pour être beau.*

Fame, like position, has its ugly side ; whatever phase of it be taken, whatever celebrity, notoriety, distinction, or fashion, it brings its own penalties with it, and it may be that these penalties underweigh its pleasures.

The most cruel of its penalties is the loss of privacy which it entails ; the difficulty which it raises to the enjoyment of free and unobserved movement. Whether the owner of a well-known name desire privacy for the rest of solitude, for the indulgence of some affection of which it is desired that the world shall know nothing, for the sake of repose and ease, or for the pursuit of some especial study, the *incognito* sighed for is almost always impossible to obtain.

Find the most retired and obscure of places, amidst hills where no foot but the herdsman's treads, and pastures which feel no step but those of the cattle, a mountain or forest nook which you fondly believe none but yourself and one other know of as existing on the face of the globe ; yet brief will be your and your companion's enjoyment of it if your life or one of your lives be famous ; the press will track you like a sleuth-hound, and all your precautions will be made as naught, and, indifferent to the harm they do or the misery they create, the Paul Prys of broadsheets will let in the glare of day upon your dusky, mossy dell.

The artist has, no doubt, in this much for which to blame himself : why does the dramatist deign to bow from his box ? why does the composer salute his audience ? why does the painter have shows at his studio ? why does the great writer tell his confidences to the newspaper hack ?

Because they are afraid of creating the enmity and the unpopularity which would be engendered by their refusal. Behind this vulgar, intrusive espionage and examination there lies the whole force of the malignity of petty natures and inferior minds —i. e., two thirds of the world. The greater is afraid of the lesser : the giant fears the sling or the stone of the pigmy ; he is alone, and the pigmies are multitudinous as the drops in the sea.

We give away the magic belt which makes us invisible, without knowing in the least all that we give away with it: all that delightful independence and repose which are the portion of the *humbles de la terre*, who, all the same, do not value it, do not appreciate it ; do not, indeed, ever cease from dissatisfaction at it. In their ignorance they think how glorious it must be to stand in the white blaze of the electric light of celebrity ; how enviable and delightful it surely is to move forever in a buzz of

wondering voices and a dust of rolling chariots, never to stir un-
chronicled and never to act uncommented. Hardly can one persuade them of the treasure which they possess in their own obscurity ? If we tell them of it, they think we laugh at them or lie.

Privacy is the necessity of good and great art, as it is the corollary of dignity and decorum in life. But it is bought with a
price ; it is bought by incurring the dislike and vindictiveness of
all who are checked in their petty malice and prying curiosity
and are sent away from closed doors.

The ideal literary life is that of Michelet ; the ideal artistic life
is that of Corot. Imagine the one leaving the song of the birds
and the sound of the seas to squabble at a Copyright Congress, or
the other leaving his green trees and his shining waters to pour
out the secrets with which nature had intrusted him in the ear
of a newspaper reporter ! If a correspondent of the press had
hidden behind an elder-bush on a grassy path at Shottery, methinks Shakespeare would have chucked him into the nearest ditch;
and if a stenographer had inquired of Dante what meats had
tasted so bitter to him at Can Grande's table, beyond a doubt the
meddler would have learned the coldness and the length of a
Florentine rápier. But then none of these men was occupied
with his own personality, none of them had the restless uneasi-
ness, the morbid fear, which besets the modern hero lest, if his
contemporaries do not prate of him, generations to come will
know naught of him.

Then, alas! oftentimes, the fox, with his pen and ink hidden
under his fur, creeps in, wearing the harmless skin of a familiar
house-dog, and the unhappy hare or pullet, who has received,
caressed, and fed him without suspicion, sees too late an account
of his good nature and of his habitation travestied and sent
flying on a news-sheet to the four quarters of the globe. Against
treachery of this kind there is no protection possible. All that
can be done is to be very slow in giving or allowing introductions ;
very wary in making new acquaintances, and wholly indifferent
to the odium incurred by being called exclusive.

Interrogation is always ill-bred ; and an intrusion that takes
the form of a prolonged interrogation is an intrusion so intolerable that any rudeness whatever is justifiable in its repression.

The man of genius gives his work, his creation, his *alter ego*,
to the world, whether it be in political policy, in literary com-

position, in music, sculpture, painting, or statuary. This the world has full right to judge, to examine, to applaud, or to con. demn ; but beyond this, into the pale of his private life it has no possible title to entry. It is said in the common jargon of criti. cism that without knowing the habits, temperament, physique, and position of the artist, it is impossible to correctly judge his creation. It is, on the contrary, a hindrance to the unbiassed judg. ment of any works to be already prejudicial *per* or *contra* by knowledge of the accidents and attributes of those who have pro. duced them. It is a morbid appetite, as well as a vulgar taste, that makes the public invade the privacy of those who lead, in. struct, or adorn their century, and these last have themselves to thank, in a great measure, for the pests which they have let loose.

Every day any one who bears a name in any way celebrated receives requests or questions from persons who are unknown to him, demanding his views on everything from Buddhism to blacking, and inquiring into every detail of his existence, from his personal affections to his favorite dish at dinner. If he deign to answer them, he is as silly as the senders.

Sometimes you will hear that a town has been named after you in America, or Australia, or Africa, with the addendum of the inevitable *ville* attached to your name : it is usually a few planks laid down in a barren plain, and you are expected to be grateful that your patronymic will be shouted on a siding as the railway train rushes by it. Sometimes an enthusiastic and un. known letter writer will implore you to tell him or her " every. thing " about yourself, from your birth onwards ; and if, as you will certainly do if you be in your senses, you consign the im. pudent appeal to the waste-paper basket, your undesired corres. pondent will probably fill up the *lacuna* from his or her own imagination. Were all this the offspring of genuine admiration, it might be in a measure excused, though it would always be ill-bred, noxious, and odious. But it is either an impertinent curiosity or a desire to make money.

The moment that your name is well known, the demands made upon you will be as numerous as they will be imperative. Though you may never have given any permission or any data for a biography, the fact will not prevent hundreds of biographies ap. pearing about you : that they are fictitious and unauthorized matters nothing either to those who publish or to those who read. Descriptions, often wholly inaccurate, of your habits, your tastes, your appearance, your manner of life, will be put in circulation, no matter how offensive or how injurious to you they may be. Your opinions will be demanded by strangers whose only object is to obtain for themselves some information which they can turn to profit. From the frequency or rarity of your dreams to the length of your menu at dinner, nothing will escape the insatiable appetite of an unwholesome and injurious inquisitiveness. Obscure nonentities called Stubbs, or Stadge, or Briggs, or Bragg, will imagine that they honor you by writing that they have baptized their brats in your name, and requesting some present or acknowledgment in return for their unwelcome effrontery in taking you as an eponymus.

It is probable, nay, I think, certain, that in no epoch of the world's history was prominence in any art or any career ever rendered so extremely uncomfortable as in ours, never so heavily handicapped with the observation and penalty-weight of inquisitive misrepresentation. All the indications of the age tend to increase a thousandfold all that minute examination of and impudent interference with others which were alive in the race in the days of Miltiades and Socrates, but which has now, in its so-called scientific toys, the means of gratifying this mischievous propensity in an infinitely greater and more dangerous degree.

The instant that any man or woman accomplishes anything which is in any way remarkable, the curiosity of the public is roused and fastens on his or her private life to the neglect and detriment of his or her creations. The composer of the " Cavalleria Rusticana," an opera which, whatever may or may not be its artistic merit, has had charm and melody enough to run like a flame of fire across Italy during the past summer, awakening the applause of the whole nation, has dwelt in obscurity and poverty up to the moment when his work arouses a fury of delight in his country people. Lo! the press immediately seizes on every detail of his hard, laborious life, and makes a jest of his long hair. What has his life or his hair to do with the score of the " Cavalleria Rusticana?" What has the fact that he has written limpid and bewitching music, which has the secret of rousing the enthusiasm of the populace, to do with the private circumstances, habits, or preferences of his daily existence? It is an intolerable impudence which can presume to pry into the latter because the former has revealed in him that magic gift of inspiration which makes him momentarily master of the souls of others.

The human mind is too quickly colored, too easily disturbed, for it to be possible to shake off all alien bias and reflected hues; and it is more just to the dead than to the living, because it is not by the dead moved either to that envy or detraction, that favor or adulation, which it unconsciously imbibes from all it hears and knows of the living.

Whoever else may deem that the phonograph, the telephone, and the photographic apparatus are beneficial to the world, every man and woman who has a name of celebrity in that world must curse them with deadliest hatred. Life is either a miserable and weak submission to their demands, or a perpetual and exhausting struggle against and conflict with their pretensions, in the course of which warfare enemies are made inevitably and continually by the tens of thousands. He who bends beneath the decrees of the sovereign spy is popular at the price of dignity and peace. Those who refuse to so stoop are marked out for abuse and calumny from all those who live by or are diverted by the results of the espionage. There is no middle way between the two ; you must be the obedient slave or the irreconcilable opponent of all the numerous and varied forms of public inquiry and personal interference. The walls of Varzin have never been high enough to keep out the interviewer, and the trees of Faringford have never been so thickly planted that they availed to screen the study of the poet. The little, through these means and methods, have found out that they can annoy, harass, torment, and turn to profit, the great. Who that knows humanity could hope that the former would abstain from the exercise of such power ?

In early youth we know not what we do, we cannot measure all we part with in seeking the publicity which accompanies success ; we do not realize that the long trumpet of our goddess Fame will mercilessly blow away our dearest secrets to the ears of all, and so strain and magnify them that they will be no more recognized by us, though become the toy of all. We do not appreciate, until we have lost it, the delightful unregarded peace with which the obscure of this world can love, hate, caress, curse, move, sit still, be sick, be sorry, be gay or glad, bear their children, bury their dead, unnoted, untormented, unobserved.

The worst result of the literary clamor for these arrays of facts, or presumed facts, is that the ordinary multitude, who have not the talent of the original seekers, imitate the latter, and deem it of more importance to know what any famous person eats, drinks, and wears, in what way he sins, and in what manner he sorrows, than it does to rightly measure and value his picture, his position, his romance, or his poem. Journalistic inquisitiveness has begotten an unwholesome appetite, an impudent curiosity, in the world, which leaves those conspicuous in it neither peace nor privacy.

The press throughout the whole world feeds this appetite, and the victims, either from timidity or vanity, do not do what they might do to condemn and resist it. The interviewer too often finds his impertinent intrusion unresented for him, or the public which employs him, to reach any consciousness of his intolerable effrontery. He has behind him those many-handed powers of anathema and misrepresentation and depreciation which are called the fourth estate, and almost all celebrity is afraid of provoking the reprisals in print which would follow on a proper and peremptory ejection of the unsought visitor.

Because a man or woman more gifted than the common multitude bestows upon the world some poem or romance, some picture, statue, or musical composition, of excellence and beauty, by what possible right can the world pry into his or her privacy and discuss his or her fortunes and character? The work belongs to the public, the creator of the work does not. The invasion of private life and character never was so great or so general as it is in the last years of this century. It is born of two despicable parents, curiosity and malignity. Beneath all the flattery, which too frequently covers with flowers the snake of inquisitiveness, the snake's hiss of envy may be plainly heard by those who have ears to hear. It is the hope to find, sometime, some flaw, some moral or physical disease, some lesion of brain or decay of fortune, in the private life of those whom they profess to admire or adore, which brings the interviewer crawling to the threshold and peering through the keyhole. What rapture for those who cannot write anything more worthy than a newspaper paragraph, to discover that the author of "Salammbo" was an epileptic! What consolation for those who cannot string rhymes together at a child's party to stand beside the bedside of Heine and watch "the pale Jew writhe and sweat!"

In Dalou's monument to Eugene Delacroix he represents the great painter with his chin sunk in the *cache-nez,* which his chilly and fragile organization led to his uncovering generally, no matter whether the weather was fine or foul. Dalou has outraged art, but he has delighted his contemporaries and crystallized their taste ; the *cache-nez* about the throat of the man of genius enchants the common herd, which catches cold perpetually, but could not paint an inch of canvas or a foot of fresco, and feels jealously, restlessly, malignantly, grudgingly, that the creator of the "Entreé des Croisé's" and the "Barque da Dante," so far above them in all else, is brought nearer to them by that folded foulard. The statue in the gardens of the Luxembourg is an epitome of the sentiment to the eye ; time, glory, and art bend before Delacroix and offer him the palms of immortality ; Apollo throws his lyre away in sympathy and ecstasy ; but what the mortal crowds see and applaud is the disfiguring neckerchief !

It is the habit of scholars to lament that so little is known of the private life of Shakespeare. It is, rather, most fortunate that we know so little, and that little but vaguely. What can we want to know more than the plays tell us ? Why should we desire to have records which, drawing earthwards the man, might draw us also downwards from that high empyrean of thought where we can dwell through the magic of the poet's incantations ?

It may be a natural instinct which leads the crowd to crave and seek personal details of the lives of those who are greater than their fellows, but it is an instinct to be discouraged and repressed by all who care for the dignity of art. The cry of the realists for *documents humains* is a phase of it ; and results from the poverty of imagination in those who require such documents as the scaffolding of their creations. The supreme gift of the true artist is a rapidity of perception and comprehension which is totally unlike the slow piecemeal observations of others. As the musician reads the page of a score at a glance, as the author comprehends the essence of a book by a flash of intelligence, as the painter sees at a glance the points and lines and hues of a landscape, whilst the ordinary man plods through the musical composition note by note, the book page by page, the landscape detail by detail, so the true artist, whether poet, painter, or dramatist, sees human nature, penetrating its disguises and embracing all its force and weakness by that insight which is within him. The catalogues, the classifications, the microscopic examinations, which are required to make up these *"documents,"* are required by those who have not that instantaneous comprehension which is the supreme gift of all supreme talent. The man who takes his notebook and enumerates in it the vegetables, the fish, the game, of the markets, missing no bruise on a peach, no feather in a bird, no stain on the slab where the perch and trout lie dying, will make a painstaking inventory, but he will not see the whole scene as Teniers or Callot saw it. When the true poet or artist takes up in his hand a single garden pear or russet apple, he will behold, through its suggestions, as in a sorcerer's mirror, a whole smiling land of orchard and of meadow ; he will smell the sweet scent of ripe fruit and wet leaves ; he will tread a thousand grassy ways and wade in a thousand rippling streams ; he will hear the matin's bell and the even song, the lowing kine and the bleating flocks ; he will think in a second of time of the trees which were in blossom when Drake and Raleigh sailed, and the fields which were green when the Tudor and Valois met, and the sunsets of long, long ago when Picardy was fierce in war and all over the Norman lands the bowmen tramped and the fair knights rode.

The phrasing of modern metaphysics calls this faculty assimilation ; in other days it has been called imagination : be its name what it will, it is the one essential and especial possession of the poetic mind, which makes it travel over space and annihilate time and behold the endless life of innumerable forests as suggested to it by a single green leaf. When the writer, therefore, asks clamorously for folios on folios of *documents humains,* he proves that he has not this faculty, and that he is making an inventory of human qualities and vices rather than a portrait of them.

OUIDA.

PROGRESS OF NATIONALISM IN THE UNITED STATES.

BY EDWARD BELLAMY, AUTHOR OF "LOOKING BACKWARD."

TECHNICALLY, the term Nationalism, as descriptive of a definite doctrine of social and industrial reform, was first used in 1888 by clubs made up of persons who sympathized with the ideas of a proper industrial organization set forth in "Looking Backward," and believed in the feasibility of their substantial adoption as the actual basis of society. Nationalism, in this strict sense, is the doctrine of those who hold that the principle of popular government by the equal voice of all for the equal benefit of all, which, in advanced nations, is already recognized as the law of the political organization, should be extended to the economical organization as well; and that the entire capital and labor of nations should be nationalized, and administered by their people, through their chosen agents, for the equal benefit of all, under an equal law of industrial service.

In this sense of a definite philosophy and a positive programme, Nationalism is a plant of very recent growth. It would, however, be quite impossible to understand the reasons for its remarkable popularity and rapid spread, and equally impossible to calculate the probabilities of its future development, without taking into account the evolutionary processes of which it is the outcome.

The very idea of the nation as an organization for the purpose of using the collective forces for the general protection and welfare, logically involved, from the beginning, the extension of that organization to the industrial as well as to the political affairs of the people. Until the democratic idea became prevalent it was, however, possible for privileged classes to hold back this evolution; and so for unnumbered ages it has been held back. From the period at which the democratic idea gained ascendancy it could be a question of but a short time before the obvious in-

terests of the majority of the people should lead to the democ-
ratizing of the national economic system to accord with the
political system.

The Nationalist movement in the United States, instead of waiting till this late day, would have arisen fifty years ago as the
natural sequence of the establishment of popular government and
of the recognition that the national organization exists wholly
and only for the promotion of the people's welfare, had it not been
for the intervention of the slavery issue. It would indeed be more
accurate to say that in a broad sense of the word the Nationalist
movement did arise fifty years ago, for in spirit if not in form it
may be said to date back to the forties. Those who are not
familiar with the history of the extraordinary wave of socialistic
enthusiam which swept over the United States at that period
and led to the Brook Farm Colony and a score of phalansteries
for communistic experiments, have missed one of the most significant as well as most picturesque chapters of American history.
Some of the most eminent persons in the country, and many who
afterwards became eminent, were connected with or in sympathy
with these enterprises. That Horace Greeley would very possibly have devoted himself to some line of socialistic agitation,
had not the slavery struggle come on, will surely be questioned by none who are familiar with his correspondence and early
writings, and in this respect he was representative of a large group
of strong and earnest spirits.

But slavery had to be done away with before talk of a closer,
kinder brotherhood of men was in order or, indeed, anything but
a mockery. So it was that presently these humane enthusiasts,
these precursors of Nationalism, were drawn into the overmastering
current of the anti-slavery agitation. Then came the war, which
should be ranked the greatest in history, not merely on account
of the extent of the territory and of the vastness of the armies involved, but far more because it issued, as such a war never did
before, in the speedy reconciliation of the foes. The reunion of
the North and South after the struggle is the best proof of the
progress of humanity that history records, the best evidence
that the Nationalist motto, "We war with systems not with
men," is not in advance of the moral sense of the nation we appeal to.

The din of the fight had barely ceased when the progress of

evolution towards economic Nationalism resumed its flow with all impetus only heightened by its interruption. But social conditions meanwhile had profoundly changed for the worse, and with them the character of the economic controversy, which now became full of rancor and bitterness. The speculative opportunities offered by the war had developed the millionaire and his shadow, the tramp. Contrasts of wealth, luxury, and arrogance with poverty, want, and abjectness, never before witnessed in America, now on every side mocked the democratic ideal and made the republic a laughing-stock.

The panic of 1873, with the seven lean years that followed in its train, ushered in the epoch of acute industrial discontent in this country. Then began the war between labor and capital. The phenomena of the period have been, on the one hand, ever-enlarging aggregations of capital, and the appropriation of the business field by groups of great monopolies ; and, on the other hand, unprecedented combinations of labor in trades-unions, federations of unions and the Knights of Labor. Both classes of phenomena, the combinations of capital and of labor, were equally significant of the evolution towards economic Nationalism. The rise of the Knights of Labor, the great trades-unions, the Federation of Trades, and, on the agricultural side, of the Grangers, Patrons of Husbandry, Farmers' Alliances, and many other organizations, were demonstrating the feasibility of organizing the workers on a scale never dreamed of; while on the other side the enormous and ever-growing trusts and syndicates were proving the feasibility of organizing and centralizing the administration of capital on a scale of corresponding magnitude. Opposed as these two tendencies seemed, they were yet destined to be combined in the synthesis of Nationalism, and were necessary stages in its evolution. Both alike, in all their phases, were blind gropings towards completer union, confessions of a necessity of organizing forces for common ends, that could find their only logical result in Nationalism, when the nation should become at once employed and employer, and labor and capital be blended in indistinguishable union.

Nor were there lacking, in the epoch spoken of, very conscious and definite appeals, although partial and inadequate ones, to the national idea as the proper line along which adequate remedies were to be sought. The greenback movement in its argument that the oppressions and inadequacies of the monetary system could only be removed by taking the issue of money wholly out of the control or influence of private persons and vesting it directly in the nation, was a distinct anticipation of Nationalism. The same idea was very evident in the proposition to reject the gold or silver standard as the basis of money and rest it broadly on the nation's assets and the nation's credit. It is true, indeed, that Nationalism, by making the nation the only storekeeper, and its relations of distribution with each citizen a direct one, excluding middlemen, will dispense with buying and selling between individuals, and render greenbacks as superfluous as other sorts of money. Nevertheless, in the spirit of its appeal to the national idea, Greenbackism was strongly tinctured with the sentiment of Nationalism.

Another of the fragmentary anticipations of Nationalism during the period referred to was the rise of the Knights of Labor. The peculiar merit of this admirable body is the broadly humane basis of its organization, which gives it an ethical distinction necessarily lacking to the mere trades-union. Its motto, "An injury to one is the concern of all," if extended to all classes, would be a good enough one for the most thorough-going Nationalist. The Knights of Labor, like the Greenbackers, believed in the national idea, and in dealing with the most formidable and dangerous class of private monopolies in this country demanded the nationalization of the railroads.

In enumerating the streams of tendency which were during this period converging towards Nationalism, mention should also be made of the various anti-monopoly parties that from time to time arose as local and more or less national parties. The platforms of some of these parties were extremely radical, and the dominant idea in the suggestion of remedies was an appeal to the nation.

Finally came the Henry George agitation. The extraordinary impression which Mr. George's book "Progress and Poverty" produced was a startling demonstration of the readiness of the public for some radical remedy of industrial evils. It is unnecessary to remind my readers that the nationalization of land was Mr. George's original proposition.

The foregoing considerations may perhaps sufficiently indicate how far back in American history the roots of Nationalism run, and how it may indeed be said to have been logically involved in the very principle of popular government on which the nation was founded.

A book of propaganda like " Looking Backward " produces an effect precisely in proportion as it is a bare anticipation in expression of what everybody was thinking and about to say. Indeed, the seeming paradox might almost be defended that in proportion as a book is effective it is unnecessary. The particular service of the book in question was to interpret the purport and direction of the conditions and forces which were tending towards Nationalism, and thereby to make the evolution henceforth a conscious, and not, as previously, an unconscious, one. The Nationalist who accepts that interpretation no longer sees in the unprecedented economical disturbances of the day a mere chaos of conflicting forces, but rather a stream of tendencies through ever larger experiments in concentration and combination towards the ultimate complete integration of the nation for economic as well as for political purposes. The sentiment of faith and good cheer born of this clear vision of the glorious end, and of the conviction that the seemingly contradictory and dangerous phenom- ena of the times are necessary means to that end, distinguishes the temper of the Nationalist as compared with that of other schools of reformers.

The first Nationalist club was organized in Boston by readers of " Looking Backward " in 1888. Almost simultaneously other clubs were organized in all parts of the country, something like one hundred and fifty having been reported within the following two years, the reporting having, however, been very laxly attended to. There never was, perhaps, a reform movement that got along with less management than that of the Nationalists. There has never been any central organization and little if any mutual organization of the clubs. Wherever in any community a few men and women have felt in sufficiently strong sympathy with the ideas of the Nationalists to desire to do something to spread them, they have formed an organization and gone ahead, with as much or little communication with other similar organizations as they have desired to have. While these clubs have been and are of the greatest use, and have accomplished remarkable results in leavening entire communities with Nationalism, there has never been any special effort to multiply them or otherwise to gather the whole body of believers into one band. We like to think that not one in a hundred who more or less fully sympathize with us is a member of a Nationalist club, or probably ever will be until the nation becomes the one Nationalist club.

The practical work of the organized Nationalists for the past four years has, of course, been chiefly educational, consisting in the effort, by lectures, books, and periodicals, to get their ideas before the people. The lack of a central organization on the part of the clubs prevents, very fortunately, the existence of any formal " official " organ. The nearest approach to such a publication was at first the *Nationalist,* a monthly, issued in Boston, which a year and a half ago was succeeded by *The New Nation,* a weekly, edited by the present writer, and devoted to the exposition of the principles and purposes of Nationalism, with the news of the movement.

In the brief period that has elapsed since the origin of the Nationalist movement, with its clearly defined philosophy and positive purpose, the growth of Nationalism in this country has been accelerated in an extraordinary manner. While it is impossible not to ascribe the acceleration largely to the literature and work of the Nationalists, it is not for a moment intended to imply that this growth is solely attributable to the strictly Nationalist propaganda. Throughout this paper the argument has been maintained that this specific movement is but the outcome of forces long in operation, which, by no means as yet wholly coalescing with strict Nationalism, continue to work consciously or unconsciously towards the same inevitable result.

It is unnecessary, surely, to do more than call attention to the great moral awakening upon the subject of social responsibilities and the ethical side, or rather the ethical soul and centre, of the industrial question, which has taken place within a very recent time. It was but yesterday that the pulpit was dumb on this class of themes, dumb because its hearers were deaf. Now, every Sunday hundreds of pulpits throughout the land are preaching social duty and the solidarity of nations and of humanity ; declaring the duty of mutual love and service, whereby the strong are made bondmen to the weak, to be the only key to the social problem. This is the very soul of Nationalism. To be able to present this theme effectively has become the best passport of the clergyman to popular success, the secret of full houses. One of the most hopeful features of the Nationalist outlook from the first has been the heartiness with which a large contingent of the clergy has enlisted in it, claiming that it was, as it truly is, nothing more than Christianity applied to industrial organization. This we hope to make so apparent that erelong all Christian men shall be obliged either to abjure Christ or come with us.

The recent change in the trend of economic discussion as to the questions involved in the proposition of Nationalism has not been less marked than the moral awakening. Until very recently this country was twenty-five years behind the intelligence and practice of Europe as to sociological questions. That there might be such awkward things as strikes we had, indeed, learned since 1873 ; but that there was any such thing as a great industrial social question, of which these were but symptoms, had not dawned upon the public or on old-fashioned economists, who supposed that wisdom had died with Adam Smith. Remember that it was only a little while ago that "the social evil" was understood to refer exclusively to a special form of vice. It was imagined that there could not be any other social evil of consequence here in America unless, perhaps, it were intemperance in the use of alcoholic stimulants or tobacco. While the "effete monarchies of Europe" might have to rectify their institutions from time to time to keep pace with human progress, we rested in the serene conviction that General Washington and Mr. Jefferson had arranged our affairs for all time, and that negro slavery was the last problem we should have to dispose of. And let it be observed, that these great patriots, in setting up popular self-government, did give us a finality of principle, but that an economic as well as a political method, in order to give effect to that principle, has now become necessary.

Where is now that easy complacency over the social situation which so recently was the prevailing temper of our people ? Economic discussion and the debate of radical social solutions absorb the attention of the country, and are the preponderating topics of serious conversations. Economic papers have the precedence in our periodicals, and, even in the purely literary magazine, they crowd the novel and the romance. Indeed, the novel with a sociological motive now sets the literary fashion, and a course in political economy has become necessary to write a successful love story.

It is not so much the increased volume of economic discussion that marks the social growth of Nationalism as the fact that its tone is chiefly given by the adherents of the new and humane schools of political economy which, until recently, had obtained but little hearing among us. Up to within a very few years the old school of political economy, although it had long before begun to fall into discredit in Europe, still held practically undisputed sway in America. To-day the new school, with its socialistic method and sympathies, is the school to which nearly all the young and rising professors of political economy belong. The definition of labor as "a commodity," would now endanger the position of an instructor in that science in any institution of learning which did not depend for its patronage upon a reputation for being behind the times. There are a few such yet despite the growth of Nationalism.

The full programme of Nationalism, involving the entire substitution of public for private conduct of all business, for the equal benefit of all, is not indeed advocated by any considerable number of economists or prominent writers. They discuss chiefly details of the general problem, but, in so far as they propose remedies, it is significant that they always take the form of state and national management of business. It would not probably be too strong a statement to say that the majority of the younger schools of political economists and economic writers on that subject now regard with favor state conduct of what they call "natural monopolies," that is to say, telegraphs, telephones, railroads, local-transit lines, water-works, municipal lighting, etc. "Natural monopolies" are distinguished by this school as businesses in which the conditions practically exclude competition. Owing to the progress of the trusts and syndicates, businesses not natural monopolies are rapidly being made artificial ones with the effect of equally excluding competition. If the economists of the "natural monopoly" school follow the logic of their method they are bound, in proportion as the progress of artificial monopolization abolishes their distinction, to become full-fledged Nationalists. I have no doubt they will soon be wholly with us, as in spirit and tendency they now are.

There is a great deal more that might be said of the recent and swiftly increasing movement of moral sentiment and scientific thought towards Nationalism, but the limits of my space compel me to pass on to the consideration of what has been accomplished in the field of politics and legislation within the four years since its rise as a definitive doctrine.

The immediate propositions of the Nationalists are on two lines. First the nationalization of inter-State business, and business in the products or service of which people in more than one State are interested. Second, the State management or municipalization of businesses purely local in their relations. In the former line the rise within two years of a third national political party, pledged to a large part of the immediate purposes of Nationalism, is certainly the most notable phenomenon. The People's Party was formed at Cincinnati on February 22, 1891, and ratified and indorsed at St. Louis, May 19, 1892, by a convention representing the great Farmers' Alliances, white and colored, of the West and South, and also the Knights of Labor and other artisans' organizations. The platform adopted at St. Louis as that on which the People's Party's Presidential candidates are to be nominated and supported by these allied organizations, demands nationalization of the issue of money, nationalization of banking by means of postal savings-banks for deposit and exchange, national ownership and operation of the telegraphs and tele phones, national ownership and operation of the railroads, and declares the land with its natural resources the heritage of the nation.

Remember that this platform voices the enthusiastic convictions and determination of many million voters belonging to organizations which have already carried several State elections, and which, as now united, may carry in the Presidential election, as their opponents concede, four or five States, and, as they themselves expect, twice or thrice that number. If you would estimate the probable growth of Nationalism in the next six months, remember that during that period the demands of this platform and the arguments for them will be stated and reiterated weekly by the eight to ten hundred farmers' papers of the South and West, and dinned into their ears by regiments of orators. About half the farmers' weeklies of the West, it should be added, not only support the St. Louis platform, but take every occasion to declare that the adoption of the whole Nationalist plan, with the industrial republic as its consummation, is but a question of time. "Talk about Nationalism," said one brawny farmer at the St. Louis convention, "why, west of the Mississippi we are all Nationalists."

In tracing the rise of this third party, it may be interesting to note that it was in the trans-Mississippi States, in the newly-admitted States and the Territories, and on the Pacific coast, where the People's Party now has its main strongholds, that the reception of "Looking Backward" was most general and enthusiastic. The growing economic distress in the great grain States had no doubt much to do with this readiness for a radical industrial solution, but the bold, adventurous temper of the people, perhaps, even more. To a race of pioneers which had hewn mighty States out of the wilderness and the desert within the lifetime of a generation, there was nothing to take the breath away in a proposal to reconstruct industry on new lines.

I have left myself little space wherein to speak of what has been done for Nationalism in the line of the municipalization of local businesses. The Nationalists of Boston and vicinity, in 1889, circulated petitions for the passage of a bill by the Legislature permitting municipalities to build and operate their own lighting plants, gas or electric. The bill failed in the Legislature of 1889–90, passing the House but being lost in the Senate. The Nationalists resumed the fight the next year on petitions bearing 13,000 names. The bill became a law after a bitter fight, in which the Nationalists, backed by the labor organizations and a strong popular sentiment, were opposed by a combination of the electric and gas companies representing $35,000,000 of capital.

Prior to that date, public lighting, although long a matter of course in Great Britain and Europe, was almost unknown in America; a striking illustration, by the way, of the incomprehensible manner in which America has lagged behind monarchical and aristocratic states in the practical application of its own patented idea of popular government.

Up to the passage of the Municipal Lighting Bill in 1891 by the Massachusetts Legislature, less than a dozen American towns had tried public lighting, and few people had even heard of their experiment. In the one year since then, sixteen towns and cities in Massachusetts alone and as many in Ohio have taken steps towards public-lighting works, while a host of municipalities in the rest of the Union are following their example.

If the Nationalists had done nothing more than point out the way of deliverance from the gas-meter, they would surely have deserved well of the American people, but in doing that they have done more—they have set the people thinking along the line of municipal self-help.

The American citizen is not unintelligent as to questions of profit and loss. Give him the A B C of a business proposition and he can usually be trusted to go through the alphabet without further assistance. Once convince him that public-light service means, as a matter of demonstration and experience, as it does, a saving to the consumer of from 30 to 50 per cent., and he will commence to scratch his head and ask why the same rule doesn't apply to water-works and transit systems.

By turning over such functions to private companies aiming only at the largest possible profits, instead of discharging them directly, cities and towns subject themselves to a needless tax, aggregating more, in many cases, than the total tax levy for nominally public purposes, as if, indeed, any purpose could be more public than lighting, water supply, and transit. Wherever a private company can make a profit on serving the community (leaving aside watered stock) the people themselves, who take no profit from themselves, can do it just so much cheaper. All we Nationalists want to do is to get people to reason along the line of their collective interests with the same shrewdness they show in pursuing their personal interests. That habit once established, Nationalism is inevitable.

EDWARD BELLAMY.

NOTES AND COMMENTS.

COLLEGE REPUBLICANS.

THE entrance of the college into politics is a feature of the Presidential campaign of 1892. The political club, however, is not a novelty in student life, nor is the organization of Republican clubs in American colleges without precedent. Hardly a campaign has passed without this sign of the interest of college students in political affairs. Formerly these clubs were organized in a spirit of fun, simply for the pleasure they afforded those who marched in torch-light processions or attended meetings held under their auspices. This year they have been formed with a more serious purpose: the students have come to realize that college thought and educated sentiment are yearly becoming a more important influence upon public opinion. As representatives of this sentiment, the attitude of college men is of some consequence. Hundreds of young men who do not go to college share, nevertheless, the college opinions and prejudices. The college graduate enjoys the reputation of being well informed on the important questions of the day, and his convictions are often of considerable weight to voters who have not enjoyed his opportunities for study. With this thought and with the purpose to extend and strengthen the principles of the party within as well as without the colleges, students have formed Republican clubs. On the 17th of May an intercollegiate convention was held at the University of Michigan, at which further organization of Republican clubs was perfected and plans adopted for active participation in the coming campaign.

These clubs will hold public meetings at which prominent men of the party will address the students on the issues of the campaign. Incidentally the members will take an active part in speaking and organizing throughout the country during the summer and fall. The political campaign has become a contest of reason, and the election an education in intelligent judgment. To no one are the problems of the currency, commerce, and government of more interest than to the student. It is natural that he should be interested in their serious consideration, and participate in the important work of their solution. Surely at no time are men more ready to listen with fairness to the exponents of the principles of both parties, and give a decision freer from selfish interest or less biassed by party prejudices, than when they are enjoying the freedom of college life. Party fealty is never weaker nor political ambition less blinding than then.

This activity of college Republicans has been the subject of criticism by the Democratic press. It is said that such organization of college students is a novelty. They doubtless have forgotten the part which Harvard University took in Massachusetts politics in the campaign of 1888. On the eve of the last Presidential election the persistent effort for four years to show that the best thought at Harvard University was Democratic culminated in the formation of a Democratic Club at Harvard, which held a mass meeting in Boston. It was there represented that the great majority of students sympathized with a movement to which they were either entirely indifferent or directly opposed. It was then that Harvard's better self realized that it could not afford to allow a few of the prominent graduates who had become disaffected from the Republican party to misrepresent the great majority of students and graduates. This large majority who had been placed in a false position resolved that if the college was to be dragged into politics it should be at least fairly represented. On November 2, 1888, there was held in Tremont Temple a Republican mass meeting which left little doubt as to the political preferences of Harvard University. At the present time a Democratic organization exists in the college which antedates the Harvard Republican Club by several years. College political clubs are not as new as the Democracy would have us think.

Our political opponents say that the college Republican clubs are a confession of the weakness of the Republican party, which they assert is in need of their aid. The students, however, are not organizing because the Republican party needs them. Their interest as young voters in the coming election is a sufficient incentive. That more than two-thirds of them are voters appears plainly from the college records. The average age of entrance at Harvard is something over nineteen years. There are 2,658 students in the University this year. Deducting from this number those in the Freshman and Sophomore years and half those classed as special students we have left 1,800 students, who in all probability are old enough to register as voters next November. Now, is there any reason why these 1,800 students should not feel as much interest in the coming election as an equal number of voters outside the college walls? An eminent Harvard professor remarked the other day: "It is the glory of the Republican party that it interests the young men." It is a sign of strength to be able to count a large majority of those who think in support of a party which believes in the principle of protection to those who work.

Perhaps no more absurd criticism has been made than that the organization of college Republican clubs is a shrewd move of the party leaders. I cannot speak definitely of other college Republican clubs, but I know that the Harvard Republican Club, the largest political college organization, was formed entirely by members of the University, independently of any party leaders or of any outside influence. For the formation, management, and the support of this club the students alone are responsible; I have no doubt this is so in other colleges. Our purpose, we are told by the writer of one attack upon us, is "to counteract the natural result of education." I presume that the natural result referred to is a belief in Free Trade. It is not true that our colleges teach Free Trade. The instructors in Political Economy are not advocates either of free trade or of protection. They lay before the student the theories, principles, and facts, and then allow him to draw his own conclusions. They seek after the truth. Every intelligent student studies the arguments of text books, listens to the lectures, and then decides for himself. If party allegiance is indicative of his decision, the Republican party needs no counteracting influence to the natural result of education. Of the 1,619 students graduating in the classes of 1885-1892 inclusive, 1,430 have expressed their political preferences. Of these 712, or 49.8 per cent., have voted for the Republican party ; 365, or 25.5 per cent., for the Democratic party; and 353, or 24.7 per cent., have been Independents. This goes to show that the believers in the party of free trade are outnumbered in the proportion of two to one. Such statistics show a remarkable lack of that "natural result of education" which our Democratic friends think we propose to counteract by our Republican Club. It is a popular impression that a vote of these same men taken several years after graduation would show still less of that heretical disloyalty to the Republican party which they would have us believe is the inevitable effect of education. Unfortunately I have no record of such a nature; but if it is fair to judge of the politics of Harvard alumni from the politics of those of them who have held prominent offices, the result would be still more satisfactory to us. For a careful examination of the roll of Harvard alumni shows that of 153 graduates who have held high office in the State and National Governments, 114 may fairly be classed as believers in the principles of the Republican party, and 39 in those of the Democratic party.

Below is a summary of offices held by Harvard graduates from 1789 to 1891. Some have held office more than once:

	Republican.	Democratic.		Republican.	Democratic.
President of the U. S....	2	0	U. S. Senators............	23	6
Vice-President of the U. S.	1	1	Congressmen..............	77	27
Cabinet Officers	10	5	Governors................	13	6
Foreign Ministers........	14	6	Total............ ...140		51

Summary, 1856–1891:

	Republican.	Democratic.		Republican.	Democratic.
Cabinet Officers...	4	2	Congressmen..............	16	8
Ministers.......	10	1	Governors................	5	1
U. S. Senators............	4	1			
Total..........			....	39	13

The last objection that I notice to the enlistment of college men in the ranks of the Republican party is that on account of their youth. Our Democratic friends characterize it as an attempt to "rob the cradle"! Such a criticism lacks none of the humor of sarcasm, coming as it does from a party whose recent success in Massachusetts is due to leaders whose youth has evidently been no serious disqualification. The jewel of consistency does not seem to glitter in the crown of the young Democracy. In answer one need only point to two of Harvard's youngest alumni, the Hon. Theodore Roosevelt and the Hon. Henry Cabot Lodge.

JOHN LOCKWOOD DODGE,
President of the Harvard Republican Club.

THE DECADENCE OF DICKENS.

MISS THACKERAY, in that indolently charming work of hers, "A Book of Sibyls," tells how a luncheon party of six, in one of the suburbs of London— "Old Kensington," it may be conjectured—talked about Jane Austen one day, and how every member of the company, save a French gentleman who knew not English, understood a chance allusion to Selina and Maple Grove. Without insisting upon Selina to the possible mortification of any readers, except to inform the uninitiated that, like Mrs. Harris and Anthony White, she was heard of but never seen, I venture to doubt whether the author of

the most famous of these three unseen characters would be found equally
familiar to a company of six well-read persons under the age of thirty-five.
I speak by the card, for the elaborate new edition of Dickens, with prefaces,
and the recent revivals at American theatres of plays founded upon the
novels, have re-stimulated discussion of the great writer whose fame was
noisier than that of any other English novelist since Walter Scott. And the
other evening "at a little dinner, not more than the muses, with all the
guests clever"—or moderately clever—"and some of them pretty,"—a condition of things which, according to the late Lord Beaconsfield, "offers
human life and human nature under very favorable circumstances"—at a
little dinner such as this, transacted in a town whose culture has acquired
the triteness of a proverb, and by persons of whom none had reached the age
of thirty-five, the subject of Dickens' novels was very thoroughly discussed.
Two of the company, a man and a woman whose researches in literature
had carried them more into the domain of French than of English fiction,
owned to never having read one of the series. Everybody else, however,
had read at least "David Copperfield," "The Pickwick Papers," "Dombey
and Son," and portions of the Christmas books; but this experience had
come to most of them in childhood; they had not refreshed their recollections,
and they betrayed little or no consciousness of the details, either humorous
or pathetic, of the volumes named. One *femme de trente ans* showed a
better knowledge of a number of the novels, including "Our Mutual
Friend," "Bleak House," and "The Old Curiosity Shop," but this lady was
in the condition of mind most hopeless to the true lover of Dickens of regarding "A Tale of Two Cities" as his masterpiece.

Not to be tedious in reporting the shortcomings of a worshipful company,
by no means without accomplishments of their own, it is interesting to
record (interesting is a word much used in their town) that the consideration of Dickens at last narrowed itself down to "Dombey and Son," apropos
of a new adaptation which had lately been seen on the stage by several of
the diners. This novel was then accepted as a test, and a man whose dreadful business it is to know all novels past and present, and to keep his
weather eye out for those to come, drew up the following examination-paper
after the ladies had left the table, and when the friends—for they are friends
—had reassembled, they addressed themselves with some zeal and a good
deal of humor to the revelation of one another's ignorance in this little game
of ten questions :—

1. How many times, by actual computation, does Joey B. announce himself as "de-vilish sly?" 2. Give a brief description of Mrs. Pipchin. 3. On
what occasion did Mrs. Blimber declare that if she "could have known
Cicero, and been his friend, and talked with him in his retirement at Tusculum (beau-ti ful Tusculum!)", she "could have died contented?". 4. Who
suggested to the first Mrs. Dombey that she should "make an effort?" 5.
What were the last words of little Paul? 6. Comment on (a) "Cleopatra,"
giving her real name; (b) Biler, giving his mother's assumed name; (c) The
Wooden Midshipman. 7. Characterize the Game Chicken and the Tutbury
Pet. 8. Analyze the effect of one or both on the career of Mr. Toots. 9.
State the relationship (if any) between Toots and the Toodles. 10. Have you
anything to say of the Nobby Shropshire One?

"State the relationship, if any, between the novels of Charles Dickens
and real life," was proposed by the man-whose-business-it-is-to-know, as an
alternative tenth question for pupils who had answered the preceding nine

questions successfully; but as only one pupil—a man—passed *cum laude*, and as even he planted himself firmly on the end of the century, and refused to consider for a moment such a proposition as the possible reality of Dickens, his unreality was tacitly admitted. Yet this tentative little examination-paper showed at least the unwieldiness, the prodigality, which belongs only to genius, the grotesque humor, and lastly and chiefly the wealth of minor characters even in one of the less good of Dickens's novels. For of all the persons and personages of "Dombey and Son" named therein—and the same might be said of more than twice as many more—not one, with the single exception of Toots, is to be found in Mr. Rose's dramatization of the novel.

It would be too hasty and too empirical to base on the true story of the defeated dinner-party the conclusion that the author of "Pickwick" is not read by the more cultivated younger people of to-day, but other straws are not lacking to show the direction of the wind. Mr. Howells frankly declares that Dickens is antiquated and impossible; and the other day an undergraduate of Harvard, on being asked whether he had read "Pendennis," answered in absolute good faith: "No, I haven't read any of Dickens yet, but I mean to." Mr. Howells ought to bestow a realistic, not to say a real, medal on a young scholar who could thus, in one direct, two edged sentence, give the cut direct to both Thackeray and Dickens. Jane, the present writer is credibly informed by this same Harvard junior—who, however, does not trouble himself more with "Emma" or "Pride and Prejudice" than with "Pendennis," but dotes instead on Rider Haggard—Jane triumphs over Dickens at Cambridge; and the whirligig of time brings in Miss Jenkyns's revenge. Her last years, as we all know, were embittered by Captain Brown's insane enthusiasm for young Mr. Dickens, then just coming into vogue, and by his preference for the interloper in literature over Dr. Johnson, whose "Rambler" was Miss Jenkyns's model of light reading. The Doctor and Mr. Boz are more evenly matched in these days, and the autocrat of Cranford, though she might not find the "Rambler" enjoying all the vogue to be desired, would rejoice in seeing "an elegant female" and a contemporary of her own hold the field against Captain Brown's upstart favorite at the most renowned seats of learning.

One other bit of testimony is worth record as a curiosity of literature. A man who teaches an humble branch of learning in the most admirable and successful of schools was instigated by the man-whose-business-it-is-to-know to inquire, on meeting his classes again after Easter, which of them enjoyed the acquaintance of Mrs. Blimber. She was unknown to each and all of thirty or more intelligent pupils, and not a ray of consciousness lighted any face when the teacher said: "Young ladies, let us resume our studies." It is scarcely probable that young gentlemen would have known better. The walls of the Tusculan villa are tottering, and there is but one hope for it, for Cicero, and for the accomplished consort of Dr. Blimber. This is the hope that Dickens may be made a fad. Thousands of people of docile tastes are now pretending to care for Miss Austen, and making the pretence plausible by a painful study of her works, simply because she is a fashion if not quite the fashion. The worthy Archdeacon Farrar, who is nothing if not literary, started the Browning boom on this continent. Will not another Captain Brown arise and boom Mr. Boz? If he will not, we may soon find in volumes of "extracts" and "selections" all that the public cares to know of Charles Dickens. And Gamp and Prig, Swiveller and the Marchioness, poor Jo and little Paul, Mr. Pickwick and

Sam Weller and David Copperfield, will appear in a detached fashion side by side with my Uncle Toby and Corporal Lefevre, poor Maria, and the starling that couldn't get out, while "Martin Chuzzlewit," "The Pickwick Papers," and "The Old Curiosity Shop," move slowly but surely towards the oblivion that has long since swallowed up "Tristram Shandy" and "A Sentimental Journey,"—the oblivion of books which no gentleman's library should be without. Whether Dickens's place in those shadowy ranks is as secure as Sterne's it is too soon to predict.

CHARLES TOWNSEND COPELAND.

WOMEN AS HUMAN BEINGS.

PEOPLE who recollect the woman's rights conventions of forty years ago have not forgotten how often the rallying-cry of these was "The Divine Right of Woman to Possess Herself."

To-day she is in full and undisputed possession of the coveted object. For good or for evil her individuality is her own. If ignorance or prejudice peeps or mutters from the dust, the remonstrance is as little heeded by her in her stately march as the chirp of a cricket or the writhing of a maimed beetle.

In this new day—the era of the coming woman, and of the woman who has come—due praise has not been awarded to the magnanimity of the men through whose graceful renunciation of preconceived ideas we have entered into the kingdom which was once held as exclusively theirs. Every door at which we have knocked has been unbolted, and courtesy that honors our common humanity has awaited us upon the threshold. More men are, in this year of Our Lord, 1892, willing to share the responsibility of suffrage with women than there are women who are willing and ready to accept the franchise. Protest against and jeremiads over the wrongs of women in the last decade of our century may rank with the tears shed by Mark Twain at the tomb of Adam. To the impartial observer, organization for armed defence against renewed tyranny would seem as senseless as Ku-Klux meetings in rural Delaware or Massachusetts.

Opposed to this array of evidence that the war is over, we have the fact that never before in the history of woman's emancipation, or of the world, have associations for the advancement of the sex—*as such*—been so rife as now. Women's corporations for every conceivable purpose—commercial, educational, religious, social, philanthropic—increase and prevail until they threaten to cover the face of the earth. We asked of man oneness and equality, and he gave it—for room to work at his side and upon his level, and he kept not back. Instead of falling into step with him, we strain ingenuity to demonstrate our unlikeness to him, and we accentuate the accident of sex until we make sex into a species. That our big brother, in surveying all this, is not betrayed into wicked gibes in the which Jeshurun might come well to the front, is referable to fear, to amazement—or to the finer attribute mentioned just now.

Our admitted claim that there is no sex in intellect is vitiated by our insistence upon feminine achievements in the realm of science and art as phenomenal. When a woman paints a picture, or sings a song, or plants an orange-grove, or opens a haberdashery, or endows a professorship, the act is catalogued among feats for the admiration of the public. " See of what a manumitted serf is capable !" is the tone, if not the language of such advertisement.

Every daily newspaper has a woman's page,—a paddock safe and clean, about which imagination constructs a fence upon the principle commended to his hired man by the thrifty Scotchman : " Use but one rail, but let that be sae high th' cawves canna loun ower it, and sae low that they canna stoop under it." Of the making of women's journals and magazines there is no end, and likely to be none. These are usually close corporations,—written by women, edited by women, and once in a good many whiles published by women. Upon the subscription books the names of men sustain in numbers the same relation to those prefixed by " Miss " or " Mrs." that bread held to sack in Falstaff's memorandum. The choice of topics is restricted to such as bear directly upon the progress of one sex ; the quality of the pabulum offered for mental digestion is warranted wholesome, but the word is open to criticism if an element of wholesomeness be the power to create intellectual brawn and moral backbone.

Let me guard what may be mistaken for sneering hypercriticism by saying that, as trade-journals, each of the legion of domestic organs devoted to the housewife, the housekeeper and the like, has in its sphere and uses a *raison d'être* as excellent as that of *The Consumer's Journal,* or *The Wheelman,* or *Outing.* It is in the realm of general literature that the distinction of sex becomes invidious. It is when gender begs the question of praise or patronage that unfairness verges upon injustice. There is, for example, no more reason why Mrs. Jones of the corner-grocery should demand custom by virtue of her sex than that Mr. Smith, on the next block, should attract trade because of a slight limp, or Mr. Robinson, across the way, because he is a married man. Each should be judged by the quality of what he offers for sale, and by his diligence in business.

Woman—with a capital letter—should by now have ceased to be a specialty. There should be no more need of " movements" in her behalf, and agitations for her advancement and development considered apart from the general good of mankind, than for the abolition of negro slavery in the United States. " For what a man "—and presumably a woman—" hath, doth he yet seek after ?" With the world of knowledge and opportunity thrown open to her, it argues little for her ambition and less for her ability to grasp cardinal principles that she elects to build fences about her reservation, and expends time and forces in patrolling precincts nobody cares to attack. "I am glad the question for discussion to-day does not contain the word ' woman,'" said a member of a celebrated literary club. " I am a weary of the pretentious dissyllable, and satiated with incessant twaddle of ' woman's progress,' ' woman's work for woman,' and the ninety-and-nine variations upon the one string. By this time we ought to be *there* if we are ever to arrive. I am half-sick of womanhood ! I want to be a human being."

A glance at the schedule of topics brought up for debate in like organizations in every township and city will justify the stricture.

(Is it a digression here to note that the Woman's Building at the Columbian Exposition is to be as distinctly separate from those in which the products of masculine brains and skill are exhibited as if what is therein collected had been sent by an alien people across the sea ?)

The " pull-all-together " that climaxes the three essentials to success in any emprise is indispensable in the upward toil of humanity towards the highest ideals.

> " You in your small corner,
> And I in mine,"

while well enough in the nursery jingle, is the extreme of puerility when applied to grown-up Christians.

Can it be—as is sometimes slyly insinuated—that the stock in trade of the pioneers in the " movement " having been distrust of the other sex, their occupation would be gone were we to deny them the harmless tilt at wind-mills in dust of their own raising? Has the habit of girding at our limita-tions in the shape of iniquitous laws and social prejudice grown so strong with the centuries that we are incapable of perceiving our altered status? In an age when we can make, keep, lose, and bequeath money as freely as our fathers and husbands; when we can be educated in the same university with our brothers; can practise medicine, law and theology; fill chairs of philosophy and literature; and travel alone and respected around the globe—our swaddling-bands are of our own making.

Is the fault in all this inherent in the texture and conditions of the femi-nine mind? It is scarcely a slur upon our sex to say that affection and ideality combine to shorten our views of certain fields of thought and action. Present a philanthropic scheme to a woman, and she forthwith sees in it her especial *protégé* of orphan, widow, or drunkard. The abstract is less to her than empty air. If she cannot lay hold of a ready-made concrete, she forms one, and takes it to her heart rather than to her head. It is altogether possible that women love women so loyally as to recognize in whatever tends to elevate humankind but another round in the ladder lately set up from earth to heaven for their feet. In politics they would be State-rights partisans instead of patriots.

A witty philanthropist said the other day that she was bound upon a mission to the neglected rich, not to the petted poor. Perhaps our appeal for a broader humanity on the part of those whose influence upon the morals and religion of the nation cannot be overestimated, might, in the like spirit, be made in behalf of our brethren and companions according to the flesh. A cogent argument of advanced thinkers who contend for higher education and political privileges for women is that she will ennoble and purify coarser natures; she is to introduce into the college the amenities of polite society; at the polls her presence will be the latter-day Una to the lion of party passion. With intellect trained to grapple with problems that tax men's best powers, she will bring her subtle intuitions to the logician's aid; the scimitar will second the cleaver's blow. Their studies and their aims will be identical; their union will accomplish the apotheosis of humanity.

With chivalry learned in an earlier, and our progressive women say a ruder age, our brothers have, in opening our ranks to us as fellow-laborers in the world's redemption, acknowledged their need of us, and proved their faith in our pledges of coöperation.

Radical and conservative may well deliberate together upon such pre-sages of the promised millenium as are offered by segregations that in tone and purpose remind the satirist of labor-unions and strikes rather than of dignified association for the elevation of a race whose destiny should be as much to women as to men.

MARION HARLAND.

A TOO-LONG VACATION.

NOT too long is vacation for the doctor, lawyer, editor, book-keeper, clerk, seamstress, or candlestick-maker. Those precious two weeks which are the standard period of annual rest for many hard workers, are altogether too short. But the thirteen weeks which represent the normal Summer vacation in college and school are long, altogether too long, for student and teacher.

The college student suffers from so long a vacation through the loss of interest in his college work. Of course he forgets his learning; this is to be expected, even desired in certain respects; but, also and more, he becomes diverted. His attention is for a whole quarter of the year directed to pursuits other than scholarly. His attention is also distracted, divided among a score of objects, frivolous, serious, wise, foolish. The influences which touch him cease to be academic, and become social and commercial. He enters into a life quite unlike his college life—which may of itself be an advantage—but of this life he does not become a vital part, which is a disadvantage. The ordering of his days becomes a disorder. His discipline is broken. He feels himself to be on a vacation, and vacation is usually intellectual vacuity. If he is obliged, through parental command or through poverty, to take up regular work a larger part of the time, he should be grateful, and he finally will be. But if he is permitted to do whatever fancy leads him to, as he too frequently is permitted, he usually does nothing though trying to do a bit of everything, reading, writing, fishing, boating, and sharing in other diversions. The vacation becomes dissipation—moral, intellectual. Forces that are needed in college are not recruited. Hardihood, endurance, concentration, pluck, grit, are not nursed through so long a period of inactivity. Laziness is the direct result of summer listlessness. Recreation does not become recreation. The student thinks himself to be in the garden of the lotos, and eating the lotos does not make a vigorous brain. The daily newspaper is the strongest regular intellectual fare; the hardest writing he does is acceptance of invitations; and the severest physical work playing tennis.

Much in all these endeavors is admirable. If such a life the reading student could have for a month, it were well, but to stretch out these methods over at least three months is not well. The proportions are bad. Resting is one thing, and a very good thing, but resting prolonged becomes rusting. Rusting eats the tool not used. Students, like tools, lose as much by August rest as by February wear. Let every student have all the rest, recreation, diversion, amusement required for keeping his forces in the finest condition ; but he does not need one-quarter of a year. A healthy student, and such as I constantly have in mind, can get as much vigor out of two months as out of three. Eight weeks in the woods will give all necessary power quite as well as thirteen. Eight weeks in the dissipating and charming enjoyments of society are better than thirteen for his college arms. A short vacation is better for a tired and healthy man than more, than a long one spent in laborious diversions.

We are trying to find a way in which college men can begin their professional career before the age of twenty-seven. "Shortening the college course" is a bad method for securing this aim. The college course is none too long, but the vacation is too long. Each student spends more than one year of his four years in vacations. He cannot afford to spend so long a time. The college period is the only period of his life when he finds so long a period of rest necessary. For the young editor or merchant, minister or lawyer, thus to rest would prove professional suicide, or rather still-birth. By transferring five weeks from the vacation to the working period of the college, and by a little extra work, we might cut the college course to three years, without a serious shortening of the time spent in study, and also with out any depreciation of the worthiness of the course itself.

The evils of the long vacation are more conspicuous in pupils of the common schools than in college students. These pupils are of the common people. More of them have parents whose purses are small than parents whose bank accounts are large. They spend their summers at home. They indulge in no outings more expensive or more prolonged than a visit to "Aunt Jane's" for a fortnight. They dwell in cities large and small, in villages large and small, and in rural desolations. But wherever they dwell, under ordinary conditions, the long vacation is no more recreative to jaded energy than a short vacation, and it is far more fraught with physical and ethical perils. Lawlessness is the general condition of boys in vacation. Every wharf and mill-pond becomes more dreadful to every parent. Apples and melons need a closer watch. They are no more inclined to "read" in the summer than our college men, and are possibly less inclined to find their happiness in harmless pleasures. They become juvenile Bohemians. They return to their books in the middle of September, not with an appetite whetted by proper abstinence, but with a distaste created by a barbarian life. Every teacher knows that at least a month is required to restore her classes to as good a working condition as was theirs at the close of school in June.   .

I might stop here. For I have said what I wanted to say as to a too-long vacation for students. The long vacation can hardly be called too long for teachers. No class of professional laborers are more laborious, none more deserving of long periods of rest, than the teachers ; and of all teachers those in the public school are most laborious and most deserving. The hours spent daily in the class-room are many,—not infrequently as many as a college professor spends in his class-room in a whole week,—and each hour is exhaustive of every form of personal energy in its severity and variety of duties. The school work which is to be done at home is considerable, especially the reading of examination papers—that bane of all teachers' lives. Their need of a long vacation is serious, yet many of them would confess that nine weeks of rest would prove to be as restful as thirteen.

For the ordinary professor of the ordinary college the vacation is too long. He has no greater need than the student of spending at least one-quarter and often one-third of the year to keep himself vigorous for working the remaining period. But, it is to be said, that to many teachers in the colleges the vacation is the occasion for doing work other and harder than that of the college routine. The reading or the writing of books or the preparation of special papers represent labors which college professors are constantly doing. I notice in particular that the professors of the natural sciences are much inclined to spend their summer in their laboratories making experiments which the broken days of the college year do not easily permit.

CHARLES F. THWING.

INDEX

TO THE

ONE HUNDRED AND FIFTY-FOURTH VOLUME

OF THE

𝕹orth 𝕬merican 𝕽eview.

Lightning Source UK Ltd.
Milton Keynes UK
UKHW040050240219
337879UK00008B/210/P